# NEWCOMER'S
# HANDBOOK

for Moving to and Living in

# Seattle

Including Bellevue, Redmond, Everett, and Tacoma

*3rd Edition*

6750 SW Franklin
Portland, OR 97223
503-968-6777
www.firstbooks.com

3rd edition

Newcomer's Handbook® and First Books® are registered trademarks of First Books.

Authors: Maria Christensen (3rd edition), Monica Fischer (2nd edition), and Amy Bellamy (1st edition)
Editors: Emily Horowitz, Linda Weinerman
Series Editor: Linda Weinerman
Cover and interior design: Erin Johnson Design
Interior layout and composition: Tricia Sgrignoli/Positive Images
Maps provided by Jim Miller/fennana design
Published by First Books®, 6750 SW Franklin Street, Portland, OR 97223-2542, 503-968-6777, www.firstbooks.com

ISBN-13: 978-0-912301-73-0
ISBN-10: 0-912301-73-2

Printed in the USA on recycled paper.

## What readers are saying about Newcomer's Handbooks:

*I recently got a copy of your Newcomer's Handbook for Chicago, and wanted to let you know how invaluable it was for my move. I must have consulted it a dozen times a day preparing for my move. It helped me find my way around town, find a place to live, and so many other things. Thanks.*

– Mike L.
Chicago, Illinois

*Excellent reading (Newcomer's Handbook for San Francisco and the Bay Area) ... balanced and trustworthy. One of the very best guides if you are considering moving/relocation. Way above the usual tourist crap.*

– Gunnar E.
Stockholm, Sweden

*I was very impressed with the latest edition of the Newcomer's Handbook for Los Angeles. It is well organized, concise and up-to-date. I would recommend this book to anyone considering a move to Los Angeles.*

– Jannette L.
Attorney Recruiting Administrator for a large Los Angeles law firm

*I recently moved to Atlanta from San Francisco, and LOVE the Newcomer's Handbook for Atlanta. It has been an invaluable resource—it's helped me find everything from a neighborhood in which to live to the local hardware store. I look something up in it everyday, and know I will continue to use it to find things long after I'm no longer a newcomer. And if I ever decide to move again, your book will be the first thing I buy for my next destination.*

– Courtney R.
Atlanta, Georgia

*In looking to move to the Boston area, a potential employer in that area gave me a copy of the Newcomer's Handbook for Boston. It's a great book that's very comprehensive, outlining good and bad points about each neighborhood in the Boston area. Very helpful in helping me decide where to move.*

– no name given (online submit form)

# TABLE OF CONTENTS

1    **Introduction**
*Local lingo, what to bring, history, Seattle address locator, getting around the Eastside*

12    ***Map of Seattle Region***

13    **Neighborhoods**

    13    *Seattle Area Counties*
        *A brief overview of King, Kitsap, Pierce, and Snohomish counties*

    16    *Seattle Neighborhoods*

    18    ***Map of Seattle***

    20    **Seattle—King County**

        20    *Downtown*
        25    *International District*
        26    *First Hill*
        28    *Capitol Hill*
        30    *Eastlake*
        32    *Queen Anne*
        34    *Magnolia*
        36    *Ballard*
        40    *Phinney Ridge/Greenwood*
        41    *Fremont*
        43    *Wallingford*
        45    *Green Lake*
        48    *University District*
        52    *Lake City*
        53    *Northgate*
        55    *Broadview*
        56    *Sand Point*
        58    *Madison Park*
        60    *Montlake*
        61    *Central District*
        63    *Madrona/Leschi*
        65    *Beacon Hill*
        66    *Rainier Valley*
        69    *Seward Park*
        70    *Duwamish District*
        72    *West Seattle*

    76    ***Eastside Map***

    78    **Surrounding Communities**

    78    *Eastern Communities (The "Eastside")—King County:*

        79    *Mercer Island*
        80    *Bellevue*
        83    *Newcastle*

# CONTENTS

84  Redmond
86  Kirkland
87  Woodinville
88  Duvall
89  Issaquah
91  Sammamish
92  North Bend/Snoqualmie
**94  North End Map**
95  Northern Communities—King County:
   95  Shoreline
   97  Lake Forest Park
   98  Bothell, Kenmore
99  Northern Communities—Snohomish County:
   99  Edmonds
   100  Mountlake Terrace
   101  Lynnwood
   102  Everett
104  Western Communities—Kitsap County:
   104  Bainbridge Island
   105  Bremerton
107  Southern Communities—King County:
   107  Renton
**108  South End Map**
   111  Kent
   112  Auburn
   113  Burien
   114  SeaTac, Tukwila
   115  Normandy Park
   116  Des Moines
   117  Federal Way
   118  Vashon Island
119  Southern Communities—Pierce County:
   119  Tacoma

**123  Finding a Place to Live**
Apartment finding tips, rental publications, listing services, roommate services; leases; rent and eviction control; renter's and homeowner's insurance; house hunting tips, real estate agencies, mortgages

**143  Moving and Storage**
Truck rentals; movers; packing, insurance; storage; children; complaints; taxes

**153    Money Matters**
*Banking; credit unions; consumer protection; credit cards; taxes; starting or moving a business*

**161    Getting Settled**
*Utilities; internet service; garbage and recycling; automobiles: driver's license, registration, emissions testing, insurance, parking, safety; social security; voter registration; library cards; passports; broadcast and cable TV; radio; local newspapers and magazines; finding a physician; pet laws & services; safety tips*

**185    Helpful Services**
*Domestic services; mail services; automobile repair; consumer protection; services for the disabled; gay and lesbian life; international newcomers*

**197    Childcare and Education**
*Childcare facilities and agencies; nanny and au pair services; public and private schools, homeschooling, online schools; higher education*

**215    Shopping for the Home**
*Malls/shopping centers, shopping districts, department stores, specialty shops, second-hand shopping; grocery stores, ethnic districts, and farmers' markets; restaurants, water, and wine*

**231    Cultural Life**
*Tickets; classical and contemporary music and dance; theater; concert facilities; comedy; museums; film houses and festivals; literary life; culture for kids*

**255    Sports and Recreation**
*Professional and college sports; participant sports, activities, and leagues; parks and recreation departments; outdoor recreation; winter sports; indoor games and recreation; health and activity clubs; sporting goods and outerwear*

**287    Greenspace and Beaches**
*Inland parks and parks with beaches: Northwest Seattle, Northeast Seattle, Southeast Seattle, Southwest Seattle, surrounding communities; state and national parks; forests; additional resources*

**297    Weather and Disaster Preparedness**
*Weather statistics; air pollution; Seasonal Affective Disorder; earthquakes; disaster preparedness*

# CONTENTS

**303 Places of Worship**
*Choosing a place of worship; historic worship centers; Buddhist, Christian, Hindu, Islamic, Jewish congregations; gay and lesbian congregations; non-traditional centers; religious studies*

**317 Volunteering**
*Volunteer centers and organizations*

**325 Transportation**
*Getting around by car, by bike, by public transportation, by regional and national transport; airlines and airports; travel resources*

**343 Temporary Lodgings**
*Hotels and motels; short-term rentals and residence hotels; bed & breakfasts; hostels and summer accommodations*

**351 Quick Getaways**
*Whidbey and San Juan Islands; Skagit Valley; British Columbia; East of the Cascades; Olympic Peninsula and Mountains; the Coast; Mount Rainier*

**357 A Seattle Year**
*January–December, annual events*

**367 A Seattle Reading List**
*Seattle architecture, art, community, family and pets; fiction; food and dining; history, outdoor guides, sports*

**371 Useful Phone Numbers and Web Sites**

**391 Index**

**401 About the Authors**

**403 Reader Response Form**

**405 Relocation Titles**

WELCOME TO SEATTLE, ONE OF THE MOST LIVABLE URBAN AREAS in the world! No doubt you've heard about the rain, but there's a lot more to the "Emerald City" than that. Part of the Pacific Northwest, Seattle is one of the most beautiful and lush regions in the United States. On a clear day, from atop every one of Seattle's many hills, you can view snow-capped mountains—including majestic Mount Rainier to the southeast—crystal-clear lakes, or the magnificent Puget Sound.

Don't be daunted by the rumors you've heard about Seattle and rain. While it's certainly true that the city has its share of rainy days, much of Seattle's rain is really a fine mist or drizzle. Often a day that starts off cloudy becomes bright and sunny by afternoon. Winters are wet but mild, averaging about five inches of rain per month from November to January, with temperatures seldom falling below the low- to mid-30s. Summers are comfortably warm, typically in the mid-70s. Spring and fall are cool but often sunny, and you'll enjoy some of the most spectacular views during these seasons, with snowy mountains set against a backdrop of radiantly clear, sunlit blue sky. Surprisingly, some residents prefer the cooler days, and as summer ends will tell you that they're relieved to be done with the weeks of "hot" temperatures. Most appreciate the rain, understanding that it is an indispensable factor in creating some of the wonderful characteristics of this area, such as the abundant green expanses, colorful rhododendrons, and plentiful lakes and waterways.

Situated between two bodies of water and two mountain ranges, Seattle has stunning vistas that can be enjoyed throughout the city. To the west is Puget Sound, an inland saltwater sea that connects to the Pacific Ocean. The Sound is what makes Washington immediately recognizable on every map of the United States, creating the Olympic Peninsula. Running along the middle of the peninsula are the Olympic Mountains (the "Olympics"), which are surrounded by forests and small logging towns. From Seattle, one can see the Olympics clearly, and recognize The Brothers, a twin-peaked mountain in the center of the range.

East of the city lies Lake Washington, 22 miles long and part of a system of lakes in the Seattle area that were formed by glaciers. Other lakes within the city include Lake Union, just north of downtown and connected by man-made channels to Lake Washington and Puget Sound, as well as Green Lake, Haller Lake, and Bitter Lake, all located in the north end of the city. All of these lakes are fed by mountain streams created by melting snow in the Cascades, a volcanic mountain range that runs the length of the state and separates Western and Eastern Washington. Mount Rainier is part of the Cascade Range, as are many smaller mountains that can be seen from vantage points throughout the city.

All of these natural wonders contribute to the abundant recreational opportunities that make Seattle a favorite of outdoor enthusiasts. From early spring to late summer, residents hike and camp in both the Cascades and the Olympics. There is water-skiing in nearby lakes, kayaking on the Sound, and fishing along the many rivers and streams. More intrepid adventurers travel to the eastern side of the Cascades for rock-climbing and bouldering, or head into the mountains for challenging mountain-climbing on Mount Rainier, Mount Baker, Mount Adams, or The Brothers. In the winter several popular ski resorts in the Cascades offer downhill skiing, snowboarding, and cross-country skiing. Those resorts on Snoqualmie Pass are just an hour drive from Seattle on I-90; others are slightly farther away on Mount Baker, Stevens Pass, and Mount Rainier.

Beneath the natural beauty, however, are problems. Puget Sound may sparkle on a clear day, but pollution is damaging the health of the waterway and its inhabitants. A large fish kill occurred during the summer of 2006 in Hood Canal, an offshoot of Puget Sound, caused in part by sewage runoff that helped to drastically drop oxygen levels. Red tide is common, which prompts shellfish harvesting bans. Puget Sound orcas (killer whales) were classified as an endangered species in 2005. Cleanup programs exist, but it remains to be seen if they will be enough to reverse the damage. If you take advantage of the many water-based recreational activities, remember to minimize your "footprint" just as you would do on land. Don't toss litter in the water or dump human waste overboard. Think about kayaking instead of power boating, and support organizations that are working to minimize pollution, such as the Puget Soundkeeper Alliance.

In addition to the mild weather and the natural beauty of the area, Seattle and its surrounding communities also share a dynamic economy. Just ten minutes east of Seattle lies the city of Bellevue, home to the world's richest man, Bill Gates, and just ten minutes east of Bellevue lies the town of Redmond, home to Gates' company, Microsoft. Other national giants headquartered here include Amazon.com, Eddie Bauer, Starbucks, and REI. While the recession of 2001 hit the Seattle area pretty hard, the economy has been on the rebound since 2003 and the Puget Sound Regional Council estimates that there will be 1.6 million jobs in the area by 2010, and more than 2 million by 2030.

Since the beginning of the new millennium, the rebounding economy and beautiful surroundings have brought thousands of newcomers to Seattle. King, Snohomish, Kitsap, and Pierce counties, which make up the Seattle metropolitan area, added over 184,500 new people since the 2000 census, for a total of 3.46 million. Seattle ended 2004 with a population of 572,600. While the pace of growth has slowed, by 2030 the expected population of the metropolitan area will be around 5 million people.

To accommodate the influx, city townhouses and condominiums have slowly replaced single-family houses with large yards. The demand for condos in downtown Seattle areas like Belltown, and the neighborhood that is still being built in South Lake Union, is high, and new condos in Ballard are being snapped up before construction is finished. According to the Census Bureau and a 2006 Associated Press article, Seattle is the country's most educated city, with a higher percentage of college graduates than any other big city. These grads are attracted to a hip, urban lifestyle in Seattle and are helping to drive the demand for downtown living. While some Seattle homes are still affordable for middle-income and first-time homebuyers, housing prices have continued their relentless upward march. With the increased demand for housing, some formerly overlooked Seattle neighborhoods, like South Park, Beacon Hill, and the Central District, are now being revitalized, with old homes remodeled and new houses built in these areas. Other newcomers, especially those with families, are opting for homes outside the city limits.

Seattle entered the national spotlight in the 1990s, making espresso (Starbucks), "grunge" music (Nirvana, Pearl Jam), microbrews (Red Hook), and software (Microsoft) a daily part of US culture. In recent years, the city's residents have added fine dining and football to their list of favorite leisure pursuits. Growth, prosperity, and an influx of young, hip college graduates have generated a wealth of highly rated new restaurants, and a berth in the 2006 Super Bowl made the Seattle Seahawks the new pride of the city. In addition, Seattle has a thriving and nationally recognized performing arts community, including the Seattle Symphony, the Seattle Opera, and the Pacific Northwest Ballet, as well as several theatrical companies including Intiman, the Seattle Repertory Theatre, and A Contemporary Theater.

As newcomers soon learn, conversations here, which used to revolve primarily around microbrews, coffee, computers, and the weather, now lament the traffic. The Texas Transportation Institute's annual study of 75 urban areas listed Seattle as having the 12th worst commute time in 2003. The institute also estimated that travelers in the region experience 47 hours of delay each year. Your daily commute is an extremely important factor to consider when choosing a place to live here, especially if your route includes either of the two bridges.

Highway 520 and Interstate 90 run along bridges that span Lake Washington, connecting Seattle with the Eastside communities, which include Bellevue, Kirkland, Issaquah, Renton, Redmond, and Woodinville. Both bridges create traffic bottlenecks during rush hour. On the bright side, the views of Lake Washington and Mount Rainier from the bridge decks are amazing!

As Seattle continues to grow, another point of concern for new and old residents alike is personal safety. In the past several years, Seattle's crime rates have remained level or have declined, due in part to strong community involvement. Exceptions, however, are auto thefts and car prowls—car break-ins and burglary—that are a serious problem throughout the state and continue to plague residents despite efforts by local police agencies. No matter which neighborhood you choose, take precautions to avoid becoming a target: lock your car and remove valuables, and park in well-lighted areas. As in any major city, be sure to take reasonable precautions when in unfamiliar surroundings. Keep money and other possessions out of sight, and avoid exploring new neighborhoods after dark. Consider getting a steering wheel locking device or a security system. (For more tips on keeping safe in Seattle, see the **Safety** section in **Getting Settled**.)

## LOCAL LINGO

While you won't hear a distinctive accent when people talk here, the Northwest is loaded with Native American place names, which can be difficult to pronounce correctly. In addition, many places have nicknames or shortened names. As with most slang, there are no general rules, but if you remember that the main freeway is "I-5" and not "the I-5" and that when people say "the mountain is out," it's a general statement about how nice the weather is, you'll be talking like a native in no time. The following list is not comprehensive, but it will give you a head start.

**Alki:** pronounced "alk-eye"; a popular beach and recreation area where the founders of the city first landed.
**The Ave:** short for University Way NE, the main business street in the University District.
**The Eastside:** encompasses all the cities east of Lake Washington, including Bellevue, Issaquah, Kirkland and Redmond.
**Geoduck:** this large clam with a long neck is pronounced "gooey-duck"
**Issaquah:** city on the Eastside pronounced "IZ-a-kwah"
**The Locks:** boats pass through the Ballard Locks to and from Puget Sound and Lake Union, officially known as the Hiram M. Chittenden Locks, which generally no one remembers.

**The Market:** the Pike Place Market. Note that it is not correct to say "Pike's" or "Pike Street" when using the full name.

**Nordy's:** affectionate shortening of Nordstrom, the department store that originated in Seattle. Note that while "Nordy's" works as a nickname, it is not correct to say "Nordstrom's."

**The Pass:** There are several passes over the Cascade Mountains, but in Seattle and the surrounding areas, if you say "the Pass," everyone will assume you're talking about Snoqualmie Pass, an hour east of the city.

**Pill Hill:** the nickname for First Hill, home to hospitals and medical clinics.

**Puyallup:** pronounced "PYEW-alup" (as in gallop), this city south of Seattle is home to the popular, annual Puyallup Fair.

**SAM:** the Seattle Art Museum, say it like the name "Sam."

**Sammamish:** pronounced "suh-MAM-ish," a lake and town on the Eastside.

**Sequim:** pronounced "Skwim," a town on the Olympic Peninsula, known for the lavender grown there and as the driest city in Western Washington.

**Snoqualmie:** pronounced "snow-KWAH-me"—you rarely hear the "l" in the word.

**The Sound:** Puget Sound is never "Puget's Sound" and saying "the Puget Sound" will rarely work in conversation. Just go with "the Sound" and people will know what you're talking about.

**UW:** Shortened, and pronounced "U-Dub," as a nickname for the University of Washington.

**WSU:** pronounced "Wa-zoo" as a nickname for Washington State University in eastern Washington, especially good to know during the Apple Cup, the annual football battle between the rivals UW and WSU.

## WHAT TO BRING

- **A detailed map**; although most of Seattle proper is on a straightforward grid, many of the major streets don't follow the rules. You can purchase a handy laminated Rand McNally fold-out map or the comprehensive Thomas Brothers Map Guide from First Books (www.firstbooks.com), publisher of this Newcomer's Handbook®.

- **A car**; public transportation (buses, monorail, ferries) is available, but it can be time consuming to explore the city without a car. Buses stop at nearly every block, and transferring buses can cause long delays. If a car is not possible, expect to spend some time getting used to the bus routes and schedules; and don't try to travel around at night by bus without checking the schedule beforehand—many buses stop running or change routes early in the evening.

- **An umbrella or rain hat**; most likely it will be raining when you arrive. Also bring a lightweight but warm jacket. Temperatures and weather conditions can vary sharply during the day, going from sunny and warm to cold and rainy within a few minutes. However, after you've been here a while, you may find yourself adopting the local disdain for umbrellas and a relaxed attitude about getting wet (it's a fact of life).
- **A cell phone,** which is convenient for contacting potential landlords from the road. If you plan to search the classifieds for your new abode, get a jump on the competition by picking up the Sunday edition of *The Seattle Times/Seattle Post-Intelligencer* on Friday night. The paper is available at most grocery and convenience stores.
- **A good attitude and a smile**; while most people in Seattle are helpful and outgoing, you'll notice a layer of reticence when meeting strangers. Some have dubbed the phenomenon the "Seattle Freeze," noting that people are very polite but not particularly friendly. A little effort can thaw the freeze, so consider joining activity or social groups as a way to meet people when you get here. With a little patience and a calm demeanor you'll be able to get help from just about anybody in Seattle. So stop in, have a café latte, and stay for a while or forever. Welcome to Seattle, a wonderful place to live!

# HISTORY

Seattle was founded on its present site in February 1852, four months after the first party of white settlers landed the schooner *Exact* on Alki Point, in what is now known as West Seattle. This group, known as the Denny Party, included Arthur Denny and his family, his brother David, as well as the Lows, the Bells, the Borens, and the Terrys. Many of the city streets are named after these founders of Seattle. In early 1852 Denny, Low, and Boren set out in a canoe to find a more sheltered area for their settlement. They crossed Elliott Bay and, measuring the depth of the bay using a piece of rope and a horseshoe, chose a harbor for their new city (Seattle) just west of what is now Pioneer Square.

Seattle is named for Chief Sealth, a Salish Indian. Dr. David "Doc" Maynard, who arrived in 1852 and started Seattle's first store and hospital, was instrumental in naming the city. Maynard was a friend of Chief Sealth's and suggested Seattle as a more easily pronounced version of the Chief's name. Maynard thought the original name for the settlement, Duwamps, a derivative of the name for one of the Indian tribes that lived around Elliott Bay, the Duwampish or Duwamish, might not attract visitors or new settlers to the area. The other nearby tribe, the Salish or Suquamish, lived between the Bay and what is now Lake Washington. There may have been additional tribes in the Seattle area, but because Native Americans around the Puget Sound were a loose-knit group, it is not clear how many separate tribes were here originally. What is clear, however, is that all of the area tribes were jointly represented by Chief Sealth. These tribes remained in the area until 1855 when, after some minor skirmishes between the settlers and the Indians, they were relocated to the Suquamish Indian Reservation across Puget Sound. Chief Sealth's farewell speech is an oft-quoted piece of Seattle history, and an inspiring reminder of the great Native American leader.

Henry Yesler, another of Seattle's most prominent and influential citizens, arrived in the fall of 1852, soon after Doc Maynard. Yesler was a tight-fisted businessman who, in 1853, built a sawmill, cookhouse, and a meeting hall, all firsts for the new city. The sawmill initially received its supply of lumber from the heavily wooded hills east of the settlement, areas that are now a part of the city. The trees were pushed to the mill down a slick wooden slipway, built into the side of a hill in downtown Seattle. The term "skid road" or "skid row," coined for this innovative contrivance, quickly became synonymous with the run-down streets and rowdy behavior of the mill workers who lived in that area.

On June 6, 1889, near what is now 1st Avenue and Madison Street, a glue pot caught fire in a carpenter's workshop, starting the Great Seattle Fire. Coming after an unusual early summer drought, the fire quickly burned down every building within a 60-acre area. Soon after the fire, city officials passed an ordinance requiring that new buildings be constructed of bricks or stone. The buildings destroyed in the fire were swiftly rebuilt under these new regulations. Surprisingly, the result of the fire was a strengthened city economy, as the rebuilding projects provided much needed business to local bricklayers and builders. The sawmill was not adversely affected because demand for lumber was still great in California, and most of what was produced at Yesler's mill was shipped to San Francisco. However, the fire and subsequent renovations did have one strange consequence. The city, taking advantage of the opportunity to correct some of the drainage problems that had plagued downtown, constructed streets at a level 12 feet higher than they had been before the fire. However, some merchants rebuilt businesses at their original level, leading to sharp inclines between the city-owned streets and the privately owned sidewalks. Eventually the city put in new sidewalks at the higher street level, and the first floors of these downtown buildings became basements and open spaces. For many years these spaces were used as an underground mall, housing legitimate businesses; they later became infamous as opium dens, brothels, and moonshine establishments. Today, the Seattle Underground Tour is a popular tourist attraction that takes visitors through some of the original labyrinthine tunnels under downtown.

During the late 1800s, gold was discovered in several nearby locations, including the Fraser River in British Columbia, Boise and Coeur d'Alene in Idaho, and the Sultan and Skagit rivers in Washington. Though gold was never present in Seattle itself, the city served many of these locations as a supplier of prospecting goods. In 1877, the Seattle & Walla Walla Railroad was constructed to transport coal (which had replaced lumber as the city's major export) from

Renton to Seattle. Then in 1893, the Great Northern Railroad placed its western terminus in Seattle, and the Northern Pacific Railroad Co. bought land in Seattle, extending its western route from Tacoma to Seattle. These events nicely positioned the manufacturers and merchants of Seattle, who were able to reap immense profits during Canada's Klondike gold rush. The rush, which officially began in the summer of 1897 when the steamer *Portland* docked in Seattle carrying "a ton of gold," brought prospectors through Seattle, many of whom geared up here for their expeditions. Seattle also benefited from the gold rush by opening its first assay office, establishing the city as a regional financial center as well as a port and manufacturing city.

By the 20th century, Seattle was a prosperous city with both an expanding population and business community. The need for more space inspired the Denny Regrade project, which began in 1907. Originally, in addition to First Hill, Capitol Hill, and Queen Anne Hill, there was another hill located at the north end of the city center, known as Denny Hill. The hill (actually a bluff overlooking Elliott Bay) prevented easy expansion of the downtown, standing, as it did, 190 feet above the level of nearby Pioneer Square. In 1898 some of the western side of the hill had been carted away to fill in around Western Avenue and Alaskan Way. In 1907, the project of regrading the entire hill began in earnest, primarily funded by private property owners. The dirt was hauled away and dumped into Elliott Bay, creating much of the current Seattle waterfront as well as the land that connects Downtown with the Duwamish River neighborhoods. Completed in 1931, the Denny Regrade is now the site of much of downtown, including the Belltown neighborhood.

The Seattle population has increased steadily since the early 1900s and the city has spread out, enveloping many communities that were originally suburbs. When Seattle hosted the World's Fair in 1962, it built a 74-acre campus that featured the Space Needle and the International Fountain. Today this site, known as Seattle Center, is home to 21 arts, science, and sports organizations, including Key Arena, the Seattle Opera, and the Pacific Science Center, as well as the monorail to downtown.

Since the 1980s the area has been regularly ranked as one of America's most livable cities, and the resulting influx of newcomers has added to an already growing population. Washington's natural resources have so far provided for such basic needs as water and electricity, and, until recently, the size of the city has provided for plenty of open space and housing, as well as a pleasant small town culture. Today, much of that is changing as Seattle braces for additional population growth and expansion issues such as adequate public transportation and affordable in-city housing.

# SEATTLE ADDRESS LOCATOR

Before going into the neighborhood profiles, we have provided tips for getting around Seattle and the Eastside, and then metro-wide county information, which should prove helpful as you begin your search for a home.

While most Seattle streets stick to a grid pattern, running east-west or north-south, others meander seemingly aimlessly through several neighborhoods. The information here will give you a good starting point for finding your way around the city, but a map or street atlas is highly recommended. The guidelines below apply only to streets within Seattle proper, or immediately north or south of the city limits. Other suburbs and communities use different methods for assigning addresses. The Thomas Guide for Metropolitan Puget Sound covers the Seattle metropolitan area, as well as cities in King, Pierce, and Snohomish counties. You can get one at a bookstore or office supply outlet, or order online at www.firstbooks.com.

The **center of the Seattle grid** is at 1st and Yesler. Street names outside downtown are provided with a North, East, South, West, NE, NW, SE, SW location tag. The tag indicates location relative to the center. Downtown streets have no location tag, and run northwest-southeast (parallel to the shore of Elliott Bay) or northeast-southwest. Outside the downtown area, most Seattle streets run north-south or east-west. Street and house numbers increase as you move away from downtown.

North-south streets are called "avenues" with the location tag at the end; for instance, 24th Avenue NW or 32nd Avenue South. Roads that run east-west are "streets" with the location tag at the beginning; for instance, NE 49th Street or SW Spokane Street. Most avenues in the city are numbered. South of the Lake Washington Ship Canal (which bisects the city north of downtown, and connects Lake Washington and Lake Union to the Puget Sound), most streets have names rather than numbers, such as Union Street or East Aloha Street. North of the ship canal, streets are numbered. Location tags are assigned as follows:

*North of Denny Way, as far as the Lake Washington Ship Canal,* streets are labeled:

- **West** if they are located west of 1st Avenue North, in Magnolia and parts of Queen Anne;
- **North** if they are located directly north of downtown, on Queen Anne and around Lake Union or between 1st Avenue North and Eastlake Avenue East;
- **East** if they are located east of Lake Union, in Eastlake and Montlake.

*North of the Lake Washington Ship Canal,* streets are labeled:

- **NW** if they are located north of the ship canal and west of 1st Avenue NW, in Ballard and Broadview;

- **North** if they are directly north of downtown between 1st Avenue NW and 1st Avenue NE, in Phinney Ridge, Green Lake, Wallingford, and Northgate;
- **NE** if they are north of the ship canal and east of 1st Avenue NE, in Lake City, the University District and Sand Point.

*South of Yesler Way*, all streets are labeled:
- **South** if they are located south of downtown and east of 1st Avenue South, in Rainier Valley, Mount Baker and Beacon Hill;
- **SW** if they are located southwest of downtown and west of 1st Avenue South, in West Seattle.

Between the Lake Washington Ship Canal and Yesler Way, and east of Lake Union, all east-west–running streets are labeled East, including those in Madrona, Leschi, the Central District, Capitol Hill, and Madison Park. However, north-south streets in this area have no location tags.

Several main thoroughfares don't follow all of the above rules. For example:

- **Martin Luther King Jr. Way**: "MLK" begins at Madison Street at the north end of the Central Area, and runs south through the Central Area, Madrona, Leschi, Beacon Hill, Mount Baker, and Rainier Valley.
- **Boren Avenue/Rainier Avenue South**: Boren Avenue runs northwest-southeast over First Hill. South of Jackson Street, Boren Avenue becomes Rainier Avenue South, and continues southeast through the south end of the Central Area and into the Rainier Valley.
- **Madison Street**: One of the city's most convenient streets, Madison Street runs east from downtown, through First Hill and Capitol Hill, and along the north end of the Central Area to Madison Park on Lake Washington.

Useful highways within Seattle are listed below. Be careful of these "thoroughfares" at rush hour:

- **Interstate 5**: I-5 runs north-south through the city and is the most commonly used thoroughfare in Seattle.
- **Interstate 90**: I-90 begins at Safeco Field in downtown Seattle and runs east. The I-90 bridge is the only roadway to Mercer Island, and has more lanes in either direction than the Highway 520 bridge to the north.
- **Highway 520**: a state highway connecting I-5 (at the north end of Capitol Hill) with the Eastside communities of Bellevue, Kirkland, and Redmond, the 520 bridge is always packed during rush hour.
- **Highway 99**: running parallel to, but west of, I-5 through Seattle, Highway 99 begins as Aurora Avenue in the north end, where it is a major thoroughfare lined with strip malls, inexpensive hotels, and other businesses. Crossing

the Lake Washington Ship Canal into the city, Highway 99 runs through the Battery Street Tunnel and becomes the Alaskan Way Viaduct, a large stacked highway along the waterfront. South of the waterfront, Highway 99 becomes East Marginal Way South and eventually Pacific Highway.

- **Highway 522**: commonly known as Lake City Way NE, Highway 522 begins at NE 75th Street, runs northeast through the Lake City neighborhood to Lake Washington, and eventually turns into Bothell Way NE at the north end of the lake.
- **West Seattle Freeway**: the West Seattle Freeway connects both I-5 (at Beacon Hill) and Highway 99 with the West Seattle peninsula.

## GETTING AROUND THE EASTSIDE

There are two highways that transport travelers from Seattle to the Eastside via a pair of floating bridges: Interstate 90, via the I-90 bridge, and Highway 520, via the Evergreen Floating Bridge. Interstate 90 brushes up against the Mount Baker neighborhood, crosses Lake Washington to Mercer Island, and passes through Bellevue, Issaquah, and Snoqualmie before crossing the Cascade Mountains into Eastern Washington. Highway 520 begins in Montlake north of downtown Seattle, crosses Lake Washington and passes through Bellevue and Kirkland before its end in Redmond.

Interstate 405 runs north-south from Renton in the south to Lynnwood in the north, and is commonly used as a connector to either I-90 or Highway 520, as well as other less traveled roads on the Eastside. Other primary thoroughfares include the Redmond–Fall City Road (Highway 202), which connects Kirkland, Redmond, Fall City, Snoqualmie and North Bend; Highway 522 runs from Bothell to Monroe and passes through Woodinville.

It's no secret that traffic in the Seattle area is a challenge. The Eastside may be worse. Dramatic growth over the last decade has flooded the community's streets and highways with commuters. There are ways to avoid the rush hour headache, however. If your employer offers flexible hours, consider working outside the standard 8 a.m. to 5 p.m. You may want to carpool with your co-workers. The diamond (carpool) lanes offer quicker commutes and relief from stop-and-go traffic. See the **Transportation** chapter for information on Metro Transit carpool programs. King County, which encompasses the Eastside, offers a comprehensive online commuting resource called "My Commute," complete with traffic cams and flow maps, at www.metrokc.gov/kcdot/mycommute. If you must drive to the city during rush hour, there isn't much you can do but grin and bear it.

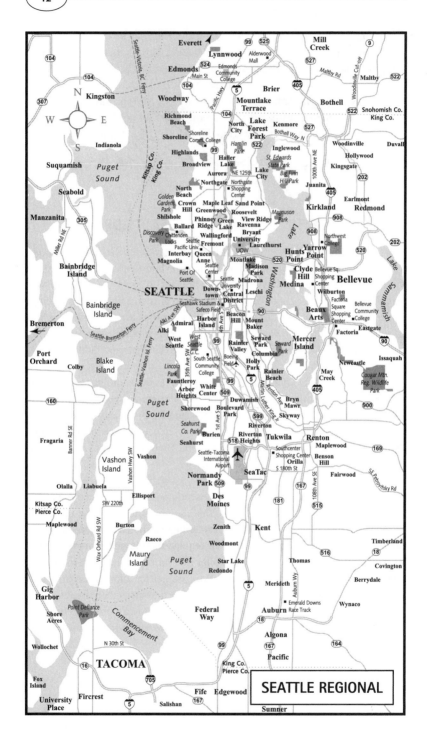

SEATTLE REGIONAL

## SEATTLE AREA COUNTIES

## KING COUNTY

KING COUNTY IS ONE OF THE LARGEST COUNTIES IN THE UNITed States, covering more than 2,200 square miles and serving 1.5 million residents. The county stretches from Bothell and Shoreline in the north to Enumclaw in the south. Bordered by Puget Sound to the west, the county includes Vashon Island. The county's eastern border abuts the Cedar and Green River watersheds, as well as the Alpine Lakes Wilderness.

Cities served by King County include, from north to south: Bothell, Kenmore, Lake Forest Park, Shoreline, Woodinville, Duvall, Skykomish, Redmond, Kirkland, Carnation, Bellevue, Seattle, Sammamish, Mercer Island, Snoqualmie, Issaquah, North Bend, Renton, Burien, Tukwila, SeaTac, Des Moines, Kent, Maple Valley, Federal Way, Black Diamond, Auburn, and Enumclaw.

Outside the cities, the county provides services to regions that lie in "unincorporated King County." In addition to what is available to all county residents, like courts, public health, and property tax appraisals, the county may also provide additional local services, like land-use regulation, emergency management, and county parks.

**County Executive:** elected to a four-year term by county voters; King County Courthouse, 516 Third Ave, Rm 400, Seattle, 206-296-4040, www.metrokc.gov/exec

**County Council:** the Metropolitan King County Council consists of 13 members who represent geographic districts throughout the county; King County Courthouse, 516 Third Ave, Rm 1200, Seattle, 206-296-1000, www.metrokc.gov/mkcc

**County Map:** www.metrokc.gov/kcmap.htm

**Government:** King County Courthouse, 516 Third Ave, Seattle, 206-296-0100, www.metrokc.gov

**Libraries:** the King County Library System is the third-largest circulating library in the United States, with 41 libraries and a traveling library center; 960 Newport Way NW, Issaquah, 425-369-3200, www.kcls.org

**Sheriff:** King County Sheriff's Office, 516 Third Ave, Room W-116, Seattle, 206-296-4155, www.metrokc.gov/sheriff

**Online:** www.metrokc.gov

## KITSAP COUNTY

Kitsap County is located on Kitsap Peninsula, across the Puget Sound from Seattle. One of the state's smallest counties, it is bordered by Hood Canal on the west, Puget Sound on the east, and Mason and Pierce counties to the south. The county seat is located in the town of Port Orchard. The city of Bremerton, home of the Puget Sound Naval Shipyard, has been undergoing a revitalization of its waterfront and downtown core and is becoming a more attractive option for those who work in Seattle but find Seattle home prices too expensive. It's a 60-minute ferry ride between Bremerton and Colman Dock on the Seattle waterfront, but many commuters take advantage of passenger-only ferries.

Bainbridge Island is only a 35-minute ride to Seattle and continues to be home to many commuters.

**County Board of Commissioners:** one commissioner is elected from each of three districts; 614 Division St, Port Orchard, 360-337-7146, www.kitsapgov.com/boc

**County Clerk:** an elected official who serves as the county's administrative and financial officer; 614 Division St, Rm 202, Port Orchard, 360-337-7164, www.kitsapgov.com/clerk

**Government:** 614 Division St, Port Orchard, 360-337-7150, www.kitsapgov.com

**Libraries:** the Kitsap Regional Library System includes nine community branches, a bookmobile and outreach services; 1301 Sylvan Way, Bremerton, 360-405-9119, www.krl.org

**Sheriff:** Kitsap County Sheriff's Office, 614 Division St, Port Orchard, 360-337-7101, www.kitsapgov.com/sheriff

**Online:** www.kitsapgov.com

## PIERCE COUNTY

South of King County is Pierce County, a region of 1,790 square miles with a population of about 713,000. The county's primary city is **Tacoma**. The northern border of Pierce County is located just south of Federal Way, and a bit north of Tacoma, about a 40-minute drive from Seattle mid-day or in the evening, and well over an hour during rush hour. For that reason, few commuters make the trek from Tacoma to Seattle each day, although more Seattleites have moved to Pierce County in recent years as they seek lower home prices.

Outside of Tacoma, Pierce County is a mix of rural communities and new housing developments. The county is also home to Fort Lewis, which consists of 87,000 acres that house and/or employ over 24,000 soldiers and civilians.

**County Council:** consists of seven members who are elected in their respective districts; 930 Tacoma Ave S, Tacoma, 253-798-7777, www.co.pierce.wa.us
**County Executive:** elected official serves as the chief executive officer of the county; 930 Tacoma Ave S, Tacoma, 253-798-7477, www.co.pierce.wa.us
**Government:** 930 Tacoma Ave S, Tacoma, 253-798-7272, www.co.pierce.wa.us
**Libraries:** the Pierce County Library System includes 20 neighborhood branches and two bookmobiles; 3005 112th St E, Tacoma, 253-536-6500, www.pcl.lib. wa.us
**Sheriff:** 930 Tacoma Ave S, Tacoma, 253-798-7530, www.co.pierce.wa.us
**Online:** www.co.pierce.wa.us

# SNOHOMISH COUNTY

Snohomish County is located north of King County. It covers just under 3,000 square miles and borders the Puget Sound to the west, Chelan County to the east, and Skagit County to the north. At its southern boundary is **Bothell**, which straddles the border of King and Snohomish counties. Other Snohomish County cities are **Edmonds**, **Mountlake Terrace**, **Lynnwood**, and **Everett**, which has served as the county seat since 1897.

Between 2000 and 2005, Snohomish County grew by 8.2%, to over 655,000 residents. By the year 2025 it is expected that the county will have grown by 49%, adding nearly 305,000 new residents.

**County Council:** the five members of the council are elected to four-year terms; 3000 Rockefeller, Everett, 425-388-3494, www1.co.snohomish.wa.us/ departments/council
**County Executive:** elected to a four-year term; 3000 Rockefeller, Everett, 425-388-3460, www1.co.snohomish.wa.us/departments/executive
**Government:** 3000 Rockefeller, Everett, 425-388-3411, www1.co.snohomish. wa.us
**Libraries:** the Sno-Isle Regional Library System serves more than half a million residents in Snohomish and Island counties through 20 community libraries,

four outreach vans and a bookmobile; 7312 35th Ave NE, Marysville, 360-651-7000, www.sno-isle.org

**Sheriff:** the Snohomish County Sheriff is elected to a four-year term; 3000 Rockefeller, Everett, 425-388-3393, www1.co.snohomish.wa.us/departments/sheriff

**Online:** www1.co.snohomish.wa.us

## SEATTLE NEIGHBORHOODS

As with many large and growing US cities, most of Seattle's neighborhoods began as small communities located outside the city limits. As Seattle expanded over the years, the city annexed many of these small mill towns and commerce centers. While the old village names survive as neighborhood monikers, so do many of the original neighborhood names. A good example of this can be seen in Ballard, where residents may refer to their homes as being in Shilshole, North Beach, Sunset Hill, Blue Ridge, or Crown Hill, all of which are located in the larger neighborhood of Ballard.

As you explore Seattle, you may notice certain repeating housing styles. Most Seattle neighborhoods have only gradually grown denser and more urban, so it is common to see several types of houses on a single residential city block. Victorians dating from the late 1800s, with their turreted front rooms and ornamented rooflines, are in most downtown neighborhoods, sitting alongside Craftsman-style bungalows, Tudors, Colonials, and Northwest Moderns.

The Northwest Modern or "Classic Box" style of architecture is one of the most plentiful, introduced in Seattle around the turn of the 20th century and instantly popular with local architects and builders. Also known as the "Capitol Hill Box" because of the number of these houses in the Capitol Hill neighborhood, this style was still being built in Seattle as late as the 1940s. Classic Box houses are large, two-story, four-square structures with symmetrical windows, front porches, hardwood floors, and high ceilings. The slope of the Classic Box roof starts above the entire square of the second story, so that the upstairs rooms are often the same in size and number as those below. Bungalows were introduced in Seattle in the early 1900s, appearing in the architectural pattern books that were a mainstay of local builders. In particular, the Arts-and-Crafts and Craftsman-style bungalows were popular in the city. Unlike the Classic Box, the bungalow is characterized by a sloped second-story roof, usually with one or two front gables and bracketed roof overhangs. These homes typically have three to four large bedrooms, oak or fir floors, and original built-in cabinetry.

Elaborate and symmetrical Colonials and Dutch Colonials, often referred to as "barn houses" for their distinctive shape, were built throughout Seattle in the decades between the two world wars. Tudors, recognizable for their steep roofs, arched doorways, and leaded windows, dot Seattle neighborhoods, as do simple Cape Cod cottages. Some north Seattle neighborhoods contain examples of the ranch house, also called ramblers. Built in the 1940s and 1950s and related to the Prairie School style created by Frank Lloyd Wright, these are sprawling single-story brick houses with giant picture windows. Olympic Manor, in the north end of Ballard, is built almost entirely in this style.

Seattleites are proud of where they live, a fact exemplified by the large number of community centers and organizations, neighborhood newspapers, and bustling corner coffee shops. Seattle's **Department of Neighborhoods** (206-684-0464, www.cityofseattle.net/neighborhoods/) runs the neighborhood service centers (listed after each profile), and administers neighborhood matching funds for local projects. Community newspapers, usually free, provide valuable information about local issues, upcoming events, and activities. Every neighborhood in Seattle has at least one coffeehouse or espresso stand, which is often a good place to start your exploration of a particular area. See the neighborhood resources that follow each neighborhood profile for information about organizations, publications, post offices, nearest emergency hospitals, and public transportation routes. (Note: only bus numbers are provided for routes running through neighborhoods. Check with Metro Transit, 206-553-3000, http://transit.metrokc.gov, for specifics on route origins and final destinations, route maps, and a trip planner.)

Unlike many other major cities, Seattle's neighborhoods do not have official borders. Those listed in this book reflect widely accepted neighborhood boundaries, many of which are guided by simple geography. For instance, many of Seattle's neighborhoods sit atop a single hill, separated by a miniature "valley" from the next neighborhood. The following neighborhood profiles are only those located within the city limits. Other communities, such as Bellevue, Redmond, Everett, and Renton are not a part of the city, but may interest newcomers; you will find these and others profiled in the **Surrounding Communities** section.

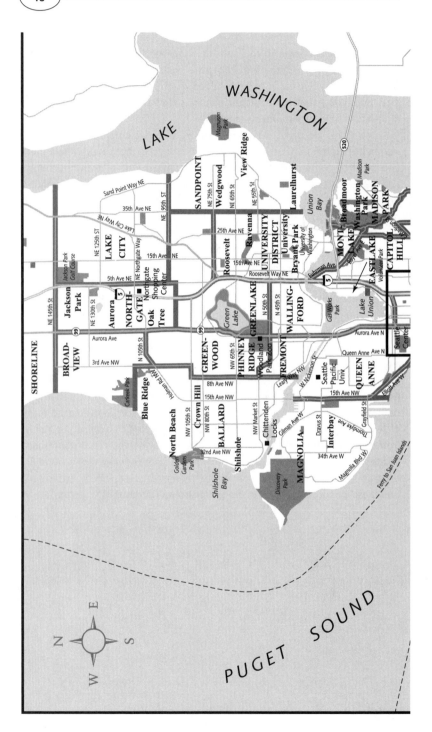

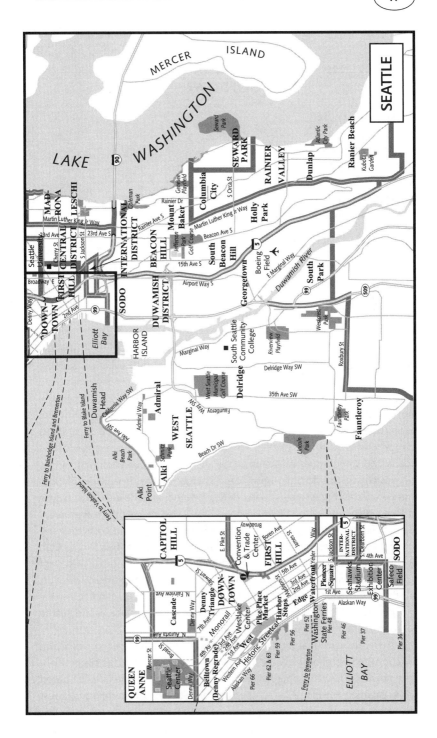

# SEATTLE—KING COUNTY

## DOWNTOWN

**PIONEER SQUARE**
**WEST EDGE**
**PIKE PLACE MARKET**
**HARBOR STEPS**
**BELLTOWN**
**WATERFRONT**
**DENNY TRIANGLE**
**CASCADE**

**Boundaries: North**: Denny Way, Mercer Street; **West**: Elliott Bay; **South**: South Royal Brougham Way, South Jackson Street; **East**: Interstate 5

**Pioneer Square** is perhaps the best-known and most historic of all districts in the Downtown area. Located near the site of Henry Yesler's sawmill and the original "skid road" (now Yesler Way), Pioneer Square was quickly rebuilt after the Great Seattle Fire of 1889 destroyed much of early Seattle. The Pioneer Building at 1st Avenue and James Street is one of the oldest buildings in Seattle, designed in 1889 by architect Elmer H. Fisher, at the request of Henry Yesler. Today, the brothels and gambling dens are long gone and Pioneer Square is a flourishing business and retail district. Small business offices are located in the upper floors of most of the old stone buildings. Oriental rug sellers, antique shops, sporting goods stores, bookstores, cafés, and art galleries fill the ground floor spaces.

Also home to a dynamic music scene, Pioneer Square's bars fill nightly with music-lovers and party-goers. Many of Seattle's influential bands have played in area clubs, such as the Central Saloon. The New Orleans Creole Restaurant features fine blues and jazz musicians; the Fenix Underground hosts rock and alternative bands; and hipsters dance the night away at the Ibiza Dinner Club or Trinity Nightclub. Joint cover is offered on the weekends for those who want to visit several bars in one evening. Fat Tuesday, Seattle's Mardi Gras celebration, fills the district with revelers for a week of music and festivities (and occasional violent clashes). Pioneer Square is also a popular meeting place before Seattle sporting events.

There are several apartment buildings in Pioneer Square, most of which are converted warehouses. While this is a busy, exciting part of the city, residentially speaking, it's most appropriate for residents comfortable in a fast-paced urban environment. In the days of the Kingdome, before Safeco Field and Qwest Field were built, this area was an inexpensive part of the city in which to live, and as a result several homeless shelters were placed here. Today, intermingled with expensive new developments and refurbished high-tech office spaces, these residences for the down-and-out remain. In less prosperous times, Pioneer Square was home to numerous artists' residences and workspaces, but many artists were squeezed out by rising rents. In early 2000, the Washington Shoe Building, which once housed five floors of galleries and artists' studios, closed its doors. The building has been transformed into an office block with a posh, top-floor penthouse. Many of the displaced residents moved south to Georgetown, but 50 artists and their families found homes in the Tashiro Kaplan Artists Lofts located on Prefontaine Place South. The two former commercial buildings were renovated as gallery and living spaces and completed in 2004.

In September of 2001, the Downtown Seattle Association and then-Mayor Paul Schell christened the new **West Edge** neighborhood, an area bordered by Lenora Street to the north, Cherry Street to the south, Second Avenue to the east, and Western Avenue to the west. Essentially a marketing tool to attract more diners and shoppers, most residents continue to use more familiar downtown neighborhood names, like Pike Place and Harbor Steps, when referring to this general area.

Established in 1907, the **Pike Place Market** is Seattle's most beloved Downtown landmark. City dwellers come here first with their out-of-town guests to see the fish-throwers at the seafood stands, sample teas at Market Spice, or listen to talented street musicians. Many Seattle residents frequent Pike Place weekly for fresh fruits and vegetables, fish and shellfish, teas and coffees, and baked goods.

Local farmers who wanted to sell their produce without the involvement of middlemen organized the market. Gradually fish and meat were added to the available goods, then bakeries and cafés moved in, soon followed by folks selling jewelry, pottery, honey, flowers, kites, and coffees. Today, you can find just about anything at the Market, from the best local tomatoes and homemade jams to kitchen wares and furniture. Many of these products are sold in shops in the blocks around the Market itself, or in the Corner Market Building, designed in 1912, and located at the corner of 1st Avenue and Pike Street. A few blocks south of Pike Place is the magnificent Seattle Art Museum with its notable "A Hammering Man" sculpture facing the waterfront.

A short stroll from Pike Place Market is **Harbor Steps**, one of Seattle's newer neighborhoods and a perfect example of Downtown's ongoing revitalization. Whereas many Seattle communities were named for their proximity to water (Green Lake, Eastlake), Harbor Steps was named for a wide outdoor staircase that climbs from Western Avenue, near the waterfront, to First Avenue at University Street. The Harbor Steps Apartments (www.harborsteps.com) opened in 1992 and now houses about 1,200 residents, with rents ranging from $1,000 to $5,000+ per month. The complex's four high-rise towers feature private balconies and expansive glass windows, offering residents sublime views of the city, sound, and mountains. Residents range from young singles to retired couples, empty nesters, and executives moving here from around the world. The small, upscale community is also home to Harbor Steps Park, the Inn at Harbor Steps, and a selection of upscale restaurants, boutiques, and galleries.

Located north of the Pike Place Market and centered around 2nd Avenue and Bell Street, **Belltown** is a part of the Denny Regrade, a section of Downtown created when Denny Hill was flattened in the early 1900s. The earth of the original steep bluff that stood in this area was carted off and dumped into Elliott Bay, creating part of what is now the Waterfront area. Like Pioneer Square, the Belltown district is a hub for Seattle's nightlife and music scene. The Crocodile Café on 2nd Avenue is a great club for new and local bands; the Moore Theater, also on 2nd Avenue, is an historic concert hall designed in 1907 by Seattle architect Edwin W. Houghton.

For most of the 1970s and '80s, Belltown was best known for its wandering homeless, drug dealers, and panhandlers, but as 2000 approached, *Sunset Magazine* declared it the "newest belle of the ball," and compared it to New York's Upper West Side. According to 2000 US Census data, in the 1990s, Belltown, along with Denny Regrade, was one of Seattle's fastest growing neighborhoods. The combined communities grew by 6,000 residents, and the number of housing units in the neighborhood jumped by nearly 2,000 units, to 7,760. Building continues at a rapid pace as Belltown has become a hip neighborhood, attractive to young professionals, and thousands of new units are planned for the coming years.

High-rise condominiums facing Elliott Bay and the Olympic Mountains can be found on 1st Avenue. These amenity-rich units (high-speed internet access, parking garages, free cable, and fitness centers) command premium rents. Condos are also pricey in trendy Belltown. *The Seattle Times* reports that at the Ellington, a 312-unit complex at First Avenue and Broad Street, condos run from $158,000 to $800,000. The units boast gas fireplaces, six telephone lines, and views of Downtown and Elliott Bay.

Only a few blocks east there are more affordable studios and one-bedrooms in buildings dating from the early 1900s. North of Pike Place, there is an assortment of apartments and low-income housing units. Like much of downtown, home and personal security issues may make Belltown an unsuitable choice for some newcomers. People interested in living Downtown should become familiar and comfortable with the area before choosing a home here. (See the end of this profile for more on safety concerns.)

The Seattle **Waterfront**, facing Elliott Bay and the craggy snow-capped Olympic Mountains, is another lively and exciting neighborhood in Downtown. Though one of the most touristy areas of Seattle, the Waterfront has many attractions for city residents. Fine restaurants featuring fresh local seafood and superior views line the piers, as do many more casual eateries and several ice cream stands.

In the past few years the city's Downtown retail district has expanded, enticing shoppers back from the suburban malls. Seattle-based Nordstrom, still the dominant player in the Downtown shopping scene, moved several years ago to the spacious and remodeled Frederick & Nelson building, and the posh Pacific Place mall attracted Coach, Tiffany & Co., and J. Crew. Nike Town, FAO Schwartz, and Kenneth Cole added stores on 6th Avenue, and Adidas and Anthropologie attract shoppers to 5th Avenue. The Fairmont Olympic Hotel, on the original site of the University of Washington, offers visitors lavish accommodations close to the City Center and Rainier Square shops.

Bounded by Denny Way, Interstate 5 and 5th Avenue, the often-overlooked **Denny Triangle** neighborhood is experiencing a renaissance, similar to the 1990s redevelopment of the Belltown and Denny Regrade neighborhoods. Development plans here include a large number of new housing units; in fact, the city's comprehensive plan for the area estimates a 450% increase by 2014, to about 5,000 units. This increase in available housing is particularly noteworthy in Denny Triangle where, for years, the only recognizable landmarks were the Greyhound Bus Station and the venerable Camlin Hotel. The area already is home to multi-use high-rises with offices, condos, apartments, and hotels, including the 31-story Metropolitan Tower Apartments, bordered by Virginia Street and Seventh and Westlake avenues, and the federal courthouse. Also new to the area, the Cornish College of the Arts expanded and created a main campus in the vicinity of Lenora and Boren avenues, as well as keeping the original campus on Capitol Hill. As in Belltown, rents here are rising, but the Denny Triangle Neighborhood Association says housing will be aimed at all income levels. The mayor is proposing zoning changes that will allow taller and narrower buildings than are now allowed in the area in exchange for developers offering some low- and middle-income housing.

Finally, northeast of Downtown, at the south end of Lake Union, the **Cascade** neighborhood, which was once primarily industrial, is enjoying the benefits of the city's plan to triple the number of residents over the next 20 years. New apartments and low-income housing units have been built in the blocks east of Fairview Avenue. In late 2000, the Low Income Housing Institute, with help from *The Seattle Times*, Fred Hutchinson Cancer Research Center, and various financial institutions, developed the Lakeview Apartments at the intersection of Harrison Street and Minor Avenue North. Sophisticated Federal-style brick buildings on Eastlake Avenue also offer affordable apartments and low-income housing opportunities.

There are also growing pains in the area, and many residents fear that the neighborhood will not remain affordable with the many new condominiums being built. Paul Allen (co-founder of Microsoft), with his company, Vulcan Northwest, has bought substantial acreage in the nieghborhood and new mixed-use buildings are sprouting. Condominiums are sold before construction is finished, and the city of Seattle has plans to revive a streetcar service that used to run around sixty years ago between Downtown and the Cascade area. The REI flagship store near I-5 has increased commercial interest here, and the neighborhood has also become the new biotech hub in the city. The ultimate goal is an urban village feel, with people living and working in the same neighborhood, and easy access to and from downtown. The Cascade P-Patch community garden at Minor Avenue North and Thomas Street, and the Cascade Playground at the corner of Harrison Street and Pontius Avenue North help maintain the feel of a liveable neighborhood.

A cautionary note, Seattle's downtown core is a varied and lively area: a mix of modern condominiums and apartments, artists' lofts, and homeless shelters amidst busy shopping and nightlife districts. Such an urban mix is a far cry from more traditional secluded neighborhoods, and is something to consider when examining the livability of the area. Violent crimes tend to be highest in Seattle's downtown core: the Pioneer Square, International District, Georgetown, Denny Regrade, Duwamish and Belltown neighborhoods. And, in other parts of Seattle, burglaries and car prowls continue to be a problem. (See **Safety and Crime** in **Getting Settled** for more information.)

**Web Site:** www.seattle.gov
**Area Code:** 206
**Zip Codes:** 98121, 98101, 98104, 98109, 98134
**Post Office:** Main Office Station, 301 Union St
**Libraries:** Central Library, 1000 4th Ave, 206-386-4636, www.spl.org; Washington Talking Book and Braille Library, 2021 9th Ave, 206-615-0400, 206-615-0419 (TTY), www.wtbbl.org
**Public Schools:** Seattle Public Schools, P.O. Box 19116, Seattle, WA 98109-1116, 206-298-7000, www.seattleschools.org
**Police:** West Precinct, 810 Virginia St, 206-615-1999, www.seattle.gov/police
**Emergency Hospital:** Harborview Medical Center, 325 9th Ave, 206-731-3074, www.uwmedicine.org/facilities/harborview
**Community Publication:** *Belltown Messenger*, 206-331-6031, www.belltownmessenger.com
**Community Resources:** Downtown Neighborhood Service Center, 820 Virginia Ave, 206-233-8560, www.seattle.gov; Downtown Seattle Association, 500 Union St, 206-623-0340, www.downtownseattle.com
**Public Transportation:** Metro Transit, 206-553-3000, http://transit.metrokc.gov; 1, 5, 10, 11, 12, 13, 14, 15, 16, 17, 18, 19, 20, 21, 22, 24, 25, 26, 27, 28, 33, 35, 36, 37, 39, 41, 42, 43, 54, 55, 56, 57, 64, 66, 70, 71, 72, 73, 74, 76, 77, 79, 81, 82, 83, 84, 85

# INTERNATIONAL DISTRICT

**Boundaries: North:** South Jackson Street; **West:** 4th Avenue South; **South:** South Dearborn Street; **East:** Rainier Avenue South

Also known as Chinatown, the International District was originally home to immigrant Chinese men who, in the late 1800s, provided an inexpensive source of labor for the railroad, fish, and lumber industries. In the early 1900s, the center of the neighborhood shifted from the waterfront to its present location, just east of the new football stadium. By then, Japanese immigrants had also moved to the area, and Filipino families soon followed. Today, a blend of Asian influences flavors the International District, with residents of Chinese, Japanese, Korean, Filipino, Vietnamese, and Southeast Asian descent sharing one bustling community.

The International District is located conveniently close to downtown, Pioneer Square, and the Central District, and I-5 passes right through the neighborhood. But, until recently, the appearance of Asian characters in shop windows was the only indication to visitors that they had come to a culturally diverse and distinct community. The neighborhood lacked a definitive entrance, like the ornamental gates of San Francisco's Chinatown. International District leaders created a neighborhood beautification and public art program that installed cheerful banners along 4th and 5th avenues and Jackson Street, as well as 11 large, vividly colored dragon sculptures at various street corners. The 12- to 18-foot dragons twine around light poles and attract the attention of tourists and locals alike.

Visitors frequent the area primarily for its Asian cuisine, with dozens of restaurants specializing in traditional Chinese, Japanese, and Vietnamese dishes. Herb stores, groceries, and bakeries line South King Street and surrounding side streets, and the king of all Asian markets, Uwajimaya, anchors the neighborhood at 600 Fifh Avenue South. The $15 million expansion and redevelopment of Uwajimaya doubled the size of the old store, and added 176 apartments and several restaurants. Rents range from just under $1,000 to nearly $2,000 per month. The huge complex serves as a bridge between the community's ancient culture and contemporary development.

The heart of the International District is the site of the old Chinatown, which lies between 4th Avenue South and I-5. The main thoroughfare is Jackson Street, although many of the historic buildings and businesses are a few blocks off Jackson. Chinatown is peppered with historic hotels, many of which have been converted into low-income housing and affordable apartments for senior citizens. There are also apartments and condominiums available for middle-income families and young professionals, similar to the units at the Uwajimaya Village Apartments. On the east side of I-5, a stretch of the International District known as **"Little Saigon"** is centered around the intersection of 12th Avenue and Jackson Street. Here you'll find an inviting selection of Vietnamese groceries and tasty take-out restaurants. The I-5 underpass on Jackson Street serves as a corridor to Little Saigon with painted and decorated freeway columns.

Crime rates here are comparable to the rest of downtown.

While most residents in the International District are of Asian or Pacific Island descent, others live here as well. An interest in downtown living seems to be attracting younger residents to a community that in recent decades had a median age in the mid-50s. According to 2000 US Census figures, the International District grew by more than 25% during the 1990s.

**Web Site:** www.seattle.gov
**Area Code:** 206
**Zip Codes:** 98134, 98144, 98104
**Post Office:** International Station, 414 6th Ave S
**Library:** Central Library, 1000 4th Ave, 206-386-4636, www.spl.org
**Public Schools:** Seattle Public Schools, P.O. Box 19116, Seattle, WA 98109-1116, 206-298-7000, www.seattleschools.org
**Police:** West Precinct, 810 Virginia St, 206-615-1999, www.seattle.gov/police
**Emergency Hospital:** Harborview Medical Center, 325 9th Ave, 206-731-3074, www.uwmedicine.org/facilities/harborview
**Community Publications:** *Northwest Asian Weekly*, 412 Maynard Ave S, 206-223-5559, www.nwasianweekly.com; *Seattle Chinese Post*, 412 Maynard Ave S, 206-223-5559, www.seattlechinesepost.com
**Community Resources:** Downtown Neighborhood Service Center, 820 Virginia Ave, 206-233-8560, www.seattle.gov; Chinatown/International District Business Improvement Area, 409 Maynard Ave S, 206-382-1197, www.seattlechinatown.org; Jackson Place P-Patch, 16th Ave S and S Weller St, 206-684-0264, www.seattle.gov/don/ppatch
**Public Transportation:** Metro Transit, 206-553-3000, http://transit.metrokc.gov

## FIRST HILL

**Boundaries: North**: East Pike Street; **West**: I-5; **South**: Yesler Way; **East**: 12th Avenue East

First Hill, commonly referred to as "Pill Hill" because of the concentration of hospitals, clinics, and medical offices in the area, lies directly east of downtown. Seattle's elite originally settled in First Hill in the mid-1800s as the city expanded beyond the downtown boundary. Later, many affluent First Hill residents moved to more distant neighborhoods, such as Madison Park and Laurelhurst. Only a few of the early homes remain, including the Tudoresque Stimson-Green Mansion built in 1898. Other remaining structures not supplanted by medical office buildings, schools, hospitals, and hotels, serve as private clubs and reception halls.

The main commercial street on First Hill is Madison Street, with an assortment of cafés, delis, hotels, and pharmacies that serve hospital and office personnel, patients, and nearby residents. The Sorrento Hotel on Madison Street is an exquisite brick building, constructed in 1907 and designed by well-known Seattle architect Harlan Thomas, designer of the 1929 Harborview Medical Center. Harborview, a few blocks south of Madison Street on First Hill, serves as the premier emergency care center in the Seattle area.

There are few single-family houses on First Hill except for those in the area south of Harborview, which tends to be noisy due to ambulance sirens and the nearby freeway. Most First Hill residents live in apartments or condominiums facing downtown to the west or Capitol Hill to the north. On the west side of First Hill, an assortment of apartment buildings bordering I-5 offer views of downtown and Elliott Bay. Although freeway noise can be distracting in these residences, there is a nice mix of high- and low-end apartments, and many downtown professionals and doctors choose to live in the area for convenience. Elegant brick apartment buildings from the early 1900s are tucked along side streets, offering secured entrances and pleasant surroundings. These buildings are only a few minutes' walk from downtown. Also, check the north end of First Hill for a selection of brick or stucco apartment buildings that date from the late 1920s.

As with nearby Capitol Hill, First Hill plays an important role in Seattle's Catholic community. Two influential Catholic schools are located here: Seattle University, a private Jesuit college on Broadway, and O'Dea Catholic High School near Madison Street.

**Web Site:** www.seattle.gov
**Area Code:** 206
**Zip Codes:** 98101, 98104
**Post Office:** Main Office Station, 301 Union St
**Library:** Central Library, 1000 4th Ave, 206-386-4636, www.spl.lib.wa.us
**Public Schools:** Seattle Public Schools, P.O. Box 19116, Seattle, WA 98109-1116, 206-298-7000, www.seattleschools.org
**Police:** East Precinct, 1519 12th Ave, 206-684-4300, www.seattle.gov/police
**Emergency Hospital:** Harborview Medical Center, 325 9th Ave, 206-731-3074, www.uwmedicine.org/facilities/harborview
**Community Publication:** *Capitol Hill Times*, 4000 Aurora Ave N, Ste 100, 206-461-1300

**Community Resource:** Yesler Community Center, 835 Yesler Way, 206-386-1245
**Public Transportation:** Metro Transit, 206-553-3000, http://transit.metrokc.gov; 2, 3, 4, 9, 12, 27, 60, 64, 84, 205, 303, 941, 942, 984

## CAPITOL HILL

**Boundaries: North:** Fuhrman Avenue East; **West:** I-5; **South:** East Pike Street; **East:** 23rd/24th Avenue East

Vibrant and diverse, Capitol Hill is one of Seattle's best-loved neighborhoods, where affordable (but rising) rents, offbeat retailers and ethnic eateries lure a rainbow of residents. It is both the center of Seattle's large gay community and a neighborhood of traditional Catholic families. At the north end, there is St. Mark's Cathedral and the Episcopal Archdiocese; at the south end is Neighbor's, a cavernous gay dance club.

Broadway is the main street of Capitol Hill. Running the length of the hill, it serves as the center of the community's commercial district. It is the place to go for lively dining or take-out; boisterous, young residents fill innumerable restaurants and bars nightly, and on summer evenings the street rings with voices late into the night. In addition to the local eateries, there are many businesses on Broadway that cater to a youthful clientele, including tattoo and body piercing shops, second-hand clothing and record stores, costume jewelers, bead shops, head shops, and gay/lesbian bookstores.

East Pike Street and East Pine Street, south of Broadway's retail core, are the center of Capitol Hill's nightlife. The area has an assortment of bars, pool halls, dance clubs, and restaurants, though this once slightly seedy district has become more refined. On East Pike Street, a collection of trendy boutiques has sprung up. A large grocery and shopping complex, featuring a QFC grocery, a Burger King, and a Great Clips hair salon takes up the corner of East Pike Street and Broadway.

Fifteenth Avenue East, five blocks east of Broadway, is another Capitol Hill retail district. This area is understated and stylish but also funky and quaint, with mod boutiques, swank eateries, and cozy pubs. Fifteenth Avenue East caters to a slightly older crowd, attracting hip baby boomers and comfortably domestic gays and lesbians. The mood here is laid-back and placid, an agreeable alternative to the constant bustle of Broadway.

To the north, Capitol Hill is filled with lovely, albeit expensive, houses, most with enchanting views. To examine the stunning vistas yourself, climb to the top of the old water tower in Volunteer Park. Homes on the eastern slope of Capitol Hill have views of the Cascades or Lake Washington; a few even offer a glimpse of Mount Rainier from a top story window. On the west side, residences look out over Lake Union, the Fremont Bridge, and the Olympic Mountains. Homes in Capitol Hill, particularly at the north end, are large and fashionable. While many are Colonials, Dutch Colonials, Victorian or Federal-style houses, the most common type of home in this area is the Northwest Modern, or "Capitol Hill Box House."

In addition to the water tower, Volunteer Park features the Seattle Asian Art Museum, a charming old water reservoir, a delightful glass conservatory, and an outdoor amphitheater for summer concerts. Homes around Volunteer Park include some of the most formal and ornate mansions in Seattle. Many are old Victorian or Federal style houses, while others are stately versions of the Northwest Modern style. Though a few homes have become unobtrusive bed and breakfasts, most are still occupied by wealthy Seattle families. Many of Capitol Hill's affluent Catholic residents live in the area and attend church at the beautiful St. Joseph's Catholic Church. Others attend St. Patrick's, at the far north end of Capitol Hill, near Roanoke Park.

South of East Aloha Street, apartments are more common and houses are smaller. Federal-style brick buildings abound in this area, subdivided into small but classic apartments, with hardwood floors and coved ceilings. Most people who live near Broadway are renters, although there are houses tucked away on the side streets that lead back toward Volunteer Park. West of Broadway, almost all of the available residences are apartments or condominiums, with many large modern apartment complexes built over I-5 and offering views of downtown and the Olympic Mountains. Rents are relatively high in this area, although many studio apartments are available. Despite its dense population, the charm of this neighborhood is that it is one of the few Seattle areas where you can walk anywhere you might need to go. In fact, having a car can be a disadvantage here, where parking is at best a challenge. In addition, several bus routes connect Capitol Hill with downtown and the University District, the major hubs of the Metro bus system.

East of Broadway, residences are a haphazard mix of houses, duplexes, and apartment buildings. Homes tend to be smaller and less ornate than those on north Capitol Hill but the styles are similar—primarily Northwest Moderns, Colonials, and Victorians. Many houses here are available as single-family or multiple-tenant rentals. Apartments in this area are generally less expensive than those on the west side of the hill, depending on the building and location. East of 15th Avenue East and south of East John Street, houses and apartments are even less expensive, particularly south of the radio towers and close to the Central District. Residents here tend to be young, a mix of artists, musicians, and college students from Seattle Central Community College or Seattle University.

**Web Site:** www.seattle.gov
**Area Code:** 206
**Zip Codes:** 98102, 98112, 98122

**Post Office:** Broadway Station, 101 Broadway

**Library:** 425 Harvard Ave E, 206-684-4715, www.spl.lib.wa.us

**Public Schools:** Seattle Public Schools, P.O. Box 19116, Seattle, WA 98109-1116, 206-298-7000, www.seattleschools.org

**Police:** East Precinct, 1519 12th Ave, 206-684-4300, www.cityofseattle.net/police

**Emergency Hospital:** Swedish Medical Center, 747 Broadway, 206-386-6000, www.swedish.org

**Community Publication:** *Capitol Hill Times*, 4000 Aurora Ave N, Ste 100, 206-461-1300

**Community Resources:** Capitol Hill Neighborhood Service Center, 501 19th Ave E, 206-684-4574; Capitol Hill Community Resource Center, 509 10th Ave E, 206-322-4567; Miller Community Center, 330 19th Ave E, 206-684-4753; Capitol Hill P-Patch, 1010 E Thomas St, 206-684-0264, www.seattle.gov/don/ppatch

**Public Transportation:** Metro Transit, 206-553-3000, http://transit.metrokc.gov; 8, 9, 10, 11, 12, 25, 43, 49, 60, 84, 984

## EASTLAKE

**Boundaries: North:** Lake Washington Ship Canal; **West:** Lake Union; **South:** East Galer Street; **East:** I-5

Just north of downtown, on the east side of Lake Union, lies the aptly named Eastlake neighborhood. Long thought of as simply an easy shortcut to downtown, Eastlake has blossomed into a charming close-knit community. Along Eastlake Avenue East are most of the retail shops and restaurants of the neighborhood, including the original Red Robin Burger & Spirits Emporium, the first of a successful local restaurant chain. Rows of houseboats share the shore of Lake Union with marine repair shops, dry docks, and National Oceanic and Atmospheric Administration (NOAA) ships. To explore the appealing houseboats in Eastlake, begin at Pete's Supermarket, located at the base of East Lynn Street then work north or south along the shore. While the houseboats vary widely in size and luxury, all share in the daily spectacle of sailboats and seaplanes on Lake Union, and the annual Independence Day fireworks display and Christmas Ship Parade.

More traditional housing is abundant in Eastlake as well. The neighborhood has an interesting mix of apartments, condominiums, duplexes, and single-family homes. Large 1970s-style apartment buildings dot the area and offer fairly inexpensive rentals, many with views of Lake Union. More traditional brick Federal-style buildings offer both apartments and condominiums. Homes in Eastlake range from turn-of-the-century Victorians to simple Northwest Moderns. Eastlake has boomed in recent years as both a commercial and residential area, and the result has been extensive new construction throughout the area. New townhouses and apartments can be found in the few blocks between Eastlake Avenue and the lake and along Franklin Avenue East, and new condo construction continues.

At the north end of Fairview Avenue, along the edge of Lake Union, are the last vestiges of the old Eastlake community. Here quaint and slightly run-down summer cottages face the lake shore. This is the site of the Eastlake P-Patch community garden, which, like the community gardens in the International District and on Capitol Hill, is a quiet treasure for those who live here. Unfortunately, what makes this area quaint—the small number of houses—also makes it difficult to find a place to live.

Eastlake is nice. It's well located with easy access to downtown and the 520 bridge, and it's friendly. Prospective neighbors might include university students in rental housing and apartment complexes along busy Boylston Avenue East; young professionals who rent and buy homes and condominiums along Franklin Avenue East, East Roanoke Street, and East Lynn Street; and well-to-do baby boomers who live west of Eastlake Avenue East, close to Lake Union. In addition, many older lifelong Eastlake residents still live in this community. While, like much of Seattle, rents here continue to rise, Eastlake is still affordable for most middle-income families. A report from Dupre + Scott Apartment Advisors (www.dsaa.com) noted that the average rent for an apartment in the Eastlake neighborhood is about 35% lower than the average rent for an apartment downtown.

**Web Sites:** www.seattle.gov, www.eastlake.oo.net
**Area Code:** 206
**Zip Code:** 98102
**Post Office:** Broadway Station, 101 Broadway
**Library:** Capitol Hill Branch, 425 Harvard Ave E, 206-684-4715, www.spl.lib.wa.us
**Public Schools:** Seattle Public Schools, P.O. Box 19116, Seattle, WA 98109-1116, 206-298-7000, www.seattleschools.org
**Police:** West Precinct, 610 3rd Ave, 206-684-8917, www.cityofseattle.net/police
**Emergency Hospital:** Harborview Medical Center, 325 9th Ave, 206-731-3074, www.uwmedicine.org/facilities/harborview
**Community Resources:** Montlake Community Center, 1618 E Calhoun St, 206-684-4736; Eastlake Community Council, 117 E Louisa St, www.eastlake.oo.net; Floating Homes Association, 2329 Fairview Ave E, 206-325-1132
**Public Transportation:** Metro Transit, 206-553-3000, http://transit.metrokc.gov; 25, 66, 70, 71, 72, 73, 83

# QUEEN ANNE

**INTERBAY**
**LOWER QUEEN ANNE**
**WESTLAKE**

**Boundaries**: **North**: Lake Washington Ship Canal; **West**: 15th Avenue West, Elliott Avenue West; **South**: Denny Way; **East**: Lake Union, Aurora Avenue North (Highway 99)

Situated on a hill towering 457 feet over downtown and Elliott Bay, Queen Anne is one of the oldest and loveliest residential areas in the city. In the 1890s, streetcar lines from downtown brought affluent residents up the south slope of the hill to their grand mansions. Since its origin, the Queen Anne neighborhood has flourished, remaining an idyllic residential area only minutes from downtown. Queen Anne Avenue North is the main commercial street, and is where residents gather for morning coffee and brunch in picturesque cafés, meet for lunch or dinner at quaint local pubs and restaurants, or shop in the upscale boutiques, specialty bakeries, and small bookstores.

Surrounding the shopping district, modest Colonials and simple bungalows are home to a mix of students, artists, professionals, and families. In addition, formal Northwest Moderns and Tudors are home to retired folks who have lived on the hill for many years. Because of the desirability of this area, many apartment and condomiunium buildings have been built in recent years, replacing some older single-family dwellings. The most affordable houses and apartments are those without a view. This is a pleasant area, with well-maintained houses surrounded by lovely lawns and beautiful nearby parks. The playground at John Hay Elementary School, east of Queen Anne Avenue North, is the site of weekend basketball games; a block west of this main thoroughfare, city ballparks are host to softball games on lazy summer afternoons.

The southwest corner of Queen Anne remains an enclave for affluent and longtime residents. The homes in this area are lavish, many glimpsed only through breaks in landscaped hedges. West Highland Drive, offering unbelievable views of downtown, Elliott Bay, Mount Rainier, and the Olympic Mountains, is lined with many of the hill's original Queen Anne–style houses. In the blocks north of West Highland Drive, homes are less expensive but still well-maintained. Most are modest Four Square or Queen Anne–style houses; a few are Craftsman-style bungalows. To see the merits of this neighborhood, walk or drive to Kerry Park, located on the south side of West Highland Drive. From this vantage point, the downtown cityscape and the shipping activities of Elliott Bay seem an arm's length away; in the distance, Mount Rainier towers over the city. The park is a favorite of nearby residents, who come after dark to admire the brilliant lights of downtown or to watch fireworks over the bay on Independence Day.

East of Queen Anne Avenue North, a variety of large and expensive homes share a lovely view of downtown and Mount Rainier. Many are elaborate Elizabethans and Colonials; others are large unadorned contemporary homes. Residents include a mix of wealthy entrepreneurs, foreign diplomats, and affluent professionals. In addition to breathtaking glimpses of Mount Rainier and downtown, the east side of the hill offers views of azure Lake Union and Capitol Hill. Many 1950s apartment buildings cling to this side of the hill, offering affordable rentals for young professionals. In addition, several houses and apartment buildings in the area have been remodeled and made into condominiums. Many of the people living in this corner of Queen Anne are middle-income professionals who work downtown. A word of advice: this is not the neighborhood to live in if your job is on the Eastside. Commuting from Queen Anne to the Eastside can take as much as an hour, sometimes more, during peak travel times.

The north and west sides of Queen Anne Hill are the best locations for reasonably priced rentals in the neighborhood. The west side of Queen Anne, including **Interbay**, a light industrial strip between Queen Anne and Magnolia, offers affordable rental apartments in modest brick and large contemporary buildings as well as rental houses and duplexes, mostly converted bungalows. Many students and faculty live in Queen Anne because Seattle Pacific University (SPU) is located at the base of the hill to the north. Around the SPU campus are numerous rentals, including unpretentious apartment buildings, modest houses, tiny houseboats, and renovated storefronts.

Apartments and condominiums are also plentiful in the **Lower Queen Anne** area, which surrounds the Seattle Center, site of the Space Needle. Built for the 1962 World's Fair, the 74-acre Seattle Center is a combination amusement park and community center. Among its many attractions are the Pacific Science Center, Opera House, Pacific Northwest Ballet, Seattle Repertory Theatre, Intiman Theater, and Key Arena, where the Seattle Sonics and Seattle Storm play. Every summer, Seattle Center is the site for Bumbershoot, a music and arts festival, as well as the Northwest Folklife Festival and the Bite of Seattle (See **A Seattle Year** for more details about these and other annual events). The Lower Queen Anne area includes retail and residential districts to the north and west. Small ethnic restaurants are located along Roy Street north of the Seattle Center, and aromatic cafés, scrumptious bakeries, old-fashioned diners, and upscale restaurants cluster around Queen Anne Avenue North. Apartment buildings of all styles fill this area, from small brick buildings on Roy Street to enormous contemporary buildings along Queen Anne Avenue North. Many of the condominiums in the area were converted from former apartment buildings.

Finally, the **Westlake** area, located at the eastern base of the hill, is a commercial district that runs along the west side of Lake Union. Westlake Avenue is lined with upscale view restaurants, private marinas, and marine shops—a combination common in Seattle's waterfront areas. A few houseboats, including the one featured in the movie *Sleepless in Seattle,* are moored here.

Though rents can vary greatly depending on which Queen Anne neighborhood you choose, figures from Dupre + Scott Apartment Advisors show that the average rent in this area for a one-bedroom apartment is about 25% lower than the average rent in Belltown. For buyers, Queen Anne remains one of the priciest neighborhoods in Seattle. Home and condominium prices continue to rise, as they have since the late 1990s.

**Web Site:** www.seattle.gov
**Area Code:** 206
**Zip Codes:** 98109, 98119
**Post Office:** Queen Anne Station, 415 1st Ave N
**Library:** 400 W Garfield St, 206-386-4227, www.spl.lib.wa.us (closed for renovation in 2007)
**Public Schools:** Seattle Public Schools, P.O. Box 19116, Seattle, WA 98109-1116, 206-298-7000, www.seattleschools.org
**Police:** West Precinct, 810 Virginia St, 206-615-1999, www.seattle.gov/police
**Emergency Hospital:** Harborview Medical Center, 325 9th Ave, 206-731-3074, www.uwmedicine.org/facilities/harborview
**Community Publication:** *Queen Anne News,* 4000 Aurora Ave N, Ste 100, 206-461-1300
**Community Resources:** Queen Anne Community Center, 1901 1st Ave W, 206-386-4240; Queen Anne Help Line, 206-282-1540, info@queenannehelpline.org; Queen Anne/Magnolia Neighborhood Service Center, 157 Roy St, 206-684-4812, www.seattle.gov
**Public Transportation:** Metro Transit, 206-553-3000, http://transit.metrokc.gov; 1, 2, 3, 4, 8, 13, 15, 16, 17, 18, 19, 24, 26, 28, 33, 45, 74, 81, 82, 994

## MAGNOLIA

**Boundaries: North:** Lake Washington Ship Canal; **West:** Puget Sound; **South:** Elliott Bay; **East:** 15th Avenue West

Just west of Queen Anne is the neighborhood of Magnolia, which like Queen Anne, is both a landmark Seattle hill and a community. Rumor has it that the hill was originally named for the distinctive Madrona trees that line the bluff, which a visiting sailor mistakenly identified as magnolias. In any case, the name stuck and now designates a charming neighborhood, which, despite its proximity to downtown, is truly a residential community. It has an interesting mix of homes, mainly

Northwest Moderns, Craftsman-style bungalows, and brick Tudors—many with views of the beautiful Puget Sound and craggy Olympic Mountains to the west, or of the downtown skyline and busy Elliott Bay to the southeast.

There are a few commercial centers on the hill that collectively serve just about every need imaginable, from medical prescriptions to pet grooming. There's even a cobbler shop for shoe repair. The heart of Magnolia is "the Village," a collection of restaurants, shops, and banks that spill over McGraw Street between 32nd and 34th avenues. Families gather here for Halloween trick-or-treating and in the summer for a children's parade. Professionals line up at one of the two coffeehouses each morning before work, or meet friends at the local pub at the end of the day. Szmania's, a critically acclaimed restaurant, is located in the Village, along with a handful of small family-friendly eateries. A marina at the south end of Magnolia is also home to several popular restaurants, which share a spectacular panorama of Elliott Bay and downtown.

Because of the extraordinary views and the easy commute to downtown, homes in Magnolia are fairly expensive. Along "the bluff," which traces the west edge of Magnolia from south to north, you will find especially lavish homes. More modestly sized and priced homes are located at the north end of the hill and in the middle valley where there is little or no view. Here homeowners tend to be a mix of young families, established professionals or senior citizens; many are longtime residents.

Renters in Magnolia represent all levels of income and occupations. Because Magnolia is not conveniently located to I-5, apartments here rent for slightly less than the Seattle average, even those with water or city views. This is particularly true for the larger, two-bedroom apartments; studio rents are comparable to other neighborhoods. You'll find many apartment buildings located at the north end of the hill, facing Ballard.

Nearby, on the Lake Washington Ship Canal, the Fisherman's Terminal is an energetic hub with constant activity from the fishing vessels that dock there. Just off West Emerson Street, part of the Fisherman's Terminal was transformed into a small shopping and dining destination, featuring Chinook's restaurant and the Bay Café, a nautical-theme gallery and gift store, and the Highliner Tavern. Continue on this route and you'll find Discovery Park and the Hiram Chittenden Locks. The locks, which separate the Lake Washington Ship Canal from the Puget Sound, offer an easy route for foot and bicycle traffic between Magnolia and Ballard. Discovery Park, in the northwest corner of Magnolia, is Seattle's largest and most verdant park, consisting of 534 acres of meadows, forest, and beach, with clay cliffs and miles of nature trails. The nearby West Point Lighthouse was built on the northwest point of the beach in 1881 and is still a popular attraction, although the attraction is now somewhat diminished by the close proximity of the West Point Sewage Treatment Plant.

Although Magnolia is not technically a peninsula, access to the hill is limited to Dravus Street, Nickerson Street, and the Magnolia Bridge. When the bridge is closed—as it has been a few times in past years due to mudslides and an earthquake—the commute to and from Magnolia lengthens considerably. Interbay, the semi-industrial area between Magnolia and Queen Anne, effectively cuts off Magnolia from the main thoroughfare of 15th Avenue West (Elliott Avenue), so only those three streets serve as overpasses into the neighborhood. Still, Magnolia is actually quite convenient to downtown and the surrounding neighborhoods, although getting to I-5 can be difficult.

**Web Site:** www.seattle.gov
**Area Code:** 206
**Zip Code:** 98199
**Post Office:** Magnolia Station, 3211 W McGraw St
**Library:** 2801 34th Ave W, 206-386-4225, www.spl.lib.wa.us
**Public Schools:** Seattle Public Schools, P.O. Box 19116, Seattle, WA 98109-1116, 206-298-7000, www.seattleschools.org
**Police:** West Precinct, 810 Virginia St, 206-615-1999, www.seattle.gov/police
**Emergency Hospital:** Swedish Medical Center Ballard, 5300 Tallman Ave NW, 206-781-6341, www.swedish.org
**Community Publication:** *Magnolia News*, 4000 Aurora Ave N, Ste 100, 206-461-1300
**Community Resources:** Queen Anne/Magnolia Neighborhood Service Center, 157 Roy St, 206-684-4812, www.seattle.gov; Magnolia Community Center, 2550 34th Ave NW, 206-386-4235; Magnolia Community Club, 206-283-1188, www.orgsites.com/wa/magnoliacommunityclub/; Magnolia Helpline, 3213 W Wheeler, 206-284-5631, admin@magnoliahelpline.org
**Public Transportation:** Metro Transit, 206-553-3000, http://transit.metrokc.gov; 19, 24, 31, 33, 994

## BALLARD

**SHILSHOLE**
**CROWN HILL**
**NORTH BEACH**
**BLUE RIDGE**

**Boundaries: North:** NW 110th Street; **West:** Puget Sound; **South:** Lake Washington Ship Canal; **East:** 3rd Avenue NW

Home to about 50,000, Ballard is a quaint and delightful neighborhood located just 15 minutes north of downtown. Originally a town made up of workers for the local Stimson Mill, Seattle annexed it in 1906 after a dead horse in the town's drinking water forced residents to turn to the city for a new water supply. In the early 1900s, Scandinavian immigrants settled in Ballard, attracted to the abundant fish in Puget Sound. Although currently commercial salmon fishing in the Sound is restricted to local Native American tribes, Ballard remains home to many professional fishermen who catch pollack, halibut, cod, and salmon along the coast of Alaska. Off-season, from the Ballard Bridge and homes in the south end of the neighborhood, are views of the colorful fishing vessels harbored at Fisherman's Terminal and along the Lake Washington Ship Canal. To learn about the boating and fishing history of Ballard, visit the Hiram Chittenden Locks and Fish Ladder, located at the west end of NW Market Street (just as the street becomes Seaview Avenue NW).

Ballard is well known as a tight-knit Scandinavian community, celebrating its heritage by hosting yearly festivals for Santa Lucia (an early saint honored during the Christmas Season), and for Syettende Mai (May 17, Norway's Constitution Day). During these celebrations, Ballard's main street, NW Market Street, is roped off from traffic and gaily decorated, and everyone is welcome to attend the festivities. Northwest Market Street is the retail section of the original town, lined with coffeehouses, bakeries, delis, and restaurants, as well as modern hobby shops, record stores, ethnic eateries, and a new, locally owned movie theatre. The Nordic Heritage Museum at 3014 NW 67th Street offers a fascinating glimpse of the Scandinavian culture that pervades the neighborhood. In contrast, one very un-Scandinavian restaurant on NW Market Street is the popular Lombardi's, famous for good Italian food, and host of an annual garlic festival. Samples from this lively event include such delicacies as garlic ice cream and garlic martinis.

Another major street in Ballard is 15th Avenue NW, which begins at the Ballard Bridge and runs north through the neighborhood. It's lined with a variety of small businesses, appliance and auto repair shops, fast-food restaurants, dry cleaners, pet shops, and antique malls. The streets off this main thoroughfare, however, are largely residential. Typically you'll find modest 1950s bungalows, brick Tudors, and simple wood-frame houses lining quiet streets. Many of these homes have views of the Olympic Mountains to the west; others overlook the boating activity along the Lake Washington Ship Canal. All homes in Ballard have easy access to downtown but, because of the longer distance to I-5, they are often less expensive than comparable houses elsewhere in the city.

In recent years, a number of hip bars, restaurants, shops, and galleries have opened in several picturesque blocks of Ballard Avenue just south of Market Street. Newcomers like Bad Albert's Tap & Grill and The Old Town Ale House present live jazz, blues, and alternative rock to complement the rockabilly and roots rock offered for years at the Tractor Tavern. This small slice of Ballard is also home to the locally famous bar and eatery Hattie's Hat. Dining and entertainment choices run the ethnic gamut from Thaiku to the Conor Byrne Pub, while the Other Coast Café serves up some of the best sandwiches in town.

East of 32nd Avenue NW, the **Shilshole** section of Ballard offers modest brick Tudors and Arts-and-Crafts-style homes with a panorama of Bainbridge Island, Puget Sound, and the Olympics. Shilshole is best known throughout the city for the seafood restaurants that line Seaview Avenue NW, like Ray's Boathouse and Anthony's Homeport, and for Golden Gardens Park. On summer evenings, visitors to the park watch in awe as the sun dips behind the Olympic Mountains. The park also attracts Seattle residents for summer picnics, swimming, and volleyball, as well as the occasional after-dark campfire. Golden Gardens is also home to one of Seattle Parks and Recreation's off-leash dog areas.

Rental homes are available throughout Ballard, particularly south of NW 65th Street, and apartment buildings line 24th Avenue NW, offering reasonable rents for studios and one- or two-bedroom units. Modest condominiums are available near NW Market Street, but recent devlopments like the Canal Street Condos on Leary Avenue are meeting the need for more urban, upscale housing choices in a neighborhood that is increasingly hip and attractive. More plush condos can be found in the Shilshole area along the waterfront. Public transportation is readily available in Ballard. Several bus routes run to downtown along 15th Avenue NW and 24th Avenue NW, and there are regular routes to Wallingford and the University District that run along NW Market Street and NW 85th Street.

One of Seattle's 12 "official" hills, **Crown Hill** begins where 15th Avenue NW meets NW 85th Street, at an intersection dominated by Safeway and QFC grocery stores. The neighborhood stretches north along 15th Avenue NW, then curves east along Holman Road. Though at first glance Crown Hill appears to be simply an accumulation of fast food outlets, auto body shops, and adult entertainment venues, the community does have its share of hidden treasures, like the Library Café and Crown Hill Hardware, which has been here for more than 80 years. Crown Hill's residential clusters are quiet, with well-tended yards and a mixture of brick Tudors and ramblers. Homes are still mostly affordable here, particularly north of NW 85th Street.

Elegant homes with views of the Puget Sound and the Olympic Mountains are situated on the northern and western hillsides of Ballard. Many of the homes in the **North Beach** area, north of NW 85th Street, are sprawling 1950s ranch houses with exquisitely landscaped yards. Other more recent additions to the neighborhood include elaborate colonials, immaculate brick Tudor cottages, and contemporary designs from the 1960s and '70s. Homes in this area have a front-row seat for breathtaking sunsets over the Olympic Mountains. In the summer months, residents watch weekend sailboat races on the sound; during the winter holidays, colorfully lighted ships follow the shoreline as part of the annual Christmas Ship Parade.

The *Seattle Post-Intelligencer* referred to the hillside community of **Blue Ridge** as one of the least known and most isolated neighborhoods in the city. Located on Puget Sound, north of Northwest 100th Street and south of Carkeek Park, Blue Ridge was developed during the Depression by William Boeing for some of his airplane company executives. Entirely residential, with less than 500 homes, the community features a club, swimming pool, tennis courts, playfields, and a private beach. Blue Ridge is a covenant community, which means there are rules and restrictions that residents are required to follow. For instance, there may be guidelines for landscaping or improvements that homeowners can make to their properties. In the past, small homes in Blue Ridge have tended to sell for about 50% higher than those in Greenview—tack on another $200,000 for a view. Larger homes, like those originally built by William Boeing, go for seven figures.

Despite the pricier accommodations of Blue Ridge, homes in Ballard generally are still affordable, especially compared to nearby neighborhoods like Queen Anne and Magnolia. Renters may also find Ballard to their liking where rents are less than those in Belltown or downtown.

While Ballard used to be known as a Nordic community, today people of many cultural backgrounds call it home. In addition to fishermen, Ballard is home to local merchants, teachers, public servants, and a flourishing senior citizen community. Young professionals are attracted to the availability of nightlife and dining and the easy distance to downtown. Shilshole and North Beach attract affluent professionals and wealthy retirees. Despite its proximity to downtown, Ballard has retained its village appeal and offers residents a close-knit community and convenient location.

**Web Sites:** www.seattle.gov, www.inballard.com
**Area Code:** 206
**Zip Codes:** 98107, 98117, 98103
**Post Office:** 5706 17th Ave NW
**Library:** 5711 24th Ave NW, 206-684-4089, www.spl.lib.wa.us
**Public Schools:** Seattle Public Schools, P.O. Box 19116, Seattle, WA 98109-1116, 206-298-7000, www.seattleschools.org
**Police:** North Precinct, 10049 College Way N, 206-684-0850, www.seattle.gov/police
**Emergency Hospital:** Swedish Medical Center Ballard, 5300 Tallman Ave NW, 206-781-6341, www.swedish.org
**Community Resources:** Ballard Community Center, 6020 28th Ave NW, 206-684-4093, www.ci.seattle.wa.us/parks; Ballard Neighborhood Service Center, 2305 NW Market St, 206-684-4060, www.cityofseattle.net; Ballard Pool, 1471 NW 67th St, 206-684-4094, www.cityofseattle.net/parks; Loyal Heights Community Center, 2101 NW 77th St, 206-684-4052, www.ci.seattle.wa.us/parks

**Public Transportation:** Metro Transit, 206-553-3000, http://transit.metrokc.gov; 15, 17, 18, 28, 31, 44, 46, 75, 81, 994

## PHINNEY RIDGE/GREENWOOD

**Boundaries: North:** Holman Road NW, North 105th Street; **West:** 8th Avenue NW, 3rd Avenue NW; **South:** North 50th Street; **East:** Aurora Avenue North (Highway 99)

The Phinney Ridge and Greenwood neighborhoods are located north of Fremont, between Ballard and Green Lake. The central feature of Phinney Ridge is the Woodland Park Zoo, located southwest of Green Lake across Aurora Avenue North. If visiting, be sure to walk through the fabulous rose garden at its 50th Street entrance. Phinney Ridge, a neighborhood known for its ever-present population of young families, is a perennial favorite of lower-middle-income, white collar professionals—teachers, public servants, non-profit organization employees, etc., creating a neighborhood reputation of liberal political views and strong community involvement. However, in more recent years, the neighborhood has become popular with more affluent professionals, and housing prices have risen accordingly.

Most Phinney Ridge residents live in Northwest Moderns or Craftsman bungalows on the west side of the hill, sharing lovely views of Ballard, the Puget Sound, and the Olympic Mountains. Apartment buildings line Phinney Avenue North along the ridge of the hill, although they taper off north of the zoo as retail shops and restaurants become more prevalent. Just north of NW 65th Street, Phinney Avenue North jogs over to become a stretch of Greenwood Avenue North and the true commercial district begins. Here the Red Mill Burger Company serves delicious burgers to people from all over Seattle; on summer evenings the line to the counter commonly stretches out the door and along the sidewalk. On Sunday mornings, another popular destination is Mae's Phinney Ridge Café at 65th Street, where hungry Seattle residents also fill the sidewalk during the brunch hour—you know you've found it by the large Holsteins painted on the bright green walls of the café. This area also offers a fun selection of ethnic and vegetarian restaurants, cozy pubs, funky coffeehouses, and card and gift shops.

The main intersection of the Greenwood neighborhood is NW 85th Street and Greenwood Avenue NW. Commercial buildings include banks, restaurants, boutiques, and well-stocked pubs, as well as the Greenwood Senior Center and the Greenwood Library. Greenwood Avenue NW is also known for its antique stores, and is a comfortable and pleasant shopping district. South of NW 85th Street, the Phinney Ridge and Greenwood neighborhoods are almost identical, with roomy bungalows and Northwest Modern homes on either side of the Greenwood Avenue NW retail core. North of NW 85th Street is a collection of more modest homes. Apartment seekers will find a selection of new apartment buildings along NW 85th Street, particularly in the few blocks just west of Aurora, and apartments circa 1970 line Greenwood Avenue NW, north of NW 90th Street. Affordable cottages, modern split-level homes, and duplexes can be found tucked away from the main streets of Greenwood Avenue North and 8th Avenue NW. Both Greenwood and Phinney Ridge are comfortable middle-class neighborhoods and many of the residents here are young professionals and their families.

Several blocks of both Greenwood and Phinney Ridge are situated close to Aurora Avenue North, a busy state highway and commercial district with a history of drugs and prostitution; prospective residents should consider this when looking at homes in the few blocks closest to Aurora Avenue North.

**Web Sites:** www.seattle.gov, www.phinneycenter.org
**Area Code:** 206
**Zip Codes:** 98103, 98107, 98117
**Post Office:** Greenwood Station, 8306 Greenwood Ave N
**Library:** 8016 Greenwood Ave N, 206-684-4086, www.spl.lib.wa.us
**Public Schools:** Seattle Public Schools, P.O. Box 19116, Seattle, WA 98109-1116, 206-298-7000, www.seattleschools.org
**Police:** North Precinct, 10049 College Way N, 206-684-0850, www.seattle.gov/police
**Emergency Hospital:** Swedish Medical Center Ballard, 5300 Tallman Ave NW, 206-781-6341, www.swedish.org
**Community Publication:** *North Seattle Herald-Outlook*, 4000 Aurora Ave N, Ste 100, 206-461-1300
**Community Resources:** Greenwood Neighborhood Service Center, 8515 Greenwood Ave N, 206-684-4096, www.seattle.gov; Greenwood Senior Center, 525 N 85th St, 206-297-0875; Phinney Neighborhood Association, 6532 Phinney Ave N, 206-783-2244
**Public Transportation:** Metro Transit, 206-553-3000, http://transit.metrokc.gov; 5, 28, 44, 48, 82, 355, 358

## FREMONT

**Boundaries**: **North**: North 46th Street/North Market Street; **East**: Stone Way North; **West**: 8th Avenue NW; **South**: Lake Washington Ship Canal and Fremont Bridge

Ten minutes north of downtown and across from the Lake Washington Ship Canal lies the picturesque Fremont district, a small Seattle neighborhood with its central core at the intersection of Fremont Avenue North, North 35th Street, and Fremont Place North, one block north of the Fremont Bridge. From here it is less than a five-minute walk to two of Seattle's most beloved sculptures, "Waiting for the Interurban" and the "Fremont Troll," as well as Seattle's most controversial statue, Emil Venkov's "Lenin," which was originally displayed in communist Slovakia in 1988.

The self-proclaimed "Center of the Universe," Fremont charms even the most cynical of Seattle residents with its mixture of inviting shops and events. It is the home of the original Red Hook Brewery, as well as several other microbreweries and pubs. There are art galleries galore, vintage clothing and "junk" stores, barber shops, and tattoo parlors. On the weekends, Seattle residents flock to the district for brunch and shopping, or for coffee and dessert at The Still Life Coffeehouse on North 35th Street. At night, Fremont's pubs overflow with a friendly and diverse crowd of locals. This area is still miraculously free of tourists, despite its proximity to downtown.

During the summer, the neighborhood hosts the Fremont Sunday Market, where residents and visitors can buy goods from local artists and artisans. Also popular is the Puget Consumers Co-op on North 34th Street, a refreshing alternative to the corporate mega-grocers. One weekend in June is devoted to the summer solstice, and includes the annual Solstice Parade and Fremont Fair. On summer Saturday evenings, a parking lot doubles as the site for the Fremont Outdoor Cinema. Moviegoers bring their own chairs to watch the flick, which is projected on the wall of a building bordering the lot.

The area is primarily residential, with a combination of artists, students, and young professionals calling Fremont home, though the last several years have seen rapid commercial growth here. The Quadrant Lake Union Center, located just east of the Fremont Bridge is home to Adobe Systems, and Getty Images plans to inhabit the Park View Building just west of the bridge. Despite the new construction, the neighborhood has maintained its delicate balance of bohemian culture and middle-class comfort. It is a close-knit community, popular among low and middle-income families, and, fortunately, still affordable for first-time homeowners.

If you'd like to rent in Fremont, your best bet is to drive, bicycle, or walk through the area looking for "For Rent" signs in windows. There is plentiful rental property here, both apartments and houses, but available units are generally snapped up before being advertised in the local newspapers. Fremont's shopping district contains some rental space, especially in the few blocks north of Fremont Place North, but don't limit your search to that area. To the east of Fremont Avenue, and across or under Aurora Avenue, there are many affordable housing opportunities. Aurora can be fairly noisy during high traffic times, so if you're sensitive to that, try to visit nearby rentals on a weekday, around 5 p.m. to experience the noise level first-hand.

A few blocks north of Fremont's shopping district is NW 39th Avenue, which is lined with large apartment buildings built during the 1950s and '60s. Since this area is along one of the main routes between Ballard, downtown, and the University District, it can be a little noisy during high traffic times. You'll find a more traditional residential area of 1920s Craftsman-style bungalows between NW 39th and NW 46th streets, and east of Fremont Avenue North. As with most Seattle neighborhoods near a university or college, the best time for renting is late April through early June, when students are making plans to head home for the summer. Fremont is 20 to 25 minutes by car or bus from the University of Washington, and a 5- to 15-minute walk from Seattle Pacific University, which is just across the Fremont Bridge on the north side of the Queen Anne neighborhood.

**Web Sites:** www.seattle.gov, www.fremont.com
**Area Code:** 206
**Zip Codes:** 98103, 98107
**Post Office:** Wallingford Station, 1329 N 47th St
**Library:** 731 N 35th St, 206-684-4084, www.spl.lib.wa.us
**Public Schools:** Seattle Public Schools, P.O. Box 19116, Seattle, WA 98109-1116, 206-298-7000, www.seattleschools.org
**Police:** North Precinct, 10049 College Way N, 206-684-0850, www.seattle.gov/police
**Emergency Hospital:** Swedish Medical Center Ballard, 5300 Tallman Ave NW, 206-781-6341, www.swedish.org
**Community Resources:** Fremont Neighborhood Council, 3518 Fremont Ave N, #111, 206-781-6624; Fremont Neighborhood Service Center, 908 N 34th St, 206-684-4054, www.seattle.gov; Fremont Public Association Community Resource Center, 1501 N 45th St, 206-694-6700, www.fremontpublic.org
**Public Transportation:** Metro Transit, 206-553-3000, http://transit.metrokc.gov; 5, 26, 28, 31, 46, 74, 82

## WALLINGFORD

**Boundaries: North:** Northeast 50th Street; **West:** Aurora Avenue North (Highway 99); **South:** Lake Washington Ship Canal; **East:** I-5

A symbol of a bygone era, the old gasworks at the north end of Lake Union marks the tip of the Wallingford neighborhood. In the early 1900s, when the plant was still operational, Wallingford was a hub of industrial activity. Now the neighborhood is predominantly residential, and the old plant is a beloved

Seattle landmark and popular public park. Gasworks Park is a favorite for kite-flying enthusiasts because of steady winds off the lake, and for bicyclists who meet to ride the Burke-Gilman trail along Lake Union and Lake Washington. In addition, Gasworks Park is the site of one of Seattle's annual Independence Day fireworks displays. Although the fireworks can be seen from anywhere around the lake, attendees here have the added benefit of watching the fireworks to the accompaniment of music and a live television broadcast.

Despite its proximity to downtown, Wallingford exudes a quiet charm. On summer evenings, couples stroll down tree-lined streets and visit with neighbors. On Sundays, people crowd into local restaurants for brunch or catch a matinee at the Guild 45th Theater. Like nearby Fremont, Wallingford is aesthetically pleasing and community focused. Elegant Wallingford Center, an old school that was re-modeled in the 1980s to become an upscale condominium and retail shopping center, is considered the crown jewel of the area. Nearby, the 45th Street Community Clinic shares a remodeled fire station with the Wallingford branch of the Seattle Public Library. Northeast 45th Street, connecting Fremont and Ballard to the University District, offers a pleasant assortment of ethnic restaurants, travel and used bookstores, and funky boutiques.

North of Gasworks Park, on the south slope of the hill, beautifully restored homes look out over the park and the downtown skyline. Many of the Victorian and Colonial houses here were built in the early 1900s. Northwest Moderns and Craftsman bungalows were added during the 1920s. Homeowners in this area tend to be young professionals, although rental opportunities attract students from the nearby UW and Seattle Pacific University. Streets here are quiet; churches and old schools dot the area, as do corner grocery stores and coffeehouses. Spectacular views of Lake Union and downtown, as well as modestly sized homes, have attracted many middle-income families to this area. That trend is changing slowly, however, as higher real estate prices have made this neighborhood less affordable for single-income families.

North of 45th Street and close to I-5, modest and more affordable homes can be found. Most are bungalows similar to those in the south end of the neighborhood, without the panoramic views of Lake Union and downtown but occasionally with views of the tips of the Cascades to the east. The area population includes young professionals and students residing in a mix of rentals and owner-occupied houses. There are few true apartment buildings in the blocks between 45th Street and Green Lake, but they become more common as one heads toward I-5 and the University District.

Wallingford is well located for those commuting to either downtown or the Eastside. Aurora Avenue North (Highway 99) runs parallel to Stone Way, just a few blocks into the Fremont neighborhood. This is generally a good route into downtown, and even to West Seattle or the Sea-Tac Airport. Savvy Eastside commuters take a shortcut along Lake Union to bypass I-5 and catch up with Highway 520 at the Montlake entrance.

**Web Sites:** www.seattle.gov, www.wallingford.org
**Area Code:** 206
**Zip Codes:** 98103, 98105
**Post Office:** Wallingford Station, 1329 N 47th St
**Library:** 1501 N 45th St, 206-684-4088, www.spl.lib.wa.us
**Public Schools:** Seattle Public Schools, P.O. Box 19116, Seattle, WA 98109-1116, 206-298-7000, www.seattleschools.org
**Police:** North Precinct, 10049 College Way N, 206-684-0850, www.seattle.gov/police
**Emergency Hospital:** University of Washington Medical Center, 1959 NE Pacific St, 206-598-3300, www.washington.edu/medical/uwmc
**Community Resources:** Wallingford Boys and Girls Club, 503 N 50th St, 206-547-2133; Wallingford Community Council, 2100-A N 45th St, 206-632-4759, www.wallingford.org; Wallingford Community Senior Center, 4649 Sunnyside Ave N, Ste 140, 206-461-7825
**Public Transportation:** Metro Transit, 206-553-3000, http://transit.metrokc.gov; 16, 26, 31, 44, 46, 74, 82

## GREEN LAKE

### MAPLE LEAF

**Boundaries: North:** NE 110th Street; **West:** Aurora Avenue North (Highway 99); **South:** North 50th Street; **East:** I-5

In the late 1800s trolleys connected Green Lake to downtown, creating a popular recreation spot for Seattle residents. An amusement park was opened on the west side of the lake and Woodland Park Zoo was developed at the south end. In the early 1900s, the city of Seattle annexed Green Lake and its surrounding lands, designating them a public space. Today, Green Lake is one of Seattle's most popular public parks. It is surrounded by a three-mile paved walkway that attracts bicyclists, in-line skaters, runners, and walkers. During the summer, fields at the east side of the lake fill with volleyball teams, and basketball courts offer informal but competitive pick-up games. At the south end of the lake, Woodland Park has baseball and soccer fields, lighted tennis courts, and a running track. A skateboard park for this area is in the planning stages.

North and east of Green Lake, cozy coffee shops, fragrant bakeries, sporting goods and bike shops provide services for visitors and residents. Most are located near the intersection of Ravenna Avenue and Green Lake Way, or a few minutes north at Green Lake Way and 80th Street. Beautiful Northwest Modern and Tudor homes line Green Lake Way, facing the lake. Even though there is heavy traffic along this main thoroughfare, the view of the lake and the popularity of the area keep up the value of these homes. Original neighborhood houses still exist, although the distance from these houses to the lake shore increased when the lake was partially drained in the early 1900s.

The neighborhood's charm and immediate accessibility to the park make Green Lake a high demand area, which is reflected in its real estate prices. According to *The Seattle Times*, the median home price in 2005 was $475,000, but it isn't difficult to find homes facing the lake that sell for over a million.

Homes just off the lake are the most expensive; many are elegant Colonial-style mansions with views of the lake and even of the Olympic Mountains. Recent construction has increased the number of condominiums and townhouses east of the lake, although the area remains primarily a mix of detached houses and apartments. More modest Northwest Modern and Craftsman homes line idyllic residential streets in the blocks southeast of Green Lake, bordering the Wallingford neighborhood. These homes have the advantage of proximity to Green Lake without the inconvenience of heavy traffic or summer parking problems. Northwest and west of the lake, particularly across Aurora Avenue North near the Phinney Ridge neighborhood, modest and affordable Craftsman-style bungalows and Cape Cod–style cottages line steep, quiet streets. There are few rentals available in this area, but prices for homes are often much lower than those closer in to the lake. Unpretentious yet comfortable homes may be found north of 80th Street. While many of these areas seem far from the lake, most are merely a few minutes' walk away. Green Lake is one of the few Seattle neighborhoods where many residents walk to do their errands. The area around the lake is flat rather than hilly and the heavy traffic in the area makes walking a pleasant alternative to driving.

While most houses around Green Lake are detached bungalows, ramblers, or duplexes, there are many options for those who would like to rent in the Green Lake area. On the southeast and east sides of the lake, particularly near Ravenna Boulevard, there are several apartment buildings and condominiums. Most are contemporary high-rise complexes; others are smaller Federal or 1950s-style apartment buildings. Many are a few blocks off the lake, surrounded by houses or other similar apartment buildings. In the smaller buildings, apartments are not often advertised in local newspapers, so prospective tenants should visit the area periodically looking for rental signs. For the best deals, try the area in the spring, when University of Washington students vacate for the summer. Dupre + Scott Apartment Advisors estimate that average monthly rent in Greenlake/ Wallingford is just over $1,000.

The Green Lake neighborhood is predominately middle-income. Southeast of the lake and across Aurora Avenue (Highway 99) to the west, couples and young families keep that part of the neighborhood hopping. These two areas have been growing rapidly as housing prices increase in the more affluent blocks north and east of Green Lake. According to the *Seattle Post-Intelligencer*, the city's Office of Management and Planning estimates that by the year 2014, the number of existing households in the Green Lake area will grow to 1,839—an increase of 400 since 1997, and a climb in density from 13.4 households per gross acre to 17.2.

Just north of Green Lake is the **Maple Leaf** neighborhood, recognizable by its blue water tower decorated with enormous white maple leaves. The small retail district runs along Roosevelt Way NE and includes coffeeshops, restaurants like the popular Judy Fu's Snappy Dragon, a hardware store, and many unique, independent stores. It is a neighborhood of quiet streets and modest but well-maintained homes. Most houses in the area are brick Tudors or contemporary split-levels, with small landscaped yards. Perched on a hill over I-5, many homes have views of the Olympics or Mount Rainier. Compared to other desirable neighborhoods in Seattle, housing prices in Maple Leaf are surprisingly affordable considering the neighborhood's proximity to Green Lake and I-5.

**Web Site:** www.seattle.gov
**Area Code:** 206
**Zip Code:** 98103
**Post Office:** Wedgwood Station, 7724 35th Ave NE
**Library:** 7364 E Green Lake Dr N, 206-684-7547, www.spl.lib.wa.us
**Public Schools:** Seattle Public Schools, P.O. Box 19116, Seattle, WA 98109-1116, 206-298-7000, www.seattleschools.org
**Police:** North Precinct, 10049 College Way N, 206-684-0850, www.seattle.gov/police
**Emergency Hospital:** Northwest Hospital, 1550 N 115th St, 206-364-0500, www.nwhospital.org
**Community Publication:** *North Seattle Herald-Outlook*, 4000 Aurora Ave N, Ste 100, 206-461-1300
**Community Resources:** Green Lake Community Center, 7201 E Green Lake Drive N, 206-684-0780, www.seattle.gov/parks; Green Lake Community Council, P.O. Box 31536, Seattle, WA 98103, www.greenlakecommunitycouncil.org; Maple Leaf Community Council, P.O. Box 75595, Seattle, WA 98125, www.ci.seattle.wa.us
**Public Transportation:** Metro Transit, 206-553-3000, http://transit.metrokc.gov; 16, 26, 48, 64, 66, 67, 68, 72, 73, 76, 77, 79, 82, 83, 242, 243, 316, 358, 372, 373

# UNIVERSITY DISTRICT

**ROOSEVELT**
**RAVENNA**
**UNIVERSITY PARK**
**BRYANT**

**Boundaries**: **North**: NE 75th Street; **West**: I-5; **South**: Lake Washington Ship Canal; **East**: NE 35th Street, Union Bay

In 1861, the University of Washington was founded on the present-day site of the Fairmont Olympic Hotel in downtown Seattle. Four Grecian pillars, all that remain of the original building, can now be seen on a small piece of land near the Paramount Theater (at the intersection of Pike Street and Boren Avenue). The university moved to its present location near Union Bay in 1895, intent upon shaking off its reputation as an elementary and high school—the UW graduated its first university student in 1876, but continued accepting pre-college students as late as 1897. Two influential Seattle citizens, Arthur Denny and Daniel Bagley, were instrumental in bringing the college to Seattle. Denny persuaded the legislature to grant Seattle the rights to the territorial university and donated 10 acres of his own property as the original site. Bagley had convinced Denny that the college would be more of an asset to the city than the other available alternatives: the state capitol, prison, or customs house. Asa Mercer, the university's first president and teacher, is best known today as the man who went east and recruited single women to move to Seattle when it was still a primarily male logging community. His substantial academic and advisory contributions to the fledgling college are largely overlooked. In 1909, the Alaska-Yukon-Pacific Exposition was held on campus, marking a turning point for the young university. Originally intended to celebrate the 10th anniversary of the Klondike Gold Rush, the event was held two years late but drew nearly four million visitors to the area. As a result of the exposition, the university received several new permanent buildings and gained national attention. Since then, annual enrollment has reached the 40,000 mark and the university has gained a reputation as a premier medical research institution. While some critics claim that the university gives special preference to its graduate and research programs, particularly the sciences over the humanities, it remains an affordable way to receive a high-quality undergraduate education.

Students, staff, and faculty of the university buzz about the campus and fill area coffeehouses at all hours of the day. On campus, be sure to visit the Burke Museum for, among other attractions, its marvelous exhibits on local Native American tribes, and the Graduate Reading Room, a beautiful cathedral-shaped room in the Suzzallo Library. For a look at one of Seattle's natural wonders, stop at "Frosh Pond" for a fabulous view of Mount Rainier over the Guggenheim Fountain.

In addition to its solid academic reputation, the University of Washington is nationally recognized for its football program. The Huskies routinely attract sold-out crowds for home games, even during disastrous seasons. Wealthy UW graduates and football fans are generous supporters of the program, and regularly generate more interest in the team than the current university students. The UW crew and basketball teams (particularly the women's) also receive local attention, although they are overshadowed by the fervent devotion of Husky football fans. All of the UW sports facilities are on the shore of Union Bay, an inlet of Lake Washington, along Montlake Avenue. Parking is scarce and traffic problems are common on football Saturdays; at other times two large parking lots north of the stadium are sufficient. City regulations benefit those who live near the stadium by assigning parking stickers and by limiting parking on most streets to neighborhood residents. Some lucky football fans come to the games by boat, tying up at the east side of the UW stadium. Others take advantage of the additional buses added to local routes on game days. For the fitness and environmentally minded, you can bike or walk to the games via the Burke-Gilman trail.

Locals and students refer to the university as the UW (pronounced "U-Dub") and to the area around it as the "U-District." Although the campus is the geographic focal point of the area, the center of the community is "the Ave." (University Way), running just a block west of the campus. A tad run-down, it's a great place to see movies, buy books and CDs, play video games, or eat at a variety of ethnic restaurants. Additional landscaping and wider sidewalks were recently added along "the Ave.," in order to improve the street surface. The Ave. is also a central location for bus service to the University District and other parts of the city, with routes to neighborhoods throughout the north end of Seattle and to downtown and Capitol Hill. Just south of NE 45th Street on the Ave., the University Bookstore carries an array of books, gifts, and art supplies, as well as required materials for UW classes. During the school year, the Ave. is a favorite student hangout. In the summer it is the site for the University District Street Fair, which takes over several blocks of the street for an entire weekend.

As one would expect, the University District is primarily a neighborhood of young people (the median age is 22). Residents include undergraduate and graduate students and university faculty members, as well as young professionals, scholars, and artists. Some families own homes in the northeast corner of the district near Ravenna Boulevard, but over 90% of U-District residents are renters. Just north of campus, 17th Avenue NE, a tree-lined avenue known informally as "Greek Row," is bordered by beautiful Colonial-style mansions. Many of these buildings, as well as those in the blocks east of 17th Avenue NE, have been converted into fraternities, sororities, and rooming houses. The north end of this area is popular with graduate students and visiting faculty, as well as long-time neighborhood residents.

West of campus you'll find apartment buildings and shared houses galore. Close to the campus there are several brick apartment buildings, offering small studios or one-bedrooms with hardwood floors and occasional views. Modern accommodations, built in the 1980s, are located near I-5 and offer multiple-bedroom apartments. Other rental opportunities are available near the University Village Mall, at the northeast corner of the UW campus. The mall includes a Starbucks and national chain stores such as The Gap, Eddie Bauer, Banana Republic, and Pottery Barn. Apartment buildings and townhouses line NE 22nd Street, and other rentals are tucked into the base of the hill behind the retail stores and strip malls that line NE 25th Street. The most affordable options here are rooms for rent in group houses—these are often listed in local papers such as *The Stranger* and the *Seattle Weekly*, and in the UW student paper *The Daily*. Rental houses are also readily available, particularly north of 50th Avenue NE. The best time for finding rentals of any kind is at the end of the school year when students head home for the summer. Many rentals are not listed in local papers, so it is generally a good idea to roam the neighborhood looking for "For Rent" signs. Additionally, the University of Washington Student Housing Affairs provides information to students and non-students alike about off-campus opportunities. Visit them in Room G20 of the Husky Union Building or call 206-543-9887.

The Roosevelt and Ravenna neighborhoods, located north of the University District, traditionally attract UW graduate students, faculty, and staff. In recent decades, professionals willing to commute to downtown or the Eastside have also moved to these areas. The center of the **Roosevelt** neighborhood is a small retail district based around the intersection of Roosevelt Avenue NE and NE 65th Street, which boasts several small ethnic restaurants, coffee shops, and bookstores. On the first Wednesday of every month, vintage motorcycle enthusiasts flock to Teddy's Bar, lining the street with bikes of all makes and models. Despite this "biker bar" tradition, the Roosevelt neighborhood is a tranquil residential community. Most houses in the Roosevelt District are Arts-and-Crafts-style bungalows and Tudor-style cottages. There are a few apartment buildings and condominiums in the neighborhoods, mostly near I-5 and Ravenna Boulevard.

The **Ravenna** neighborhood is named for the ravine that runs through the area, at one time connecting Green Lake with Union Bay and Lake Washington. Water still flows in the ravine, fed by underground streams and Seattle's ubiquitous rain. Ravenna Park follows the ravine, winding northwest toward the Green Lake area. It is a beautiful and lush city park with trails, tennis courts, and picnic areas. There are a variety of architectural styles in Ravenna, including modest Tudors, roomy Arts-and-Crafts homes, and 1960s bungalows. There are occasional opportunities for renting houses here, and a few apartments and townhouses line 25th Avenue East. Recent changes to Ravenna include the move of the familiar Honey Bear Bakery from its North 55th Street location to Northeast 65th Street and 20th Avenue.

The **University Park** neighborhood ranges from 16th Avenue NE in the west to 21st Avenue NE in the east. Its northern border is Ravenna Park, and NE 50th Street marks its southern edge. The tiny neighborhood is home to Park Drive, known as "Candy Cane Lane" during the Christmas holidays because of the profusion of lights and decorations that draw visitors from all over the city. The neighborhood consists primarily of well-preserved Arts-and-Crafts homes.

The **Bryant** neighborhood, east of University Village, has much in common with Ravenna. Houses here are mainly modest bungalows and Tudors, with a few scattered brick ranch houses. Ravenna and Bryant attract families, UW faculty and staff members, and professionals who work downtown or on the Eastside. Commuters to the Eastside have few choices on their route to the 520 bridge from here, so the drive at rush hour can be time-consuming. Beyond that, you can't beat its offer of quiet streets and friendly neighbors.

**Web Site:** www.seattle.gov

**Area Code:** 206

**Zip Codes:** 98105, 98115

**Post Office:** University Station, 4244 University Way NE

**Library:** 5009 Roosevelt Way NE, 206-684-4063, www.spl.lib.wa.us

**Public Schools:** Seattle Public Schools, P.O. Box 19116, Seattle, WA 98109-1116, 206-298-7000, www.seattleschools.org

**Police:** North Precinct, 10049 College Way N, 206-684-0850, www.seattle. gov/police

**Emergency Hospital:** University of Washington Medical Center, 1959 NE Pacific St, 206-548-4000, www.washington.edu/medical/uwmc

**Community Publication:** *North Seattle Herald-Outlook*, 4000 Aurora Ave N, Ste 100, 206-461-1300

**Community Resources:** University District Neighborhood Service Center, 4534 University Way NE, 206-684-7542, www.seattle.gov; Ravenna-Bryant Community Association, 6535 Ravenna Ave NE, 206-528-0329, www.scn.org/ neighbors/rbca; Ravenna Eckstein Community Center, 6535 Ravenna Ave NE, 206-684-7534; Roosevelt Neighbors' Alliance, 4534 University Way NE, 206-632-7760, www.scn.org/neighbors/rna; University Park Community Club, www.upcc.org

**Public Transportation:** Metro Transit, 206-553-3000, http://transit.metrokc.gov; 25, 31, 43, 44, 45, 46, 48, 49, 64, 65, 66, 67, 68, 70, 71, 72, 73, 74, 75, 76, 79, 83, 133, 167, 197, 205, 243, 271, 272, 277, 301, 316, 372, 373

# LAKE CITY

**Boundaries: North:** NE 145th Street; **West:** 5th Avenue NE; **South:** NE 95th Street; **East:** Lake Washington

Lake City is located near the north end of Lake Washington, just inside the city limits. When Seattle annexed Lake City in 1957, it was a quiet lakefront suburb with a small retail core along Lake City Way, a branch of the state highway system also known as Highway 522. Much of that small town character remains in Lake City, which attracts a mix of low- and middle-income families and professionals. The residential streets of Lake City are sheltered from the busy traffic of the highway, resulting in a slice of seclusion and a friendly, small-town atmosphere.

Those looking to live in Lake City will find affordable homes and ample rental apartments. Homes here are modest, predominantly bungalows or modern split-levels; many are on unusually large lots. Those east of Lake City Way may have views of Lake Washington and the Cascades. The Lake Washington waterfront in Lake City used to be lined with small weekend cottages, but as property values have soared many of those have been replaced with large, contemporary homes. Because of the distance from downtown and the Eastside, real estate prices and rents are generally lower here than in other residential neighborhoods in Seattle. However, living in Lake City makes for an easy commute to the north end of Lake Washington, Bothell, and Kenmore. Most apartment buildings are located in the few blocks to either side of Lake City Way and along NE 125th Street. Nearly half of the residents of Lake City rent apartments or houses, though new, modern condominium complexes on Lake City Way—with retail spaces at street level—are beginning to change that.

Lake City Way has changed significantly since it became part of Seattle; a small, tree-lined and pedestrian-friendly section of the "old town" still exists, with restaurants and small, locally owned retail businesses, but a major part of the highway is crowded with strip malls, gas stations, and auto lots. Adult bookstores and strip clubs have given Lake City Way a slightly seedy reputation, although the businesses have had little impact on the residential areas of the neighborhood. The community has experienced some problems with criminal activity near the highway, but community watch groups and patrols have substantially reduced crime along Lake City Way and throughout the neighborhood.

This is a culturally diverse community, and the meld of cultures and languages is reflected in the assortment of new businesses that have sprouted up along Lake City Way, including ethnic art shops and restaurants. Because of the affordable rents and homes, residents are primarily blue-collar workers and their families. More recently, the area has begun to attract artists and college-educated professionals, as well as retirees with modest incomes. The neighborhood particularly appeals to renters because of its wide variety of housing and affordability.

**Web Site:** www.seattle.gov
**Area Code:** 206
**Zip Code:** 98125
**Post Office:** Lake City Station, 3019 NE 127th St
**Library:** 12501 28th Ave NE, 206-684-7518, www.spl.lib.wa.us
**Public Schools:** Seattle Public Schools, P.O. Box 19116, Seattle, WA 98109-1116, 206-298-7000, www.seattleschools.org
**Police:** North Precinct, 10049 College Way N, 206-684-0850, www.seattle.gov/police
**Emergency Hospital:** Northwest Hospital, 1550 N 115th St., 206-364-0500, www.nwhospital.org
**Community Publication:** *North Seattle Herald-Outlook*, 4000 Aurora Ave N, Ste 100, 206-461-1300
**Community Resources:** Lake City Community Center, 12531 28th Ave NE, 206-362-4378; Lake City Neighborhood Service Center, 12707 30th Ave NE, 206-684-7526, www.seattle.gov; Meadowbrook Community Center, 10517 35th Ave NE, 206-684-7522, www.seattle.gov/parks;
**Public Transportation:** Metro Transit, 206-553-3000, http://transit.metrokc.gov; 41, 64, 65, 72, 75, 79, 243, 306, 312, 330, 372

# NORTHGATE

**JACKSON PARK**
**OAK TREE**
**AURORA**

**Boundaries: North**: North 145th Street; **West**: Aurora Avenue North (Highway 99); **South**: NE 92nd Street; **East**: 5th Avenue NE

Northgate is a large neighborhood centered around the Northgate Mall, which opened in 1950 and claims to be the oldest shopping mall in North America. The mall itself is rather small by current standards, and the businesses located there tend to be scaled-down versions of their downtown or Bellevue Square counterparts. Nevertheless, ample parking around the mall, as well as its close proximity to I-5, makes it a popular shopping destination. The mall and surrounding areas are currently undergoing renovations, including an expansion of the mall, and a large parking garage that is being added to address the increased traffic in the area. A new branch of the Seattle Public Library on Fifth Avenue NE facing the mall was completed in 2006, along with a new community center and park.

While the immediate area around the Northgate Mall is filled with small retail businesses that benefit from the mall traffic—restaurants, drug stores, banks, and sporting goods stores—the heart of Northgate's residential community is north of the mall, stretching as far as the Jackson Park neighborhood at the city boundary. Houses in this area are 1950s brick ranch houses or modest split-levels on large lots, popular with first-time homebuyers. There are also a number of duplexes, townhouses, apartment buildings, and condominiums, as well as an increasing number of senior citizen residences. While real estate and rental prices are lower here than in other parts of the city, this is a close-knit community, complete with freshly painted houses, well-kept lawns, and friendly neighbors. Many contemporary apartments and condominiums are just off the main streets in the area surrounding Northgate Mall.

West of I-5, the **Oak Tree** area runs along Aurora Avenue, north of Green Lake. The Oak Tree Shopping Center, which gave this area its name, has a Starbucks, several good restaurants, a large multiplex theater, and a supermarket. Nearby North Seattle Community College, an imposing concrete structure that resembles a small penitentiary, has a solid reputation, attracting students of all ages. The area around the college includes several small government agencies as well as the North Precinct for the Seattle Police Department. Also located in Oak Tree are a cultural center—formerly a public school—and a collection of modest homes and brightly painted townhouses.

North of Oak Tree is **Aurora**, which includes the area north of Northgate Way (105th Street) between Aurora Avenue North and I-5. Aurora Avenue North is a major business district, with a seemingly endless series of strip malls, car dealerships, small hotels, taverns, and appliance stores. While Aurora Avenue North has a reputation for petty crime and prostitution, residents who live even a few blocks off this main street rarely encounter any problems. A block or two east of Aurora Avenue North is a selection of modest split-level and contemporary brick homes. Real estate and rental prices in this area tend to be slightly lower than in those neighborhoods closer to downtown.

**Web Site:** www.seattle.gov
**Area Code:** 206
**Zip Codes:** 98133, 98125
**Post Office:** Northgate Station, 11036 Eighth Ave NE
**Library:** Lake City Library, 12501 28th Ave NE, 206-684-7518, www.spl.lib.wa.us
**Public Schools:** Seattle Public Schools, P.O. Box 19116, Seattle, WA 98109-1116, 206-298-7000, www.seattleschools.org
**Police:** North Precinct, 10049 College Way N, 206-684-0850, www.seattle.gov/police
**Emergency Hospital:** Northwest Hospital, 1550 N 115th St, 206-364-0500, www.nwhospital.org
**Community Publication:** *North Seattle Herald-Outlook*, 4000 Aurora Ave N, Ste 100, 206-461-1300
**Community Resource:** Bitter Lake Community Center, 13035 Linden Ave N, 206-684-7524, www.seattle.gov/parks

**Public Transportation:** Metro Transit, 206-553-3000, http://transit.metrokc.gov;
5, 16, 41, 66, 67, 68, 73, 75, 77, 242, 303, 304, 308, 345, 346, 347, 348, 373

# BROADVIEW

## THE HIGHLANDS

**Boundaries: North:** NW 145th Street; **West:** Puget Sound; **South:** NW 110th Street; **East:** Aurora Avenue North (Highway 99)

Located in the northwest corner of Seattle, Broadview, with its quiet residential streets and unremarkable commercial district, is really more of a suburban community than an urban neighborhood. Most of the area bears a close similarity to the suburban Shoreline community located just north of the city.

Greenwood Avenue North is the commercial street in this neighborhood and is lined with a variety of retail businesses, restaurants, and several small strip malls. This avenue also serves as a dividing line down the center of the neighborhood, with more affluent residents to the west and working-class families to the east. Bitter Lake, just northeast of the intersection of 130th and Greenwood, is surrounded by single-family homes that attract middle-income professionals. There are some apartments and condominium complexes between Greenwood Avenue and Aurora Avenue North, particularly south of 130th Street. Because this area is not so close to downtown or I-5, these generally rent for less than comparable in-city units.

Houses in the Broadview neighborhood are mainly modern bungalows, ramblers, and split-levels, although the homes grow grander as you progress north along 3rd Avenue NW, especially on the west side of the street. Many of these homes have splendid views of the Puget Sound and the Olympic Mountains, similar to the more expensive homes just south in the North Beach area.

At the far north end of 3rd Avenue NW, the Seattle Golf Club and the entrance to **The Highlands** present a glimpse of one of the most exclusive developments in Seattle. The Highlands, designed in 1909 by the Olmsteds (who also designed Seattle's park system), remain an exclusive and private enclave for the very wealthy. Although the lots are smaller now than the original minimum of five acres, the winding wooded roads and gated entrance have preserved the quiet seclusion of this community.

Houses and apartments close to Aurora Avenue North offer the least expensive prices and rents, while still providing the comforts of a close-knit residential community. A variety of modest and affordable houses for young families and middle-income professionals can be found north of 130th Street between 3rd Avenue NW and Greenwood Avenue NW, and in the vicinity of Carkeek Park.

While Broadview does not attract tourists, nor promise adventurous living, it will satisfy those looking for a stable suburban-style community within the city.

**Web Site:** www.seattle.gov
**Area Code:** 206
**Zip Code:** 98177
**Post Office:** Greenwood Station, 8306 Greenwood Ave N
**Library:** 12755 Greenwood Ave N, 206-684-7519, www.spl.lib.wa.us
**Public Schools:** Seattle Public Schools, P.O. Box 19116, Seattle, WA 98109-1116, 206-298-7000, www.seattleschools.org
**Police:** North Precinct, 10049 College Way N, 206-684-0850, www.seattle.gov/police
**Emergency Hospital:** Northwest Hospital, 1550 N 115th St, 206-364-0500, www.nwhospital.org
**Community Resource:** Bitter Lake Community Center, 13035 Linden Ave N, 206-684-7524, www.seattle.gov/parks
**Public Transportation:** Metro Transit, 206-553-3000, http://transit.metrokc.gov; 5, 28, 304, 345, 355

## SAND POINT

**LAURELHURST**
**VIEW RIDGE**
**WEDGWOOD**

**Boundaries: North:** NE 95th Street; **West:** 35th Avenue NE, Lake City Way; **South:** Union Bay; **East:** Lake Washington

On the shore of Lake Washington, the Sand Point neighborhood is best known as the location of the National Oceanic and Atmospheric Administration (NOAA) and Children's Hospital & Regional Medical Center. NOAA, a federal research facility that studies the weather and its impact upon the ocean and coastlines, shares a base with the Sand Point Naval Station on Lake Washington. Children's Hospital and Regional Medical Center, located on Sand Point Way, is a regional pediatric referral center that serves the special health care needs of children and their families.

Sand Point also features two public parks, both with access to the Lake Washington waterfront. Matthews Beach, located north of NOAA, is a summer favorite of sunbathers, picnickers, and swimmers. The Burke-Gilman trail stops off at Matthews Beach as it follows the edge of Lake Washington, giving bicyclists and in-line skaters easy access to the park. South of NOAA, Magnuson Park offers visitors the use of several sports fields, a swimming beach, kite hill, off-leash dog park, trails, public art, and a boat launch. Recently renovated, Magnuson Park is also the home of a new community garden and outdoor amphitheater.

**Laurelhurst**, on the southern hill of the Sand Point neighborhood, is a quiet and determinedly private neighborhood. Residents here tend to be affluent professionals and retirees living in homes with incredible views of Lake Washington and Union Bay, with Mount Rainier and the snow-capped Cascades providing a stunning backdrop. Laurelhurst is a neighborhood of expensive homes with appropriately manicured lawns and private waterfront access. Most houses are single-family residences, ranging in style from modest brick Tudors to palatial Georgians and Colonials. The border of Laurelhurst, along Sand Point Way, includes a thriving upscale retail district, as well as Children's Hospital and other clinics. At the top of the hill, the Laurelhurst park and community center serves as a hub for neighborhood activities, including softball games, summer picnics, aerobics, and pottery classes. The few rental opportunities to be found in this neighborhood are in the handful of apartment buildings located along Sand Point Way.

**View Ridge**, north of Laurelhurst, tends to attract wealthy professionals, affluent retirees, and UW professors. Homes in this area are modest brick Tudors and 1950s ranch houses with well-kept lawns; many have panoramic views of the sun rising over Lake Washington and the Cascades. Near Matthews Beach are renovated beach cottages, a reminder of an earlier time when this area was an out-of-town destination for Seattle residents. There are several newer "view" condominiums in this area as well. As with Laurelhurst, most rentals are limited to apartment buildings on busy Sand Point Way.

Located between Sand Point Way and 25th Avenue NE, **Wedgwood** offers a mix of affordable single-family homes, duplexes, townhouses, and apartment buildings with occasional views of the Cascade Mountains. Though homes in this neighborhood can't be considered cheap, they are less expensive here than elsewhere in the Sand Point area. Most homes are Cape Cod and Saltbox-style cottages, or Craftsman bungalows. The rental market is dominated by Wedgewood Estates, a large, nicely tended complex owned by the City of Seattle to ensure that mid-range housing remains available in this increasingly expensive part of town. Residents tend to be middle-income professionals and young families, as well as UW faculty and staff. Wedgwood has a strong and active Jewish community, with three synagogues located in the neighborhood. The retail district centers on two intersections along 35th Avenue NE, at NE 75th and NE 85th Streets, with grocery stores, medical offices, coffeeshops and bakeries, restaurants, and a few locally owned businesses.

**Web Sites:** www.seattle.gov, www.northeastseattle.com
**Area Code:** 206
**Zip Codes:** 98105, 98115

**Post Office:** Wedgwood Station, 7724 35th Ave NE
**Library:** North East Library, 6801 35th Ave NE, 206-684-7539, www.spl.lib.wa.us
**Public Schools:** Seattle Public Schools, P.O. Box 19116, Seattle, WA 98109-1116, 206-298-7000, www.seattleschools.org
**Police:** North Precinct, 10049 College Way N, 206-684-0850, www.seattle.gov/police
**Emergency Hospital:** University of Washington Medical Center, 1959 NE Pacific St, 206-548-4000, www.washington.edu/medical/uwmc
**Community Publication:** *North Seattle Herald-Outlook*, 4000 Aurora Ave N, Ste 100, 206-461-1300
**Community Resources:** Laurelhurst Community Center, 4554 NE 41st St, 206-684-7531; Sand Point Community Housing Association, 6940 62nd Ave NE, 206-517-5499; View Ridge Community Council, P.O. Box 15218, Seattle, WA 98115, www.scn.org/neighbors/viewridge
**Public Transportation:** Metro Transit, 206-553-3000, http://transit.metrokc.gov; 64, 65, 68, 71, 74, 75, 76, 83, 243, 372, 986, 987, 988, 989, 994, 995

## MADISON PARK

### WASHINGTON PARK
### DENNY BLAINE
### BROADMOOR

**Boundaries: North:** Union Bay; **West:** Lake Washington Boulevard; **South:** Lake Washington Boulevard; **East:** Lake Washington

On the shore of Lake Washington, the community of Madison Park lies just south of Union Bay and the 520 floating bridge. During the late 1800s, Madison Park was a beachfront resort town frequented by Seattle residents. Many took the cable car from downtown Seattle to the shore to spend the day or rented a nearby cottage for the week. Festivities in the summer included a carnival with food and games, and a Ferris wheel.

Today, Madison Park is an affluent community with a small-town feel. Shop owners know the names of their local customers, traffic is slow and leisurely, people stroll the sidewalks and smile at one another. It's one of the few Seattle neighborhoods that is not on a shortcut route to other parts of the city, so it is spared the traffic problems of other less fortunate neighborhoods.

One-of-a-kind restaurants and cafés, fashionable boutiques, and fragrant bakeries offering scrumptious goodies line East Madison Street, Madison Park's main thoroughfare. Nowhere will you find sprawling supermarkets, warehouse stores, chain restaurants or fast food joints. Although First Hill and Capitol Hill, with their mainstream business districts, are only ten minutes away, many Madison Park residents do most of their shopping locally.

Near the east end of East Madison Street, Colonial and Northwest Modern homes intermingle with more modest Cape Cods, reminiscent of the beach cottages that lined the shore in early Madison Park. Two traditionally expensive and fashionable Madison Park neighborhoods, **Washington Park** and **Denny Blaine**, lie further south along the shore of Lake Washington and on the hill facing the lake. Homes in these areas are an interesting mix, primarily Colonials and Northwest Moderns, as well as a few Elizabethan or Tudor homes. Many of the stately homes here were built when Seattle's wealthiest migrated to this area and other posh neighborhoods, such as Queen Anne and Capitol Hill, away from downtown and First Hill. Finally, the section called **Broadmoor** offers a variety of elegant homes in an ultra-exclusive golf and country club setting, tucked between Lake Washington and the Arboretum.

Just south of East Madison Street, high-rise condominiums face Lake Washington. Since these were completed, local zoning restrictions have changed, preventing other similar buildings from crowding out the homes that are the core of Madison Park. These condos offer the neighborly appeal of Madison Park and spectacular views of Lake Washington, the Cascades, and imposing Mount Rainier. On the north shore of the Madison Park peninsula, other contemporary and Colonial-style condominiums offer views of Lake Washington and the 520 Bridge.

Madison Park continues to be a neighborhood of wealthy and influential Seattle citizens. The community has a median income more than twice that of the rest of the city, and the homes here are some of the more expensive in Seattle; even modest Cape Cod cottages run in the several-hundred-thousand-dollar range. Though they rarely appear on the market, the grand residences in Broadmoor and Denny Blaine often break the million-dollar mark.

**Web Site:** www.seattle.gov
**Area Code:** 206
**Zip Codes:** 98112, 98122
**Post Office:** East Union Station, 1110 23rd Ave
**Library:** Montlake Library, 2300 24th Ave E, 206-684-4720, www.spl.lib.wa.us
**Public Schools:** Seattle Public Schools, P.O. Box 19116, Seattle, WA 98109-1116, 206-298-7000, www.seattleschools.org
**Police:** East Precinct, 1519 12th Ave, 206-684-4300, www.cityofseattle.net/police
**Emergency Hospital:** Swedish Medical Center, 747 Broadway, 206-386-2573, www.swedish.org
**Community Publication:** *Madison Park Times*, 4000 Aurora Ave N, Ste 100, 206-461-1300

**Community Resources:** Denny-Blaine Park, 200 Lake Washington Blvd E, www. seattle.gov/parks; Madison Park, 2300 43rd Ave E, www.seattle.gov/parks

**Public Transportation:** Metro Transit, 206-553-3000, http://transit.metrokc.gov; 11, 84, 988

# MONTLAKE

## PORTAGE BAY

**Boundaries**: **North**: Lake Washington Ship Canal; **West**: Fuhrman Avenue East; **South**: Boyer Avenue East; **East**: Lake Washington Boulevard

The Montlake Cut is a small, man-made waterway that connects Lake Union and Lake Washington. Each year on the first Saturday in May, the annual Opening Day celebration of boating season is celebrated here. Spectators, boating enthusiasts, and crew teams fill the cut for a day of races and boats on parade. The event's highlight is the Windermere Cup, the final race of the day that features the men's and women's Husky crew teams. Just south of the UW Husky Stadium, the Montlake Bridge crosses the cut, connecting Montlake Avenue to 24th Avenue East. The Montlake neighborhood includes all of the homes to the south side of this bridge and to either side of 24th Avenue East, which divides the community into east and west. Highway 520 further divides the area into north and south halves. Because it is located at the crossroads of two major thoroughfares, Montlake suffers from heavy traffic, particularly at rush hour. Despite this, the neighborhood feels tucked away from the cares of the city.

Homes in Montlake are a mix of imposing mansions, exquisite cottages, brick Tudors and elaborate Colonials. Winding streets and culs-de-sac add to the feeling of privacy in the neighborhood, though navigating the streets can be confusing. With the Montlake Cut to the north and the Arboretum to the east, Montlake's only close neighbor is **Portage Bay**, itself a tiny residential offshoot of the Eastlake and Capitol Hill neighborhoods. There are no shopping centers or malls, only a couple of small corner grocers and a freeway on-ramp gas station. University Village, an upscale outdoor shopping center located just north of Montlake on 25th Avenue NE, offers everything from a Banana Republic and Eddie Bauer to a huge QFC Grocery. The neighborhood is home to two of Seattle's premier yacht clubs, the Seattle Yacht Club and Queen City Yacht Club, giving members easy access to both Lake Union and Lake Washington. Also, the Museum of History and Industry is here, as well as beautiful Foster Island Park, a popular place to rent canoes, rowboats or sailboats and paddle or sail through the Arboretum.

On the south side of Highway 520 and west of 24th Avenue East, the Montlake Playfield is a center of activity for the neighborhood, with quiet tennis courts and a popular activity center. Just across 24th Avenue East, Montlake homes brush up against the Washington Park Arboretum, a 200-acre public park with 5,500 different trees and shrubs and a stunning Japanese Garden. A quick drive through the Arboretum brings you to the edge of the Madison Park neighborhood, and provides access to the heavenly bakeries, elegant salons, and excellent restaurants that line Madison Street.

Most Montlake residents are middle- or high-income professionals who work downtown or on the Eastside. When lucrative high-tech jobs on the Eastside, including those at Microsoft, increased in the late 1990s, Montlake became a popular neighborhood for successful software engineers and other technical workers. Other residents include current and retired UW professors and UW Medical Center doctors. Convenient access to I-5 and the Highway 520 Bridge—as well as the secluded and quiet nature of the residential areas—makes Montlake an attractive and sought-after location.

**Web Sites:** www.seattle.gov, www.montlake.net
**Area Code:** 206
**Zip Code:** 98112
**Post Office:** East Union Station, 1110 23rd Ave
**Library:** 2300 24th Ave E, 206-684-4720, www.spl.lib.wa.us
**Public Schools:** Seattle Public Schools, P.O. Box 19116, Seattle, WA 98109-1116, 206-298-7000, www.seattleschools.org
**Police:** East Precinct, 1519 12th Ave, 206-684-4300, www.cityofseattle.net/police
**Emergency Hospital:** University of Washington Medical Center, 1959 NE Pacific St, 206-548-4000, www.washington.edu/medical/uwmc
**Community Resources:** Montlake Community Center, 1618 E Calhoun St, 206-684-4736, www.seattle.gov/parks; Northeast Neighborhood Service Center, 4534 University Way NE, 206-684-7542, www.seattle.gov
**Public Transportation:** Metro Transit, 206-553-3000, http://transit.metrokc.gov; 25, 43, 44, 48, 167, 242, 243, 250, 252, 255, 256, 257, 260, 261, 265, 266, 268, 271, 272, 277, 280, 311

## CENTRAL DISTRICT

### JUDKINS PARK

**Boundaries:** **North:** East Madison Street, **West:** 12th Avenue East; **South:** I-90; **East:** Martin Luther King Jr. Way

The Central District or Central Area, referred to as "the CD" by most Seattle residents, cuts a long narrow swath through the center of Seattle. Most retail enterprises in the CD are located along 12th Avenue East and on 23rd Avenue East; many are family-owned restaurants and shops, including small African- or Asian-American groceries.

Sandwiched between Capitol Hill, First Hill, and the International District to the west, and Madison Park, Madrona, and Leschi to the east, the CD has long had an uneasy relationship with the rest of Seattle. Homes here are not all that different from those at this end of Capitol Hill—most are charming turn-of-the-century Victorians, 1920s Colonials, and Craftsman bungalows. Nevertheless, housing prices in the Central District, especially the eastern portion, have historically lagged behind prices in the rest of Seattle, in part because of geography. Steep slopes in the area slowed development and served as dividers from the rest of the city; the CD was further cut off by the expansion of I-90. Between 1970 and 1990, many homes in the area were neglected or even abandoned as residents moved out to the suburbs.

In recent years, however, housing prices in the CD have risen as more affluent residents have moved to the area, particularly in the north end of the neighborhood. Although many houses in the CD are still run-down from years of neglect, many are being refurbished by newcomers and longtime residents. In fact, home prices in the central section of Seattle rival those in the Ballard/ Greenlake region.

Bordered by I-90 to the south, 20th Avenue South to the west, Yesler Way to the north, and Martin Luther King Jr. Way to the east, **Judkins Park** is a one-mile rectangle in the southeast corner of the Central Area. Once a neglected neighborhood decimated by the expansion of I-90 in the 1960s, Judkins Park, like much of the rest of the Central District, is now flourishing. Residents can buy freshly baked bread from Gai's Northwest Bakery Thrift on South Weller Street. At the corner of South Jackson Street and 23rd Avenue South, there is a Walgreen drugstore, Starbucks, Hollywood Video, and a Red Apple market.

At the center of the Central District is Garfield High School, which consistently produces National Merit Scholars, and boasts a number of famous former students, including Jimi Hendrix, Bruce Lee, Quincy Jones, and Ernestine Anderson. Other notable Central Area institutions include Providence Medical Center and Seattle University.

An analysis of census data showed that in 1980 the area was more than 80% African-American and about 11% white. By 2000, *The Seattle Times*, reporting on the changing demographics of the CD, declared that the area had become home to fewer African-Americans than at any other time in the previous 30 years; census figures from the same year put the residential mix at 43% white, 32% African-American, 10% Asian or Pacific Islanders, and 8% Hispanic. Economic change is also being felt in the Central District. Millions of dollars of new construction is under way or planned, including a four- to six-story building at 2211 East Madison Street that now houses a Safeway supermarket, upper-level residential units, and an underground parking garage.

Prospective residents should be aware that racial tensions do exist in the Central District. The general target of the neighborhood's anger, however, is the city and its law enforcement, and steps have been taken to improve relations, including the formation of a civilian-led Office of Professional Accountability.

**Web Sites:** www.seattle.gov, www.centralarea.org
**Area Code:** 206
**Zip Codes:** 98122, 98144
**Post Office:** East Union Station, 1110 23rd Ave
**Library:** Douglass-Truth Library, 2300 E Yesler Way, 206-684-4704, www.spl.lib. wa.us
**Public Schools:** Seattle Public Schools, P.O. Box 19116, Seattle, WA 98109-1116, 206-298-7000, www.seattleschools.org
**Police:** East Precinct, 1519 12th Ave, 206-684-4300, www.cityofseattle.net/police
**Emergency Hospital:** Swedish Medical Center, 747 Broadway, 206-386-2573, www.swedish.org
**Community Resources:** Central Area Development Association, 2515 S Jackson St, 206-328-2240, www.seattle.gov; Central Area Motivation Program, 722 18th Ave, 206-329-4111, www.seattle.gov; Central Area Youth Association, 119 23rd Ave, 206-322-6640; Central Neighborhood Association, www. centralarea.org; Central Neighborhood Service Center, 1825 S Jackson St, Ste 208, 206-684-4767, www.seattle.gov; Garfield Community Center, 2323 E Cherry St, 206-684-4788, www.seattle.gov/parks; Langston Hughes Cultural Arts Center, 104 17th Ave S, 206-684-4757; Yesler Community Center, 835 E Yesler Way, 206-386-1245, www.seattle.gov/parks

## MADRONA/LESCHI

**Boundaries**: **North**: Denny Way; **West**: Martin Luther King Jr. Way; **South**: I-90; **East**: Lake Washington

The Madrona and Leschi neighborhoods lie along Lake Washington, east of the Central District and the International District. While Madrona sits atop the hill facing west, Leschi, named for a Nisqually Indian executed for resisting the whites, faces east toward Lake Washington. Some consider Madrona and Leschi part of the Central District, but both neighborhoods are quite different from the CD. While the CD historically has been a neighborhood for those with moderate means, both Madrona and Leschi started out as affluent neighborhoods. It wasn't until after the 1960s when many of its wealthy residents moved to other areas of Seattle and outside Seattle that Madrona/Leschi declined. Fortunately for many, this shift made the area more affordable, and allowed for an influx of people from varied backgrounds. The result is that today these neighborhoods are a welcoming blend of various ethnic groups and income levels with both longtime residents and newcomers.

Madrona's center is the lively intersection of 34th Avenue East and East Union Street. Clustered here are the popular cafés and trendy shops. The few blocks surrounding this intersection create an idyllic urban village, with people sitting on storefront steps and at restaurant tables along the sidewalks. There are several small eateries here that cater to a Sunday brunch crowd. In Leschi, most businesses are located on the lake, and are primarily view restaurants and boat-related ventures, including the Corinthian Yacht Club. A condominium and retail complex, Lakeside at Leschi, is located on the shore of Lake Washington. To the south, Leschi Park features Victorian-style grounds, towering sequoias, and colorful tulip trees. Atop the hill, Frink Park offers lovely walking trails under grand maples.

Residents of Madrona and Leschi range from artists and artisans to young professionals, from retirees to families with young children. Homes also run the gamut in size and style, from opulent turn-of-the-century Victorians and Colonials to narrow abodes that were once corner groceries. Many of the splendid homes in Leschi have spectacular views of Lake Washington, the Cascade Mountains, and Mount Rainier. Other homes in both Madrona and Leschi share a view of downtown and the Olympics to the west.

Security concerns are evidenced by the bars on the windows on some businesses and houses in these neighborhoods. While there is a strong sense of community here, proximity to higher crime neighborhoods such as Rainier Valley and the Central District make both Madrona and Leschi more vulnerable than other Seattle neighborhoods. However, the crime rates are trending down in these areas and local neighborhood watch groups are organized and effective.

**Web Site:** www.seattle.gov
**Area Code:** 206
**Zip Codes:** 98122, 98144
**Post Office:** East Union Station, 1110 23rd Ave
**Libraries:** Douglass-Truth Library, 2300 E Yesler Way, 206-684-4704, www.spl.lib.wa.us; Madrona-Sally Goldmark Library, 1134 33rd Ave, 206-684-4705, www.spl.lib.wa.us
**Public Schools:** Seattle Public Schools, P.O. Box 19116, Seattle, WA 98109-1116, 206-298-7000, www.seattleschools.org
**Police:** East Precinct, 1519 12th Ave, 206-684-4300, www.cityofseattle.net/police
**Emergency Hospital:** Harborview Medical Center, 325 9th Ave, 206-731-3074, www.uwmedicine.org/facilities/harborview
**Community Resources:** Central Area Motivation Program, 722 18th Ave, 206-329-4111, www.seattle.gov; Garfield Community Center, 2323 E Cherry St,

206-684-4788, www.seattle.gov/parks; Madrona Community Council, 206-287-4837, www.madrona.org

**Public Transportation:** Metro Transit, 206-553-3000, http://transit.metrokc.gov; 2, 3, 27, 84, 988

## BEACON HILL

### SOUTH BEACON HILL
### HOLLY PARK
### MOUNT BAKER

**Boundaries**: North: I-90; **West**: I-5; **South**: South Ryan Street (to Martin Luther King Jr. Way South), South Genesee Street; **East**: Lake Washington

From the top of Beacon Hill, the Amazon.com Building looms over the city like a huge gothic castle, and the internet giant has helped to change the face of this south Seattle community. While Beacon Hill has been overlooked by prospective homeowners or tenants in the past, it is now a growing, flourishing, ethnically diverse neighborhood with a strong sense of community and comfortable homes that are among the most affordable in the city.

North of Spokane Street, quiet streets are lined with 1940s tract houses and modest bungalows on small but well-kept lots. Residents include middle-income families and young or retired couples. Apartment buildings in the area offer studio, one-, and two-bedroom units for rents slightly below the city average. Many streets have views of downtown, the Cascades, or the Olympics, and a small park on 12th Avenue South has provided memorable postcard pictures of Seattle and Elliot Bay. A new light rail line will connect north Beacon Hill to downtown and Sea-Tac Airport by the end of 2009, but be aware that the construction of a tunnel under Beacon Hill, and the new station, will affect the neighborhood for some years.

South of Spokane Street, small bungalows and contemporary split levels sell for slightly less than comparable homes at the north end of the hill. New townhomes have subdivided several of the larger lots in the neighborhood. Small family businesses such as Asian groceries and restaurants dot the neighborhood, and the beautiful Jefferson Park and Public Golf Course is located here.

Farther south, New Holly and Othello Station— pioneering mixed income developments—contain new single-family homes and townhomes interspersed with small parks. The area is racially and economically diverse and offers housing for low and middle-income families as well as market rate homes. Othello Station will also be a stop on the future light rail line.

Clinging to the east slope of the hill, the Mount Baker neighborhood is the most affluent section of Beacon Hill. Most homes here have spectacular views of the south end of Lake Washington and the Cascades. Many wealthy professionals live in this area, and it is certainly one of the most racially diverse of Seattle's affluent neighborhoods.

Crime may be a concern on some parts of Beacon Hill, particularly in the southeast section, as gang-related activities occasionally encroach from nearby Rainier Valley. Local crime prevention groups have been increasingly successful in mobilizing the community and in cleaning up public spaces, but newcomers should be aware of the neighborhood dynamics before choosing a home here.

**Web Site:** www.seattle.gov

**Area Code:** 206

**Zip Codes:** 98118, 98144

**Post Offices:** Columbia Station, 3727 S Alaska St; International Station, 414 6th Ave S

**Library:** 2519 15th Ave S, 206-684-4711, www.spl.lib.wa.us

**Public Schools:** Seattle Public Schools, P.O. Box 19116, Seattle, WA 98109-1116, 206-298-7000, www.seattleschools.org

**Police:** South Precinct, 3001 S Myrtle St, 206-386-1850, www.seattle.gov/police

**Emergency Hospital:** Harborview Medical Center, 325 9th Ave, 206-731-3074, www.uwmedicine.org/facilities/harborview

**Community Publication:** *Beacon Hill News*, 4000 Aurora Ave N, Ste 100, 206-461-1300

**Community Resources:** Greater Duwamish Neighborhood Service Center, 3801 Beacon Ave S, 206-233-2044, www.seattle.gov; Jefferson Community Center, 3801 Beacon Ave S, 206-684-7481, www.seattle.gov/parks

**Public Transportation:** Metro Transit, 206-553-3000, http://transit.metrokc.gov; 14, 27, 32, 36, 38, 39, 42, 48, 60, 106

# RAINIER VALLEY

**COLUMBIA CITY**
**RAINIER BEACH**
**DUNLAP**

**Boundaries: North:** South Genesee Street; **West:** Martin Luther King Jr. Way South; **South:** South Juniper Street, South 116th Street; **East:** 48th Avenue South, Lake Washington

Until the construction of I-90 through the Central District, what is now Rainier Valley was a southerly extension of the CD. Today, Rainier Valley is one of Seattle's most ethnically diverse neighborhoods, with a large minority and immigrant population. Unfortunately, it has a higher percentage of residents living in poverty than other neighborhoods and more problems with crime than many other areas of the city. Perhaps because of its physical isolation from the rest of Seattle, Rainier Valley has not received the attention that might have prevented or lessened many of its current socioeconomic problems.

Residents believe the neighborhood is a better place to live in now than it was a decade ago. Their optimism is well-founded. According to the Seattle Police Department, the crime index for the South Precinct, which includes Rainier Valley, dropped 8% in the first ten months of 2006. Notably, auto thefts decreased by nearly 30%, and total thefts decreased by 22%. Robbery, however, rose 38%, and gang activity is still occasionally reported in Rainier Valley. Despite the mixed statistics, there are still hopeful signs that this is a community on the mend.

The new mixed-use Rainier Court development at 3700 Rainier Avenue South will provide 500 housing units and retail space on a formerly contaminated industrial site. The buildings are filling with residents and the final two phases of the project should be developed by 2008. The city estimates that the valley's industrial north end will employ about 5,000 people by 2014.

The retail district is located along Rainier Avenue South, and is Rainier Valley's main thoroughfare. It is home to small, locally owned shops, delis, bakeries, and take-out restaurants. The renowned Borracchini's Bakery has been in the neighborhood for more than 70 years, and attracts people from all over Seattle with its delicious decorated-while-you-wait sheet cakes. It's one of the few reminders of Rainier Valley's Italian heritage—the area was settled almost a century ago by Italian immigrants, and was referred to as "Garlic Gulch." Once the exclusive province of ethnic shops and eateries, national chain retailers have recently come this way, allowing residents to meet almost all of their shopping needs without leaving the neighborhood. The Mutual Fish Company is one of the best places in the city for fresh seafood; for the alternative-minded, the neighborhood offers a PCC Natural Market (bordering the Seward Park neighborhood), specializing in organic produce, natural foods, and freshly baked treats. Overall, Rainier Valley seems to be benefiting from both the hard work of committed community groups and the increased prosperity of the greater Seattle area.

Columbia City, in the heart of Rainier Valley, is also experiencing revitalization. Beginning in 1995, residents joined together to fight increasing crime through an innovative crime-stopping dog walk. Several nights a week, residents and their pets would stroll through the community. The idea was to get people out of their homes, allow them to meet their neighbors, and send a message to criminals that they were not welcome. This, combined with other efforts, including those by the Columbia City Revitalization Committee, worked. As crime decreased, the commercial district, centered at Rainier Avenue South and South Ferdinand Street, began to expand to include new restaurants, coffee shops, an art gallery, and offices. A farmers' market at the corner of Rainier Avenue South and South Edmunds, and live-music walks are other popular attractions. The Rainier Valley Cultural Center offers a wide variety of performing arts in a classic building. Homes in Columbia City range from turn-of-the-century Victorians to modest bungalows. While homes here are slightly more expensive than those in the rest of Rainier Valley, the prices are still well below the city average.

Rainier Beach and Dunlap, located on the Lake Washington waterfront, offer lovely old homes, ranging from modest 1920s bungalows to stately turn-of-the-century mansions, most with spectacular views of Lake Washington and the Cascades. Crime rates in this part of the Rainier Valley are at or below the Seattle average. Seward Park Estates, once one of the most run-down apartment complexes in Seattle, now provides quality low-income housing just steps from Lake Washington. In general, real estate prices in this neighborhood remain slightly lower than they are for comparable view homes in other parts of the city.

Rainier Beach reflects the racial diversity of the entire Rainier Valley, with a mixture of whites, African-Americans, Asian/Pacific Islanders, and Hispanics. Such diversity is reflected in the tiny business district (characterized by the popular King Donut, at 9232 Rainier Avenue South), where you'll find a Filipino-owned, coin-operated laundry, a Vietnamese jewelry store, a Mexican restaurant, and a Japanese teriyaki shop.

Newcomers to Seattle looking into Rainier Valley should keep in mind that gang-related activities and violent crimes are more common here than elsewhere in the city. Although most residents are respectable, hard-working folks, and there are many wonderful streets in Rainier Valley, pockets of criminal activity may be only a block or two away.

**Web Site:** www.seattle.gov
**Area Code:** 206
**Zip Codes:** 98118, 98178
**Post Office:** Columbia Station, 3727 S Alaska St
**Libraries:** Columbia Library, 4751 Rainier Ave S, 206-386-1908, www.spl.lib.wa.us; New Holly Library, 6805 32nd Ave S, 206-386-1905, www.spl.lib.wa.us; Rainier Beach Library, 9125 Rainier Ave S, 206-386-1906, www.spl.lib.wa.us
**Public Schools:** Seattle Public Schools, P.O. Box 19116, Seattle, WA 98109-1116, 206-298-7000, www.seattleschools.org
**Police:** South Precinct, 3001 S Myrtle St, 206-386-1850, www.seattle.gov/police
**Emergency Hospital:** Harborview Medical Center, 325 9th Ave, 206-731-3074, www.uwmedicine.org/facilities/harborview
**Community Resources:** Central Area Motivation Program, 77919 Rainier Ave S, 206-722-2417, www.seattle.gov; Southeast Neighborhood Service Center,

4859 Rainier Ave S, 206-386-1931, www.seattle.gov; Rainier Community Center, 4600 38th Ave S, 206-386-1919, www.seattle.gov/parks; Rainier Beach Community Center, 8825 Rainier Ave S, 206-386-1925, www.seattle.gov/parks; Van Asselt Community Center 2820 S Myrtle St, 206-386-1921, www.seattle.gov/parks; Rainier Valley Cultural Center, 3515 S Alaska St, 206-760-4288, www.seedseattle.org/arts/rvcc

**Public Transportation:** Metro Transit, 206-553-3000, http://transit.metrokc.gov; 7, 8, 9, 32, 34, 36, 38, 39, 42, 48, 51, 106, 107, 987

## SEWARD PARK

**Boundaries: North**: South Genesee Street; **West**: 48th Avenue South; **South**: South Holly Street; **East**: Lake Washington

The Seward Park neighborhood is located just south of Mount Baker, on Lake Washington. The park from which this community takes its name is a 277-acre peninsula filled with lush vegetation, including cherry trees, lofty Douglas firs, and silvery madrona trees. Whether or not you choose to live here, Seward Park is always worth a visit: during the summer the park hosts jazz concerts and the annual Seafair celebration; and, in addition to nature trails and the lake, it is one of the best places in the city to savor breathtaking views of Mount Rainier. Residents take advantage of the Seward Park Art Studio, located in the original 1927 bathhouse, which offers pottery classes for all levels of students and serves as a workshop for several professional artists. And, residents and visitors alike line the streets for the annual Danskin Triathlon for women, held at either Seward Park or nearby Stan Sayres Park.

Residents of Seward Park are mostly affluent professionals, including local politicians and judges, and plenty of seniors, some of whom reside in the Kline Galland nursing home. While nearly half of Seward Park residents are Asian-American or African-American, the neighborhood is best known for its strong Jewish community. In fact, most of Seattle's Orthodox Jews live in or near Seward Park, attending one of the many synagogues located here. Bikur Cholim Machzikay, the oldest synagogue in Washington, is located at 5145 South Morgan Street.

Homes in Seward Park range from 1950s brick ranch houses to stately modern mansions. Most have views of Lake Washington and Mount Rainier; many have waterfront access. While homes here are expensive due to the panoramic views, the neighborhood's proximity to Rainier Valley has kept real estate prices slightly lower than other Seattle neighborhoods.

**Web Site:** www.seattle.gov
**Area Code:** 206

**Zip Code:** 98178

**Post Office:** Columbia Station, 3727 S Alaska St

**Library:** Rainier Beach Library, 9125 Rainier Ave S, 206-386-1906, www.spl.lib.wa.us

**Public Schools:** Seattle Public Schools, P.O. Box 19116, Seattle, WA 98109-1116, 206-298-7000, www.seattleschools.org

**Police:** South Precinct, 3001 S Myrtle St, 206-386-1850, www.seattle.gov/police

**Emergency Hospital:** Harborview Medical Center, 325 9th Ave, 206-731-3074, www.uwmedicine.org/facilities/harborview

**Community Resources:** Southeast Neighborhood Service Center, 4859 Rainier Ave S, 206-386-1931, www.seattle.gov; Rainier Beach Community Center, 8825 Rainier Ave S, 206-386-1925, www.seattle.gov/parks; Seward Park, 5902 Lake Washington Blvd S, (Environmental Learning Center, 206-684-4396, Art Studio, 206-722-6342); Lakewood Seward Park Community Center, 4916 S Angeline St, 206-722-9696; Bikur Cholim Machzikay Hadath Congregation, 5145 S Morgan, 206-721-0970, bikurcholim@qwest.net

## DUWAMISH DISTRICT

### SOUTH PARK
### GEORGETOWN
### SODO

**Boundaries: North**: South Royal Brougham Way, South Dearborn Street; **West**: Duwamish Waterway, Highway 509; **South**: South Barton Street; **East**: I-5

The Duwamish District is a primarily industrial area that starts just south of Safeco Field and follows the Duwamish River south to the city limits. Originally the land on either side of the river was fertile farmland, but eventually the farms were displaced by industries that used the river for shipping and, unfortunately, dumping. Today, most of the district remains strictly industrial, although there are pockets of residential and retail activity in the South Park and Georgetown areas. Boeing Field is located in the vicinity, but most employees commute to the area rather than live here. People from other parts of the city visit the Gai's Bakery outlet store and the nearby Museum of Flight at Boeing Field, or use the through streets in this neighborhood as shortcuts to the SeaTac Airport, Burien, and West Seattle.

**South Park** is a small community at the south end of this district, near the Duwamish River. This is a neighborhood of extremely modest bungalows, many of which are rentals. Quickly becoming known as "Little Tijuana," South Park is the only neighborhood in Seattle where Hispanic residents are heavily concentrated, 37% according to the 2000 census. Anchoring the neighborhood's four-block retail core on 14th Avenue South is the Mexi-Mart, a Mexican grocery, bakery, take-out restaurant, clothing, and music store. The residential face of the neighborhood is slowly changing, however, as more middle-class Seattle residents are finding South Park one of the most affordable areas in the city.

The **Georgetown** neighborhood, in the area around South Michigan Street, is an odd assortment of simple frame houses, breakfast cafés, warehouses, and other industrial buildings. Residents of Georgetown tend to be blue collar workers who appreciate the lower housing prices. A growing number of artists have discovered Georgetown's affordable studio space, including several who collaborate and share resources in the former Rainier Brewery on Airport Way South, now home to artist live/work spaces and Tully's Coffee headquarters. The Seattle Design Center, a 360,000-square-foot complex of 60 designer showrooms on Sixth Avenue South, provides many of the city's contractors and homeowners with furnishings, fabrics, and accessories.

The **SODO** (South of the Dome/South of Downtown) area borders downtown at Royal Brougham Street, south of the former Kingdome area. It's an industrial area, filled with warehouses and small manufacturing plants. The historic Sears building—now headquarters to Starbucks Coffee—is located here, as well as a sprawling new Home Depot. Few people actually live in SODO, but many of those who do are artists, residing in spacious lofts tucked inside converted warehouses. Though there are no grocery stores here, and the noise from passing cargo and passenger trains can be unbearable at times, creative types appreciate the lofts' high ceilings and plentiful elbowroom. City planners are considering new zoning laws that would allow higher buildings in the area to pave the way for future development of condominiums and apartment buildings in a plan to remake this area into a mixed-use urban neighborhood.

**Web Site:** www.seattle.gov
**Area Code:** 206
**Zip Codes:** 98108, 98168, 98106
**Post Office:** Georgetown Station, 620 S Orcas St
**Library:** Delridge Library, 5423 Delridge Way SW, 206-937-7680, www.spl.lib. wa.us
**Public Schools:** Seattle Public Schools, P.O. Box 19116, Seattle, WA 98109-1116, 206-298-7000, www.seattleschools.org
**Police:** West Precinct, 610 3rd Ave, 206-684-8917, www.seattle.gov/police
**Emergency Hospital:** Harborview Medical Center, 325 9th Ave, 206-731-3074, www.uwmedicine.org/facilities/harborview
**Community Resources:** Duwamish Coalition, 516 3rd Ave, www.ci.seattle.wa. us/business/dc; Georgetown Crime Prevention and Community Council, P.O. Box 80021, Seattle, WA 98108, www.ci.seattle.wa.us/commnty/georgetown;

Greater Duwamish Neighborhood Service Center, 3801 Beacon Ave S, 206-233-2044, www.seattle.gov; SODO Business Association, 2728 3rd Ave S, 206-292-7449, www.seattle.gov

**Public Transportation:** Metro Transit, 206-553-3000, http://transit.metrokc.gov; 21, 22, 23, 32, 35, 38, 39, 56, 57, 60, 85, 101, 106, 113, 116, 118, 119, 121, 122, 123, 131, 132, 133, 134, 150, 152, 170, 174, 177, 190, 191, 194, 196, 280

## WEST SEATTLE

**ADMIRAL**
**ALKI**
**FAUNTLEROY**
**DELRIDGE**

**Boundaries: North**: Puget Sound, Elliott Bay; **West**: Puget Sound; **South**: Seola Beach Drive SW, SW Roxbury Street; **East**: Duwamish Waterway, Highway 509

In 1851, the schooner *Exact* landed on Alki Beach in what is now West Seattle, bringing the Denny party to the Puget Sound. Charles Terry, a member of the original party, remained behind while the rest of the group moved on to what is now the Seattle waterfront. By 1897, the peninsula had a large enough population to merit a ferry between downtown and West Seattle. Today, West Seattle is a comfortable residential hill connected to the rest of the city by the West Seattle Freeway, which bridges the Duwamish Waterway and the man-made Harbor Island.

Atop the hill, the West Seattle Junction at SW Alaska Street and California Avenue SW is a commercial center for West Seattle. Clothing boutiques, bookstores, small diners, and drug stores fill the ground floor retail space around "the Junction." Young couples and singles rent the quaint apartments above the storefronts. East of the junction, auto dealerships and ethnic take-out restaurants cluster around the intersection of SW Alaska Street and Fauntleroy Way SW.

With housing prices lower than in similar neighborhoods closer to the city, West Seattle continues to gain in popularity. Homes can be found in the $300,000 to $400,000 range here.

The intersection of SW Admiral Way and California Avenue SW is the second retail core on the hill. Here, the historic Admiral Theater presides over the intersection, which is lined with small shops, espresso joints, and funky restaurants. The **Admiral** district, which surrounds this intersection, is one of the more affluent areas in West Seattle. Homes at the top of the hill, mainly Craftsman bungalows and Northwest Moderns, have views of downtown to the northeast or of the Olympics to the west. Residents of the Admiral area tend to be middle- to upper-income professionals and their families.

The Admiral business district enjoys a magnificent Thriftway grocery store, filled with gourmet cheeses, fresh flowers, and fine wines, but suffers from a shortage of parking. Residents here lobbied for a parking garage near the Admiral Theatre, but the city council refused to approve funding. Instead, a local developer agreed to add an extra floor of parking to a condominium project. Nonetheless, parking on a Saturday night, when the district is filled with diners and moviegoers, continues to present a challenge.

**Alki** is a long, narrow beach neighborhood that stretches along the north and west sides of the peninsula and offers the atmosphere of an ocean resort town. In the summer, the beach is crowded with sunbathers, in-line skaters, bicyclists, and volleyball players. In the spring and fall, residents meet for coffee and dessert at the Alki Bakery, or stop for dinner at Spuds Fish & Chips or Pegasus Pizza. Although development has begun to change the face of this area, many 1960s condominiums and beach cottages are still located just a short walk or bicycle ride from the beach. Residents are generally middle-income service professionals, many of whom are longtime West Seattle residents. Alki has extraordinary views of both downtown Seattle and the Olympic peninsula. The most spectacular views of the Olympics come during early spring or late fall, when the sun is bright and the snow has not yet melted in the mountains. The Alki beachhead is a popular destination for couples watching the sunset during the summer, and many intrepid Seattle residents brave inclement winter weather to watch the waves crash against the shore. Salty's on Alki, at 1936 Harbor Avenue SW, is one of the city's favorite view restaurants and a popular spot for wedding receptions and Sunday brunch. If there is a downside to Alki, it is the waves of tourists, short-term renters, and sun-worshippers who crowd the neighborhood during the summer. The city's anti-cruising ordinance stopped most of the circling of cars and motorcycles, but traffic on sunny days still slows to a crawl on Harbor Avenue SW.

Comparing Alki's views to those of Manhattan from Hoboken, NJ, the *Seattle Post-Intelligencer* calls this one of Seattle's hottest condo markets, with units selling for $275,000 to $1 million.

The **Fauntleroy** neighborhood lies along the southwest slope of the hill in West Seattle, facing the Puget Sound. Though Fauntleroy is best known throughout the rest of Seattle for its ferry dock, with services to Vashon Island and the Olympic Peninsula, it is also a comfortable, secluded neighborhood. Beautiful brick Tudors, classic Northwest Modern homes, and modest bungalows line winding streets and quiet culs-de-sac. Fauntleroy was home to some of Seattle's original families, like the Colmans, who built the city's first brick building and its downtown ferry terminal. Another famous resident, Jim Whittaker, who was the first American to stand atop Mount Everest, grew up playing in the woods in Fauntleroy. Homes here have unparalleled views of Puget Sound, Vashon Island,

and the Olympics. Lincoln Park, at 8011 Fauntleroy Way SW, has grills for summer barbecuing, and a heated Olympic-size salt-water pool right on the edge of the sound for spectacular summer swimming. Fauntleroy's tiny commercial district is easy to miss, and that suits residents just fine. A Greek restaurant, neighborhood bakery, gift shop, and beauty salon are concentrated in a single building at SW Wildwood Place and 45th Avenue SW.

As Fauntleroy's popularity grows, modest homes belonging to low- and middle-income families are being sold to wealthy retirees and professionals, though turnover is occurring less quickly here than in other West Seattle neighborhoods. Interestingly, the transfer of property within families is not unusual, according to one local real estate agent.

In the southeast quarter of West Seattle, Delridge is a neighborhood of simple 1950s ramblers, contemporary split-levels, and tract houses. On its eastern edge near West Marginal Way, Delridge is primarily industrial. To the west, residential areas offer modest homes and modern apartment complexes. The median income in this neighborhood is lower than most of West Seattle; rents and real estate prices tend to be much lower as well. Community groups in Delridge work to improve the quality of life here. One such effort was the Delridge Neighborhoods Development Association's proposal to include affordable apartments on the top two floors of the new library. The impressive result is the full service Delridge Public Library, 5423 Delridge Way SW, which opened in June 2002 and features 19 low-income housing units on the upper two floors. The High Point section of Delridge was formerly a sprawling low-income housing development that was razed to the ground and rebuilt as a mixed-income community, including market rate housing, rental units, a senior center, and retail space. The first phase of the project was completed in 2006 and the final phase will be finished in 2009.

Though West Seattle is only a 20-minute drive from downtown, the neighborhood is not as convenient for those working on the Eastside. The commute covers the West Seattle Freeway, I-5, and I-90, all of which have heavy traffic during rush hour. However, for people working downtown who would like to live in a neighborhood that feels utterly removed from the city, West Seattle may be the perfect spot.

**Web Sites:** www.seattle.gov, www.wschamber.com
**Area Code:** 206
**Zip Codes:** 98106, 98116, 98126, 98136
**Post Office:** West Seattle Station, 4412 California Ave SW
**Libraries:** Delridge Library, 5423 Delridge Way SW, 206-937-7680, www.spl.lib.
    wa.us; High Point Library, 6338 32nd Ave SW, 206-684-7454, www.spl.lib.wa.us;
    Southwest Library, 9010 35th Ave SW, 206-684-7455, www.spl.lib.wa.us; West
    Seattle Library, 2306 42nd Ave SW, 206-684-7444, www.spl.lib.wa.us

**Public Schools:** Seattle Public Schools, P.O. Box 19116, Seattle, WA 98109-1116, 206-298-7000, www.seattleschools.org

**Police:** South Precinct, 3001 S Myrtle St, 206-386-1850, www.seattle.gov/police

**Emergency Hospital:** Harborview Medical Center, 325 9th Ave, 206-731-3074, www.uwmedicine.org/facilities/harborview

**Community Publication:** *West Seattle Herald*, 2604 California Ave SW, 206-932-0300, www.westseattleherald.com

**Community Resources:** Alki Community Center, 5817 SW Stevens St, 206-684-7430, www.seattle.gov/parks; Delridge Community Center, 4501 Delridge Way SW, 206-684-7423, www.cityofseattle.net/parks; Delridge Neighborhood Service Center, 5405 Delridge Way SW, 206-684-7416, www.seattle.gov; Hiawatha Community Center, 2700 California Ave SW, 206-684-7441, www.cityofseattle.net/parks; High Point Community Center, 6920 34th Ave SW, 206-684-7422, www.seattle.gov/parks; Southwest Community Center, 2801 SW Thistle St, 206-684-7438, www.seattle.gov/parks; West Seattle Junction Association, 4210 SW Oregon St, Ste A, 206-935-0904, www.wsjunction.com; West Seattle Neighborhood Service Center, 4205 SW Alaska, 206-684-7495, www.seattle.gov

**Public Transportation:** Metro Transit, 206-553-3000, http://transit.metrokc.gov; 22, 37, 51, 53, 54, 55, 56, 57, 85, 116, 118, 119, 128, 773

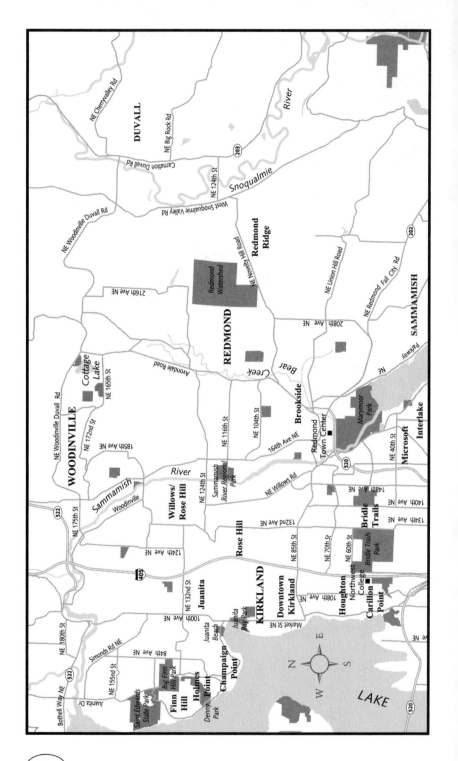

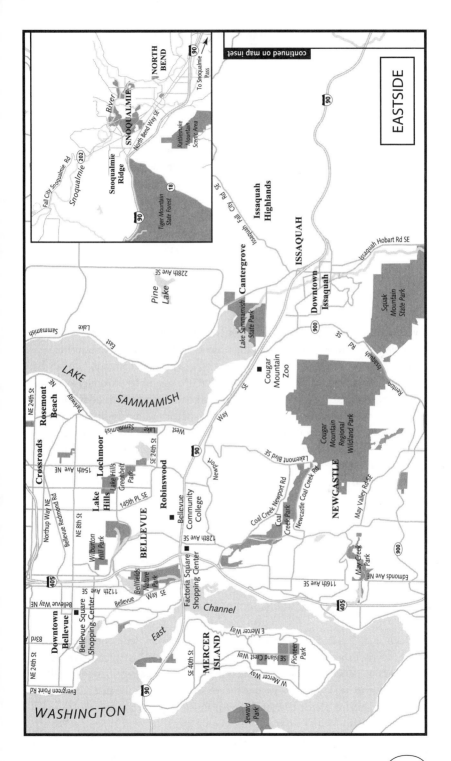

EASTSIDE

continued on map inset

**NORTH BEND**

To Snoqualmie Pass

Snoqualmie River

North Bend Way SE

**SNOQUALMIE**

Fall City Snoqualmie Rd

Snoqualmie (202)

**Snoqualmie Ridge**

Rattlesnake Mountain Scenic Area

Tiger Mountain State Forest

Issaquah Fall City Rd SE

**Issaquah Highlands**

**Cantergrove**

228th Ave SE

Pine Lake

Lake Sammamish State Park

**ISSAQUAH**

**Downtown Issaquah**

Squak Mountain State Park

Issaquah Hobart Rd SE

Renton Issaquah Rd SE

Sammamish

LAKE

East Lake Sammamish Parkway NE

SAMMAMISH

NE 24th St

**Rosemont Beach**

**Crossroads**

**Lochmoor**

154th Ave NE

Lake Hills Greenbelt Park

SE 24th St

**Lake Hills**

145th Pl SE

**Robinswood**

Cougar Mountain Zoo

SE Way

West Lake Sammamish Parkway

Way

Newport

**NEWCASTLE**

Cougar Mountain Regional Wildland Park

Lakemont Blvd SE

Coal Creek Newport Rd

Coal Creek Park

Newcastle Coal Creek Rd

May Valley Rd SE

Northup Way NE

Bellevue Redmond Rd

NE 8th St

Wilburton Hill Park

**BELLEVUE**

Bellevue Community College

128th Ave SE

(900)

Edmonds Ave NE

May Creek Park

116th Ave SE

(405)

(900)

(405)

Bellevue Way NE

83rd

NE 24th St

**Downtown Bellevue**

Bellevue Square Shopping Center

112th Ave SE

Bellfields Nature Park

Bellevue Way SE

Factoria Square Shopping Center

East Channel

SE 40th St

**MERCER ISLAND**

SE Island Crest Way

Pioneer Park

E Mercer Way

W Mercer Way

Evergreen Point Rd

(90)

**WASHINGTON**

Seward Park

77

## SURROUNDING COMMUNITIES

Today, Seattle is composed of much more than simply the city itself. Beyond the city limits, many communities benefit from and contribute to Seattle's economy. A good number of Seattle residents go to work each day on the Eastside, to communities such as Bellevue, Kirkland or Redmond (where Microsoft is based). Both Seattle and Eastside residents commute to jobs in Tacoma to the south or Everett to the north. Many catch a ferry from Bainbridge Island west of downtown, or from towns and cities on the Olympic Peninsula.

According to local real estate agents, many newcomers arrive in Seattle with hopes of living in the city or very close to the city, only to find that housing prices are higher than they expected, or lot sizes smaller than they had hoped. Many choose to expand their search to include the Eastside, the north or south sides of greater Seattle, or along the I-5 corridor. When choosing a community outside Seattle, there are a few things to think about beyond housing prices. Consider if you want a suburban or rural environment—some make their homes in traditionally rural communities beyond the suburbs, including Duvall, Snoqualmie, and Woodinville. Do you want new construction in a planned community, or an older home in a more established neighborhood? Do you prefer proximity to water or to mountains? Exclusive planned neighborhoods in some Eastside suburbs, particularly those with views of Lake Washington or Lake Sammamish, attract affluent residents looking for a suburban lifestyle. Communities like Issaquah and Redmond are filled with new developments, while mature communities like Burien or Shoreline offer established neighborhoods with spectacular views. And, perhaps most important, how much time do you want to spend in your car every day, commuting to work? Long commutes can negatively affect one's personal and professional life, not to mention harm done to the environment.

# EASTERN COMMUNITIES (THE "EASTSIDE")—KING COUNTY

*Mercer Island, Bellevue, Newcastle, Redmond, Kirkland,*
*Woodinville, Duvall, Issaquah, Sammamish, North Bend/Snoqualmie*

A decade ago, "The Eastside" consisted primarily of Bellevue, Redmond, and Kirkland. Today, just about any city east of Seattle to Snoqualmie Pass is referred to as being on the Eastside. With the exception of Mercer Island, which has a limited amount of land available for new construction, the Eastside is the place to turn if you're looking for a large new home in a planned or gated community. Many eastern cities also feature wooded or semi-rural areas—a rarity in Seattle. The Eastside has always been known as an upscale region, so it's not surprising that Bill Gates—the world's richest man—lives here, in the affluent suburb of Medina.

# MERCER ISLAND

## ROANOKE

Located at the south end of Lake Washington, Mercer Island is an established, upscale community. While only minutes away from downtown Seattle, it feels miles away from the urban hubbub. This insular city with beautiful view homes, plentiful opportunities for recreation, and a compact but comprehensive commercial district, attracts affluent professionals and entrepreneurs. Though small, the city boasts numerous parks, including Luther Burbank Park at the north end of the island. A popular summer recreation area, Luther Burbank offers swimming, boating, a playground, and an off-leash dog area. During the summer months, performances are held at its small outdoor amphitheater. Not surprisingly, Mercer Island's school district is well-known for its academic accomplishments, and each year sends 95% of its seniors on to college. And, the cherry on the top, because Mercer Island is situated between Seattle and the Eastside, it's an easy commute for professionals in both regions—perfect for two-career couples. The island measures 5 miles long and 2 1/2 miles wide, and in 2005 reported a population of just under 22,000 residents.

As you would expect, housing prices and rents on the island are high. Many of the homes here are sprawling estates and modern mansions, but there are a few modest houses around, mostly built between the 1950s and the 1980s. Houses in the half million-dollar range are the norm, and rents are expensive, just a bit higher than those in downtown Seattle.

Mercer Island's primary artery is Mercer Way—East Mercer Way on the eastern half of the island and West Mercer Way on the western side. The winding road hugs the lakeshore, and seemingly is used as much by runners and bicyclists as by cars. (In fact, Mercer Island is a fantastic place to train for triathlons or races, because of its opportunities for swimming, running and biking.) Island Crest Way bisects the island, running north/south. The community's commercial district is located adjacent to the freeway at the north end of the island, and is bounded by 27th and 32nd streets, Island Crest Way and 77th Avenue SE.

At the northern tip of Mercer Island is the **Roanoke** neighborhood. This is where you'll find two of Mercer Island's historic landmarks, the Roanoke Inn and the VFW Hall. The Roanoke Inn, at 72nd Avenue SE and North Mercer Way, is a homey little tavern and eatery smack-dab in the middle of a residential community. Established in 1914,"the Roanoke" served as a speakeasy during Prohibition. Today, the restaurant is popular with both islanders and city folk for its weeknight dinner specials, cozy atmosphere, and patio dining during the summer. The VFW Hall, which began its history as the Keewaydin ("the north wind") Club and later the Mercer Island Community Club, was built by Mercer Island residents in 1922 to host social events.

**Web Site:** www.ci.mercer-island.wa.us
**Area Code:** 206
**Zip Code:** 98040
**Post Office:** 3040 78th Ave SE
**Library:** 4400 88th Ave SE, 206-236-3537, www.kcls.org
**Public Schools:** Mercer Island School District, 4160 86th Ave SE, 206-236-3330, www.misd.wednet.edu
**Police:** City Hall, 9611 SE 36th St, 206-236-3500, www.ci.mercer-island.wa.us
**Emergency Hospitals:** Harborview Medical Center, 325 9th Ave, 206-731-3074, www.uwmedicine.org/facilities/harborview; Overlake Hospital Medical Center, 1035 116th Ave NE, 425-688-5000, www.overlakehospital.org
**Community Publication:** *Mercer Island Reporter*, 7845 SE 30th St, 206-232-1215, www.mi-reporter.com
**Community Resources:** Community Center at Mercer View, 8236 SE 24th St, 206-236-3545, www.ci.mercer-island.wa.us; Mercer Island Beach Club, 8326 Avalon Dr, 206-232-3125; Mercer Island Boys' & Girls' Club, 2825 West Mercer Way, 206-232-4548, www.pos-itiveplace.org; Mercer Island Chamber of Commerce, 7613 SE 27th St, 206-232-3404, www.mercerislandchamber.org; Mercer Island Country Club, 8700 SE 71st St, 206-232-5600, www.mercerislandcc.com; Mercer Island Historical Society, 206-232-1263, www.mihistory.org; Mercerwood Shore Club, 4150 East Mercer Way, 206-232-1622, www.mercerwood.com; Stroum Jewish Community Center of Greater Seattle, 3801 East Mercer Way, 206-232-7115, www.sjcc.org
**Public Transportation:** Metro Transit, 206-553-3000, http://transit.metrokc.gov; 201, 202, 203, 204, 205, 213, 216, 891, 892, 942, 989; Sound Transit, 206-398-5000, www.soundtransit.org

# BELLEVUE

**DOWNTOWN BELLEVUE**
**BRIDLE TRAILS**
**BROOKSIDE**
**CROSSROADS**
**ROSEMONT BEACH**
**INTERLAKE**
**LOCHMOOR**
**ROBINSWOOD**
**LAKE HILLS**

A decade ago, Bellevue was a small city best known to Seattle residents as home to Bellevue Square, an upscale mall. Today, Bellevue is the state's fifth-largest city, and enjoys a thriving downtown, excellent schools, and abundant parks. While the area has a reputation of being home to wealthy residents (the cost of living here tops the national average by more than 50%, according to Bestplaces.net), you'll find people of various incomes living in Bellevue. Suburban housing developments filled with modest split-level and contemporary homes dot the area, and homes close to Lake Washington to the west or Lake Sammamish to the east are more elegant and expensive. Most houses to the east are on the newer side, and range in style from traditional brick ranch houses to angular art deco homes to lavish new brick Tudors. Home prices in Bellevue range from the $300,000s to the millions.

According to the City of Bellevue, the region's largest employers are Bellevue Community College, Boeing, Microsoft, PACCAR, Nordstrom, Safeway, Puget Sound Energy, and Overlake Hospital. Along with Microsoft, many high-tech companies are located in the Eastside. In fact, high-tech jobs account for about 20% of all Eastside jobs. Bellevue is also a popular choice for professionals who work in Seattle, as evidenced by the heavy morning and evening traffic across both bridges.

Though Bellevue is primarily a city of unassuming neighborhoods, **Downtown Bellevue** has become a hip place to live, with several thousand residents now calling it home. Several condominiums have been erected here, more are being constructed, and a host of new shops and restaurants have been added to the area near Bellevue Square. A recent addition to the area, Lincoln Square is a soaring skyscraper with condos, retail and office space, restaurants, and the four-star Westin Bellevue Hotel. Also fairly new, the Bellevue Arts Museum, located at 510 Bellevue Way NE, is the site of the city's annual arts and crafts fair.

Most of Bellevue's neighborhoods offer a range of housing styles and prices, though properties near the water will generally cost more than those inland. If you're looking for seclusion and large lots, consider the Bridle Trails community in northern Bellevue. Most homes in the neighborhood rely on septic tanks instead of sewers, but property is at a premium, and there are some incredible new estates peeking through the pines. The median home price here is $519,000. To the southeast are the **Brookside** and **Microsoft** neighborhoods, popular options for many Microsoft employees. Homes here are large and comfortable, and sell for prices comparable to Bridle Trails.

**Crossroads** is one of Bellevue's most culturally diverse neighborhoods. About 8,000 people live here and you are just as likely to hear residents speaking Russian, Spanish, or Chinese as English. Crossroads Shopping Center, at NE 8th Street and 156th Avenue NE, is a popular meeting place for members of the East European, Hispanic, and Asian communities. The mall frequently hosts live music and community celebrations. Also at the mall is the Library Connection, a public library with multi-language programs and materials, and internet access. In northeast Bellevue, near Lake Sammamish, are the **Rosemont Beach**, **Interlake** and **Lochmoor** neighborhoods. Homes in these communities have risen sharply in value in recent years, with the median price at just over $450,000 in 2005, though those with views are considerably more expensive. Most houses are large ramblers built in the mid- to late-1970s.

The **Robinswood** and **Lake Hills** communities are located in southeast Bellevue, near Bellevue Community College. There are a variety of rentals in this area, which are popular with students and employees of nearby Factoria Mall. Most homes here are more affordable than other areas of Bellevue. The exception is the area overlooking the Glendale Golf & Country Club, where newly constructed homes can cost up to a million. Robinswood Community Park, at 148th Avenue SE and SE 22nd Street, is a favorite local attraction. It features soccer and baseball fields, and a quaint cottage for party and banquet rentals.

**Web Site:** www.ci.bellevue.wa.us

**Area Code:** 425

**Zip Codes:** 98004, 98005, 98006, 98007, 98008, 98009, 98015

**Post Offices:** 1171 Bellevue Way NE; 11405 NE 2nd Pl; 15731 NE 8th St

**Libraries:** 1111 110th Ave NE, 425-450-1765; 15228 Lake Hills Blvd, 425-747-3350; 14250 SE Newport Way, 425-747-2390, www.kcls.org

**Public Schools:** 12111 NE 1st St, 425-456-4000, www.belnet.bellevue.k12.wa.us

**Police:** City Hall, 11511 Main St, 425-452-6917, 877-881-2731; Factoria Substation, 4098 Factoria Square Mall SE, 425-452-2891; Crossroads Substation, 15600 NE 8th St, 425-452-2891; Spiritwood Substation, 1424 148th Ave SE D-9, 425-452-6971, www.ci.bellevue.wa.us

**Emergency Hospital:** Overlake Hospital Medical Center, 1035 116th Ave NE, 425-688-5000, www.overlakehospital.org

**Community Publication:** *King County Journal*, 11400 SE 8th St, 425-455-2222, www.kcjn.com

**Community Resources:** Bellevue Chamber of Commerce, 10500 NE 8th St, Ste 212, 425-454-2464, www.bellevuechamber.org; Bellevue Community College, 3000 Landerholm Circle SE, 425-564-1000, www.bcc.ctc.edu; Bellevue Downtown Association, 500 108th Ave NE, Ste 210, 425-453-1223, www.bellevuedowntown.org; Bellevue Historical Society, 425-450-1046, www.scn.org/bellehist; Crossroads Community Center, 16000 NE 10th St, 425-452-4874; Highland Park Community Center, 14224 NE Bel-Red Rd, 425-452-7686; North Bellevue Community Senior Center, 4063 148th Ave NE, 425-452-7681; Northwest Community Center, 9825 NE 24th St, 425-452-4106

**Public Transportation:** Metro Transit, 206-553-3000, http://transit.metrokc.gov; 167, 212, 217, 220, 222, 225, 229, 230, 232, 233, 234, 237, 240, 243, 245, 247, 249, 253, 256, 261, 271, 272, 280, 342, 630, 885, 886, 889, 890, 921, 942; Sound Transit, 206-398-5000, www.soundtransit.org

# NEWCASTLE

## CHINA CREEK

Situated between the cities of Bellevue, Renton, and Issaquah, Newcastle is a new community (incorporated as a city in 1994), with a population of about 8,000. Depending on whom you ask, Newcastle is either an Eastside neighborhood or a South End neighborhood. In fact, it is located southeast of Seattle, so both descriptions are accurate. But, Newcastle's numerous planned housing communities, like China Creek, and the public—but nonetheless swanky—Golf Club at Newcastle, give the city a distinctly Eastside feel. In general, homes in Newcastle are more expensive than in Renton to the south, ranging from $400,000 to $800,000. Many have views of the mountains, Lake Washington or the golf course. Condos and townhouses can be found for just over $300,000.

Despite its proximity to the much larger city of Bellevue, Newcastle's leaders and residents take pride in the city's small-town feel and strong sense of community. Each year in September, the city hosts Newcastle Days. This two-day celebration is at Lake Boren Park, a 20-acre park located on SE 84th Avenue just off Coal Creek Parkway, one of Newcastle's major thoroughfares. Another impressive local treasure is Cougar Mountain Regional Wildland Park, the biggest park in King County, with more than 3,000 acres of trails and wildlife habitat.

**Web Site:** www.ci.newcastle.wa.us
**Area Code:** 425
**Zip Codes:** 98056, 98059
**Post Office:** 4301 NE 4th St, Renton
**Libraries:** 14250 SE Newport Way, Bellevue, 425-747-2390, www.kcls.org; 2902 NE 12th St, Renton, 425-430-6790, www.ci.renton.wa.us
**Public Schools:** Issaquah School District, 565 NW Holly St, 425-837-7000, www.issaquah.wednet.edu; Renton School District, 300 SW 7th St, 425-204-2300, www.renton.wednet.edu
**Police:** 13020 SE 72nd Pl, 425-649-4444, www.ci.newcastle.wa.us
**Emergency Hospital:** Overlake Hospital Medical Center, 1035 116th Ave NE, 425-688-5000, www.overlakehospital.org
**Community Resources:** China Creek Homeowner's Association, 6947 Coal Creek Pkwy SE #146, www.chinacreek.org; Cougar Mountain Regional Wildland Park, 18201 SE Cougar Mountain Dr, 206-296-4145; www.metrokc.gov/parks; The Golf Club at Newcastle, 15500 Six Penny Lane, 425-793-5566, www.newcastlegolf.com; Greater Newcastle Chamber of Commerce, 425-641-7590; Newcastle Historical Society, 425-226-4328

# REDMOND

## REDMOND RIDGE
## WILLOWS/ROSE HILL

Though it is known as the bicycle capital of the Pacific Northwest, Redmond certainly is best known as the home of technology powerhouse Microsoft and renowned game maker Nintendo. Once a sleepy farming community, Redmond today is a thriving city of more than 47,000 residents. Most are in the middle- to upper-income bracket; many are affiliated with Microsoft or Nintendo. According to Bestplaces.net, Redmond's cost of living is 47% higher than the national average. Redmond increasingly attracts professionals and their families who seek larger homes and acreage that can't be found in the city.

Even before Redmond became a popular place to live, a variety of local attractions drew thousands of visitors to the city each year. Marymoor Park, along West Lake Sammamish Parkway, is one of the region's best parks. Along with the most popular off-leash dog area in Western Washington, the 640-acre park features a velodrome (hence the city's cycling moniker), numerous sports fields, tennis courts, and a venue designated specifically for remote-controlled airplanes. Numerous festivals, concerts, sporting, and community events take place here.

At the southern tip of Marymoor Park is Lake Sammamish, which covers almost 4,900 acres to touch the cities of Sammamish, Bellevue, and Issaquah. Idylwood Park, south of Marymoor on West Lake Sammamish Parkway NE, is a popular summertime recreation area on the western shore of the lake, and features picnic tables, outdoor grills, and a dock. The homes along the lakefront are a mix of summer cottages and large contemporary houses. Most have beach access and moorage. During the summer, the lake is busy with water skiers and boaters.

State Route 520 is the primary route in and out of Redmond, and ends at the city's southeastern border. Unfortunately, traffic jams on the highway are notorious, and Redmond residents can do little to avoid them. However, Redmond's explosive population growth over the past decade has delivered lots of new amenities and commercial endeavors to its confines, and unless you work in Seattle, you may never feel the need to leave. A modern new downtown has grown up around its original core, and stylish brick mixed-use buildings now surround the quaint city center. Residents no longer need trek to Bellevue Square now that the massive, open-air Redmond Town Center, comprised of 120 acres of stores, restaurants and offices, is right in their own backyards.

Though much of it looks new, Redmond is one of the Eastside's oldest communities, and despite traffic and parking issues here, there is a lovely small-town feel. Perhaps that stems from its deep agricultural roots, or from efforts to preserve open spaces. In **Redmond Ridge**, a popular planned community in the northeast part of the city, developers preserved 600 acres of forest, wetlands, and parks. The insular neighborhood has its own community center and parks, and will eventually have its own elementary school. In tune with the technology needs of Redmond's residents, the Ridge offers residents three internet and two cable television options. Single-family homes in this development start around $400,000 and reach well over a million. Condominiums don't cost much less, with the average price in 2005 coming in at over $600,000.

To the west of Redmond Ridge is the **Willows/Rose Hill** neighborhood, which borders Kirkland to the west and the Willows Run Golf Course to the east. Numerous high-tech offices are located along the community's eastern edge, including 3-Com, Nextel, and Metawave. Like many Eastside neighborhoods, old meets new here, with small ramblers on large lots perched next to contemporary planned communities. Along the neighborhood's outer edges are townhomes and apartment and condominium complexes which are popular with students attending nearby Lake Washington Technical College.

**Web Site:** www.ci.redmond.wa.us

**Area Code:** 425

**Zip Codes:** 98052, 98053, 98073, 98074

**Post Office:** 16135 NE 85th St

**Library:** 15990 NE 85th, 425-885-1861, 425-895-7951 (TTY), www.kcls.org

**Public Schools:** Lake Washington School District, 16250 NE 74th St, 425-702-3200, www.lkwash.wednet.edu

**Police:** 8701 160th Ave NE, 425-556-2500, www.ci.redmond.wa.us

**Emergency Hospital:** The Eastside Hospital (Group Health Cooperative), 2700 152nd Ave NE, 425-888-5151, www.ghc.org

**Community Publication:** *King County Journal*, 11400 SE 8th St, 425-455-2222, www.kcjn.com

**Community Resources:** Friends of Marymoor Park, 206-205-8751, www.marymoor.org; Old Redmond Schoolhouse Community Center, 16600 NE 80th St, 425-556-2300, www.ci.redmond.wa.us; Redmond Ridge, 10735 Cedar Park Crescent NE, 888-820-8188, www.redmondridge.com; Senior Center, 15670 NE 85th St, 425-556-2314, 425-556-2906 (TTD), www.ci.redmond.wa.us; Serve Our Dog Areas, 425-881-0148, www.soda.org

**Public Transportation:** Metro Transit, 206-553-3000, http://transit.metrokc.gov; 216, 220, 230, 232, 233, 245, 247, 249, 250, 251, 253, 254, 265, 266, 268, 269, 291, 644, 922, 929, 997; Sound Transit, 206-398-5000, www.soundtransit.org

# KIRKLAND

**DOWNTOWN**
**HOUGHTON**
**CARILLON POINT**
**JUANITA**
**CHAMPAGNE POINT**
**HOMES POINT**
**FINN HILL**
**ROSE HILL**

Kirkland is a small town on the shore of Lake Washington, just north of Highway 520. Real estate prices here are expensive, as many homes have views of the lake. In fact, some of the most spectacular views on the Eastside are found in Kirkland, with Lake Washington, the Seattle skyline, and Mount Rainier all visible from a few fortunate neighborhoods. The influx of nearby technology companies helped to fuel Kirkland's housing boom. Many choose to live here because of the short drive to Redmond, and because Kirkland is close to Highway 520 and Interstate 405, some residents commute west to Seattle or north to Everett.

Housing styles in Kirkland are a mixed bag, from turn-of-the-century homes like those on Seattle's Queen Anne Hill to ultra-modern condominiums to 1960s ramblers. Because land is scarce in Kirkland, short-platting—the practice of building multiple homes on a piece of property that used to contain just one house—is increasingly common. Many neighborhoods offer an odd combination of homes; it's not uncommon to find quaint Craftsman bungalows rubbing elbows with massive, newly built houses.

The **Downtown** area is a sophisticated shopping district with a colorful marina, cozy cafes, trendy boutiques, and unique gift shops. This neighborhood also supports several bars that are popular with the early-20s crowd. Condos are the norm in downtown Kirkland, and can cost as little as $250,000 or as much as $2.5 million. Young professionals and empty-nesters alike live along the city's waterfront and in the **Houghton** area, just south of downtown. A handful of small beachfront parks cozy up to the lakeshore, and the upscale Woodmark Hotel perches on **Carillon Point**. If you're not ready to buy, or if you plan to rent until you find the perfect house, this area offers lots of rental properties, from apartments to condominiums to small houses. The eastern section of Houghton, near Northwest College, offers more affordable homes, but homes with views can still garner up to $3 million.

The **Juanita** neighborhood, north of downtown Kirkland, is an up-and-coming community anchored by the Juanita Village mixed-use property. Modeled after the village centers in northern Europe, the pedestrian-friendly project combines shops, banks, and restaurants with apartments, condominiums, and townhomes. West of Juanita, the **Champagne Point** and **Homes Point** neighborhoods are private, funky communities with incredible views of Lake Washington. Homes are anywhere from 60 years old to brand new, and prices are high. Residents here can just as easily go for a sheltered walk in the woods or take a leisurely stroll along the beach.

For affordable homes, newcomers should look to the Finn Hill and Rose Hill neighborhoods. **Finn Hill** is located northwest of downtown and **Rose Hill** is situated to the northeast. Newcomers should be aware, however, that while most of Kirkland is free from traffic congestion except during rush hour, the area surrounding Rose Hill is frequently backed up along NE 85th Street.

**Web Site:** www.ci.kirkland.wa.us
**Area Code:** 425
**Zip Codes:** 98033, 98034, 98083
**Post Office:** 721 4th Ave
**Libraries:** 308 Kirkland Ave, 425-822-2459; 12315 NE 143rd, 425-821-7686, www. kcls.org
**Public Schools:** Lake Washington School District, 16250 NE 74th St, 425-702-3200, www.lkwash.wednet.edu
**Police:** 123 5th Ave, 425-828-1183, www.ci.kirkland.wa.us
**Emergency Hospital:** Evergreen Hospital Medical Center, 12040 NE 128th St, Kirkland, 425-899-1000, www.evergreenhealthcare.org
**Community Publication:** *King County Journal*, 11400 SE 8th St, 425-455-2222, www.kcjn.com
**Community Resources:** Greater Kirkland Chamber of Commerce, 401 Parkplace, Ste 102, 425-822-7066, www.kirklandchamber.org; Kirkland Arts Center, 620 Market St, 425-822-7161, www.kirk-landartscenter.org; Kirkland Heritage Society, 1032 4th St, 425-828-4095, www.historylink.org/khs; North Kirkland Community Center, 12421 103rd Ave NE, 425-828-1105, www.ci.kirkland. wa.us; Senior Center, 352 Kirkland Ave, 425-828-1223, www.ci.kirkland.wa.us; Teen Center, 348 Kirkland Ave, 425-822-3088, www.ci.kirkland.wa.us
**Public Transportation:** Metro Transit, 206-553-3000, http://transit.metrokc.gov; 220, 230, 234, 236, 237, 238, 245, 251, 252, 254, 255, 256, 257, 260, 265, 277, 291, 342, 630, 644, 935, 952, 986; Sound Transit, 206-398-5000, www.soundtransit. org

## WOODINVILLE

Woodinville is a close neighbor of Redmond, attracting many Microsoft employees and their families. The city is located in the north central region of King County, just east of the intersection of State Route 522 and Interstate 405. Most homes in Woodinville are large contemporary structures in suburban developments or modest farmhouses on acreage. The city epitomizes the goal of many formerly rural Eastside communities, which is to blend city living with a country attitude. With an excellent school system, this city is popular with young families.

Formerly a heavily forested region of King County, Woodinville became an incorporated city in 1993. The community is comprised primarily of single-family homes, with about 40% of dwellings designated for multi-family use. Generally, older, modest homes dating from before Woodinville's housing boom of the late 1990s have a median price of $300,000. Most new properties sell for more than a half-million dollars, and larger palatial estates are priced in the millions.

Residents have access to the usual suburban shopping centers, grocery stores, fast food restaurants, and chain stores, plus the country's largest single-outlet garden center, Molbak's. This local gem serves as Woodinville's commercial hub, taking up 15 acres on NE 175th Street. The company also has a high-tech, 42-acre greenhouse complex near NE 124th Street and State Route 202. The city is also home to two wineries, Chateau St. Michelle and Columbia, and the Redhook Brewery's restaurant and bottling facility.

**Web Site:** www.ci.woodinville.wa.us
**Area Code:** 425
**Zip Code:** 98072
**Post Office:** 17610 Woodinville Snohomish Rd
**Libraries:** Woodinville Library, 17105 Avondale Rd NE, 425-788-0733; Kingsgate Library, 12315 NE 143rd, 425-821-7686, www.kcls.org
**Public Schools:** Northshore School District, 18315 Bothell Way NE, 425-489-6000, www.nsd.org
**Police:** 13203 NE 175th St, 425-489-2700, www.metrokc.gov/sheriff
**Emergency Hospital:** Evergreen Hospital Medical Center, 12040 NE 128th St, Kirkland, 425-899-1000, www.evergreenhealthcare.org
**Community Publication:** *The Woodinville Weekly*, 13342 NE 175th St, 425-483-0606, www.nwnews.com
**Community Resources:** Woodinville Chamber of Commerce, 13205 NE 175th St, 425-481-8300, www.woodinvillechamber.org; Woodinville Community Center, 13203 NE 175th St, 425-398-9327, www.ci.woodinville.wa.us
**Public Transportation:** Metro Transit, 206-553-3000, http://transit.metrokc.gov; 236, 237, 251, 311, 372; Sound Transit, 206-398-5000, www.soundtransit.org

## DUVALL

Duvall is a farming community in the valley east of Redmond and Bothell. The city offers country homes and a half-hour commute to Redmond or Bellevue. Many of the houses are hidden in wooded hills; some have views of the Snoqualmie River, lush farmland or the Cascades.

Despite its proximity to the larger cities of the Eastside, Duvall is a rural community. At the height of the 1990s' high-tech boom, families flocked to Duvall for its short commute to Microsoft, but that influx has now tapered off. Today Duvall has fewer than 6,000 residents, and the city's commercial district consists of about three blocks on Main Street, home to city hall, the public library, restaurants, grocery stores, and gas stations.

Short-platting—building multiple homes on a piece of property that used to contain just one house—is common in Duvall. As demand for housing in Duvall grew, property owners, many of them farmers, realized they could make more money by dividing and selling off pieces of land than by farming it. In some cases, this has resulted in a patchwork effect in the community, with small clusters of homes popping up next to large farms.

Duvall's demographics are diverse and reflect the area's home prices, which range from inexpensive mobile homes to several thousand dollars for new construction. The average sales price of a home in 2006 was just over $450,000, while the average price of a condominium was $300,000. Newcomers should be able to find a home for less than in other Eastside communities.

**Web Site:** www.cityofduvall.com
**Area Code:** 425
**Zip Codes:** 98014, 98019
**Post Office:** 26400 NE Valley St
**Library:** 15619 NE Main St, Duvall, 425-788-1173, www.kcls.org
**Public Schools:** Riverview School District, 32240 NE 50th St, 425-844-4500, www.riverview.wednet.edu
**Police:** 15535 Main St NE, Duvall, 425-788-1519, www.cityofduvall.com
**Emergency Hospital:** Overlake Hospital Medical Center, 1035 116th Ave NE, 425-688-5000, www.overlakehospital.org
**Community Resources:** Duvall Arts Commission, 425-788-2983, www.cityofduvall.com/DAC.html; Sno-Valley North Little League, 425-844-1991, www.svnll.org
**Public Transportation:** Metro Transit, 206-553-3000, http://transit.metrokc.gov; 232, 311, 929

# ISSAQUAH

### CANTERGROVE
### ISSAQUAH HIGHLANDS
### DOWNTOWN

If location is the most important tenet in real estate, then it is no wonder Issaquah's housing market is booming. Nestled midway between Seattle and Snoqualmie Pass, the once-sleepy town is ideally located to take advantage of the best the city and the mountains have to offer. Unfortunately, the city's rapid growth has had a less-than-ideal side effect: some of the worst traffic on the Eastside.

In the last several years, Issaquah saw more than a million square feet of commercial space added, including a popular Krispy Kreme outlet. There is also a Costco, Lowe's Home Improvement Center, a movie theater, and numerous restaurants. The concentration of retail businesses just off the freeway results in frequent congestion in the downtown core. But, once you leave downtown, it is still possible to find the quieter rural atmosphere that attracted residents to Issaquah decades ago, although it's hard to look at the hills surrounding the city without seeing a housing development. Suburban neighborhoods are becoming more the norm.

Issaquah is the community of choice for many of Seattle's highly paid athletes. Former Mariners Ken Griffey Jr. and Jay Buhner lived here, and at least one Seahawk has been in residence. Planned communities, like **Cantergrove** in eastern Issaquah, offer million-dollar homes with huge, wooded lots and mountain views. Nearby, the **Issaquah Highlands** neighborhood resembles a movie set, rising above the city and surrounded by spectacular views that reach all the way to Bellevue. The Highlands community is a mix of new condos and homes situated around a village green complete with its own cash machine and nearby shopping center. Homes start at about a half-million dollars, with condos selling for around $350,000 and up.

In **Downtown** Issaquah is a small collection of historic homes and buildings, and most of the city's apartments. On Front Street, quaint brick buildings house shops and theatres; also in downtown are the police department and library, and every year Front Street hosts the large and popular Issaquah Salmon Days Festival.

**Web Site:** www.ci.issaquah.wa.us
**Area Code:** 425
**Zip Codes:** 98027, 98029, 98075
**Post Office:** 400 NW Gilman Blvd
**Libraries:** 10 W Sunset Way, 425-392-5430; 960 Newport Way NW, 425-369-3200, www.kcls.org
**Public Schools:** Issaquah School District, 565 NW Holly St, 425-837-7000, www.issaquah.wednet.edu
**Police:** 130 E Sunset Way, 425-837-3200, www.ci.issaquah.wa.us
**Emergency Hospitals:** Overlake Medical Center at Issaquah, 6520 226th Pl SE, 425-688-5777, www.overlakehospital.org; Valley Medical Center, 400 S 43rd St, Renton, 425-228-3450, www.valleymed.org
**Community Publication:** *Issaquah Press*, P.O. Box 1328, Issaquah, 425-392-6434
**Community Resources:** Issaquah Community Center, 301 Rainier Blvd S, 425-837-3300, www.ci.issaquah.wa.us; Issaquah Historical Society, 425-392-3500, www.issaquahhistory.org; Issaquah Little League, 425-391-9747, www.

issaquahlittleleague.org; Issaquah Valley Senior Center, 105 2nd Ave NE, 425-392-2381

**Public Transportation:** Metro Transit, 206-553-3000, http://transit.metrokc.gov; 200, 209, 210, 214, 216, 217, 218, 269, 271, 927; Sound Transit, 206-398-5000, www.soundtransit.org

# SAMMAMISH

## SAMMAMISH PLATEAU

With Redmond to the north and Issaquah to the south, the newest city in King County is ideally situated for commuters to those cities, though traffic can be very difficult during rush hour. Incorporated in 1999, with a population of over 36,000, Sammamish hugs the shores and hills east of Lake Sammamish. The majority of the population lives on the **Sammamish Plateau** to the east of the lake. Rapid growth and numerous new housing developments cause traffic headaches, but the area still retains a rural feeling. Homes here run between $400,000 and $1,300,000. Homes on the lake or with lake views can sell for considerably more.

Sammamish is a young city with many parts still in the planning stages. A new city hall opened on the Plateau in 2006 in an area known as the Commons, that now includes a civic plaza, parking, and greenspaces. The schools are split between the Lake Washington School District and the Issaquah School District. The pleasant and safe neighborhoods and good schools make the city popular with families.

**Web Site:** www.ci.sammamish.wa.us
**Area Code:** 425
**Zip Codes:** 98074, 98075
**Post Offices:** 400 NW Gilman Blvd, Issaquah; 15731 NE 8th St, Bellevue
**Library:** 825 228th Ave NE, 425-836-8793, www.kcls.org
**Public Schools:** Lake Washington School District, 16250 NE 74th St, Redmond, 425-702-3200, www.lkwash.wednet.edu; Issaquah School District, 565 NW Holly St, 425-837-7000, www.issaquah.wednet.edu
**Police:** 801 228th Ave SE, 425-295-0770, www.ci.sammamish.wa.us
**Emergency Hospitals:** Overlake Medical Center at Issaquah, 6520 226th Pl SE, 425-688-5777, www.overlakehospital.org; The Eastside Hospital (Group Health Cooperative), 2700 152nd Ave NE, 425-888-5151, www.ghc.org
**Community Publication:** *Sammamish Review*, PO Box 1328, Issaquah, 425-392-6434, www.sammamishreview.com
**Community Resources:** Sammamish Chamber of Commerce, 704 228th Ave NE #123, 425-681-4910, www.sammamishchamber.org; Sammamish Community Service Center, 486 228th Ave NE, 206-205-8380; Sammamish Heritage Society,

704 228th Ave NE, 425-281-0170, www.sammamishheritage.org; Sammamish Symphony Orchestra, 206-517-7777, www.sammamishsymphony.org

**Public Transportation:** Metro Transit, 206-553-3000, http://transit.metrokc.gov; 216, 269, 927; Sound Transit, 206-398-5000, www.soundtransit.org

# NORTH BEND/SNOQUALMIE

## SNOQUALMIE RIDGE

Located approximately 30 miles east of Seattle, the communities of North Bend and Snoqualmie are in the Snoqualmie Valley, surrounded by mountains and lush pasture. Before the area's high-tech boom in the 1990s, which brought tremendous growth here, the two towns were primarily a stop on the way to the mountain passes and to Eastern Washington.

It was in the early 1990s when the North Bend/Snoqualmie area was thrust into the limelight as the backdrop for David Lynch's groundbreaking television show, "Twin Peaks." (The region still hosts an annual Twin Peaks Festival each August). At the time, the area was rural, and the pace of life here was slower than in established suburbs like Bellevue. For that reason, although these two towns certainly lie to Seattle's east, North Bend and Snoqualmie were not generally included in the blanket description of "Eastside." That changed in the late 1990s, when high-tech employees and first-time homebuyers began moving to the region in droves. Today, North Bend and Snoqualmie are known as much for their housing developments as they once were for winter recreation.

In theory, North Bend and Snoqualmie are about a half-hour drive from Seattle and 20 minutes from Bellevue, but heavy traffic on Interstate 90 usually makes for a much longer commute. A trip to downtown Seattle during rush hour will take at least 45 minutes.

Despite the drive, both North Bend and Snoqualmie are well on their way to becoming suburban bedroom communities, as developments like **Snoqualmie Ridge** continue to attract families looking to buy bigger houses and pay lower prices. Snoqualmie Ridge is a sprawling, 1,300-acre community that boasts its own golf course and more than 500 acres of preserved open space. Homes in the mixed-use development sell for between $350,000 and $1 million.

**Web Sites:** www.ci.north-bend.wa.us; www.ci.snoqualmie.wa.us
**Area Code:** 425
**Zip Codes:** 98045, 98065, 98068
**Post Offices:** 451 E North Bend Way, North Bend; 8264 Olmstead Lane SE, Snoqualmie

**Libraries:** North Bend Library, 115 E 4th, 425-888-0554; Snoqualmie Library, 38580 SE River St, 425-888-1223, www.kcls.org

**Public Schools:** Snoqualmie Valley Public Schools, P.O. Box 400, 425-831-8000, www.snoqualmie.wednet.edu

**Police:** 1550 Boalch Ave NW, North Bend, 206-296-0612, www.metrokc.gov/sheriff; 34825 SE Douglas St, Snoqualmie, 425-888-3333, www.ci.snoqualmie.wa.us

**Emergency Hospital:** Snoqualmie Valley Hospital, 9575 Ethan Wade Way SE, 425-831-2300,

**Community Resources:** Northwest Railway Museum, 38625 SE King St, Snoqualmie, 425-888-3030, www.trainmuseum.org; Upper Snoqualmie Valley Chamber of Commerce, 425-888-4440, www.snovalley.org

**Public Transportation:** Metro Transit, 206-553-3000, http://transit.metrokc.gov; 209, 214, 929

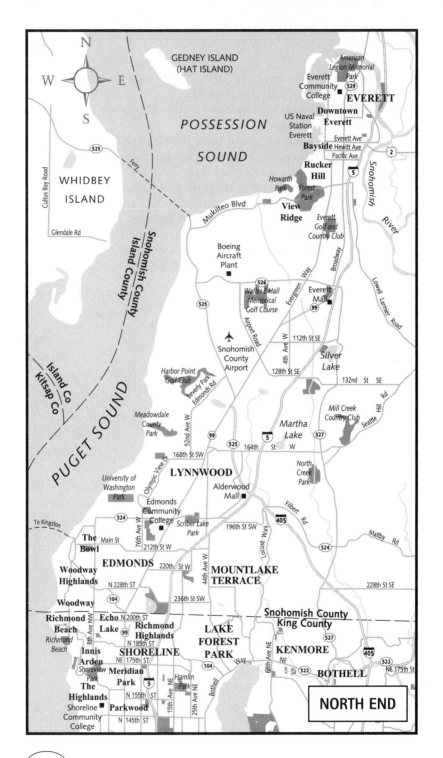

N

W    E

S

GEDNEY ISLAND
(HAT ISLAND)

*POSSESSION*

*SOUND*

WHIDBEY

ISLAND

Glendale Rd

Cultus Bay Road

(525)

Ferry

Snohomish County
Island County

Island Co
Kitsap Co

*PUGET SOUND*

American
Legion Memorial
Park

Everett
Community
College

(529)

**EVERETT**

US Naval
Station
Everett

**Downtown
Everett**

**Bayside**

Everett Ave
Hewitt Ave
Pacific Ave

(2)

**Rucker
Hill**

*Howarth
Park*

*Forest
Park*

(5)

Snohomish

River

**View
Ridge**

*Everett
Golf and
Country Club*

Mukilteo Blvd

Boeing
Aircraft
Plant

(526)

*Walter E Hall
Memorial
Golf Course*

(525)

Airport Road

Evergreen Way

Broadway

Lowell Larimer Road

Everett
Mall

(99)

Snohomish
County
Airport

4th Ave W

112th St SE

128th St SE

*Silver
Lake*

132nd St SE

*Harbor Point
Golf Club*

*Beverly Park*

Edmonds Rd

*Meadowdale
County
Park*

52nd Ave W

Seattle Hill Rd

*Mill Creek
Country Club*

(99)

(525)

164th

*Martha
Lake*

St W

(527)

168th St SW

Olympic View Dr

(5)

*North
Creek
Park*

**LYNNWOOD**

*University of
Washington
Park*

Alderwood
Mall

Filbert Rd

(405)

Edmonds
Community
College

(524)

*Scriber Lake
Park*

196th St SW

Locust Way

(524)

Maltby Rd

To Kingston

76th Ave W

Main St

212th St W

220th St W

44th Ave W

**MOUNTLAKE
TERRACE**

228th St SE

**The
Bowl**

**EDMONDS**

N 228th ST

236th SW

**Woodway
Highlands**

**Woodway**

(104)

**Snohomish County
King County**

**Richmond
Beach**

Echo
Lake

N 200th ST

N 185th ST

**Richmond
Highlands**

**LAKE
FOREST
PARK**

(527)

**KENMORE**

*Richmond
Beach*

8th Ave NW

(99)

NE 175th ST

(104)

Way

68th Ave NE

NE

(405)

(522)

NE 175th ST

**Innis
Arden**

*Shoreview
Park*

**Meridian
Park**

**SHORELINE**

(5)

*Hamlin
Park*

15th Ave NE

25th Ave NE

Bothell

(522)

**BOTHELL**

**The
Highlands**

Shoreline
Community
College

N 155th ST

**Parkwood**

N 145th ST

**NORTH END**

# NORTHERN COMMUNITIES—KING COUNTY

*Shoreline, Lake Forest Park, Bothell, Kenmore*

The communities north of Seattle are often collectively referred to as the "North End." For the most part, homes in these cities are more affordable than in Seattle or the Eastside. The North End is popular with Boeing employees who commute to Everett, and with first-time homebuyers looking for less expensive housing than what can be found in Seattle. The North End is varied; with charming seaside communities like Edmonds just a few miles away from high-tech suburbs like Lake Forest Park.

## SHORELINE

**RICHMOND BEACH**
**INNIS ARDEN**
**THE HIGHLANDS**
**RICHMOND HIGHLANDS**
**ECHO LAKE**
**MERIDIAN PARK**
**PARKWOOD**

Shoreline, home to over 53,000, is a growing community just north of Seattle. Known for its excellent schools and affordable contemporary homes, Shoreline is popular with young families increasingly priced out of Seattle and the Eastside. Before becoming a city in 1995, Shoreline was an unincorporated region of King County. It is surrounded by Edmonds and Woodway to the north, Lake Forest Park to the east, and Seattle to the south.

As its name implies, the city hugs the Puget Sound shoreline, offering spectacular sound and mountain views from expensive waterfront homes. Further inland, local architecture is best described as a mix of older split-levels, colonials, mid-century ramblers, and modern new construction. As you travel east toward I-5, homes in Shoreline become even more affordable. Neighborhoods east of Aurora Avenue offer smaller fixer-uppers and rental homes. Generally, home prices in Shoreline range from the low $200,000s to just over $400,000, depending on the neighborhood. Exceptions include **Richmond Beach**, in the northwest corner of the city, where most homes start at $500,000, with view properties costing even more. Lots here are larger than those in Seattle, and charm and privacy are abundant. Not surprisingly, there is little turnover. The same is true for upscale **Innis Arden**, just south of Richmond Beach. Residents here are working and retired professionals who value the protections of covenant communities and the generous greenbelt. Lots are spacious and housing prices begin around the half-million-dollar mark. South of Innis Arden is **The Highlands**, where some of Seattle's wealthiest families have lived since the turn of the century. The gated waterfront/golf-course community is filled with multi-million-dollar mansions and sprawling estates. Some of the region's most incredible sound and mountain views are from the homes in this community that is so exclusive the houses don't have addresses.

A good bet for newcomers seeking moderately priced housing is the central Shoreline area, which includes the **Richmond Highlands**, **Echo Lake**, **Meridian Park**, and **Parkwood** neighborhoods. Situated between Aurora Avenue and I-5, these communities offer affordable homes typically built during the 1920s to 1930s, or during the post–World War II expansion of the 1950s and '60s. Many have been painstakingly restored or remodeled, but others could use a little TLC.

Shoreline boasts one of the region's most popular two-year colleges: Shoreline Community College, at Greenwood Avenue North and Arden Way, just east of The Highlands. About 14,000 students attend the college, which also offers adult continuing education classes.

Shoreline doesn't really have a city center, but Aurora Avenue North's sprawling commercial district cuts through the city and offers ample opportunities for commerce, including Sears at North 155th Street, Fred Meyer and QFC at North 185th Street, and Home Depot and Costco at North 205th Street.

Just 15 miles north of downtown Seattle, Shoreline offers a relatively easy commute to the city. Both I-5 and Highway 99 connect Shoreline and Seattle, so drivers have two options when traveling between the two cities. An average commute takes about 20 minutes.

**Web Site:** www.cityofshoreline.com

**Area Code:** 206

**Zip Codes:** 98133, 98155, 98177

**Post Offices:** Bitter Lake Station, 929 N 145th St, Seattle; Gateway QFC Contract Station, 18300 Midvale Ave N, Shoreline; North City Branch, 17233 15th Ave NE, Shoreline; Richmond Beach Foods Contract Station, 2002 NW 196th St, Shoreline

**Libraries:** 19601 21st Ave NW, Shoreline, 206-546-3522; 345 NE 175th, 206-362-7550, Shoreline, www.kcls.org

**Public Schools:** Shoreline School District, 18560 1st Ave NE, Shoreline, 206-361-4412, 206-418-3386, www.shorelineschools.org

**Police:** Shoreline Police Station, 1206 N 185th St, 206-546-6730; Eastside Police Center, 521 NE 165th St, 206-363-8424; Westside Police Center, 630 NW Richmond Beach Rd, 206-546-3636, www.cityofshoreline.com

**Emergency Hospital:** Northwest Hospital, 1550 N 115th St, Seattle, 206-364-0500, www.nwhospital.org

**Community Resources:** Center for Human Services, 17018 15th Ave NE, 206-362-7282 (Voice/TDD), www.chs-nw.org; Richmond Highlands Recreation Center, 16554 Fremont Ave N, 206-542-6511; Shoreline Community College, 16101 Greenwood Ave N, 206-546-4101, www.shoreline.ctc.edu; Shoreline–Lake Forest Park Arts Council, P.O. Box 55304, 206-542-6511, www.slfparts.org; YMCA, 1220 NE 175th St, 206-364-1700, www.seattleymca.org

**Public Transportation:** Metro Transit, 206-553-3000, http://transit.metrokc.gov; 5, 77, 242, 301, 303, 304, 308, 316, 330, 331, 342, 345, 346, 347, 348, 355, 358, 373; Sound Transit, 206-398-5000, www.soundtransit.org

## LAKE FOREST PARK

Lake Forest Park, located north of Seattle and east of Shoreline, is a small community of fewer than 13,000 residents. It has a mix of contemporary single-family homes on large lots, with a median home price of a little over $455,000. People choose Lake Forest Park as much for its lack of excitement as for its tree-covered hillsides. This is a quiet place, where kids play in the street and residents are surprised when they don't run into a friend or acquaintance at the grocery store.

The city's social and commercial center is the Lake Forest Park Towne Center, near the intersection of Bothell Way NE and Ballinger Way NE. The mall includes Third Place Books, a huge retail space that combines books, food, and entertainment, as well as Third Place Commons, a large indoor park-like space where many community groups meet. The mall is also home to a branch of Shoreline Community College.

**Web Site:** www.cityoflfp.com
**Area Code:** 206
**Zip Code:** 98155
**Post Office:** 17233 15th Ave NE, Seattle
**Library:** 17171 Bothell Way NE, 206-362-8860, www.kcls.org
**Public Schools:** Shoreline School District, 18560 1st Ave NE, Shoreline, 206-367-6111, 206-367-4111, www.shorelineschools.org
**Police:** 17425 Ballinger Way NE, 206-364-8216, www.cityoflfp.com
**Emergency Hospital:** Northwest Hospital, 1550 N 115th St, 206-364-0500, www.nwhospital.org
**Community Publication:** *Shoreline/Lake Forest Park Enterprise*, 425-673-6500, www.enterprisenewspapers.com
**Community Resources:** Lake Forest Park Stewardship Foundation, 17171 Bothell Way NE, 206-361-7076, www.lfpsf.org; Shoreline Community College at Lake Forest Park, 17171 Bothell Way NE, 206-533-6700, www.success.shoreline.edu/scclfp; Shoreline–Lake Forest Park Senior Center, 18560 1st Ave NE, Shoreline, 206-365-1536; Third Place Commons, 17171 Bothell Way

NE, 206-366-3302, www.thirdplacecommons.org; YMCA, 1220 NE 175th St, Shoreline, 206-364-1700, www.seattleymca.org

**Public Transportation:** Metro Transit, 206-553-3000, http://transit.metrokc.gov; 306, 308, 312, 331, 342, 372; Sound Transit, 206-398-5000, www.soundtransit. org; 522

## BOTHELL, KENMORE

**Bothell** is no longer just a bedroom community for Seattle and Eastside employees. More than 20,000 people now work in Bothell, instead of commuting to jobs in other areas. Major employers include high-tech, communications, medical equipment companies, and a regional University of Washington campus. Located just 12 miles north of Seattle, the city is home to about 30,000 residents. It straddles both King and Snohomish counties.

With median home prices of just under $260,000, the city is a popular choice for young families and early career professionals. Though the city has grown considerably in the past decade, it retains a friendly downtown core that revolves around sleepy Main Street. Here you'll find cozy cafes and restaurants, plus furniture, retail, and antique stores. Another popular spot with residents is Bothell Landing, at 9919 NE 180th Street, just south of the city center. The site features playground equipment, a pedestrian bridge to the Sammamish River Trail, fishing, and small-boat mooring. It is also the site of the city's first schoolhouse and a log cabin.

West of Bothell is **Kenmore**. Incorporated in 1998, Kenmore is a growing city, with a population of nearly 20,000. Kenmore is also home to Bastyr University, an acclaimed college of natural medicine. Housing options include spacious homes overlooking Lake Washington, as well as more modest dwellings, some along partially forested hills. Housing prices are comparable to those in Bothell, making it a good bet for first-time homebuyers. Key to the city's future is a proposed development called Lakepointe, a 45-acre site at the northeast end of Lake Washington, which would include 1,200 condos, a marina, a lakefront park, pedestrian walkways, an amphitheater, and 600,000 square feet of commercial space. In January 2002, the project's development partnership dissolved because of concerns about the economy. According to the City of Kenmore, the property owner is still committed to completing the project, but for now, plans are on hold.

**Web Sites:** www.ci.bothell.wa.us; www.cityofkenmore.com
**Area Code:** 425
**Zip Codes:** 98011, 98012, 98021, 98028, 98041, 98082
**Post Offices:** Bothell Main Office, 10500 Beardslee Blvd, Bothell; Kenmore Branch, 6513 NE 181st, Kenmore

**Libraries:** Bothell Library, 18215 98th Ave NE, Bothell, 425-486-7811, 425-402-7071 (TTY); Kenmore Library, 18138 73rd NE, Kenmore, 425-486-8747, www.kcls.org

**Public Schools:** Northshore School District, 18315 Bothell Way NE, Bothell, 425-489-6000, www.nsd.org

**Police:** 18410 101st Ave NE, Bothell, 425-486-1254, www.ci.bothell.wa.us; 18118 73rd Ave NE, Kenmore, 206-296-4480, www.metrokc.gov/sheriff

**Emergency Hospital:** Northwest Hospital, 1550 N 115th St, Seattle, 206-364-0500, www.nwhospital.org

**Community Resources:** Bothell Historical Museum, 9919 NE 180th St, Bothell, 425-486-1889; Cascadia Community College, 18345 Campus Way NE, Bothell, 425-352-8000, www.cascadia.ctc.edu; Kenmore Heritage Society, 8124 NE 166th St, Kenmore, 425-488-2818, www.scn.org/civic/kenmoreheritage; Northshore Chamber of Commerce, 18414 103rd Ave NE, Ste A, Bothell, 425-486-1245, www.solveris.com/nshore; South Snohomish County Chamber of Commerce, 3500 188th St SW, Ste 490, Lynnwood, 425-774-0507, www.sscchamber.org

**Public Transportation:** Metro Transit, 206-553-3000, http://transit.metrokc.gov; 234, 236, 238, 251, 306, 312, 331, 342, 372, 644, 935; Sound Transit, 206-398-5000, www.soundtransit.org

# NORTHERN COMMUNITIES—SNOHOMISH COUNTY

*Edmonds, Mountlake Terrace, Lynnwood, Everett*

## EDMONDS

### THE BOWL
### WOODWAY
### WOODWAY HIGHLANDS

Edmonds, overlooking Puget Sound just north of Seattle, is a peaceful village with a quaint shopping district. The Edmonds-Kingston Ferry Terminal, once the central attraction of the city, is now overshadowed by the popular downtown waterfront amenities, including restaurants, chic clothing boutiques, and funky gift shops. While there is tremendous wealth in Edmonds, you have to look hard to find it. This is a decidedly low-key community where residents are friendly and unpretentious and consider Edmonds the gem of Puget Sound.

The neighborhood that encompasses downtown and the surrounding hillside is **The Bowl**. The architecture here is varied, with a mix of Victorian homes, small bungalows, new condominiums, and older apartment buildings. Houses are staggered along the hillside for optimal views, and housing prices often depend on how much of the mountains and water you can glimpse—median price in 2006 was a little over $400,000. Most city services are located right in downtown Edmonds, including the police and fire stations, civic center, city hall, and museum. Condos are abundant in downtown Edmonds. Many are occupied by snowbirds who spend the spring and summer in the Northwest, and fly to warmer climes for fall and winter.

South of downtown is the community of **Woodway**, a secluded, woodsy neighborhood of expensive homes on large lots—one to five acres, due to the restrictions on short-platting here. Home prices range from $800,000 to two million. Also in Woodway is one of Edmonds' only planned communities, **Woodway Highlands**, which is similar to new developments on the Eastside: large homes nestled close together.

**Web Site:** www.ci.edmonds.wa.us
**Area Code:** 425
**Zip Codes:** 98020, 98026
**Post Office:** 201 Main St
**Library:** 650 Main St, 425-771-1933, www.sno-isle.org
**Public Schools:** Edmonds School District, 20420 68th Ave W, Lynnwood, 425-670-7000, www.edmonds.wednet.edu
**Police:** 250 5th Ave N, 425-771-0200, www.ci.edmonds.wa.us
**Emergency Hospital:** Stevens Memorial Hospital, 21601 76th Ave W, Edmonds, 425-640-4000, www.stevenshealthcare.org
**Community Resources:** Edmonds Art Commission, 700 Main St, 425-771-0228, www.ci.edmonds.wa.us/artscomm; Edmonds Chamber of Commerce, 121 5th Ave N, 425-670-1496, www.edmondswa.com/Chamber; Edmonds Community College, 20000 68th Ave W, 425-640-1459, www.edcc.edu; Frances Anderson Cultural and Leisure Center, 700 Main St, 425-771-0230, www.ci.edmonds.wa.us; South County Senior Center, 220 Railroad Ave, 425-774-5555, www.ci.edmonds.wa.us/senior
**Public Transportation:** Community Transit, 425-353-RIDE, 800-562-1375, www.commtrans.org

## MOUNTLAKE TERRACE

Like Lake Forest Park in King County, Mountlake Terrace has a mix of contemporary single-family homes on large lots. This is a family-oriented community, with some of the city's most popular attractions revolving around children and recreation: Lake Ballinger is flanked by golf courses, and features a boat ramp and fishing pier; the city's public pavilion includes a swimming pool, racquetball courts, a weight room, and a preschool facility; next to the pavilion are outdoor playing fields, tennis courts, and a park. There are also a few casinos in the city for adult entertainment.

When you consider the city's kid-friendly attitude it's easy to understand why Mountlake Terrace is a good choice for young families. While home prices have appreciated significantly in recent years, the median price of a home in 2005 was $265,000. Major employers include Blue Cross of Washington and Alaska, and the Edmonds School District.

**Web Site:** www.ci.mountlake-terrace.wa.us
**Area Code:** 425
**Zip Code:** 98043
**Post Office:** 6817 208th St SW, Lynnwood
**Library:** 23300 58th Ave W, 425-776-8722, www.sno-isle.org
**Public Schools:** Edmonds School District, 20420 68th Ave W, Lynnwood, 425-670-7000, www.edmonds.wednet.edu
**Police:** 5906 232nd St SW, 425-670-8260, www.ci.mountlake-terrace.wa.us
**Emergency Hospital:** Stevens Memorial Hospital, 21601 76th Ave W, Edmonds, 425-640-4000, www.stevenshealthcare.org
**Community Resources:** Edmonds Community College, 20000 68th Ave W, Lynnwood, 425-640-1459, www.edcc.edu; Mountlake Terrace Historical Committee, www.snonet.org/loscho/mlthc; South Snohomish County Chamber of Commerce, 3500 188th St SW, 425-774-0507, www.sscchamber.org
**Public Transportation:** Community Transit, 425-353-RIDE, 800-562-1375, www.commtrans.org

## LYNNWOOD

For those who live outside it, Lynnwood is best known as the home of Alderwood Mall. But, if you can get beyond the sprawling shopping center and surrounding strip malls, you may find a gem of a home in the residential areas of Lynnwood. Tranquil suburban streets with modest affordable homes make Lynnwood the choice of many middle-income families and first-time homebuyers. Most residents either work in one of the community's numerous retail outlets, or commute south to Seattle or north to Everett. Lynwood's proximity to major thoroughfares, including I-5 and Highway 99, is advantageous for commuters.

Though about midway between Seattle and Everett, Lynnwood's residents generally turn to Seattle for attractions not found in their community. Lynnwood does boast the Interurban Trail which offers 4 miles of trails for biking and walking, as well as hundreds of park acres in the city limits.

In Lynnwood, you can still find homes in the mid- to upper-$200,000s, though they don't linger on the market. There is a pleasant mix of older construction and new developments, plus numerous condominiums and apartments, particularly near Edmonds Community College, which is actually located in Lynnwood.

**Web Site:** www.ci.lynnwood.wa.us
**Area Code:** 425
**Zip Codes:** 98036, 98037, 98046
**Post Offices:** 6817 208th St SW; 3715 196th St SW, Ste A; 800-275-8777, www.usps.com
**Library:** 19200 44th Ave W, 425-778-2148, www.sno-isle.org
**Public Schools:** Edmonds School District, 20420 68th Ave W, Lynnwood, 425-670-7000, www.edmonds.wednet.edu
**Police:** 19321 44th Ave W, 425-744-6900, www.ci.lynnwood.wa.us
**Emergency Hospital:** Stevens Memorial Hospital, 21601 76th Ave W, Edmonds, 425-640-4000, www.stevenshealthcare.org
**Community Resources:** Recreation Center, 18900 44th Ave W, 425-771-4030, www.ci.lynnwood.wa.us; Senior Center, 5800 198th St SW, 425-744-6464, www.ci.lynnwood.wa.us; South Snohomish County Chamber of Commerce, 3500 188th St SW, Ste 490, Lynnwood, 425-774-0507, www.sscchamber.org
**Public Transportation:** Community Transit, 425-353-RIDE, 800-562-1375, www.commtrans.org

## EVERETT

**BAYSIDE**
**DOWNTOWN**
**RUCKER HILL**
**VIEW RIDGE**
**THE PRESERVE**

Everett, a large city about forty minutes north of Seattle, was established in the late 1800s to support the infamous Monte Cristo gold mines. Although the mines never produced the expected amount of gold, the city continued as an industrial center. Today, Boeing and Naval Station Everett are the primary employers in Everett, although many other companies, including a sawmill, are also located here. As with Seattle, many distinct neighborhoods exist in Everett, each worth exploring if you are considering making your home here.

Broadway divides Everett into western and eastern halves, and is the city's major north-south thoroughfare. In the northern end of the city, west of Broadway, you'll find **Bayside**, a classic Everett neighborhood of turn-of-the-century homes, some with fantastic views of Possession Sound, the naval station, and the marina. Many of the houses here are handed down from generation to genera-tion but when they do come on the market, they are usually more affordable than the Craftsman and Victorian homes for sale in Seattle's view neighbor-hoods. As you travel south along Marine View Drive toward downtown Everett, you'll find that many of these historic homes have been turned into multi-family rental units.

To fill Everett's growing need for affordable housing, a number of develop-ers built new condominiums in **Downtown Everett** and apartment buildings are still being converted to condominiums. These new dwellings offer proximity to law firms, banks, and government buildings, some shops and restaurants, his-toric theatres, and the city's performing arts center. City planners worked hard to transform a less-than-exciting reputation by overhauling Everett's sleepy down-town. Hewitt Avenue was made more pedestrian-friendly, and, in 2003, the new Everett Events Center provided a concert venue and ice skating rink, the home of the Silvertips hockey team. While the city's waterfront district lacks housing options, it does feature a small shopping center, a hotel, a marina, and the Everett Yacht Club.

Though Everett certainly claims its share of view properties and esteemed neighborhoods, newcomers will find a good selection of quiet, comfortable areas with affordable houses. **Rucker Hill** and **View Ridge** are attractive neigh-borhoods with many view homes and nearby parks. Houses are priced from about $350,000. **The Preserve** is a new community, complete with sidewalks and underground power lines; prices start at around $300,000.

It is unlikely that you will choose to commute from Everett to Seattle each day, but if your job takes you north of Seattle or if you plan to work from home and want a little more bang for your buck, Everett is worth considering. The city offers many of the same attractions as Seattle, including performing arts, sport-ing events, a shopping mall, and popular city parks.

**Web Site:** www.everettwa.org
**Area Code:** 425
**Zip Codes:** 98201, 98203, 98204, 98205, 98206, 98207, 98208
**Post Office:** 3102 Hoyt Ave
**Libraries:** 2702 Hoyt Ave, 425-257-8000; 9512 Evergreen Way, 425-257-8250, www.epls.org
**Public Schools:** Everett Public Schools, 4730 Colby Ave, 425-745-1993, www.everett.k12.wa.us
**Police:** 3002 Wetmore Ave, 425-257-8400, www.everettwa.org
**Emergency Hospital:** Providence Everett Medical Center, 1321 Colby Ave, 425-261-2000, www.providence.org/everett

**Community Resources:** Boeing Everett Tour Center, 800-464-1476, www.boeing.com; The Children's Museum in Snohomish County, 3013 Colby Ave, 425-258-1006, www.childs-museum.org; Downtown Everett Association, P.O. Box 5267, Everett, 98206, info@downtowneverett.org, www.downtowneverett.com; Everett Area Chamber of Commerce, 11400 Airport Rd, 425-438-1487, www.snobiz.org; Everett Center for the Arts at Monte Cristo, 1507 Wall St, 425-257-8380, www.everettwa.org; Everett Community College, 2000 Tower St, 425-388-9100, www.evcc.ctc.edu; Everett Performing Arts Center, 2710 Wetmore Ave, 425-257-8600, www.everettwa.org; Port of Everett, P.O. Box 538, Everett, 98206, 800-729-7678, www.portofeverett.com

**Public Transportation:** Community Transit, 425-353-RIDE, 800-562-1375, www.commtrans.org

## WESTERN COMMUNITIES—KITSAP COUNTY

*Bainbridge Island, Bremerton*

### BAINBRIDGE ISLAND

#### WINSLOW

As Seattle residents search out alternatives to the bustle of living in the city, Bainbridge Island becomes more popular. A 30-minute ferry ride from the Seattle waterfront, Bainbridge Island is a community of lawyers, doctors, successful artisans, architects, and others, many of them ex-Seattleites.

At just under 28 square miles, the island is comparable in size to Manhattan, but residents and real estate agents say it more closely resembles the idyllic California seaside communities of Sausalito or La Jolla. Many homes on the island have stunning views of Puget Sound or the distant Seattle skyline, and as in any community with a good location and spectacular views, housing prices can be steep. In fact, home values have skyrocketed in recent years, with the median home price in 2005 reaching over $430,000, and the housing market remains strong. Rentals are scarce, except for seasonal accommodations during the summer months.

The **Winslow** neighborhood, adjacent to the ferry terminal, is the current hot spot, offering shops, restaurants, and the island's few condominiums. The community resembles Seattle's Madison Park neighborhood, with its spectacular water views and upscale boutiques. The neighborhood is popular with young professionals, who commute to the city and appreciate the short walk to the ferry terminal. Winslow is also where you'll find the island's only movie theater.

Despite its explosive growth, Bainbridge Island has managed to hang on to its rural feel, with abundant trees, parks, ponds, and beaches. Equestrian trails wind through the community, and many of the island's kids take riding lessons in addition to golf and swimming instruction. Like Mercer Island to the east of Seattle, Bainbridge is known for its excellent schools. The island also offers golf and country clubs, quaint restaurants, and homey bed and breakfast inns.

So what are the drawbacks? Cell phone reception can be iffy on Bainbridge, island kids may suffer from a bit of pre-adolescent claustrophobia, some people find the lack of diversity a drawback, and residents are dependent on the state ferry system. But, with Seattle's heavy traffic, Bainbridge Islanders are happy to forgo the messy daily grind of the Seattle expressways. In emergency situations, island patients are airlifted to Seattle's Harborview Medical Center in minutes.

**Web Site:** www.ci.bainbridge-isl.wa.us

**Area Code:** 206

**Zip Code:** 98110

**Post Office:** 10355 NE Valley Rd

**Library:** 1270 Madison Ave N, 206-842-4162, www.krl.org

**Public Schools:** Bainbridge Island School District, 8489 Madison Ave NE, 206-842-4714, www.bainbridge.wednet.edu

**Police:** 625 Winslow Way E, 206-842-5211, www.ci.bainbridge-isl.wa.us

**Emergency Hospital:** Harborview Medical Center, 325 9th Ave, 206-731-3074, www.uwmedicine.org/facilities/harborview

**Community Publication:** *Bainbridge Island Review*, 206-842-6613, www.bainbridgereview.com

**Community Resources:** Bainbridge Island Chamber of Commerce, 590 Winslow Way E, 206-842-3700, www.bainbridgechamber.com; Bainbridge Island Racquet Club, 8520 Renny Ln NE, 206-842-5661; Bainbridge Island Senior Center, 370 Brien Dr, 206-842-1616, www.bainbridgeseniors.org; Wing Point Golf & Country Club, 811 Cherry Ave, 206-842-2688, www.wingpointgolf.com

**Public Transportation:** Washington State Ferries, 206-464-6400, 888-808-7977, www.wsdot.wa.gov/ferries

## BREMERTON

The largest city on the west side of Puget Sound, Bremerton has a population of nearly 40,000 anchoring the Kitsap Peninsula. An hour's ferry ride away from Seattle, and a half hour drive to Tacoma, puts Bremerton within easy reach of Puget Sound's other largest cities. Best known as the home of the Puget Sound Naval Shipyard, which employs 8,000 civilians and the same amount of military,

Bremerton long had a slightly dingy, navy town reputation. Things have changed in recent years, with a revitalization of the downtown core. Restaurants, art galleries, art walks, and shops lure residents to downtown, while historic ships, a Naval Museum, festivals, and a waterfront boardwalk lure tourists. A 60-minute ferry ride to the Seattle waterfront is daunting to some, but more and more people are finding the lower home prices in Bremerton a sufficient reason to endure the commute to jobs in Seattle.

The city of Bremerton is divided by the Port Washington Narrows and connected by two bridges which help to create distinct neighborhoods within the city. Median home prices are half of what they are in Seattle, and homes with water views, or even waterfront property, sell for less than they do on the east side of the Sound. New waterfront condominiums with spectacular views are comparable in price to Tacoma and Seattle, starting around $350,000 and running over a million. As in most towns with a military base, rentals are plentiful, from older apartment buildings to spacious houses. A one-bedroom apartment averages around $700 a month.

**Web Site:** www.ci.bremerton.wa.us

**Area Code:** 360

**Zip Codes:** 98310, 98311, 98312, 98314, 98337

**Post Offices:** 1281 Sylvan Way; 602 Pacific Ave; 200 National Ave S

**Libraries:** 612 5th St, 360-377-3955; 1301 Sylvan Way, 360-405-9100, www.krl. org

**Public Schools:** Bremerton School District, 134 N Marion Ave, 360-473-1026, www.bremertonschools.org

**Police:** 239 4th St, 360-473-5220, www.ci.bremerton.wa.us

**Emergency Hospital:** Harrison Medical Center, 2520 Cherry Ave, 360-377-3911, www.harrisonhospital.org

**Community Publication:** *The Kitsap Sun*, 545 5th St, 888-377-3711, www. kitsapsun.com

**Community Resources:** Chamber of Commerce, 286 4th St, 360-479-3579, www. bremertonchamber.org; Olympic College, 1600 Chester Ave, 360-792-6050, www.olympic.edu; Kitsap County Department of Emergency Management, 911 Carver St, 360-307-5870, www.kitsapdem.org; Bremerton Naval Museum, 402 Pacific Ave, 360-479-7447

**Public Transportation:** Washington State Ferries, 206-464-6400, 888-808-7977, www.wsdot.wa.gov/ferries; Kitsap Transit, 360-377-2877, 800-501-7433, www. kitsaptransit.org

# SOUTHERN COMMUNITIES—KING COUNTY

*Renton, Kent, Auburn, Burien, SeaTac, Tukwila,*
*Normandy Park, Des Moines, Federal Way, Vashon Island*

The communities south of Seattle are often collectively referred to as the "South End." For the most part, homes in these cities are more affordable than in Seattle or the Eastside. Many years ago, the common perception was that these areas were less desirable because they were further away from big city attractions like professional sports, theater, museums, and fine dining. Today, however, many of these communities have revitalized downtown cores, complete with nice restaurants and evening entertainment, and are increasingly attracting singles, couples, and young professionals and their families. Many neighborhoods to the west offer fantastic views of the sound and mountains, and most have thriving shopping centers. Today, the remaining drawback to the South End is airplane noise from nearby Sea-Tac Airport.

## RENTON

**DOWNTOWN**
**TALBOT**
**BENSON**
**FAIRWOOD**

Renton has always been best known as the home of Boeing's commercial airplane factory. However, at the cusp of 2007, major new developments, in varying stages of planning and activity, are beginning to shake the heavily industrial perception of this town on the south end of Lake Washington. The *New York Times* has reported on the Seattle Seahawks' plans to build a new headquarters and training facility on 19 acres of Lake Washington shore, already purchased by the football team's owner—and Microsoft co-owner—Paul Allen, while a major shopping center is in development on 46 acres just across from the Boeing factory.

Traditionally home to middle-income Boeing employees and a healthy working class population, Renton has already been attracting a crowd of young professionals. For the price of a small Seattle home on a tiny lot, prospective homeowners can buy a large, modern home in Renton, although that is changing in certain neighborhoods.

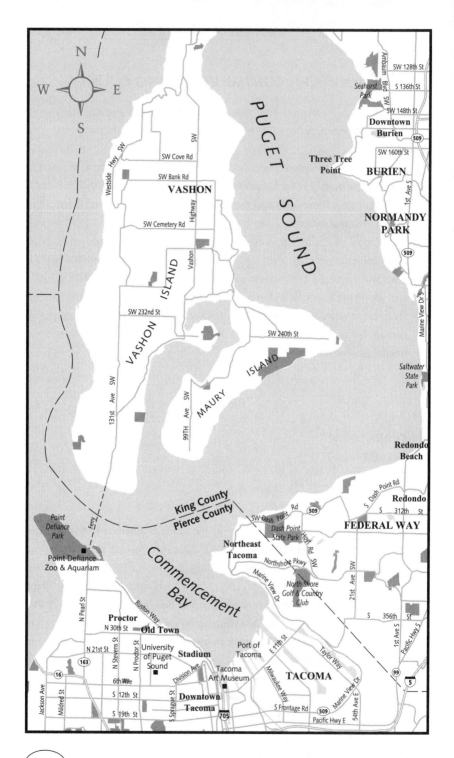

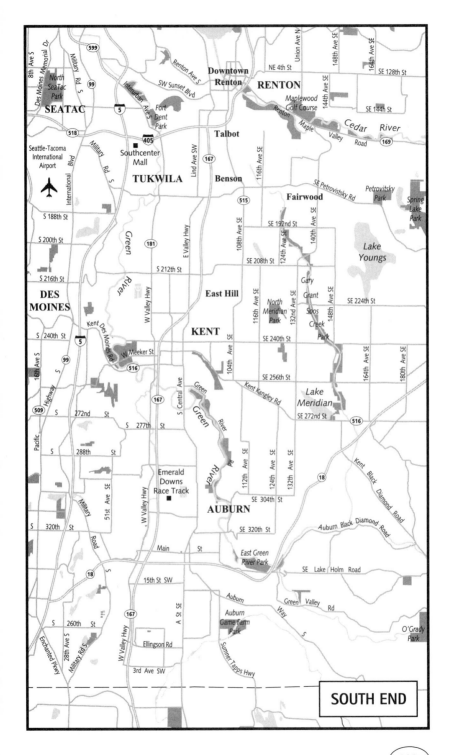

SOUTH END

Shopping centers or small business districts anchor most of Renton's mature neighborhoods. **Downtown**, mom-and-pop stores and restaurants occupy historic brick structures, while large chain stores like IKEA and Fry's Electronics dominate vast parking lots and strip malls. Housing here is limited to small bungalows, ramblers, and rental houses, and home prices are low. Fixer-uppers can be had for less than any other area in Renton. Downtown residents are close to the city's main library, a popular walking trail along the Cedar River, and the sport stadium shared by all three city high schools.

Above downtown is the **Talbot** or **Benson** area, which is popular with employees of Valley Medical Center. There is a good selection of condominiums and apartments in this neighborhood, as well as affordable homes built in the 1980s. New developments here are small because they are limited by the hillside and I-405, and some have views of downtown. This is a good area for entry-level homebuyers.

**Fairwood** is an established, upscale community that revolves around the Fairwood Golf and Country Club. Built in the late 1960s and early 1970s, the neighborhood is a mix of colonials, brick ramblers, and contemporary homes. In most of the neighborhood, power lines are hidden underground, and many of the houses abut the golf course.

New housing developments began to spring up around Renton in the early 1990s. With names like Summerwind, The Orchards, Windwood, and Stonegate, they feature large homes in safe communities. There are houses in just about every price range, from the $300,000s to half a million dollars, depending on construction, views, and lot size, and 2007 has already seen ground broken for a site of luxury lakefront homes ($800,000 – $3 million) in keeping with Renton's large-scale economic development.

**Web Site:** www.ci.renton.wa.us
**Area Code:** 425
**Zip Codes:** 98055, 98056, 98057, 98058, 98059
**Post Offices:** 17200 116th Ave SE; 314 Williams Ave S; 4301 NE 4th St
**Libraries:** 17009 140th SE, 425-226-0522, www.kcls.org; 100 Mill Ave S, 425-235-2610
**Public Schools:** Renton School District, 300 SW 7th St, 425-204-2300, www.renton.wednet.edu
**Police:** 1055 S Grady Way, 425-430-7500, www.ci.renton.wa.us
**Emergency Hospital:** Valley Medical Center, 400 S 43rd St, Renton, 425-228-3450, www.valleymed.org
**Community Resources:** Greater Renton Chamber of Commerce, 300 Rainier Ave N, 425-226-4560, www.renton-chamber.com; Renton Community Center, 1715 Maple Valley Hwy, 425-430-6700; Renton Community Foundation, 300 Rainier Ave N, 425-235-2356, www.rentonfoundation.org; Renton Historical Museum, 235 Mill Ave S, 425-255-2330; Renton Senior Activity Center, 211 Burnett Ave N, 425-430-6633; Renton Technical College, 3000 NE 4th St, 425-235-2352, www.renton-tc.ctc.edu

**Public Transportation:** Metro Transit, 206-553-3000, http://transit.metrokc.gov; 101, 105, 106, 107, 110, 140, 143, 148, 149, 153, 155, 161, 167, 169, 240, 247, 280, 342, 908, 909, 952

# KENT

## EAST HILL

Formerly a rich agricultural valley, Kent today is one of the country's busiest distribution centers. It is the fourth-largest city in King County and the 9th largest in the state, and it's growing.

There is an abundance of designated parks and greenspace in Kent, ranging in size from the one-tenth of an acre Gowe Street Mini Park (Kennebeck Avenue and Titus Street) to the 310-acre Green River Natural Resources Area, a wetland and wildlife refuge at 22000 Russell Road, in the Kent Valley. The Green River Trail, a popular path for walking, running and biking, follows the east bank of the river from south Seattle through Kent and on into Auburn.

In Kent, renters outnumber homeowners, nearly two to one. There are dozens of multiple-family housing units, particularly on its East Hill, which is home to many strip malls and fast-food restaurants. Traffic in the teeming East Hill area is a constant challenge, as commuters headed toward Tacoma, Seattle, and Everett converge on the arterials and freeways.

This is a popular community for first-time homebuyers looking for new construction. The median home price in 2005 barely topped $250,000, making Kent one of the most affordable cities in the greater Seattle area. Likewise, apartments here are reasonably priced, averaging less than $900 per month.

**Web Site:** www.ci.kent.wa.us
**Area Code:** 253
**Zip Codes:** 98031, 98032, 98035, 98046, 98064
**Post Office:** 10612 SE 240th
**Library:** 212 2nd Ave N, 253-859-3330, 253-854-1050 (TTY), www.kcls.org
**Public Schools:** Kent School District, 12033 SE 256th St, 253-373-7000, www.kent.wednet.edu
**Police:** 220 4th Ave S, 253-856-5800, www.ci.kent.wa.us
**Emergency Hospital:** Valley Medical Center, 400 S 43rd St, Renton, 425-228-3450, www.valleymed.org
**Community Resources:** Kent Chamber of Commerce, 524 W Meeker St, Ste 1, 253-854-1770, www.kentchamber.com; Kent Commons, 525 4th Ave N, 253-856-5000, www.ci.kent.wa.us; Resource Center, 315 E Meeker St, 253-856-5030, www.ci.kent.wa.us; Senior Activity Center, 600 E Smith St, 253-856-5150, www.ci.kent.wa.us

**Public Transportation:** Metro Transit, 206-553-3000, http://transit.metrokc.gov; 150, 153, 154, 158, 159, 161, 162, 164, 166, 168, 169, 173, 174, 175, 180, 183, 190, 191, 192, 194, 197, 247, 912, 914, 916, 918, 941, 952

# AUBURN

South of Kent, the city of Auburn is located on the Green and White Rivers with grand views of Mt. Rainier. Billing itself as "the world's biggest small town," Auburn boasts a population of nearly 50,000 people. Now more of an industrial town, the area has a long history as a farming center and has preserved many of its historic sites, including the Neely Mansion which is listed on the National Register of Historic Places. Olson Farm is the only intact family farm in King County, and offers tours of its 60 acres and historic buildings.

Downtown Auburn still has a picturesque, small town feeling, but this city is also the home of the Auburn SuperMall, the largest outlet mall in the Northwest. The Muckleshoot Casino, run by the Muckleshoot Indian tribe, is a major entertainment draw, as is the Emerald Downs horse racing track, and the Auburn Performing Arts Center is an important part of the cultural life.

The small town feeling of Auburn draws families, as does an average home price of less than $300,000. Despite the rural feeling of much of the area, and the feeling of being far from the "big city," the Sounder train travels to both Seattle and Tacoma, a convenience for commuters.

**Web Site:** www.auburnwa.gov
**Area Code:** 253
**Zip Codes:** 98001, 98002, 98003, 98023, 98047, 98063, 98071, 98092, 98093
**Post Offices:** 120 Cross St SE; 11 3rd St NW
**Library:** 1102 Auburn Way S, 253-931-3018, www.kcls.org
**Public Schools:** Auburn School District, 915 4th St NE, www.auburn.wednet. edu
**Police:** 340 E Main St, 253-931-3080, www.ci.auburn.wa.us
**Emergency Hospital:** Auburn Regional Medical Center, 202 N Division St, 253-833-7711, www.armcuhs.com
**Community Publication:** *Auburn Reporter*, http://reporternewspapers.com
**Community Resources:** Auburn Performing Arts Center, 700 E Main St, 253-931-4827, Chamber of Commerce, 108 S Division St, 253-833-0700, www. auburnareawa.org; Green River Community College, 12401 SE 320th St, 253-833-9111, www.greenriver.edu; Auburn Senior Activity Center, 808 9th St SE, 253-931-3016
**Public Transportation:** Metro Transit, 206-553-3000, http://transit.metrokc.gov; 152, 154, 164, 180, 181, 915, 917, 919, 952; Sound Transit, 206-398-5000, www. soundtransit.org

# BURIEN

## DOWNTOWN
## THREE TREE POINT

Like many south-end cities, Burien often hides its charms among strip malls and busy intersections. But, a closer look at this diverse community reveals sound and mountain views, saltwater beaches, affordable housing, and easy commutes to Seattle and Sea-Tac Airport. Burien is popular with medical professionals who work at Highline Community Hospital, pilots and flight attendants, and Weyerhaeuser employees.

The quickest route to Burien from downtown Seattle is Highway 509, a road much less traveled than the better-known I-5. Unfortunately, the route ends at the intersection of 1st Avenue South and Highway 518, a conglomeration of fast food restaurants and auto dealerships that doesn't give visitors a terribly good first impression of Burien. City planners are hoping to change that impression by renovating the downtown core and adding a large, pedestrian-friendly town square complex that will include over 400 new condominiums and townhomes, stores, restaurants, a new park, and library. Construction is slated for completion in 2009.

Rentals are plentiful in and around downtown, with a mix of old and new apartment buildings, condominiums, and senior housing units. First-time homebuyers may be interested in areas east of downtown, like Chelsea Park, where post–World War II homes go for less than $300,000.

Three Tree Point is the jewel of Burien, an entirely residential neighborhood of artists, writers, doctors, and lawyers, among others, who seek privacy and spectacular Puget Sound views. The homes perched along the bluff and waterfront are varied, ranging from beach bungalows to turn-of-the-century farmhouses. The neighborhood is also popular with scuba divers, who come to explore underwater shipwrecks, and hikers and history buffs, who climb the old Indian trail that winds up the hillside from the beach.

**Web Site:** www.burienwa.gov
**Area Code:** 206
**Zip Codes:** 98146, 98148, 98166, 98168
**Post Offices:** Burien Station, 609 SW 150th, Seattle; Seahurst Main Office, 2116 SW 52nd St, Burien
**Library:** 14700 6th Ave SW, 206-243-3490, www.kcls.org
**Public Schools:** Highline School District, 15675 Ambaum Blvd SW, 206-433-0111, www.hsd401.org
**Police:** 14905 6th Ave SW, 206-296-3333, www.ci.burien.wa.us

**Emergency Hospital:** Highline Community Hospital, 16251 Sylvester Rd SW, 206-244-9970, www.hchnet.org

**Community Resources:** Burien Community Center, 425 SW 144th St, 206-988-3700; Burien Community Computer Center, 653 SW 152nd St, 206-241-3551, www.burien.org; Burien Little Theatre, 206-242-5180, SW 146th and 4th Ave S, www.burienlittletheatre.com; Southwest King County Chamber of Commerce, 16400 Southcenter Pkwy #210, Tukwila, 206-575-1633, www.swkcc.org

**Public Transportation:** Metro Transit, 206-553-3000, http://transit.metrokc.gov; 120, 121, 122, 123, 131, 132, 133, 134, 139, 140, 180

## SEATAC, TUKWILA

SeaTac (named for the Seattle-Tacoma International Airport) is a modest middle-class suburb with pleasant and inexpensive contemporary homes. Airline and Boeing employees live in this area, but other local businesses employ many residents as well. SeaTac, and its neighbor, Tukwila, are subject to heavy airport noise. In fact, many homes have been vacated or torn down to make way for the airport's third runway. But, both communities enjoy a wealth of starter homes and apartments, and easy access to shopping and banking.

Tukwila is best known as the site of Southcenter Mall, (now officially known as the Westfield Shoppingtown Southcenter) a popular shopping center anchored by Nordstrom and Macy's, as well as other big-name department stores. There are numerous restaurants and strip malls surrounding Southcenter, and many industrial buildings. Because of the wealth of retail and industry, taxes in Tukwila are low, making the community attractive to young families and first-time homebuyers. Houses here range from the high $100,000s for older, smaller homes, to $600,000 and up for new subdivisions.

The city of Tukwila provides a "welcome packet" on its web site at www.ci.tukwila.wa.us/infopack/intro.htm.

**Web Sites:** www.seatac.wa.gov; www.ci.tukwila.wa.us

**Area Code:** 206

**Zip Codes:** 98108, 98138, 98148, 98158, 98168, 98178, 98188, 98198

**Post Offices:** 15250 32nd Ave S; 225 Andover Park W

**Libraries:** 17850 Military Rd S, 206-242-6044, 206-242-4335 (TTY); 4060 S 144th, 206-242-1640; 14475 59th S, 206-244-5140, www.kcls.org

**Public Schools:** Highline School District, 15675 Ambaum Blvd SW, 206-433-0111, www.hsd401.org; Tukwila School District, 4640 S 144th St, 206-901-8000, www.tukwila.wednet.edu

**Police:** 17900 International Blvd, Ste 401, 206-241-9100, www.metrokc.gov/sheriff; 6200 Southcenter Blvd, 206-433-1808, www.ci.tukwila.wa.us

**Emergency Hospital:** Highline Community Hospital, 12844 Military Rd S, 206-248-4730, www.hchnet.org

**Community Resources:** North SeaTac Park Community Center, 13735 24th Ave S, 206-439-9273; Southwest King County Chamber of Commerce, 16400 Southcenter Pkwy #210, Tukwila, 206-575-1633, www.swkcc.org; Tukwila Community Center, 12424 42nd Ave S, 206-768-2822, www.ci.tukwila.wa.us; Tukwila Golf Course, 13500 Interurban Ave, 206-242-4221

**Public Transportation:** Metro Transit, 206-553-3000, http://transit.metrokc.gov; 126, 128, 140, 150, 154, 155, 161, 174, 180, 191, 194, 280, 600, 941

## NORMANDY PARK

About 20 miles south of Seattle is Normandy Park, a timeless seaside community between Burien and Des Moines. The city's location, small size, and reputable police force make it a popular choice with middle- to upper-income families and older residents. It lacks the suburban sprawl of other south end communities, and enjoys lots of greenspace and water views. There is little commerce here, however, so residents rely on nearby Burien or Des Moines.

As with any city situated on the water, Normandy Park offers a range of housing, from multi-million-dollar estates with commanding views to large ramblers that sell for less than half a million. Because lot and home sizes are larger here than in most Seattle suburbs, affording residents much treasured privacy, you won't find much for less than $300,000. Those lucky enough to land a beachfront home have access to The Cove, a parcel of jointly owned property that includes the beach, a playground, tennis and volleyball courts, and a community center. Beachfront property owners pay a small annual fee and split the property taxes for the privilege.

Normandy Park is known for its speeding restrictions, so if you come looking here, be sure to keep it to 25 miles per hour. The speed limit is in effect throughout the city, not just in the residential areas.

**Web Site:** www.ci.normandy-park.wa.us
**Area Code:** 206
**Zip Codes:** 98148, 98166, 98198
**Post Offices:** 609 SW 150th St, Seattle; 2003 S 216th St, Des Moines
**Library:** 21620 11th Ave S, Des Moines, 206-824-6066, www.kcls.org
**Public Schools:** Highline School District, 15675 Ambaum Blvd SW, Burien, 206-433-0111, www.hsd401.org

**Police:** 801 SW 174th St, 206-248-7600, www.ci.normandy-park.wa.us
**Emergency Hospital:** Highline Community Hospital, 16251 Sylvester Rd SW, Burien, 206-244-9970, www.hchnet.org
**Community Resources:** Des Moines Senior Center, 22030 Cliff Ave S, Des Moines, 206-878-1642, www.ci.des-moines.wa.us; Normandy Park Community Club, 17655 12th Ave SW, 206-242-3778
**Public Transportation:** Metro Transit, 206-553-3000, http://transit.metrokc.gov; 121, 122, 131, 132

# DES MOINES

Des Moines (pronounced De Moin) is a peaceful town located midway between Seattle and Tacoma. Marine View Drive, the primary artery through town, hugs the shoreline and meanders through the city's small commercial district.

Commerce revolves around the marina and waterfront, where a handful of seafood restaurants attract diners from all over the South End. The waterfront promenade is a safe and popular spot for walkers and runners and the pier is usually full of people fishing and crabbing. There is a dense concentration of condominiums near the Des Moines waterfront, many with gorgeous views. Like Edmonds to the north, Des Moines is popular with retirees who spend summers in the Northwest and escape to warmer climates during the winter.

Most homes in Des Moines are mature, comfortable ramblers and split levels built in the 1950s and later. There are small pockets of newer construction, but development is limited by geography.

**Web Site:** www.ci.des-moines.wa.us
**Area Code:** 206
**Zip Codes:** 98148, 98198
**Post Office:** 2003 S 216th St
**Libraries:** 21620 11th Ave S, 206-824-6066; 26809 Pacific Hwy S, 253-839-0121, www.kcls.org
**Public Schools:** Highline School District, 15675 Ambaum Blvd SW, Burien, 206-433-0111, www.hsd401.org
**Police:** 21900 11th Ave S, 206-878-3301, www.ci.des-moines.wa.us
**Emergency Hospital:** Highline Community Hospital, 16251 Sylvester Rd SW, Burien, 206-244-9970, www.hchnet.org
**Community Resources:** Des Moines Senior Center, 22030 Cliff Ave S, 206-878-1642, www.ci.des-moines.wa.us; Greater Des Moines Chamber of Commerce, 206-878-7000; Mt. Rainier Pool, 22722 19th Ave S, 206-296-4278, www.metrokc.gov/parks
**Public Transportation:** Metro Transit, 206-553-3000, http://transit.metrokc.gov; 121, 122, 131, 132, 166, 173, 174, 175, 191

# FEDERAL WAY

## REDONDO BEACH
## REDONDO

Federal Way is a modest middle-class suburb with pleasant and inexpensive (compared to Seattle) contemporary homes. Airline, Boeing, and Weyerhaeuser employees live in this area, but other area businesses employ many residents as well. The median house price in 2005 was around $264,000, making it one of the area's most affordable communities. There are lots of nice starter homes here, many of them older ramblers and/or fixer-uppers that sell for less than the median price. There are also many pockets of planned communities, like Steel Lake and Twin Lakes, with gorgeous homes on large lots. Adding to the city's diversity is a variety of apartments, condominiums, and rental homes. The location, between Seattle and Tacoma, makes sense for couples needing easy access to both communities.

As with many of the region's communities that hug Puget Sound, Federal Way also has a handful of waterfront communities that offer panoramic views. **Redondo Beach** is one such neighborhood. Formerly a vacation spot, the community is now a mix of beach bungalows, contemporary new homes, and condominiums. In **Redondo**, the community above the beach, you'll find large homes with partial views that sell in the half-million dollar range.

Like Lynnwood to the north of Seattle, Federal Way serves as a retail center for residents of many South End communities. SeaTac Mall is located here, along with numerous chain stores and restaurants. Other sources of local pride are the King County Aquatic Center, which was built for the 1990 Goodwill Games, and the rhododendron and bonsai garden, owned by Weyerhaeuser Co.

**Web Site:** www.ci.federal-way.wa.us
**Area Code:** 253
**Zip Codes:** 98001, 98003, 98023, 98063, 98093
**Post Office:** 32829 Pacific Hwy S
**Libraries:** 34200 1st Way S, 253-838-3668; 848 S 320th St, 253-839-0257, 206-296-5203 (TTY), www.kcls.org
**Public Schools:** Federal Way Public Schools, 31405 18th Ave S, 253-945-2000, www.fwsd.wednet.edu
**Police:** 34008 9th Ave S, 253-661-4600, www.ci.federal-way.wa.us
**Emergency Hospital:** St. Francis Hospital, 34515 9th Ave S, 253-927-9700, www.fhshealth.org
**Community Publication:** *Federal Way Mirror*, 1414 S 324th St, Ste B210, 253-946-2890, www.fedwaymirror.com

**Community Resources:** Federal Way Chamber of Commerce, 34004 16th Ave S, Ste 101, 253-838-2605, www.federalwaychamber.com; King County Aquatic Center, 650 SW Campus Dr, 206-296-4444, www.metrokc.gov/parks

**Public Transportation:** Metro Transit, 206-553-3000, http://transit.metrokc.gov; 173, 174, 175, 177, 179, 181, 182, 183, 187, 190, 191, 192, 194, 196, 197, 901, 903; Sound Transit, 206-398-5000, www.soundtransit.org; Pierce Transit, 253-581-8000, www.piercetransit.org

## VASHON ISLAND

Out in the middle of Puget Sound, between Seattle and Tacoma, lies rural Vashon Island. If you decide to move there and commute to a job off the island, be aware that the only way on and off the island is by ferry boat. Islanders are fiercely proud of their independence, so don't count on there ever being a bridge built to the mainland. The ferry docks in West Seattle in less than thirty minutes, but a passenger-only ferry goes to the Colman Dock on the downtown Seattle waterfront.

Vashon is actually comprised of two islands, Vashon and Maury Islands, connected by a narrow land bridge. It isn't an official city, but part of unincorporated King County. It's roughly the size of Manhattan Island, but only has a population of around 11,000. That number grows a bit in summer, as summer houses for city residents are popular here, but due to zoning restrictions and the water table, there will never be a population explosion. Most of the island is very rural, with plenty of undeveloped land, beaches, and parks. Homes range from very old farmhouses to million-dollar waterfront mansions, and prices are comparable to Seattle. There is one apartment complex in town, but rentals are hard to come by.

The town of Vashon is roughly in the middle of the island on the main north/south highway that connects the ferry docks on each end of the island. There are a number of restaurants and shops and it is possible to get all of your necessities without leaving the island, but you won't find many chain stores. Many artists, activists, and wealthy retirees call the island home and families tout the excellence of the schools. If you're an independent type looking for a rural, small town atmosphere fairly close to city amenities, and don't mind a little isolation, Vashon might be perfect.

**Web Site:** www.vmicc.org
**Area Code:** 206
**Zip Code:** 98070
**Post Offices:** 10005 SW 178th St; 23830 Vashon Hwy SW
**Library:** 17210 Vashon Hwy SW, 206-463-2069, www.kcls.org
**Public Schools:** Vashon Island School District, 18850 103rd Ave SW, 206-408-8100, www.vashonsd.wednet.edu

**Police:** King County Sheriff's Office, 19021 Vashon Hwy S, 206-463-3618, www. metrokc.gov/sheriff

**Emergency Hospital:** Harborview Medical Center, 325 9th Ave, 206-731-3074, www.uwmedicine.org/facilities/harborview

**Community Publication:** *Vashon-Maury Island Beachcomber*, www.vashon beachcomber.com

**Community Resources:** VashonIsland.net, www.vashonisland.net; Chamber of Commerce, 19021 Vashon Hwy SW, 206-463-6217, www.vashonchamber. com; Vashon Island Community Service Center, Courthouse Square, 19021 Vashon Hwy SW, 206-296-4510, www.metrokc.gov; Vashon Health Center, 10030 SW 210th St, 206-463-3671; Vashon-Maury Senior Center, 10004 SW Bank Rd, 206-463-5173, www.seniorservices.org/sc/vashon.asp; Vashon Allied Arts, 206-463-5131, www.vashonalliedarts.org

**Public Transportation:** Washington State Ferries, 206-464-6400, 888-808-7977, www.wsdot.wa.gov/ferries; Metro Transit, 206-553-3000, http://transit. metrokc.gov

# SOUTHERN COMMUNITIES—PIERCE COUNTY

## TACOMA

### NORTHEAST TACOMA
### DOWNTOWN
### STADIUM DISTRICT
### OLD TOWN
### PROCTOR

As the second largest city in Western Washington (population 193,600), Tacoma doesn't quite count as a suburb, although some residents do commute to Seattle for work. An industrial and port city, Tacoma remains a less expensive alternative to Seattle. To truly appreciate Tacoma, you must get off I-5. Otherwise, it's easy to assume that the city's only attraction is the famous Tacoma Dome, the only dome remaining in Western Washington.

A decade ago, parts of Tacoma were troubled by gang activity, but efforts by the city and local community action groups have done much to contain and improve the situation. Today, home and personal security concerns for Tacoma residents are comparable to those in Seattle.

Tacoma has its own $100-million fiber optics network under the city, making it the most wired city in the country—according to its economic development director. So, it's not surprising that the city has been able to lure high-tech companies from other parts of the US, including Seattle. Other major employers in Tacoma include the Tacoma School District, the Frank Russell Company, University of Washington at Tacoma, Regence Blue Shield, DaVita Inc, and local hospitals. Cultural attractions include the Museum of Glass and the Tacoma Art Museum next to Union station. In addition, the city zoned warehouse district space for artists, and boasts a fine arts high school (grades 10-12), the Tacoma School of the Arts, located at 1950 Pacific Avenue.

There are many distinct neighborhoods in Tacoma. If you're looking for new construction and a neighborhood of young, professional families, check out **Northeast Tacoma**, a conglomeration of planned developments staggered along the hillside. Homes started going up in the early 1980s, and construction continues; prices range from $250,000 to $400,000. There is no real commercial center here, but the conveniences of Federal Way and downtown Tacoma are just a short drive away.

**Downtown Tacoma** is experiencing a major revitalization. You will find hundreds of refurbished and new apartments, condominiums and artists' lofts, quaint pubs, historic theaters, a gorgeous new art museum, the Washington State History Museum and a burgeoning night life. Similar to Seattle's Belltown neighborhood, downtown Tacoma has become a hip spot to live, particularly for employees of the city's growing banking and finance community.

Some of Tacoma's most attractive neighborhoods are located in the city's northern sector. The **Stadium District** is home to Stadium High School and a nearly century-old French Renaissance castle, originally intended as a luxury hotel. The Stadium neighborhood is an eclectic mix of condominiums, turn-of-the-century Victorians, Craftsman bungalows, and mansions. Lively and diverse, the Stadium District is home to Tacoma's gay community, young professionals, and long-time residents. The neighborhood boasts spectacular views, good schools and wide, tree-lined streets. Except for the occasional mansion, homes here cost less than $700,000, and many go for under $400,000.

**Old Town**, above the city's bustling waterfront, is a former fishing village that offers modest homes at affordable prices. Tacoma's waterfront is a popular recreation area, with numerous docks and walkways, restaurants, and a new hotel. In the works is a planned community at the site of the former ASARCO smelter at the end of Ruston Way. The plan includes a mix of housing, parks, and retail space, and is sure to raise property values in the area. **Proctor**, again in North Tacoma, is also popular with young professionals. With a quaint commercial district, Proctor offers the convenience of a small downtown with the charm of a residential neighborhood. Well-kept Craftsman homes line the quiet streets. Prices begin at around $200,000.

Tacoma has an expansive parks system, including a series of greenspaces and trails along the Commencement Bay waterfront. On sunny days, the area resembles Seattle's Alki shorefront, with walkers, runners, and rollerbladers jostling for position on the sidewalks—there's no place better for people-watching during the summer. Also in Tacoma are Point Defiance Park and Point Defiance Zoo & Aquarium, two of the South End's premier weekend destinations. At 698 acres, Point Defiance Park is among the 20 largest urban parks in the United States. It includes a replica of Fort Nisqually, a logging museum, rose and Japanese gardens, and 14 miles of hiking trails.

**Web Site:** www.cityoftacoma.org

**Area Code:** 253

**Zip Codes:** 98401, 98402, 98403, 98404, 98405, 98406, 98407, 98408, 98409, 98411, 98412, 98413, 98415, 98416, 98418, 98421, 98422, 98424, 98430, 98431, 98433, 98438, 98439, 98442, 98443, 98444, 98445, 98446, 98447, 98450, 98455, 98460, 98464, 98465, 98466, 98467, 98471, 98477, 98481, 98492, 98493, 98497, 98498, 98499

**Post Offices:** 1220 Martin Luther King Jr. Way; 1102 A St; 3801 N 27th St, 3705 S "G" St, 3503 S 56th St; 4001 S Pine St; 5431 Pacific Ave; 8235 S Park Ave; 3002 6th Ave; 320 Garfield St S

**Libraries:** 1102 Tacoma Ave S, 253-591-5666; 765 S 84th St, 253-591-5620; 1902 S Cedar St, 253-591-5166; 212 Brown's Point Blvd NE, 253-591-5630; 215 S 56th St, 253-591-5650; 3523 E "G" St, 253-591-5660; 3411 S 56th St, 253-591-5670; 3828 Portland Ave, 253-594-7805; 7001 6th Ave, 253-591-5680; 3722 N 26th St, 253-591-5640, www.tpl.lib.wa.us; 13718 Pacific Ave S, 253-531-4656; 5107 112th St E, 253-536-6186; 14916 Washington Ave SW, 253-588-1014; 3605 Bridgeport Way W, 253-565-9447, www.pcl.lib.wa.us

**Public Schools:** Tacoma School District, 601 S 8th St, 253-571-1000, www.tacoma. k12.wa.us

**Police:** 3701 S Pine St, 253-591-5900, www.tacomapolice.org

**Emergency Hospital:** Tacoma General Hospital, 315 Martin Luther King Jr. Way, 253-403-1000, www.multicare.org

**Community Publications:** *The News Tribune*, 1950 S State St, 253-597-8742, www. thenewstribune.com; *Tacoma Daily Index*, 1019 Pacific Ave, Ste 1216, 253-627-4853, www.tacomadailyindex.com

**Community Resources:** Beacon Senior Center, 415 S 13th St, 253-591-5083; Lighthouse Senior Center, 5016 A St, 253-591-5080; Point Defiance Zoo & Aquarium, 5400 N Pearl St, 253-591-5337, www.pdza.org; Port of Tacoma, One Sitcum Plaza, 253-383-5841, www.portoftacoma.com; Tacoma Art Museum, 1123 Pacific Ave, 253-272-4258, www.tacomaartmuseum.org; University of Washington at Tacoma, 1900 Commerce St, 253-692-4000, www.tacoma. washington.edu; YMCA of Tacoma-Pierce County, 1002 S Pearl St, 253-564-9622; 9715 Lakewood Dr SW, 253-584-9622; 1144 Market St, 253-597-6444, www.tacomaymca.org

**Public Transportation:** Pierce Transit, 3701 96th St SW, 253-581-8000, 800-562-8109, www.ptbus.pierce.wa.us

A DECADE AGO, FINDING A PLACE TO LIVE IN SEATTLE WAS EASY. Today, it will take persistence and some luck to find what you want. Situated between two bodies of water, with only narrow bridges and ferries to connect it to surrounding communities, Seattle faces the challenges of a growing population and substantial geographical constraints. Couple these factors with rising home prices and a growing population of well over half a million people in 2004, and it's easy to understand the high price of area real estate.

Leveling off in the early 1990s, housing prices rose again in the mid 1990s, accounting for Seattle's listing by the National Association of Realtors and the Washington Center for Real Estate Research as being among the country's most expensive places to buy residential real estate. Though the national and regional economies slowed after 2000, home prices in King County continued to rise. As of September 2006, the median price for a single-family home in King County was $425,000, according to the Northwest Multiple Listing Service. (More about Seattle's cost of living can be found at www.BestPlaces.net, a non–ad-driven site with information and statistics for 3,000 US cities and towns.)

In 2006, as more people became priced out of the homebuying market, rental units became much more in demand and are now more difficult to find and offer fewer incentives to new renters. Job growth in the region and apartments converting to condominiums contributed to a decreasing vacancy rate, which stood at 4.2% in King County in the fall of 2006.

Once a city primarily of single-family homes, the creation of duplexes and triplexes from older homes is now common. Condominiums and apartment buildings account for a large portion of current building projects, as do townhouses and multi-family houses. Rental rates in Seattle are high. Recent figures from Dupre + Scott Apartment Advisors (www.dsaa.com) listed $920 as the average rent in King County. At the same time, many of the neighborhoods surveyed had rents that topped $1,100. Keep in mind that competition for rental properties—particularly for houses—is stiff. A landlord-hosted open house often attracts numerous applicants, and the event takes on the air of a job interview, with well-dressed renters vying for the landlord's attention. To get an edge over the competition, bring a prepared rental application with you, along with a list of references, and be ready to write a check for first and last month's rent and a damage deposit. If you are moving from out of state, you may be required to get a cashier's check or money order.

## APARTMENT HUNTING

## DIRECT ACTION

To find an apartment in Seattle on your own, consider a strategy using several methods. Searching the local classifieds, either online or in print, is the best way to begin. An early edition of the *Sunday Seattle Times/Seattle Post-Intelligencer* arrives in stores on Friday night, allowing you to call landlords first thing Saturday morning. The listings should give you a good sense of prices in various neighborhoods. Since many local landlords don't run advertisements in the paper it's also a good idea to drive through the neighborhoods you're interested in, looking for posted rental notices. Many rentals offered by owners can be found on http://seattle.craigslist.com.

If you'd like to be near a local university or college, late spring is the best time to look for vacancies. These neighborhoods include Fremont, Wallingford, or North Queen Anne near Seattle Pacific University; the University District, Green Lake and Ravenna near the University of Washington; or Capitol Hill and the Central Area, which border the Seattle University campus.

Wherever you set your sights, check out www.seattlerentals.com, which lists vacancies in Seattle and surrounding communities. The site also includes neighborhood descriptions, pictures, and maps, as well as moving resources. You can find listings for apartments, condos, and houses offered through landlords and property management firms, and use tools to save your favorites and get e-mail listing updates.

Also, don't forget **word of mouth**. Some of the best apartments are found through the grapevine. Even if you are new to the area and haven't yet established such connections, you can still put the word out. Check college/university, coffee shop, and grocery bulletin boards (see below). When you call about vacancies, ask about any others that may be opening up in the neighborhood. Chances are, even if the apartment you are calling about has been taken, someone knows someone up the street who is moving on. In addition, the neighborhood profiles include a list of neighborhood organizations, which may be a good resource for finding out about available apartments, as well as area safety and neighborhood events.

## CLASSIFIED ADVERTISEMENTS

In **Seattle**, check out these news sources for the best selection of classified ads:

- *Seattle Post-Intelligencer/The Seattle Times*; get the joint Sunday edition, which has the most comprehensive rental and real estate listings for Seattle and surrounding communities. Rentals are divided into apartments and houses in the "NWclassifieds" section, and further subdivided by location. Houses for sale are listed in the "Home/Real Estate" section, also organized by location. The newspapers share an online classifieds section at http:// classifieds.nwsource.com/classified. New listings appear daily in both the print and online versions.
- *Seattle Weekly*; a free newspaper, the *Weekly* is distributed on Thursdays and is available in newspaper vending boxes, cafés, bars, and convenience and grocery stores. The paper often lists rental opportunities not found in the larger publications. To view ads online, visit www.seattleweekly.com. New ads are posted to the web site every day.
- *The Stranger*; a free weekly newspaper that can be found in restaurants and bars throughout Seattle. *The Stranger* is distributed on Thursdays, and contains rental and real estate classifieds. Online ads, which are updated daily, can be found at www.thestranger.com.

Community newspapers are excellent avenues for finding an apartment; many run local classifieds that will give you first crack at vacancies that may not appear in the citywide papers. These papers are usually available free of charge at neighborhood businesses and cafés.

- *Ballard News Tribune*, www.ballardnewstribune.com
- *Beacon Hill News & South District Journal*, www.zwire.com/site/news. asp?brd=855
- *Capitol Hill Times*, www.zwire.com/site/news.asp?brd=855
- *Madison Park Times*, www.zwire.com/site/news.asp?brd=855
- *Magnolia News*, www.zwire.com/site/news.asp?brd=855
- *North Seattle Herald-Outlook*, www.zwire.com/site/news.asp?brd=855
- *Queen Anne News*, www.zwire.com/site/news.asp?brd=855
- *West Seattle Herald*, www.westseattleherald.com
- *White Center News*, www.robinsonnews.com

To find housing in Seattle's surrounding communities, check out the classified ads in these major newspapers:

- *Federal Way News*, www.federalwaynews.net
- *The Herald*, www.heraldnet.com
- *Highline Times*, www.highlinetimes.com
- *Issaquah Press*, www.issaquahpress.com
- *King County Journal*, www.kingcountyjournal.com
- *Kirkland Courier*, www.zwire.com/site/news.asp?brd=855
- *Mercer Island Reporter*, www.mi-reporter.com
- *Tacoma News Tribune*, www.tribnet.com

All of the newspapers listed above have "roommate wanted" or "room available" sections, worth a look if you're on a limited budget. Shared houses are common in some areas of Seattle, particularly in the University District and the southeast side of Capitol Hill. These can be a good option if you plan to move again in several months, as many do not require a long-term lease.

## OTHER RENTAL PUBLICATIONS

Several companies publish free rental guides. Most list newer apartment complexes or apartments that are maintained by large property management companies. You can pick up rental guides at most grocery or convenience stores.

- *Apartment Guide*, www.apartmentguide.com
- *For Rent*, www.forrent.com

## BULLETIN BOARDS

Check out bulletin boards on college campuses, or in laundromats, coffee shops, and convenience stores in the neighborhoods that interest you.

- **Bellevue Community College**: housing opportunities are posted in the college cafeteria.
- **North Seattle Community College**: housing information can be found on campus at Baxter Center.
- **Seattle Central Community College**: two community bulletin boards are available in the Broadway Edison Building.
- **Seattle Pacific University**: bulletin boards can be found on campus at Weter Hall and in the Student Union Building.

- **Seattle University**: a classifieds ads bulletin board is located on the first floor of the Student Union Building.
- **South Seattle Community College**: a student bulletin board is located in the Jerry Brockey Building.
- **University of Washington**: off-campus housing information is available in Room G20 of the Husky Union Building.

## ONLINE RESOURCES

These local and national apartment-listing and roommate referral sites may be worth a look. Each lists vacancies in the Seattle area.

- **Apartment Rental Guide.com**, www.apartmentrentalguide.com
- **Rentals.com**, www.rentals.com
- **Roommate Express**, www.e-roommate.com
- **Roommates.com**, www.roommates.com
- **Seattle Apartment Finders**, www.seattleapartmentfinders.com
- **Seattle Rentals**, www.seattlerentals.com
- **SeattleRenter.com**, www.seattlerenter.com

## APARTMENT SEARCH FIRMS

One way to find an apartment, particularly if your time is limited, is to use an apartment search firm. These can be especially helpful if you want to set up your rental before arriving in town, as most agents will do a lot of the legwork for you. When speaking to an apartment search firm agent, be specific about your needs and budget. The following firms offer free search services.

- **Apartment Finders of Seattle**, 206-213-0127, 800-473-3733, www.seattleapartmentfinder.com
- **Apartment Hunters**, 206-770-0111, 888-772-0111, www.apthunters.com

## CHECKING IT OUT

You're on your way to the day's first rental appointment, you haven't had breakfast, the old college friends you're staying with are getting restless, your back is aching from a bad night's sleep on their sofa-bed, and twenty other people are waiting outside the prospective apartment when you drive up. You panic, take a quick glance around, like what you see, and grab an application. Three months later you're wondering how you landed in such a dump.

To avoid this scenario, tour each apartment with a clear idea of what you want. Beyond personal likes and dislikes, there are some specific things to check for as you look:

- Is the apartment on the first floor? If so, does it have burglar bars? First floor apartments are easy targets for burglary.
- Are the appliances clean and in good working order? Test all of the stove's burners. Does the kitchen sink have one or two basins? Is there sufficient counter space? Is the freezer compartment of the refrigerator a frost-free variety?
- Check the windows to make sure they open, close, and lock. Do the windows, especially the bedroom windows, open onto a busy street or alley? Alleys are especially notorious for late-night car horns and loud early morning trash removal.
- Are there enough closets? Are the closets big enough to accommodate your belongings?
- Is there private storage space in a secure area?
- Is there adequate water pressure for the shower, the sink, and the toilet? Turn them on and check.
- Flush all toilets and check for leaks or unusual noises.
- Check the number of electrical outlets. In older buildings it is common to have one or two outlets per room. Are there enough outlets for all your plug-in appliances?
- Are there laundry facilities in the building? Is there a laundromat within walking distance?
- How close is the building to public transportation and grocery stores?
- If you are looking at a basement apartment, check to see if there are any water stains along the walls. They're a sure sign of flooding.
- Does it smell funny? They may have sprayed the apartment for bugs. You should think twice before taking it.
- Is there a smoke and/or carbon monoxide detector in the apartment?

Ed Sacks' *Savvy Renter's Kit* contains a thorough renter's checklist for those interested in augmenting theirs.

If it all passes muster, be prepared to stake your claim without delay!

## STAKING A CLAIM

When you view a unit, come prepared. Bring your checkbook. If you are moving from out of state, you may be required to provide a cashier's check or money order instead of a personal check. Have cash on hand in case you cannot get to the bank and need to purchase a money order from a convenience store or check-cashing outlet. Also bring a copy of your credit report for the building manager. Prepare a renter's resume with addresses of your last three residences, including the names, phone numbers, fax numbers, and e-mail addresses of your previous landlords, building managers, and roommates. Better yet, before you come to the Seattle area, bring letters of recommendation from the aforementioned that vouch for your sterling qualities. Employment information may also be helpful. If you have secured a job, ask your employer to write a letter on company stationary that verifies your start date and salary.

It won't hurt to mention casually that you don't have a dog, cat or monkey, and that you don't smoke or play the drums. Feel free to rave about the unit and how great it feels (after all, a landlord is human, too). If there is a garden, mention that you love gardening and have a very green thumb. If you do have a pet, ask former landlords to write letters praising its good behavior. If your dog is well behaved, you may want to bring him with you to show how well trained he is (if, of course, he actually is well trained).

When applying for a place, consider that landlords will want your monthly earnings to be equal to at least three times the monthly rent. They can request only non-smokers, they can prohibit pets other than a working dog, and they can bar you from having overnight guests for more than a certain number of nights per year. (If you think you'll have lots of visitors, watch out for a lease containing such a clause, as this may not bode well for your tenant/landlord relationship.)

In Seattle's competitive job market, it isn't just the early bird that gets the worm, it can also be the polite worm, the well-dressed worm, and the worm with the highest bid. Treat the open house or appointment like a job interview. If competition is particularly stiff, you may want to offer to sign a lease for longer than the required time period.

According to The Tenants Union (see below), the renter's most powerful moment is right before the rental agreement is signed. Once you sign an agreement, you will be bound by its terms, except for provisions that are illegal under the Landlord-Tenant Act. The union says these issues should be discussed before you agree to move in:

- How much is the rent, and when is it to be paid?
- Are there any rate charges for delinquent payments?
- Who will pay for the utilities?
- Is the tenancy for a fixed period, like one year, or is it for an indefinite period?
- What are the rules on guests, pets, parking, etc.?
- What repairs or cleaning has your landlord agreed to complete before you move in? (Get all promises in writing.)
- Is there a deposit? If so, how much, and when will it be refunded? (A non-refundable fee may not be called a deposit.

## TENANT/LANDLORD RELATIONS

### LEASES/RENTAL AGREEMENTS AND SECURITY DEPOSITS

Most landlords in Seattle require your first month's rent, a security or "damage" deposit, and a signed lease agreement prior to moving in. Many also require the last month's rent to be paid either prior to renting or within the first three months of tenancy. Make sure that you read your lease agreement before signing, and before paying anything. Check to see how and when the rent can be increased and by how much; don't assume that it can't be increased during the initial term of your lease. Such details should be negotiated before you sign the lease.

In Washington, the type of your tenancy (month-to-month or fixed period) will determine your rights and duties under the Landlord-Tenant Act, according to The Tenants Union. If you have an agreement with your landlord to stay for a fixed period at the same rent, you have a lease. To be valid, it must be in writing. If it is to be in effect for more than one year, it must not only be in writing, but it must also be signed by the landlord before a notary public. Rent cannot be increased during the fixed period, and the tenancy rules cannot be changed, unless both you and your landlord agree about it. At that time, says The Tenants Union, you must initial any changes that are made.

In the city of Seattle, month-to-month rental agreements are legal but a minimum stay requirement or penalties for not fulfilling a minimum stay on a month to month agreement are illegal. (These agreements usually state that if the tenant does not stay for a minimum number of months, usually six, he/she forfeits the deposit.) If a tenant loses a deposit because of such illegal provisions, the tenant is entitled to collect from the landlord double the deposit, plus actual damages incurred and attorney's fees and costs. Before a tenant sues in small claims court, he/she must request that the landlord return the deposit. For more information, contact **The Tenants Union** at 206-723-0500 or visit www.tenantsunion.org.

If a landlord charges a deposit, the lease or rental agreement must be in writing, and must include the terms under which any of the deposit will be returned. A deposit cannot be withheld for normal wear and tear, according to the Washington State Bar Association. If a tenant pays a deposit, the landlord must provide a written document describing the condition of the rental unit, and keep the deposit in a trust account. The landlord has 14 days after a tenant moves out to return a deposit, or give a written explanation why it was not refunded.

### RENT AND EVICTION CONTROL

There is no rent control in Washington State. In fact, a state law prohibits cities and counties from passing any kind of rent control measure. According to The

Tenants Union, a tenant's only protection against a rent increase is a lease. In a month-to-month agreement, a landlord can raise the rent as often as he/she pleases, but must give 30 days written notice. Landlords are prohibited from raising rent as a means of either discrimination or retaliation.

In Seattle, landlords are required to give tenants a minimum of 60 days written notice when rent is to be increased by 10% or more during a 12-month period. The same rule applies to other housing costs like water or sewage. The notice must coincide with the beginning of the rental period, usually the first day of the month.

The landlord-tenant rules in Washington tend to favor landlords. A landlord can issue a three day notice to pay rent or vacate to a tenant who is only one day late with the rent. If the tenant pays rent after the three days given on the notice, the landlord is not obliged to accept payment. Landlords are also not obligated to accept partial payments. Many landlords will accept rent within five days of the date it is due, but may charge a late fee. Emergencies that prevent a tenant from paying rent on time should be discussed with the landlord, who may agree to accept partial payment or to set up a payment plan. If alternate terms are agreed upon, tenants should be sure to get them in writing, and ask the landlord to sign and date them. If additional assistance is necessary, contact The Tenants Union.

In 1996, Seattle passed a Just Cause Eviction Ordinance that prohibits landlords from evicting tenants without a court order. For the full text of the law, visit The Tenants Union web site at www.tenantsunion.org.

## LANDLORD/TENANT RIGHTS AND RESPONSIBILITIES

Washington landlords have a list of obligations that they must fulfill, including being accessible to their tenants and obeying the rules of the rental agreement. In addition, they must keep the rental property up to code, maintain the roof, walls, and structural components of the building, keep common areas safe and clean, provide a pest-control program, and provide the facilities necessary to supply heat, electricity, and hot and cold water. They must also provide adequate locks and maintain the appliances that come with the rental unit.

Contrary to what some believe, a landlord may not enter your apartment whenever he/she wishes. A landlord must have tenant consent to inspect the premises, make repairs, supply necessary services, or show the unit to a prospective renter. The time of entry must be reasonable, and he/she must notify you two days in advance. Of course, in an emergency, your landlord can enter your apartment without notice or permission.

A tenant must also meet a series of legal responsibilities. He/she must pay rent, keep his/her dwelling clean and sanitary, dispose of garbage, and properly use fixtures and appliances. He/she must not damage or permit damage to the property, and property must be restored to its original condition, except for normal wear and tear, before moving out. He/she must also comply with the rental agreement.

The Federal Fair Housing Act of 1968 makes it illegal for a landlord to discriminate based on a person's race, sex, national origin or religion. In addition, various local laws forbid discrimination against unmarried persons, children, gays, and disabled persons.

If you have any problems with your landlord while you're renting, or if you feel that you were discriminated against while you were hunting for an apartment or house, the resources listed below may help:

- **City of Seattle Office for Civil Rights**, 206-684-4500, 206-684-4503 (TTY), www.seattle.gov/civilrights
- **City of Seattle Office of Housing**, 206-684-0721, www.seattle.gov/housing
- **The Tenants Union**, 206-723-0500, 206-723-0523 (TDD), www.tenantsunion. org
- **Washington State Attorney General's Office**, 206-464-6684, 800-551-4636, www.atg.wa.govconsumer/lt
- **Washington State Bar Association**, 206-448-WSBA, 800-945-WSBA, www. wsba.org

## RENTER'S/HOMEOWNER'S INSURANCE

You've moved into your new apartment, and the last boxes have been cleared away. Take a look around and ask yourself, "How much would it cost to start over if everything I own was destroyed by fire?" Probably more than you might think. Imagine having to replace your clothing, television, stereo, furniture, computer and other accumulations of a lifetime. No small bill.

Typically, with renter's insurance you are protected against fire, hail, lightning, explosion, aircraft, smoke, vandalism, theft, building collapse, frozen plumbing, defective appliances, and sudden electrical damage. Renter's insurance also may cover personal liability as well as damage done (by you) to the property of others.

By now you should be convinced that renter's insurance is a good idea, especially because your belongings would not be insured under your landlord's policy. The good news about renter's insurance is that it is not a huge expense. For $20,000 in coverage your annual rate may run between $150 to $200 if you live in an apartment, and $200 to $250 if you live in a house.

When shopping for renter's insurance, be sure to ask whether the insurance company pays as soon as the claim is filed and whether it pays cash-value or replacement value. If you have a cash-value policy, you will only be paid what your five-year-old television is worth, not what it costs to replace it. Some big-ticket items, such as computers or jewelry, are insured only to a certain amount. Find out what these limits are. A higher deductible usually gives you a lower premium. You can purchase renter's insurance through almost any insurance agency.

Web sites worth investigating as you search for renter's insurance are Insure. com, www.insure.com, which offers instant quotes from more than 300 insurance companies; QuickenInsurance, www.insuremarket.com, which is good for finding inexpensive insurance rates online; and InsureMe, www.insureme.com, which offers online quotes from several companies for you to choose from.

Whether you get renter's insurance or not, it's a good idea to keep an inventory of all items of value and record their serial numbers. You may also want to take photographs of your belongings, or walk through your apartment with a video camera and record them on tape. Make a copy of these records and keep one at a friend's house or in a safe deposit box.

Below is a list of some of the major insurers in the Seattle area:

- **Allstate**, www.allstate.com
- **Farmers Insurance Group**, www.farmersinsurance.com
- **MetLife**, www.metlife.com
- **Pemco**, www.pemco.com
- **Safeco**, www.safeco.com
- **State Farm Insurance**, www.statefarm.com
- **Unigard**, www.unigard.com

## BUYING

Many people come to Seattle intending to buy a house in the city, but find that the cost of a home is just too high. Newcomers can avoid sticker shock by thoroughly researching home prices and neighborhoods before they arrive, and by keeping an open mind about the types of housing and the locations they are willing to consider. For instance, you will get more bang for your buck in Renton or Snoqualmie, but your commute to the city will be longer. Or, maybe you had your heart set on living in Queen Anne or Magnolia, but you find a really wonderful Craftsman home in the Central Area that's in your price range. It's important to determine your priorities ahead of time, but to be flexible when possible.

Most streets in Seattle are lined with single-family homes on roomy lots. Over the last decade, home values grew steadily with the economy, and in the late 1990s the Seattle housing market exploded. Homes were on the market for just days before selling, and bidding wars were common. The pace slowed somewhat with the 2001 recession, but has picked back up in recent years, with affordable housing becoming rare, and even million dollar (and upwards) homes are snapped up quickly. Home prices are slightly less expensive in nearby suburbs, such as Renton, Bothell, and Edmonds.

Property taxes are another expense to consider. The **King County Department of Assessments** is responsible for collecting property taxes in Seattle and most surrounding communities. You can estimate your annual property taxes if you know the assessed value of your property and your tax levy rate. Divide the value of your home by 1,000 and multiply by the tax levy rate. In Seattle in 2006, the tax levy rate was $9.63. Thus, for a home valued at $300,000, property taxes would be about $2,889. The tax levy rate varies by city; to find the rate in the city of your choice, visit the Department of Assessments web site at www.metrokc.gov/Assessor.

Before buying a house, it's a good idea to hire an independent building inspector or engineer to examine the foundation and overall structure, heating and plumbing systems, and the roof. Also request that the inspector check for mold, particularly if the roof has been replaced recently or if there are signs of water damage in the basement. Your lender will appraise the house, but only to determine if its value will safely secure the loan. If possible, you should include language in your purchase offer that allows you to take back the offer if your inspection uncovers a serious problem. At the very least, your real estate agent should be willing to negotiate with the seller on any major flaws turned up during the inspection. For more see below under **Purchase Agreements**.

How should you go about finding a home to buy in Seattle? Any good real estate agent will tell you there are three things to consider when purchasing a house: location, location, location. The **Neighborhoods** chapter of this book will give you a good overview of the neighborhoods in Seattle, as well as profiles of many of the city's suburbs. From there, visit the neighborhood(s) you're considering. Get a general feel for the area; visit the schools and parks; drive to or from the neighborhood during rush hour to evaluate traffic flow and freeway noise. Attend a few open houses to find a realtor that knows the area. The *Seattle Times/Seattle Post-Intelligencer* Sunday edition has a Home/Real Estate section that lists many of the open houses in Seattle and surrounding communities. The paper is available on Friday evenings, so you can get a drive-by preview. Or, visit the classifieds' web site at http://classifieds.nwsource.com; new open house announcements are added daily. Additional newspaper sites are listed previously in this chapter under **Classified Advertisements**.

The **Washington State Housing Finance Commission** offers free home ownership programs and homebuyer education seminars (see below under **Additional Resources**). For more information, visit the agency's web site at www.wshfc.org or call 206-464-7139 (in Seattle) or 800-767-4663. You can also find information on buying or selling a home at the **National Association of Realtors** web site, www.realtor.com.

## CONDOMINIUMS, CO-OPS, AND CO-HOUSING

Buying a home in Seattle doesn't necessarily mean buying a traditional single-family house. Condominiums, co-ops, and co-housing projects are all options, depending on your needs. All three are usually less expensive than traditional houses, and may be a good first step for first-time homeowners. Condominiums in particular have become a popular housing choice in places like Downtown and Ballard, where many new buildings are going up, and units are often sold before construction is complete.

A **condominium** is a type of joint ownership. Each housing unit is individually owned and residents collectively own the common areas—grounds, lobbies, elevators, hallways, surrounding property, and recreational facilities. You own the apartment outright, so you can usually make improvements to it, rent it out, or resell it as you see fit. However, some restrictions apply to condo ownership. Generally, a condo association oversees the rules of the complex, making decisions about building repairs, external improvements and landscaping. Some condo associations impose rules on subletting. Be sure to review, with your real estate lawyer, the association rules and regulations, and the current operating budget. Consider any major improvements or repairs that will be required in the next few years, and see if the budget will be able to cover most of the cost.

If your building has jointly owned amenities, such as a hot tub, rooftop deck or pool, the association coordinates maintenance on those facilities as well. All of these services come at a cost; expect to pay anywhere between $100 to several hundred dollars in monthly association dues, as well as a one-time fee for capital improvements or emergency repairs, such as a new roof. While these dues may add up over time to little more than the maintenance on your own house, you'll need to factor them in when evaluating your monthly house payments.

A co-op (cooperative apartment) is another option for home ownership in Seattle. When you buy a co-op, you are buying shares in the ownership of a building. Co-ops tend to be much less expensive than comparable condominiums, but there are some important trade-offs. Co-ops are tightly controlled by the shareholders in the building—in other words by all of the co-op owners. This can make it difficult to buy a cooperative apartment, since the co-op board will interview you, consider both your financial status and neighborly qualities, and may require several letters of reference. You may not have the option to remodel your unit, rent it out, or even sell it quickly, should you need to (as the co-op board must approve prospective buyers). If you're short on cash, buying into a co-op can be challenging because many lenders will not approve mortgages for them. Unfortunately, many co-ops do not accept anything but a full cash payment at the time of purchase. Co-ops are most common in the Capitol Hill, Eastlake, and First Hill neighborhoods.

Those thinking about buying a condominium or co-op should seriously consider that owning a condo or co-op obligates you socially a bit more than does a freestanding house. While your co-op or condo neighbors could turn out to be great friends and neighbors, the opposite could also be true.

Co-housing projects are catching on in Seattle as residents seek to recapture the aura of a close-knit neighborhood in a rapidly growing city. Also called "intentional communities," co-housing projects offer communal living with affordable condo-style ownership opportunities. Each household owns its own unit, but shares communal space such as a "common house." Co-housing residents often prepare and eat meals together, share gardening responsibilities, and environmental initiatives like recycling and composting are common. For more information on co-housing, visit The Co-housing Network at www.cohous ing.org, or contact one of the co-housing communities listed here:

- **Duwamish Cohousing**, Seattle, 206-767-7726, www.duwamish.net
- **Jackson Place Cohousing**, 206-784-5619, www.seattlecohousing.org
- **Puget Ridge Cohousing**, 206-763-3450, www.scn.org/pugetridgecohousing
- **Sharingwood Co-housing**, Snohomish County, 360-668-1439, http://sharingwood.org
- **Songaia Cohousing Community**, Snohomish County, 425-486-2035, www.songaia.com
- **Vashon Co-housing**, Vashon Island, 206-463-4053, www.vashoncohousing.org
- **Winslow Cohousing Group**, Bainbridge Island, 206-780-1323, www.winslowcohousing.org

## WORKING WITH REALTORS

If you are unfamiliar with the city, it may be helpful to find a real estate agent or broker to help you with your search. Friends or co-workers may be able to recommend someone, or consider the agents who host open houses in your neighborhood of choice. The agent should be someone you trust, who listens to you, knows the city and the neighborhoods you like, and understands the market. A good realtor will not expect you to pay more than you can afford, although you may find that the house you can afford and the house you want are very different things.

Generally, homebuyers in Seattle do not use a real estate lawyer. Often the only lawyer involved is an employee of the escrow company. Nevertheless, it is a good idea to have the name of a real estate attorney available just in case. Ask friends or co-workers for recommendations, or ask your agent to suggest a reputable attorney.

The major national and regional real estate companies offer online lists of agents. To begin your search you may want to visit one of the realtor web sites listed below, or go to HomeGain (www.homegain.com), a company that offers free tools for estimating the value of a home; finding a real estate agent or a home; and getting a mortgage.

- **Coldwell Banker**, www.coldwellbanker.com
- **Prudential**, www.prudential.com/realestate
- **RE/MAX**, www.remax.com
- **John L. Scott**, www.johnlscott.com
- **Windermere**, www.windermere.com

If you already have a chosen area, consider contacting one of the agents listed here.

## SEATTLE

- **Cynthia Creasey and Mack McCoy**, Lake & Company Real Estate, 7801 Green Lake Drive N, 206-276-8292, www.seattlehomes.net
- **Val Ellis**, Coldwell Banker Bain Associates, 1200 Westlake Ave N #406, 206-216-3461, www.valellis.com
- **Mary Jereczek**, Keller Williams Realty, 12535 15th Ave NE, 206-407-1000, http://169552.yourkwagent.com
- **Maury King**, Windermere Real Estate, 4919 S Genesee St, 206-954-9010, www.realestateseattle.com
- **Virginia Mason and Whitney Mason**, Coldwell Banker Bain Associates, 1200 Westlake Ave N #406, 206-216-3418, www.soldinseattle.com
- **Jim Reppond**, Coldwell Banker Bain Associates, 1200 Westlake Ave N #406, 206-295-1771, www.seattle-realestate.com
- **Eileen Tefft**, LTD Real Estate, 222 Wall St, Ste 110, 206-441-1850, www.seattlenumber1homesite.com

## EASTSIDE

- **Ardell DellaLoggia**, Sound Realty, 116 Central Way, Kirkland, 425-822-8226, http://searchingseattle.com
- **Oscar Diaz**, Windermere Real Estate, 13000 NE 20th St, Bellevue, 425-883-1800, http://oscardiaz.mywindermere.com
- **Dianne Girard**, Windermere Real Estate, 4055 Lake Washington Blvd NE, 425-822-5100, www.diannegirard.com
- **Stan Mackey**, Coldwell Banker Bain Associates, 150 Bellevue Way SE, 425-450-5227, www.stanmackey.com
- **Michael Smith Realtors**, Prudential, 1008 140th Ave NE, Bellevue, 425-453-9100, http://prumsr.com

## WEST
- **Beverly Green,** Windermere Real Estate, 840 Madison Ave N, Bainbridge Island, 206-780-7678, www.realestateonbainbridgeisland.com
- **Peggy Lee,** Windermere Real Estate, 9939 Mickelberry Rd NW, Silverdale, 360-692-6102, www.realestatebremerton.com
- **Jim Lundwall**, 840 Madison Ave N, Bainbridge Island, 206-780-7699, www.bainbridgeandkitsap.com
- **Carol Sue Rogers,** Windermere Real Estate, 600 Park Ave, Bremerton, 360-479-7004, www.bremertonhomes.com

## NORTH
- **Susan Funk**, Keller Williams Realty, 111 SE Everett Mall Way, Ste C-101, Everett, 425-422-3365, www.susanfunk.com
- **Hal and Sharon Howard**, Prudential Northwest Realty Associates, 18551 Aurora Ave N, #100, Shoreline, 206-546-4124, www.halhoward.com
- **Chantel Keller**, Re/Max Real Estate, P.O. Box 1809, Stanwood, 425-293-6699, www.everettrealestatewa.com
- **Chris Mattix,** Windermere Real Estate, 4211 Alderwood Mall Blvd, Ste 110, Lynnwood, 425-954-4020, www.onlinehomesnw.com
- **Patrick and Tonya Tye**, Windermere Real Estate, 4211 Alderwood Mall Blvd, Ste 110, Lynnwood, 206-793-7996, www.seattleabodes.com
- **Jim Wold**, Windermere Real Estate, 210 5th Ave S, Ste 102, Edmonds, 425-530-2700, www.edmondsrealestate.com

## SOUTH
- **Lauri Amandus**, John L Scott Real Estate, 4735 NE 4th St, Renton, 206-718-7355, www.laurisells.com
- **Sharon Benson**, Coldwell Banker Bain, 5929 Westgate Blvd, Ste A, Tacoma, 253-381-7447, www.sharonbenson.com
- **Crist Granum**, John L Scott Real Estate, 13401 Vashon Hwy SW, Vashon Island, 206-419-3661, www.vashondreams.com
- **Robbie Howell**, Windermere Real Estate, 401 SW 152nd St, 206-241-6837, www.homesbyrobbie.com
- **Shelley Propernick**, John L Scott Real Estate, 20632 108th Ave SE, Kent, 206-920-0244, www.shelleypropernick.com
- **Brian Stoll**, Re/Max, 33915 1st Way S, Ste 114, Federal Way, 253-569-0406, www.bstoll.com

## PURCHASE AGREEMENTS, CREDIT, MORTGAGES, INSURANCE

The purchase agreement is a legally binding document signed by the buyer and seller that states the price and all the terms of the sale. It is the most negotiable, variable, and important document produced in the homebuying process. The purchase agreement is the document to which a buyer may attach contingencies. Such contingencies can protect you, the buyer, from being legally bound by the purchase agreement if, for example, you cannot sell the house you live in now, the house you are buying does not pass mechanical and structural inspection, the seller is not able to give you possession by a certain date, or you cannot qualify for a loan.

Washington does not regulate purchase agreements, but it does require Form 22J, the disclosure of lead-based paint. If a seller does not give a buyer this form, the buyer can rescind the sale up until the closing date. The state also requires the seller to deliver to the buyer a property disclosure statement (Form 17). The statement provides the buyer with information about the condition of the property, and may outline known or potential problems, like a leaky roof or drainage problems.

It's a good idea to get pre-approved for a loan before looking for houses in earnest. Most sellers will not seriously consider an offer from a buyer who is not pre-approved. The pre-approval process should not commit you to a particular lender or interest rate. It is simply a document that indicates to the seller that when you formally apply for a loan, you will most likely qualify to purchase the home. Most banks or mortgage brokers will process a pre-approval application without a fee. In addition to making your offer more attractive to the seller, the pre-approval process gives you, the buyer, an accurate idea of how much you can spend on a house.

A key factor when seeking a loan is your credit history. Check your credit report to make sure it is accurate before meeting with a loan officer. You can check your credit report with all three national credit bureaus listed here. You will need to provide your name, address, previous address, and Social Security number with your request. Check with each company for specific instructions. Reports are free if you have been denied credit based on your credit report within the last 30 days, otherwise, expect to pay a fee. You can also request a free credit report from each of the three national credit bureaus once every year at www.annualcreditreport.com. The national credit bureaus are:

- **Equifax**, P.O. Box 105873, Atlanta, GA 30348, 800-685-1111, www.equifax.com
- **Experian**, P.O. Box 2104, Allen, TX 75002-2104, 888-397-3742, www.experian.com
- **TransUnion Corporation**, P.O. Box 390, Springfield, PA 19064-0390, 800-916-8800, www.transunion.com

When contemplating buying a house, you'll want to evaluate your personal finances. How much can you afford to pay up front, and how much will you then be able to pay per month? Generally, you will be able to qualify for a loan of about three or four times your yearly income, depending on your credit record and other debts. The loan won't cover your down payment and closing costs, however. In most cases closing costs, which are in addition to the down payment, run 3 to 7% of the purchase price. These can include loan origination fees, attorney's fees, title search, title insurance, inspections, and tax and insurance premiums held in escrow. As a buyer you will probably not be expected to pay the broker's fees, which are commonly paid by the seller. Expect your down payment to be 10% to 20% of the price of the home. Additional fees, such as mortgage insurance or higher loan origination fees, are often required if the down payment is less than 20%.

Finally, a few words about getting a loan: it may be most convenient to get your pre-approval from a local bank, but shop around before you sign for your loan. While many banks offer competitive interest rates, mortgage brokers can often match or beat their best offers. Make sure you ask about loan origination fees (points) when requesting interest rate quotes. Usually the lowest interest rate includes a hefty one-time fee, one that may not be mentioned until you're ready to sign the papers. The Bank Rate Monitor web site (www.bankrate.com) provides mortgage and interest rate data on over 2,000 lending institutions.

Major banks and mortgage-lending institutions usually have web sites, and most now allow you to get pre-approved online. See **Mortgages** below for a list.

Once your loan is approved, your lender will require you to buy **homeowner's insurance** to protect their investment (your home). Be sure the policy you choose covers the house, its contents and outbuildings, and includes earthquake coverage. Depending on where your new home is located, you may want to explore the option of flood insurance as well. You'll also want to protect yourself in case of liability. Policies vary, so check restrictions and exclusions carefully to make sure you have the coverage you need. A basic homeowner's policy includes liability insurance to protect you if someone is injured on your property; property protection, which insures your house and personal belongings against damage or loss; and living expense coverage that will pay for you to live elsewhere while repairs are being made.

You may also need mortgage insurance, which is required by many lenders as well as the FHA to cover them if you default on your loan, and title insurance, which protects the lender in case the legal title to the property isn't clear. It doesn't protect you though, so, in addition, you may want to buy an owner's title insurance policy, or get an attorney's opinion on your title. If the seller has purchased title insurance in recent years, you may be able to get the same title company to issue you a new policy at a lower cost, so be sure to ask for a re-issue credit. See **Renter's Insurance** above for a list of insurance companies.

## ONLINE RESOURCES—HOUSE HUNTING

You can start your search on the internet before you arrive in Seattle. While searching the web probably won't get you a house—many are sold shortly after they are listed—it will give you a good idea about what's on the market, where you should look once you get here, and about how much you can expect to pay. One company, **ZipRealty** (www.ziprealty.com) harnesses the power of the internet to offer buyers a 20% rebate of the company's commission if a home is bought through one of their agents. The service is only available in metropolitan areas of 13 states, but Seattle is one of them. Not every site lists every home in the Seattle area, but most homes will be listed on at least one site. Also, don't forget the newspaper classifieds (see above under **Apartment Hunting**).

- **Cyberhomes**, www.cyberhomes.com
- **HomeSeekers.com**, www.homeseekers.com
- **Homestore.com**, www.homestore.com
- **National Association of Realtors**, www.realtor.com
- **Real Estate.com**, www.realestate.com
- **Realty Locator**, www.realtylocator.com
- **Trulia Real Estate Search**, www.trulia.com
- **Yahoo! Real Estate**, http://realestate.yahoo.com
- **ZipRealty**, www.ziprealty.com

## FOR SALE BY OWNER

If you prefer to buy or sell a home without an agent, check out the sites below; they specialize in home listings by owners:

- **FiSBO Registry Inc.**, www.fisbos.com
- **ForSaleByOwner.com**, www.forsalebyowner.com
- **HomesByOwner.com**, www.homesbyowner.com
- **Owners.com**, www.owners.com

## MORTGAGES

The following sites might be useful:

- **CitiMortgage**, www.citimortgage.com; CitiMortgage's site lets visitors pre-qualify for loans, shop and compare rates, and apply for loans online.
- **Countrywide**, www.countrywide.com; includes a section for buyers with less-than-perfect credit.
- **E-Loan**, www.eloan.com; find loans with low rates and low origination fees.
- **Freddie Mac**, www.freddiemac.com; offers information on current mortgage averages.

- **Home Finance of America**, www.bestrateloans.com; offers competitive home financing rates.
- **Interest.com**, www.interest.com; includes a section for first-time homebuyers, details on how to find a lender close to home, and mortgage rate comparisons.
- **Mortgage-calc.com**, www.mortgage-calc.com; find several simple, free online calculators for mortgages, amortization, refinancing and more.
- **Quicken Loans**, www.quickenmortgage.com; easy-to-use calculators help expedite and clarify the finance process.

## ADDITIONAL RESOURCES

If you want to buy a house, especially if you are a first-time homebuyer, consider taking a real estate class, often available at area colleges. The **Washington State Housing Finance Commission** offers free home ownership programs and homebuyer education seminars. For more information, visit the agency's web site at www.wshfc.org or call 206-464-7139 (in Seattle) or 800-767-HOME. If you don't have the time or inclination for a class, but are willing to conduct your own research, look for a book on homebuying how-tos. An invaluable resource is the **Washington Center for Real Estate Research (WCRER)**, 800-835-9683 or www.cbe.wsu.edu/~wcrer. The WCRER, a division of the Washington State University College of Business and Economics, provides research and education materials to consumers.

The following resources may be of interest for those in the market for a new home:

- *100 Questions Every First Time Homebuyer Should Ask* by Ilyce R. Glink
- *Opening the Door to a Home of Your Own*, a pamphlet published by the Fannie Mae Foundation for first-time homebuyers, can be obtained by calling 800-834-3377.
- **Rain City Guide**, www.raincityguide.com, a Seattle real estate blog with helpful, relevant and constantly updated information on the local real estate market.
- **www.scorecard.org**—Check here if you are concerned about toxic waste issues in or near your prospective neighborhood. This site is sponsored by the Environmental Defense Fund.
- **The U.S. Department of Housing and Urban Development** offers an online tutorial on the homebuying process at www.hud.gov/buying.
- *Your New House: the Alert Consumer's Guide to Buying and Building a Quality New Home*; now in its fourth edition, a very helpful resource, especially for those building a new home.
- **Zillow.com**, www.zillow.com, offers estimates of what your home is worth, as well as comparisons with comparable homes in your neighborhood. Search for any address, for free, and get aerial maps, home info, charts, graphs and more.

**B**EFORE YOU CAN START YOUR NEW LIFE IN SEATTLE, YOU AND YOUR worldly possessions have to get here. How difficult that will be depends on how much stuff you've accumulated, how much money you're willing or able to spend on the move, and where you're coming from.

## TRUCK RENTALS

The first question you need to answer: am I going to move myself or will I have someone else do it for me? If you're used to doing everything yourself, you can rent a vehicle and head for the open road. Look in the Yellow Pages under "Truck Rental," and call around and compare; also ask about any specials. Below we list four national truck rental firms and their toll-free numbers and web sites. For the best information, you should call a local office. Note: most truck rental companies now offer "one-way" rentals (don't forget to ask whether they have a drop-off/return location in or near your destination), as well as packing accessories and storage facilities. Of course, these extras are not free. If you're cost-conscious you may want to scavenge boxes in advance of your move and, if you haven't yet found your new residence, make sure you have a place to store your belongings upon arrival. Also, if you're planning to move during the peak moving months of May through September, call well in advance of when you'll need the vehicle—a month at least.

Once you're on the road, keep in mind that your rental truck may be a tempting target for thieves. If you must park it overnight or for an extended period (more than a couple of hours), try to find a safe spot, preferably a well-lit place you can easily observe.

- **Budget**, 800-283-4382, www.budget.com
- **Penske**, 888-996-5415, www.penske.com

- **Ryder**, 800-297-9337, www.ryder.com
- **U-HAUL**, 800-468-4285, www.uhaul.com

Not sure if you want to drive the truck yourself? Commercial freight carriers, such as **ABF**, offer an in-between service: they deliver a 28-foot trailer to your home, you pack and load as much of it as you need, and they drive the vehicle to your destination (usually with some commercial freight filling up the empty space). Available through their web site at www.upack.com.

## MOVERS

Surveys show that most people find movers through the Yellow Pages. If that's too random for you, probably the best way to find a mover is through a personal recommendation. Absent a friend or relative who can point you to a trusted moving company, try some of the internet personal recommendation sites like www.citysearch.com, www.yelp.com and www.judysbook.com. It's not a good idea to merely do an internet search for movers, as you'll likely be taken to web sites for online moving brokers, who do not have a good track record for steering customers to reputable movers. For long distance or interstate moves, the **American Moving and Storage Association's** site (www.moving.org) identifies member movers both in Washington and across the country. In the past, *Consumer Reports* (www.consumerreports.org) has published useful information on moving. Members of **AAA** can call their local office and receive discounted rates and service through AAA's Consumer Relocation Service.

Disagreeable moving experiences, while common, aren't obligatory. To aid you in your search for a hassle-free mover, we offer a few general recommendations. First and foremost, make sure any moving company you consider hiring is **licensed by the appropriate authority**:

- **The Washington Utilities and Transportation Commission (WUTC) regulates intrastate moves**. All movers operating within the state of Washington are required to have a valid state UTC permit. The permit number must appear on the mover's vehicles, advertisements, correspondence, business cards, and web site. A licensed mover must comply with UTC safety, insurance, and service standards, and must perform its services at reasonable rates and within a reasonable time. WUTC offers a free "Moving Survival Kit" on its web site (www.wutc.wa.gov) where you also will find a list of registered movers. To check on your mover by phone, call WUTC consumer information at 800-562-6150 (toll-free in Washington), or 360-664-1160. When you call, you will be informed if the moving company is registered, and whether there have been complaints lodged against it.
- **Interstate moves** are regulated by the US Department of Transportation's **Federal Motor Carrier Safety Administration (FMCSA)**. When reviewing

prospective carriers, make sure the carrier has a Department of Transportation MC ("Motor Carrier") or ICC MC number that should be displayed on all advertising and promotional material as well as on the truck. With the MC number in hand, you can contact the Washington office of FMCSA at 360-753-9875 or check www.fmcsa.dot.gov to see if the carrier is licensed and insured. You can also learn how to protect yourself from scams by downloading brochures from the web site. Before a move takes place, federal regulations require interstate movers to furnish customers with a copy of "Your Rights and Responsibilities When You Move." If they don't give you a copy, ask for one. FMCSA's role in the regulation of interstate carriers concerns safety issues, not consumer issues. To find out if any complaints have been filed against a prospective mover, check with the Better Business Bureau (www.bbb.org) in the state where the moving company is licensed, as well as with that state's Consumer Protection Office.

## ADDITIONAL RECOMMENDATIONS

- If someone recommends a mover to you, get names (the salesperson or estimator, the drivers, the loaders). To paraphrase the NRA, moving companies don't move people, people do.
- Once you've narrowed your search down to two or three companies, ask a mover for references, particularly from customers who recently did moves similar to yours. If a mover is unable or unwilling to provide such information or tells you that it can't give out names because their customers are all in the federal Witness Protection Program … perhaps you should consider another company.
- Even though movers will put numbered labels on your possessions, you should make a numbered list of every box and item that is going in the truck. Detail box contents and photograph anything of particular value. Once the truck arrives on the other end, you can check off every piece and know for sure what did (or did not) make it. In case of claims, this list can be invaluable. Even after the move, keep the list; it can be surprisingly useful.
- Be aware that during the busy season (May through September), demand can exceed supply and moving may be more difficult and more expensive than during the rest of the year. If you must relocate during the peak moving months, call and book service well in advance, a month, at least, ahead of your moving date. If you can reserve service way in advance, say four to six months early, you may be able to lock in a lower winter rate for your summer move. Keep in mind that Saturdays are usually busy moving days and you might have better luck moving on a less busy day of the week.

- Whatever you do, do *not* mislead a salesperson about how much and what you are moving. And make sure you tell a prospective mover how far they'll have to transport your stuff to and from the truck as well as any stairs, driveways, obstacles or difficult vegetation, long paths or sidewalks, etc. The clearer you are with your mover, the better he or she will be able to serve you.
- You should ask for and receive a written estimate of the probable cost of your move. The estimate should clearly and accurately describe all charges. In Washington, there are two types of estimates: A **non-binding estimate** is an educated guess of what your move would cost based on the mover's survey of your belongings. In this scenario your final cost can exceed the non-binding estimate—though there is a limit on how much over the estimate the company can charge. A **binding estimate** is a written agreement that guarantees the price you pay based on the items to be moved and the services listed on the estimate, inventory or tally sheet.
- Remember that price, while important, isn't everything, especially when you're entrusting all of your worldly possessions to strangers. Choose a mover you feel comfortable with.
- Think about packing. Depending on the size of your move and whether or not you do the packing yourself, you may need a lot of boxes, tape, and packing material. Boxes provided by the mover, while not cheap, are usually sturdy and the right size. Sometimes a mover will give a customer free used boxes. It doesn't hurt to ask. Liquor stores and grocery stores are also good places to ask for boxes. Also, *don't* wait to pack until the last minute. If you're doing the packing, give yourself at least a week to do the job, two is better.
- Listen to what the movers say; they are professionals and can give you expert advice about packing and preparing. Also, be ready for the truck on both ends—don't make them wait. Not only will it irritate your movers, but it may cost you. Understand, too, that things can happen on the road that are beyond a carrier's control (weather, accidents, etc.) and your belongings may not get to you at the time or on the day promised. (See note about insurance below.)
- Treat your movers well, especially the ones loading your stuff on and off the truck. Offer to buy them lunch, and tip them if they do a good job.
- Ask about insurance; the "basic" 60 cents per pound industry standard coverage is not enough. If you have homeowner or renter's insurance, check to see if it will cover your belongings during transit. If not, consider purchasing "full replacement" or "full value" coverage from the carrier for the estimated value of your shipment. Though it's the most expensive type of coverage offered, it's probably worth it. Trucks get into accidents, they catch fire, they get stolen—if such insurance seems pricey to you, ask about a $250 or $500 deductible. This can reduce your cost substantially but still give you much better protection in the event of a catastrophic loss. Transport irreplaceable items, such as jewelry, photographs or key work documents, yourself.

- Be prepared to pay the full moving bill upon delivery. Cash or bank/cashier's check may be required. Some carriers will take VISA and MasterCard but it is a good idea to get it in writing that you will be permitted to pay with a credit card since the delivering driver may not be aware of this and may demand cash. Unless you routinely keep thousands of dollars of greenbacks on you, you could have a problem getting your stuff off the truck.
- Above all, ask questions, and if you're concerned about something, ask for an explanation in writing.
- Finally, before moving pets, attach a tag to your pet's collar with your new address and phone number in case your pet accidentally wanders off in the confusion of moving.

Those **moving within the Seattle area** with minimal belongings probably won't need a huge truck to complete the task. If you (and your friends) are not interested in loading and unloading a rented truck, you may consider hiring one of the following local movers. All were registered with the WUTC and held current permits at the time of publication:

- **All My Sons Moving & Storage**, 206-444-9000; Eastside: 425-373-9000; South King County: 253-859-8000, www.allmysons.com
- **Crown Moving Company**, 1071 Andover Park W, 206-274-7081, 866-728-2008, www.crownmoving.com
- **Hansen Bros. Moving & Storage**, 12645 Stone Ave N, 206-365-4454, www.hansenbros.com
- **Neighbors Moving & Storage**, 206-381-1234; Eastside: 425-614-0100; South King County: 253-872-9400, www.neighborsmoving.com
- **University Moving & Storage**, 905 N 128th, 206-362-0508, www.universitymovingandstorage.com

According to the WUTC, moving costs in Washington are calculated in one of two ways, depending on the distance. For moves of 35 miles or more, rates are based on the weight of your goods and the distance hauled. For moves of less than 35 miles, rates are based on the number of workers used, the amount of time necessary to load, move, and unload your goods, and the mover's hourly rate. The UTC sets maximum rates that a mover can charge, but it can be worth your while to shop around among legitimate, trustworthy movers, as many will charge less than the maximum rates to get your business.

## CONSUMER COMPLAINTS—MOVERS

If you have a problem with your mover that you haven't been able to resolve directly, you can file a complaint about an intrastate move with the **Washington Utilities and Transportation Commission**. Call the Consumer Affairs Section at

800-562-6150, or use the online complaint form at www.wutc.wa.gov. If yours was an interstate move, your options for government intervention or assistance are limited. Years ago the now-defunct Interstate Commerce Commission (ICC) would log complaints against interstate movers. Today, you're pretty much on your own. The Federal Motor Carrier Safety Administration recommends that you contact the Better Business Bureau in the licensing state, as well as that state's consumer protection office to register a complaint. If satisfaction still eludes you, begin a letter writing campaign: to the state Attorney General, to your congressional representative, to the newspaper, the sky's the limit. Of course, if the dispute is worth it, you can hire a lawyer and seek redress the all-American way.

# STORAGE

If you and your belongings are going to arrive at your destination at different times, you have a few options. Many movers have their own warehouses for storage, or contract out with other warehouse companies. If your mover is going to handle storage for you for up to 90 days, it is considered **storage in transit** and is regulated by the WUTC. Any storage after 90 days is considered **permanent storage** and is no longer regulated. The WUTC web site provides more information at www.wutc.wa.gov.

If you discover that your new abode is too small for all of your stuff, or it's taking longer than expected to get permanently settled and you need storage beyond 90 days, you'll want to explore a couple of options. You can go the **Self Storage** route (see below) or rent a container from a portable storage company. These companies will deliver as many 5' by 8' wooden containers as you need to your home, where you will pack them. When you're finished packing, the company will come to pick the containers up and store them in their secured facilities until you need them. A good rule of thumb is that two containers will generally store the contents of a studio or one bedroom home or apartment. Five containers will hold the contents of a two or three bedroom home. Some companies offer their services nationally, so you can pack your belongings in one state and have them delivered to your new home for less than hiring a traditional mover. Other companies only service local regions so this may be an alternative to traditional self-service storage.

- **Door to Door Storage & Moving**, several locations in the Puget Sound area, 888-366-7222, www.dtdstorage.com
- **PODS**, Portable On Demand Storage, 888-776-PODS, www.pods.com
- **PortaBox Storage**, multiple locations, 888-269-8646, www.portabox.com

## SELF STORAGE

If you prefer a do-it-yourself approach and need a temporary place to store your stuff while you find a new home, self-storage is the answer. Most units are clean, secure, insured, and inexpensive, and you can rent anything from a locker to your own mini-warehouse. You'll need to bring your own padlock and be prepared to pay first and last month's rent up front. Many will offer special deals to entice you, such as second month free. Probably the easiest way to find storage is to look in the Yellow Pages under "Storage—Household & Commercial." To conduct your search online, visit the site of local yellow pages provider QwestDex at www. qwestdex.com.

Keep in mind that demand for storage surges in the prime moving months (May through September), so try not to wait until the last minute to rent storage. If you don't care about convenience, your cheapest storage options may be out in the boonies. You just have to figure out how to get your stuff there and back.

A word of warning: unless you no longer want your stored belongings, pay your storage bill and pay it on time. Storage companies may auction the contents of delinquent customers' lockers.

- **12th & Madison Self Storage**, 1111 E Madison St, 206-381-1236, www.12th andmadisonselfstorage.com
- **Belltown Self Storage**, 1915 3rd Ave, 206-903-1785, www.belltownselfstorage. com
- **Lake City Mini Storage**, 3116 NE 130th St, 206-447-0198, www.lakecity ministorage.com
- **Magnolia Bridge Self Storage**, 1900 15th Ave W, 206-583-8981, www. magnoliabridgeselfstorage.com
- **Market Street Self Storage**, 2811 NW Market St, 206-789-8080, www. marketstreetstorage.com
- **Public Storage**, 800-447-8673, www.publicstorage.com
- **Roosevelt Self Storage**, 6910 Roosevelt Way NE, 206-583-8972, www. rooseveltselfstorage.com
- **Seattle Self Storage**, 1100 Poplar Place S, 206-323-3000, www.seattle-selfstorage.com
- **Shurgard Self Storage**, 800-748-7427, www.shurgard.com
- **Vine Street Storage**, 11 Vine St, 206-443-3500, www.vinestreetstorage.com

# CHILDREN

Studies show that moving can be hard on children. According to an American Medical Association study, children who move often are more likely to suffer from such problems as depression, worthlessness, and aggression. Often their academic performance suffers as well. If you must move, there are a few things you can do to help your children through this stressful time:

- Talk about the move with your kids. Be honest but positive. Listen to their concerns. To the extent possible, involve them in the process.
- Make sure the child has his/her favorite possessions on the trip; don't pack "blankey" in the moving van.
- Make sure you have some social life planned on the other end. Your child may feel lonely in your new home and such activities can ease the transition.
- Keep in touch with family and loved ones as much as possible. Photos and phone calls are important ways of maintaining links to the important people you have left behind.
- If your child is of school age, take the time to involve yourself in his/her new school.

There are many good books and resources to help children adjust to moving. First Books (www.firstbooks.com) offers *The Moving Book: A Kids' Survival Guide* by Gabriel Davis; *Max's Moving Adventure: A Coloring Book for Kids on the Move*, by Danelle Till; and a Kid's Moving Kit—a colorful backpack filled with fun activities. Other good publications include, *Alexander, Who's Not (Do You Hear Me? I Mean It!) Going to Move* by Judith Viorst; and *Smart Moves: Your Guide through the Emotional Maze of Relocation* by Nadia Jensen, Audrey McCollum, and Stuart Copans.

## TAXES

If your move is work-related, some or all of your moving expenses may be tax-deductible—so you will want to keep those receipts. Though eligibility varies, depending, for example, on whether you have a job or are self-employed, the cost of moving yourself, your family, and your belongings is generally tax deductible, even if you don't itemize. The criteria: in order to take the deduction your move must be employment-related, your new job must be more than 50 miles away from your current residence, and you must be at your new location for at least 39 weeks during the first 12 months after your arrival. If you take the deduction and then fail to meet the requirements, you will have to pay the IRS back, unless you were laid off through no fault of your own, or transferred again by your employer. It's probably a good idea to consult a tax expert regarding IRS rules related to moving. If you're a confident soul, get a copy of IRS Form 3903 (www.irs.gov) and do it yourself!

## ONLINE RESOURCES—RELOCATION

- **www.firstbooks.com**: relocation resources and information on moving to Atlanta, Boston, Chicago, Los Angeles, Minneapolis-St. Paul, New York City, San Francisco and the Bay Area, and Washington, D.C., as well as London, England. The *Newcomer's Handbook for Moving to and Living in the USA* is also available.
- **www.homefair.com**: realty listings, moving tips, and more.
- **www.moving.com**: comprehensive web portal featuring a tool that lets you compare movers' rate quotes online.
- **www.moving.org**: American Moving and Storage Association site; referrals to interstate movers, local movers, storage companies, and packing and moving consultants.
- **www.movingscam.com**: provides helpful articles, volunteer-staffed message boards, and a list of "blacklisted" movers.

## BANKING

A S SOON AS YOU FIND A PLACE TO HANG YOUR HAT, YOU WILL WANT to find a home for your money. For major deposits, shop around for interest rates, but for routine checking and savings, you'll be more interested in ATM fees, online banking options, and direct deposit services—an increasingly common alternative to getting a paycheck in the mail or on your desk. Although opening an account is fairly simple, it's a good idea to keep your old checking account current until you've completed the task of setting up a new one here. This can be particularly important if you're going to try to rent a home or apartment before opening a local account; many landlords won't accept a tenant who doesn't have a bank account.

You'll probably want to call around to find out about special promotions; many banks offer special deals or extra perks for opening a checking account. But be sure to find out when the promotion ends and what the normal rates are. Ask if a debit card is available to use with your account. Debit cards, often displaying a VISA or MasterCard symbol, take the place of a written check, deducting the amount of your purchase directly from your checking account, usually at no charge. They can be used as an ATM card for cash withdrawals and deposits, but be aware that using ATM machines that are not owned by your bank can often incur fees. Most banks in the Seattle area charge non-members a fee to use their ATM machines. This charge can range from $1.00 to $2.00. Exceptions are Washington Mutual, Frontier Bank, and First Mutual Bank.

To open a checking account, you'll need to apply at the bank's web site, or visit a local branch office and bring the minimum deposit required (this amount varies from bank to bank, so call ahead). You will also need photo ID and proof of address (a letter or utility bill mailed to your new address, or your rental contract).

You may also want to open a savings account in addition to your checking account. With some banks, you will save on fees by having two accounts at the same location. Other services offered by banks include credit cards, loans, mortgages, lines of credit, and online bill paying.

The largest Seattle banks offer the convenience of branches throughout the Puget Sound area. There are also many smaller community banks offering competitive rates and services. You may find membership in a credit union more appealing, with better interest rates, lower loan fees, and low-fee checking. Most of the following area banks have several branch offices in the city and surrounding communities:

- **Bank of America,** 800-442-6680, www.bankofamerica.com
- **Banner Bank,** 800-527-6435, www.bannkerbank.com
- **Cascade Bank,** 800-326-8787, www.cascadebank.com
- **CityBank,** 425-745-5933, www.citybank.com
- **Columbia Bank,** 800-305-1905, www.columbiabank.com
- **First Mutual Bank,** 800-735-7303, www.firstmutual.com
- **Frontier Bank,** 888-779-4801, www.frontierbank.com
- **HomeStreet Bank,** 800-719-8080, www.homestreet.com
- **KeyBank,** 800-539-2968, www.key.com
- **Peoples Bank,** 800-584-8859, www.peoplesbank-wa.com
- **Seattle Savings Bank,** 888-262-7562, www.seattlesavingsbank.com
- **Sterling Savings Bank,** 800-772-7791, www.sterlingsavingsbank.com
- **US Bank,** 800-872-2657, www.usbank.com
- **Viking Community Bank,** 206-297-4200, www.vikingbank.com
- **Washington Federal Savings Bank,** 206-624-7930, www.washingtonfederal.com
- **Washington First International Bank,** 206-292-8880, www.wfib.com
- **Washington Mutual,** 800-788-7000, www.wamu.com
- **Wells Fargo,** 800-869-3557, www.wellsfargo.com

## CREDIT UNIONS

A low-cost alternative to a bank checking account is a similar type of account at a credit union, where rates are often higher and fees lower. Formerly, you had to belong to a union or an employee organization to have access to these consumer-friendly nonprofits, but recent rule changes have relaxed membership requirements to allow wider access to credit unions. In many cases, all you need is to be a state or county resident. Contact information for local credit unions is listed here:

- **Alaska USA Federal Credit Union,** 800-525-9094, www.alaskausa.org
- **Boeing Credit Union,** 800-233-2328, www.becu.org
- **Cascade Federal Credit Union,** 800-562-2853, www.cascadefcu.org

- **Group Health Credit Union,** 800-562-5515, www.ghcu.org
- **King County Credit Union,** 800-248-6928, www.kccu.com
- **Qualstar Credit Union,** 800-848-0018, www.qualstarcu.com
- **School Employees Credit Union of Washington,** 888-628-4010, www.secuwa.org
- **Seattle Metropolitan Credit Union,** 800-334-2489, www.smcu.com
- **Verity Credit Union,** 800-444-4589, www.veritycu.com
- **Washington State Employees Credit Union,** 800-562-0999, www.wsecu.org

## INTERNET AND ONLINE BANKING

While online banking has been provided by traditional brick and mortar banks for years, there is a new breed of institutions, the internet-only banks. These are banks without brick and mortar counterparts, and while some believe they are the future of banking, traditional institutions don't seem to be in immediate danger. While many people still like knowing that their bank has a branch in their neighborhood or city, they also take advantage of the online banking services provided by their bank. In fact, according to the Pew Research Center, 43% of internet users use online banking.

Even if you choose to do most of your banking at a traditional bank, it might be worth your while to investigate an internet bank for high interest rate products like CDs, though be sure to read the fine print carefully. Most offer introductory rates that will change after your account has been established for a specified time. Also be aware that internet banking can be convenient if you have payroll direct deposit, but if you need to deposit checks you will have to send them in by mail in pre-paid envelopes and wait for your funds to be available. The following are some of the institutions that offer interest bearing checking and savings accounts:

- **Bank of Internet USA,** 877-541-2634, www.bankofinternet.com
- **EverBank,** 888-882-3837, www.everbank.com
- **Imperial Capital Bank,** 866-413-5626, www.imperialcapitalbank.com
- **ING Direct,** 800-464-3473, www.ingdirect.com
- **NetBank,** 888-256-6932, www.netbank.com

## CONSUMER PROTECTION

If you have a problem with your financial institution, first try to resolve the issue through their customer service department or with a bank officer. If the matter concerns a discrepancy on your statement, time is usually important. Find out how long you have to resolve the situation, and file a written complaint with the bank as soon as possible. If attempts to resolve the issue are unsuccessful, call the

Washington State Attorney General's Office, Consumer Protection Division complaints hotline at 206-464-6684, or visit www.wa.gov/ago/consumer. Another good resource for banking regulations and how to protect yourself from fraud is the Washington State Department of Financial Institutions, which regulates banks, credit unions, mortgage lenders and other financial services providers. You can also file a complaint about a company by calling 877-746-4334 or visiting www.dfi.wa.gov.

## CREDIT CARDS

As soon as you've established a new address in Seattle, chances are you'll start receiving plenty of credit card offers in the mail. In the unlikely event they don't find you, here are credit card companies you can contact:

- **American Express,** 800-528-4800, www.americanexpress.com
- **Department store credit cards,** check at the customer service counter or at the checkout counter, or apply online. Many stores offer a discount on your first purchase, with some restrictions. Department store cards are sometimes easier to qualify for than traditional credit cards, and can be used to establish a credit history if you have none. Seattle-area department stores that offer credit cards include Macy's (www.macys.com), Nordstrom (www.nordstrom.com), Mervyn's (www.mervyns.com), JC Penney (www.jcpenney.net), Sears (www.sears.com), Gottschalks (www.gottschalks.com), and Target (www.target.com).
- **Diner's Club,** 800-234-6377, www.dinersclub.com
- **Discover Card,** 800-347-2683, www.discovercard.com
- **MasterCard and VISA,** www.mastercard.com, www.visa.com; most banks offer one or both of these two major credit cards, and you can sign up for the card when opening your bank account. However, you may be able to find a more competitive interest rate by shopping around. See **Additional Credit Card Resources** below.

A word of warning to credit card users: the biggest revenue sources for credit card issuers are penalty charges for late credit card payments. If you want to avoid high finance charges, determine your grace period—the period between the end of a billing cycle and the payment due date—and pay off your balance within this period. For some cards, grace periods have been eliminated (often the case for cards issued with rewards programs, such as university cards or frequent-flyer cards). Another method to calculate finance charges compounds interest daily instead of monthly. Called "daily periodic rate" billing, this may only squeeze a few extra pennies out of you, but they're still your pennies. Since credit card issuers are always coming up with new ways to improve their profits, be sure to read the fine print in your contract. For additional consumer information, access CardWeb, 800-344-7714, www.cardweb.com, or the Consumer Action Organization, www.consumer-action.org.

## ADDITIONAL CREDIT CARD RESOURCES

A list of low-rate card issuers can be found on the internet at CardWeb, the Consumer Action Organization site, BankRate.com (www.bankrate.com), and iMoneynet.com (www.imoneynet.com).

To see your personal credit report, go to www.annualcreditreport.com. At this site, you can receive a free copy of your credit report from the three main credit bureaus once a year. You can also visit each credit bureau individually:

- **Equifax,** 800-685-1111, www.equifax.com
- **Experian,** 888-397-3742, www.experian.com
- **Trans Union Corporation,** 800-322-8228, www.transunion.com

## PREPAID DEBIT CARDS

An alternative to credit cards that is gaining popularity is prepaid debit cards. These are cards with a MasterCard or Visa logo that are bought online, at banks, or at retailers like Rite-Aid or Walgreens, and are also called "stored value" cards. You load money on the card, depending on the limits set by the issuer, and use the card the same way you would any debit or credit card. You can reload money at any time, but shop around for the best fees as most cards have a monthly charge, as well as fees, to reload money. For the credit challenged, most of these cards don't require credit checks. The major advantage is not being able to spend what you don't have, and some issuers target parents of teens, touting the advantage of using a prepaid card over handing out a cash allowance. The following are some of the better known prepaid cards:

- **Allow Card,** 877-725-5698, www.allowcard.com
- **Green Dot,** 877-434-3578, www.greendotonline.com
- **Western Union PrePaid MasterCard,** 800-792-8700, www.westerunion.com

# TAXES

## SALES TAX

Washington state residents do not pay a state income tax. Instead, there is a high sales tax (7% to 8.9%) that is charged on all purchases other than food and most prescription drugs. The sales tax is a combination of state and local taxes, so the rate varies by municipality and region. In Seattle, the sales tax rate is 8.8% (6.5% for the state, 1.9% for the city and .4% for the Regional Transit Authority.) After you've lived here for a while, you'll get used to paying more than the listed price for most items.

## FEDERAL INCOME TAX

The IRS's Live Telephone Assistance, 800-829-1040, is available for consumers with questions and/or in need of forms or help with forms. For free publications about IRS tax services, call 800-829-3676. During tax season, IRS forms are available at local libraries and post offices. You can also find forms online at www.irs. gov. When filing federal tax forms, the following numbers may be useful:

- **Where's My Refund?,** 800-829-4477
- **Washington State Department of Revenue,** 800-647-7706

If you need more help than you think you can get online or over the phone, you can go to a local Taxpayer Assistance Center. While you can call ahead for an appointment, taxpayers are welcome to drop in any time during business hours, from 8:30 am to 4:30 pm. Centers in the Puget Sound area:

- **Seattle,** 915 2nd Ave, 206-220-6015
- **Bellevue,** 520 112th Ave NE, 425-468-6036
- **Everett,** 3020 Rucker Ave, 425-304-6811
- **Tacoma,** 1201 Pacific Ave, 253-428-3518

## ELECTRONIC INCOME TAX FILING

Record numbers of taxpayers took advantage of e-filing in 2006, according to the IRS. Over 72 million tax returns were filed electronically, and 20 million of those were filed by people using their home computers. With tax software, such as TurboTax, widely available, and many online options for filing, e-filing has never been more convenient, or so heavily encouraged by the IRS. The IRS web site offers links to authorized providers, payment and direct deposit options, calculators, and more. You can even check the status of your refund online. Telephone filing is no longer available, but in its place is a new service called Free File. Companies listed on the IRS site offer free online filing for taxpayers with an Adjusted Gross Income of $50,000 or less. Eligibility and services vary from company to company, so be sure to read their guidelines carefully to find out if you qualify and if the services are right for you. Visit www.irs.gov for more information.

## STARTING OR MOVING A BUSINESS

When Boeing decided to move its corporate headquarters from Seattle to Chicago in 2001, the company cited traffic, education, and taxes as its top complaints. However, according to the Small Business Survival Index released by the Small Business Survival Committee in 2005, Washington is the fourth most entrepreneur-friendly state. In 2006, the Seattle-Bellevue-Everett area was 28th on Inc. com's national list of Best Large Cities for Doing Business. Smaller Puget Sound cities fared even better on the Overall Best Cities list, with Bellingham coming in 8th and Bremerton-Silverdale at 13th.

Business owners in Washington are subject to a business and occupation tax and/or a public utility tax. These are based on the gross receipts of the business and the rates vary depending on the type of business. The tax can be manageable for established companies, but hard on start-up companies that have yet to show a profit. The Washington Alliance for a Competitive Economy notes that business taxes are high, and a 2003 study for the Council on State Taxation found that "Washington business paid 54 percent of state and local taxes, compared with a U.S. average of 43 percent." One bright note is that the state lacks a corporate and a personal income tax.

If you do choose to start a business in Washington, the state has created a simple, one-stop system called the Master License Service that will walk you through the process, with all of the checklists, forms, and resources you'll need. For details, visit the Department of Licensing at www.dol.wa.gov, or call 360-664-1400. Other good resources for starting, operating, expanding, or relocating a business within Washington include:

- **Washington Small Business Development Center,** 509-358-7765, www.wsbdc.org
- **Washington State Business and Project Development,** 360-725-4100, www.choosewashington.com/business_resources

ONCE YOU'VE FOUND A PLACE TO CALL HOME, YOU'LL NEED TO arrange phone service, electric and/or gas accounts, trash pick-up, and so on. Most of your utilities can be hooked up with a phone call, although in some cases you may be required to mail or fax documents. Other services in this chapter, such as auto registration or photo ID, will require a visit to an office but you can probably live without these for a few days or even weeks. Also included in this chapter: a list of broadcast media; passport, voter, and library registration details; assistance with finding a doctor and/or vet; and consumer protection and safety information.

## UTILITIES

### ELECTRICITY

**Seattle City Light** (206-684-3000, 206-684-3225 [TTY], www.seattle.gov/light) supplies electricity for all residences within the city limits. Seattle City Light offers four ways to open a new account. You can handle it by phone using one of the following numbers: 206-684-3000, 800-862-1181, 206-684-3225 (TTY); or download a form online and fax it to 206-684-3347 or mail it to P.O. Box 34023, Seattle, 98124. You can also set up your new account completely online, where you can also transfer service and close accounts. You will also need to get a meter reading at your new address. You can do this by reading the meter yourself, paying a fee to have Seattle City Light do it for you, or let them estimate the reading for free.

Outside the Seattle city limits, **Puget Sound Energy** (888-225-5773, 800-962-9498 [TTY], www.pse.com) provides electrical service for the remainder of King County and much of Pierce County. Customer service is accessible at the above number from 7:30 a.m. to 6:30 p.m., Monday through Friday. Multi-lingual representatives are available.

In Tacoma, electric service is provided by **Tacoma Power** (253-502-8600, 253-502-8343 [TTY], www.ci.tacoma.wa.us/power). Tacoma Power also covers Fircrest, University Place, Fife, and parts of Steilacoom, Lakewood, and unincorporated Pierce County. In **Snohomish County**, including Everett, contact the Snohomish County Public Utility District (www.snopud.com, 425-783-1000; 425-783-8660 [TTY], or toll free in Western Washington at 877-783-1000), Monday through Friday, 8 a.m. to 5:30 p.m.

## NATURAL GAS OR OIL HEAT

In Seattle, heating options are electric, natural gas, or oil. Most likely you will go with whatever is already at your new house, apartment, or condominium. Unless the cost is included in your rent or condominium dues, you will be responsible for setting up a new account and for filling the existing tank (if using oil). If you decide to install a new furnace, water heater, or stove, you must be home for the line hook-up. If you choose the same fuel as the previous resident, just call for service; the gas or oil company will handle the rest. Natural gas is supplied to Seattle and Seattle suburbs by **Puget Sound Energy**, 888-225-5773, www.pse.com.

Heating oil may be purchased from any of several local companies; a few are listed here. Check the Yellow Pages for additional companies.

- **Ballard Oil Co.**, 206-783-0241, www.ballardoil.com
- **Cascade Oil Company**, 206-323-6050, 800-823-6050, www.cascadeoil.com
- **Glendale Heating**, 206-243-7700, 800-392-7687, www.glendaleheating.com
- **Laurelhurst Oil**, 206-523-4500, www.laurelhurstoil.com
- **Olson Energy Service**, 206-782-5522, www.olsonenergy.com
- **Pacific Northwest Energy Company**, 800-735-7137, www.heatingoil.com

## TELEPHONE

You'll need a home phone number for most applications so you'll want to get your residential telephone service established before anything else. **Qwest** provides local telephone service in Seattle. Call 800-244-1111 (TTY), 800-223-3131, 7 a.m. to 7 p.m., weekdays to set up your account, or go to www.qwest.com, to order service online. Be prepared with the following information: home address, preferred long distance company, and information on your previous phone account (including your former address and telephone number). A deposit may be required when you set up service depending on your credit status and previous telephone service history.

## AREA CODES

The area code in Seattle, and just north and south of the city limits, is 206. A large block of cities located to the north, east, and south of Seattle use the 425 area code. In cities farther south, like Kent and Tacoma, the area code is 253. Other areas in Western Washington use 360 (both north and south of Seattle). East of the Cascades the area code is 509. Long distance calls require 11 digits (1 + area code + number).

The following area codes represent the Seattle local calling area and surrounding communities:

- **206**: Bainbridge Island, Des Moines, Richmond Beach, Seattle, Vashon
- **253**: Auburn, Des Moines, Kent, Tacoma
- **425**: Ames Lake, Bellevue, Bothell, Duvall, Everett, Halls Lake, Issaquah, Kirkland, Maple Valley, North Bend, Redmond, Renton, Snoqualmie

## LONG DISTANCE

Long distance service providers frequently advertise very low per-minute rates, but be sure to read the fine print. If you have to pay $5.95 a month to get the five-cents per minute deal, and you don't make many long distance calls, it may make more sense for you to use a prepaid calling card—or even your cell phone for long distance. For help comparing long distance and wireless calling plans, visit the **Telecommunications and Research and Action Center (TRAC)** (not affiliated with the telecommunications industry), at www.trac.org. Major long distance service providers include:

- **AT&T**, 800-222-0300, www.att.com
- **MCI**, 800-955-0925, www.mci.com
- **Sprint**, 800-877-4000, www.sprint.com

## CELLULAR PHONES

There are many choices for cellular service in Seattle. Shop around, as rates and telephone prices can vary widely, and always ask about current promotions or discounts before committing yourself to a contract. If you will be working for a large company or government agency, ask your employer whether there is a company service plan. Often these offer much lower rates than you could get on your own. Listed here are some cellular companies that serve the Seattle area:

- **Cingular Wireless**, 866-246-4852, www.cingular.com
- **Qwest Wireless**, 800-222-3772, www.qwest.com/wireless
- **Sprint PCS**, 800-480-4727, www.sprint.com
- **T-Mobile**, 800-T-MOBILE, www.t-mobile.com
- **Verizon Wireless**, 866-256-4646, www.verizonwireless.com

## PREPAID CELLULAR PHONE SERVICE

With only slightly higher rates and no yearly contracts, prepaid cellular phone service is catching on with those who need mobile phone service. Simply purchase a phone that comes with prepaid service and activate the service online or with a phone call. When minutes run out the service is easily replenished with a payment. Some of the bigger cellular companies like Cingular (www.cingular.com) and T-Mobile (www.t-mobile.com) offer prepaid plans, and other companies like TracFone (www.tracfone.com) are exclusively prepaid. Phone may be bought online or at hundreds of retail stores like drugstores and grocery stores.

## DIRECTORY ASSISTANCE

In today's web-oriented world, directory assistance need no longer be fee-laden. An online Yellow Pages directory is available from Qwest (www.qwestdex.com) and numerous sites are dedicated to providing telephone listings and web sites, including the following:

- www.411.com
- www.anywho.com
- www.superpages.com
- www.switchboard.com
- www.whitepages.com
- www.yellowbook.com

Of course, you can still pay to access a local or national number by dialing 411. In Washington, a directory assistance call will cost you $1.25, for both local and national numbers.

## ONLINE SERVICE PROVIDERS

There are many online service providers that offer basic internet access and e-mail service via existing phone lines. Some of these provide free service but often bombard you with advertisements. For a complete list of internet service providers located near you, check the Yellow Pages under "Internet Access Providers."

For high-speed internet access, consider signing up for service on a digital subscriber line (known as DSL), or via cable modem access. DSL runs over copper wires like those used for telephone calls, but on a separate line. Unlike a dial-up option, a DSL connection is always on, so logging onto the internet is nearly instantaneous. Cable internet access is available from cable TV providers. Like DSL, the cable modem is always on. One possible disadvantage with cable modem is that your access speed may decrease if your neighbors also use cable. Before you sign up for cable modem, ask the provider what speed they guarantee.

Whatever type of connection you select, here are a few questions you may want to ask:

- What must the provider do to your home when installing the system?
- Does the provider offer technical support?
- What are the tech support hours?
- What is the average wait on the telephone for technical support? How long is it before tech support e-mail is answered?
- Does the provider offer e-mail accounts?
- Will the provider host your web site?
- What is the monthly fee?

Here are a few companies that offer dial-up access, DSL, and/or cable modem:

- **America Online**, 888-265-8003, www.aol.com
- **AT&T Worldnet Service**, 800-967-5363, www.att.com
- **Comcast**, 800-COMCAST, www.comcast.com
- **Compuserve**, 800-848-8199, www.compuserve.com
- **Earthlink**, 800-511-2041, www.earthlink.com
- **Qwest Internet Services**, 877-660-6342, www.qwest.com/internet
- **Seanet**, 800-973-2638, www.seanet.com
- **Verizon**, 877-863-0151, www.verizon.net

## WATER

**Seattle Public Utilities** supplies drinking water to more than 1.3 million people in the Seattle/King County area. If you are renting, the property owner must notify the utility of changes in occupancy, but it's likely you will be responsible for the monthly bill. If you have purchased a home, you must change the current service to your name. Call 206-684-3000, Monday through Friday, 7:30 a.m. to 6 p.m., Saturday, 8 a.m. to 5 p.m., or visit www.seattle.gov/util.

According to Seattle Public Utilities, the water it provides—which is supplied by the Cedar River and Tolt River watersheds—meets or exceeds all federal drinking water quality standards. The Cedar River Watershed, 141 square miles in size, at an elevation ranging from 538 feet to 5,447 feet, collects between 57 and 140 inches of precipitation each year and supplies over 65% of the area's drinking water. The South Fork Tolt River in the foothills of the Cascades east of

Carnation at an elevation ranging between 760 and 5,535 feet, collects between 90 and 160 inches of precipitation each year and supplies about 30% of Seattle's drinking water.

Like electricity, water service outside Seattle is provided by local public utility districts or private companies. If you live outside the Seattle Public Utilities district, the Department of Ecology recommends that you call the city nearest you to determine your supplier. See the **Useful Phone Numbers and Web Sites** chapter to contact your local government office.

If you have questions or concerns about water quality, call the King County **Department of Health** (206-296-4932) or the state **Department of Ecology** (360-407-6000). For current reports on water quality and legislative activity related to the state's water supply, visit www.wa.gov.

## GARBAGE AND RECYCLING

Seattle Public Utilities provides trash and recycling services. The Seattle Municipal Code requires that all residents have garbage containers and pay for garbage collection. Charges appear every other month on a combined utility bill, along with water and sewer fees. Garbage is collected once a week on an assigned day. The cost of the service depends on the number and size of garbage containers. It is important to note that recycling is mandatory in Seattle and the city will provide recycling containers and pickup at no charge. You can be fined for putting recyclables in your regular garbage. Call 206-684-3000 for customer service or recorded information on rates and services. To view a rate table, visit www.seattle.gov/util/services.

For most apartments and condominiums, sanitation and recycling fees are included in your monthly rent or dues. For single-family residences, you must buy a garbage can from the city or from a hardware store, and you must set up service with the city. There are a number of different-sized containers varying in price from $10.20 to $49.05. Backyard collection is also available at higher rates. There are also charges for additional garbage collected beyond your usual level of service. Yard waste is collected every other week, on the same day of the week as your garbage. The city requires that yard waste be contained in rigid cans, placed in Kraft paper or reusable polyethylene bags, or bundled with twine. A monthly charge of $4.30 covers the 96-gallon container provided by the city plus another container up to 32 gallons and a four-foot by two-foot bundle. Some food scraps and food-soiled paper are allowed in yard waste containers.

The city also offers recycling pick-ups every other week at both houses and apartments in the city, scheduled on the same day as your garbage collection day. (Yard waste and recycling alternate weeks.) One recycling container is provided for newspapers, mixed papers, aluminum, plastic and tin. Glass must be collected in a separate container. Recycling is free in Seattle, and should go a long way toward reducing what you pay for garbage. Again, call 206-684-3000 for customer service or recorded information on services. If you live in an apartment or condominium, these services should be provided for all tenants. If you are renting or have purchased a house, the recycling containers should be with the house.

The City of Seattle runs two recycling and disposal stations. Both transfer stations are open seven days a week, except for Thanksgiving, Christmas, and New Year's Day. Go to www.ci.seattle.wa.us/util for hours or directions.

- **North Recycling and Disposal Station**, 1350 N 34th St
- **South Recycling and Disposal Station**, 8105 Fifth Ave S (south of First Ave South Bridge)

Residents outside Seattle should check with their local municipality regarding trash pick-up and recycling.

## CONSUMER PROTECTION—UTILITY COMPLAINTS

It's always a good idea to try to resolve billing or other disputes directly with the utility company. If that fails you can file a formal complaint with the appropriate consumer complaint office. A division of the Department of Neighborhoods, the **Citizens Service Bureau** fields all complaints about city departments. According to the City of Seattle, the office responds to more than 54,000 citizen questions and complaints annually. Call the Citizens Service Bureau at 206-684-8811, or send an e-mail to city.action@ci.seattle.wa.us.

To file a complaint about a state department or independent company, contact the state **Consumer Protection Division** (800-551-4636). You may also file a complaint online, or download a complaint form at www.atg.wa.gov/consumer.

## AUTOMOBILES

Details about licensing, operating and parking a car in Seattle, auto insurance, and seatbelt laws are covered here. For information about auto repair and consumer protection related to automobiles, check the **Helpful Services** chapter. Additional auto-related listings, such as auto impound numbers, parking tickets and traffic violations line, and who to call about illegally parked and/or abandoned vehicles are in the **Useful Phone Numbers and Web Sites** chapter.

## DRIVER'S LICENSE, STATE IDENTIFICATION

You must apply for a Washington State driver's license within 30 days of becoming a resident. You are considered a resident when you establish a permanent home in the state, register to vote, receive state benefits, apply for any state license, or seek in-state tuition fees. To obtain a license for the first time, you must pass a written exam, a vision test, and a driving skills test. The fee is $45. If you have a valid driver's license from another state, bring proof of identification, fill out an application, and pay a fee to receive a Washington license. You will have to surrender your out-of-state license. If you currently live out of state, you can order a *Washington State Driver's Guide* by phone, or find it on the **Department of Licensing** web site (www.dol.wa.gov; click on "Driver License," then "Getting a License," then "Driver License Testing"). The cost of a state photo ID is $20.

You must visit a department of licensing to obtain your license, temporary permit, or photo ID card. Recent customer service improvements have greatly increased the efficiency of these offices, but you're still better off going on a weekday rather than a Saturday when the lines are longer. Bring your current (valid or expired) license, other proof of identification, and proof of state residence, such as a utility bill or rental agreement. If you've recently been married and need your name changed on your driver's license, bring your marriage certificate. Finally, don't forget to bring cash or a personal check. The Department of Licensing does not accept credit cards. Most offices are open Tuesday, Wednesday, Friday, and Saturday from 8:30 a.m. to 4:30 p.m. and Thursday from 9:30 a.m. to 4:30 p.m., but office hours vary by location. Call to confirm hours of operation before you visit, or check their web site (www.dol.wa.gov).

- **Auburn**, 3310 Auburn Way N, Ste H, 253-931-3940
- **Bellevue**, 525 156th SE, 425-649-4281
- **Bothell**, 18132 Bothell Way NE, Ste B6, 425-483-1739
- **Bremerton**, 1550 NE Riddell Rd, 360-478-6975
- **Downtown Seattle** (renewals only), 380 Union St, 206-464-6845
- **East Seattle**, 5811 Rainier Ave S, 206-721-4560
- **Everett**, 5313 Evergreen Way, 425-356-2967
- **Federal Way**, 1617 324th St, 253-661-5001
- **Greenwood**, 320 N 85th St, 206-706-4268
- **Kent**, 25410 74th Ave S, 253-872-2782
- **Kirkland**, 10639 NE 68th St, 425-827-0318
- **Lynnwood**, 18023 Hwy 99, Ste E, 425-672-3406
- **North Bend**, 402 Main Ave S, 425-888-4040
- **North Seattle**, 907 N 135th St, 206-368-7261
- **Renton**, 1314 Union Ave NE, 425-277-7231
- **Tacoma South**, 6402 S Yakima Ave, Ste C, 253-593-2990
- **Tacoma West**, 8313 27th St W, 253-534-3218
- **West Seattle**, 8830 25th Ave SW, 206-764-4144

Low-income seniors and disabled persons may apply for a City of Seattle identification card, entitling them to discounts in the Seattle area. Call the **Mayor's Office for Senior Citizens** (206-684-0500) for more information.

## AUTO REGISTRATION

You must license your automobile or motorcycle within 30 days of becoming a Washington resident, even if the tabs from your previous state of residence are still valid. The fine for driving an unregistered vehicle is a minimum of $330.

To license your automobile in Washington you will pay a basic license fee of $30. In addition, you will pay various filing, county, and state fees totaling approximately $30. You may pay a $10 surcharge if you get your registration from a sub-agent (often worth the additional charge for the added efficiency; see below), and a $15 emissions test charge (for vehicles manufactured after 1967; see below). The **State of Washington Department of Licensing** web page (www.dol.wa.gov) offers tips on vehicle, vessel, and driver's licensing; contact them at 1125 Washington Street SE, Olympia, 360-902-3600, 360-664-8885 (TDD). For more information on vehicle licensing in Washington, contact the **King County License and Regulatory Service Division** (500 4th Avenue Room 401, 206-296-4000, www.metrokc.gov/lars/autoboat).

## VEHICLE/VESSEL LICENSE SUB-AGENTS

- **Bellevue**: Alpine Management Services, 3927 Factoria Blvd SE, Ste D-5, 424-747-2816; Bel-Red Auto License, 15600 NE 8th Ste O-14, 425-747-0444
- **Bothell**: Canyon Park Vehicle Licensing Agency, 20631-D Bothell-Everett Hwy, 425-481-7113; Worthington Brokerage, 10035 NE 183rd St, 425-481-1644
- **Edmonds**: Edmonds Auto License Agency, 550 5th Ave S, 425-774-6657
- **Everett**: Bev's Auto Licensing Inc., 9111 Evergreen Way, 425-353-5333; Claremont Vehicle Licensing, 5319 Evergreen Way, 425-353-5557; Julie's Licensing Service, 1001 N Broadway, Ste A-7, 425-252-3518; Snohomish County Auditor Auto License, 3000 Rockefeller Ave, 425-388-3371; Village Licensing, 9327 4th St NE, Ste 7, 425-334-7311
- **Federal Way**: Federal Way Auto License Agency, 32610 17th Ave S, Ste C4, 253-874-8375
- **Kent**: Kent Licensing Agency, 331 Washington Ave S, 253-852-3110
- **Kirkland**: Lee Johnson Auto License, 12006 NE 85th St, 425-828-4661
- **Lakewood**: Active Military/Civilian Agency, 12500 Bridgeport Way SW, 253-588-7786; Military Retired Bureau, 10644 Bridgeport Way SW, 253-588-9049
- **Lynnwood**: Lynnwood Auto License Agency, Fred Meyer, 4615 196th St SW, Ste 150, 425-774-7662

- **Mountlake Terrace**: McMahan License Agency, 22911 56th Ave W, 425-670-3874
- **Renton**: Fairwood/Maple Valley License Agency, 14276 SE 176th St, 425-228-7234; Renton License Agency, 329 Williams Ave S, 425-228-5640
- **Seattle**: Ballard Licensing Agency, 2232 NW Market St, 206-781-0199; Bill Pierre License Agency, 12531 30th Ave NE, 206-361-5505; Georgetown License Agency, 5963 Corson Ave S, 206-767-7782; Puget Sound License Agency, 3820 Rainier Ave S, Ste C, 206-723-9370; Siler Licensing, 628 SW 151st St, 206-243-8222; University License Agency, 5615 Roosevelt Way NE, 206-522-4090; Wendels License and Service, 13201 Aurora Ave N, Ste 2, 206-362-6161; West Seattle Licenses, 5048 California Ave SW, 206-938-3111; White Center License Agency, 10250 16th Ave SW, 206-763-7979
- **Snoqualmie**: Sno Falls Credit Union, 9025 Meadow Brook Way SE, 425-888-8705
- **Tacoma**: North Pacific Financial Service Inc., 5442 S Tacoma Way, 253-475-4112; Western Auto Licensing Inc., 215 S Garfield St (Parkland), 253-537-3112; Pierce County Auditor Auto License, 2401 S 35th St, Ste 200, 253-798-3649; Quik Stop Licensing II, 6722 W 19th St (University Place), 253-564-6555
- **Woodinville**: Woodinville License Agency, 17403 139th Ave NE, 425-486-0289

## EMISSIONS TEST INFORMATION

In Clark, King, Pierce, Snohomish, and Spokane counties, most vehicles must pass an emissions test every two years, even if the vehicle is certified in another state. The fee for testing is $15 and must be paid in cash. Testing station hours are Monday through Friday, 9 a.m. to 5 p.m., and Saturday, 9 a.m. to 1 p.m. The list below is for testing stations in King County. For additional sites and more information, call the state **Department of Ecology** at 800-272-3780 or visit the agency's web site: www.ecy.wa.gov.

- **Auburn**, 3002 "A" St SE, 253-939-1225
- **Bellevue**: 15313 SE 37th St, 425-644-1803
- **Redmond**: 18610 NE 67th Ct, 425-882-3317
- **Renton**: 805 SW 10th St, 425-228-6453
- **Seattle**: 12040 Aurora Ave N, 206-362-5173; 3820 6th Ave S, 206-624-1254

## AUTOMOBILE INSURANCE

The State of Washington requires drivers to have automobile insurance for all owned or leased vehicles, providing liability coverage for damage to the other driver's vehicle, as well as bodily damage to the driver and passengers of the other car. Minimum requirements are $25,000 for bodily injury to the other driver; $50,000 for total bodily injury to driver and all passengers; and $10,000 for property damage to the other driver's car. The fines for not carrying automobile insurance are steep, close to $400. You are required to show proof of insurance if stopped for a moving violation or if involved in an automobile accident. Coverage is available from area and national insurance companies. Contact your homeowners' insurance agent first, and ask about a possible discount for carrying multiple policies with the same company. Check the Yellow Pages under "Insurance" for listings of area companies. The **Washington State Insurance Commissioner** provides a free online consumer guide to auto insurance at www.insurance.wa.gov.

## AUTOMOBILE SAFETY

Washington is a pretty safe place for drivers. According to the state Traffic Safety Commission, that's largely due to the region's reliance on freeways, which are roughly three times safer than other roads and city streets. When highway accidents do occur, they are often caused by the combination of drinking and driving.

In 2005, alcohol-related deaths accounted for 45% of the state's traffic fatalities. In comparison, the national percentage for alcohol-related fatalities was 39%. While dropping the legal blood alcohol level for drivers to 0.08% in 1999, and enacting new laws slowed the rate of deaths, driving under the influence remains a problem.

According to the Washington State Patrol, the new laws give police more power when arresting people charged with DUI (Driving Under the Influence), allowing them to suspend driver's licenses, impound vehicles, and pursue drivers across state lines. The rules also require breath-triggered ignition locks, for at least a year, for those drivers convicted of DUI with alcohol levels above 0.15%, and limit to once in a lifetime the opportunity to avoid DUI prosecution by entering an alcohol-treatment program.

Washington also regulates the use of seat belts and child restraints. Every person riding in a motor vehicle must wear a seat belt. Driving without a seat belt is considered a primary offense, meaning officers can pull you over for that reason alone. The fine for driving without a seat belt is $101. Child guidelines are: kids under one year or less than 20 pounds must ride in a rear-facing infant seat; kids between one and four years, or up to 40 pounds, must be in a forward-facing safety seat; and kids between four and six, or up to 60 pounds, must ride in a booster seat. For tips on properly installing car seats check with your local fire department or go to www.safekids.org.

## PARKING

Parking in Seattle can be challenging at times, but if you're moving here from another large city you may be pleasantly surprised. While parking for a few hours in the business district can be very expensive, there are affordable lots in some parts of downtown. Street parking is also available throughout downtown, at a cost of $1.50 per hour, but be sure to read the signs carefully. Some streets restrict parking during the busiest traffic hours; other parking meters have special time restrictions or fees. Parking fines are not insignificant: $35 for a street parking infraction. (See below for more about parking tickets.) The good news on street parking downtown is that you only need to pay between 8 a.m. and 6 p.m. Monday-Saturday. Meters are also free on holidays.

If you'll be commuting to downtown Seattle, your least expensive—and possibly most convenient—option may be to take the bus. If that's not practical, consider setting up or joining a carpool and take advantage of reduced parking fees. Call **City of Seattle Commuter Services** (206-684-0816) to arrange for a carpool parking permit. The cost for downtown carpool parking is $250 per quarter (three months) for a two-person carpool or $125 per quarter for a three-person carpool. (See **Transportation** for more information.) Your employer may offer discounts at nearby parking lots or offer incentives to carpool or ride mass transit.

If you prefer to drive to work by yourself, arrange to rent a space in a parking lot or garage. Street parking is too expensive and inconvenient for all-day parking. Here is a partial list of downtown parking garages.

- **1111 3rd Avenue Garage**, 1111 3rd Ave, 206-623-0226
- **4th & Columbia Parking**, 723 4th Ave, 206-622-7373
- **520 Pike Building Garage**, 520 Pike St, 206-340-8803
- **Harbor Steps Garage**, 1200 Western Ave, 206-622-4846
- **IBM Building Garage**, 1200 5th Ave, 206-623-2675
- **Key Tower Garage**, 700 5th Ave, 206-628-9042
- **King Street Garage**, 83 S King St, 206-340-0738
- **Norton Building Garage**, 800 1st Ave, 206-622-2870
- **Parking at Pacific Place**, 600 Pine St, 206-652-0416
- **Public Market Parking**, 1531 Western St, 206-621-0469
- **Seattle Tower Garage**, 3rd Ave at University St, 206-624-2473
- **Securities Building Garage**, 1922 3rd Ave, 206-623-9937; 1913 4th Ave, 206-269-0762
- **Third Avenue Building Garage**, 1111 Third Ave, 206-623-0226
- **U-Park**: Tower Lot, 1825 7th Ave; 7th Ave & Marion St; 100 4th Ave S, 206-284-9797
- **Union Square Garage**, 601 Union St, 206-447-5664
- **Union Station Parking Garage**, 550 4th Ave S, 206-652-4602

- **United Airlines Building Garage**, 2020 5th Ave, 206-448-9992

## RESIDENTIAL PARKING PERMITS

In Seattle proper, residential neighborhood parking can be a problem in some areas. Although there is still free street parking in residential neighborhoods, restrictions are common. Restricting parking on busy streets is done to keep traffic flowing, and parking time limits keep spaces available for shoppers. Other restrictions that limit parking on residential streets during certain hours of the day target habitual long-term parking by people who do not live in the area. For instance, neighborhoods with popular theaters and restaurants may have evening parking restrictions; areas with office buildings or hospitals nearby may have daytime parking restrictions. If your neighborhood has restricted parking, you'll want to get a residential parking permit. These permits cost $35 and are usually good for two years. Call **Seattle Transportation** at 206-684-5086 for more information, or visit www.seattle.gov/transportation/parking.

## PARKING TICKETS

If you get a parking ticket, you must pay it within 15 days, or you'll be charged a penalty. The city will also notify the state Department of Licensing and a collection agency. To pay in person, visit the Municipal Court of Seattle in the Public Safety Building, 600 3rd Avenue: 8 a.m. to 5 p.m. Monday–Friday. The court will accept cash, cashier's check, money order, VISA or MasterCard. If you can't get away during business hours, there is a green deposit box in front of the building, but only cashier's checks or money orders are accepted. Finally, you can mail payments to the Municipal Court of Seattle, 600 3rd Avenue, Room 100, Seattle, WA 98104. For more information about parking tickets, call 206-684-5600 or visit www.seattle.gov/courts.

## TOWED OR STOLEN CARS

There are tow-away zones and red curbs throughout the city where you may not park, even temporarily, or you will be subject to immediate towing. There are three towing companies that provide towing service and impound lots in Seattle. If you believe that your vehicle has been impounded by order of the police department, call 206-684-5444 (have your license number ready) and you will be directed to the appropriate lot. Sometimes it can take several hours for information to reach the police department, so if you want to take immediate action you can try calling the towing companies to discover which has your vehicle.

- **ABC Towing**, 206-682-2869
- **E T Towing**, 206-622-9188

- **Lincoln Towing**, 206-364-2000

If your car was towed while on private property, call the owner or manager of that property or the posted towing company number. To report a stolen vehicle, call the Seattle Police Department non-emergency line at 206-625-5011.

# SOCIAL SECURITY

It is the rare American citizen who does not have a Social Security number. Non-citizens who are working or studying here will also need a number. This can be done by mail, by first calling 800-772-1213 and answering five automated questions, then mailing a completed application form with the necessary documents (the form will be sent after the initial telephone interview); or go online to www.ssa.gov. You may also visit the nearest Social Security office (see the telephone book or get the address from the 800 number above or at www.ssa.gov), no appointment necessary.

Bring with you a certified birth certificate and two other pieces of identification: passport, driver's license, school or government ID, health insurance card, military records, an insurance policy. A Social Security employee will complete the application, and you should receive a card with your number within several weeks.

Non-citizens need a birth certificate and/or a passport and a green card or student documentation, as well as whatever immigration documents you have. It may take a month or more to receive a card.

If you already have a number but have lost your card, call the number above to apply for a new card.

# VOTER REGISTRATION

To register to vote in Seattle, you must be at least 18 years old, a citizen of the United States, and a legal resident of the state of Washington. To vote in an upcoming election, you must register at least 30 days prior. You may register to vote online, at government offices, schools, and public libraries. You can also register through the mail or through the "Motor Voter" program. "Motor Voter" registration is completed when you apply for or renew your driver's license. It takes only an extra minute or two. You need not declare your political affiliation or party membership when you register. Any registered voter can receive an absentee ballot in Washington, and the option is becoming more popular. To request an absentee ballot, contact your county auditor or elections department. For more information, or to register by mail, call the Secretary of State's **Voter Information and Elections Hotline** (800-448-4881, 800-422-2683 [TTY]) or go to www.secstate.wa.gov/elections/register.aspx.

## LIBRARY CARDS

The Seattle metropolitan area has two overlapping library systems, the Seattle Public Library and the King County Library System. Both libraries offer an extensive selection of books and other materials and, upon request, will reserve books at other libraries in their system for your use.

The **Seattle Public Library** free service area includes the City of Seattle, the City of Bothell, and most of King County. The exceptions are the cities of Enumclaw, Renton, Yarrow Point, and Hunts Point. Anyone who lives, works, attends school, or owns property within the service area qualifies for a free library card. Seattle Public Library cards are available at any neighborhood library. Check the **Neighborhoods** chapter for listings of Seattle libraries near you. You must show identification, such as a driver's license or passport. If you live outside the library's free service area, you can purchase a non-resident library card for an annual fee of $55. For more information, call Borrower Services at 206-386-4190.

To borrow books from the **King County Library System (KCLS)**, you must apply for a King County Library card, which is available to anyone who lives in the KCLS service area, or in the service area of another library system that has a reciprocal borrowing agreement. This includes residents of Seattle, Renton, and Enumclaw. The KCLS service area consists of unincorporated King County and just about every city in the county. For the complete list, visit www.kcls.org. You can apply for a card at any King County Library branch or online at www.kcls.org. You must provide ID and verification of your address. Call the following for more information:

- **Seattle Public Library, Central Library**, 800 Pike St, 206-386-4636, www.spl.lib.wa.us
- **King County Library System**, Main Office, 960 NW Newport Way, 800-462-9600, www.kcls.org

Seattle residents also benefit from proximity to the University of Washington and its libraries. Free services to visitors include in-library use of most materials, limited access to library computers, reference assistance, tours, and classes. Call 206-543-0242 or visit www.lib.washington.edu for more information. See the **Literary Life** section of the **Cultural Life** chapter for a list of UW libraries.

## PASSPORTS

In Seattle, passports are processed at the **Seattle Passport Agency**, located downtown at the US Department of State, 915 2nd Avenue, Suite 992, 877-487-2778 (appointment line). This office serves only those customers who are traveling within two weeks or who need foreign visas, and is by appointment only. Hours are Monday–Friday, 8 a.m. to 3 p.m. Travelers not meeting those criteria may pick up passport applications at the Lake City, University District, Ballard, Delridge, West Seattle, Southeast, or Central neighborhood service centers. Check the **Neighborhoods** chapter for locations. Bring two standard passport photos, a picture ID, and proof of US citizenship, such as a previous US passport, certified birth certificate, naturalization certificate or certificate of citizenship. The cost is $97 for a new passport for those 16 and older, $82 for those under 16, and $67 to renew a passport issued less than 15 years earlier. The standard turnaround time for a new passport is 25 days, but an expedited three-day passport can be requested for an additional $60 fee. For appointments and recorded information, call the Seattle Passport Agency office. To use the internet for your passport application, go to the web site for the **Bureau of Consular Affairs** (www.travel.state.gov).

## TELEVISION

### CABLE

**Comcast** provides cable television service to all of Seattle except for some parts of the Central District, where residents are served by **Millennium Digital Media** (800-829-2225, www.mdm.net). Millennium also serves Duvall, the Sammamish Plateau (east of Redmond and north of Issaquah), Redmond, Issaquah, and Bellevue. Comcast currently offers hundreds of digital cable channels in Seattle, with similar lineups in King, Pierce, and Whatcom counties. The company also offers high speed cable internet access and digital phone service. Installation fees and monthly rates vary depending on which package you choose, but the company frequently offers special packages to new customers. Prices can vary widely depending on service, and the company offers discounts when you "bundle" services, such as having your cable TV, high speed internet, and phone service all through Comcast. To order new service, call 800-COMCAST, or visit www.comcast.com. Comcast office locations are listed here:

- **Auburn**, 4020 Auburn Way N
- **North Seattle**, 1140 N 94th St
- **Redmond**, 14870 NE 95th St
- **South Seattle**, 15241 Pacific Hwy S

### LOCAL STATIONS

If you signed up for cable or satellite service, the local broadcast stations listed here may differ:

- Channel 4, KOMO-TV, ABC
- Channel 5, KING-TV, NBC
- Channel 6, KONG-TV, NBC
- Channel 7, KIRO-TV, CBS
- Channel 9, KCTS-TV, PBS
- Channel 11, KSTW-TV, CW
- Channel 13, KCPQ-TV, FOX

## RADIO STATIONS

Seattle area residents love their music! Here's a guide to local radio stations:

### ADULT CONTEMPORARY
- KBKS, 106.1 FM
- KLSY, 92.5 FM
- KMIH, 104.5 FM
- KMTT, 103.7 FM
- KPLZ, 101.5 FM
- KYPT, 96.5 FM

### ALTERNATIVE/MODERN ROCK
- KEXP, 90.3 FM
- KGRG, 89.9 FM
- KKBY, 104.9 FM
- KNDD, 107.7 FM

### CHRISTIAN
- KCIS, 630 AM
- KCMS, 105.3 FM
- KGNW, 820 AM
- KLFE, 1590 AM

### CLASSIC SOUL
- KSRB, 1150 AM

### CLASSICAL
- KING, 98.1 FM

### PUBLIC AFFAIRS
- KSER, 90.7 FM

### COUNTRY
- KMPS, 94.1 FM

### JAZZ
- KBCS, 91.3 FM
- KPLU, 88.5 FM
- KWJZ, 98.9 FM

### KIDS
- KKDZ, 1250 AM

### KOREAN
- KSUH, 1450 AM
- KWYZ, 1230 AM

### NEWS, NPR
- KIRO, 710 AM
- KNWX, 770 AM
- KOMO, 1000 AM
- KPLU, 88.5 FM
- KRKO, 1380 AM
- KUOW, 94.9 FM

### OLDIES
- KBSG, 97.3 FM
- KBSG, 1210 AM

## ROCK

- KISW, 99.9 FM
- KIXI, 880 AM
- KRWM, 106.9 FM
- KZOK, 102.5 FM

## SPORTS

- KIRO, 710 AM
- KJR, 950 AM

## TALK RADIO

- KJR, 950 AM
- KKOL, 1300 AM
- KOMO, 1000 AM
- KPTK, 1090 AM

- KQBZ, 100.7 FM
- KRKO, 1380 AM
- KVI, 570 AM

## TOP 40/DANCE

- KNHC, 89.5 FM

## URBAN CONTEMPORARY

- KRIZ, 1420 AM
- KUBE, 93.3 FM
- KYIZ, 1620 AM

## WORLD MUSIC AND FOLK

- KBCS, 91.3 FM
- KCMU, 90.3 FM

# LOCAL NEWSPAPERS AND MAGAZINES

In March 2000, the **Seattle Post-Intelligencer** and **The Seattle Times**, the city's two metropolitan daily newspapers, squared off in head-to-head competition as *The Times* moved from afternoon publishing to morning. *The Seattle Times*, locally owned by the Blethen family since 1896, and the *Post-Intelligencer*, founded in 1863 and now part of the Hearst Corporation, though separately owned and managed, share a joint operating agreement that allows *The Times* to handle advertising, circulation, production and promotion for both. News and editorial functions remain separate. In 2003 *The Seattle Times* challenged the joint operating agreement, which the *Post-Intelligencer* maintains is necessary for it to stay in business, and after a series of ugly legal battles, both sides agreed to private arbitration. A final decision in the case is expected in the spring of 2007.

The following newspapers and magazines serve Seattle and surrounding communities:

- **The Herald**, 1213 California Ave, Everett, 425-339-3000, www.heraldnet.com
- **Issaquah Press**, 425-392-6434, www.issaquahpress.com
- **King County Journal**, 11400 SE 8th, Bellevue, 425-455-2222, www.king countyjournal.com
- **The Kitsap Sun**, 545 5th St, Bremerton, 888-377-3711, www.kitsapsun.com
- **Mercer Island Reporter**, 7845 SE 30th St, 206-232-1215, www.mi-reporter. com
- **Newcastle News**, P.O. Box 1328, Issaquah, 98027, 425-392-6434, www. newcastle-news.com

- **Puget Sound Business Journal**, 720 Third Ave, Ste 800, 206-583-0701, www. bizjournals.com/seattle
- **Seattle Daily Journal of Commerce**, 83 Columbia St, 206-622-8272, www.djc. com
- **Seattle Homes and Lifestyles**, 1221 E Pike St, 206-322-6699, www. seattlehomesmag.com
- **Seattle Magazine**, 423 3rd Ave W, 206-284-1750, www.seattlemag.com
- **Seattle Metropolitan Magazine**, 1201 Western Ave, Ste 425, 206-957-2234, www.seattlemet.com
- **Seattle Post-Intelligencer**, 101 Elliott Ave W, 206-464-2121, www. seattle-pi.com
- **The Seattle Times**, 1120 John St, 206-464-2111, www.seattletimes.com
- **Seattle Weekly**, 1008 Western Ave, Ste 300, 206-623-0500, www.seattleweekly. com
- **Snoqualmie Valley Record**, 8124 Falls Ave SE, Snoqualmie, 425-888-2311, www.valleyrecord.com
- **The Stranger**, 1535 11th Ave, 3rd Flr, Seattle, 206-323-7101, www.thestranger. com
- **Tacoma News Tribune**, 1950 S State St, 253-597-8742, www.tribnet.com
- **Vashon-Maury Island Beachcomber**, 17502 Vashon Hwy SW, 206-463-9195, www.vashonbeachcomber.com
- **Washington CEO**, 200 W Thomas St, Seattle, 206-441-8415, ww.washingtonceo. com

## FINDING A PHYSICIAN

When searching for a doctor in Seattle you will find plenty of options. Begin by determining your needs: are you looking for a general family practitioner or a specialist? An MD or a naturopath? Do you prefer the comforts of a small clinic or the more extensive services of a large hospital? And perhaps most importantly, does your health plan limit who you can see? Many new residents rely on recommendations from friends or co-workers when looking for a doctor. Another option is to contact the **King County Medical Society** at 206-621-9396 or www. kcmsociety.org. Their web site allows you to search by physician's last name, zip code, specialty, or language. Or, call a physician referral line or local hospital. Here is a list of local referral lines, many of which are affiliated with major area hospitals:

- **Children's Hospital and Regional Medical Center**, 866-987-2500, www. seattlechildrens.org
- **King County Medical Society**, 206-621-9396, www.kcmsociety.org
- **Northwest Hospital Physician Referral**, 206-633-4636, www.nwhospital.org

- **Overlake Hospital Medical Center**, 425-688-5211, www.overlakehospital. org
- **PacMed Clinics**, 888-472-2633, www.pacmed.org
- **Swedish Medical Center**, 800-793-3474, www.swedish.org
- **UW Physicians**, 800-852-8546, www.uwphysicians.org
- **Valley Medical Center**, 425-656-4636, www.valleymed.org
- **Virginia Mason**, 888-862-2737, www.virginiamason.org
- **Washington Association of Naturopathic Physicians**, 206-547-2130, www. wanp.org
- **Washington Osteopathic Medical Association**, 206-937-5358, www.woma. org

Should you have a **serious complaint** about a medical provider, which you cannot resolve directly with your provider, contact the **Washington Medical Quality Assurance Commission**, P.O. Box 47865, Olympia, WA 98504, 360-236-4700, or the **Washington State Board of Osteopathic Medicine and Surgery** (same address and phone number).

The Office of the Washington State Insurance Commissioner assists consumers with questions about health insurance concerns, from Medicare to HMOs to long-term care, through their **Statewide Health Insurance Benefits Advisors (SHIBA)**. Call their 24- hour consumer hotline, 800-562-6900.

## PET LAWS & SERVICES

Pets in Seattle must be licensed annually, even those that generally are kept inside. A dog license costs $40.00 ($20.00 if the dog is spayed or neutered); cats are $25.00 ($15.00 if the cat is spayed or neutered). Two-year licenses are available for a discount. To qualify your pet for a license, you must provide proof that your pet has received a current rabies vaccination. The reduced license fee for a spayed or neutered pet requires a copy of a veterinarian's spay or neuter certificate. Low-income senior citizens and disabled persons with a City of Seattle ID card qualify for a 50% discount on all fees. (See the **Driver's License, State Identification** section of this chapter for more information about ID cards.)

All four-legged pets (except cats) must be on a leash or held by the owner when in public places in Seattle, including sidewalks. In addition, Seattle has strict "scoop laws" that require the person in charge of the animal to clean up after the pet.

Eleven city parks have "off-leash" areas where pets are allowed to roam freely, but there are a few rules. Owners must have voice control over their pets, dogs must be licensed, and poop must be scooped.

- **"Blue Dog Pond,"** Martin Luther King Jr. Way S and S Massachusetts

- **Genesee Park**, 46th Ave S and S Genesee St
- **Golden Gardens Park**, 8498 Seaview Place NW
- **I-5 Colonnade**, beneath I-5, south of E Howe St, between Lakeview Blvd and Franklin Ave E
- **Jose Rizal Park**, 1008 12th Ave S
- **Magnuson Park**, 7400 Sandpoint Way NE
- **Northacres Park**, west of I-5 at N 130th St
- **Plymouth Pillars Park**, Boren Ave between Pike and Pine Sts
- **Regrade Park**, 2251 3rd Ave
- **Westcrest Park**, 8806 8th Ave SW
- **Woodland Park**, W Greenlake Way

**Luther Burbank Park** on Mercer Island also has a popular off-leash area at 2040 84th Ave SE. One of the area's most popular dog parks is located outside the city limits in Redmond. This off-leash area at **Marymoor Park** covers over 40 acres and provides dogs with swimming and fetching opportunities. A non-profit group, **Serve Our Dog Areas**, is dedicated to its maintenance and preservation. To volunteer, call 425-881-0148 or visit www.soda.org.

If you're interested in adopting an animal, you can visit the **Seattle Animal Control Center** at 2061 15th Avenue West (in the Interbay area), 206-386-4254. Fees range from $82 to $165 depending on the size, gender, and type of animal. You must provide current photo ID, and your landlord's name and phone number if you live in a rental property. For more information about Seattle Animal Control and pets available for adoption, visit the SAC web site at www.seattle. gov/animalshelter.

Organizations that may prove useful for those who have lost a pet or have found a stray are:

- **Humane Society for Seattle/King County**, 13212 SE Eastgate Way, Bellevue, 425-641-0080, www.seattlehumane.org
- **King County Animal Control Enforcement**, 206-296-7387
- **King County Animal Control Shelter**, 821 164th Ave NE, Bellevue, 206-296-3940; 21615 64th Ave S, Kent, 206-296-7387, www.metrokc.gov/lars/animal
- **Progressive Animal Welfare Society (PAWS)**, 15305 44th Ave W, Lynnwood, 425-787-2500, www.paws.org
- **Seattle Animal Control Hotline** (Lost Pets), 206-386-4254, www.seattle. gov/rca/animal
- **Seattle Animal Control Shelter**, 2061 15th Ave W, 206-386-4254, www.seattle. gov/rca/animal

## PET CARE SERVICES

If the off-leash areas in the city's parks aren't enough to convince you that Seattle has gone to the dogs in recent years, consider the rise in the canine comfort industry, and the increase in pet-sitting and dog-walking providers. If you must leave your dog or cat home alone for the day—or for weeks—consider hiring a surrogate or sending your pet to daycare.

- **Adventures in Sitting Kitties**, 206-595-7473, www.sittingkitties.com
- **Bone-A-Fide Dog Ranch**, 206-501-9247, www.bone-a-fide.com
- **Central Bark**, 206-325-3525, www.central-bark.com
- **Great Dog Daycare**, 206-526-1101, www.gogreatdog.com
- **Happy Camper Pet Service**, 206-784-5291, www.happycamperpets.com
- **Hillrose Pet Resort**, 206-241-0880, www.petresort.com
- **Kitty Luv Cat Sitting Service**, 206-260-3112, www.kittyluv.com
- **Lap of Luxury**, 206-217-0317, www.lapofluxury.info
- **The Pet Au Pair**, 206-200-5357, www.mypetaupair.com
- **Pet Sitters of Puget Sound**, www.psps.org

Does your dog or cat need a ride to daycare, the vet, or a groomer? One service in town offers pet transport for a variety of needs. Try **Seattle Dog Taxi**, 206-853-5944, www.seattledogtaxi.com.

## SAFETY AND CRIME

According to statistics compiled by the Seattle Police Department, in 2005, 47,555 major crimes were reported in Seattle, a 2% increase from the previous year, but a 4.4% decrease for the period of 1999-2005. 4,110 were violent crimes, with aggravated assault leading the way with 2,343. The murder rate saw a significant decrease in the 1999-2005 period, down 44% with 25 homicides reported in 2005. In fact, the two-year period of 2004-2005 posted the lowest murder rate of any time since 1964-1965. Property crimes—burglary, larceny, and auto theft—increased by 1.5% from 2004 to 2005, but decreased 4.7% over the 1999-2005 period. Mere numbers don't tell the whole picture, and the Seattle Police Department reports that among the 25 largest cities in the country, Seattle is the 8th safest.

If the state of Washington and the city of Seattle have an Achilles heel when it comes to crime, it is auto thefts, which have plagued the region for more than a decade. There were 9,558 reported thefts in 2005, a 3.2% increase from 2004; however, the news isn't all bad. With a new focus on enforcement, public awareness campaigns, and stiffer penalties for offenders, the numbers for the first half of 2006 show a marked decrease in auto thefts.

Auto theft is a crime of opportunity, so your best defense is to deny a thief the opportunity to take your automobile. Also protect yourself from car prowls or smash and grabs by not leaving anything in the car. Valuable or not, items left in cars are tempting to thieves. The Seattle Police Department Car Prowl Task Force recommends the following preventive measures:

- Always lock your car, and remove valuables when parking.
- Park in well-lighted areas, even at home.
- Park in areas of busy pedestrian traffic.
- Install an anti-theft device.
- Call 911 to report suspicious activity.

Auto thefts and car prowls notwithstanding, most Seattle neighborhoods are safe. Take precautions, however, especially in unfamiliar areas. The following safety tips may be helpful: walk quickly and with a purpose, especially at night; don't dawdle or slow your pace, even when approached, and keep clear of alleyways, deserted areas, and dead ends. If riding in a bus, stay close to the front, near the driver. Most of all, trust your instincts. If you feel uneasy about a person or situation, there may be a good reason for it. For more personal safety tips, visit the Seattle Police Department's crime page at www.seattle.gov/police.

Many neighborhoods participate in **Block Watch**, a free crime prevention and emergency preparedness program sponsored by the Seattle Police Department. Overseen by precinct coordinators, there are currently over 38,000 registered "block watches" operating throughout the city. To participate, or for more information go to www.seattle.gov/police/prevention/Blockwatch/.

NOW THAT YOU HAVE A PLACE TO CALL HOME, AND HAVE TAKEN CARE of the basics like setting up electricity and gas accounts, you might have time to investigate and benefit from some of the area's helpful services. Services such as **Housecleaning**, **Pest Control** or **Automobile Repair** can make your life a bit simpler. Other sections in this chapter include **Postal and Shipping Services**, **Consumer Protection**, **Services for People with Disabilities**, **Gay and Lesbian Life** and help for **International Newcomers**.

## DOMESTIC SERVICES

For those who need a little extra help around the house, the following services might be of interest. Check the Yellow Pages for more listings.

### DIAPER SERVICES

- **Baby Diaper Service**, 206-634-2229, www.seattlediaper.com
- **Sunflower Diaper Service**, 206-782-4199

### DRY CLEANING DELIVERY

- **Four Seasons Cleaners**, 2800 15th Ave W, 206-286-9696, www.fourseasonscleaners.com
- **Jay's Dry Cleaners**, 2350 24th Ave E, 206-328-8158, www.jaysdrycleaners.com
- **Stadium Cleaners**, 3307 NE 65th St, 206-522-9125, www.stadiumcleaners.com

- **Village Cleaners**, 2620 NE 46th St, University Village Mall, 206-522-1033, www. stadiumcleaners.com

## HOUSECLEANING

You may decide to use a housecleaning service before you move into your new home or for routine chores on an ongoing basis. A few housecleaning businesses are listed below. As with all lists in this guide, inclusion does not indicate endorsement. If you are not satisfied with the service you receive from a company during the initial cleaning, request that they clean again at no charge.

- **April Lane's Homecleaning**, Seattle: 206-527-4290; Eastside: 425-649-8600, www.aprillaneshc.com
- **Attention to Detail**, 206-621-7421, 425-353-2850, www.attentiontodetailnw. com
- **Dana's Housekeeping–Housekeeper Referral Service**, Seattle/South Snohomish County: 206-368-7999; South King County/West Seattle: 253-433-0070; Newport Hills/Greater Eastside: 425-827-2220; www.housecleaning. com
- **Maid Brigade**, 888-222-6243, www.maidbrigade.com
- **Maid in the Northwest**, Seattle: 206-622-7783; North Seattle: 206-365-5087; Federal Way/Kent: 253-859-9029; Bellevue/Eastside: 425-455-0655; Edmonds/ Lynnwood: 425-775-3888; Des Moines/Tacoma: 425-927-4122; www. maidinthenw.com
- **Merry Maids**, Seattle/University District: 206-527-2984; West Seattle: 206-937-7083; North Seattle/South Snohomish County: 425-778-3355; Eastside: 425-881-6243; South King County: 253-833-6171; www.merrymaids.com
- **Mighty Maids**, West Seattle: 206-938-9662; Eastside/Renton: 425-226-1614; South King County: 253-630-2799, www.mightymaidswa.com
- **Rent-A-Yenta House Cleaning Service**, Seattle: 206-325-8902; Eastside: 425-454-1512; www.renta-yenta.com

## PEST CONTROL

Rats have long been a problem in Seattle, and the pesky rodents are an increasing nuisance in the suburbs as well. If setting traps yourself hasn't worked or is not an option, consider calling an exterminator, or visit www.pestweb.com to find tips for dealing with unwelcome house "guests." These local pest control experts can also help you with carpenter ants (another local problem), as well as hornets, termites, and other pests that might be bugging you.

- **Aard Pest Control**, 206-575-3319, 425-776-3662, www.aardpestcontrol.com
- **Able Pest Control**, 206-575-9877, 253-867-5990, www.ablepestcontrol.net

- **Cascade Pest Control**, South Seattle: 206-244-0356, Central/North Seattle: 206-525-0882, www.cascadepest.com
- **Eden Advanced Pest Technologies**, Seattle: 206-219-5787; Bellevue: 425-882-3205; Everett: 425-357-8282; 800-401-9935; www.edenpest.com
- **Integrity Pest Control**, Seattle: 206-264-9554; Kirkland: 425-827-2484; Renton: 425-228-2127, www.integritypestcontrol.com
- **Orkin**, 800-562-5610, www.orkin.com
- **Redi National Pest Eliminators**, Seattle: 206-633-1234; Eastside: 425-454-8500; South King County: 253-838-8806; Lynnwood: 425-742-7433
- **Terminix**, Seattle/Bothell/Kirkland: 425-487-6643; Mercer Island: 206-232-4704; Renton: 425-251-5943; Kent/Auburn: 253-872-3462; Des Moines/Federal Way: 253-839-0808; Bellevue/Redmond: 425-451-7876; North Bend: 425-888-4474; www.terminix.com

## POSTAL AND SHIPPING SERVICES

If you are between addresses and in need of a place to receive mail, you can rent a box at a local post office or choose a private receiving service. Many of the private services allow call-in mail checks and mail forwarding, but they are often more expensive than the post office.

### MAIL RECEIVING SERVICES

- **The Mail Box**, Seattle: 300 Lenora St, 206-728-1228; 300 Queen Anne Ave N, 206-285-0919; 6201 15th Ave NW, 206-789-7564; Bellevue: 10020 Main St, 425-453-9019
- **The UPS Store**, 1700 7th Ave, 206-624-1550; 4616 25th Ave NE, 206-524-2558; 4742 42nd Ave SW, 206-933-3038; 1037 NE 65th, 206-528-7447; 10002 Aurora Ave N, 206-527-5065; 410 Broadway Ave E, 206-860-0818; 1425 Broadway, 206-324-5600; 3518 Fremont Ave N, 206-547-4410; 24 Roy St, 206-282-2288, www.theupsstore.com

### PACKAGE DELIVERY SERVICES

- **DHL Worldwide Express**, 800-225-5345, www.dhl-usa.com
- **FedEx**, 800-463-3339, www.fedex.com/us
- **United Parcel Service (UPS)**, 800-742-5877, www.ups.com
- **US Postal Service Express Mail**, 800-275-8777, www.usps.com

## JUNK MAIL

To curtail the deluge of mail you surely will receive after relocating, register on-line with the **Direct Marketing Association's Mail Preference Service**. There is a $1 fee for having your name removed from marketing lists and you can also print out a form and mail it in. Visit the web site at www.dmaconsumers.org. This should help, but you will have to contact some catalog companies directly with a purge request, and it won't affect companies who are not members of the DMA. (Keep in mind: you might actually appreciate some of the mass-market mail, as many retailers and household service providers welcome new residents with coupons and special offers.)

## AUTOMOBILE REPAIR

Finding a mechanic you can trust is often difficult. The most popular way to find a shop is to ask around—co-workers, neighbors, and friends. Though often pricey, auto dealers are generally reliable, and will have the right equipment and parts to work on your car. Check the Yellow Pages for listings.

Those considering an independent mechanic shop may want to check with the **Better Business Bureau** to determine if any complaints have been filed against it. The local chapter serves Alaska, Oregon, and Western Washington, and is located at 1000 Station Drive, Suite 222, in DuPont. Call 206-431-2222 or visit www.thebbb.org.

If it's just "advice" you need, consider tuning your radio to NPR's "Car Talk." Locally, the program can be heard on KUOW, 94.9 FM, on Saturday from 9 to 10 a.m.

If the question isn't who will repair your car, but rather who to call to have it towed, your best resource may be an automobile club like the **American Automobile Association**. For information about membership benefits and services, visit www.aaawa.com, or call 800-222-4357. There are three Seattle offices, located at: 4554 9th Avenue NE, 206-633-4222; 1523 15th Avenue West, 206-218-1222; and 4701 42nd Avenue SW, 206-937-8222. Additional locations are Bellevue, Bremerton, Everett, Federal Way, Issaquah, Lynnwood, Redmond, Renton, and Tacoma.

## CONSUMER PROTECTION—AUTOMOBILES

If you are looking for a new car, Washington has a lemon law to protect owners who have "substantial or continuing problems with warranty repairs." A lemon is defined as a vehicle that has one or more substantial defects, which has been subject to a "reasonable number of attempts" to diagnose or repair the problem(s) under the manufacturer's warranty. The law does not cover problems caused by owner abuse or negligence, or any unauthorized modifications made to the vehicle. Nor does it cover some motorcycles and large commercial trucks, motor homes used as homes, office or commercial space, or vehicles purchased as part of a fleet of 10 or more. The law allows the owner to request an arbitration hearing through the office of the **Washington Attorney General** within 30 months of the vehicle's original retail delivery date. If you are not the original owner, you can still apply the lemon law if the vehicle was purchased within two years of delivery to the original retail consumer, and within the first 24,000 miles of operation. For more details, visit the Attorney General's Consumer Protection web site at www.atg.wa.gov/consumer, or call 800-551-4636.

Information about vehicle recalls and crash tests can be found at the **US Department of Transportation's Auto Safety Hotline**, 888-327-4236, or visit www.nhtsa.dot.gov.

## CONSUMER PROTECTION—RIP-OFF RECOURSE

Got a beef with a merchant or company? There are a number of agencies that monitor consumer-related businesses and will take action when necessary. The best defense against fraud and consumer victimization is to avoid it—read the contracts down to the smallest print, save all receipts and canceled checks, get the name of telephone sales and service people with whom you deal, check a contractor's license number with the state's Consumer Protection Division for complaints. Despite such attention to details, sometimes you still get stung. A dry cleaner returns your blue suit, but now it's purple and he shrugs. A shop refuses to refund, as promised, on the expensive gift that didn't suit your mother. After $898 in repairs to your engine, your car now vibrates wildly, and the mechanic claims innocence. Negotiations, documents in hand, fail. You're angry, and embarrassed because you've been had. There is something you can do.

- **Attorney General's Office**, Consumer Protection Division, 900 4th Ave, Ste 2000, 800-551-4636, www.atg.wa.gov/consumer; in 2005, problems with telecommunications and online services, retail business, collection agencies, and auto sales companies topped the list of consumer complaints received by the Attorney General's Office. The Consumer Protection Division web site outlines how to resolve and file complaints. Seven neighborhood consumer resource centers are also available throughout the state.
- **Better Business Bureau**, 1000 Station Dr, Ste 222, DuPont, 206-431-2222, www.thebbb.org; the local chapter serves both Western Washington, Oregon, and Alaska. The BBB can supply you with a reliability report for a business. The agency also accepts complaints when a breakdown in communication occurs between you and a business.
- **City of Seattle Department of Neighborhoods, Citizens Service Bureau**, 600 Fourth Ave, Rm 105, 206-684-2489; www.seattle.gov/citizenservice; the Citizens Service Bureau employs four full-time complaint investigators who provide investigation, mediation, and assistance for questions and complaints about city services.

- **King County Office of Citizen Complaints**, 400 Yesler Way, Rm 240, 206-296-3452, www.metrokc.gov/ombuds; if your dispute is with a county agency, contact the county Ombudsman's Office. Though the office cannot take legal action on your behalf, they can generally resolve the matter through a fact-finding effort with the agency involved.
- **King County Small Claims Court**, King County Courthouse, 516 Third Ave, Rm W-1034, 206-205-9200, 206-205-2820, www.metrokc.gov/KCDC; with some exceptions, an individual, business, partnership or organization can bring a small claims suit for the recovery of money only, up to $4,000. The filing fee is $25.
- **The Tenants Union**, 5425B Rainier Ave S, 206-723-0500, www.tenantsunion. org; their web site provides a series of online brochures to answer renters' commonly asked questions. Phone calls and walk-ins to the office are taken on Monday and Wednesday between 3 p.m. and 6 p.m., and Thursday, 12 a.m. to 4 p.m.

## MEDIA-SPONSORED CONSUMER ADVOCACY PROGRAMS

The following consumer advocacy and assistance programs are operated by Seattle area television stations.

- **KOMO 4 Buyer Beware**, 206-404-4799, 140 4th Ave N, www.komotv. com/buyerbeware
- **KING 5 Legally Speaking**, 206-448-5555, 333 Dexter Ave N, www.king5. com/localnews/legallyspeaking
- **KIRO 7 Consumer Alert Team**, 206-728-7777, 2807 3rd Ave, www.kirotv. com/consumer

## LEGAL RESOURCES

- **Columbia Legal Services**, 101 Yesler Way, 206-464-5911, 800-542-0794
- **King County Lawyer Referral Service**, 206-267-7010, www.kcba.org
- **Northwest Justice Project**, 401 Second Ave S, 206-464-1519, 888-201-1012, www.nwjustice.org
- **Senior Rights Assistance**, 2208 2nd Ave, 206-448-5720, www.seniorservices. org
- **Washington State Bar Association**, 206-443-9722, 800-945-9722, 2101 4th Ave, www.wsba.org

## SERVICES FOR PEOPLE WITH DISABILITIES

There are a number of organizations in the Seattle area that serve as resources for disabled persons. The **Washington Coalition of Citizens with Disabilities**

**(WCCD)** offers legal services concerning civil rights violations; an employment program, which provides assistance in finding a job; a travel training program, to help disabled persons use the Metro bus system; a technical assistance program, providing job training; and a self-advocacy program, to teach disabled persons how to speak up for their rights. The **Northwest Disability and Business Technical Assistance Center (NWDBTAC)** supports the integration of all persons with disabilities into the community and provides publications on workplace accessibility and other topics. The **Washington Assistive Technology Alliance (WATA)** increases access to and awareness of technologies that provide assistance and accessibility for people with disabilities. The **University of Washington's Assistive Technology Resource Center (ATRC)** provides information, referral services, training, and consultation regarding assistive technology devices, services, and funding. The **Easter Seal Society of Washington** provides housing assistance programs and vocational rehabilitation, including interview skills training, job search techniques, and on-the-job support. They also publish a pamphlet listing accessible sites in the Seattle area.

**Metro Transit** issues Regional Reduced Fare Permits to individuals with disabilities. The permit costs $3 and is valid for Metro transportation, Washington State Ferries, Community Transit, Pierce Transit, and most other bus agencies in the region. Buses are equipped with wheelchair lifts and special seating. For those individuals who require assistance in riding the bus, a special Personal Care Attendant permit allows the disabled person's escort to ride free. Depending on the nature of the disability, a letter of certification from a physician, psychiatrist, psychologist or audiologist is required. Call Metro Transit at 206-553-3060, 206-684-1739 (TTY) for more information and to receive a copy of the certification form.

Here's a list of addresses and phone numbers for the above centers and some other national and local organizations:

- **Alliance of People With Disabilities**, 4649 Sunnyside Ave N, Ste 100, 206-545-7055, 206-632-3456 (TTY), www.disabilitypride.org
- **Center for Technology and Disability Studies**, University of Washington, 206-685-4181 (Voice), 206-616-1396 (TTY), 800-841-8345 (Voice/TTY), http://uwctds.washington.edu
- **Community Service Center for the Deaf and Hard of Hearing**, 1609 19th Ave, 206-322-4996 (Voice/TTY), 877-301-0006 (Voice/TTY), www.cscdhh.org
- **Community Services for the Blind and Partially Sighted**, 9709 3rd Ave NE, Ste 100, 206-525-5556, 800-458-4888, www.csbps.com
- **Deaf–Blind Service Center**, 1620 18th Ave, Ste 200, 206-323-9178 (Voice/TTY)
- **Easter Seals Washington**, 157 Roy St, 206-281-5700, www.wa.easterseals.com

- **Hearing Loss Association of Washington**, P.O. Box 4025, Kent, WA 98032, 360-871-0997 (Voice), www.hearingloss-wa.org
- **Hearing, Speech and Deafness Center**, 1625 19th Ave, 206-323-5770 (Voice), 206-388-1275 (TTY) www.hsdc.org
- **Learning Disabilities Association of Washington**, 16315 NE 87th St, Redmond, 425-882-0820, www.ldawa.org
- **Metro Transit**, 206-553-3060, 206-684-1739 (TTY), http://transit.metrokc.gov
- **Northwest ADA/IT Center**, P.O. Box 574, Portland, OR 97207-0574, 800-949-4232, www.nwada.org
- **Washington Assistive Technology Act Program (WATAP)**, University of Washington, Box 357920, 800-214-8731, 866-866-0162 (TTY), http://watap.org
- **Washington Protection and Advocacy System**, 315 5th Ave S, Ste 850, 800-562-2702, 800-905-0209 (TTY), www.wpas-rights.org
- **Washington State Department of Social and Health Services, Deaf Services**, 1115 Washington St SE, Olympia, 360-902-8000 (Voice/TTY), 800-422-7930 (Voice/TTY)
- **Washington Telecommunications Relay Services**, dial 711, or 800-833-6384, 800-833-6388 (TTY), 800-833-6385 (Telebraille)

## GAY AND LESBIAN LIFE

When the census counted same-sex partners for the first time in 2000, figures indicated that Seattle has one of the nation's highest percentages of gay households. At the count, one out of every 21 couples living together in Seattle listed themselves as homosexual. Of 15,900 same-sex pairs in Washington, about half resided in King County, and nearly one-fifth lived in Seattle. While this may be news to some, it is not news to Seattle's thriving and well-established gay community. There are numerous organizations, businesses, and publications that address the concerns and interests of Seattle's lesbian, gay, bisexual, and transgender community—too many to detail here. We mention the following as starting points.

- **City of Seattle Commission for Sexual Minorities**, 700 3rd Ave, Ste 750, 206-684-4500, 206-684-4503 (TTY), www.seattle.gov/scsm
- **Dignity Seattle**, 206-325-7314, www.dignityseattle.org, is the country's largest and most progressive organization of gay, lesbian, bisexual and transgender Catholics.
- **Greater Seattle Business Association**, 2150 N 107th St, Ste 205, 206-363-9188, www.thegsba.org; GSBA's goal is to strengthen and expand business and career opportunities in the gay and lesbian community.

- **Lambert House Gay Youth Center**, 1818 15th Ave, 206-322-2515, www. lamberthouse.org; an activities and resource center for lesbian, gay, bisexual, transgender, and questioning youth ages 22 and under.
- **Lesbian Resource Center**, 227 S Orcas St, 206-322-3953, www.lrc.net; established in Seattle in 1971, LRC promotes empowerment, visibility, and social change.
- **Parents, Families and Friends of Lesbians and Gays (PFLAG)**, Seattle Chapter, 1122 E Pike St, 206-325-7724, www.seattle-pflag.org, promotes the health and well-being of sexual minorities through support, education, and advocacy.
- **Seattle Gay Couples**, www.seattlegaycouples.com, provides a comfortable environment to meet other couples, strengthen relationships, and explore gay-related issues.
- **Seattle LGBT Community Center**, 1115 E Pike St, 206-323-5428, www. seattlelgbt.org
- **Seattle Out and Proud**, 1605 12th Ave, Ste 2, 206-322-9561, www.seattlepride. org, FDC organizes and promotes the annual Seattle Pride parade and march.

## NEWSPAPERS

- *Seattle Gay News*, 1605 12th Ave, Ste 31, 206-324-4297, www.sgn.org
- *The Stranger*, 1535 11th Ave, 206-323-7101, www.thestranger.com

## ENTERTAINMENT

Most of Seattle's gay bars and restaurants are located in the Capitol Hill neighborhood.

- **C.C. Attle's**, 1501 E Madison, 206-726-0565
- **Changes**, 2103 N 45th, 206-545-8363
- **The Cuff**, 1533 13th Ave, 206-323-1525, www.cuffcomplex.com
- **Elite**, 622 Broadway E, 206-324-4470
- **Madison Pub**, 1315 E Madison, 206-325-6537
- **Manray**, 514 E Pine St, 206-568-0750, www.manrayvideo.com
- **Neighbours Disco**, 1509 Broadway, 206-324-5358, www.neighboursnightclub. com
- **Purr Cocktail Lounge**, 1518 11th Ave, 206-325-3112, www.purrseattle.com
- **R Place**, 619 E Pine, 206-322-8828, www.rplaceseattle.com
- **Re-Bar**, 1114 Howell St, 206-233-9873, www.rebarseattle.com
- **Sea Wolf Saloon**, 1413 14th Ave, 206-323-2158
- **Thumper's**, 1500 E Madison, 206-328-3800
- **Timberline Tavern**, 2015 Boren Ave, 206-622-6220
- **Wild Rose**, 1021 E Pike St, 206-324-9210, www.thewildrosebar.com

# INTERNATIONAL NEWCOMERS

According to the 2000 Census, foreign born people make up 16.9% of Seattle's population. While the city is a desirable place to live, since 9/11 government regulations have made it a little more difficult to relocate here from abroad. Visit the U.S. consulate in your home country to learn the steps you will need to take depending on your relocation status. Rules are different for permanent residency, students, guest workers, etc.

You can find comprehensive information and help on the **US Citizen and Immigration Services** web site at http://uscis.gov. There you can learn about the different types of immigrant and visa classifications, regulations, and the forms you will need. The USCIS strongly urges people to download forms from their web site, but if you need to have forms mailed to you, call 800-870-3676. For more general questions and help, call 800-375-5283 or 800-767-1833 (TTY).

If you are already in Seattle and need to contact the USCIS, the local office is at 12500 Tukwila International Blvd. To make an appointment to speak with an Immigration Information Officer you must use an online service called INFOPASS, www.infopass.uscis.gov. Call 800-375-5283 for details.

Contacting the consulate of your home country can be a good starting point for adjusting to your new home in Seattle. The area is home to five official consulates and many honorary consulates. While honorary consulates may not be able to handle issues like visas and passports, they often provide resources for newcomers, and can connect you with local organizations.

## OFFICIAL CONSULATES

- **Consulate General of Canada**, 1501 4th Ave, Ste 600, 206-770-4060, www,seattle.gc.ca
- **Consulate General of Japan**, 601 Union St, Ste 500, 206-682-9107, www.seattle.us.enb-japan.go.jp
- **Consulate General of the Republic of Korea**, 2033 6th Ave, Ste 1125, 206-441-1011
- **Consulate of Mexico**, 2132 3rd Ave, 206-448-3526
- **Consulate General of the Russian Federation**, 2323 Westin Bldg, 2001 6th Ave, 206-728-1910

## HONORARY CONSULATES

- **Consulate of Australia**, 401 Andover Park E, 206-575-7446
- **Consulate of Austria**, 416-A E Morris St, La Conner, 360-466-1100
- **Consulate of Belgium**, 2200 Alaskan Way, Ste 470, 206-728-5145

- **Consulate of Bolivia**, 15215 52nd Ave S, Park Ridge, Bldg #100, 206-244-6696
- **Consulate of Cambodia**, 1818 Westlake Ave N, Ste 315, 206-217-0830
- **Consul of the Republic of Croatia**, 7547 S Laurel St, 206-772-2968
- **Consulate of Cyprus**, 5555 Lakeview, Ste 200, Kirkland, 425-827-1700
- **Consulate of Denmark**, 6204 E Mercer Way, Mercer Island, 206-230-0888
- **Consulate of Estonia**, 8 Lindley Rd, Mercer Island, 206-467-1444
- **Consul General of Ethiopia**, 2200 Alaskan Way, Ste 300, 206-364-6401
- **Consulate of Finland**, 17102 NE 37th Pl, Bellevue, 425-451-3983
- **Consulate of France**, 2200 Alaskan Way, Ste 490, 206-256-6184
- **Consulate of Germany**, 1750 112th Ave NE, Ste B-217, Bellevue
- **Consul of Hungary**, PO Box 578, Kirkland, 98083, 425-739-0631
- **Consulate of Iceland**, 5610 20th Ave NW, 206-783-4100
- **Consulate of Jamaica**, 8223 S 222nd St, Kirkland, 253-872-8950
- **Consulate of Lithuania**, 5919 Wilson Ave S, 206-725-4576
- **Consulate of Luxembourg**, 725 1st St S, Apt 202, Kirkland, 425-822-4607
- **Consulate of New Zealand**, 10649 North Beach Rd, Bow, 360-766-6791
- **Consulate of Norway**, 1402 3rd Ave, #806, 206-623-3957
- **Consulate of Peru**, 3717 NE 157th St, Ste 100, 206-714-9037
- **Consulate General of the Seychelles**, 3620 SW 309th St, Federal Way, 253-874-4579
- **Consulate of Spain**, 4709 139th Ave SE, Bellevue, 425-237-9373
- **Consulate of Sweden**, 1215 4th Ave, Ste 1019, 206-622-5640
- **Consulate of The Netherlands**, 4609 140th Ave NE, Bellevue, 425-861-4437
- **Consulate General of Turkey**, 12328 NE 97th St, Kirkland, 425-739-6722
- **Consulate of Uruguay**, 1420 5th Ave, Ste 4100, 206-223-7000
- **Consulate General of Uzbekistan**, 800 5th Ave, Ste 4000, 206-625-1199

## PUBLICATIONS

The USCIS has a free, online brochure called ***Welcome to the United States: A Guide for New Immigrants*** that can help you get settled, find resources, and learn about your rights and responsibilities. It's located at www.uscis.gov/graphics/citizenship/imm_guide.htm

- ***Newcomer's Handbook for Moving to and Living in the USA***, by Mike Livingston, published by **First Books**, 503-968-6777, www.firstbooks.com

## MOVING PETS TO THE USA

- ***The Pet-Moving Handbook***, by Carrie Straub, published by **First Books**, 503-968-6777, www.firstbooks.com

- **Air Animal Pet Movers**, 800-635-3448 (U.S.), 813-879-3210 (International), www.airanimal.com
- **Cosmopolitan Canine Carriers**, 800-243-9105, www.caninecarriers.com

ONE OF THE MOST CHALLENGING AND OVERWHELMING TASKS parents face when moving to a new area is finding good childcare and/ or schools for their kids. While the process is not an easy one, with time and effort it is possible to find what is best for your children, whether it be in-home or on-site daycare, an after-school program, or a good public or private school. In addition, the possibilities presented by homeschooling and online schools are addressed in this chapter. The wide variety of opportunities available for higher education is also presented. Of course the keys to success in all of these areas are research and persistence.

Note: mention in this book of a particular childcare organization or business is not an endorsement. We recommend that you scrutinize any persons or organizations before entrusting your youngster(s) to them.

## CHILDCARE

## DAYCARE

Often, the best advice when looking for childcare is to ask for referrals from friends or co-workers. For newcomers who may be lacking such resources, a good place to start is the **Washington State Child Care Resource & Referral Network**, 800-446-1114, www.childcarenet.org. This private, non-profit agency will send you a packet of age-specific childcare, health, and parenting information, and tell you about a local referral program in your area. In the city of Seattle, that program is **Child Care Resources**, 206-329-5544, www.childcare.org. Based on your criteria, Child Care Resources will give you a list of providers from its database of more than 2,000 facilities in King County. While referrals are for state-licensed facilities, be sure to visit prospective sites and interview caregivers, regardless of any recommendations you may receive about an organization. Many local employers offer a benefits package that includes a similar service; check with your place of work for details.

Childcare in Washington is regulated by the new state **Department of Early Learning (DEL)** (formerly the Division of Child Care & Early Learning), www.del.wa.gov. The agency offers several helpful publications on its web site, including "Child Care Options for Parents" and "Choosing Child Care." The staff at the division of Child Care & Early Learning is responsible for licensing more than 2,000 childcare homes and centers, which provide care for approximately 50,000 children in King County. Licensers process background checks, inspect and monitor facilities, investigate complaints, and take corrective action when necessary. While most agree the current level of supervision is not sufficient, there is hope that with the restructuring and creation of the new Department of Early Learning positive changes will be made. Furthermore, a facility that is under investigation for licensing violations or allegations of abuse/neglect is not required to report the investigation to inquiring parents. Add to this the current shortage of trained teachers and aides in King County and it's easy to understand why diligent and thorough research is in order when looking for childcare.

In Washington, a license is required for anyone paid to care for children on a regular basis (unless the children are related to the caregiver). The state imposes minimum licensing requirements for three different types of childcare facilities: licensed childcare centers; licensed school age centers; and licensed family homes. A **childcare center** is a facility that provides regularly scheduled care for a group of children age one month through age 12. A **school age center** is a program operating in a facility other than a private residence, accountable for school age children when school is not in session. The program must provide adult-supervised care and a variety of developmentally appropriate activities. A **licensed family home** is a facility in the family residence of the licensee that provides regularly scheduled care for 12 or fewer children from birth to age 11. Before receiving a license from Child Care & Early Learning, a prospective daycare provider must have a business license, undergo a criminal history background check, attend a first aid/CPR class that includes infant/child CPR and pediatric first aid, attend an HIV/AIDS awareness class, and pass a state licensing inspection at the place of business. Only licensed daycare providers qualify for liability insurance. However, because liability insurance is not required by the state, you must ask the daycare providers you interview if their business is covered. You can check the license status of your childcare provider through the DEL web site at www.del.wa.gov, or call 866-48-CHECK.

The **Service Employees International (SEIU)** Local #925, the local union for childcare workers, may be able to offer some help in your search for good childcare. The SEIU district office is located at 2900 Eastlake Avenue East, #230. Call 206-322-3010 or go to www.seiu925.org for more information.

- **Child Care Resources**, Seattle, 253-329-5544; Eastside, 425-865-9350
- **City of Seattle Child Care Information and Referral**, 206-461-3207, 206-461-4571 (TTY)
- **South King County Family Child Care Association**, Child Care Referral Line, 253-639-1417
- **Southwest King County Family Child Care Association**, 253-854-7869

## WHAT TO LOOK FOR IN DAYCARE

When searching for the best place for your child, be sure to visit prospective daycare providers—preferably unannounced. In general, look for a safe environment and caring attitude. Check that the kitchen, toys, and furniture are clean and safe. Observe the other kids at the center. Do they seem happy? Are they well behaved? Are the teacher/child ratios acceptable? Ask for the telephone numbers of other parents who use the service and talk to them before committing. It's a good idea to request a daily schedule—look for both active and quiet time, and age-appropriate activities. In the winter months, weather in Seattle doesn't allow for a lot of outdoor activities, but make sure that sports, games, and field trips are still included in the curriculum.

Keep in mind that a license does not guarantee the service of the quality you may want. If you think a provider might be acceptable, call the Licensed Child Care Information System at 866-48-CHECK to determine their licensing status, and call on parent referrals.

## ONLINE RESOURCES—DAYCARE

The state Department of Early Learning suggests the following child-related online resources:

- **Consumer Product Safety Commission**, www.cpsc.gov
- **National Association of Childcare Professionals**, www.naccp.org
- **Office of the Superintendent of Public Instruction**, www.k12.wa.us
- **Washington State's Infant Toddler Early Intervention Program**, www1.dshs.wa.gov/iteip

## NANNIES

A number of agencies match families with nannies. Although these services tend to be pricey, some include background checks or psychological testing during the applicant screening process. Nannies are not licensed by the state, and screening processes vary among agencies, so you may want to ask for interview specifics at the various agencies. That said, a nanny can be a wonderful addition to your family. Whether you're employed outside your home or simply need some assistance while working at home, a considerate and hard-working nanny may be the best option for your childcare needs. Area nanny services include:

- **A Nanny for U**, 206-525-1510, 425-745-9882, www.anannyforu.com
- **Annie's Nannies**, 206-784-8462, www.anihouseholdstaffing.com
- **CareWorks**, 206-325-9985, www.careworkseattle.com
- **Home Details**, 206-285-7656, www.homedetailsinc.com
- **Judi Julin, RN, Nannybroker Inc.**, Seattle, 206-624-1213, Eastside, 425-392-5681, www.nannybroker.com
- **Keepsake Nannies**, 253-845-2202, www.keepsakenannies.com
- **The Perfect Nanny**, 425-971-4566, www.theperfectnanny.com
- **The Seattle Nanny Network Inc.**, Eastside, 425-803-9511, www.seattlenanny.com

Be sure to check all references before hiring a nanny. These companies offer pre-employment screening services, and can provide criminal background checks, driving records, and credit reports:

- **Active Employment Screening**, 800-555-1420
- **Alliance Credit Services Inc.**, 877-333-5897, www.alliancecredit.com
- **Background Investigations Inc.**, 888-338-1550, www.wedobackground checks.com
- **Sound Screening Services Inc.**, 800-300-0138, www.soundscreening.com

For those hiring a nanny without an agency, there are certain taxes that must be paid: Social Security and Medicare, and possibly unemployment. For assistance with such issues, check the **Nanitax** web site, www.4nannytaxes.com, or call them at 800-NANITAX.

## AU PAIRS

If you'd like the convenience of a nanny at a considerably lower cost, or if you're simply interested in a cultural exchange, consider the services of an au pair. Young women (and a few men), usually from Europe, provide a year of childcare and light housekeeping in exchange for airfare, room and board, and a small stipend. Au pairs work up to 45 hours a week, and often go to school or sightsee during their time off.

It is a good program for those families and au pairs who understand the trade-offs of the system. Nevertheless, you may want to confirm that you and the au pair have mutual expectations for your year together. The au pair will be in a foreign country and interested in traveling and meeting people her age. While most agencies outline specific responsibilities, make sure the au pair understands what is expected during her year of employment; your au pair may not have fully considered how restricted her free time will be. Additionally, some parents may have unrealistic expectations of an au pair, assuming that she will be a combination nanny, babysitter, and full-time housekeeper, with few social interests. That said, if you and your au pair come to an agreement early in the relationship, and follow the guidelines detailed by the agency, most likely you will be very pleased with the au pair experience.

The US Department of State **Bureau of Educational and Cultural Affairs** is responsible for authorizing the organizations that conduct au pair exchange programs. For answers to frequently asked questions, visit http://exchanges.state. gov/education. The following organizations administer the au pair program:

- **American Institute for Foreign Study**, Au Pair in America, 800-727-2437, www.aifs.org
- **AYUSA International**, AuPairCare, 800-428-7247, www.aupaircare.com
- **EF Au Pair**, 800-333-6056, www.efaupair.org
- **Euraupair Intercultural Child Care Programs**, 800-333-3804, www.euraupair. com
- **Go Au Pair**, 800-574-8889, www.goaupair.com
- **InterExchange Au Pair**, 800-287-2477, www.interexchange.org

## BABYSITTERS

If you haven't found a reliable babysitter in your neighborhood, or the one you found just called and cancelled, the following companies offer babysitting services. Be prepared to pay more for immediate response.

- **Annie's Nannies**, 206-784-8462, www.anihouseholdstaffing.com
- **Best Sitters, Inc.**, 206-682-2556, 425-455-5533, www.bestsittersinc.com
- **Judi Julin, RN, Nannybroker Inc.**, Seattle, 206-624-1213, Eastside, 425-392-5681, www.nannybroker.com
- **The Seattle Nanny Network Inc.**, Seattle, 206-374-8688, Eastside, 425-803-9511, www.seattlenanny.com

## CHILD SAFETY

Numerous public agencies, private organizations, and hospitals offer resources to help keep your kids safe. The **Seattle Public Library** provides parents and teachers with a list of internet safety organizations on its web site, www.spl.org/children/safety. **Public Health of Seattle & King County** will deliver health and safety news alerts via e-mail; to subscribe, visit www.metrokc.gov/health. The **Seattle Fire Department** offers a program for children called Fire Stoppers—call 206-386-1338 for details. Several hospitals offer infant and child CPR programs, including **Children's Hospital & Regional Medical Center**, 206-789-2306, www. seattlechildrens.org, and **Swedish Medical Center**, 206-386-3606, www.swedish.org.

## SCHOOLS

## SEATTLE PUBLIC SCHOOLS (K–12)

In recent years, public schools in Seattle have faced a series of serious problems, approaching crisis level, including a huge budget deficit, low enrollment and graduation rates, and high dropout rates. To correct the budget deficit, projected to be around $20 million in 2007-2008 and nearly $40 million the following school year, Superintendent Raj Manhas pushed through a painful plan to close some schools and reorganize the transportation system, which the School Board approved in 2006. No schools have been closed in Seattle since 1989, but drastic drops in student enrollment and the condition of some of the aging buildings necessitated the plan. Some students will be reassigned to other schools and some programs will be moved to other existing schools or buildings. In addition to the chaos created by the announcement of school closures, Superintendent Raj Manhas announced his resignation in October 2006. The search for a new superintendent will likely last well into 2007.

In addition to the financial problems faced by the School District, the state of academics has come under fire. The graduation rate is low at 59%, and the dropout rate is high at 22%; although new plans are being formed to address this situation, the new requirement of passing the WASL test in order to graduate from high school may make it a slow climb out of the academic doldrums. The **Washington Assessment of Student Learning** is a series of standards-based tests that must be passed in 10th grade as a graduation requirement. Students who fail are given four more opportunities to re-take the test, as well as tutoring help, and there are other graduation options for those who fail the WASL at least twice. The class of 2008 will be the first students to be affected by the new requirement, which means passing the reading, writing, and math tests. The classes of 2010 and beyond will have science added to that list. Students start taking the WASL in 3rd grade, and while average scores have historically been low, they are starting to rise.

Although the news is grim, there are a few bright spots. In the fall of 2000 students of the K-8 African American Academy (www.seattleschools.org/schools/aaa) moved into a new $24 million facility on Beacon Hill. The school's mission is to help African-American children meet and exceed Seattle public schools' academic standards. The three-story building houses a science lab, photo darkroom, art room, music room, gymnasium, and 90-seat lecture hall. Another development in Seattle Public Schools is the addition of The Center School (www.seattleschools.org/schools/thecenterschool), the district's newest high school, and the only school located in downtown Seattle. In fact, the small high school enjoys a home on the grounds of the Seattle Center, where seniors can take advantage of internships. While core academics are strong and technology is used throughout the curriculum, the school's focus is on the arts. All electives are based on the arts, and portfolios are a graduation requirement.

Other notable public school programs include **TOPS** (www.topsk8.org), a K–8 program known for its strong parent involvement and state-of-the-art school building, and **Summit** (www.seattleschools.org/schools/summitk-12), Seattle's only K–12 school, which prides itself on utilizing the cross-age learning opportunities that arise from having kids of all ages in the same building.

For younger students, Seattle Public Schools offers both half-day and full-day kindergarten. There is a huge demand for full-day programs, and some are fee-based. Check with area schools for more information. The Seattle school district also offers Montessori programs at two schools—**Graham Hill Elementary** (www.seattleschools.org/area/main/ShowSchool?sid=220) and **Daniel Bagley Elementary** (www.seattleschools.org/area/cac/schoolprofiles/bagley.pdf). (See below for a list of private Montessori programs.)

For more information about these schools and to see which schools are being closed or moved, go to www.seattleschools.org.

## ENROLLMENT—SEATTLE PUBLIC SCHOOLS

The Seattle Public Schools enrollment process is a bit complicated—and not without controversy—but most parents consider it a vast improvement over the former school assignment program. The old system did not allow voluntary school selection and involved busing large numbers of students throughout the city to improve the racial balance at each school. While busing successfully integrated the schools, it also took its toll on the overall well-being of the public school community. With bus rides as much as 90 minutes each way, many students found it difficult to get to and from school, let alone participate in after-school sports and activities. With such inconveniences, those who could afford to chose private schools instead.

In 1993, the school district offered the community a voluntary school selection process, which is limited only by space and the racial integration standards set by the state. The goal is to give all students their first-choice school. The district has consistently come close to the goal. Slight changes are made to the program each year, but generally the enrollment guidelines are as follows. Each elementary school has a "reference area." Your child's reference area school is determined by your address. Further, elementary schools are grouped into geographic clusters—nine groups of schools defined by location (North, Northeast, Northwest, Queen Anne/Magnolia, Central, South, Southeast, West Seattle North, and West Seattle South). Elementary school students may choose any school in the district, but your child will receive priority assignment only when you choose your reference area school and register on time (dates vary according to school year, generally it's some time in February for elementary, and in March for middle and high schools). When more children apply to a school than space allows, students are assigned based on a series of "tiebreakers." In this order, a child will get priority if he/she has a sibling at the same school, lives in the school's reference area, positively impacts the school's racial integration, lives closer to the school than other students who have applied, or wins a random lottery.

In middle school and high school, students are also assigned reference areas, and schools are grouped into geographic regions. Middle and high school students may also choose any school, and receive priority assignment if they register on time, as long as there are enough spots to accommodate all the students who want to go there. If too many students choose a particular school, the following tiebreakers are applied in this order: the student has a sibling at the same school, the student lives in the region (middle school only), the student positively impacts racial integration, the student lives closer to the school than another waiting student, or the student wins a random lottery.

To enroll your child in Seattle Public Schools, you must obtain a registration form by visiting one of the enrollment service centers or by calling 206-252-0760. You can also print the application from the district's web site at www.seattle schools.org. The centers can provide you with your child's reference area or cluster assignment. To complete the registration process, you must bring two proofs of address, such as a rent receipt, driver's license, or preprinted check, and your child's immunization records.

- **Bilingual Family Center**, Aki Kurose Middle School, 3928 S Graham St, Rm 104, 206-252-7750
- **North Enrollment Service Center**, Wilson Pacific Bldg, 1330 N 90th St, 206-252-4765
- **South Enrollment Service Center**, Columbia Annex Bldg, 3100 S Alaska St, 206-252-6800

If you can register your child for school during the regular enrollment period (February for elementary, March for middle and high school), you have a much better chance to receive your first choice school assignment. All applications received before the period deadline are processed together and each carries equal weight. After the regular enrollment period ends, applications are processed on a "first-come, first-served" basis. Some schools fill up quickly based on special programs or popularity; others simply have smaller buildings and cannot accommodate as many students. Alternative schools and classes, such as honors, special education, multi-cultural or bilingual programs, often have additional requirements that restrict enrollment.

An important element of the registration program is the appeals process. If your child does not receive his/her first-choice school, you may appeal to the school district and, if necessary, request a hearing before the Student Assignment Appeals Board. It is always worth taking this step if you are truly dissatisfied with your child's school assignment. Grounds for appeal include medical or psychological concerns, extreme hardship, and district failure to follow district guidelines.

While the Enrollment Service Centers can provide information on any of the Seattle Public Schools, another excellent resource for statistics and information on schools and programs is *The Seattle Times School Guide*, which contains information on more than 600 private and public schools in the greater Seattle area. The guide is on the web at http://community.seattletimes.nwsource.com/ schoolguide. In addition, you may want to contact SchoolMatch in Westerville, Ohio, to request its report on Seattle schools. The report, which costs $34, will include information on student-teacher ratios, test scores, and even property values in your chosen neighborhood.

All of the above mentioned resources, as well as some other Seattle Public Schools resources, are listed here.

- **SchoolMatch**, 800-992-5323, 614-890-1573, www.schoolmatch.com
- **Seattle Public Schools**, P.O. Box 19116, Seattle, WA 98109-1116, 206-252-0010, www.seattleschools.org
- **Advanced Learning**, 206-252-0130
- **Automated Enrollment Services Line**, 206-252-0410
- **Appeals**, 206-252-0586
- **Bilingual Services**, 206-252-7750
- **Special Education Services**, 206-252-0055
- **Transportation Services**, 206-252-0900
- **Wait List Automated Info Line**, 206-252-0212

## SURROUNDING COMMUNITIES

For information on public schools outside the city of Seattle, contact your local school district, or visit its web site. A selection of districts is listed here:

- **Auburn School District**, 915 4th St NE, Auburn, WA 98002, 253-931-4900, www.auburn.wednet.edu

- **Bellevue Public Schools**, P.O. Box 90010, Bellevue, WA 98009-9010, 425-456-4000, www.bsd405.org
- **Bremerton School District**, 134 N Marion Ave, Bremerton, WA 98132, 360-478-5151, www.bremertonschools.org
- **Edmonds School District**, 22901 106th Ave W, Lynnwood, WA 98036, 425-670-7000, www.edmonds.wednet.edu
- **Everett Public Schools**, 4730 Colby Ave, Everett, WA 98203, 425-385-4000, www.everett.k12.wa.us
- **Federal Way Public Schools**, 31405 18th Ave S, Federal Way, WA 98003, 253-945-2000, www.fwsd.wednet.edu
- **Highline Public Schools**, 15675 Ambaum Blvd SW, Burien, WA 98166, 206-433-0111, www.hsd401.org
- **Issaquah School District**, 565 NW Holly St, Issaquah, WA 98027, 425-837-7000, www.issaquah.wednet.edu
- **Kent School District**, 12033 SE 256th St, Kent, WA 98031, 253-373-7000, www.kent.wednet.edu
- **Lake Washington School District**, P.O. Box 97039, Redmond, WA 98073, 425-702-3200, www.lkwash.wednet.edu
- **Mercer Island School District**, 4160 86th Ave SE, Mercer Island, WA 98040, 206-236-3330, www.misd.k12.wa.us
- **Northshore School District**, 18315 Bothell Way NE, Bothell, WA 98011, 425-489-6000, www.nsd.org
- **Renton School District**, 700 SW 7th St, Renton, WA 98055, 425-204-2300, www.renton.wednet.edu
- **Shoreline Public Schools**, 18560 1st Ave NE, Shoreline, WA 98155, 206-361-4412, www.shorelineschools.org
- **Tacoma Public Schools**, P.O. Box 1357, Tacoma, WA 98401-1357, 253-571-1000, www.tacoma.k12.wa.us
- **Tahoma School District**, 25720 Maple Valley-Black Diamond Rd SE, Maple Valley, WA 98038, 425-413-3400, www.tahoma.wednet.edu
- **Tukwila School District**, 4640 S 144th St, Tukwila, WA 98168, 206-901-8000, www.tukwila.wednet.edu
- **Vashon Island School District**, 18850 103rd Ave SW, Vashon, WA 98070, 206-408-8100, www.vashonsd.wednet.edu

## PRIVATE SCHOOLS

If you are considering a private school there are many options in the greater Seattle area, most of which provide bus service. A few of the private schools in Seattle and its surrounding communities are listed here; check the Yellow Pages for more. Entrance requirements vary widely. Be sure to call or visit the school for more information.

- **Annie Wright School** (P–12), 827 N Tacoma Ave, Tacoma, 253-272-2216, www. aw.org; situated on Commencement Bay, Annie Wright is a co-ed day school through grade 8 and an all-girls' boarding/day school grades 9 through 12.
- **Bellevue Christian School** (P–12), 1601 98th Ave NE, Bellevue, 425-454-4402, www.bellevuechristian.org; with a comprehensive program that serves preschool through 12th-grade students, Bellevue Christian educates close to 1,350 children, and promotes socioeconomic and religious diversity.
- **Bishop Blanchet High School** (9–12), 8200 Wallingford Ave N, 206-527-7711, www.blanchet.k12.wa.us; a Catholic, college preparatory school, Bishop Blanchet sends approximately 98% of its graduates on to higher education. The north Seattle high school is a member of the Class AAA division of the Seattle Metro League.
- **Bush School** (K–12), 405 36th Ave E, 206-326-7736, www.bush.edu, commands nine acres in the Madison Valley neighborhood. Emphasis is placed on cooperative learning, with students working in groups to reach common goals.
- **Cascade Christian Schools** (P–12), 815 21st St SE, Puyallup, 253-841-1776, www.cascadechristianschool.org, support early childhood centers and elementary schools in Puyallup, Spanaway, and Tacoma, as well as Cascade Christian Junior/Senior High School in Puyallup.
- **Charles Wright Academy** (K–12), 7723 Chambers Creek Rd W, Tacoma, 253-620-8300, www.charleswright.org, is located on 90 acres in suburban Tacoma. The school provides a challenging college-prep curriculum at all grade levels.
- **The Clearwater School** (ages 4–19), 11006 34th Ave NE, 206-306-0060, www. clearwaterschool.com, is part of a national network of Sudbury Schools, modeled after the Sudbury Valley School in Massachusetts. Students direct their own activities and engage in a participatory democracy.
- **Concordia Lutheran School** (K–8), 7040 36th Ave NE, 206-525-7407, http:// concordia.seattle.wa.us; owned and operated by the Lutheran School Association of Greater Seattle, Concordia offers a strong Christian atmosphere where children develop academically, socially, and physically.
- **Holy Family School** (K–8), 505 17th St SE, Auburn, 253-833-5130, www. hfsauburn.com; the philosophy of this Catholic school is that parents have the primary responsibility for their child's education, and that the church, school, and community complement this role.
- **Holy Names Academy** (9–12), 728 21st Ave E, 206-323-4272, www.holynames-sea.org; a Catholic, college preparatory school for girls, is a three-time winner of the US Department of Education's blue ribbon of excellence. Athletes compete in the Class AAA division of the Seattle Metro League.

- **Islamic School of Seattle** (P–6), 720 25th Ave, 206-329-5735, www.iss-chm. com; founded in 1980, the Islamic School has since added an accredited Montessori preschool and a full-immersion Arabic program.
- **The Jewish Day School of Metropolitan Seattle** (P–8), 15749 NE 4th St, Bellevue, 425-460-0200, www.jds.org; the Jewish Day School provides a challenging curriculum of general and Jewish studies, along with enrichment opportunities.
- **King's School** (P–12), 19303 Fremont Ave N, Seattle, 206-546-7218; King's West (P–12), 4012 Chico Way NW, Bremerton, 360-377-7700, www.kingsschools.org, serves Seattle and Kitsap families seeking a college preparatory program that emphasizes strong academics, positive discipline, and Christian faith.
- **Lakeside School** (5–12), 14050 1st Ave NE, 206-368-3600, www.lakesideschool. org, is a co-ed school that enrolls about 700 students, with an average student to teacher ratio of 7.5 to 1, and an average class size of just 16 students. The school's most famous alumni are Microsoft co-founders and Seattle residents Bill Gates and Paul Allen.
- **Meridian School** (K–5), 4649 Sunnyside Ave N, 206-632-7154, www. meridianschool.edu; located in the Wallingford neighborhood, Meridian School combines its academic curriculum with thematic studies like raising salmon or recreating a pioneer encampment.
- **The Northwest School** (6–12), 1415 Summit Ave, 206-682-7309, www. northwestschool.org, is a college preparatory day and boarding school that offers cross-disciplinary study in the humanities, sciences, and performing and fine arts.
- **St. Edward** (P–8), 4212 S Mead St, 206-725-1774, www.saintedwardseattle. org; instruction at St. Edward takes place in multi-age, non-graded classrooms. Catholic values and church teachings permeate all aspects of the school community.
- **St. Joseph School** (K–8), 700 18th Ave E, 206-329-3260, www.stjosephsea.org; classrooms at this Catholic school are all equipped with e-mail and internet capabilities.
- **Seattle Jewish Community School** (K–5), 7330 35th Ave NE, 206-522-5212, www.sjcs.net; at SJCS, girls and boys participate equally in all areas of academics and Jewish ritual. The school stresses parental involvement and a non-competitive environment.
- **Seattle Lutheran High School** (9–12), 4141 41st Ave SW, 206-937-7722, www. seattlelutheran.org; the mission of this Lutheran high school in West Seattle is to prepare students for a lifetime of learning, service, and leadership.
- **Seattle Preparatory School** (9–12), 2400 11th Ave E, 206-324-0400, www. seaprep.org, provides college preparatory instruction in the Jesuit tradition. Known for its athletic success, the school is a member of the Class AAA division of the Seattle Metro League.

- **Seattle Urban Academy** (9–12), 3800 S Othello Ave, 206-723-0333, www. seattleurbanacademy.org; specializes in meeting the needs of at-risk students, helping them earn full or partial credit toward their high school diploma.
- **Shoreline Christian School** (P–12), 2400 NE 147th St, Shoreline, 206-364-7777, www.shorelinechristian.org, is a multi-denominational Christian school.
- **Soundview School** (P–8), 6515 196th St SW, Lynnwood, 425-778-8572, www. soundview.org; in 2001 Soundview added five acres to its campus, and built a separate middle school to accommodate the upper grades.
- **University Preparatory Academy** (6–12), 8000 25th Ave NE, 206-525-2714, www.universityprep.org; with fewer than 500 students, University Prep stresses small classes, a commitment to diversity, and a balanced curriculum.

## MONTESSORI SCHOOLS

Dr. Maria Montessori developed the Montessori theory of education in the early 1900s. The Montessori Foundation estimates that there are more than 4,000 schools in the United States that follow her strategies. For information about the Montessori philosophy, visit the Pacific Northwest Montessori Association's web site at www.pnma.org, or call 800-550-PNMA. The following is a partial list of Montessori schools in Seattle:

- **Chelsea House Montessori**, 13742 30th Ave NE, 206-363-5212, http:// chelseahouse.tripod.com
- **Children's Niche Montessori**, 1412 NW 67th St, 206-782-1886
- **Learning Tree Montessori**, 1721 15th Ave, 206-324-4788
- **Mary's Montessori Preschool**, 7925 10th Ave SW, 206-767-4314
- **Montessori Garden**, 8301 5th Ave NE, 206-524-8307, http://montessorigarden. qwestdex.com
- **Montessori School of Seattle**, 720 18th Ave E, 206-325-0497, www. montessorischoolofseattle.com
- **Mt. Baker Montessori**, 2714 34th Ave S, 206-723-8265
- **Northwest Montessori School**, 7400 25th Ave NE, 206-524-4244; 4910 Phinney Ave N, 206-634-1347; 8443 34th Ave SW, 206-933-8557; 8501 SE 40th, Mercer Island, 206-232-4595, www.northwestmontessori.org
- **Pacific First Montessori**, 1420 5th Ave, #300, 206-682-6878, www. pacificfirstmontessori.com
- **Sunnyside Montessori**, 3939 S Americus St, 206-725-5756
- **Veranda Montessori School**, 526 N 105th St, 206-782-5250
- **Wedgewood Montessori Preschool**, 6556 35th Ave NE, 206-525-4432
- **West Seattle Montessori** (K–8), 4536 38th Ave SW, 206-935-0427, www. westseattlemontessori.com

## WALDORF SCHOOLS

Waldorf education is based on the philosophy of Austrian philosopher Rudolf Steiner. For more information on the Waldorf method, visit the Association of Waldorf Schools of North America at www.awsna.org. The following is a list of Waldorf schools in Western Washington:

- **Hazel Wolf High School**, 160 John St, 206-522-2644, www.hwhs.org
- **Madrona School**, 105 Winslow Way W, Bainbridge Island, 206-855-8041, www.madronaschool.org
- **Seattle Waldorf School**, 2728 NE 100th St, 206-524-5320, www.seattlewaldorf.org
- **Three Cedars School**, 556 124th Ave NE, Bellevue, 425-401-9874, www.threecedars.org

## HOMESCHOOLING

For a variety of reasons, homeschooling is attractive to many parents, and the state of Washington makes it fairly easy to choose that option. All you'll need to do is file a Declaration of Intent with your local school district and be sure you meet the qualifications for homeschooling. To qualify you must teach only your own child(ren) and have completed one year, or 45 credits, of college. If you don't have the college education you can be supervised by a qualified teacher for an hour a week, or complete a course in home-based instruction or be deemed qualified by your local school district superintendent. You will be required to have your children tested or assessed once a year and to meet the minimum hours for instruction, though how you construct those hours is up to you. You can request information and a forms packet from the Seattle School District's **Homeschool Resource Center** by calling 206-252-4720, or download the declaration of intent from the web site at www.seattleschools.org/schools/hrc. The center also provides classes that homeschoolers can attend, a computer lab, library, gym and many other resources for support, encouragement and guidance for homeschooling families.

There are many homeschool support groups in the area with many different philosophies, as well as online sources of information. A few of these are listed here:

- **Washington Homeschool Association**, 6632 S 191st Pl, Ste E100, Kent, 425-251-0439, www.washhomeschool.org
- **Homeschool Resource Center**, 1330 N 90th St, Bldg 200, 206-252-4720, www.seattleschools.org/schools/hrc
- **Home Education Magazine**, 800-236-3278, www.homeedmag.com
- **Homeschoolers' Support Association**, 425-687-1449, www.hsa-wa.org

# ONLINE SCHOOLS

Once the sole domain of higher learning, online schools are slowly gaining ground at the high school, middle school, and even elementary school level. Some offer courses designed to supplement enrollment in a traditional school, or for homeschoolers, and some are completely online public schools offering valid high school diplomas. Depending on enrollment status and type of school, fees may be charged. There are no fees to attend public schools, even virtually.

- **Digital Learning Commons**, 4507 University Way NE, Ste 204, Seattle, 206-616-9940, www.learningcommons.org; grades 9–12
- **Evergreen Internet Academy**, 13501 NE 28th St, Vancouver, 360-604-4057, http://eia.egreen.wednet.edu; grades 7–12
- **Insight School of Washington**, 12011 Bel-Red Rd, Bellevue, 866-800-0017, www.go2ischool.net; grades 9–12
- **Internet Academy**, 32020 1st Ave S, Ste 109, Federal Way, 253-945-2230, www.iacademy.org; grades K–12
- **Washington Virtual Academy**, 1584 McNeil St, Ste 200, DuPont, 253-964-1068, www.wava.org; grades K–8

# HIGHER EDUCATION

In some ways, Seattle is one big college town. It is the site of the state's largest public university, the University of Washington, and home to many other well-known private and community colleges. You can become a doctor, a diver, a lawyer, or a massage therapist without ever leaving the city limits. Educational programs abound outside the city as well.

The state's Direct Transfer Agreement makes it convenient for students to transfer from any Washington community college to one of the state's six four-year universities. The system works well for students who prefer to earn an Associate's degree before choosing a university, or who need to improve their grades a bit before applying to a four-year school. The agreement isn't a guarantee of admission, however, so it's best to check with the four-year college of your choice to discover any additional admission requirements.

In addition to traditional colleges, there are many special interest, vocational, and technical programs. Here is a partial list of schools located in the Seattle area.

## SEATTLE

- **Antioch University**, 2326 6th Ave, 206-441-5352, www.antiochsea.edu, is a five-campus system that emphasizes an interdisciplinary curriculum. In addition to undergraduate courses, the college offers graduate programs in environment and community, management, whole systems design, and organizational psychology.

- **Art Institute of Seattle**, 2323 Elliott Ave, 206-448-0900, 800-275-2471, www. ais.edu; students here learn from artists and professionals in a hands-on environment. AIS offers either Associate of Applied Arts degrees or diploma certificates through the schools of design, fashion, culinary arts, and media arts.
- **Ashmead College**, 2111 N Northgate Way, 206-527-0807, www. ashmeadcollege.com, provides instruction in massage and fitness training, as well as a new program for aromatherapy and spa treatments. Campuses are also located in Everett, Tacoma, and Vancouver.
- **City University**, 2150 N 107th St, 206-364-4228, www.cityu.edu, serves working adults who want to continue their education without interrupting their careers. CU offers more than 50 undergraduate and graduate programs, and has campuses in Bellevue, Everett, Renton, and Tacoma.
- **Cornish College of the Arts**, 1000 Lenora St, 206-726-5151, www.cornish.edu, offers Bachelor of Fine Arts and Bachelor of Music degrees in art, dance, design, music, theater, performance production, and humanities and sciences.
- **North Seattle Community College**, 9600 College Way N, 206-527-3600, www. northseattle.edu; located in a pleasant concrete building near Northgate Mall, NSCC is a versatile community college that offers day and evening classes for undergraduates and professionals. The school's continuing education program offers a variety of computer courses for all levels of users.
- **Seattle Central Community College**, 1701 Broadway, 206-587-3800, http:// seattlecentral.org; a school of 10,000 students, SCCC is located in the Capitol Hill neighborhood, offering both undergraduate and professional education classes. In 2001, *TIME* magazine named SCCC as one of its four "Colleges of the Year" for its success in helping first-year students make the transition into college life.
- **Seattle Pacific University**, 3307 3rd Ave W, 206-281-2000, www.spu.edu; located at the north end of Queen Anne, SPU is a private Christian university with a picturesque campus, offering degrees in liberal arts, fine arts, business, and education, among others.
- **Seattle University**, 900 Broadway, 206-296-6000, www.seattleu.edu; an independent Jesuit university located on First Hill, SU offers courses in a wide variety of subjects, including graduate programs in law, nursing, and software engineering, as well as undergraduate degrees in philosophy, theology, and the sciences.
- **South Seattle Community College**, 6000 16th Ave SW, 206-764-5300, www. southseattle.edu; located in West Seattle, SSCC offers both vocational and academic classes. The college's Duwamish Center provides apprentice-related training and first aid instruction. The Home and Family Life department is here as well.

- **University of Washington**, 17th Ave NE and NE 45th St, 206-543-2100, www. washington.edu; founded in 1861, the University of Washington is a public research university attended by about 40,000 students. Known internationally for its biomedical research, the UW also has outstanding graduate programs in business and law, and is a respected undergraduate institution. The university hosts guest speakers, dance troupes, and musicians throughout the year. In the fall, the Husky football team attracts alumni and sports fans from across the state.

## EASTSIDE

- **Bastyr University**, 14500 Juanita Dr N, Kenmore, 425-823-1300, www.bastyr. edu; a renowned natural medicine university offering undergraduate and graduate degrees in fields ranging from naturopathic medicine and nutrition to acupuncture and oriental medicine and exercise science.
- **Bellevue Community College**, 3000 Landerholm Circle SE, Bellevue, 425-564-1000, www.bcc.ctc.edu; one of western Washington's most popular two-year colleges, BCC offers A.A., A.S., and A.A.S. degrees in a variety of academic programs.
- **Lake Washington Technical College**, 11605 132nd Ave NE, Kirkland, 425-739-8100, www.lwtc.ctc.edu, offers job-training and professional development programs, and serves as a community resource, featuring a job placement center, library, dental clinic, and arboretum.

## NORTH

- **Cascadia Community College**, 18345 Campus Way NE, Bothell, 425-352-8000, www.cascadia.ctc.edu, is the state's newest community college, offering two-year degrees, certificate programs, and continuing education.
- **Edmonds Community College**, 20000 68th Ave W, Lynnwood, www.edcc. edu; ECC's 50-acre campus is located just 15 miles north of Seattle. The college allows students the opportunity to combine weekend, online, and evening classes to fit busy schedules.
- **Everett Community College**, 2000 Tower St, Everett, 425-388-9100, www. evcc.ctc.edu; in 1999, ECC added a state-of-the-art instructional technology center to its campus, which also includes a fitness and sports center and an applied technology training center.
- **Shoreline Community College**, 16101 Greenwood Ave N, Shoreline, 206-546-4101, www.shoreline.edu; boasts a gorgeous, 83-acre campus just 10 miles north of downtown Seattle. More than 12,000 full- and part-time students benefit from small classes and the surrounding recreational and cultural opportunities.

- **Western Washington University**, 516 High St, Bellingham, 360-650-3000, www.wwu.edu; just 90 miles north of Seattle, WWU commands 200 acres in scenic Bellingham, a bayside city of 65,000. Specializing in the liberal arts, WWU consistently ranks high on *U.S. News & World Report*'s list of regional public universities.

## SOUTH

- **Evergreen State College**, 2700 Evergreen Pkwy NW, Olympia, 360-866-6000, www.evergreen.edu; with a reputation as the state's most liberal and laid-back college, Evergreen State offers team-taught, multi-disciplinary programs that draw from many areas of study.
- **Green River Community College**, 12401 SE 320th St, Auburn, 253-833-9111, www.greenriver.edu, offers A.A. degrees in a variety of disciplines, from accounting to wastewater technology.
- **Highline Community College**, 2400 S 240th St, Des Moines, 206-878-3710, www.highline.ctc.edu; Highline's courses of study are divided into academic transfer, professional/technical, pre-college study, and extended learning.
- **Pacific Lutheran University**, Tacoma, 253-531-6900, www.plu.edu; located in Tacoma's suburban Parkland neighborhood, PLU includes a College of Arts and Sciences, professional schools of the arts, business, education, nursing and physical education, and both graduate and continuing education programs.
- **Tacoma Community College**, 6501 S 19th St, 253-566-5000, www.tacomacc.edu, offers a range of academic and occupational degrees, worker retraining programs, and continuing education classes.
- **University of Puget Sound**, 1500 N Warner St, Tacoma, 253-879-3100, www.ups.edu; UPS is a private liberal arts college with less than 3,000 students, mostly undergraduates.

## CONTINUING EDUCATION

Seattle is the most educated city in the US, according to figures released in 2006 by the Census Bureau, but the learning doesn't stop here with a college degree. Non-degree continuing education classes are very popular and offered by most of the community colleges, as well as individuals and studios all over the city. You can take a class on everything from biodiesel basics and bookkeeping to Thai cooking and tying knots. Two good sources of continuing education classes are:

- **ASUW Experimental College**, University of Washington Husky Union Building, G-10, 206-543-4375, http://depts.washington.edu/asuwxpcl
- **Discover U**, 2150 N 107th St, 206-365-0400, www.discoveru.org

S HOPPING IS GOOD IN SEATTLE AND MADE EVEN BETTER IN RECENT years with the addition of upscale stores to newly remodeled malls and shopping squares. Bellevue Square and University Village in particular have become destinations for the fashionable and affluent. Seattle's downtown shopping core also has been made more cosmopolitan with the arrival of stores like Kenneth Cole, Coach, Tommy Hilfiger, and Tiffany & Co. Heady espresso stands, swank cocktail lounges, and trendy eateries complete the day out.

Most of the shopping locations listed in this chapter are found in Seattle or in nearby towns such as Lynnwood, Tukwila or the Eastside, but some may be in surrounding communities just a bit farther away, like the bargain-filled outlet malls in North Bend and Mount Vernon. Unless otherwise noted, all of the following are Seattle addresses.

## SHOPPING DISTRICTS

While nearly every neighborhood in Seattle has its own small retail core, the following **Seattle districts** are well known for their shopping opportunities.

- If you are in a spending mood, some of the best shopping **downtown** can be found in and around the soaring Pacific Place mall at the intersection of 6th Avenue and Pine Street, and just west is the equally impressive Nordstrom flagship store. Westlake Center at 4th Avenue and Pine Street offers four floors of shopping and dining as well as a popular outdoor plaza. For over a decade this area of downtown has been undergoing a concerted and expensive retail makeover as many upscale, locally owned retailers, as well as big names in international fashion and entertainment, have located here.
- Originally a simple farmers' market, the popular and famous **Pike Place Market** is located downtown at 1st Avenue and Pike Street. In addition to the traditional fish, meats, fruits and vegetables, stalls are filled with local

arts, crafts, flowers, teas, and clothing. Surrounding the marketplace, unique clothing shops, gardening and home decorating stores, antique malls and importers share space with tiny restaurants and fragrant bakeries.

- Located at the north end of Fremont Bridge, the **Fremont** shopping district is known for unique boutiques, vintage clothing stores, funky bakeries, and the local Red Hook Brewery. Fremont is a great location to visit for a strong cup of coffee and enjoyable window shopping. Every Sunday the Fremont Market offers a European-style flea market that attracts treasure hunters from all over the city.

- Capitol Hill's busy **Broadway** shopping district runs along Broadway, from East Roy Street to Madison Street. Usually crowded until late at night, the district has almost as many restaurants, cafes, and bakeries as retail stores. Shops cater to a young crowd, with several new and used music stores, bookstores such as the popular Bailey-Coy Books, costume jewelry and bead shops, tattoo and body-piercing parlors, movie theaters, and funky clothing stores.

## MALLS

Most Seattle-area malls offer a combination of shopping options, from reasonably priced, practical stops, to high-end department stores, to one-of-a-kind boutiques—though not much in the way of discount stores. In the last decade, specialty retailers and popular national chains replaced many of the malls' bargain-oriented shops and dollar stores, which are now often located outside the malls.

- **Alderwood Mall**, I-5 and Alderwood Mall Blvd; 184th St SW, Lynnwood, 425-771-1121, www.alderwoodmall.com
- **Bellevue Square**, NE 8th St and Bellevue Way; 302 Bellevue Square, Bellevue, 425-454-8096, www.bellevuesquare.com
- **Crossroads Shopping Center**, NE 8th St and 156th Ave NE; 15600 NE 8th St, Bellevue, 425-644-1111, www.crossroadsbellevue.com
- **Everett Mall**, I-5 and Everett Mall Way; 1402 SE Everett Mall Way, Everett, 425-355-1771, www.everettmall.org
- **Factoria Mall**, I-405 and I-90; 4055 Factoria Mall SE, Bellevue, 425-641-8282
- **Lakewood Towne Center**, 5731 Main St SW, Lakewood, 253-584-6191
- **Northgate Mall**, I-5 and Northgate Way; 401 NE Northgate Way, Seattle, 206-362-4777, www.northgateshoppingctr.com
- **Pacific Place**, 6th Ave and Pine St; 600 Pine St, Seattle, 206-405-2655, www.pacificplaceseattle.com
- **Redmond Town Center**, NE 74th St and 164th Ave NE; 16945 NE 74th St, Redmond, 425-867-0808, www.shopredmondtowncenter.com

- **SeaTac Mall**, S 320th St and Pacific Highway S; 1928 S SeaTac Mall, Federal Way, 253-839-6150, www.seatacmall.com
- **University Village**, 25th Ave NE and Montlake Ave NE; 2673 University Village, Seattle, 206-523-0622, www.uvillage.com
- **Westfield Shoppingtown Southcenter** (formerly named and still referred to as the Southcenter Mall), I-5 and I-405; 633 Southcenter Mall, Tukwila, 206-246-7400, http://westfield.com/southcenter
- **Westlake Center**, 4th Ave and Pine St; 400 Pine St, Seattle, 206-467-1600, www.westlakecenter.com

## FACTORY DISCOUNT STORES AND OUTLET MALLS

Great bargains can be found in factory discount stores, which often stock over-runs and imperfect goods. Pay attention to price and merchandise quality. Most of these malls are quite a drive from Seattle, so check the locations on a map or call ahead for directions before you leave the city.

- **Centralia Factory Outlet Center**, 1342 Lum Rd, Centralia, 360-736-3327, www.centraliafactoryoutlet.com
- **Factory Stores at North Bend**, 461 South Fork Ave SW, North Bend, 425-888-4505
- **Birch Bay Square**, 3400 Birch Bay–Lynden Rd, Custer, 360-366-3128, www.birchbaysquare.com
- **Prime Outlets at Burlington**, 448 Fashion Way, Burlington, 360-757-3548, www.primeoutlets.com
- **SuperMall of the Great Northwest**, Hwy 18 and Hwy 167, Auburn, 253-833-9500, www.supermall.com

## WAREHOUSE STORES

Warehouse stores now offer good deals on just about anything, from clothing and groceries to furniture and appliances. One caveat: you have to buy many items in bulk, so unless you have room for 100 rolls of toilet paper... Both of the warehouse chains listed here have membership requirements; call for more details.

- **Costco**, 4401 4th Ave S, 206-622-3136; 1175 N 205th St, 206-546-0480; 10200 19th Ave SE, Everett, 425-379-7451; 35100 Enchanted Parkway S, Federal Way, 253-874-3652; 3900 20th St E, Fife, 253-719-1953; 1801 10th Ave NW, Issaquah, 425-313-0965; 8629 120th Ave NE, Kirkland, 425-827-1693; 19105 Hwy 99, Lynwood, 425-640-7700; 1201 39th SW, Puyallup, 253-445-7543; 10000 Mickleberry Rd NW, Silverdale, 360-692-1140; 2219 S 37th St, Tacoma, 253-475-

2093; 1160 Saxon Dr, Tukwila, 206-575-9191; 24008 Snohomish-Woodinville Rd SE, Woodinville, 425-806-7700, www.costco.com
- **Sam's Club**, 13550 Aurora Ave N, 206-362-6700; 1101 Super Mall Way, Auburn, 253-333-1026; 901 S Grady Way, Renton, 425-793-7443, www.samsclub.com

## DEPARTMENT STORES

Nordstrom (not Nordstroms) originated in Seattle, and still dominates the local market for high-end clothing and shoes. However, Seattle offers many alternatives for both home and personal shopping. A few of the largest stores are here:

- **Macy's**, 1601 3rd Ave, 206-506-6000; 7400 166th Ave NE, Redmond, 425-498-6000; Alderwood Mall, 425-712-6000; Bellevue Square, 425-688-6000; Northgate Shopping Center, 206-440-6000; Southcenter Mall, 425-656-6000, www.macys.com
- **Gottschalks**, Northgate Mall, 206-367-7690, www.gottschalks.com
- **Nordstrom**, 500 Pine St, 206-628-2111; Alderwood Mall, 425-771-5755; Bellevue Square, 425-455-5800; Northgate Shopping Center, 206-634-8800; Southcenter Mall, 206-246-0400, www.nordstrom.com
- **JC Penney**, Alderwood Mall, 425-771-9555; Bellevue Square, 425-454-8599; Northgate Shopping Center, 206-361-2500; Puyallup, 253-845-6669; Southcenter Mall, 206-246-0850, www.jcpenney.com
- **Sears Roebuck & Co.**, 76 S Lander, 206-344-4830; 15711 Aurora Ave N, 206-440-2000; Everett, 425-355-7070; Federal Way, 253-529-8200; Lynnwood, 425-771-2212; Puyallup, 253-770-5700; Redmond, 425-644-6749; Tukwila, 206-241-3422, www.sears.com

## DISCOUNT DEPARTMENT STORES

Discount chains, such as Kmart, Target, and Wal-Mart, do business throughout the Seattle area. Check the Yellow Pages for the nearest location of your favorite. Below are a few of the discount department stores in the region.

- **Fred Meyer**, 18325 Aurora Ave N, 206-546-0720; 100 NW 85th St, 206-784-9600; 915 NW 45th St, 206-297-4300; 13000 Lake City Way NE, 206-440-2400; 12221 120th Ave NE, Kirkland, 425-820-3200, www.fredmeyer.com
- **Kmart**, 13200 Aurora Ave N, 206-363-6319; Bremerton, 360-377-3872; Everett, 425-353-8103; Kent, 253-852-9071, www.kmart.com
- **Marshalls**, 15801 Westminster Way N, 206-367-8520; 2600 SW Barton St, 206-933-3055; Lynnwood, 425-771-6045; Redmond, 425-644-2429, www.marshallsonline.com

- **Mervyn's**, Bellevue, 425-643-6554; Lynnwood, 425-672-7765; Redmond, 425-558-9500, www.mervyns.com
- **Ross Dress for Less**, 301 Pike St, 206-623-6781; 13201-B Aurora Ave N, 206-367-6030; 332 NE Northgate Way, 206-364-2111; Bellevue, 425-644-2433; Everett, 425-356-9970; Federal Way, 253-941-2122; Kent, 253-852-6442; Kirkland, 425-814-9798; Issaquah, 425-313-9616; Tukwila, 206-575-0110, www.rossstores. com
- **Target**, 302 NE Northgate Way, 206-494-0897; 2800 SW Barton, 206-932-1153; Bellevue, 425-562-0830; Everett, 425-353-3167; Federal Way, 253-839-3399; Issaquah, 425-392-3357; Kent, 253-850-9710; Lynnwood, 425-670-1435; Redmond, 425-556-9533; Tukwila, 206-575-0682; Woodinville, 425-482-6410, www.target.com
- **Wal-Mart**, Auburn, 253-735-7855; Bremerton, 360-698-2889; Everett, 425-923-1740; Federal Way, 253-941-9974; Lynnwood, 425-741-9445; Renton, 425-227-0407, www.walmartstores.com

# HOUSEHOLD SHOPPING

## APPLIANCES/ELECTRONICS/COMPUTERS & SOFTWARE

For your stereo, television, cellular phone, home theater, and technology purchases, there is a wide variety of electronics and computer stores in Seattle. Large department and warehouse stores such as Sears and Costco are worth a visit when shopping for home audio or video options and major appliances. All of the big box chain stores are represented, such as **Best Buy** (www.bestbuy.com), **Circuit City** (www.circuitcity.com), **Radio Shack** (www.radioshack.com), **Comp USA** (www.compusa.com), **Magnolia Hi-Fi** (www.magnoliahifi.com), and **Fry's Electronics** (www.frys.com). One Seattle location well known for its concentration of electronics stores is just north of the University District on Roosevelt Way NE, between NE Ravenna Boulevard and NE 65th Street. The following list is a sampling of specialty electronics and appliance stores in the area:

- **Albert Lee Appliances**, 1476 Elliott Ave W, 206-282-2110, www.albertlee appliance.com
- **The Audio Connection**, 5621-A University Way NE, 206-524-7251, www. audioconnectionseattle.com
- **Definitive Audio**, 6206 Roosevelt Way NE, 206-524-6633; 14405 NE 20th, Bellevue, 425-746-3188, www.definitive.com
- **Direct Buying Service,** 1749 1st Ave S, 206-783-2980, www.directbuying service.com
- **Hawthorne Stereo**, 6303 Roosevelt Way NE, 206-522-9609, www.haw thornestereo.com

- **The Mac Store**, 815 NE 45th St, 206-522-0220, www.thecomputerstore.com
- **Re-PC**, 1565 6th Ave S, 206-623-9151, www.repc.com
- **SpeakerLab**, 6220 Roosevelt Way NE, 206-523-2269, www.speakerlab.com
- **Stereo Warehouse**, 13728 Aurora Ave N, 206-365-5622, www.superstereowarehouse.com
- **Wiseman's Appliance & TV**, 2619 California Ave SW, 206-937-7400, www.wisemanappliance.com

## BEDS, BEDDING & BATH

Some area department stores sell bedding as well as beds. For their names, locations and phone numbers, see the previous entries under **Department Stores**.

- **All About Down**, 352 N 78th St, 206-784-3444, www.allaboutdown.com
- **Bed Bath & Beyond**, multiple locations, www.bedbathandbeyond.com
- **Bedrooms and More**, 300 NE 45th St, 206-633-4494, www.bedroomsandmore.com
- **Comfort by Akiko**, 705 E Pike St, 206-328-3173, www.comfortbyakiko.com
- **Feathered Friends**, 119 Yale Ave N, 206-292-2210, www.featheredfriends.com
- **French Quarter Linens**, 903 Western Ave, 206-223-9700, www.frenchquarterlinens.com
- **Linens 'n' Things**, multiple locations, www.lnt.com
- **Mattress Depot**, 823 NE Northgate Way, 206-361-4561
- **Sleep Country USA**, multiple locations, www.sleepcountry.com
- **Soaring Heart Futons**, 101 Nickerson St, Ste 400, 206-282-1717, www.soaringheart.com
- **Yves Delorme**, 2629 NE University Village, 206-523-8407, www.yvesdelorme.com

## CARPETS & RUGS

Carpet and flooring companies abound. Check the Yellow Pages for a complete listing. If it's an Oriental rug you need, a fun place to begin your search is in the many galleries and shops in the Pioneer Square area of downtown.

- **Carpet World**, 917 NW 49th St, 206-782-4856
- **The Color Store**, 1122 E Madison St, 206-328-3908
- **Consolidated Carpets**, 200 N 85th St, 206-789-7737, www.consolidatedcarpets.com
- **Driscoll Robbins Oriental Carpets**, 1002 Western Ave, 206-292-1115, www.driscollrobbins.com

- **Pande Cameron**, 333 Westlake Ave N, 206-624-6263; 13013 NE 20th, Bellevue, 425-885-1816, www.pande-cameron.com
- **Pitcher Brothers House of Carpets**, 5034 University Way NE, 206-522-4611, http://pitcherbrothers.com
- **Ravenna Interiors**, 2251 NE 65th St, 206-525-5794, http://ravennainteriors.com
- **Turabi Rug Gallery**, 112 1st Ave S, 206-624-7726; 7321 Greenwood Ave N, 206-782-9205, www.turabirugs.com
- **Yam Oriental Rugs**, 627 1st Ave, 206-622-2439, www.yamorientalrugs.com

## FURNITURE

A home furnishings store may be one of the first places you visit as you try to fill your new home or apartment. For a huge selection of reasonably priced contemporary furnishings, check out the IKEA store in Renton, south of Seattle. Many department stores offer good selections of traditional home furnishings. Call ahead for details, or check the newspaper for sales and special promotions. Catalog favorites, such as Pottery Barn, Restoration Hardware, and Crate and Barrel, allow consumers to shop in-person, by mail, or online.

- **Dania Home and Office**, 825 Western, 206-524-9611, www.daniafurniture.com
- **Deep Interior**, 1006 Western, 206-621-1380, www.deepinterior.com
- **Ethan Allen Home Interiors**, 2209 NE Bel-Red Rd, Redmond, 425-641-3133; 4029 Alderwood Mall Blvd, Lynnwood, 425-775-1901; 17333 Southcenter Pkwy, Tukwila, 206-575-4366, www.ethanallen.com
- **IKEA Home Furnishings**, 600 SW 43rd, Renton, 425-656-2980, www.ikea.com
- **Levitz Furniture**, 17601 Southcenter Pkwy, Tukwila, 206-575-0510, www.levitz.com
- **Masins Furniture**, 220 2nd Ave S, 206-622-5606; 10708 Main St, Bellevue, 425-450-9999, www.masins.com
- **McKinnon Furniture**, 1201 Western Ave, Ste 100, 206-622-6474, www.mckinnonfurniture.com
- **Miller-Pollard Interiors**, 2624 NE University Village, 206-527-8478, 206-325-3600, www.millerpollard.com
- **Norwalk–The Furniture Idea**, 1010 Western Ave, 206-622-0282, www.norwalkfurnitureidea.com
- **Olsen Furniture**, 5354 Ballard Ave NW, 206-782-6020, www.olsenfurniture.com

- **Pottery Barn**, 600 Pine St, 206-621-0276; 4645 University Village, 206-522-6860; 600 Pine St, 206-621-0276; 212 Bellevue Square, Bellevue, 425-451-0097; 3000 184th St SW, Lynnwood, 425-774-5441, www.potterybarn.com
- **Restoration Hardware**, 600 Pine St, 206-652-4545; 4635 University Village, 206-522-2775, www.restorationhardware.com

## HOUSEWARES

- **The Container Store**, 700 Bellevue Way NE, Bellevue, 425-453-7120, www.containerstore.com
- **Cost Plus Imports**, multiple locations, www.worldmarket.com
- **Crate and Barrel**, 2680 NE 49th St, 206-937-9939; 555 Bellevue Square NE, Bellevue, 425-646-8900, www.crateandbarrel.com
- **Mrs. Cooks**, 2685 NE University Village, 206-525-5008, www.mrscooks.com
- **Pier 1 Imports**, 905 Bellevue Way NE, Bellevue, 425-451-8002; 15725 Westminster Way N, 206-361-0984; 7231 170th Ave NE, Redmond, 425-882-2565, www.pier1.com
- **Pottery Barn**, 600 Pine St, 206-621-0276; 4645 University Village, 206-522-6860; 600 Pine St, 206-621-0276; 212 Bellevue Square, Bellevue, 425-451-0097; 3000 184th St SW, Lynnwood, 425-774-5441, www.potterybarn.com
- **Restoration Hardware**, 600 Pine St, 206-652-4545; 4635 University Village, 206-522-2775, www.restorationhardware.com
- **Sur La Table**, 84 Pine St, 206-448-2244; 90 Central Way, Kirkland, 425-827-1311, www.surlatable.com
- **Williams Sonoma**, 600 Pine St, 206-621-7405; 2530 NE University Village, 206-523-3733; 216 Bellevue Square, Bellevue, 425-454-7007, www.williamssonoma.com

## LAMPS & LIGHTING

- **Antique Lighting Company**, 8214 Greenwood Ave N, 206-622-8298, www.antiquelighting.com
- **Hansen Lamp and Shades**, 6510 Phinney Ave N, 206-783-6859; 10706 Lake City Way NE, 206-363-1635, www.hansenlamp.com
- **Harold's Lighting**, 1912 N 45th St, 206-633-2557, www.haroldslamps.com
- **Highlights**, 905 Western Ave, 206-382-9667, www.highlightslighting.com
- **Lamps Plus**, 11919 NE 8th St, Bellevue, 425-688-1033; 3611 196th St SW, Lynnwood, 425-775-4320; 16839 Southcenter Pkwy, Tukwila, 206-575-9110, www.lampsplus.com
- **Lighting Supply Inc.**, 2729 2nd Ave, 206-441-5075, www.lightingsupply.net

- **Seattle Lighting**, 222 2nd Ave S, 206-622-4736; 14505 NE 20th St, Bellevue, 425-455-2110; 6710 Tacoma Mall Blvd, Tacoma, 253-475-8730, www.seattlelighting.com

## HARDWARE & GARDEN CENTERS

For paint and wallpaper, light fixtures, landscaping supplies, and anything else you might need for your Saturday projects, the following list might be useful.

- **City People's**, 500 15th Ave E, 206-324-9510; 5440 Sand Point Way NE, 206-524-1200
- **Five Corners Hardware**, 305 W McGraw St, 206-282-5000
- **Hardwick's**, 4214 Roosevelt Way NE, 206-632-1203, www.ehardwicks.com
- **The Home Depot**, multiple locations, www.homedepot.com
- **Junction True Value Hardware**, 4747 44th Ave SW, 206-932-0450
- **Lowe's Home Improvement Warehouse**, multiple locations, www.lowes.com
- **Madison Park Hardware**, 1837 42nd Ave E, 206-322-5331
- **Magnolia Ace Hardware**, 2420 32nd Ave W, 206-282-1916
- **Magnolia Garden Center**, 3213 W Smith St, 206-284-1161, www.magnoliagarden.com
- **Molbak's**, 13625 NE 175th St, Woodinville, 425-483-5000, www.molbaks.com
- **Sky Nursery**, 18528 Aurora Ave N, 206-546-4851, www.skynursery.com
- **Stewart Lumber & Hardware**, 1761 Rainier Ave S, 206-324-5000
- **Swansons**, 9701 15th Ave NW, 206-782-2543, www.swansonsnursery.com
- **Stoneway Hardware & Supply**, 4318 Stone Way N, 206-545-6910
- **Tweedy & Popp Ace Hardware**, 1916 N 45th St, 206-632-2290
- **University Hardware**, 4731 University Way NE, 206-523-5353

## SECOND-HAND SHOPPING

Second-hand shopping is a favorite pastime of many Seattle residents. What better way to spend a drizzly afternoon than digging for treasures that cost so little? There are many antique and vintage stores in Seattle, particularly near the Pike Place Market and in the Greenwood, Ballard, and Fremont neighborhoods. Several towns beyond the city limits, most notably Duvall, Issaquah, and Snohomish, are known for their many antique stores. Also, check the Sunday newspapers for estate sales or auctions. Most are open to the public, and some also hold previews so you can judge whether to arrive early.

- **Area 51**, 401 E Pine St, 206-568-4782
- **Antika**, 8421 Greenwood Ave N, 206-789-6363

- **Antique Mall of West Seattle**, 4516 California Ave SW, 206-935-9774
- **Antiques at Pike Place**, 92 Stewart St, 206-441-9643
- **Aurora Antique Pavilion**, 24111 Hwy 99, Edmonds, 425-744-0566
- **Bogart Bremmer, & Bradley Antiques**, 8000 15th Ave NW, 206-783-7333, www.bbbantiques.com
- **Children's Hospital Thrift Stores**, 15835 Westminster Way N, 206-448-7609; 303 W Meeker, Kent, 253-850-8216; 15137 NE 24th, Redmond, 425-746-3092
- **Collective**, 5323 Ballard Ave NW, 206-782-1900, www.collectiveinballard.com
- **Goodwill**, multiple locations, www.seattlegoodwill.org/retail
- **Fremont Antique Mall**, 3419 Fremont Place N, 206-548-9140
- **Funtiques**, 1512 NE 65th St, 206-527-9575
- **Gilman Antique Gallery**, 625 NW Gilman Blvd, Issaquah, 425-391-6640
- **Pelayo Antiques**, 7601 Greenwood Ave N, 206-789-1999, www.pelayoantiques.com
- **Seattle Antique Market**, 1400 Alaskan Way, 206-623-6115, www.seattleantiquesmarket.com
- **Value Village**, multiple locations, www.valuevillage.com

# FOOD

Now comes the fun part, eating! Seattle has a great selection of eateries, ranging from greasy spoons to elegant seafood restaurants. Almost every neighborhood in Seattle has at least one espresso stand, a cafe or bakery, and a local pub or micro-brewery. Ask your neighbors for recommendations, check the newspapers for restaurant write-ups, or visit one of the web sites offering reviews by locals, such as **Yelp** (www.yelp.com), **Judy's Book** (www.judysbook.com), or **Citysearch** (www.seattle.citysearch.com).

At-home chefs are in luck too. In addition to the well-stocked supermarkets common in any city, Seattle has a nice selection of specialty grocers, food co-ops, farmers' markets, and fresh seafood markets.

## GROCERY STORES

Many of the large grocery stores in the city are open 24 hours, and most feature well-stocked delis and on-site bakeries. The current trend in the new and remodeled stores is to offer an in-house floral department, espresso stand, and a take-out food counter with sandwiches, salads, sushi, and hot entrees. Many have adjoining businesses such as bakery, bagel or coffee shops, and small bank branches. **Trader Joes** (www.traderjoes.com), **Thriftway** (www.thriftway.com), and **Albertson's** (www.albertsons.com), each have several locations throughout the city, but the predominant chains are **QFC** (www.qfconline.com) and **Fred**

**Meyer** (www.fredmeyer.com), both owned by food giant Kroger, and **Safeway** (www.safeway.com). Selection, good sales, and convenience are consumers' oft-sited reasons for shopping at large chains; some even have in-store pharmacies. But don't miss out on the unique offerings at the smaller grocers. **Ballard Market** and **Greenwood Market** (http://townandcountrymarkets.com), both owned by Town and Country Markets, Inc., are popular for their large bulk selections, organic goods, and great weekly specials.

Two warehouse stores in the Seattle area offer good deals on bulk foods and other household items. These are **Costco** (www.costco.com) and **Sam's Club** (www.samsclub.com). See above under **Warehouse Stores** for locations. Both have membership requirements. Call ahead for details.

## SPECIALTY/HEALTH FOOD GROCERS

- **Madison Market**, 1600 E Madison St, 206-329-1545, www.madisonmarket. com
- **Metropolitan Market**, 1908 Queen Anne Ave N, 206-284-2530; 2320 42nd Ave SW, 206-937-0551; 5250 40th Ave NE, 206-938-6600, 100 Mercer St, 206-213-0778, www.metropolitan-market.com
- **Mother Nature's Natural Foods**, 516 1st Ave N, 206-284-4422
- **Phinney Market**, 5918 Phinney Ave N, 206-789-3663, www.phinneymarket. com
- **Pioneer Organics**, 901 NW 49th St, 206-632-3424, http://pioneerorganics. com
- **Rainbow Grocery**, 417 15th Ave E, 206-329-8440
- **Small Potatoes Urban Delivery**, 2232 1st Ave S, 206-621-7783, www.spud. com
- **Whole Foods**, 6400 Roosevelt Way NE, 206-985-1500; www.wholefoods.com

Another grocery shopping option is the food cooperative. With eight neighborhood stores, Seattle's largest is **PCC (Puget Consumers Co-Op)**, which offers a wide selection of natural and organic foods. Visit www.pccnaturalmarkets.com or call your nearest store for membership information.

- **PCC Fremont**, 716 N 34th St, 206-632-6811
- **PCC Greenlake**, 7504 Aurora Ave N, 206-525-3586
- **PCC Issaquah**, 1810 12th Ave NW, 425-369-1222
- **PCC Kirkland**, 10718 NE 68th St, 425-828-4622
- **PCC Redmond**, 11435 Avondale Rd NE, 425-285-1400
- **PCC Seward Park**, 5041 Wilson Ave S, 206-723-2720
- **PCC View Ridge**, 6514 40th Ave NE, 206-526-7661
- **PCC West Seattle**, 2749 California Ave SW, 206-937-8481

## ETHNIC DISTRICTS AND MARKETS

Small grocery stores specializing in delicacies from other parts of the world are scattered throughout the Seattle area and surrounding communities. Immigrants and natives alike are attracted to these unique stores.

### AFRICAN
- **Kilimanjaro Market**, 12515 Lake City Way NE, 206-440-1440
- **West African Market**, 5997 Rainier Ave S, 206-723-6218
- **Zuma Grocery & Deli**, 129 NW 85th St, Ste A, 206-781-8600

### ASIAN
There are numerous Asian markets in Seattle's International District, also known as Chinatown. Start at the intersection of 4th Avenue South and Jackson Street and head east. Don't miss Uwajimaya, the biggest Asian store in the West. You will also find a collection of Asian groceries along Aurora Avenue in North Seattle and on Beacon Hill.

- **Asia Market**, 9615 15th Ave SW, 206-762-8658
- **Cambodian Market**, 9419 16th Ave SW, 206-767-0531
- **Center Oriental Grocery**, 9641 15th Ave SW, 206-762-5620
- **Foulee Market**, 2050 S Columbian Way, 206-764-9607
- **Hop Thanh Supermarket**, 1043 S Jackson St, 206-322-7473
- **Phnom Penh Market**, 7123 Martin Luther King Jr. Way S, 206-723-4341
- **Uwajimaya**, 4601 6th Ave S, Seattle, 206-624-3215; 15555 NE 24th, Bellevue, 425-747-9012
- **Vientian Asian Grocery**, 6059 Martin Luther King Jr. Way S, 206-723-3160
- **Viet Wah Super Foods**, 6040 Martin Luther King Jr. Way S, 206-760-8895
- **Vina Supermarket**, 6951 Martin Luther King Jr Way S, 206-722-3918

### GREEK-MIDDLE EASTERN
- **Aladdin Gyro-Cery**, 4139 University Way NE, 206-632-5253
- **Zizo Market**, 10204 Main St, Bellevue, 425-646-9496, www.zizomarket.com

### INDIAN-PAKISTANI
- **Bharat Groceries**, 14340 NE 20th St, Bellevue, 425-746-0857
- **Pakistani and Indian Grocery**, 12325 Roosevelt Way NE, 206-368-7323
- **R&M Videos and Grocery**, 5501 University Way NE, 206-526-1793
- **Mayuri Food & Video**, 2560 152nd Ave NE, Redmond, 425-861-3800

## ITALIAN
- **Borracchini's Bakery & Market**, 2307 Rainier Ave S, 206-325-1550
- **De Laurenti Specialty Food and Wine**, 1435 1st Ave, 206-622-0141, www. delaurenti.com
- **Salumi**, 309 3rd Ave S, 206-621-8772, www.salumicuredmeats.com

## SPANISH-MEXICAN-LATIN AMERICAN
- **El Mercado Latino**, 1514 Pike Pl, 206-623-3240
- **La Bodeguita Specialty Foods**, 2528A Beacon Ave S, 206-329-9001
- **Mexican Grocery**, 1914 Pike Pl, 206-441-1147
- **Tienda Latina Mexican & Latin Grocery**, 16716 Hwy 99, Lynnwood, 425-745-3472

# FARMERS' MARKETS

If you're searching for the highest quality in fruits and vegetables, your best bet is to buy right from the growers. During the summer, you can often find corn, cherries, raspberries, strawberries, apples, and peaches sold from truck beds on city street corners. For a bigger selection, try one of the farmers' markets in Seattle. The largest is Pike Place Market, in downtown Seattle at the west end of Pike Street. Don't be fooled by the fact that Pike Place is a popular tourist attraction; it is also a year-round destination for locals in search of fresh produce—succulent nectarines, perfect tomatoes or flavorful Walla Walla sweet onions. You can also find fresh fish and shellfish, homemade jams, jellies and honey, and brilliantly colored tulips, daffodils and dahlias. Neighborhood farmers' markets are open either on weekends or on an assigned weekday, and offerings include fresh produce from local farmers, and arts and crafts. Except for the year-round Pike Place Market, the Fremont Market, and the Ballard Market, all the markets here are open from late spring to early fall. The markets in the University District and West Seattle are open through December.

## SEATTLE
- **Ballard Farmers' Market**, Ballard Ave, Sundays, 10 a.m. to 4 p.m.
- **Broadway Farmers' Market**, Broadway & E Thomas St, Sundays, 11 a.m. to 3 p.m.
- **Columbia City Farmers' Market**, 4801 Rainier Ave S, Wednesdays, 3 to 7 p.m.
- **Fremont Sunday Market**, 400 N 34th St, Sundays, 10 a.m. to 4 p.m.
- **Lake City Farmers' Market**, NE 127th & 30th NE, Thursdays, 3 p.m. to 7 p.m.
- **Magnolia Farmers' Market**, 2550 34th Ave W, Saturdays, 10 a.m. to 2 p.m.

- **Pike Place Market**, 1st Ave and Pike St, Monday-Saturday, 9 a.m. to 6 p.m.; Sunday 10 a.m. to 5 p.m.
- **University District Farmers' Market**, NE 50th St and University Way NE, Saturdays, 9 a.m. to 2 p.m.
- **Wallingford Farmers' Market**, 4400 Wallingford Ave N, Wednesdays, 3 p.m. to 7 p.m.
- **West Seattle Farmers' Market**, SW Alaska St and California Ave SW, Sundays, 10 a.m. to 2 p.m.

## SURROUNDING COMMUNITIES
- **Bothell Country Village Farmers' Market**, 23732 Bothell-Everett Hwy, Fridays, 10 a.m. to 3 p.m.
- **Edmonds Museum Summer Market**, Bell St between 5th and 6th Aves, Saturdays, 9 a.m. to 3 p.m.
- **Everett Farmers' Market**, Everett Marina at Port Gardner Landing, Sundays, 11 a.m. to 4 p.m.
- **Issaquah Public Market**, SE 56th and 10th Ave NW, Saturdays, 9 a.m. to 2 p.m.
- **Kirkland Farmers' Market**, Park Lane E, between 3rd and Main, Wednesdays, 1 to 7 p.m.
- **North Bend Farmers' Market**, Main and Park at State Route 202, Saturdays, 9 a.m. to 1 p.m.
- **Redmond Saturday Market**, 7730 Leary Way, Saturdays, 8 a.m. to noon
- **Vashon Island Growers Association Farmers' Market**, 1/2 block north of Bank Rd on Vashon Hwy SW, Saturdays, 9 a.m. to 1 p.m.
- **Woodinville Farmers' Market**, 17301 133rd Ave NE, Saturdays, 9 a.m. to 4 p.m.

## COMMUNITY GARDENS

For the ultimate in freshness you could grow your own herbs and veggies. It doesn't take much space; a window box will do for many herbs. If you prefer a little more growing room when you garden, but don't have the space in your own backyard, consider a community garden. In Seattle, residents of 44 neighborhoods share "P-Patches," community gardens that boast more than 1,900 plots on 12 acres of land. **P-Patch** gardeners supply seven to ten tons of fresh organic vegetables to Seattle food banks each year. Many gardens have waiting lists—some up to three years long. According to the Seattle Department of Neighborhoods, only 10% to 20% of plots turn over each year, so you might want to get on the list as soon as you are settled into your new neighborhood. To sign up, or for more information, call the P-Patch Program at 206-684-0264, or visit www.seattle.gov/neighborhoods/ppatch.

## RESTAURANTS

Depending on your degree of interest in food, dining out here can be a convenience, a diversion, a hobby, a sport, a religion or a vocation. Offering every cuisine imaginable, Seattle is beginning to catch up to food meccas like San Francisco and New York City. To find popular eateries in your neighborhood, visit www.seattle.citysearch.com, www.yelp.com, or www.zagat.com. For helpful printed guides, consider buying the *Zagat Survey, Seattle/Portland Restaurants* or *The Food Lover's Guide to Seattle* by Katy Calcott.

Thanks to a cookbook from authors Cynthia Nims and Kathy Casey, Seattle's cooks can reproduce their favorite restaurant meals at home: *Best Places Seattle Cookbook: Recipes from the City's Outstanding Restaurants and Bars* features 125 recipes and 24 essays about local food and drink.

If you're tired after a long day of work and prefer to eat in without the hassle of cooking, consider picking up some food to go. Nearly all restaurants and most local grocery stores and specialty food shops offer take-out. If you can't even muster the energy to pick up a meal, a company called **Restaurants To Go** (www. restaurantstogo.com) will pick up a meal you order online from area restaurants and deliver it to you. Minimum orders and delivery fees apply, but it can be convenient, especially if you're craving food from a restaurant clear across town. Call 206-443-8646 for more information, or visit the web site to place your order.

## MAKE-AND-TAKE MEAL ASSEMBLY

An option that might be more of a bargain than you'd expect is make-and-take meal assembly, where the store does the prep and all you do is the assembly. The now popular national concept actually originated in Seattle in 2002. A few of the more popular companies, all with multiple Seattle-area locations, follow. You can also go to the Easy Meal Prep Association's web site, www.easymealprep.com, for updated lists and locations.

- **Designed Dinners,** www.designeddinners.com
- **Dinners Done Right,** www.dinnersdoneright.com
- **Dinners Ready,** www.dinnersready.com
- **Dream Dinners,** www.dreamdinners.com

## DRINKING WATER

Many Seattle residents drink plain tap water, though some use a simple home filtering system, such as a Brita water pitcher. For less trusting souls, some companies will deliver drinking water to your home or business:

- **Allwater Corp**, 206-624-3266, 425-451-0610, www.allwatercorp.com
- **Crystal Springs**, 800-453-0293, www.crystal-springs.com
- **Culligan**, 888-575-0234, www.culligan.com
- **Mountain Mist**, 877-233-5204, www.mountainmist.com

## WINES

Just north of Seattle, Woodinville is home to two wineries, **Chateau Ste. Michelle** (www.ste-michelle.com) and **Columbia Winery** (www.columbiawinery.com). Both offer tours and tastings. If you want to experience a wine country tour without traveling to California, you're in luck. Eastern Washington has its own wine country with dozens of nationally and internationally known wineries. Visit the web site of **Washington Wine Country** (www.winecountrywashington.org) to plan your trip.

- **Champion Wine Cellars**, 108 Denny Way, 206-284-8306, www.championwinecellars.com
- **City Cellars Fine Wines**, 1710 N 45th St, 206-632-7238, www.citycellar.com
- **Esquin Wine Merchants**, 2700 4th Ave S, 206-682-7374, www.esquin.com
- **La Cantina Wine Merchants**, 5436 Sandpoint Way NE, 206-525-4340
- **Madison Park Cellars**, 4227 E Madison, 206-323-9333, www.madisonparkcellars.com
- **Pike and Western Wine Merchants**, 1934 Pike Pl, 206-441-1307, www.pikeandwestern.com
- **Portalis Wine Shop**, 5205 Ballard Ave NW, 206-783-2007, www.portaliswines.com
- **Seattle Cellars Ltd.**, 2505 2nd Ave, #102, 206-256-0850, www.seattlecellars.com
- **West Seattle Cellars**, 6026 California Ave SW, 206-937-2868, www.westseattlecellars.com

THOUGH SEATTLE LANDED ON THE WORLD MUSIC MAP AS THE birthplace of grunge, it is not just a music mecca for alternative rock and its fans. Seattle is home to big and small arts venues that offer top-notch live performances in classical music, opera, comedy, and theater. Area residents flock to film openings, improvisational theater, traveling Broadway shows, art walks and galleries, and readings by visiting authors. The months of inclement winter weather guarantee large audiences for most performances. In the summer, entertainers simply move to the enticing outdoors. Music concerts are held in local parks, on the waterfront, and in concert halls. Another concert venue about two and a half hours east of Seattle is "The Gorge," a huge amphitheater with a stunning view of the Columbia River that attracts big names in contemporary and classic rock, blues, and jazz. Located in George, Washington, it has been called the best outdoor concert venue in the country. Several summer festivals feature fabulous musical and theatrical performances; see **A Seattle Year** for more details.

Also covered in this chapter: **Museums, Literary Life**, and **Culture for Kids**. Unless otherwise noted, the following establishments are in Seattle.

## TICKETS

Like nearly every major city in the US, tickets to most shows in Seattle can be bought through **Ticketmaster**: 206-628-0888 or online at www.ticketmaster. com. For especially popular events, such as rock concerts and professional sports playoffs, you may have no choice but to buy from Ticketmaster. However, for many events and performances you can avoid paying the extra Ticketmaster fees by purchasing tickets directly at the event venue's box office. Many area Fred Meyer stores have a Ticketmaster outlet, but check the web site for retail locations.

Several local live entertainment venues, including the Crocodile Café, Comedy Underground, and Tractor Tavern, use the online ticket service **TicketWeb**, www.ticketweb.com. Still other attractions, like the Showbox Theater, use **TicketsWest**; go to www.ticketswest.com or call 800-992-8499 for a list of venues using this service. **TicketWindow**, 206-325-6500, www.ticketwindowonline.com, is a local online box office that provides tickets to dozens of smaller venues and offers discount walk-up service at four locations. The outlets, located in Capitol Hill's Broadway Market, at the Pike Place Market information booth, in the Pacific Place Mall in downtown, and at Bellevue's Meydenbauer Center, offer half-price, day-of-show tickets to a variety of arts events; sales are cash and walk-up only, and there is no service charge. Call 206-324-2744 to find out what events are available.

If you have your heart set on a sold-out performance, a broker can usually provide a ticket, but expect to pay dearly for the opportunity. Broker services can charge top dollar because they operate outside the city and avoid Seattle's anti-scalping ordinance. Look in the Yellow Pages under "Ticket Sales—Entertainment & Sports."

## CLASSICAL MUSIC AND DANCE

## PROFESSIONAL—SYMPHONIC, CHORAL, OPERA, CHAMBER MUSIC

- **Seattle Choral Company**, 1518 NE 143rd St, 206-363-1100, www.seattlechoralcompany.org; performances are held December through June at various venues.
- **Seattle Men's Chorus**, 319 12th Ave, 206-323-0750, www.flyinghouse.org/smc; the largest community choir in North America and the largest gay men's choir in the world, the Seattle Men's Chorus offers lavish performances, often with nationally famous guest artists. Under the same production umbrella is the **Seattle Women's Chorus**, formed in 2002, http://www.flyinghouse.org/swc; both groups offer five concerts per season.
- **Seattle Opera**, 1020 John St, 206-389-7676, www.seattleopera.org; world renowned, the Seattle Opera features five productions from August to May, as well as a bi-yearly summer presentation of "The Ring" cycle by Wagner. A typical season includes several traditional performances of popular operas, as well as contemporary works and fresh takes on old standards. The opera routinely attracts international stars for lead roles, and longtime patrons recognize the local performers filling out each performance, held in the Marion Oliver McCall Hall.

- **Civic Light Opera**, 7400 Sand Point Way NE #101N, 206-363-4807, www.clo-musicaltheatre.org; for 28 years this group has provided local audiences with professional musical theater. Performances are from September through May at the Magnuson Community Center.
- **Seattle Pro Musica**, 1756 NW 56th St, 206-781-2766, www.seattlepromusica.org; this award-winning group performs a three-concert season that ranges from medieval chant to the works of living composers.
- **Seattle Symphony**, 200 University St, 206-215-4700, www.seattlesymphony.org; presents weekly performances, September through June, in Benaroya Hall, an acoustic masterpiece with seating for 2,500.
- **Seattle Baroque Orchestra**, 2366 Eastlake Ave E, Ste 406, 206-322-3118, www.seattlebaroque.org; this popular orchestra performs 17th- and 18th-century music from October through April in Benaroya Hall and the Kirkland Performance Center, using historical—or replicas of historical—instruments.
- **Northwest Sinfonietta**, PO Box 1154, Tacoma, WA 98401, 253-383-5344, www.nwsinfonietta.org; Tacoma's classical chamber orchestra performs in the Rialto Theater in Tacoma as well as Town Hall in Seattle.
- **Tacoma Opera**, 917 Pacific Ave, Ste 407, Tacoma, WA 98402, 253-627-7789, www.tacomaopera.com; performances are held at the Pantages Theater in downtown Tacoma.
- **Bellevue Opera**, 8726 NE 11th St, Bellevue, WA 98004, 425-454-1906, www.bellevueopera.org; offers two productions per year in Bellevue's Meydenbauer Center.
- **Bellevue Philharmonic**, PO Box 1582, Bellevue, WA 98009, 425-455-4171, www.bellevuephil.org; professional orchestra for the eastside, performing October through April in the Meydenbauer Center.

## COMMUNITY—SYMPHONIC, CHORAL, OPERA, CHAMBER MUSIC

For a list of all Puget Sound choral groups, from small neighborhood groups to large-scale community choruses, visit the web site of **Open Harmony**, www.openharmony.org

- **Choral Arts**, PO Box 9009, 877-404-2269, www.choral-arts.org; this 30-member choir presents concerts in Seattle and Tacoma.
- **Federal Way Symphony**, P.O. Box 4513, Federal Way, WA 98063, 253-529-9857, www.federalwaysymphony.org; performances take place at St. Luke's Church, 515 S 312th St, in Federal Way.
- **Lake Union Civic Orchestra**, PO Box 75387, 206-343-5826, www.luco.org; comprised of all volunteers, this chamber orchestra offers four performances from October to June in Seattle's Town Hall.

- **Masterworks Choral Ensemble**, P.O. Box 1091, Olympia, WA 98507, 360-491-3305, www.mce.org; presents five concerts from October to June at the Washington Center for the Performing Arts in Olympia.
- **Northwest Symphony Orchestra**, PO Box 116231, 206-242-6321, www.northwestsymphonyorchestra.org; performs works by Pacific Northwest composers, as well as classical pieces.
- **Rainier Symphony**, PO Box 58182, 206-781-5618, www.rainiersymphony.org; serving up classical and pops to South King County audiences in the Foster Performing Arts Center in Tukwila and the Renton IKEA Performing Arts Center.
- **Thalia Symphony Orchestra**, 3307 3rd Ave W, 206-281-2048, www.thaliasymphony.org; Seattle Pacific University's orchestra-in-residence performs October through June.
- **Everett Symphony**, 1507 Wall St, Everett, WA 98201, 425-257-8382, www.everettsymphony.org; for over 65 years this North Sound orchestra has been holding performances from October through June.

## DANCE

- **ARC Dance Company**, PO Box 9997, 206-352-0798, www.arcdance.org; a repertory dance company presenting a variety of dance styles, including modern, ballet, and jazz.
- **Evergreen City Ballet**, 710 S 2nd St, Renton, WA 98055, 425-228-6800, www.evergreencityballet.org; performances are held October through June in the Auburn Performing Arts Center, 700 E Main St, Auburn, WA 98002.
- **On the Boards**, 100 W Roy St, 206-217-9888, www.ontheboards.org; approximately 200 experimental and contemporary performances are presented October through December in two theaters at the Behnke Center for Contemporary Performance, and at theaters throughout Seattle.
- **Pacific Northwest Ballet (PNB)**, 301 Mercer St, 206-441-9411, www.pnb.org; presents six programs, September through June, including several performances of short contemporary works and one or two longer traditional pieces. Also offers lectures and community outreach events. The annual Christmas show is a beloved version of The Nutcracker, featuring sets designed by author and illustrator Maurice Sendak. Performances are in the Marion Oliver McCaw Hall.
- **Spectrum Dance Theater**, 800 Lake Washington Blvd, 206-325-4161, www.spectrumdance.org; Seattle's premier contemporary dance company draws on influences from swing to scat and tango to blues. Performances are held at a variety of venues throughout Seattle and the Eastside.
- **UW World Dance Series**, 4001 University Way NE, 206-543-4880, www.uwworldseries.org; as part of the UW World Series, Meany Theater presents a selection of dance performances from around the globe. The series runs from

October to May. Meany Theater is located on the UW campus, at 15th Ave NE and Campus Parkway.

## CONTEMPORARY MUSIC

Seattle burst onto the national music scene in the early 1990s as the home of "grunge" rock. While bands like Pearl Jam, Soundgarden, Alice In Chains, and Nirvana put the city on the map for alternative music, other musical genres likewise thrive in Seattle. The following bars, clubs, and concert halls are best known for the category under which they are listed, but many book a variety of acts. Check out the *Seattle Weekly* (www.seattleweekly.com) or *The Stranger* (www. thestranger.com)—both free local newspapers found in bars, cafes, and music stores—to find out each venue's schedule.

## CONCERT VENUES

- **Benaroya Hall**, S. Mark Taper Auditorium, 200 University St, 206-215-4747, www.benaroyahall.com
- **Chateau Ste. Michelle Winery**, 14111 NE 145th St, Woodinville, 425-488-3300, www.ste-michelle.com
- **Gorge Amphitheatre**, 754 Silica Rd NW, George, 206-628-0888, www.hob. com
- **Key Arena**, Seattle Center, 206-684-7200, www.seattlecenter.com
- **Memorial Stadium**, Seattle Center, 206-956-3270, www.seattlecenter.com
- **Paramount Theatre**, 911 Pine St, 206-467-5510, www.theparamount.com
- **Summer Nights at Gasworks Park**, 2101 N Northlake Way, 206-281-7788, www.summernights.org
- **Tacoma Dome**, 2727 East "D" St, Tacoma, 253-272-3663, www.tacomadome. org
- **Everett Events Center**, 2000 Hewitt Ave, Everett, 425-322-2600, www. everetteventscenter.com

## BARS AND NIGHTCLUBS

### ALL AGES

- **Paradox Theater**, 5510 University Way NE, 206-524-7677, www.theparadox. org
- **Studio Seven**, 110 S Horton St, 206-286-1312, www.studioseven.us
- **The Vera Project**, 1621 12th Ave, 206-956-8372, www.theveraproject.org

## ALTERNATIVE, INDUSTRIAL, ROCK

- **Central Saloon**, 207 1st Ave S, 206-622-0209, www.centralsaloon.com
- **Chop Suey**, 1325 E Madison St, 206-324-8000, www.chopsuey.com
- **Crocodile Café**, 2200 2nd Ave, 206-441-5611, www.thecrocodile.com
- **Doc Maynard's**, 610 1st Ave, 206-682-3705, www.docmaynards.com
- **El Corazon**, 109 Eastlake Ave E, 206-381-3094
- **Fenix Underground**, 109 S Washington, 206-405-4323, www.fenixunder ground.com
- **FunHouse**, 206 5th Ave N, 206-374-8400, www.thefunhouse.com
- **The Heavens Nightclub**, 172 S Washington St, 206-622-1863
- **King Cat Theatre**, 2130 6th Ave, 206-269-7444
- **Moore Theatre**, 1932 2nd Ave, 206-467-5510, www.themoore.com
- **Neumos**, 925 E Pike St, 206-709-9467, www.neumos.com
- **Rocksport**, 4209 SW Alaska St, 206-935-5838, www.rocksport.net
- **Showbox**, 1426 1st Ave, 206-628-3151, www.showboxonline.com
- **Sunset Tavern**, 5433 Ballard Ave, 206-784-4880
- **Waldo's**, 12657 NE 85th St, Kirkland, 425-827-9292, www.waldosbarandgrill. com

## BLUES, JAZZ

- **Bad Albert's**, 5100 Ballard Ave NW, 206-782-9623
- **Dimitriou's Jazz Alley**, 2033 6th Ave, 206-441-9729, www.jazzalley.com
- **Highway 99 Blues Club**, 1414 Alaskan Way, 206-382-2171, www. highwayninetynine.com
- **Larry's Greenfront Restaurant and Lounge**, 209 1st Ave S, 206-624-7665
- **Latona by Green Lake**, 6423 Latona Ave NE, 206-525-2238
- **New Orleans Restaurant**, 114 1st Ave S, 206-622-2563, www.neworleans creolerestaurant.com
- **Old Timer's Café**, 620 1st Ave S, 206-623-9800
- **The Triple Door**, 216 Union St, 206-838-4333
- **Tula's Restaurant and Jazz Club**, 2214 2nd Ave, 206-443-4221

## COUNTRY

- **Cowgirls, Inc.**, 421 First Ave S, 206-340-0777, www.cowgirlsinc.com
- **Little Red Hen**, 7115 Woodlawn Ave NE, 206-522-1168, www.littleredhen. com
- **McCabes American Music Café**, 3120 Hewitt Ave, Everett, 425-252-3082, www.mccabeseverett.com

## DANCE, DJs

- **Baltic Room**, 1207 Pine St, 206-625-4444
- **Belltown Billiards**, 90 Blanchard St, 206-448-6779, www.belltownseattle.com
- **Club Noc Noc**, 1516 2nd Ave, 206-223-1333, www.clubnocnoc.com
- **Contour**, 807 1st Ave, 206-447-7704
- **Down Under**, 2407 1st Ave, 206-728-4053, www.downundernightclub.com
- **Element**, 332 5th Ave N, 206-441-7479, www.elementseattle.com
- **Last Supper Club**, 124 S Washington St, 206-748-9975, www.lastsupperclub.com
- **Neighbours**, 1509 Broadway, 206-324-5358, www.neighborsnightclub.com
- **Paragon Restaurant and Bar**, 2125 Queen Anne Ave N, 206-283-4548, www.paragonseattle.com
- **Re-bar**, 1114 Howell St, 206-233-9873, www.rebarseattle.com
- **The Ballroom**, 456 N 36th St, 206-634-2575
- **Trinity**, 111 Yesler Way, 206-447-4140, www.trinitynightclub.com
- **Venom**, 2218 Western Ave, 206-448-8887, www.venomseattle.com
- **Vogue**, 1516 11th Ave, 206-324-5778, www.vogueseattle.com

## FOLK, ROCKABILLY, SWING

- **Fiddler's Inn**, 9219 35th Ave NE, 206-525-0752
- **Tractor Tavern**, 5213 Ballard Ave NW, 206-789-3599, www.tractortavern.com

## FUNK, HIP HOP, R&B, SOUL

- **Vito's Madison Grill**, 927 9th Ave, 206-682-6959, www.vitosmadisongrill.com
- **The War Room**, 722 E Pike St, 206-328-7666, www.thewarroomseattle.com

## IRISH AND CELTIC

- **The Celtic Swell**, 2722 Alki Ave SW, 206-932-7935, www.celticswell.com
- **Conor Byrne Pub**, 5140 Ballard Ave NW, 206-784-3640, www.conorbyrnepub.com
- **The Dubliner Pub**, 3515 Fremont Ave N, 206-548-1508
- **Fado Irish Pub**, 801 1st Ave, 206-264-2700, www.fadoirishpub.com
- **The Irish Emigrant**, 5260 University Way NE, 206-525-2955, www.irishemigrant.net
- **Kells**, 1916 Post Alley, 206-768-728-1916, www.kellsirish.com
- **Mulleady's Irish Pub**, 3055 21st Ave W, 206-283-8843
- **The Owl 'n' Thistle**, 808 Post Ave, 206-621-7777, www.owlnthistle.com

## LATIN

- **Century Ballroom**, 915 E Pine St, 206-324-7263, www.centuryballroom.com
- **Mojito Café**, 181 Western Ave W, 206-217-1180, www.mojitocafe.com

## THEATER AND FILM

While many residents become season ticket subscribers, you'll find this is a city of last-minute ticket buyers. Even the most popular shows may not sell out until the day of the performance, though it's always good to call ahead and check availability.

## PROFESSIONAL THEATER

- **A Contemporary Theater (ACT)**, 700 Union St, 206-292-7676, www.acttheatre. org; referred to as "ACT theater" or "the ACT," presents contemporary works by both established and little-known playwrights.
- **Empty Space Theatre**, 901 12th Ave, 206-547-7500, www.emptyspace.org; located in the Lee Center for the Arts at Seattle University, the Empty Space Theatre has been producing contemporary shows in Seattle since 1970. The Empty Space is a favorite of Seattle theatergoers, who enjoy the boisterous comedies and cutting edge dramas performed (and often written) by talented local players.
- **The 5th Avenue Musical Theatre Company**, 1308 5th Ave, 206-625-1418, www.5thavenuetheatre.org; the opulent and Chinese inspired 5th Avenue produces musical theater and hosts traveling productions of major Broadway shows, as well as concerts, lectures, and films.
- **Intiman Theatre**, Playhouse, Seattle Center, 201 Mercer St, 206-269-1900, www.intiman.org; this outstanding theater won the 2006 Tony Award for the best U.S. regional theater. Presenting a variety of modern and classic works, the Intiman addresses contemporary issues with ambitious and dynamic interpretations of new and established plays.
- **Paramount Theater**, 911 Pine St, 206-467-5510, www.theparamount.com; the magnificent Paramount Theater hosts traveling productions of Broadway shows, as well as concerts, dance performances, and outreach programs. The plush lobby and ornate performance hall, which can be converted into a dinner theater, make this an elegant venue for any play or musical.
- **Seattle Public Theater**, 7312 W Green Lake Dr N, 206-524-1300, www. seattlepublictheater.org; the company performs at the Greenlake Bathhouse, a cozy brick building which used to serve as the lake's bathhouse. The theater produces classic shows with a good dose of humor.

- **Seattle Repertory Theatre**, Bagley Wright Theater, Seattle Center, 155 Mercer St, 206-443-2222, www.seattlerep.org; perhaps Seattle's best-known theater, "The Rep" presents a mix of classical and contemporary plays each season, from October to April. The theater often performs plays that have recently completed successful Broadway runs, but never hosts touring shows.
- **Seattle Shakespeare Company**, Center House Theater, Seattle Center, 206-733-8222, www.seattleshakespeare.org; professional theater company highlighting the works of Shakespeare, often with a contemporary twist. Occasionally offers a non-Shakespearean classic play.
- **SecondStory Repertory**, Redmond Town Center, 16587 NE 74th St, Redmond, 425-881-6777, www.secondstoryrep.org; a non-profit, professional ensemble, SecondStory presents comedies, revues, dramas, and musicals year-round. The company also offers musicals for children through the Sprouts Children's Theater series.
- **Tacoma Actors Guild (TAG)**, Theatre on the Square, 915 Broadway, Tacoma, 253-272-2145, www.tacomaactorsguild.com; productions range from classic to contemporary, serious drama to light-hearted comedy. The *San Francisco Chronicle* described TAG as "… an asset as rare as Tacoma's zoom lens view of Mount Rainier."
- **Taproot Theatre Company**, 204 N 85th St, 206-781-9707, www.taproottheatre. org; celebrating their 30th anniversary in 2006, the popular Taproot produces musicals, comedies, and dramas that celebrate theater and reflect their values of faith and respect.

## COMMUNITY THEATER

- **Annex Theatre**, 1122 E Pike St, 206-728-0933, www.annextheatre.org
- **Bellevue Civic Theatre**, Meydenbauer Center, 11100 6th St, Bellevue, 425-235-5087, http://www.bellevuecivic.org
- **Book-It Repertory Theatre**, 305 Harrison St, 206-216-0833, www.book-it.org
- **Centerstage Theater Arts**, 3200 SW Dash Point Rd, Federal Way, 253-835-2000, www.centerstagetheatre.org
- **Driftwood Players**, Wade James Theatre, 950 Main St, Edmonds, 425-774-9600, www.driftwoodplayers.com
- **Lakewood Playhouse**, 5729 Lakewood Towne Center Blvd, Lakewood, 253-588-0042, www.lakewoodplayhouse.org
- **The Mercer Island Players**, 8805 SE 40th St, Mercer Island, 206-339-7785, www.islandplayers.org
- **Renton Civic Theatre**, 507 S Third St, Renton, 425-226-5529, www.renton civictheater.org
- **Theater Schmeater**, 1500 Summit Ave, 206-324-5801, www.schmeater.org

- **Valley Community Players**, Carco Theatre, 1717 Maple Valley Hwy, Renton, 425-226-5190, www.valleycommunityplayers.org
- **Village Theatre**, Francis J. Gaudette Theatre, 303 Front St N, Issaquah, 425-392-2202; Everett Performing Arts Center, 2710 Wetmore Ave, Everett, 425-257-8600, www.villagetheatre.org
- **Woodinville Repertory Theatre**, 7026 240th St SE, Woodinville, 425-481-8502, www.woodinvillerep.org

## IMPROV

A combination of stand-up comedy and acting, improvisational theater uses audience suggestions to create a scene, which is then played for laughs. Most improv groups perform only on the weekends; make sure you call ahead as times and locations change.

- **Jet City Improv**, 5510 University Way NE, 206-781-3879, www.jetcityimprov.com
- **TheatreSports**, 1428 Post Alley, 206-587-2414, www.unexpectedproductions.org

## COMEDY

- **Comedy Underground**, 222 S Main St, 206-628-0303, www.comedyunderground.com
- **Giggles Comedy Nite Club**, 5220 Roosevelt Way NE, 206-526-5653, www.gigglescomedyclub.com

## FILM

There are numerous movie theatres in Seattle, and multi-screen outlets continue to rise in developing areas outside of Seattle. For general multi-screen movie complexes, visit www.movies.com or check the Yellow Pages under "Theatres-Movies." The following is a list of alternative and fine art movie houses.

- **Central Cinema**, 1411 21st Ave W, 206-686-6684, www.central-cinema.com
- **Columbia City Cinema**, 4816 Rainier Ave S, 206-721-3156, www.columbiacitycinema.com
- **Crest Cinema Center**, 16505 5th Ave NE, 206-781-5755, www.landmarktheatres.com
- **Egyptian Theatre**, 805 E Pine St, 206-781-5755, www.landmarktheatres.com
- **Grand Illusion Cinema**, 1403 NE 50th St, 206-523-3935, www.grandillusioncinema.org

- **Guild 45th Theatre**, 2115 N 45th, 206-781-5755, www.landmarktheatres.com
- **Harvard Exit**, 807 E Roy, 206-781-5755, www.landmarktheatres.com
- **Neptune Theatre**, 1303 NE 45th St, 206-781-5755, www.landmarktheatres. com
- **Northwest Film Forum**, 1515 12th Ave S, 206-329-2629, www.nwfilmforum. org
- **Seven Gables Theater**, 911 NE 50th St, 206-781-5755, www.landmarktheatres. com
- **Varsity Theatre**, 4329 University Way NE, 206-781-5755, www.landmark theatres.com

## FILM FESTIVALS

- **The Langston Hughes African American Film Festival**, 104 17th Ave S, 206-684-4757, www.langstonblackfilmfest.org
- **Northwest Asian American Film Festival**, 409 7th Ave S, 206-340-1445, www. nwaaff.org
- **Seattle Arab & Iranian Film Festival**, 206-322-0882, www.saiff.com
- **Seattle International Film Festival**, 400 9th Ave N, 206-324-9997, www. seattlefilm.com
- **Seattle Jewish Film Festival**, 1402 3rd Ave, Ste 1415, 206-622-6315, www. ajcseattle.org
- **Seattle Lesbian and Gay Film Festival**, 1122 E Pike St, #1313, 206-323-4274, www.seattlequeerfilm.org

## MUSEUMS

Rainy days are perfect for strolling through the quiet (and dry) halls of fine museums—and Seattle has plenty of both! From art and science to culture and history, area museums offer interesting and diverse exhibitions, and many host traveling exhibits. Be sure to call ahead or go online to find out about the latest offerings and to check on days and hours of operation (several museums are closed on Monday and most have free admission days).

## ART

- **Bellevue Arts Museum**, 510 Bellevue Way NE, 425-519-0770, www.bellevue arts.org; located across the street from Bellevue Square, the Eastside's most popular shopping mall. A 2005 building renovation and a change in the museum's mission statement resulted in a cutting edge museum focused on crafts and design. Offering lectures, workshops and demonstration, it also sponsors the yearly Bellevue Arts and Crafts Fair. Hours are Tuesday–Thursday, 10 a.m.–5:30 p.m., Friday, 10 a.m.–9 p.m., Saturday, 10 a.m.–5:30 p.m., and Sunday, 11 a.m.–5:30 p.m. Admission is $7 for adults, $5 for seniors and students. Kids under 6 are free.

- **Frye Art Museum**, 704 Terry Ave, 206-622-9250, www.fryeart.org; located on First Hill in an International Style building designed in 1952 by Paul Thiry, the Frye Art Museum houses a collection of 19th century paintings by European artists, as well as a large collection of works by 18th century German artists. It also offers art classes and art history courses. Open Tuesday–Saturday, 10 a.m.–5 p.m., until 8 p.m. on Thursday, and Sunday noon–5 p.m. Free admission.
- **Henry Art Gallery**, University of Washington, 15th Ave NE and NE 41st St, 206-543-2280, www.henryart.org; the 19th century and early 20th century American and European works originally donated by local businessman Horace C. Henry are still the backbone of this museum's collection, however, the museum also offers modern and multidisciplinary art and design and innovative programs. Open Tuesday–Sunday, 11 a.m.–5 p.m., until 8 p.m. on Thursdays. No charge for high school and college students, UW faculty and staff, and kids 13 and younger. Thursdays are free.
- **Museum of Glass**, 1801 Dock St, Tacoma, 253-284-4750, 866-4-MUSEUM, www.museumofglass.org; devoted to the exhibition and interpretation of contemporary art with a focus on the medium of glass. A 500-foot pedestrian tunnel crafted by legendary glass artist Dale Chihuly links the museum to downtown Tacoma. Check the web site or call for hours. Admission is $10 for adults, $8 for seniors, $4 for children, 6–12. Free every third Thursday of the month.
- **Museum of Northwest Art (MoNA)**, 121 S 1st St, LaConner, 360-466-4446, www.museumofnwart.org; the Skagit Valley, north of Seattle, has long been a haven for Northwest artists. MoNA opened in 1981 to present the works of these artists, and to serve as a source of education. The museum's small permanent collection consists of paintings, sculpture, glass and works on paper. Open daily, 10 a.m.–5 p.m. Admission is $5 for adults, $4 for seniors, $2 for students, and free for children 12 and under.
- **Seattle Art Museum (SAM)**, 100 University St, 206-654-3100, www.seattleartmuseum.org; located near the Pike Place Market, the Seattle Art Museum houses an exceptional collection, which includes a variety of African, Chinese, and Native American pieces, as well as European and American art. SAM is Seattle's preeminent art museum, showcasing international traveling exhibits of photography, painting, and sculpture. Closed in 2005 for major renovation and expansion, SAM reopens with a dramatic new space in May 2007. Broadening the museum's scope, the **Olympic Sculpture Park** at 2910

Western Ave opened in January 2007. This waterfront park, a transformed nine-acre industrial site, features over 20 sculptures along with a series of gardens as well as spectacular views of Puget Sound and the Olympic Mountains. Free admission.

- **Seattle Asian Art Museum**, Volunteer Park, 1400 E Prospect St, 206-654-3100, www.seattleartmuseum.org; housed in a 1933 Art Deco building flanked by two popular replicas of Ming Dynasty camels, this gallery presents art from all over Asia. The museum is a focal point of Volunteer Park, located at the northeast corner of Capitol Hill. Open Tuesday–Sunday, 10 a.m.–5 p.m., Thursday until 9 p.m. Admission for adults is $5; $3 for seniors, youths 13–17, and students with ID; those 12 and under are admitted free. Admission on the first Thursday and first Saturday of the month is free.

- **Tacoma Art Museum (TAM)**, 1701 Pacific Ave, Tacoma, 253-272-4258, www.tacomaartmuseum.org; TAM's exhibits emphasize art and artists from the Northwest. A collection of Dale Chihuly's glass works is a permanent fixture. Every other summer the museum hosts the Northwest Biennial, a juried competition for artists from Washington, Oregon, Idaho, and Montana. Hours are Tuesday–Saturday, 10 a.m.–5 p.m., every third Thursday, 10 a.m.–8 p.m., and Sunday, noon–5 p.m. Admission is $7.50 for adults, $6.50 for seniors and students, and free for kids 5 and under. Admission on the third Thursday of each month is free.

## ART GALLERIES

A vibrant art scene thrives in Seattle, with many galleries receiving national and international attention and acclaim. Dozens of galleries showcase everything from traditional to cutting edge art by both local artists and those outside the Northwest. Check the Art Guide Northwest web site for listings of galleries, artists, and events around Puget Sound, www.artguidenw.com. Listed below are just some of the galleries to be found in Seattle.

- **Azuma Gallery**, 530 1st Ave S, 206-622-5599, www.azumagallery.com
- **Benham Gallery**, 1216 1st Ave, 206-622-2480, www.benhamgallery.com
- **Patricia Cameron Gallery**, 234 Dexter Ave N, 206-343-9647, www.patricia camerongallery.com
- **Center on Contemporary Art**, 410 Dexter Ave N, 206-728-1980, www.cocaseattle.org
- **Davidson Galleries**, 313 Occidental Ave S, 206-624-1324; Davidson Contemporary, 310 S Washington St, 206-624-7684 www.davidsongalleries.com
- **Foster/White Gallery**, 220 3rd Ave S, 206-622-2833; 1331 5th Ave, 206-583-0100, www.fosterwhite.com

- **Friesen Gallery**, 1210 2nd Ave, 206-628-9501, www.friesengallery.com
- **Garde Rail Gallery**, 110 3rd Ave S, 206-621-1055, www.garde-rail.com
- **G. Gibson Gallery**, 300 S Washington St, 206-587-4033, www.ggibsongallery. com
- **Grover/Thurston Gallery**, 309 Occidental Ave S, 206-223-0816, www. groverthurston.com
- **James Harris Gallery**, 309A 3rd Ave S, 206-903-6220, www.jamesharrisgallery. com
- **Lisa Harris Gallery**, 1922 Pike Pl, 206-443-3315, www.lisaharrisgallery.com
- **Linda Hodges Gallery**, 316 1st S, 206-624-3034, www.lindahodgesgallery. com
- **Howard House**, 604 2nd Ave, 206-256-6399, www.howardhouse.net
- **Greg Kucera Gallery**, 212 3rd Ave S, 206-624-0770, www.gregkucera.com
- **Jeffrey Moose Gallery**, 1333 5th Ave, 206-467-6951, www.jeffreymoosegallery. com
- **Bryan Ohno Gallery**, 155 S Main St, 206-667-9572, www.bryanohnogallery. com
- **Pacini Lubel Gallery**, 207 2nd Ave S, 206-326-5555, pacinilubel.com
- **Catherine Person Gallery**, 319 3rd Ave S, 206-763-5565, www. catherinepersongallery.com
- **Platform Gallery**, 114 3rd Ave S, 206-323-2808, www.platformgallery.com
- **Roq La Rue Gallery**, 2312 2nd Ave, 206-374-8977, www.roqlarue.com
- **Francine Seders Gallery**, 6701 Greenwood Ave N, 206-782-0355, www. sedersgallery.com
- **Soil Art Gallery**, 112 3rd Ave S, 206-264-8061, www.soilart.org
- **Stonington Gallery**, 119 S Jackson St, 206-405-4040, www.stoningtongallery. com
- **William Traver Gallery**, 110 Union St, 206-587-6501, www.travergallery.com

## ART WALKS

Each month, various communities in the Puget Sound region host monthly "art walks," where neighborhood galleries stay open late and often provide food and live music. This is a great way to see the exhibits without fighting daytime traffic and crowds. Look in weekly newspapers for information or call participating galleries.

### First Thursday
- **Pioneer Square**, 6 p.m.–8 p.m.

### First Friday
- **Fremont Art About**, 206-632-4848, 6 p.m.–9 p.m.
- **Anacortes Gallery Walk**, Anacortes, 360-293-6938, 6 p.m.–9 p.m.

- **Bainbridge Island Art Walk**, Bainbridge Island, 6 p.m.–8 p.m.
- **Bremerton Gallery Walk**, Bremerton, 5 p.m.–8 p.m.
- **Vashon Island Gallery Cruise**, Vashon Island, 206-463-5131, 6 p.m.–9 p.m.

*Second Thursday*
- **Kirkland Art Walk**, Kirkland, 425-889-8212, 6 p.m.–9 p.m.

*Second Saturday*
- **Ballard Art Walk**, 206-789-1490, 6 p.m.–9 p.m.

*Third Thursday*
- **Edmonds Art Walk**, Edmonds, 425-776-3778, 5 p.m.–8 p.m.
- **Tacoma Art Walk**, Tacoma, 253-272-4258, 5 p.m.–8 p.m.

## CULTURE, HISTORY

- **Burke Museum of Natural History and Culture**, University of Washington, NE 45th St and 17th Ave NE, 206-543-5590, www.washington.edu/burkemuseum; the Burke Museum houses fascinating exhibits on Pacific Rim geology, natural history, and anthropology. Native American artifacts—including masks, beads, and totem poles—and displays of dinosaur skeletons and fossils, are especially popular with children. Open seven days a week, 10 a.m.–5 p.m., the first Thursday of the month until 8 p.m. General admission for adults is $8, $6.50 for seniors, $5 for students and youths over 5, and free for children 5 and under. Free for UW staff, faculty, and students.
- **Coast Guard Museum Northwest**, Pier 36, 1519 Alaskan Way S, 206-217-6993, www.uscg.mil/mlcpac/iscseattle; Coast Guard memorabilia, photographs, model ships and other nautical items are on display at this museum. Tours of Coast Guard cutters are available on weekends. Open Monday, Wednesday, and Friday, 9 a.m.–3 p.m., Saturday and Sunday, 1 p.m.–5 p.m. Free admission.
- **Experience Music Project (EMP)**, 325 5th Ave N, 877-367-5483, www.emp live.org; Microsoft co-founder Paul Allen envisioned EMP as a place for music enthusiasts to explore and celebrate musical history and diversity. The 140,000-square-foot building (either a masterpiece or an eyesore, depending on who you ask), is home to interactive exhibits, unique artifacts, and performance spaces. Open daily, 10 a.m.–8 p.m. Admission is $19.95 for adults 18 to 64, $15.95 for seniors and members of the military, $14.95 for youths 7–17, and free for children 6 and under.
- **History House of Greater Seattle**, 790 N 34th St, 206-675-8875, www. historyhouse.org; through photographs and documents, History House displays the pictorial history of Seattle and its neighborhoods. Open Wednesday–Sunday, 12 p.m.–5 p.m. Admission is $1.

- **Museum of History and Industry**, McCurdy Park, 2700 24th Ave E, 206-324-1126, www.seattlehistory.org; local Northwest history is presented in this museum near the University of Washington. A museum popular with children, exhibits include old-fashioned fire engines, model ships, and figureheads. History buffs will enjoy the large collection of archival photographs and the many artifacts of Seattle's fishing, lumber, and shipping industries. Hours are daily, 10 a.m.–5 p.m., first Thursday of the month from 10 a.m. to 8 p.m. Admission is $7 for adults, $5 for seniors and for kids 5–17, and free for children under 5. No admission fee on first Thursday.
- **Nordic Heritage Museum**, 3014 NW 67th St, 206-789-5707, www.nordicmuseum.org; this museum chronicles the history of the Scandinavian immigrants who settled in the Ballard neighborhood and other areas of the Pacific Northwest. The museum offers Nordic dance and language classes, Scandinavian films, and lectures. Hours are Tuesday–Saturday, 10 a.m.–4 p.m., Sunday, noon–4 p.m. Admission is $6 for adults, $5 for seniors and college students, $4 for youths over 5, and free for children under 5.
- **Science Fiction Museum and Hall of Fame**, 325 5th Ave N, 206-724-3428, www.sfhomeworld.org; housed in the same building as the EMP, this is the first museum devoted to the genre of science fiction and its creators. Interactive exhibits explore literature, movies, and art, and this is now the permanent physical home of the Sci-Fi Hall of Fame. Open Monday–Thursday, 10 a.m.–5 p.m., Friday–Sunday 10 a.m.–6 p.m. Admission is $12.95 for adults 18-64, $8.95 for seniors and youths 7-17, $10.95 for military, and free to kids 6 and under.
- **Seattle Metropolitan Police Museum**, 317 3rd Ave S, 206-748-9991; located in Pioneer Square, the museum is the largest police museum in the western United States, combining historical displays with an interactive learning area for children and adults. The museum is open Tuesday–Saturday, 11 a.m.–4 p.m. Admission is $3 for adults and $1.50 for kids 12 and under. Seniors and the disabled receive a 10% admission discount.
- **Wing Luke Asian Museum**, 407 7th Ave S, 206-623-5124, www.wingluke.org; housed in a converted garage in the historic International District, the nationally recognized Wing Luke Asian Museum showcases pan-Asian culture, history, and art. Open Tuesday–Friday, 11 a.m.–4:30 p.m., Saturday and Sunday, noon–4 p.m. Admission is $4 for adults, $3 for students and seniors, and $2 for kids 5 to 12.

## SCIENCE

- **Museum of Flight**, 9404 E Marginal Way S, 206-764-5720, www.museumofflight.org; located on the original site of the Boeing Company, the museum presents a complete history of flight and aviation technology. This is a great museum for kids and adults alike, with interactive exhibits, archival film footage, and colorful full-scale reproductions of some of Boeing's first airplanes—early bi-planes and military jets among them—hanging from the ceiling. The Red Barn, which housed the first Boeing airplane factory, is also part of the exhibit. Open daily from 10 a.m. to 5 p.m., first Thursdays until 9 p.m. General admission is $14, $13 for seniors, $7.50 for children ages 5–17, and free for those 4 and under.

- **Odyssey Maritime Discovery Center**, 2205 Alaskan Way, Pier 66, 206-374-4000, www.ody.org; explore the maritime history, present, and future of Puget Sound and the North Pacific. Enjoy hands-on, interactive exhibits on commercial fishing, shipping, recreation, and marine protection. Open Tuesday–Thursday, 10 a.m.–3 p.m., Friday 10 a.m.–4 p.m., and Saturday, 10 a.m.–5 p.m. Admission is $7 for adults, $4 for seniors and students 5–18, $2 for children 2–4, and free for children under 2.
- **Pacific Science Center**, Seattle Center, 200 2nd Ave, 206-443-2001, www.pacsci.org; not your traditional museum by any means, the Pacific Science Center has more than 200 interactive exhibits on science and nature. Children in particular enjoy the hands-on activities, which approach learning in fun and creative ways. Open Monday–Friday, 10 a.m.–5 p.m., weekends and holidays, 10 a.m.–6 p.m. General admission ranges from $10 for adults to free admission for those under 3.

## LITERARY LIFE

With its rainy days and coffee worship, Seattle is a great bookstore town, and in 2005 was named as America's most literate city. Area residents flock to fiction and poetry readings, book groups, and book-signings. Seattle is even home to that bookstore without shelves, Amazon.com. While the city has chain stores like Barnes & Noble and Borders, many residents are fiercely loyal to Seattle's independent booksellers. Used bookstores do a roaring trade, and twice a year the Friends of the Seattle Public Library hold a popular book sale in a huge warehouse at Magnuson Park. See the *Seattle Weekly*, *Seattle Post-Intelligencer* and *The Seattle Times* for listings of upcoming readings and author signings, or contact your local bookstore for its calendar of events.

# BOOKSTORES

## GENERAL INTEREST

- **B. Dalton Bookseller**, Northgate Mall, 206-364-5810
- **Bailey-Coy Books**, 414 Broadway E, 206-323-8842

- **Barnes & Noble Booksellers**, 2675 NE University Village St, 206-517-4107; 600 Pine St, 206-264-0156; 2600 SW Barton St, 206-932-0328, www.barnesandnoble. com
- **Borders Books & Music**, 1501 4th Ave, 206-622-4599, www.borders.com
- **City Books**, 1305 Madison St, 206-682-4334
- **Elliott Bay Book Company**, 101 S Main St, 206-624-6600, www.elliottbay book.com
- **Fremont Place Book Company**, 621 N 35th St, 206-547-5970, www.fremont placebooks.com
- **Island Books**, 3014 78th Ave SE, Mercer Island, 206-232-6920, www.mercer islandbooks.com
- **M. Coy Books & Espresso**, 117 Pine St, 206-623-5354
- **Magnolia's Book Store**, 3206 West McGraw St, 206-283-1062
- **Queen Anne Books**, 1811 Queen Anne Ave N, 206-283-5624, www.queenanne books.com
- **Santoro's Books**, 7216 Greenwood Ave N, 206-784-2113
- **Seattle University Book Store**, Seattle University, 823 12th Ave, 206-296-5820, www.seattleubookstore.edu
- **Secret Garden Bookshop**, 2214 NW Market St, 206-789-5006, www.secret gardenbooks.com
- **Square One Books**, 4724 42nd Ave SW, 206-935-5764, square1books.com
- **Third Place Books**, 17171 Bothell Way NE, Lake Forest Park, 206-366-3333, www.thirdplacebooks.com; **Ravenna Third Place Books**, 6504 20th Ave NE, 206-525-2347, www.ravennathirdplace.com
- **University Bookstore**, 4326 University Way NE, 206-634-3400; 990 102nd Ave NE, Bellevue, 425-462-4500; 18325 Campus Way NE, Ste 102, Bothell, 425-352-3344; 15311 Main St, Mill Creek, 425-385-3530; 1754 Pacific Ave, Tacoma, 253-272-8080, www.bookstore.washington.edu

## SPECIAL INTEREST

- **Aviation Book Company**, 7201 Perimeter Rd S, Ste C, Boeing Field, 206-767-5232, www.aviationbook.com
- **Cinema Books**, 4753 Roosevelt Way NE, 206-547-7667, cinemabooks.net
- **East West Bookshop**, 6500 Roosevelt Way NE, 206-523-3726, 800-587-6002, www.ewbookshop.com
- **Flora & Fauna Books**, 121 1st Ave S, 206-623-4727, www.ffbooks.net
- **Left Bank Books**, 92 Pike St, 206-622-0195, www.leftbankbooks.com
- **Mountaineers Bookstore**, 300 3rd Ave West, 206-284-6310, www.mountain eersbooks.org
- **Open Books: A Poem Emporium**, 2414 N 45th St, 206-633-0811, www.open poetrybooks.com

- **Seattle Mystery Bookshop**, 117 Cherry St, 206-587-5737, www.seattlemystery.com
- **Wide World Books & Maps**, 4411-A Wallingford Ave N, 206-634-3453, www.wideworldtravels.com
- **SeaOcean Book Berth**, 3534 Stone Way N, 206-675-9020, www.seaoceanbooks.com

## USED BOOKSTORES

- **Cat and Cannon Books**, 12513 Lake City Way, 206-367-6370, www.catandcannon.com
- **Couth Buzzard Used Books**, 7221 Greenwood Ave N, 206-789-8965
- **Epilogue Books**, 2005 NW Market St, 206-297-2665, www.epiloguebooks.com
- **Globe Bookstore**, 5220 University Way NE, 206-524-2480
- **Half Price Books**, 4709 Roosevelt Way NE, 206-547-7859, www.halfpricebooks.com
- **Horizon Books**, 425 15th Ave E, 206-329-3586; 6512 Roosevelt Way NE, 206-523-4217
- **Magus Bookstore**, 1408 NE 42nd St, 206-633-1800
- **Ophelia's Books**, 3504 Fremont Ave, 206-632-3759, www.opheliasbooks.com
- **Seattle Book Center**, 3530 Stone Way N, 206-547-7870, www.seattlebookcenter.com
- **Twice Sold Tales**, 905 E John St, 206-324-2421; 1311 NE 45th St, 206-545-4226; 3504 Fremont Ave N, 206-632-3759; 7 Mercer St, 206-282-7687, www.twicesoldtales.com

## LIBRARIES

In addition to the bookstores mentioned above, the Seattle area is fortunate to have two strong public library systems—Seattle Public and King County—an extensive university library network, and a handful of specialty collections. In 1998, Seattle voters approved a $196.4 million bond measure for building new libraries, and to improve or replace existing branches. Project completion is expected some time in 2007.

## PUBLIC LIBRARIES

In Seattle, most residents borrow their books from the Seattle Public Library system, a network of 23 neighborhood branches, plus the Washington Talking Book and Braille Library, and the central downtown branch. The Central Library, designed by renowned architect Rem Koolhaas and completed in 2004, is a modern architectural masterpiece that receives 8,000 visitors a day. For a public library branch near you, see the community resources listed at the end of each neighborhood profile.

The King County Library System (KCLS) complements the Seattle network. It is composed of 42 community branches from Kenmore to Muckleshoot, and Vashon Island to North Bend. KCLS also offers a number of traveling library services that allow trained library staff to visit senior centers, social service agencies, community centers, and childcare centers to bring books and computer training to those who can't always get to a library. For a list of neighborhood branches, visit www.kcls.org.

- **King County Library System**, 960 Newport Way NW, Issaquah, 425-369-3200, www.kcls.org
- **Seattle Public Library**, 1000 4th Ave, 206-386-4636, www.spl.lib.wa.us
- **Washington Talking Book and Braille Library**, 2021 9th Ave, 206-615-0400, TTY 206-615-0418, www.wtbbl.org

## SPECIALTY

- **Jewish Public Library**, 3502 NE 65th St, 206-290-6301
- **Karpeles Manuscript Library**, Tacoma Museum, 407 S "G" St, Tacoma, 206-383-2575, www.rain.org/~karpeles
- **The Mountaineers Library**, The Mountaineers Club, 300 3rd Ave W, 206-284-6310, http://mountaineers.library.net
- **Railway Library**, Northwest Railway Museum, 38625 SE King St, Snoqualmie, 425-888-3030, www.trainmuseum.org
- **Seattle Metaphysical Library**, 2220 NE Market St, L-05, 206-329-1794, www.seattlemetaphysical.org
- **Walter Johnson Memorial Library**, Nordic Heritage Museum, 3014 NW 67th St, 206-789-5707, www.nordicmuseum.org

## UNIVERSITY OF WASHINGTON LIBRARIES

The University of Washington maintains 21 libraries, from general undergraduate to specialized academic. Below is a list of available libraries. For more information, call or visit the web site, 206-543-0242, www.lib.washington.edu: Architecture & Urban Planning, Art, Chemistry, Drama, East Asia, Engineering, Fisheries-Oceanography, Business, Friday Harbor Library, Law, Health Sciences, K.K. Sherwood Library, Mathematics Research, Horticultural, Natural Sciences, Odegaard Undergraduate Library, Physics-Astronomy, Social Work, Suzzallo & Allen Library, UW Bothell Library, UW Tacoma Library.

## CULTURE FOR KIDS

In Seattle, there are so many cultural opportunities for kids they may grow up before they can see or do everything. Besides numerous musical and outdoor opportunities, there are museums, dance and theatre performances, and puppet shows all aimed at or comprised of children. Several print and online publications offer calendars of events for family and kids' events. In print, check the calendar listings in the Thursday editions of *The Seattle Times* (www.seattletimes.com) and the *Seattle Post-Intelligencer* (www.seattle-pi.com). *ParentMap Magazine* is issued monthly and offers a complete calendar of events and activities on its web site at www.parentmap.com. Online, visit the ParentCafe web site at www.parentcafe. org or Northwest Baby & Child at www.nwbaby.com for child-focused articles and listings of upcoming events. The Seattle Center, a popular family venue, hosts a variety of colorful festivals and cultural events throughout the year, www.seattle center.com.

The following child-oriented listing of events and places represents only a part of what the Emerald City has to offer. For more ideas on how to entertain the kids, including a cornucopia of family and holiday festivals, see **A Seattle Year**.

## MUSIC

- **Bellevue Youth Symphony Orchestra**, 400 108th Ave NE, #204, Bellevue, 425-467-5604, www.byso.org; there are no age requirements for the four orchestras and the flute ensemble, just one year of school or private instruction. Students come from over 20 communities in King, Snohomish, and Pierce counties and offer several performances throughout the school year.
- **Columbia Choirs**, 425-486-1987, 866-486-1987, www.columbiachoirs.com; the Columbia Choirs program trains kindergarten through adult singers. The organization operates several choirs for different youth levels, as well as women's and men's choirs. Performances are held throughout the Puget Sound region.
- **Northwest Girlchoir**, 6208 60th Ave NE, 206-985-3969, www.northwestgirl choir.org; offering five choir divisions for girls grades 3–12. Five mainstage concerts are produced each year, as well as several community performances and national and international tours.
- **Pacifica Children's Chorus**, 11342 17th Ave NE, 206-527-9095, www. pacificachoirs.org; over 100 young singers are given music education and the opportunity to join one of four performing choirs. Two or three concerts are offered each year in a variety of musical styles, and at least one performance is multi-disciplinary, combining music, dance, poetry, prose, and drama.

- **Seattle Girls' Choir**, 433 Tog Rd, Brinnon, WA 98320, www.seattlegirlschoir. org; performances include an annual SGC concert series, collaborative events with the Seattle Opera and Seattle Symphony, and tours, festivals, and competitions across the country and internationally. Students ages 6 to 18, from 35 communities around Puget Sound, participate in six different choirs, and receive instruction in vocal technique, music theory, and composition.
- **Seattle Youth Symphony Orchestras (SYSO)**, 11065 5th Ave NE, Ste A, 206-362-2300, www.syso.org; operates five full orchestras during the school year, summer music festivals, and extensive outreach programs, including the Endangered Instruments Program. Each of the five orchestras performs three concerts during the academic year.

# MUSEUMS

- **The Children's Museum**, Center House, Seattle Center, 206-441-1768, www. thechildrensmuseum.org; intended for children ages one to eight, this delightful interactive museum also presents special multi-cultural programs in the lower level of the Center House. Open Monday–Friday, 10 a.m. to 5 p.m., Saturday and Sunday, 10 a.m.–6 p.m. Admission is $5.50.
- **Northwest Railway Museum**, 38625 SE King St, Snoqualmie, 425-888-3030, www.trainmuseum.org; the Snoqualmie Depot, the centerpiece of the Northwest Railway Museum, is on the National Register of Historic Places. The museum's collection includes steam locomotives, passenger and freight cars, and railway artifacts. This is the largest railway museum in Washington. Open Thursday–Monday, 10 a.m. to 5 p.m. No charge for admission.
- **Rosalie Whyel Museum of Doll Art**, 1116 108th Ave NE, Bellevue, 425-888-3030, www.dollart.com; a premier collection of over 3,000 dolls, from antique to modern, as well as dollhouses, miniatures, and teddy bears, and exhibits on the history of doll making. Open Monday–Saturday, 10 a.m.–5 p.m., Sunday, 1 p.m.–5 p.m. Admission is $7 for adults, $6 for seniors, $5 for kids 5–17, and free for children 4 and under.

# OUTDOOR

- **Cougar Mountain Zoological Park**, 19525 SE 54th, Issaquah, 425-391-5508, www.cougarmountainzoo.org; this unique zoo has the largest herd of Siberian reindeer in the country, places in the top three for cougar facilities in the country, and offers the world's only wildlife tracks library.
- **Northwest Trek**, 11610 Trek Dr E, Eatonville, 360-832-6117, www.nwtrek.org; located in Eatonville, southeast of Seattle, the Northwest Trek wildlife park features up-close views of cougars, eagles, grizzly and black bears, and wolves,

among others. A tram tour is included in the admission price. Park hours vary depending on the time of year, so call or visit their web site before you visit. Admission is $12 for adults, $11 for seniors, $8 for kids 5–12, $5 for 3- and 4-year-olds, and free for kids 2 and under. Admission is less for Pierce County residents.

- **Point Defiance Zoo & Aquarium**, 5400 N Pearl St, Tacoma, 253-591-5337, www.pdza.org; a favorite among residents south of Seattle, Point Defiance Zoo & Aquarium puts kids eye-to-eye with beluga whales, pachyderms, sharks, and reptiles. The zoo opens at 9 a.m. year-round; closing time varies from 4 p.m. in winter to 6 p.m. in summer. Admission is $10 for adults, $9 for seniors, $8 for kids 4–12, and free for kids under 3. Admission is lower for residents of Pierce County.
- **Seattle Aquarium**, Pier 59, 1483 Alaskan Way, 206-386-4300, www.seattleaquarium.org; the star attractions at the Seattle Aquarium are the adorable sea otters and the underwater viewing dome, but kids also love the jellyfish tank and the giant octopus. A major expansion is scheduled to open in spring 2008, but the aquarium remains open during construction. Open daily, 10 a.m.–5 p.m. in the fall and winter; 9:30 a.m.–5 p.m. in the spring; 9:30 a.m.–7 p.m. in the summer. Admission is $12.50 for adults, $8.50 for kids 6–12, $5.50 for children 3–5, and free for kids 2 and under.
- **Woodland Park Zoo**, 5500 Phinney Ave N, 206-684-4800, www.zoo.org; in November 2000, the Woodland Park Zoo welcomed Hansa, a newborn Asian elephant. The youngster is now a zoo favorite, along with popular exhibits like the African Village and Butterflies & Blooms. Scheduled feeding times around the zoo are also a big hit. Hours vary, depending on the season, but the zoo is open every day of the year, including holidays. Call or visit the web site for specifics. Admission is $10.50 for adults, $8.50 for seniors, $7.50 for kids 3–12, and free for kids 2 and under.

## THEATER AND DANCE

- **Kaleidoscope Dance Company**, 12577 Densmore Ave N, 206-363-7281, www.creativedance.org/kaleidoscope; the only modern dance company in the world composed of 8 to 14 year olds. Offers two performances a year in winter and spring.
- **Northwest Puppet Center**, 9123 15th Ave NE, 206-523-2579, www.nwpuppet.org; the only permanent puppet theater in the region features the Carter Family Marionettes and hosts guest artists from around the world. Also offers a museum and archival library.
- **Seattle Children's Theatre**, Charlotte Martin Theater, 201 Thomas St, Seattle Center, 206-441-3322, www.sct.org, offers seven productions each season,

plus school matinees and two school touring productions. The season runs from September to June.

- **Youth Theatre Northwest**, 8805 SE 40th St, Mercer Island, 206-232-4145, www.youththeatre.org; teaches theater skills to kids 3–18 and presents five productions during the school year, as well as three summer stock performances.

S EATTLE HAS MUCH TO OFFER IN THE WAY OF SPORTS AND RECRE-
ation. For weekend warriors who enjoy playing games as much as they like
watching them, there are plenty of indoor and outdoor activities available,
from a recreational pick-up game at one of Seattle's many parks to participation
in an organized league. For avid spectators, there is professional and college action galore.

Health clubs are listed at the end of this chapter.

These **sports publications** offer in-depth coverage of local sporting events
and activities:

- *48 Degrees North*, 6327 Seaview Ave NW, 206-789-7350, www.48north.com
- *Fishing & Hunting News*, P.O. Box 3010, Bothell, WA 98041, 360-282-4200, www.fishingandhuntingnews.com
- *Northwest Runner*, 6310 NE 74th St, Ste 217E, 206-527-5301, www.nwrunner.com
- *Northwest Yachting Magazine*, 7342 15th Ave NW, 206-789-8116, www.nwyachting.com
- *Outdoors NW*, 10312 Wallingford Ave N, 206-418-0747, www.sportsetc.com

## TICKETS

If you follow sports at all, you already know that Seattle has professional basketball, baseball, and football teams. What you may not realize until you live here
is that fans in the Pacific Northwest tend to be of the fair-weather variety, both
figuratively and literally. While that can be upsetting to the players, it is often
good news for die-hard fans, because during mediocre seasons, tickets generally
can be purchased without much advance notice. In boom years, however, like the

Seattle Seahawks' 2005 season leading up to their appearance in SuperBowl XL, tickets are hard to come by.

Tickets for all Seattle professional sporting events can be purchased by phone or online at **Ticketmaster** (206-628-0888, www.ticketmaster.com) or in person at Ticketmaster outlets at most Fred Meyer stores. Or, you can visit the venue's box office. The Seattle Sonics and Storm play at Key Arena, the Seattle Mariners play at Safeco Field, and the Seattle Seahawks play at Qwest Field. See below under **Professional Sports** for web addresses and contact information for each team.

With the repeal of Seattle's anti-scalping ordinance in 2005, tickets to sold-out events are a little easier to come by than in years past, when your only recourse would be a high-priced ticket broker. Brokers are still an option, especially if you're wary of buying tickets online from individuals through web sites like eBay.com and craigslist.org. You can find brokers in the Yellow Pages under "Ticket Sales—Entertainment & Sports," or typing the search phrase "online ticket broker" into Google.com will result in pages of online brokers. As a last resort you can usually find people selling tickets near event venues, though you may be limited in availability and price. It's a seller's market.

## PROFESSIONAL AND COLLEGE SPORTS

## PROFESSIONAL SPORTS

### BASEBALL

Seattle is home to the Seattle Mariners, which after many years of being a sub-500 team, earned fan love and loyalty through a series of winning streaks and play-off berths. Also in the Seattle area are two minor league teams, the Tacoma Rainiers and the Everett AquaSox.

- The American League's **Seattle Mariners** play approximately 80 home games. They play in the highly touted Safeco Field, a ballpark admired for its easy viewing of baseball and a retractable roof for those notorious Seattle rain showers. You can order tickets by calling 206-622-HITS or online, where you can also print your tickets after purchasing. Visiting one of the Mariner stores, located in most area malls, is another option for ticket purchase. For a Mariners schedule and more information, go to http://seattle.mariners.mlb.com.
- The **Tacoma Rainiers** are a Triple-A club in the Pacific Coast league. A farm team for the Mariners, the Rainiers play during the spring and summer in Cheney Stadium. There are usually several fun theme nights throughout the

season with extra entertainment and prizes. For a schedule or tickets call 253-752-7700, or visit www.tacomarainiers.com.

- The **Everett AquaSox** host their home games at Everett Memorial Stadium in downtown Everett. The AquaSox are a Single-A farm team for the Seattle Mariners, and offer many exciting games during the summer. Contact their office at 425-258-3673, or visit www.aquasox.com.

## BASKETBALL

- The National Basketball Association's **Seattle SuperSonics** have played their home games at Key Arena, located at the Seattle Center, but 2006 found the team with problems over their Key Arena lease, and owner Howard Schultz, CEO of Starbucks, sold the team to an Oklahoma City group. The Sonics will continue to play the 2006-2007 season in Key Arena, and the new owners offered assurances that the Sonics will remain a Seattle team. In February 2007, the owners decided on Renton as the site for a new arena, but unless funding is approved by the Washington legislature, a move out of the area could still be in the future. For tickets, call 206-283-DUNK, or visit www.nba.com/sonics.
- The **Seattle Storm** joined the Women's National Basketball Association for the 2000 season. Like most expansion teams, the Storm struggled in their first season, but rapidly improved, and in 2004 they won the WNBA Championship and the continued adoration of fans. The Storm was sold along with the SuperSonics, so while they will play out the 2007 season in Key Arena, their future remains just as cloudy. For tickets and information, call 206-217-WNBA or visit www.wnba.com/storm.

## FOOTBALL

In 2002, the National Football League's **Seattle Seahawks** moved into their new, state-of-the-art stadium at Qwest Field—and into a new division, the NFC West. The team went on to a championship 2005 season and an appearance in Super Bowl XL, where they suffered a heartbreaking loss to the Steelers. Disappointed fans all over the city rallied around the cry "next year." For more about the Seahawks, go to www.seahawks.com. For tickets, call 888-NFL-HAWK.

## HOCKEY

- Key Arena is also home to the **Seattle Thunderbirds**, a Western Hockey League team. The Thunderbirds always draw a large and enthusiastic crowd for competitive games and the occasional brawl. Tickets and information are at 206-448-PUCK or www.seattle-thunderbirds.com.

- The **Everett Silvertips** made their Western Hockey League debut in the 2003-2004 season and two years later reached the final 4 in the WHL Playoffs. They play before enthusiastic fans in the Everett Events Center. For more information call 425-252-5100 or visit www.everettsilvertips.com.

## HORSE RACING

Northwest thoroughbred racing enthusiasts trek to Auburn to catch the action at **Emerald Downs**. For more information call 253-288-7000 or visit www. emdowns.com.

## SOCCER

- The **Seattle Sounders** are Seattle's professional soccer team. Part of the USL First Division League, they play their home games at Qwest Field. Though soccer is usually less popular than other major league sports in most US cities, the Sounders have a loyal following of boisterous fans. Call 800-796-KICK for tickets, or visit www.seattlesounders.net.
- Women's soccer in Seattle is represented by the **Seattle Sounder Saints**, a member of the USL W-League. They play at the Starfire Sports complex in Tukwila. For information call 206-431-3232 or visit www.starfiresports.com

## COLLEGE SPORTS

Many sports fans prefer college games to professional contests. For reasons of convenience, cost, or alum loyalty, it's true that the frenzied fans and the youthful energy found at college events make for an exciting experience. The area's largest draw for college sports is the University of Washington, which offers many first class sporting events. The ticket office is at 101 Graves Building on the UW campus. For more information about UW athletics see below or visit http://go huskies.cstv.com. To find out more about the sports programs of other nearby colleges or universities, call their information desk. (See **Childcare and Education** for a list of area schools.)

## UW BASEBALL

The Huskies have a men's baseball team and a women's softball team. Both play at Husky Ballpark. Call 206-543-2200 or go to http://gohuskies.fansonly.com for more information.

## UW BASKETBALL

The Husky Women's Basketball team is a frequent contender in the NCAA championship tournament, and the Husky Men's team made the NCAA championship tournament in 2005 and 2006. Both play their home games at Bank of America Arena on the UW campus. Check http://gohuskies.cstv.com on the web or call 206-543-2200 for tickets and information.

## UW FOOTBALL

The University of Washington's Husky Football team has a long list of national championships. Games are played at Husky Stadium, which is one of the best college football venues in the nation. Not only does the stadium offer great seating for the game, it provides fans a panoramic view of Lake Washington and snow-capped Mount Rainier. Football games are popular with students, and many alumni are season ticket holders, so it's often difficult to get tickets. Call 206-543-2200 or go to http://gohuskies.cstv.com for more information.

## PARTICIPANT SPORTS AND ACTIVITIES

Ask residents what they love most about the Puget Sound area, and a common response will be the great selection of outdoor recreation opportunities. From watching the sunset over the Olympics in a nearby neighborhood park, to climbing to the summit of Mount Rainier, there are hundreds of activities for every level of athlete throughout the four seasons.

If you're looking for general information on local parks, kiddie pools, tennis courts or community programs start with the **Seattle Parks and Recreation Department** (206-684-4075, www.cityofseattle.net/parks) or your local community center (listed after the neighborhood profiles). In addition to playgrounds, ball fields, swimming pools, and basketball and tennis courts, neighborhood community centers offer fitness classes, dance lessons, pottery and art classes, and other activities. **King County Parks** can be reached at 206-296-4232 or www.metrokc.gov/parks, and the **Kitsap County Department of Facilities, Parks and Recreation** can be reached at 360-337-5350 or www.kitsapgov.com/parks.

## PARKS AND RECREATION DEPARTMENTS

- **Auburn**, 910 9th St SE, 253-931-3043, www.ci.auburn.wa.us
- **Bainbridge Island**, 7666 NE High School Rd, 206-842-2306, www.biparks.org
- **Bellevue**, 450 110th Ave NE, 425-452-6881, www.ci.bellevue.wa.us
- **Bothell**, 18305 101st Ave NE, 425-486-7430, www.ci.bothell.wa.us

- **Bremerton**, 680 Lebo Blvd, 360-473-5305, www.ci.bremerton.wa.us
- **Burien**, 415 SW 150th St, 206-988-3700, www.burienparks.net
- **Des Moines**, 1000 S 220th St, 206-870-6527, www.desmoineswa.gov
- **Duvall**, 14701 Main St, Ste A-1, 425-788-3434, www.cityofduvall.com
- **Edmonds**, 700 Main St, 425-771-0230, www.ci.edmonds.wa.us
- **Everett**, 802 E Mukilteo Blvd, 425-257-8300, www.ci.everett.wa.us
- **Federal Way**, 33325 8th Ave S, 253-835-6901, www.cityoffederalway.com
- **Issaquah**, 301 Rainier Blvd S, 425-837-3300, www.ci.issaquah.wa.us
- **Kenmore**, 6700 NE 181st St, 425-398-8900, www.cityofkenmore.com
- **Kent**, 220 4th Ave S, 253-856-5100, www.ci.kent.wa.us
- **Kirkland**, 505 Market St, Ste A, 425-587-3300, www.ci.kirkland.wa.us
- **Lake Forest Park**, 17425 Ballinger Way NE, 206-368-5440, www.cityoflfp.com
- **Lynnwood**, 18900 44th Ave W, 425-771-4030, www.ci.lynnwood.wa.us
- **Mercer Island**, 9611 SE 36th St, 206-236-3545, www.ci.mercer-island.wa.us
- **Mountlake Terrace**, 23204 58th Ave W, 425-776-9173, www.ci.mountlake terrace.wa.us
- **Newcastle**, 13020 Newcastle Way, 425-649-4444, www.ci.newcastle.wa.us
- **North Bend**, 211 Main Ave N, 425-888-0486, www.ci.north-bend.wa.us
- **Redmond**, 16600 NE 80th St, 425-556-2300, www.ci.redmond.wa.us
- **Renton**, 1055 S Grady Way, 425-430-6600, www.ci.renton.wa.us
- **Sammamish,** 801 228th Ave SE, 425-898-0660, www.ci.sammamish.wa.us
- **SeaTac**, 4800 S 188th St, 206-973-4670, www.ci.seatac.wa.us
- **Seattle**, 100 Dexter Ave N, 206-684-4075, www.cityofseattle.net/parks
- **Shoreline**, 17544 Midvale Ave N, 206-546-5041, www.cityofshoreline.com
- **Snoqualmie**, 38194 SE Stearns Rd, 425-831-5784, www.ci.snoqualmie.wa.us
- **Tacoma**, 4702 S 19th St, 253-305-1000, www.metroparkstacoma.org
- **Tukwila**, 12424 42nd Ave S, 206-767-2342, www.ci.tukwila.wa.us
- **Vashon Island**, 17130 Vashon Hwy SW, 206-463-9602, www.vashonpark district.org
- **Woodinville**, 17301 133rd Ave NE, 425-489-2700, www.ci.woodinville.wa.us

## ADVENTURE RACING/ORIENTEERING

- Adventure racing is a multi-discipline sport that usually involves paddling, mountain biking, and trekking, as well as navigating a course through wilderness, and can take anywhere from hours to days. Sometimes other disciplines like horseback riding and fixed rope are involved. Some teams offer training to those new to the sport, but you may have to find other like-minded individuals and form your own team. The **Pacific Northwest Adventure Racing Community** offers links to teams, events, and a forum, and can be reached at 253-709-8232 or www.pnwar.com.

- Orienteering is a fast-growing sport in the area involving navigating a course through sometimes difficult terrain with a map and compass. The **Cascade Orienteering Club** offers events, training, and maps, as well as permanent orienteering courses around the area. They can be reached at 425-778-7202 or www.cascadeoc.org.

## BASEBALL/SOFTBALL

Every spring, as the cherry trees blossom, Seattle residents flock to local fields to play baseball or softball. Call one of the area parks and recreation departments listed above to reserve a field for a casual game between friends, or put together your own team and participate in a league. Most leagues are organized privately or through local community centers (listed after the neighborhood profiles). The following resources may also be helpful:

### ADULT LEAGUES

- **Bellevue Baseball/Softball Athletic Association**, 425-746-4592
- **Puget Sound Senior Baseball League**, 425-957-1430, www.pssbl.com

### YOUTH LEAGUES

- **Little League,** www.littleleague.org; every city and town in the Puget Sound region offers Little League baseball and softball. Larger cities like Seattle and Bellevue have several leagues. To find a league near you visit the official web site.
- **United States Amateur Baseball Association**, 425-776-7130, www.usaba. com

If you're simply in the mood for an impromptu game with friends or for some casual batting practice, ball fields are available. To reserve a field, call the **Seattle Parks and Recreation Individual Field Reservation Line** at 206-684-4077. For parks in surrounding communities, contact the city parks and recreation departments listed previously in this chapter.

## BASKETBALL

Considering Seattle's unpredictable weather, you might think that basketball would be near the bottom of the list as a favorite sport. That's definitely not the case. Lively pick-up games are common in Seattle's playgrounds and community centers, and there are many organized leagues at gyms and athletic clubs. If you're interested in league play or workshops, consider the health clubs listed later in this chapter, or call one of the area's parks and recreation departments (see above). For a casual but competitive pick-up game in Seattle call your local community center (see **Community Resources** following each neighborhood write-up in the **Seattle Neighborhoods** chapter) or call the **Seattle Parks and Recreation Department** at 206-684-4075.

# BICYCLING

In Seattle, cycling is popular as both a sport and a means of transportation. Despite the unpredictable weather and hilly topography, many residents bike to work and school, and to do errands. Bicycle lanes have become more common on major thoroughfares throughout the city and its surrounding communities. (For more information on commuting by bike, see the **Transportation** chapter.)

Green Lake is a popular destination for recreational cyclists, as are many locations along the **Burke-Gilman Trail**. For a fun and scenic ride, bike the Burke-Gilman Trail from Gasworks Park on Lake Union to Kenmore on Lake Washington. This trail is also used as a shortcut for many UW students riding to school each morning.

**Cascade Bicycle Club (CBC)**, the largest cycling club in the United States, is based in Seattle. With over 6,500 members, CBC sponsors several rides each day, for riders of all skill levels, as well as several annual events. Contact CBC at 206-522-BIKE, or check out their comprehensive web site at www.cascade.org. Those interested in track racing should contact the **Marymoor Velodrome Association** at 206-957-4555, or go to http://marymoor.velodrome.org. Racing events are held regularly at Marymoor Park in Redmond.

The following are a few of the most popular annual street rides in the Seattle area:

- **The Cannonball**, held in late June and organized by the Redmond Cycling Club, is a one-day trek from Seattle to Spokane along I-90. Call 425-739-8609 or visit www.redmondcyclingclub.org.
- **Chilly Hilly**, held in late February and sponsored by CBC, is a 33-mile bicycle tour around Bainbridge Island. It marks the official opening of bicycle season in the Pacific Northwest.
- **The Daffodil Classic**, an annual ride sponsored by the **Tacoma Wheelmen's Bicycle Club**, is held in mid-April. There are several routes, ranging from 20 to 100 miles. Call 253-759-2800 or visit www.twbc.org.
- **The Kitsap Color Classic**, a ride through Kitsap County on the Olympic Peninsula, is held in early October when the leaves begin to turn. CBC sponsors this ride.
- **The RAMROD (Ride Around Mount Rainier in One Day)** is sponsored by the Redmond Cycling Club and takes place in late July. It is a 150+ mile race around Mount Rainier, and is perhaps the most challenging in the area, with 10,000 feet of climbing during the race.

- **STP (Seattle-to-Portland)** is a two-day non-competitive bike ride from Seattle to Portland, sponsored by the CBC. Riders can choose to participate for one or two days; those riding for two days stay overnight midway. The STP takes place in mid-July and is the best-known bicycling event in the area.

Just as popular as traditional bicycling, mountain biking is a favorite recreational activity for many Seattle residents. Seattle's hills provide great practice routes, and there are several scenic and challenging mountain-bike trails just a short drive out of the city. An excellent resource for local mountain-biking information is the **Backcountry Bicycle Trails Club** (206-524-2900, www.bbtc.org). If you're new to the sport, the club offers a "boot camp" for first-time trail riders. For information on nearby trails, check out a copy of the *King County Bicycling Guidemap*, available at King County Public Libraries; it can also be ordered by phone or online: 206-263-4741, www.metrokc.gov/kcdot/tp.

## BIRD WATCHING

Though bird watching may not rank high on Seattle's list of popular pursuits, the region does include its fair share of birders. In Seattle, the **National Audubon Society** recommends Discovery and Green Lake parks, the Montlake Wetlands, Washington Park Arboretum, and in West Seattle, Alki Beach and Lincoln Park. To find bird watching spots in surrounding communities, visit http://wa.audubon. org.

- **East Lake Washington Audubon Society**, 308 4th Ave S, Kirkland, 425-576-8805, www.elwas.org
- **National Audubon of Washington**, 1411 4th Ave S, Ste 920, Seattle, 206-652-2444, http://wa.audubon.org
- **Pilchuck Audubon Society**, 2928 Rockefeller, Everett, 425-252-0926, www.pilchuckaudubon.org
- **Seattle Audubon Society**, 8050 35th Ave NE, 206-523-4483, www.seattleaudubon.org
- **Washington Ornithological Society**, P.O. Box 3178, Seattle, WA 98103, www.wos.org

## BOATING

It's no surprise that Seattle residents love their watercraft. Even on cloudy days, you'll see several boats out on the lakes or in Puget Sound. Colorful spinnakers dot the Sound each weekend, as sailing races are held near Shilshole Bay. On sunny days, floatplanes arriving at Lake Union dodge the many sailboats that crowd the lake, and the early-morning calm of Lake Washington entices crowds of skiers.

## ROWING, CANOEING, AND KAYAKING

- **Everett Rowing Association**, P.O. Box 1774, Everett, 98206, 425-257-8337, www.everettrowing.com
- **Green Lake Small Craft Center**, 5900 W Green Lake Way N, 206-684-4074, www.seattle.gov/parks/boats
- **Lake Union Crew Rowing Club**, 11 E Allison St, 206-860-4199, www.lakeunioncrew.com
- **Lake Washington Rowing Club**, 910 N Northlake Way, 206-547-1583, http://lakewashingtonrowing.com
- **Moss Bay Rowing & Kayaking Center**, 1001 Fairview Ave N, 206-682-2031, www.mossbay.net
- **Mount Baker Rowing and Sailing Center**, 3800 Lake Washington Blvd S, 206-386-1913, www.seattle.gov/parks/boats
- **Northwest Outdoor Center**, 2100 Westlake Ave N, 206-281-9694, www.nwoc.com
- **Sammamish Rowing Association**, 5022 W Lake Sammamish Pkwy, Redmond, 425-653-2583, www.srarowing.com
- **Seattle Canoe and Kayak Club**, 5900 W Green Lake Way N, 206-684-4074, www.scn.org/skcc
- **Washington Kayak Club**, P.O. Box 24264, Seattle, WA 98124, 206-433-1983, www.wakayakclub.org

## SAILING

- **Mount Baker Rowing and Sailing Center**, 3800 Lake Washington Blvd S, 206-386-1913, www.seattle.gov/parks/boats
- **Renton Sailing Club**, 425-235-0952, www.rentonsailing.org
- **Sail Sand Point**, 7777 62nd Ave NE, #101, 206-525-8782, www.sailsandpoint.org
- **Seattle Sailing Club**, 7001 Seaview Ave NW, Ste 125, 206-782-5100, www.seattlesailing.com
- **Wind Works Sailing Center**, 7001 Seaview Ave NW, Ste 204, 206-784-9386, www.windworkssailing.com

## YACHT CLUBS

- **Corinthian Yacht Club of Seattle**, 7755 Seaview Ave NW, 206-789-1919, http://cycseattle.org
- **Edmonds Yacht Club**, 456 Admiral Way, Edmonds, 425-778-5499, www.edmondsyachtclub.com

- **Meydenbauer Bay Yacht Club**, P.O. Box 863, Bellevue, WA 98009, 425-454-8880, www.mbycwa.org
- **Queen City Yacht Club**, 2608 Boyer Ave E, 206-709-2000, www.queencity.org
- **Rainier Yacht Club**, 9094 Seward Ave S, 206-722-9576, www.rainieryachtclub.com
- **Seattle Yacht Club**, 1807 E Hamlin St, 206-325-1000, www.seattleyachtclub.org
- **Tyee Yacht Club**, 3229 Fairview Ave E, 206-324-0200, www.tyeeyachtclub.org
- **Washington Yacht Club**, University of Washington, 206-543-2219, http://students.washington.edu/sailing

## OTHER BOATING RESOURCES

- **Boating Safety Classes,** 800-336-BOAT
- **Seattle Police Harbor Patrol Unit,** 206-684-4071
- **Seattle Boat Ramp Supervisor,** 206-684-7249
- **US Coast Guard 24-hour Emergency,** 800-982-8813

# BOWLING

Bowling is most popular during Seattle's wet, gray winter months. The following bowling alleys organize leagues regularly, but also welcome amateur and first-time bowlers.

- **Imperial Lanes**, 2101 22nd Ave S, 206-325-2525, www.amf.com/imperiallanes
- **Hi-Line Lanes**, 15733 Ambaum Blvd SW, Burien, 206-244-2272, www.hilinelanes.com
- **Magic Lanes**, 10612 15th Ave SW, 206-244-5060, www.magiclanes.com
- **Roxbury Lanes**, 2823 SW Roxbury St, 206-935-7400, http://roxburylanes.com
- **Sun Villa Lanes**, 3080 148th SE, Bellevue, 425-455-8155, www.amf.com/sunvillalanes
- **Sunset Bowl**, 1420 NW Market St, 206-782-7310, www.sunsetbowl.com
- **West Seattle Bowl**, 4505 39th Ave SW, 206-932-3731, www.wsbowl.com

# CHESS

- **America's Foundation for Chess**, 3720 Carillon Point, Kirkland, 425-216-0051, www.af4c.org
- **Seattle Chess Club**, 17517 15th Ave NE, 206-417-5405, www.seattlechessclub.org

# DANCE

- **Arthur Murray Dance Studios**, 530 Dexter Ave N, 206-447-2701, www.wash ingtondancesport.com
- **Century Ballroom**, 915 E Pine St, 206-324-7263, www.centuryballroom.com
- **DanceSport International**, 12535 Lake City Way NE, 206-361-8239, www. dancesportseattle.com
- **Fifth Avenue Dance Studios**, 2211 3rd Ave, 206-621-9824
- **Sharon Ardelle's Dance Factory**, 327 NE 91st, 206-522-0575
- **Washington Dance Club**, 1017 Stewart St, 206-628-8939, www. washingtondance.com

# FENCING

- **Fleur de Lys Fencing Club**, 2550 34th Ave W, 206-782-1165, www. fleurdelysfencing.org
- **Rain City Fencing Center**, 12368 Northup Way, Bellevue, 425-497-8897, www. raincityfencing.com
- **Salle Auriol Seattle**, 760 Harrison St, 206-623-8357, www.salleauriol.com

# FIELD HOCKEY/LACROSSE

- **Coopers Lacrosse Club**, 8065 Lake City Way NE, 206-522-2923, www. cooperslacrosse.com
- **Seattle Lacrosse Club**, www.seattlelacrosseclub.com
- **Seattle Women's Field Hockey Club**, www.seattlefieldhockey.org

# FISHING AND SHELLFISH GATHERING

The fishing and shellfishing opportunities in Washington are nothing short of amazing. Although the area is famous for salmon and Dungeness crab, you'll also find clams, mussels, oysters, trout, and steelhead. If you're gathering shellfish with a local, you may even get a glimpse of a geoduck. Geoduck, pronounced "gooey-duck," are huge razor clams indigenous to Washington's ocean beaches. Like clams, you'll need to dig for geoduck, but they're fast and a lot tougher to catch!

There is one thing to be aware of before heading to a beach with bucket and shovel in hand—beaches are periodically closed due to algae blooms and/or pollution. The summer of 2006 saw the worst Red Tide in a decade and most Puget Sound beaches were closed to shellfish harvesting. Some of the toxins affecting shellfish can cause paralytic shellfish poisoning in humans and can't be cooked out, so it's always a good idea to check with the **Washington Department of**

**Fish and Wildlife** first. You can reach their shellfish hotline at 800-562-5632 or visit the web site. Contact information is below.

Several types of salmon and trout migrate through the waters of western Washington. Chinook are the largest of the Pacific salmon and spawn in the Columbia and Snake rivers, as well as other small rivers and streams. Coho or silver salmon are a popular sport fish in the Puget Sound, and can also be found in coastal tributaries. Sockeye salmon are a flavorful salmon, found in Lake Washington, Baker Lake, Quinault Lake, Ozette Lake, and Lake Wenatchee. Pink salmon, or humpback salmon, spawn only every other year, so they appear in Washington waters during odd-numbered years only. Chum salmon can be found in small coastal streams, but are not particularly tasty and so are not popular as a sport fish. Steelhead and cutthroat trout, named for the red markings just below the head of the fish, live in freshwater streams and Puget Sound bays. Although cutthroats are common throughout North America, those in Washington are the only ones that spend the warm summer months in saltwater.

Lakes and rivers in Washington yield an unusual catch of fish, including many non-native species. When settlers arrived here in the mid-1800s, they caught trout, char, whitefish and a few other small fish in the freshwater lakes and streams. As more people moved to the area and the trout population began to dwindle, additional species of fish were imported. While trout (including cutthroat, steelhead, brook and brown trout) are still the most popular fish in Washington's many rivers, the state's lakes and rivers are now stocked with a variety of fish, from sunfish and catfish, to perch and pike.

Favorite locations for trout fishing near the Puget Sound are the Skagit, Snoqualmie, Skykomish and Green rivers. Other plentiful rivers in the state include the Columbia, Cowlitz, Kalama and Hoh. Bottomfish such as halibut, cod, and rockfish are common in Neah Bay, the Hood Canal, and around the San Juan Islands. Lake Washington and the Puget Sound have limited numbers of sturgeon, which are more numerous in the Columbia and Snake Rivers. If you're looking for largemouth bass, try Moses Lake, Silver Lake, Long Lake, Sprague Lake or the Columbia River. Smallmouth bass are commonly found in the Columbia, Snake, and Yakima rivers, and in Lake Washington, Lake Sammamish, and Lake Stevens. You may catch yellow perch in Lake Washington, Lake Sammamish or Lake Stevens. You're more likely to find walleye in eastern Washington lakes such as Moses Lake, Lake Roosevelt or Soda Lake. If you're a fan of catfish, you'll find brown bullheads in Lake Washington, Moses Lake or Liberty Lake, and channel catfish in Fazon Lake and Sprague Lake. Tiger muskies (pike) are commonly found in Mayfield Lake in Lewis County, while northern pikes swim in Long Lake near Spokane.

The **Washington Department of Fish and Wildlife (WDFW)** regulates fishing and shellfish gathering throughout the state, acting as both conservation and licensing entity. The agency provides many helpful publications on a variety of fish and wildlife subjects, which can be ordered by phone or downloaded from the department's web site (see below). Recreational fishing licenses are required for all state residents 15 and over, and for all non-residents, regardless of age. Licenses are divided into three categories: freshwater, saltwater, and shellfish/seaweed. Licenses are valid for a variety of time periods, from one day to one year, and must be displayed at all times while fishing or gathering shellfish. License fees and restrictions vary according to the fish or shellfish collected; fees range from $4.93 to $41.61 for residents. Licenses may be purchased from most sporting goods stores, or online at http://fishhunt.dfw.wa.gov.

- **Washington State Department of Fish and Wildlife**, 1111 Washington St SE, Olympia, 360-902-2200, http://wdfw.wa.gov

## FRISBEE

While many Seattle parks have adequate open spaces for a game of frisbee, a few parks are especially popular with enthusiasts. Gasworks Park, at the north end of Lake Union, combines a wide expanse of green lawn with pleasant breezes off the lake. Discovery Park in Magnolia has a good-sized grassy meadow in which to play, and Woodland Park near Green Lake offers a quiet shady expanse. The Seattle area also features several disc golf courses, including Lakewood King County Park, North Park, Juel Community Park, and Lake Fenwick. For more information, go to www.pdga.com.

If ultimate frisbee is your game of choice, you may want to try one of several regular pick-up games in the area. Common locations are Volunteer Park, Lincoln Park in West Seattle, and Marymoor Park in Redmond. League play is organized privately or through the **Northwest Ultimate Association**, P.O. Box 85112, Seattle, WA 98145, 206-781-5840, www.discnw.org.

## GOLF

Three public golf courses, run by the City of Seattle Parks and Recreation Department, are listed below, along with public courses in surrounding communities. In addition, the parks department offers a short course near Green Lake, the **Green Lake Pitch and Putt** (walk-ons only), and near Queen Anne, the **Interbay Golf Center**, with miniature golf course and driving range (reservations taken up to seven days in advance). While there are many other golf courses in the greater Seattle area, most are private or semi-private courses. Check the local Yellow Pages for more information.

- **Classic Country Club**, 4908 208th St E, Spanaway, 253-847-4440, www.classicgolfclub.net
- **The Golf Club at Newcastle**, 15500 Six Penny Lane, 425-793-5566, www.newcastlegolf.com
- **Green Lake Pitch and Putt**, 5701 W Green Lake Way N, 206-632-2280, www.seattle.gov/parks/athletics

- **Harbour Pointe Golf Club**, 11817 Harbour Pointe Blvd, Mukilteo, 206-355-6060, www.harbourpointegolf.com
- **Interbay Golf Center**, 2501 15th Ave W, 206-285-2200, www.seattlegolf.com/interbay.php
- **Jackson Park Golf Club**, 1000 NE 135th St, 206-363-4747, www.seattlegolf.com/jackson.php
- **Jefferson Park Golf Club**, 4101 Beacon Ave S, 206-762-4513, www.seattlegolf.com/jefferson.php
- **Kayak Point Golf Course**, 15711 Marine Dr, Stanwood, 360-652-9676, www.kayakpoint.com
- **Meadow Park Golf Course**, 7108 Lakewood Dr, Tacoma, 253-473-3033, www.metroparkstacoma.org
- **West Seattle Golf Club**, 4470 35th Ave SW, 206-935-5187, www.seattlegolf.com/west.php

## GYMNASTICS

Most community centers and YMCAs offer gymnastics and tumbling classes, but there are a few gyms in the area devoted exclusively to the sport:

- **Emerald City Gymnastics Academy**, 17969 NE 65th, Redmond, 425-861-8772
- **Gymnastics East**, 13425 SE 30th St, Ste 2A, Bellevue, 425-644-8117, www.gymeast.com
- **Gymnastics Unlimited**, 34016 9th Ave S, D-5, Federal Way, 253-815-0998, www.gymnasticsunlimitedus.com
- **Metropolitan Gymnastics**, 6822 S 190th St, Kent, 206-575-4138, www.metropolitangym.com
- **Northshore Gymnastics Center**, 19460 144th Ave NE, Woodinville, 425-402-6602, www.northshoregymnastics.com
- **Northwest Aerials**, 12440 128th Lane NE, Kirkland, 425-823-2665, www.nwaerials.com

## HANG GLIDING/PARAGLIDING

Most of the Puget Sound region is an hour or less from the foothills of the Cascade Mountains, which are an ideal place for hang gliding and paragliding, offering spectacular scenery on long, slow descents.

- **AAAA Hang Gliding School**, 11345 Sand Point Way NE, 206-363-3680
- **Cloudbase Country Club**, P.O. Box 629, Issaquah, 98027, 425-703-2382, www.cloudbase.org
- **The Northwest Paragliding Club**, P.O. Box 2265, Issaquah, 98027, www.nwparagliding.com

- **Parafly Paragliding**, 10534 157th Ave NE, Redmond, 425-605-0433, www. paraflyparagliding.com
- **The Paragliding Center**, 11206 Issaquah-Hobart Rd SE, Issaquah, 206-387-3477, www.seattleparagliding.com
- **Paraglide Washington**, 5500 S Juniper St, 206-328-1104, www.paraglide washington.com
- **SkyCo Sports**, 70 E Sunset Way, Issaquah, 425-890-0265, www.skycosports. com

## HIKING

If you like to hike, you'll love living in Seattle. Not only are there several short hikes in local parks, such as Discovery Park and Seward Park, but just outside of the city there are hundreds of trails for hikers of all fitness levels. Mountaineers Books publishes a series of useful books that describe nearly every trail in Washington. The following resources may be helpful when choosing a trail.

- **Mountaineers Books**, 1011 SW Klickitat Way, 206-223-6303, www.mountain eersbooks.org
- **National Park Service**, 909 1st Ave, 206-220-4000, www.nps.gov
- **The Mountaineers Club**, 300 3rd Ave W, 206-284-6310, www.mountaineers. org
- **Seattle Post Intelligencer**, http://seattlepi.nwsource.com/getaways/hike
- **WashingtonHikes.com**, www.washingtonhikes.com
- **Washington Trails Association**, 2019 3rd Ave S, Ste 100, 206-625-1367, www. wta.org

## HORSEBACK RIDING

Horseback rides and lessons are available in many of Seattle's surrounding rural communities. Check with the following, or look in the Yellow Pages under "Horse Rentals & Riding" for more listings.

- **Creekside Stables**, 17513 51st Ave SE, Bothell, 425-485-6040, www.geocities. com/creekside_stables
- **Elk Run Stables**, 45004 SE 161st Pl, North Bend, 425-888-4341
- **Gold Creek Equestrian Center**, 16528 148th Ave NE, Woodinville, 425-806-4653, www.gold-creek.com
- **Phoenix Farm**, 8832 222nd St SE, Woodinville, 425-486-9395, www.phoenix farm.com
- **Tiger Mountain Outfitters**, 24508 SE 133rd, Issaquah, 425-392-5090

## ICE SKATING/HOCKEY

Most bodies of water in Seattle never freeze, but there are plenty of ice skating opportunities available, albeit the indoor kind. Most rinks offer skate rentals, lessons, hockey leagues and open ice sessions. During the holiday season, an ice rink at **Seattle Center** is open to the public. Call 206-684-7200 for details. Year-round rinks include:

- **Castle Ice Arena**, 12620 164th SE, Renton, 425-254-8750, www.castleice.com
- **Highland Ice Arena,** 18005 Aurora Ave N, Shoreline, 206-546-2431, www.highlandice.com
- **Kingsgate Ice Arena**, 14326 124th Ave NE, Kirkland, 425-823-1242
- **Lynnwood Ice Center**, 19803 68th Ave W, Lynnwood, 425-640-9999, www.lynnwoodicecenter.com
- **Olympic View Arena**, 22202 70th Ave W, Mountlake Terrace, 425-672-9012, www.olyview.com

## IN-LINE/ROLLER SKATING AND SKATEBOARDING

In-line skating is a popular activity on Seattle's paved paths, particularly at Green Lake, Alki Beach, and on the Burke-Gilman Trail. Some skaters even turn vacant parking lots into impromptu rinks for trick skating or pick-up hockey games. Several sporting goods stores offer in-line skating rentals. **Gregg's Greenlake Cycle**, 7007 Woodlawn Ave NE, 206-523-1822, www.greggscycles.com, offers easy access to a paved path.

For in-line skating lessons, try **Get Your Bearings Inline Skate School** at the **Lynnwood Roll-A-Way Skate Center**, 6210 200th St SW, Lynnwood, 206-300-3919, www.getyourbearings.com, or Skate Journeys, 206-276-9328, www.skatejourneys.com. For inline hockey leagues and drop-ins, go to **Arena Sports** at Magnuson Park, 7727 63rd Ave NE, Ste 101, 206-985-8990, www.arenasports.net. A good roller rink for family skating is the **Skate King**, 2301 140th Ave NE, Bellevue, 425-641-2047, www.bellevueskateking.com.

If skateboarding is your thing, try the **Inner Space Skatepark** at 3506-1/2 Stone Way N, 206-634-9090. www.innerspaceskateboarding.com, or the outdoor skate park at **Ballard Commons Park**, 5701 22nd Ave NW.

## MARTIAL ARTS

Every style of martial arts is represented by dozens of schools and dojos in the Seattle area and surrounding communities. The martial arts have a long history in Seattle, where the first U.S. judo dojo was founded in 1907. Bruce Lee, who attended the University of Washington, developed his style of kung-fu here and is buried in Lake View Cemetery on Capitol Hill. Whether you're looking for simple self defense instruction or advanced karate moves, you're sure to find a sensei (instructor) to suit your needs. Many community centers offer classes, and the following are just a sampling of the martial arts schools in the area. For a complete listing, check the Yellow Pages under "Martial Arts Instruction".

- **Aikido of West Seattle**, 4421 Fauntleroy Way SW, 206-938-5222, www.aikidows.com
- **Chinese Wushu and Tai Chi Academy**, 709-1/2 S King St, 206-749-9513, www.yijiaowushu.com
- **Greenlake Martial Arts**, 319 NE 72nd St, 206-522-2457, www.newkungfu.com
- **Minakami Karate Dojo**, 3000 NE 125th St, 206-363-7717; 15230 Lake Hills Blvd, Bellevue, 206-356-1720, www.minakamikarate.com
- **MKG Martial Arts International**, 8310 Greenwood Ave N, 206-789-2411, www.mkgseattle.com
- **Two Cranes Aikido**, 7110 Woodlawn Ave NE, 206-523-5503, www.twocranesaikido.com
- **Washington Karate Association**, 8618 3rd Ave NW, 206-784-3171; 14906 Bel-Red Rd, Bellevue, 425-641-8123; 8015 Steilacom Blvd SW, Lakewood, 253-589-6924, www.washingtonkarate.com
- **World Martial Arts & Health**, 2002 Market St, 206-782-7000; 12402 SE 38th St, Ste 103, Bellevue, www.yunsmartialarts.com

## RACQUET SPORTS

## TENNIS

Outdoor public tennis courts dot the city and are generally open on a first-come, first-served basis, although reservations may be requested through the Seattle Parks and Recreation Department. The Amy Yee Tennis Center in the Mount Baker neighborhood, also run by the Seattle Parks and Recreation Department, offers lessons and indoor and outdoor courts. For tennis courts in surrounding communities, contact one of the parks and recreation departments listed previously in this chapter.

- **Seattle Parks and Recreation Department**, Outdoor Court Information/Reservations, 206-684-4062, www.seattle.gov/parks/athletics
- **Amy Yee Tennis Center**, 2000 Martin Luther King Jr. Way S, 206-684-4764, www.seattle.gov/parks/athletics

## RACQUETBALL

A few racquetball courts in the greater Seattle area are open to the public:

- **Kent Commons**, 525 4th Ave N, Kent, 253-856-5000, www.ci.kent.wa.us
- **Lynnwood Recreation Center,** 18900 44th Ave W, Lynnwood, 425-771-4030, www.ci.lynnwood.wa.us
- **Mountlake Terrace Recreation Pavilion**, 5303 228th St SW, Mountlake Terrace, 425-776-9173, www.cityofmlt.com
- **White Center Park**, 1321 SW 102nd St, Seattle, 206-205-5275, www.metrokc. gov

## CLUBS

Private racquet clubs and health clubs offer lessons and court rentals for a variety of games, including tennis, racquetball, and squash. Call for details, as activities and services vary.

- **Central Park Tennis Club**, 12630 NE 59th, Kirkland, 425-822-2206, www. centralparktennisclub.com
- **Edgebrook Club**, 13454 SE Newport Way, Bellevue, 425-746-2786, www. edgebrookclub.org
- **Forest Crest Tennis Club**, 4901 238th St SW, Mountlake Terrace, 425-774-0014, www.forestcrest.com
- **Gold Creek Tennis & Sports Club**, 15327 140th Pl NE, Woodinville, 425-487-1090, www.goldcreektennis.com
- **Mercer Island Country Club**, 8700 SE 71st St, Mercer Island, 206-232-5600, www.mercerislandcc.com
- **Olympic Athletic Club**, 5301 Leary Way NW, 206-789-5010, www.olympic athleticclub.com
- **Seattle Tennis Club**, 922 McGilvra Blvd E, 206-324-3200, www.seattletennis club.org
- **Silver Lake Tennis & Fitness Club**, 505 128th St SE, Everett, 425-745-1617, www.columbiaathletic.com

## ROCK CLIMBING

Rock climbing is a popular sport in Washington, with several local climbing clubs and walls, as well as many nearby outdoor destinations. Closest perhaps is Little Si, near North Bend along I-90. Leavenworth, a Bavarian-style village on Highway 2, attracts a variety of climbers. If you're new to the sport, visit the Leavenworth area and start with the boulders near Icicle Creek; many of them have bars embedded in the rock for easy top-roping. More difficult climbs near Leavenworth can be found at Castle Rock and the Peshastin Pinnacles. Near Stevens Pass, the Index Town Wall provides challenging routes for climbers of all levels. Close to the town of Vantage, basalt columns near the Columbia River offer good climbing for experienced climbers only. Nearby, an area known as The Feathers is appropriate for beginners. In the Olympics, Flapjack Lakes Trail leads to challenging rock-climbing.

If you've never tried rock-climbing before, or if you're an experienced climber who wants to stay in practice without leaving the city, the following climbing walls and clubs offer a variety of rock-climbing experiences. Most of the clubs offer rock-climbing lessons, as do those organizations listed under "Lessons and Guide Resources" below.

## CLIMBING WALLS

- **REI Pinnacle** (indoor), 222 Yale Ave N, 206-223-1944, www.rei.com
- **University of Washington Climbing Rock** (outdoor), south of Husky Stadium on Montlake Ave NE, 206-543-9433
- **Schurman Rock** (outdoor), Camp Long, 5200 35th Ave SW, 206-684-7434, www.ci.seattle.wa.us
- **Marymoor Climbing Structure** (outdoor), east end of Marymoor Park, Redmond, 206-296-2964

## ROCK-CLIMBING CLUBS

- **Stone Gardens**, 2839 NW Market St, 206-781-9828, www.stonegardens.com
- **Vertical World**, 2123 W Elmore St, Seattle, 206-283-4497; 15036-B NE 95th Street, Redmond, 425-881-8826; 5934 State Hwy 303 NE, Bremerton, 360-373-6676, www.verticalworld.com

## LESSONS AND GUIDE RESOURCES

- **Alpine Ascents International**, 121 Mercer St, 206-378-1927, www.alpine ascents.com
- **Cascade Alpine Guides & Adventures**, 5103 190th Pl NE, Sammamish, 425-898-7329, 800-981-0381, www.cascadealpine.com
- **Mountain Madness**, 3018 SW Charlestown St, 206-937-8389, www.moun tainmadness.com
- **The Mountaineers**, 300 3rd Ave W, 206-284-6310, www.mountaineers.org
- **REI**, 222 Yale Ave N, 206-223-1944; 7500 166th Ave NE, Redmond, 425-882-1158; 3000 184th St SW, Lynnwood, 425-640-6200; 240 Andover Park W, Tukwila, 206-248-1938; 3825 S Steele St, Tacoma, 253-671-1938, www.rei.com

# RUGBY/GAELIC FOOTBALL

- **Eastside Rugby Football Club**, 206-388-3217, www.seattlerugby.com
- **The Seattle Gaels**, www.seattlegaels.com
- **The Seattle Quake Rugby Football Club**, 1122 E Pike St, #1124, 206-337-1346, www.quakerugby.org
- **Seattle Rugby Club**, P.O. Box 85282, Seattle, 98145, 206-781-3690, www.seattlerugbyclub.org
- **Tacoma Nomads Rugby Football Club**, 3513 E Portland Ave, Tacoma, www.tacomarugby.com
- **Valley Rugby Football Club**, P.O. Box 58551, Tukwila, 98138, 206-382-7299, www.valleyrugby.com

# RUNNING

Considering the weather in Seattle, you might think that running wouldn't be a favorite sport in the city. For some reason, though, the rain just seems to make area runners more determined. The most popular running locations in Seattle are Green Lake (the inner loop is 2.8 miles, the outer loop is slightly over 3 miles), the Burke-Gilman Trail, Myrtle Edwards Park, and Alki Beach in West Seattle. Listed below are several running clubs in Seattle, which sponsor weekly club runs and annual events:

- **Club Northwest**, P.O. Box 31958, Seattle, 98103, 206-729-9972, www.clubnorthwest.org
- **Eastside Runners**, P.O. Box 2616, Redmond, WA 98073, www.eastsiderunners.com
- **Seattle Frontrunners** (Gay/Lesbian), P.O. Box 31952, Seattle, WA 98103, www.seattlefrontrunners.org
- **Seattle Running Club**, 919 E Pine St, 206-329-1466, www.seattlerunningcompany.com/Club
- **West Seattle Runners**, 206-938-2416, www.westseattlerunners.org

Many races are held annually throughout Seattle. Some of the most popular are the St. Patrick's Day Dash (4 miles) held in March, the Jingle Bell Run (5K) held in early December, and the Race for the Cure (5K) held in mid-October. The Torchlight Run (8K), held in August as part of the Seafair celebration, is both a run and a parade event, with prizes given for best costume and group theme. The Beat the Bridge Run (8K) is a favorite local run, so named because the object is to cross the University Bridge before the bridge goes up. Comedians and musicians entertain those runners who get stuck behind the bridge until the bridge is lowered again. The Seattle Marathon and Half-Marathon are held each year in November. The best option for getting information on upcoming races is to contact a local running club or running store. The following stores advertise races and also sponsor weekly group runs:

- **Seattle Running Company**, 919 E Pine St, 206-329-1466, www.seattle runningcompany.com; race hotline, 206-325-4800
- **Super Jock 'n Jill**, 7210 E Green Lake Dr N, 206-522-7711, www.superjocknjill. com; runners' hotline, 206-524-7876

## SCUBA DIVING

If you think that scuba diving is a purely tropical pastime, think again! Puget Sound may be cold and a bit murky, but with the proper equipment it can be a diver's paradise. Depending on the time of year, you'll probably want a drysuit and gloves, but once you're in the water, with the abundance of fish and sights, you won't mind the extra weight. You can find octopus, wolf eels and the occasional sixgill shark among many other natural wonders. There are plenty of dive schools and supply shops in the area.

- **A2Z Scuba**, 1109 River Rd, Puyallup, 253-840-DIVE, www.a2zscuba.com
- **Bubbles Below Diving**, 17315 140th Ave NE, Woodinville, 425-487-2822, www. bubblesbelow.com
- **Lighthouse Diving Center**, 8215 Lake City Way, 206-524-1633; 5421 196th St SW, #6, Lynnwood, 425-771-2679; 2502 Pacific Ave, Tacoma, 253-627-7617, www.lighthousediving.com
- **Northwest Sports Divers**, 8030 NE Bothell Way, Kenmore, 425-747-8842, www.nwsportsdivers.com
- **Silent World Scuba Diving**, 13600 NE 20th St, Bellevue, 425-747-8842, www. silent-world.com
- **Sound Dive Center**, 5000 Burwell St, Bremerton, 360-373-6141, www. sounddive.com
- **Tacoma Scuba**, 1602 Center St, Ste C, Tacoma, 253-238-1754, www.tacoma scuba.com
- **TL Sea Diving**, 23405 Pacific Hwy S, Des Moines, 206-824-4100
- **Underwater Sports**, 10545 Aurora Ave N, 206-362-3310; 264 Railroad Ave, Edmonds, 425-771-6322; 205 E Casino Rd, Everett, 425-355-3338; 11743 124th Ave NE, Kirkland, 425-821-7200; 12003 NE 12th, Bellevue, 425-454-5168; 34428 Pacific Hwy S, Federal Way, 253-874-9387; 9606 40th Ave SW, Tacoma, 253-588-6634

## SKIING AND SNOWBOARDING

The highways over the Cascade Mountains lead to several ski resorts that are not too far. Whistler, a few hours' drive north of Vancouver, BC, is considered one of the best ski resorts in North America. Skiing and snowboarding are both popular activities at nearby resorts, which usually offer lessons for all levels of skiers. Call ahead for details and lodging reservations.

## WASHINGTON STATE SKI AREAS

- **Crystal Mountain**, near Mount Rainier, 33 miles east of Enumclaw on Highway 410, 360-663-2265, snow-line 888-754-6199, www.crystalmt.com
- **Mission Ridge**, 12 miles east of Wenatchee on Highway 2, 509-663-6543, snow-line 509-663-3200, www.missionridge.com
- **Mount Baker**, 56 miles east of Bellingham on Highway 542, 360-734-6771, www.mtbakerskiarea.com
- **Stevens Pass**, 65 miles east of Everett on Highway 2, 206-812-4510, snow-line 206-634-1645, www.stevenspass.com
- **The Summit at Snoqualmie** (includes Alpental, Hyak, Ski Acres and Snoqualmie ski areas), 60 miles east of Seattle on I-90, 425-434-7669, snow-line 206-236-1600, www.summit-at-snoqualmie.com
- **White Pass**, near Mount Rainier, 50 miles west of Yakima on Highway 12, 509-672-3101, snow-line, 509-672-3100, www.skiwhitepass.com

## OUT-OF-STATE SKI AREAS

- **Mount Bachelor**, 22 miles southwest of Bend, OR, 541-382-2442 or 800-829-2442, www.mtbachelor.com
- **Mount Hood Meadows**, 80 miles east of Portland near Hood River, OR, 503-337-2222 or 800-SKI-HOOD, www.skihood.com
- **Mount Washington**, located 80 miles north of Nanaimo on Vancouver Island, BC, 888-231-1499, www.mtwashington.bc.ca
- **Silver Mountain**, located 70 miles east of Spokane in Kellogg, ID, 208-783-1111 or 800-204-6428, www.silvermt.com
- **Schweitzer**, located 86 miles northeast of Spokane near Sandpoint, ID, 208-263-9555, 800-831-8810, www.schweitzer.com.
- **Whistler** (includes Whistler and Blackcomb ski areas), 75 miles north of Vancouver, BC, 866-218-9690, www.whistler-blackcomb.com

## SKI/SNOWBOARD RENTALS

- **All About Bike and Ski**, 3615 NE 45th St, 206-524-2642, www.allaboutbike andski.com

- **REI**, 222 Yale Ave N, 206-223-1944; 7500 166th Ave NE, Redmond, 425-882-1158; 3000 184th St SW, Lynnwood, 425-640-6200; 240 Andover Park W, Tukwila, 206-248-1938; 3825 S Steele St, Tacoma, 253-671-1938, www.rei.com
- **Seattle Ski and Snowboard**, 14915 Aurora Ave N, 206-548-1000, www.seattleski.com
- **Woodinville Ski Rentals**, 15606 Woodinville-Duvall Rd, Woodinville, 425-485-7547, www.wood-ski.com

## SNOWMOBILING

In Washington, snowmobiling is allowed on many forest and park trails. Snowmobiles are available for rent near most ski areas and in other wilderness areas throughout the state. Check the Yellow Pages. Rentals generally include a short lesson that covers riding techniques and safety tips. The following resources may be helpful if you're planning a day of snowmobiling:

- **Washington State Parks and Recreation Commission**, 800-233-0321, www.parks.wa.gov
- **Washington State Snowmobile Association**, 1690 Winona Lane, Walla Walla, 800-783-9772, www.wssa.us

## WASHINGTON STATE SNOWMOBILE SNO-PARK INFORMATION

- **Apple Country Snowmobile Club**, 509-662-2351
- **Blue Mountain SnoMo Club**, 509-382-2002
- **Chelan Ranger District**, 509-682-2576
- **Cle Elum Ranger District**, 509-852-1100
- **Colville National Forest**, 509-684-7000
- **Cowlitz Valley Ranger District**, 360-497-1100
- **Entiat Ranger District**, 509-784-1511
- **Lake Wenatchee Ranger District**, 509-763-3103
- **Mount Adams Ranger District**, 509-395-3400
- **Mount Baker Ranger District**, 360-856-5700
- **Mount St. Helens Ranger District**, 360-449-7800
- **Okanogan County**, 509-422-7324
- **Naches Ranger District**, 509-653-1400
- **Pomeroy Ranger District**, 509-843-1891
- **Snoqualmie Ranger District**, 360-825-6585
- **Spokane County Parks and Recreation**, 509-477-4730, www.spokanecounty.org/parks
- **Tonasket Ranger District**, 509-486-2186

- **Wenatchee River Ranger District**, 509-763-3106
- **White River Ranger District**, 360-825-6585

# SOCCER

While a few high schools have teams, most children and adults play competitive soccer in private leagues. The following soccer resources are in the greater Seattle area:

- **Ballard Youth Soccer**, 6201 15th Ave NW, www.ballardsoccer.org
- **Beacon Hill Soccer Club**, 206-322-1156
- **Capitol Hill Soccer Club**, 3809 Corliss Ave N, 206-322-7673, www.capitolhillsoccer.org
- **Co-Rec Soccer Association**, P.O. Box 22064, Seattle, 98122, 206-329-1548, www.co-recsoccer.com
- **Eastside Youth Soccer Association**, 15600 NE 8th St, Ste B1, Bellevue, 425-462-6616, www.eysa.org
- **Emerald City Football Club**, P.O. Box 85505, Seattle, 98145, 206-619-4016, http://emeraldcityfc.org
- **Greater Seattle Soccer League (GSSL)**, 9750 Greenwood Ave N, 206-782-6831, www.gssl.org
- **Hillwood Soccer Club**, 206-542-3353, www.sysa.org/hillwoodsoccer
- **Lake City Soccer Club**, 12345 Lake City Way NE, #401, 206-365-7684, www.lkcitysoccer.org
- **LVR Youth Soccer Club** (Laurelhurst, View Ridge, Ravenna), P.O. Box 15923, Seattle, WA 98115, 206-525-6045, www.lvr-soccer.org
- **Lake Washington Youth Soccer Association**, 12525 Willows Rd NE, Ste 100, Kirkland, 425-821-1741, www.lwysa.org
- **Liga Hispana del Noroeste**, 11401 Rainier Ave S, 206-772-3785, www.ligahispana.com
- **Liga Hispana Rainier Youth Soccer Club**, 11401 Rainier Ave S, 206-772-3785, www.laligayayouthsoccerclub.org
- **Magnolia Soccer Club**, 3213 W Wheeler St, 206-274-1280, www.magnoliasoccerclub.com
- **McGilvra Youth Soccer Club**, P.O. Box 22996, Seattle, 98122, 206-860-2488, www.mcgilvrasoccerclub.com
- **Mount Baker/Lakewood Youth Soccer Club**, 2945 36th Ave S, 206-725-2286, www.mblsoccer.org
- **Queen Anne Soccer Club**, 2212 Queen Anne Ave N, www.qasoccer.org
- **Seattle Youth Soccer Association**, 206-835-5522, www.sysa.org
- **Shorelake Soccer Club**, P.O. Box 55472, Shoreline, 98155, 206-362-3594, www.shorelakesoccer.com

- **Silver Lake Soccer Club**, P.O. Box 12543, Mill Creek, 98082, 425-481-2665, www.silverlakesoccerclub.com
- **TOPSoccer**, 19808 13th Dr SE, Bothell, 206-486-7673, http://eteamz.active.com/sysatopsoccer
- **Washington State Soccer Association**, 7802 NE Bothell Way, Kenmore, 425-485-7855, www.wssa.org
- **Washington State Women's Soccer Association**, P.O. Box 50305, Bellevue, 98015, 206-626-6750, www.wswsa.org
- **Washington State Youth Soccer Association**, 500 S 336th St, Ste 100, Federal Way, 253-4-SOCCER, www.wsysa.com
- **Woodinville Indoor Soccer Center**, 12728 NE 178th St, Woodinville, 425-481-5099, www.woodinvilleindoor.com
- **Woodland Soccer Club**, 206-632-1930, www.woodlandsoccer.org

## SWIMMING

When hot weather hits Seattle, folks head in droves to the few swimming beaches in the city. Lifeguards are generally on duty at Seattle beaches 11 a.m. to 8 p.m., from June 20 through Labor Day (except in inclement weather). To find beaches in communities outside Seattle, contact one of the parks and recreation departments listed previously in this chapter. The following are Seattle parks with swimming areas (call Seattle Parks and Recreation's general information line at 206-684-4075 for more information):

- **Green Lake Park**: 7201 E Green Lake Dr and 7312 W Green Lake Dr
- **Madison Park**, 1900 43rd Ave E
- **Madrona Park**, 800 Lake Washington Blvd S
- **Magnuson Park**, 7400 Sand Point Way NE
- **Matthews Beach Park**, 9300 51st Ave NE
- **Mount Baker Park**, 2301 Lake Washington Blvd S
- **Pritchard Beach**, 8400 56th Ave S
- **Seward Park**, 5900 Lake Washington Blvd S

Wading pools are open for the little ones in many parks, playgrounds, and community centers in Seattle. Park wading pools are open daily (provided the temperature is over 70 degrees), from 11 a.m. to 8 p.m. Community center and playground wading pools are open weekdays only, and hours vary. Call the city's **Aquatic Information Hotline** at 206-684-7796 for more information. Here are the city's three biggest wading pools:

- **Green Lake Park**, 7312 W Green Lake Dr
- **Lincoln Park**, 8600 Fauntleroy Way SW
- **Volunteer Park**, 1400 E Galer St

For those interested in year-round swimming, Seattle city pools offer a variety of open swim sessions, lessons and lap-swimming options. Many host swim club practices for Masters and all ages programs. To find pools in communities outside Seattle, contact one of the parks and recreation departments listed previously in this chapter.

- **Ballard Pool**, 1471 NW 67th St, 206-684-4094
- **Colman Pool** (outdoor), 8603 Fauntleroy Way SW, 206-684-7494
- **Evans Pool**, 7201 E Green Lake Dr N, 206-684-4961
- **Madison Pool**, 13401 Meridian Ave N, 206-684-4979
- **Meadowbrook Pool**, 10515 35th Ave NE, 206-684-4989
- **Medgar Evers Pool**, 500 23rd Ave, 206-684-4766
- **Mounger Pool** (outdoor), 2535 32nd Ave W, 206-684-4708
- **Queen Anne Pool**, 1920 1st Ave W, 206-386-4282
- **Rainier Beach Pool**, 8825 Rainier Ave S, 206-386-1944
- **Southwest Pool**, 2801 SW Thistle St, 206-684-7440

Several swim clubs hold regular practices at pools around Seattle, many offering a variety of practices for all levels of experience. Call for details, as prices and entrance requirements vary widely. An excellent resource for competitive swimming information in Washington is **Pacific Northwest Swimming (PNS)**, 753 North Central Avenue, Kent, 253-852-0680. The organization maintains a comprehensive web site at www.pns.org that includes swim club directories. Some local swim clubs are listed below. Because many practice at multiple locations, business office addresses are given for some clubs.

- **Cascade Swim Club**, P.O. Box 77043, Seattle, 98177, 206-546-1036, www.cascadeswimclub.org
- **Chinook Aquatic Club**, P.O. Box 59384, Renton, 98058, 206-230-5812, www.chinookaquaticclub.org
- **Salmon Bay Aquatics**, P.O. Box 17442, Seattle, 98127, www.salmonbay.org
- **Swim Seattle**, P.O. Box 22505, Seattle, 98122, 206-575-0808, www.swimseattle.org

# VIDEO ARCADES

- **Chuck E. Cheese's**, 2239 148th Ave NE, Bellevue, 425-746-5000; 25817 104th Ave SE, Kent, 253-813-9000; 3717 196th St, Lynnwood, 425-771-1195; 4911 Tacoma Mall Blvd, Tacoma, 253-473-3078, www.chuckecheese.com
- **Fun Forest**, Seattle Center, 206-728-1585, www.funforest.com
- **Gameworks**, 1511 7th Ave, 206-521-0952, www.gameworks.com
- **Illsionz Magical Center**, 1025 NW Gilman Blvd, Issaquah, 425-427-2444, www.illusionz.com

- **Quarters**, Pier 57, 1301 Alaskan Way, 206-625-9196

## VOLLEYBALL

You might think that volleyball would be a purely indoor sport in Western Washington, and while there are many indoor leagues, summertime finds players on the sands of Alki Beach and Golden Gardens Park enjoying beach volleyball. North Beach Volleyball even offers indoor beach volleyball in a spacious warehouse at Magnuson Park. Many local community centers offer drop-in volleyball, and a good place to find resources is the web site of **Seattle Volleyball.Net**, www.seattlevolleyball.net, a site devoted to connecting people to all things volleyball. The following organizations offer league play for different ages and skill levels nearly year round.

- **Adult Volleyball Education**, P. O. Box 30789, Seattle, 98103, 206 783-9580
- **A/E Volleyball Association**, 6724 2nd Ave NW, 206-782-8030, www.aevolleyball.net
- **Jet City Sports**, PO Box 31272, Seattle, 98103, 206-706-2661, www.jetcitysports.com
- **Moxie Volleyball**, 770 122nd Ave NE, Bellevue, 98005, 425-985-0540, www.moxievolleyball.com
- **North Beach Volleyball**, Seattle, 7727 63rd Ave NE, Bldg #2, 206-624-2899, www.sandboxsports.net
- **Northwest Volleyball**, 15821 NE 8th St, Ste W-200, Bellevue, 98008, 425-497-1051, www.volleyballnw.com
- **Seattle Volleyball Club**, 2202 29th Ave S, www.svcvball.homestead.com
- **Strike Force Volleyball**, PO Box 3073, Redmond, 98052, 425-867-0489, www.sfvbclub.org
- **Underdog Sports Leagues Volleyball**, 206-320-8326, www.underdogseattle.com

## WATER-SKIING

During the summer, there are hundreds of people water-skiing on Lake Washington. Many skiers launch their boats early in the morning from Magnuson Park in Sand Point and head out to the middle of the lake. Other lakes in Washington popular with water-skiers are Lake Sammamish in Bellevue and Lake Chelan, north of Wenatchee. For equipment and supplies, try the following resources:

- **Adrenaline Water Sports**, 13433 NE 20th Ave, Ste C, Bellevue, 425-746-9253, www.adrenalinewatersports.com
- **Bakes ProShop**, 6424 E Lake Sammamish Pkwy SE, Issaquah, 425-392-8595, www.bakesmarine.com

- **Extremely Board**, 1175 NW Gilman Blvd, Ste B-7, Issaquah, 425-391-4572, www.extremelyboard.com
- **Pro Tour Watersports**, 13131 NE 124th St, Ste A, Kirkland, 425-814-1395, www.protourwatersports.com
- **Seattle Watersports**, 6820 NE 175th St, Bothell, 888-481-2754, www.seattlewatersports.com
- **Straight-Line Water Sports**, 9660 153rd Ave NE, Redmond, 425-881-3377
- **Sturtevant's Sports**, 1100 Bellevue Way NE, Bellevue, 425-454-6465 or 888-454-7669, www.sturtevants.com
- **Wiley's Ski Shop**, 1417 S Trenton St, 206-762-1300, www.wileyski.com

## WIND-SURFING

While Green Lake, Lake Union, Puget Sound, and Lake Washington are all popular destinations for windsurfing enthusiasts, the Columbia River Gorge is the ultimate thrill for experienced wind-surfers. Located on the southern border of Washington near Hood River, OR, the gorge is challenging and exciting for veteran surfers, but can be rough and even dangerous for beginners. The following resources provide information and lessons for both experienced wind-surfers and beginners:

- **Columbia Gorge Windsurfing Association**, 202 Oak St, Ste 150, Hood River, OR, 541-386-9225, http://windsurf.gorge.net/cgwa
- **Urban Surf**, 2100 N Northlake Way, 206-545-9463, http://urbansurf.com

## YOGA

Yoga has become enormously popular in Seattle, with studios popping up all over the city, and health clubs rushing to add classes. Here are a few Seattle yoga studios:

- **8 Limbs Yoga Centers**, 500 E Pike St, 206-325-1511; 7345 35th Ave NE, 206-523-9722; 4546-1/2 California Ave SW, 206-933-YOGA, www.8limbsyoga.com
- **The Ashtanga Yoga School**, 2420 E Union St, 206-261-1711, www.aysyoga.com
- **Bikram's Yoga College of India,** 1054 N 34th St, 206-547-0188, www.bikramyogaseattle.com
- **The Center for Yoga in Seattle**, 2261 NE 65th St, 206-526-9642, www.yogaseattle.com
- **Hatha Yoga Center**, 4550 11th Ave NE, 206-632-1706, www.hathayogacenter.com
- **Inside Out Yoga**, 8016 Dayton Ave N, 206-729-2199, www.kimtrimmer.com
- **Lotus Yoga**, 4860 Rainier Ave S, 206-760-1917, www.lotusyoga.biz

- **Planet Earth Yoga Center**, 418 N 35th St, 206-365-1997, www.planetearthyoga. com
- **Santosha Yoga**, 2812 E Madison St, 206-264-5034, www.yoga4everyone.com
- **Seattle Holistic Center**, 7700 Aurora Ave N, 206-525-9035, www.seattle holisticcenter.com
- **Seattle Yoga Arts**, 109 15th Ave E, 206-440-3191, www.seattleyogaarts.com
- **Sound Yoga**, 5639 California Ave SW, 206-938-8195, www.soundyoga.com
- **Two Dog Yoga Studio**, 12549 28th Ave NE, 206-367-9608, www.twodogyoga. com
- **Whole Life Yoga**, 8551 Greenwood Ave N, Ste 2, 206-784-2882, www. wholelifeyoga.com
- **The Yoga Tree**, 3601 Fremont Ave N, #315, 206-545-0316, www.yogatree.com

## HEALTH CLUBS

Whether you're trying to stay in shape during the off-season, get in shape for spring break, or simply prefer group fitness or weight-lifting to outdoor sports, Seattle is full of health clubs and gyms. Most offer conditioning classes, as well as personal training programs. Some clubs also offer yoga, spinning, swimming workouts, and nutrition and health classes. Call or visit the club you're interested in to get details on their programs.

- **24 Hour Fitness**, multiple locations, 800-432-6348, www.24hourfitness.com
- **Allstar Fitness**, 330 2nd Ave W, 206-282-5901; 509 Olive Way, Ste 213, 206-292-0900; 2629 SW Andover St, 206-932-9999; 700 5th Ave, 14th floor, 206-343-4692, www.allstarfitness.com
- **Anderson's Nautilus Fitness Center**, 7203 Woodlawn Ave NE, 206-524-7000, www.andersonsnautilus.com
- **Aqua Dive Swim & Fitness Club**, 12706 33rd Ave NE, 206-364-2535
- **Ballard Health Club**, 2208 NW Market St, 206-706-4882, www.ballardhealth club.com
- **Bally Total Fitness**, multiple locations, 800-515-2582, www.ballyfitness.com
- **Cross Train Concepts Conditioning Studio**, 1446 NW 53rd St, 206-782-2199
- **Curves**, multiple locations, 800-848-1096, www.curvesinternational.com
- **Gold's Gym**, multiple locations, www.goldsgym.com
- **Magnolia Athletic Club**, 3320 W McGraw St, 206-283-1490
- **Mieko's Fitness**, 2438 32nd Ave W, 206-286-9070; 12015 31st Ave NE, 206-417-4715; 8401 Main St, Edmonds, 425-712-0363, 13018 39th Ave SE, Everett, 425-385-8038, www.miekosfitness.com
- **Olympic Athletic Club**, 5301 Leary Ave NW, 206-789-5010, www. olympicathleticclub.com

- **Pro-Robics**, 1530 Queen Anne Ave N, 206-283-2303; 3811 NE 45th St, 206-524-9246, www.prorobics.com
- **Pro Sports Club**, 501 Eastlake Ave, 2nd Flr, 206-332-1873; 4455 148th Ave NE, Bellevue, 425-885-5566, www.proclub.com
- **Pure Fitness**, 808 2nd Ave, 888-415-9204; 1275 Westlake Ave N, 888-415-9198, www.purefitnessclubs.com
- **Seattle Athletic Club**, 2020 Western Ave, 206-443-1111; 333 NE 97th St, 206-522-9400, www.sacdt.com/main.html
- **Seattle Fitness Club**, 83 S King St, 206-467-1800, http://seattlefitness.com
- **Sound Mind & Body**, 437 N 34th St; 206-547-3470, www.smbgym.com
- **University Fitness**, 4511 Roosevelt Way NE, 206-632-3460, www.university fitnessseattle.com
- **Washington Athletic Club**, 1325 6th Ave, 206-622-7900, www.wac.net
- **Westlake Club**, 1275 Westlake Ave N, 206-283-9320
- **X GYM**, 2505 2nd Ave, Ste 100, 206-728-XGYM; 3213 Harbor Ave SW, 206-938-XGYM; 126 Central Way, Ste 150, Kirkland, 425-822-XGYM, www.xgym.com

## ACTIVITY CLUBS

- **Events and Adventures**, 2122 112th Ave NE, #B-100, Bellevue, 425-882-0838, www.eventsandadventures.com
- **The Mountaineers**, 300 3rd Ave, 206-284-6310, www.seattlemountaineers. org
- **Sierra Club**, Cascade Chapter, 180 Nickerson St, Ste 202, 206-378-0114, http:// cascade.sierraclub.org

## SPORTING GOODS AND OUTDOOR WEAR STORES

Whether you're heading out of town for a rugged hike or spending an hour at the park with a Frisbee, you may need to go shopping first. Seattle is the birthplace of sporting goods giant REI, and residents take their sports and recreational activities seriously, so there are dozens of places to find just the right equipment. Check the Yellow Pages under "Sporting Goods—Retail" for everything from boots and bicycling to fleece and fishing.

SEATTLE'S LANDSCAPE IS THE RESULT OF VARIOUS GEOLOGIC FORCES: the hills and mountains created by shifting plates far beneath the earth's surface, the lakes and waterways carved out by a great system of glaciers and several ice ages. Add to this a rainy climate broken by bright sunlight, throw in lush indigenous evergreens and colorful rhododendrons, and it is no wonder that Seattle residents spend so much time outdoors. The city's park system, which includes many lakes and beaches, provides abundant opportunities for enjoying the area's natural beauty.

In 1903, J.C. Olmsted designed most of Seattle's park system. The Seattle park board hired Olmsted to design a boulevard system that would link much of the city's parkland, which had been purchased between 1897 and 1903. The result is impressive, with approximately 20 miles of winding parkway connecting many of Seattle's major greenspaces. The following is a brief description of Seattle's most popular parks, although in addition to those listed here, many neighborhoods also have small parks, athletic fields, and playgrounds. To get more information on any of the parks listed here, call the **Seattle Parks and Recreation Department** at 206-684-4075 or visit www.cityofseattle.net/parks.

## NORTHWEST SEATTLE PARKS

### INLAND PARKS

- **Green Lake** is perhaps Seattle's most popular public park. It is surrounded by almost three miles of paved walkway, attracting bicyclists, in-line skaters, runners, and strolling couples. In Seattle, where locals are undaunted by drizzle and early winter darkness, Green Lake has become a year-round mecca for early-morning and late-evening walkers and joggers. During the summer, fields at the east side of the lake fill with volleyball teams, the basketball courts host informal but competitive pick-up games, and in the evenings, in-line skaters can be found playing hockey in the drained kiddie pool. The Seattle Parks Department's Green Lake Small Craft Center, 206-684-4074, sponsors rowing classes as well as novice sailing classes at the south end of the lake, and beginning wind-surfers set sail from the eastern shore. Another Seattle tradition, the annual Seafair Milk Carton Derby, launches from the shore each July, and there are many other events held on Green Lake throughout the year.

- **Kerry Park**, on the southwest corner of Queen Anne Hill, overlooks Elliott Bay and the downtown skyline, providing a spectacular view of the city.
- **Woodland Park**, at the south end of Green Lake, offers tennis courts, lawn bowling, and grassy picnic areas, as well as the Woodland Park Zoo, a seasonal favorite of adults and kids alike. One particularly popular program is the Bird of Prey program, where kids delight in watching trained raptors in flight. Small children enjoy the petting zoo and pony rides in the summer. The zoo is located in the Phinney Ridge neighborhood, at Phinney Avenue North and North 50th Street. Call 206-684-4800 for hours. Also worth a visit is the spectacular Rose Garden, just outside the zoo's south gate. Call 206-684-4863 for details and special events information.

## PARKS WITH BEACHES

- **Carkeek Park,** north of Golden Gardens, offers stunning vistas of Puget Sound from bluff trails, an Environmental Learning Center and, at the right time of year, glimpses of salmon in Piper Creek, which runs through the park. A trail through wetlands leads to the beach, accessed by a footbridge over the railroad tracks.
- **Discovery Park,** on the western point of Magnolia, is the largest of the Olmsted-designed parks. Its over-500 acres of wooded trails and flowery meadows, towering sea cliffs, and windy beaches provide everyone with something to do. Visit in the evening to watch the sun set over the Olympics, or come during the day for a pleasant hike down to the beach. Clay cliffs overhang the rocky beach, furnishing hours of fun for kids. Nearby quiet meadows are great places for picnics or impromptu bird watching. You may see bald eagles, hawks, falcons or even an osprey. From the beach you may catch sight of migrating seabirds and views of the West Point Lighthouse. The Daybreak Star Cultural Center, in the center of the park, celebrates Native American culture with art exhibits and special programs. Call 206-285-4425 for details.
- **Gasworks Park**, at the north end of Lake Union, is built around the dramatic skeleton of the old gasworks factory and offers stunning views of the

downtown skyline. The park attracts kite-flyers and Frisbee players, and is a starting point for the Burke-Gilman Trail, a paved walkway that heads east from Gasworks to Lake Washington, then along the lake shore to the Eastside. The giant sundial atop the park's central hill is always worth a visit. Gasworks Park hosts an annual Independence Day celebration, complete with a spectacular fireworks display over Lake Union.

- **Golden Gardens Park**, which is not a part of the Olmsted plan, is located at the north end of Ballard. The park features one of Seattle's few truly sandy beaches, luring swimmers, picnickers, and volleyball players through the summer months, and is one of the few public parks in the city that allow bonfires.

## NORTHEAST SEATTLE PARKS

### INLAND PARKS

- **Ravenna Park**, north of the University of Washington, follows a steep ravine northwest to Cowen Park. It features a wading pool and wooded trails and is a favorite for picnics.

### PARKS WITH BEACHES

- **Magnuson Park** is the second largest park in the city, with sports fields and a boat launch to Lake Washington. It features Kite Hill, for, you guessed it, kite flying, as well as outdoor art installations, an outdoor amphitheater hosting theater productions in the summer, a community garden, a swimming beach with lifeguard on duty during the summer, plenty of trails, and one of the best off-leash dog parks. The site of a former naval station, many of the large, old buildings are now used as headquarters for community organizations, and large events like the Friends of the Seattle Public Library Book Sale and a popular plant sale are held here.
- **Matthews Beach Park**, on the Lake Washington waterfront near Sand Point, is a popular summer destination for sunbathers and swimmers, and is also a stop on the Burke-Gilman Trail.

## SOUTHEAST SEATTLE PARKS

### INLAND PARKS

- **Volunteer Park**, on the northeast corner of Capitol Hill, also provides incredible views of downtown, as well as Puget Sound and the Olympic Mountains. For an even more dazzling view, climb to the top of the 75-foot water tower. In

Volunteer Park you'll also find the Seattle Asian Art Museum, and a 1912 conservatory filled with orchids and other tropical plants. Just north of the park, the Lake View Cemetery contains the graves of several prominent Seattle citizens, including "Doc" Maynard and Bruce Lee.

- **Jefferson Park** on Beacon Hill, with sweeping views of the city, is also home to the Jefferson Park Golf Course. A major expansion to the park is planned, with construction beginning spring 2007 and finishing in 2009. When it is finished, the park will be home to sports courts, a skateboard park, community center, large lawns, gardens, and meadows.

## PARKS WITH BEACHES

- **Madison Park** is located on Lake Washington at the far east end of Madison Street. Although not part of the Olmsted plan, it originated in the 1890s as the site of a summer amusement park. Today it is a popular sunny-day hangout, offering the perennial summer favorites of picnicking, swimming, and sunbathing.

- **Mount Baker Park** is north of Seward Park, near the site of the Seafair hydroplane races that take place each August. The Mount Baker Rowing and Sailing Center hosts beginning rowing and sailing classes, and is home to both an adult and a high school crew team. Call the center at 206-386-1913 for details.

- **Seward Park**, in the southeast corner of Seattle, is located on the 277-acre Bailey Peninsula. In addition to a beach, the park has a system of nature trails perfect for solitary walks or bird-watching (bald eagles are occasionally sighted here). Also enticing, the 1920s bathhouse now serves as an artists' studio, offering a variety of ceramics classes for adults and children; call 206-722-6342 for class availability.

- **The Washington Park Arboretum**, along Madison Avenue, picks up the Olmsted planned parkway in Madrona. The Arboretum is a 255-acre woodland managed by the University of Washington. Though it was a part of the Seattle park system as early as 1904, it was developed by the university as an arboretum in 1936. Originally filled with native Northwest plants and trees, today the Washington Park Arboretum is home to more than 5,500 flowers, trees, and shrubs from all over the world. It includes the beautifully sculptured Japanese Tea Garden, designed in 1960 by Japanese architect Juki Iida. At the north end of the Arboretum, the Museum of History and Industry hosts fascinating exhibits of Seattle's industrial history and maritime heritage.

# SOUTHWEST SEATTLE PARKS

## INLAND PARKS

- **Schmitz Preserve Park** in West Seattle is a 53-acre haven of old-growth forest and hiking trails lovingly tended by neighborhood groups, with very little change over the last century.
- **Westcrest Park** is a large park wrapped around the West Seattle Reservoir with a great view of the city, paths, a playground, and an off-leash dog park.

## PARKS WITH BEACHES

- **Alki Beach Park** in West Seattle is a great place to watch sunsets over the Olympics or enjoy a spectacular view of downtown Seattle. During the summer, in-line skaters, bicyclists, and serious beach volleyball players flock to this park. The beach resort atmosphere adds to the charm of this narrow strip of land along the northwest shore of West Seattle.
- **Lincoln Park,** in West Seattle's Fauntleroy neighborhood, is one of Seattle's most popular parks, with bluffs overlooking Puget Sound, miles of trails through dense woods, and a paved walking path along the beach. There's a large wading pool, and the city's only saltwater swimming pool. Colman pool is an outdoor heated pool on the beach, only open in the summer and popular with generations of Seattleites. With ball fields, picnic shelters, beachcombing, and watching ferries plying the waters just south of the park, this is easily a daylong destination.

# SURROUNDING COMMUNITIES

Several Seattle-area parks are owned or maintained by the **King County Park System**, a vast network of lakes and green spaces. They operate 180 parks, 175 miles of trails, and pools and sports fields all over the county. To find a county park in your neck of the woods, call 206-296-4232 or visit www.metrokc.gov/parks.

## MERCER ISLAND

- **Luther Burbank Park**, on the northeast end of Mercer Island, commands 77 acres and a three-quarters-of-a-mile stretch of Lake Washington waterfront. Nearly three miles of trails provide opportunities for walks and bird watching. Other amenities include tennis courts, a group picnic area, a grassy amphitheater, and daily moorage. Luther Burbank's off-leash dog area offers pets the rare opportunity to swim legally in a public park. 206-236-3545, www. ci.mercer-island.wa.us

## BELLEVUE

- **Cougar Mountain Regional Wildland Park** is surrounded by the cities of Bellevue, Newcastle, and Issaquah, just minutes from downtown Seattle. The park covers more than 3,000 acres, making it the largest park in the King County system. More than 36 miles of trails are for hikers, and 12 miles are devoted to equestrians. Fourteen creeks originate within the park, including three salmon-spawning creeks: Coal Creek, May Creek, and Tibbett's Creek. 206-296-4232, www.metrokc.gov/parks
- **Kelsey Creek Park** consists of 150 acres of wetland and forest habitat. The park boasts numerous hiking and jogging trails, including a gravel loop trail that circles picturesque barns and pastures. The highlight of the park is Kelsey Creek Farm, which is home to a variety of animals, and offers several children's programs. 425-452-7688, www.ci.bellevue.wa.us
- **Robinswood Community Park** is the setting for Robinswood House, one of the area's most popular wedding reception and private-party sites. For rental information, call 425-452-7850. The park also features four indoor and four outdoor tennis courts, a pond and playground, and a fully equipped baseball field with scoreboard. 425-452-6881, www.ci.bellevue.wa.us
- **Wilburton Hill Park**, which includes the Bellevue Botanical Garden, features ball fields, hiking trails, and a children's play area. The Botanical Garden contains 36 acres of lush flower gardens and landscaping. Guided tours of the grounds are available. 425-452-6881, www.ci.bellevue.wa.us

## KIRKLAND

- **Juanita Bay Park** offers numerous opportunities to view a variety of wildlife, including songbirds, waterfowl, raptors, shorebirds, turtles, and beavers. The 144-acre park's paved trails and boardwalks make self-guided tours easy, but volunteer park rangers also offer interpretive tours on the first Sunday of the month at 1 p.m. 425-828-2237, www.ci.kirkland.wa.us

## REDMOND

- **Marymoor Park** is the crown jewel of the King County Park System and one of the most popular parks in the entire Puget Sound region, particularly among dog owners, soccer players, bicycle racers, rock climbers, and model airplane enthusiasts. Covering 640 acres, the park is visited by more than a million people each year. Annual events at Marymoor include King County's Heritage Festival and several music events. Notable attractions at Marymoor include a 40-acre off-leash dog area, the Marymoor Velodrome, Willowmoor Farm, and the Marymoor Climbing Rock. 206-296-4232, www.metrokc.gov/parks

## RENTON

• **Gene Coulon Memorial Beach Park** was originally named Lake Washington Beach Park because of its location on the southeast shore of the region's most popular recreational lake. The park consists of 53 acres, and encourages several aquatic activities, including swimming, boating, water skiing and windsurfing. Gene Coulon is home to two commercial quick-service restaurants, Kidd Valley and Ivar's, a rarity at area parks. 425-430-6700, www.ci.renton. wa.us/commserv/parks

## TUKWILA

• **Fort Dent Park** is best known for its plentiful softball fields. The park hosts dozens of tournaments each year, including state and national competition. Fort Dent also features soccer fields and a kids' play area, along with a variety of birds and animals that flock to the park's wetlands. The 54-acre park is located adjacent to the Green River Trail, a regional pathway that winds 14 miles through South King County. 206-768-2822, www.ci.tukwila.wa.us

## BURIEN

• **Seahurst Park** is popular with divers and beachcombers. The 185-acre park was owned by the King County Park System, until it was given to the new city of Burien in 1996. The park's main attraction is the 2,000-foot-long saltwater beach. Other highlights include picnic shelters and tables, a play area, and numerous trails. 206-988-3700, www.burienparks.net

## TACOMA

• **Point Defiance Park** is among the 20 largest urban parks in the United States, and is the setting for one of Tacoma's most popular destinations, the Point Defiance Zoo and Aquarium. About two million people visit the 698-acre park each year to stroll through gardens and old-growth forests, travel back in time at Fort Nisqually, ride behind an authentic locomotive at Camp 6 Logging Museum, or bike along Five Mile Drive. 253-305-1000, www.tacomaparks.com

- **Wright Park**, just north of Tacoma's city center, is one of the few Washington parks listed on the National Register of Historic Places. The park's centerpiece is the glass-domed W.W. Seymour Botanical Conservatory, which was built in 1908. The conservatory presents seasonal floral displays in addition to its permanent collection of exotic tropical plants. Other attractions include walking and jogging paths, a children's play area and wading pool, lawn bowling, horseshoes and a community center. 253-305-1000, www.tacomaparks.com

## BAINBRIDGE ISLAND

- **Gazzam Lake Park and Wildlife Preserve**, on the southwest corner of the island, is Bainbridge's second-biggest area of undeveloped land. The 318-acre park includes 13 acres of freshwater wetlands, home to a variety of wildlife, including deer and birds. An interpretive center is planned for the park, as well as a trail to Puget Sound. 206-842-2306, www.biparks.org
- **Grand Forest** consists of 240 acres spread over three plots on central Bainbridge Island. The property includes second-growth forests plus wetlands and wildlife habitat. Thanks to the Eagle Scouts, the former Department of Natural Resources land now features trails and trail signs. 206-842-2306, www.biparks.org
- **Manzanita Park**, at the north end of Bainbridge Island, is popular with hikers and horseback riders because its 120 acres are ribboned with hiking and equestrian trails. 206-842-2306, www.biparks.org

## MOUNTLAKE TERRACE

- **Terrace Creek Park** is Mountlake Terrace's largest park, occupying 60 acres in the center of the city. Amenities include barbecues, picnic areas, trails, play equipment, and playfields. 425-776-9173, www.ci.mountlake-terrace.wa.us/departments/parks

## EDMONDS

- **Underwater Park** is located just north of the ferry dock, at the foot of Main Street in downtown Edmonds. One of the first underwater parks on the West Coast, Underwater Park is 27 acres of tide and bottom lands with artificial reefs and an abundance of marine life. Designated as a marine preserve and sanctuary in 1970, the park attracts scuba divers from across the state. 425-771-0230, www.ci.edmonds.wa.us/parks.stm

## VASHON ISLAND

- **Dockton Park**, sheltered by Quartermaster Harbor, offers boat moorage, a swimming beach, picnic areas and playground, and hiking trails. 206-463-9602, www.vashonparkdistrict.org
- **Ober Park** in downtown Vashon is popular for outdoor concerts, picnics, its playground and meeting spaces. The park district headquarters are located here, as is the library, and the grassy lawns and earthen berms play host to the annual Strawberry Festival. 206-463-9602, www.vashonparkdistrict.org
- **Pt. Robinson Park** on the eastern tip of Maury Island is home to the historic Pt. Robinson Lighthouse, which offers free tours, as well as trails, picnic areas and beachcombing. 206-463-9602, www.vashonparkdistrict.org

## STATE AND NATIONAL PARKS

If you're in the mood for something slightly more adventurous than a city outing, consider a trip to one of Washington's many state or national parks.

- **Mount Rainier National Park** activities include skiing, hiking, camping, and mountain climbing. For more information, see the **Quick Getaways** chapter, call 360-569-2211 for more information, or visit www.nps.gov/mora.
- **Olympic National Park** on the Olympic Peninsula (about two hours northwest of Seattle) also offers hiking, camping, and mountain-climbing opportunities. For an up-close look at the mountains without the hike, visit Hurricane Ridge near Port Angeles. You can drive to the ridge and view the mountains from the comfort of the visitors' center. Also worth a visit is Sol Duc Hot Springs, in the center of the park. For more information on the Olympic National Park, see the **Quick Getaways** chapter, call 360-565-3130, or visit www.nps.gov/olym.
- **North Cascades National Park** offers stunning views, hundreds of hikes and an outstanding museum. 360-856-5700, www.nps.gov/noca.

To receive information on any of Washington's 125 state parks, call the **Washington State Parks and Recreation Commission** at 360-902-8844, or visit their web site at www.parks.wa.gov.

## FORESTS

Surrounding Olympic National Park, on the Olympic Peninsula, is **Olympic National Forest**. Its 632,000 acres are shared by outdoor enthusiasts and wildlife, and are managed for timber, mining, grazing, oil and gas, watershed, and wilderness. Twenty campgrounds pepper the land, and 266 miles of trails wind through the area. For more information, call 360-956-2402 or visit www.fs.fed.us/r6/olympic.

## ADDITIONAL RESOURCES

For comprehensive recreation information for the entire state, visit **Washington State Tourism** at www.experiencewashington.com or call a state travel counselor, 800-544-1800, Monday through Friday, from 8 a.m. to 5 p.m. If you're heading for one of the region's mountain passes, call the **Washington State Department of Transportation** highway information line at 511, or check the pass report online at www.wsdot.wa.gov/traffic. For additional outdoor recreation ideas, read the **Quick Getaways** and **Sports and Recreation** chapters of this book.

"THE BLUEST SKIES YOU'VE EVER SEEN ARE IN SEATTLE," SANG Perry Como, "and the hills the greenest green…" The late crooner was right. On a sunny summer day, the city is wrapped in aquamarine and the landscape glows green. Such brilliantly lush environs led in part to the city's nickname of the Emerald City. But, Como forgot to mention the rain, and the accompanying mudslides, the frequent windstorms, occasional earthquakes and, every now and then, a drought; such are some of the challenges that Gore-Tex-clad residents contend with every year.

In Seattle, jokes about the perpetual precipitation are as constant as the rain. One holds that residents of Seattle don't tan—they rust. Then there's the one that asks, "What do you call two straight days of rain in Seattle?" A weekend. While rainfall here isn't actually relentless, at times it does feel like Noah and his ark are about to sail into town, especially during winters like 2005-2006 when it rained for 27 days in a row, not quite beating the 1953 record of 33 straight days of rain.

The soggiest time in Seattle is November through February, with an average rainfall of nearly 22 inches during those four months. In 1996—a notorious year in the area's weather history—nearly 52 inches of rain fell in the region, close to the record 55 inches set in 1950. While waterlogged years like 1996 stand out because they are extraordinary, Seattle is, generally, a soggy city throughout the winter, though stories of nine months of solid rain should be discounted.

When heavy rains do arrive, they are sometimes accompanied by damaging mudslides and floods. The same hills that offer residents spectacular views render homes, trees, and roads vulnerable in extreme weather. In the aftermath of heavy rains and snowstorms residents face mudslides and sinkholes that damage houses and wash out roads, a fact that new residents should keep in mind when searching for a new home. Though mudslides certainly aren't an everyday occurrence during the rainy months, they happen often enough to cause concern. Geologists recommend that homeowners try to determine if they are at risk for a slide by understanding how water causes damage and what triggers slides. According to experts, steep bluffs and hillsides where earth movement has occurred in the past or where the geology favors such movement, are most at risk. That includes the bluffs that encircle Puget Sound and parts of Lake Washington, like West and North Seattle, Magnolia, and Bainbridge Island. With this in mind, folks should search a prospective property for signs of earth movement or signs that the property is getting a lot of water. Indicators include leaning or bent trees, and cracks in the yard, the foundation, driveway or patio. A property that is getting a lot of water may have spots on the lawn that stay greener or that are continually wet, and/or mossy. If you find potential problems, you may want to hire a civil or geo-technical engineer to analyze the drainage situation and make recommendations. Both can be found in the Yellow Pages.

Despite its proximity to both the Cascade and Olympic mountain ranges, Seattle is not a snowy city, receiving on average only 7.1 inches per year, though years without any measurable snowfall in the urban areas are common. Communities to the east, like Issaquah, North Bend, and Snoqualmie, get a little more snowfall. Of course, there are exceptions, like the winter of 1999, when record snow levels were recorded in the Northwest and more than 300 inches piled up at the base of the Mount Baker Ski Area.

If you are looking for sun, you may have to drive to find it in abundance. According to the Western Regional Climate Center, Seattle enjoys only 71 days of clear skies. In comparison, Yakima, about two and a half hours east of the city, experiences 109 clear days. The WRCC defines a clear day as one that sees zero to 3/10 average cloud cover. The clearest months here are in July, with 12 days, August, with 10 days, and September, with nine days. November through February average just three clear days each month. The mixed blessing is that there are also 93 partly cloudy days a year, defined by the WRCC as days with 4/10 to 7/10 cloud cover. Breaks in the clouds can send people racing outdoors to enjoy a couple of hours of sun, regardless of the time of year.

Because sunshine is not a daily occurrence, and weeks can pass without a break in the clouds, about ten percent of the region's residents suffer from **Seasonal Affective Disorder**, according to David Avery, a professor of psychiatry and behavioral sciences at the University of Washington. Another ten percent experience milder forms of depression. The National Mental Health Association says that as the seasons change, a shift occurs in our internal biological clocks that can cause us to be out of step with our daily schedules. Symptoms include sadness, sluggishness, change in appetite, and excessive sleeping. If you are moving from a sunny state like California or Florida, you should be aware of possible seasonal depression. Many people affected by the disorder have found relief using portable light boxes, like the ones sold by The SunBox Company (www. sunbox.com).

Washington does occasionally experience drought conditions, which in turn set the stage for dangerous wildfires. During drought years, local governments usually ask resident to limit yard watering, and farming communities may impose rolling dry-outs to conserve irrigation water. Wildfires generally are confined to the eastern part of the state, though forested neighborhoods like those in southeast King County also can be at risk. The National Fire Protection Association offers tips on protecting your home from wildfire at its web site, www. firewise.org.

Though Seattle's weather picture can seem bleak, its bane—the rain—is also its blessing. If it weren't for the rain the hills wouldn't grow nearly as green and the deep blue skies wouldn't be so revered.

## WEATHER STATISTICS

Despite the clouds, a reputation for rain and occasional extreme weather, Seattle has a mild, temperate climate, receiving 37.07 average inches of rain in a year, far less than some other areas of the country. According to the **Western Regional Climate Center** (www.wrcc.dri.edu), the average minimum and maximum temperatures at Sea-Tac Airport are as follows: **January** 38-46° F; **February** 37-50° F; **March** 39-53° F; **April** 42-58° F; **May** 47-64° F; **June** 52-70° F; **July** 55-75° F; **August** 56-76° F; **September** 52-70° F; **October** 46-60° F; **November** 40-51° F; **December** 36-45° F.

## AIR POLLUTION

Most of Seattle's air quality problems are seasonal. In summer, the region's traffic congestion, and the emissions from gas engines on boats, jet skis, and lawnmowers, creates smog or ozone problems. To help combat the problem, vehicle emission tests are required every other year in King, Pierce, and Snohomish counties. In winter, particles associated with smoke from wood stoves and fireplaces build up. For the most part, Seattle meets national standards for clean air. High levels of benzene, however, which stem from high concentrations of benzene in gasoline sold in the region, do present an increased cancer risk. New EPA requirements to take effect between 2009 and 2011 should reduce toxic emissions significantly over the next 20 years.

The **Puget Sound Clean Air Agency**, which is charged with enforcing federal, state, and local air quality laws, provides current air quality reports and forecasts at its web site, www.pscleanair.org. You can also view images from its Seattle visibility camera and receive information about local burn bans. The agency recommends the following tips for improving air quality:

- Use an efficient EPA-certified pellet or wood stove. Uncertified wood stoves are illegal to use during a burn ban.
- Burn manufactured logs or pellets.
- Dry firewood at least six months before using it.
- Give your fire lots of air for optimum heat and minimum smoke.
- Drive less.
- When the weather is hot, refuel your vehicle during cooler evening hours.
- Make sure your gas cap seals properly.
- Wait until temperatures decrease and breezes pick up before mowing the lawn or using gas-powered garden equipment.
- Consider using non–gasoline-powered equipment, like a sailboat instead of a motorboat or a manual push mower instead of a gas-powered lawn mower.

## DISASTER PREPAREDNESS

A federal study released in 2000 found that Washington is the nation's second-most-vulnerable state to costly damage from earthquakes. Seattle ranks seventh in the nation among major cities that could expect severe quake damage. Knowing this, it was nonetheless shocking when the 6.8-magnitude Nisqually Earthquake struck the Puget Sound region on February 28, 2001. It was the biggest quake to rattle the area in more than half a century. It caused 410 injuries, and damage statewide was estimated at $2 billion. Experts agree that Seattle was lucky. The quake was buried 32 miles deep, so its effects were muted. Experts also agree that the Nisqually Earthquake was not the "Big One" that the region can expect. The Seattle Fault Line, which runs east-west through the heart of downtown Seattle, Bellevue, and Bainbridge Island, is a shallow fault that would cause severe damage if it's the cause of the next big earthquake. It's overdue, but experts can't predict if it will happen tomorrow or a hundred years from now.

Aside from luck, the secret to surviving a major earthquake, or any other major disaster, is found in the time-proven Boy Scout adage, "be prepared." There are dozens of good books about how to get ready for a seismic onslaught, and plenty of free information available from local, state, and federal agencies. You should prepare to be on your own for three to seven days, as it may take that long for emergency crews to restore power, water, and telephone service to affected areas.

The **King County Office of Emergency Management** maintains a 3 Days 3 Ways web site (www.3days3ways.org) which provides links to disaster preparedness resources and recommends a simple 3 step approach to any disaster: make a plan; build a kit; get involved. You can get in-depth information about local hazards, learn how to develop communication and evacuation plans and what kind of supplies to keep in a disaster kit. The basic rule of thumb is to keep enough water and food on hand to supply your family for three days. For a major disaster, however, supplies for seven days are strongly urged. You'll want supplies like flashlights, a battery-operated radio, and a first aid kit as well. Don't forget about medications and providing for your pets.

The **Red Cross of Seattle King County** (www.seattleredcross.org) also offers plans and resources for disaster preparation. Both sites urge people to get training in CPR and basic first aid, and outline ways to get involved with helping your neighbors and community. The **City of Seattle** sponsors SDART (Seattle Disaster Aid and Response Teams), a program in which the city trains groups of local people to respond to the needs of their neighbors and coordinate with officials during a crisis. To get more information or to find a group near you, call 206-233-7123 or visit www.ci.seattle.wa.us.

Here are a few additional resources for disaster preparedness:

- **American Red Cross**, Seattle King County Chapter, 206-323-2345, www.seattleredcross.org
- **Cascadia Region Earthquake Workgroup**, 206-328-2533, www.crew.org
- **Federal Emergency Management Agency**, 425-487-4600, www.fema.gov
- **King County Office of Emergency Management**, 206-296-3830, www.metrokc.gov/prepare
- **Pierce County Department of Emergency Management**, 253-798-7470, www.co.pierce.wa.us
- **Seattle Emergency Management**, 206-233-5076, www.cityofseattle.net/emergency_mgt
- **Snohomish County Department of Emergency Management**, 425-388-3411, www1.so.snohomish.wa.us
- **US Geological Survey Geologic Hazards Program**, http://geohazards.cr.usgs.gov

One final note: be sure to purchase a homeowner's insurance policy that covers quake damage. Generally, earthquake coverage is not part of a standard policy. See **Finding a Place to Live** for a list of area insurers.

## CHOOSING A PLACE OF WORSHIP

FINDING A PLACE OF WORSHIP CAN BE AS SIMPLE AS SOLICITING THE suggestion of a co-worker or neighbor, or as intensely personal and complex as choosing a spouse. If you belong to a congregation in your old hometown, your religious leader might be able to refer you to a kindred congregation in Seattle. If you don't have a referral, pick up a copy of the Saturday edition of *The Seattle Times,* which publishes a "Religion Digest" in the local section. Or check the Yellow Pages under "Churches," "Synagogues" and "Mosques." The phone book listings are arranged by denomination and include sections for nondenominational, interdenominational, and independent churches, as well as metaphysical centers.

These interfaith agencies, representing congregations working together to address hunger, homelessness, and other urban problems, might be able to refer you to a congregation:

- **The Church Council of Greater Seattle**, 4 Nickerson, Ste 300, 206-525-1213, www.churchcouncilseattle.org
- **The Interfaith Council of Washington**, P.O. Box 31005, Seattle, 98103, 206-547-4077 www.interfaithcouncil.com
- **Washington Association of Churches**, 419 Occidental Ave S, 206-625-9790, www.thewac.org

Online directories—generally limited to Christian denominations—include **Net Ministries**, http://netministries.org, **Churches Dot Net**, http://churches.net, **USA Church**, www.usachurch.com, and **For Ministry**, www.forministry.com. Synagogues serving all branches of Judaism are listed at **Jewish.com**, www.jewish.com.

## BUDDHISM

The non-sectarian **Northwest Dharma Association** publishes the *Northwest Dharma News* and organizes multi-tradition events. The organization's web site provides a calendar of Buddhist retreats, classes and events, and links to other Buddhist sites. For more information visit their office at 158 Thomas St #17, 206-441-6811, or visit www.nwdharma.org.

The **Seattle Buddhist Center**, 3315 Beacon Ave South, is affiliated with the international movement known as the Friends of the Western Buddhist Order. The center offers shrine rooms for meditation, Dharma book sales and merchandise, a lending library, and conversation areas. Call 206-726-0051 or visit www. seattlebuddhistcenter.org.

- **Sakya Monastery of Tibetan Buddhism**, 108 NW 83rd St, 206-789-2573, www.sakya.org
- **Seattle Buddhist Temple**, 1427 S Main St, 206-329-0800, www.seattlebetsuin. com
- **Seattle Shambhala Center**, 3017 E Harrison St, 206-860-4060, www. shambhala.org
- **Vajralama Buddhist Center**, 6556 24th Ave NW, 206-526-9565

## CHRISTIANITY

If you are looking for a church that is convenient to where you live, start your search at the **Seattle Area Churches and Places of Worship** web site, www. hostfororgs.com/churches/seattle.html, which provides links to area churches, organized by location. The **National Council of the Churches of Christ in the USA**, 212-870-2227, www.ncccusa.org, publishes the *Yearbook of American & Canadian Churches*, a directory that lists thousands of Christian churches in North America. Order one for $50 at 888-870-3325 or browse the directory links at www.electronicchurch.org.

The list of churches below is just a sampling of places of worship in Seattle. For a more thorough selection, check the Yellow Pages under "Churches."

### HISTORIC AND NOTABLE CHURCHES

- **First African Methodist Episcopal Church**, 1522 14th Ave, 206-324-3664, www.fameseattle.org; First AME Church Seattle is the oldest congregation in the Pacific Northwest to be established by African-Americans. Founded in 1886, the church is an historical landmark. In August 2001, the church welcomed Bishop Vashti McKenzie, the first woman ever appointed bishop in the AME Church.

- **Mount Zion Baptist Church**, 1634 19th Ave, 206-322-6500, www.mountzion. net; founded in 1890, Mount Zion Baptist Church is one of the city's oldest continuously active places of worship. It is perhaps best known to those outside its congregation for its annual Martin Luther King Jr. celebration. The church is also active in community outreach, and serves as a meeting place for a variety of local organizations and committees.
- **St. James Cathedral**, 804 9th Ave, 206-622-3559, www.stjames-cathedral. org; the century-old St. James is the cathedral for the Catholic Archdiocese of Seattle, as well as an active parish church for the Capitol Hill community. Check the schedule for outstanding classical musical events throughout the year, including a popular New Year's Eve gala.
- **Seattle First United Methodist Church**, 811 5th Ave, 206-622-7278, www. firstchurchseattle.org; recognizable for its terra cotta dome, the First United Methodist Church came to a difficult decision in 2006 to sell its historic building, which was in desperate need of repairs the congregation could not afford. A new church will be built downtown in Belltown so that vital programs like meal service and a homeless shelter can be continued where the need is greatest. The old structure will be replaced with an office tower.
- **Temple of The Church of Jesus Christ of Latter-day Saints**, 2808 148th SE, Bellevue, 425-643-5144; the 110,000-square-foot temple attracted its share of controversy when it was built in the late 1970s, from environmentalists who balked at its size and location, to women's rights activists who opposed the church's stand on the Equal Rights Amendment. Today, the temple's lofty gold leaf statue of the angel Moroni is a familiar local beacon.

# CATHOLIC

## BYZANTINE CATHOLIC

- **St. John Chrysostom Byzantine Catholic Church**, 1305 S Lander St, 206-329-9219

## ROMAN CATHOLIC

The **Archdiocese of Seattle** encompasses all of western Washington, and includes more than 160 parishes and missions that serve over half a million Catholics. In addition to managing more than 60 ministries and programs that serve the Catholic community, the Archdiocese runs a library/media center and publishes the *Catholic Northwest Progress*. The Archdiocese offices are located at 710 9th Ave. For more information, call 206-382-4560, or visit www.seattlearch.org.

- **Holy Family Church**, 9622 20th SW, 206-767-6220

- **Immaculate Conception Church**, 820 18th, 206-322-5970
- **Our Lady of Guadalupe Church**, 7000 35th Ave SW, 206-935-0358
- **Our Lady of the Lake Church**, 3517 NE 89th, 206-523-6776
- **Sacred Heart Church of Seattle**, 205 2nd Ave N, 206-284-4680
- **St. James Cathedral**, 804 9th Ave, 206-622-3559, www.stjames-cathedral.org
- **St. Peter Catholic Church**, 2807 15th Ave S, 206-324-2290

## ORTHODOX

- **Russian Orthodox Cathedral of St. Nicholas**, 1714 13th Ave, 206-322-9387
- **St. Demetrios Greek Orthodox Church**, 2100 Boyer Ave E, 206-325-4347, www.saintdemetrios.com
- **St. Nectarios American Orthodox Church**, 10300 Ashworth Ave N, 206-522-4471
- **St. Spiridon Cathedral**, 1310 Harrison, 206-624-5341

## PROTESTANT

### AFRICAN METHODIST EPISCOPAL

- **First AME Church**, 1522 14th Ave, 206-323-9642, www.fameseattle.org
- **Walker Chapel AME Church**, 800 28th Ave S, 206-325-8468, www.ame-church.com

### AFRICAN METHODIST EPISCOPAL ZION

- **Ebenezer AME Zion Church**, 1716 23rd Ave, 206-322-6620

### ANGLICAN

- **St. Barnabas Anglican Church**, 2340 N 155th St, Shoreline, 206-365-6565, www.stbarnabas-anglican-wa.org
- **St. Paul Anglican Church**, 1040 NE 95th St, 206-526-9020

### APOSTOLIC

- **The Apostolic Faith**, 7420 9th Ave NE, 206-522-1350, www.apostolicfaith.org
- **Faith Deliverance Assembly**, 2642 S 138th, 206-762-2684
- **Jesus the Rock**, 555 16th Ave, 206-325-4358

## ASSEMBLIES OF GOD

- **All Saints Church**, 1716 2nd Ave N, 206-285-3866, www.believedoubtseek. org
- **Calvary Christian Assembly**, 6801 Roosevelt Way NE, 206-525-7474, www. ccassembly.org
- **Creekside Church**, 12345 8th Ave NE, 206-367-6500, http://thecreeksidechurch. org
- **Latin American Assemblies of God Temple El Redentor**, 5500 17th Ave S, 206-768-1868
- **Westminster Community Church**, 14550 Westminster Way N, 206-364-5200
- **Westwood Christian Assembly**, 9252 16th Ave SW, 206-763-0585

## BAPTIST

- **Queen Anne Baptist Church**, 2011 1st Ave N, 206-282-7744, www. queenannebaptist.org
- **Rosehill Missionary Baptist Church**, 7550 Martin Luther King Jr. Way S, 206-721-0426

### AMERICAN BAPTIST
- **Beacon Hill First Baptist Church**, 1607 S Forest St, 206-324-3350
- **Chinese Baptist Church**, 5801 Beacon Ave S, 206-725-6363, http://seattlecbc. org
- **Damascus Baptist Church**, 5237 Rainier Ave S, 206-725-9310
- **Fremont Baptist Church**, 717 N 36th St, 206-632-7994
- **Mount Zion Baptist Church**, 1634 19th Ave, 206-322-6500, www.mountzion. net
- **Seattle First Baptist**, 1111 Harvard Ave, 206-325-6051, www.seattlefirstbaptist. com
- **Tabernacle Missionary Baptist Church**, 2801 S Jackson, 206-329-9794
- **Wedgwood Community Church**, 8201 30th Ave NE, 206-522-5778, www. wedgwoodchurch.org

### GENERAL CONFERENCE BAPTIST
- **Ballard Baptist Church**, 2004 NW 63rd St, 206-784-1554, www.ballardbaptist. org
- **Haller Lake Baptist Church**, 14054 Wallingford Ave N, 206-364-1811

## SOUTHERN BAPTIST

- **Anchor Baptist Church**, 3524 NE 95th St, 206-525-5646
- **Korean-American Calvary Baptist Church**, 7817 S 125th St, 206-772-4371, www.kacbc.org
- **Northgate Baptist Church**, 10510 Stone Ave N, 206-525-5699

## CHRISTIAN SCIENCE

- **First Church of Christ-Scientist**, 1801 16th Ave, 206-324-3020
- **Third Church of Christ-Scientist**, 5208 19th Ave NE, 206-522-5755
- **Sixth Church of Christ-Scientist**, 4310 SW Oregon St, 206-932-6004
- **Seventh Church of Christ-Scientist**, 2555 8th Ave W, 206-282-9255
- **Thirteenth Church of Christ-Scientist**, 3500 NE 125th St, 206-362-7646

## CHURCH OF CHRIST

- **Church of Christ Iglesia Ni Cristo**, 6020 Rainier Ave S, 206-723-0346
- **Church of Christ North Seattle**, 13315 20th Ave NE, 206-367-9232
- **Church of Christ West Seattle**, 4220 SW 100th St, 206-938-0212
- **Holgate Street Church of Christ**, 2600 S Holgate St, 206-324-5530, www.holgatecoc.org
- **Madison Park Church of Christ**, 1115 19th Ave, 206-324-6775

## CHURCH OF GOD IN CHRIST

- **Berean Church of God in Christ**, 3417 Rainier Ave S, 206-725-0745
- **Greater Glory Church of God in Christ**, 6419 Martin Luther King Jr. Way S, 206-723-6419, www.greaterglorycogic.org
- **Madison Temple Church of God in Christ**, 2239 E Madison St, 206-323-4900
- **Smith Temple Church of God in Christ**, 1516 30th Ave, 206-329-3829
- **Survival Church of God in Christ**, 8459 50th Ave S, 206-725-9366

## CHURCH OF JESUS CHRIST OF LATTER-DAY SAINTS (MORMON)

- **Seattle Fifth Ward**, 5701 8th Ave NE, 206-524-5414, www.lds.org
- **Seattle First Ward**, 2415 31st Ave W, 206-285-5343, www.lds.org

## COVENANT

- **Interbay Covenant Church**, 3233 15th Ave W, 206-283-9660, www.interbaycov.org

## EPISCOPAL

- **Downtown Trinity Episcopal Church**, 609 8th Ave, 206-624-5337, www.trinityseattle.org
- **St. Andrew's Episcopal Church**, 111 NE 80th St, 206-523-7476, www.saintandrewsseattle.org
- **St. John the Baptist Episcopal Church**, 3050 California Ave SW, 206-937-4545, www.sjbws.org
- **St. Mark's Episcopal Cathedral**, 1245 10th Ave E, 206-323-0300, www.saintmarks.org
- **St. Paul's Episcopal Church**, 15 Roy St, 206-282-0786, www.stpaulseattle.org

## EVANGELICAL

- **Evangelical Chinese Church**, 651 NW 81st St, 206-789-6380, www.eccseattle.org
- **Maple Leaf Evangelical Church**, 1059 NE 96th St, 206-525-3707, www.mapleleafchurch.org
- **Medhane-Alem Evangelical Church (Ethiopian)**, 8445 Rainier Ave S, 206-720-0181, www.medhanealem.com

## FOURSQUARE GOSPEL

- **Living Way Foursquare Church**, 400 N 105th St, 206-367-9600
- **New Hope Seattle**, 16101 Greenwood Ave, Shoreline, 206-713-5040, www.newhopeseattle.org
- **Shorewood Foursquare Church**, 10300 28th Ave SW, 206-932-0186

## FRIENDS (QUAKERS)

- **North Seattle Friends Church**, 7740 24th Ave NE, 206-525-8800, www.northseattlefriends.org
- **University Friends Meeting**, 4001 9th Ave NE, 206-547-6449

## INTERDENOMINATIONAL

- **Church of Mary Magdalene**, 811 5th Ave, 206-621-8474, www.churchofmarymagdalene.org

## JEHOVAH'S WITNESSES

- **Central and Spanish Congregation**, 333 19th Ave E, 206-325-4192
- **Ballard and North Park Congregation**, 9240 6th Ave NW, 206-783-9940

- **Queen Anne Congregation**, 3626 34th Ave W, 206-285-7986
- **Rainier Congregation**, 5933 39th Ave S, 206-722-1250
- **Southwest Cambridge and White Center Congregation**, 2121 SW Cambridge St, 206-762-5486

# LUTHERAN

## ELCA

- **Bethel Chinese Lutheran Church**, 6553 40th Ave NE, 206-524-7631
- **Central Lutheran Church of the Holy Trinity**, 1710 11th Ave, 206-322-7500
- **Crown Lutheran Church**, 1501 NW 90th St, 206-784-1930
- **First Lutheran Church of West Seattle**, 4105 California Ave SW, 206-935-6530, www.flcws.org
- **Gethsemane Lutheran Church**, 911 Stewart St, 206-682-3620, www.urbanfaith.org
- **Luther Memorial Church**, 13047 Greenwood Ave N, 206-364-2510
- **Queen Anne Evangelical Lutheran Church**, 2400 8th Ave W, 206-284-1960, www.qaelc.org
- **University Lutheran Church**, 1604 NE 50th St, 206-525-7074, www.ulcseattle.org

## MISSOURI SYNOD

- **Beacon Lutheran Church**, 1720 S Forest St, 206-322-0251
- **Hope Lutheran Church**, 4456 42nd Ave SW, 206-937-9330, www.hopeseattle.org
- **Messiah Lutheran Church**, 7050 35th Ave NE, 206-524-0024, www.messiahseattle.org
- **Zion Evangelical Lutheran Church**, 7109 Aurora Ave N, 782-6734

# MENNONITE

- **Seattle Mennonite Church**, 3120 NE 125th St, 206-361-4630, http://seattle.wa.us.mennonite.net

# METHODIST

## CHRISTIAN METHODIST EPISCOPAL
- **Curry Temple**, 172 23rd Ave, 206-325-9344

## FREE METHODIST
- **Ballard Free Methodist Church**, 1460 NW 73rd St, 206-784-6111
- **First Free Methodist Church**, 3200 3rd Ave W, 206-281-2240, www.ffmc.org

• **Rainier Avenue Free Methodist Church**, 5900 Rainier Ave S, 206-722-5616

## UNITED METHODIST
• **Beacon United Methodist Church**, 7301 Beacon Ave S, 206-722-5042, www.gbgm-umc.org/beaconumc
• **Green Lake United Methodist Church**, 6415 1st Ave NE, 206-526-2900
• **Haller Lake United Methodist Church**, 13055 1st Ave NE, 206-362-5383, www.hallerlakeumc.org
• **Magnolia United Methodist Church**, 2836 34th Ave W, 206-282-3266
• **Seaview United Methodist Church**, 4620 SW Graham St, 206-932-7609
• **Trinity United Methodist Church**, 6512 23rd Ave NW, 206-784-2227, www.tumseattle.org

## NAZARENE

• **Ballard Church of the Nazarene**, 6541 Jones Ave NW, 206-784-1418
• **Beacon Hill Church of the Nazarene**, 4352 15th Ave S, 206-762-2136,
• **North Seattle Church of the Nazarene**, 13130 5th Ave NE, 206-367-5955
• **Seattle First Church of the Nazarene**, 4401 2nd Ave NE, 206-632-4560
• **West Seattle Church of the Nazarene**, 4201 SW Juneau St, 206-932-4581

## NON-DENOMINATIONAL

• **Christian Faith Center**, 21024 24th Ave S, 206-824-8188, www.caseytreat.com
• **Emmanuel Bible Church**, 503 N 50th St, 206-632-5539, www.ebcseattle.org
• **Faith Bible Church**, 128 18th Ave, 206-322-8044, www.fbcseattle.org
• **Mars Hill Church**, 1401 NW Leary Way, 206-706-6641, www.marshillchurch.org
• **New Covenant Christian Center**, 7930 Rainier Ave S, 206-725-6222, www.ncccministry.org
• **Vineyard Christian Fellowship of Seattle**, 4142 Brooklyn Ave NE, 206-547-4354, www.seattlevineyard.org
• **Westside Church**, 7758 Earl Ave NW, 206-781-5154, www.westsidechurch.com

## PENTECOSTAL

• **Bethany Temple Church**, 1122 26th Ave S, 206-328-1816
• **Full Gospel Pentecostal Federated Church**, 5071 Delridge Way SW, 206-935-1511
• **Holy Ground Pentecostal Tabernacle Church**, 3425 Martin Luther King Jr Way S, 206-723-1809

## PRESBYTERIAN

- **Beacon Hill Presbyterian Church**, 1625 S Columbian Way, 206-762-0870
- **Bethany Presbyterian Church**, 1818 Queen Anne Ave N, 206-284-2222, www. bethanypc.org
- **Bethel Presbyterian Church**, 11002 Greenwood Ave N, 206-362-3600
- **Japanese Presbyterian Church**, 1801 24th Ave S, 206-323-5990, www.jpresby. org
- **Lake City Presbyterian Church**, 3841 NE 123rd St, 206-362-6878, www. lakecitypres.org
- **Northminster Presbyterian Church**, 7706 25th NW, 206-783-3402, www. northminsterpres.org
- **Seattle First Presbyterian Church**, 1013 8th Ave, 206-624-0644, www. firstpres.org
- **Wallingford Presbyterian Church**, 1414 N 42nd St, 206-632-0263, www. wallpc.org
- **West Side Presbyterian Church**, 3601 California Ave SW, 206-935-4477, www. wspc.org

## SEVENTH-DAY ADVENTIST

- **Breath of Life Seventh-day Adventist Church**, 9807 26th Ave SW, 206-762-0333
- **Green Lake Seventh-day Adventist Church**, 6350 E Green Lake Way N, 206-522-1330, www.greenlakesda.org
- **West Seattle Seventh-day Adventist Church**, 7901 35th Ave SW, 206-932-4211

## UNITARIAN UNIVERSALIST

- **University Unitarian Church**, 6556 35th Ave NE, 206-525-8400, www. uuchurch.org

## UNITED CHURCH OF CHRIST

- **Admiral Congregational United Church of Christ**, 4320 SW Hill St, 206-932-2928, www.admiralchurch.org
- **Broadview Community United Church of Christ**, 325 N 125th St, 206-363-8060, www.broadviewucc.org
- **Plymouth Congregational Church**, 1217 6th Ave, 206-622-4865, www. plymouthchurchseattle.org

- **University Congregational United Church of Christ**, 4516 16th Ave NE, 206-524-2322, www.universityucc.org

## UNITY

- **Seattle Unity Church**, 200 8th Ave N, 206-622-8475, www.seattleunity.org

## WESLEYAN

- **Crown Hill Wesleyan Church**, 9204 11th Ave NW, 206-783-6400

## HINDUISM

The **Vedanta Society of Western Washington** is a branch of the Ramakrishna Order of India, which was established by Swami Vivekananda in 1894. The main temple and bookshop are located at 2716 Broadway East, on Capitol Hill, and the Tapovan Retreat is at 23217 27th Avenue NE, in Arlington, north of Seattle. On Sundays at 11 a.m., the society presents a lecture on the Vedanta philosophy and religion. A second class is conducted Tuesdays at 7:30 p.m. For more information, call 206-323-1228 or visit www.vedanta-seattle.org.

- **Hindu Temple and Cultural Center**, 3818 212th St SE, Bothell, 425-483-7115

## ISLAM

The **Islamic Educational Center** of Seattle is located in Mountlake Terrace at 23204 55th Avenue West. The center offers religious, educational and cultural services, including Persian school and a library. For details, call 206-547-1990 or visit www.ershad.org.

- **Islamic (Idriss) Mosque**, 1420 NE Northgate Way, 206-363-3013
- **Islamic Center of Eastside**, 14700 Main St, Bellevue, 425-746-0398, www.bellevuemosque.com
- **Jamaatul Ikhlas**, 1350 E Fir St, 206-322-6246
- **West Seattle Masjid**, 1022 SW Henderson, 206-763-2239

## JUDAISM

The **Jewish Federation of Greater Seattle**, 2031 3rd Avenue, which coordinates and funds Jewish projects, provides leadership, and supports educational programs, is a substantial resource for the Jewish community. The organization's comprehensive web site, www.jewishinseattle.org, provides links to Jewish resources, lists holidays and Shabbat candle-lighting occasions, and offers reprints of the *Guide to Jewish Washington*, which is published each year by Seattle's only Jewish newspaper, the *Jewish Transcript*. For more information, call 206-443-5400.

The **Samuel and Althea Stroum Jewish Community Center of Greater Seattle** promotes intergenerational Jewish events, informal education programs and activities, and social services, including a childcare center and senior adult programs. The JCC's primary facility on Mercer Island, 3801 East Mercer Way, features a state-of-the-art fitness center. The Center also has facilities at 8606 35th Avenue NE. Call 206-232-7115 or visit www.sjcc.org.

## REFORM

- **Temple Beth Am**, 2632 NE 80th St, 206-525-0915
- **Temple de Hirsch Sinai**, 1511 E Pike St, 206-323-8486, http://tdhs-nw.org
- **Temple B'nai Torah** 15727 NE 4th St, Bellevue, 425-603-9677, www. templebnaitorah.org

## CONSERVATIVE

- **Congregation Beth Shalom**, 6800 35th Ave NE, 206-524-0075

## ORTHODOX

- **Bikur Cholim-Machzikay Hadath**, 5145 S Morgan St, 206-721-0970, www. ou.org/network/shuls/bikurcholim
- **Chabad-Lubavitch Chabad House**, 4541 19th Ave NE, 206-527-1411
- **Congregation Ezra Bessaroth**, 5217 S Brandon St, 206-722-5500, www. ezrabessaroth.org
- **Sephardic Bikur Holim Congregation**, 6500 52nd Ave S, 206-723-3028, www. sbhseattle.org

## PROGRESSIVE

- **Kol HaNeshamah**, 6115 SW Hinds St, 206-935-1590, www.kol-haneshamah. org

## RECONSTRUCTIONIST

- **Kadima**, 2366 Eastlake Ave E, 206-547-3914, www.kadima.org

## RENEWAL

- **Bet Alef Meditative Synagogue**, 8511 15th Ave NE, Ste 102, 206-527-9399, www.betalef.org
- **Congregation Eitz Or**, 6556 35th Ave NE, 206-467-2617, www.eitzor.org

# GAY & LESBIAN

For information on gay-friendly churches visit the web site of **Gay Church** at www.gaychurch.com. The following is a sampling of gay-friendly Seattle area congregations:

## CHRISTIAN

- **All Pilgrims Christian Church**, 500 Broadway E, 206-322-0487, www.allpilgrims.org
- **Central Lutheran Church**, 1710 11th Ave, 206-322-7500, www.loveiscentral.org
- **Dignity Seattle**, 206-325-7314, www.dignityusa.org, is the country's largest and most progressive organization of gay, lesbian, bisexual and transgender Catholics.
- **Gethsemane Lutheran Church**, 911 Stewart St, 206-682-3620, www.urbanfaith.org
- **Grace Gospel Chapel**, 2052 NW 64th St, 206-784-8495, www.gracegospelwa.org
- **Keystone Congregational Church**, 5019 Keystone Pl N, 206-632-6021
- **Mt. Baker Park Presbyterian Church**, 3201 Hunter Blvd S, 206-722-5884, www.mtbakerchurch.org
- **St. Joseph Catholic Church**, 700 18th Ave E, 206-324-2522, www.stjosephparish.org
- **St. Patrick's Catholic Church**, 2702 Broadway E, 206-329-2960, www.stpatsseattle.org
- **St. Mark's Episcopal Cathedral**, 1245 10th Ave E, 206-323-0300, www.saintmarks.org
- **Seattle First Baptist Church**, 1111 Harvard Ave, 206-325-6051, www.seattlefirstbaptist.org
- **Wallingford United Methodist Church**, 2115 N 42nd St, 206-547-6945, www.wallingfordumc.org
- **University Baptist Church**, 4554 12th Ave NE, 206-632-5188, www.ubcseattle.org

## JEWISH

- **Congregation Tikvah Chadashah**, 1122 E Pike St, 206-355-1414, www.tikvahchadashah.org
- **Congregation Eitz Or**, 6556 35th Ave NE, 98115, 206-467-2617, www.eitzor.org
- **Kol HaNeshamah**, 6115 SW Hinds St, 206-935-1590, www.kol-haneshama.org

## SPIRITUALITY/ETHICS

- **Ethical Culture Society of Puget Sound**, 425-562-8740, www.ethicalculturesociety.org
- **Theosophical Society in Seattle**, 717 Broadway Ave E, 206-323-4281, http://seattle-ts.org

## RELIGIOUS STUDIES

The following colleges and universities offer graduate degree programs in religious studies:

- **Mars Hill Graduate School**, 2525 220th St SE, Bothell, 425-415-0505, www.mhgs.edu
- **Northwest Baptist Seminary**, 4301 N Stevens St, Tacoma, 253-759-6104
- **Seattle University**, Theology and Ministry, 206-296-5330, www.seattleu.edu
- **University of Washington**, Jackson School of International Studies, Comparative Religion Program, 206-543-4370, www.washington.edu
- **Western Reformed Seminaries**, Pastoral Studies, 5 S "G" St, Tacoma, 253-272-0417, www.wrs.edu

WHEN YOU'RE NEW IN TOWN, VOLUNTEERING MAY PROVIDE the perfect opportunity to get acquainted with the community and to make new friends in the process. In addition to meeting people with similar interests, you'll be helping organizations that are often short on cash and resources. Seattle has many charitable and philanthropic organizations that offer a variety of services, from the basics of food and clothing, to counseling, to funding education or medical research.

## VOLUNTEER PLACEMENT

If you're not sure where to begin, the following volunteer placement services can point you in the right direction:

- **Seattle Works**, 312 1st Ave N, Ste 200, 206-324-0808, www.seattleworks.org
- **United Way of King County**, 720 2nd Ave, 206-461-3655, www.uwkc.org
- **Volunteers of America**, 6559 35th Ave NE, 206-523-3565, www.voa.org
- **VolunteerMatch**, www.volunteermatch.org

## ORGANIZATIONS

Volunteer opportunities also can be found in the Yellow Pages, in newspaper advertisements, and online at craigslist.org. The following is a sample of possibilities, listed by category:

### AIDS

- **Bailey-Boushay House**, 2720 E Madison St, 206-322-5300, www.virginiamason.org/dbbailey-boushay
- **Dunshee House**, 303 17th Ave E, 206-322-2437, www.dunsheehouse.org

- **Gay City Health Project**, 511 E Pike, 206-860-6969, www.gaycity.org
- **Lifelong AIDS Alliance**, 1002 E Seneca, 206-328-8979, www.lifelongaids alliance.org
- **Multifaith Works**, 1801 12th Ave, Ste A, 206-324-1520, www.multifaith.org
- **People of Color Against AIDS Network**, 2200 Rainier Ave S, 206-322-7061, www.pocaan.org

## ALCOHOL AND DRUG DEPENDENCY

- **Salvation Army Adult Rehabilitation Center**, 1000 4th Ave S, 206-587-0503, www.nwarmy.org

## ANIMALS

- **The Humane Society for Seattle/King County**, 13212 SE Eastgate Way, Bellevue, 425-641-0080, www.seattlehumane.org
- **Pasado's Safe Haven**, P.O. Box 171, Sultan, 98294, 360-793-9393, www. pasadosafehaven.org
- **Progressive Animal Welfare Society (PAWS)**, 15305 44th Ave W, Lynnwood, 425-787-2500, www.paws.org
- **Seattle Animal Control**, 2061 15th Ave W, 206-615-0820, www.cityofseattle. net/animalshelter

## CHILDREN

- **Big Brothers Big Sisters of King County**, 1600 S Graham St, 206-763-9060, 877-700-2447, www.bbbs.org/pugetsound
- **Big Brothers Big Sisters of Pierce County**, 1501 Pacific Ave, Ste 310C, Tacoma, 253-396-9630, www.bbbs.org/pugetsound
- **Boys and Girls Clubs of King County**, 603 Stewart, #300, 206-461-3890, www. positiveplace.org
- **Catholic Community Services**, 100 23rd Ave S, 206-328-5696, www.ccsww. org
- **Childhaven**, 316 Broadway, 206-624-6477, www.childhaven.org
- **Children's Home Society of Washington**, 3300 NE 65th St, 206-695-3200, www.chs-wa.org

## CRIME PREVENTION

- **Seattle Police Department Volunteer Alliance**, 206-615-0892, www. cityofseattle.net/police

## CULTURAL IDENTITY

- **Chinese Information and Service Center**, 409 Maynard Ave S, Ste 203, 206-624-5633, www.cisc-seattle.org
- **El Centro de la Raza**, 2524 16th Ave S, 206-329-9442, www.elcentrodelaraza.com
- **Filipino Youth Activities**, 810 18th Ave, Rm 108, 206-461-4870, www.fya-pinoy.org
- **Japanese American Citizens League**, 316 Maynard Ave S, 206-622-4098, www.jaclseattle.org
- **Jewish Family Service**, 1601 16th Ave, 206-461-3240; 15821 NE 8th St, Ste 210, Bellevue, 425-643-2221; 1215 Central Ave S, Ste 131, Kent, 253-850-4065; www.jfsseattle.org
- **Jewish Federation of Greater Seat**tle, 2031 3rd Ave, 206-443-5400, www.jewishinseattle.org
- **Korean Community Counseling Center**, 302 N 78th St, 206-784-5691; 23830 Hwy 99, Edmonds, 425-697-5642
- **Seattle Indian Center**, 611 12th Ave S, 206-329-8700, www.seattleindiancenter.org
- **Seattle Samoan Center**, 2524 16th Ave S, #201, 206-322-0284
- **Society of African Americans USA**, 1218 E Cherry St, 206-860-0531
- **United Indians of All Tribes Foundation**, Daybreak Star Art & Cultural Center, Discovery Park, 206-285-4425, www.unitedindians.com
- **Urban League of Metropolitan Seattle**, 105 14th Ave, 206-461-3792, www.urbanleague.org

## CULTURE AND THE ARTS

- **Northwest Programs for the Arts**, 1319 Dexter Ave N, 206-632-4545, www.northwestarts.org
- **Pacific Northwest Ballet**, 301 Mercer St, 206-441-2427, www.pnb.org

## DISABILITY ASSISTANCE

- **Catholic Community Services**, 100 23rd Ave S, 206-328-5696, www.ccsww.org
- **Community Services for the Blind and Partially Sighted**, 9709 3rd Ave NE, 206-525-5556, www.csbps.com
- **Deaf-Blind Service Center**, 1620 18th Ave, Ste 200, 206-323-9178, www.seattledbsc.org
- **Easter Seal Society of Washington**, 157 Roy St, 206-281-5700, http://wa.easterseals.com

## ENVIRONMENT

- **EarthCorps**, 6310 NE 74th St, Ste 201E, 206-322-9296, www.earthcorps.org
- **Earth Ministry**, 6512 23rd Ave NW, Ste 317, 206-632-2426, www.earthministry.org
- **Earth Share of Washington**, 1402 3rd Ave, 206-622-9840, www.esw.org
- **Friends of the Earth**, 4512 University Way NE, 206-633-1661, www.foe.org
- **Seattle Audubon Society**, 8050 35th Ave NE, 206-523-4483, www.seattleaudubon.org
- **Sierra Club, Cascade Chapter**, 180 Nickerson St, Ste 202, 206-378-0114, http://cascade.sierraclub.org
- **WashPIRG**, 3420 Eastlake Ave E, Ste 100, 206-568-2850, www.washpirg.org

## FOOD DISTRIBUTION

- **Auburn Food Bank**, 930 18th Pl NE, Auburn, 253-833-8925, www.skcfc.org/theauburnfoodbank
- **Beacon Avenue Food Bank**, 6230 Beacon Ave S, 206-722-5105
- **Bothell Food Bank**, 18220 96th Ave NE, Bothell, 425-485-6521
- **Des Moines Area Food Bank**, 22225 9th Ave S, Des Moines, 206-878-2660, www.myfoodbank.org
- **Downtown Food Bank**, 1531 Western Ave, 206-626-6462, www.pikemarketseniorcenter.org
- **Edmonds Food Bank**, 828 Caspers St, Edmonds, 425-778-5833, www.edmondsumc.org/carol_rowe_memorial.htm
- **Federal Way Food Bank**, 1200 S 336th St, Federal Way, 253-838-6810, www.multi-servicecenter.com
- **Food Lifeline**, 1702 NE 150th St, Shoreline, 800-404-7543, www.foodlifeline.org
- **Highline Food Bank**, 18300 4th Ave S, 206-433-9900
- **Issaquah Food Bank**, 179 1st Ave SE, Issaquah, 425-392-4123, http://issaquahfoodbank.org
- **Kent Food Bank**, 515 W Harrison St, Kent, 253-856-5180
- **Lynnwood Food Bank**, 5320 176th St SW, Lynnwood, 425-745-1635, www.lynnwoodfoodbank.org
- **Northwest Harvest**, P.O. Box 12272, Seattle, 98102, 206-625-0755, www.northwestharvest.org
- **Redmond Food Bank**, 16225 NE 87th St, Redmond, 425-869-6000
- **Renton Food Bank**, 221 Morris St, Renton, 425-255-5969
- **Tukwila Food Pantry**, 3118 S 140th St, Tukwila, 206-431-8293, www.tukwilapantry.org
- **University District Food Bank**, 4731 15th Ave NE, 206-523-7060, www.udistrictfoodbank.org

- **West Seattle Food Bank**, 3518 SW Genesee St, 206-932-9023, www.west seattlefoodbank.org
- **White Center Food Bank**, 9700 8th SW, 206-762-2848, www.skcfc.org/white centerfoodbank

## GAY AND LESBIAN

- **Seattle Out and Proud**, 1605 12th Ave, Ste 2, 206-322-9561, www.seattlepride. org
- **Lambert House**, 1818 15th Ave, 206-322-2515, www.lamberthouse.org
- **Lesbian Resource Center**, 227 S Orcas St, 206-322-3953, www.lrc.net
- **The Pride Foundation**, 2014 E Madison, Ste 300, 206-323-3318, www. pridefoundation.org

## HEALTH AND HOSPITALS

Most hospitals welcome volunteers—just give the nearest one a call. For specific health issues, contact one of the following organizations:

- **Alzheimer's Association**, Western and Central Washington State Chapter, 12721 30th Ave NE, Ste 101, 206-363-5500, www.alzwa.org
- **American Cancer Society**, 2120 1st Ave N, 206-283-1152; 1001 N Broadway, Everett, 425-339-4141, www.cancer.org
- **American Heart Association**, 710 2nd Ave, Ste 900, 206-632-6881, www. americanheart.org
- **American Lung Association**, 2625 3rd Ave, 206-441-5100, www.alaw.org
- **March of Dimes Birth Defects Foundation**, 1904 3rd Ave, Ste 230, 206-624-1373, www.modimes.org
- **National Multiple Sclerosis Society**, Greater Washington Chapter, 192 Nickerson St, Ste 100, 206-284-4236, www.nmsswas.org

## HOMELESS SERVICES

- **Family Services**, 615 2nd Ave, Ste 150, 206-461-3883
- **Jubilee Women's Center**, 620 18th Ave E, 206-324-1244, www.jwcenter.org
- **Millionair Club**, 2515 Western Ave, 206-728-5600, www.millionairclub.org
- **Real Change**, 2129 2nd Ave, 206-441-3247, www.realchangenews.org
- **Sacred Heart Shelter**, 232 Warren Ave N, 206-285-7489, http://sacredheart. catholiccharitiesseattlearch.org
- **Salvation Army**, 811 Maynard Ave S, 206-621-0145, www.nwarmy.org
- **Union Gospel Mission**, Department of Volunteer Efforts, 3800 S Othello, 206-723-0767, www.ugm.org
- **YouthCare**, 2500 NE 54th St, 206-694-4500, www.youthcare.org

## HUMAN SERVICES

- **American Red Cross**, 1900 25th Ave S, 206-323-2345; 811 Pacific Ave, Bremerton, 360-377-3761; www.seattleredcross.org
- **Catholic Community Services**, 100 23rd Ave S, 206-328-5696, www.ccsww.org
- **Habitat for Humanity**, 15439 53rd Ave S, Ste B, Tukwila, 206-292-9617, www.seattle-habitat.org
- **Salvation Army**, 1101 Pike St, 206-442-9944, www.nwarmy.org
- **Seattle Goodwill**, 1400 S Lane St, 206-329-1000, www.seattlegoodwill.org

## LEGAL AID

- **American Civil Liberties Union of Washington**, 705 2nd Ave, 206-624-2184, www.aclu-wa.org
- **Catholic Community Services**, 100 23rd Ave S, 206-328-5696; 12828 Northup Way, Ste 100, Bellevue, 425-284-2238, www.ccsww.org
- **Volunteer Legal Services**, 900 4th Ave, #600, 206-267-7100
- **Washington State Bar Association**, 2101 4th Ave, Ste 400, 800-945-9722, 206-443-9722, www.wsba.org

## LITERACY

- **Friends of the Seattle Public Library**, 1000 4th Ave, 206-523-4053, www.splfriends.org
- **King County Library System**, 960 Newport Way NW, Issaquah, 425-369-3275, www.kcls.org
- **Literacy Action Center**, 8016 Greenwood Ave N, 206-782-2050,
- **Literacy Council of Seattle**, 811 5th Ave, 206-233-9720, www.literacyseattle.org

## MEN'S SERVICES

- **DADS America**, P.O. Box 65131, Shoreline, 98155, 206-623-DADS, www.dadsamerica.org

## POLITICS—ELECTORAL

- **Freedom Socialist Party**, New Freeway Hall, 5018 Rainier Ave S, 206-722-2453, www.socialism.com
- **Green Party of Seattle**, 206-524-3377, www.seattlegreens.org
- **International Socialist Organization**, 206-931-2922, www.internationalsocialist.org

- **King County Democratic Central Committee**, 616 1st Ave, Ste 350, 206-622-9157, www.kcdems.net
- **Labor Party**, 206-382-5712, www.thelaborparty.org
- **League of Women Voters of Washington**, 4710 University Way NE, Ste 214, 206-622-8961, www.lwvwa.org
- **Libertarian Party of Washington State**, 15831 NE 8th, Ste 210, Bellevue, 425-641-8247, www.lpwa.org
- **King County Republican Party**, 845 106th Ave NE, Ste 110, Bellevue, 425-990-0404, www.kcgop.org

## POLITICS—SOCIAL

- **American Veterans Association**, 915 2nd Ave, 206-220-6244, www.amvets.org
- **Amnesty International Seattle**, 206-622-2741, www.scn.org/amnesty
- **Blacks in Government**, 810 3rd Ave, 206-624-4870, www.bignet.org

## REFUGEE ASSISTANCE

- **International Rescue Committee**, 318 1st Ave S, Ste 200, 206-623-2105, www.theirc.org/seattle
- **Lutheran Refugee Program**, 206-694-5700, www.lirs.org
- **Refugee Women's Alliance**, 4008 Martin Luther King Jr Way S, 206-721-0243, www.rewa.org

## SENIOR SERVICES

- **Auburn Senior Center**, 809 9th St SE, Auburn, 253-931-3016
- **Bellevue Senior Center**, 4063 148th Ave NE, Bellevue, 425-455-7681
- **Catholic Community Services**, 100 23rd Ave S, 206-328-5696, www.ccsww.org
- **Central Area Senior Center**, 500 30th Ave S, 206-726-4926
- **Federal Way Senior Center**, 4016 S 352nd, Auburn, 253-838-3604, www.federalwayseniorcenter.org
- **Greenwood Senior Center**, 525 N 85th St, 206-297-0875, www.greenwoodseniorcenter.org
- **Highline Senior Center**, 1210 SW 136th St, Burien, 206-244-3686
- **Issaquah Valley Senior Center**, 105 2nd Ave NE, Issaquah, 425-392-2381
- **Lynnwood Senior Center**, 5800 198th St SW, Lynnwood, 425-744-6464
- **Northshore Senior Center**, 10201 E Riverside Dr, Bothell, 425-487-2441
- **Northwest Senior Activity Center**, 5429 32nd Ave NW, 206-461-7811
- **Pike Market Senior Center**, 1931 1st Ave, 206-728-2773
- **Redmond Senior Center**, 8703 160th Ave NE, Redmond, 425-556-2314

- **Renton Senior Center**, 211 Burnett Ave N, Renton, 425-130-6633
- **Senior Center of West Seattle**, 4217 SW Oregon St, 206-932-4044
- **Senior Services of Seattle/King County**, 2208 2nd Ave, 206-448-5757, www. seniorservices.org
- **Shoreline Senior Activity Center**, 18560 1st Ave NE, 206-365-1536
- **Southeast Seattle Senior Center**, 4655 S Holly St, 206-722-0317
- **Tukwila Senior Program**, 12424 42nd Ave S, Tukwila, 206-768-2822
- **Vashon-Maury Senior Center**, 10004 SW Bank Rd, Vashon Island, 206-463-5173

## WOMEN'S SERVICES

- **FaithTrust Institute**, 2400 N 45th St, #10, 206-634-1903, www.faithtrustinstitute.org
- **Catherine Booth House (Salvation Army Shelter for Abused Women)**, 206-324-4943, www.nwarmy.org
- **Junior League of Seattle**, 4119 E Madison St, 206-324-3638, http://jrleagueseattle.org
- **New Beginnings for Battered Women and Their Children**, 206-926-3016, www.newbegin.org
- **Refugee Women's Alliance**, 4008 Martin Luther King Jr Way S, 206-721-0243, www.rewa.org

## YOUTH

- **Central Area Youth Association**, 119 23rd Ave, 206-322-6640, www.seattle-caya.org
- **Central Youth and Family Services**, 1901 Martin Luther King Jr. Way S, 206-322-7676
- **Friends of Youth**, 16225 NE 87th St, Ste A-6, Redmond, 425-869-6490, www.friendsofyouth.org
- **Ruth Dykeman Children's Center**, 1033 SW 152nd St, 206-242-1698, www.rdcc.org
- **Southwest Youth and Family Services**, 4555 Delridge Way SW, 206-937-7680, www.swyfs.org
- **University District Youth Center**, 4516 15th Ave NE, 206-526-2992
- **Youth Care**, 2500 NE 54th St, 206-694-4500, www.youthcare.org

## GETTING AROUND BY CAR

**D**ESPITE EFFORTS BY THE CITY AND KING COUNTY TO REDUCE THE number of single-occupancy vehicles on the road, I-5, I-405, and both bridges to the Eastside are always crowded during rush hour. According to the 2000 census, the number of people in the state of Washington commuting an hour or more to work increased 73% from 1990 to 2000! Despite this knowledge, many Seattle residents still drive everywhere—to work, to church, to the grocery store. There are alternatives. Buses, carpools, and ride-sharing programs are viable options for many residents. The city offers incentives to businesses that encourage their employees to share the commute, walk or bicycle to work—something you may want to investigate at your office. If you must drive, here are a few tips for making your commute a little easier.

- **Metered ramps** are freeway on-ramps equipped with traffic lights to control the flow of traffic. Most in-city ramps to I-5 are now metered, although the lights operate only during high-volume hours. Metered ramps usually have an H.O.V. (high occupancy vehicle) on-ramp lane, which allows carpool vehicles on without stopping.
- **Traffic reports** are available on all major radio and television stations during rush hour, and on news radio station KIRO 710 AM every 10 minutes weekday mornings and afternoons. These reports can be invaluable once you've identified a few routes to your usual destinations. Or call the new **Washington State Department of Transportation (WSDOT)** traffic line at 511 to get information on current traffic conditions, including traffic flow statistics and accident and construction reports. Transportation trouble spots are listed on the *Seattle Post-Intelligencer's* web site at http://seattlepi.nwsource.com/transportation. This is also the site to visit for more information about local transportation issues and concerns, including a weekly question/answer section.

- **Traffic webcams** and traffic flow maps for freeways and major highways are available from the WSDOT and are updated every few minutes at www.wsdot. wa.gov/traffic/seattle. You can also access ferry webcams and webcams in the mountain passes and at the Canadian border crossing. The City of Seattle also maintains webcams of city streets and traffic hotspots at www.seattle.gov/ trafficcams, and the City of Bellevue does the same at www.cityofbellevue. org/trafficcam. King County offers cameras in outlying communities at www. metrokc.gov/kcdot/mycommute.
- **Electronic signs** placed over freeways alert drivers to accidents and, during rush hours, will give point-to-point commute times. This may not help you plan in advance, but if you're late for a meeting it's helpful to know that it will take 21 minutes to drive from downtown Seattle to Lynnwood.
- **Travel Times** for 32 different commute routes around Puget Sound are updated every five minutes on the DOT web site at www.wsdot.wa.gov/ traffic/seattle/traveltimes. The table shows distance, average commute time and current commute time.

## MAJOR EXPRESSWAYS

As you get to know Seattle, you'll establish alternatives to the major freeways, highways, and thoroughfares. Until then, here are some of the main arteries:

- The main north-south freeway is **Interstate 5**. Running smack through the middle of the city, this freeway is both a blessing and a curse for those living near it. If you're running errands, and if I-5 is moving at all, it is usually the quickest way to other neighborhoods in the city. However, if you're more than ten minutes from the freeway, it's often quicker to take local streets across town.
- Another north-south thoroughfare in the city is **Highway 99** (Aurora Avenue), which parallels I-5 as far as the Seattle Center, then cuts under the city and follows the waterfront. The section of Highway 99 along the waterfront is a stacked freeway known as "the viaduct." North of the Green Lake area, Highway 99 can be fairly slow because of the traffic lights. South of the lake and through the downtown area, Highway 99 is a reliable alternative to I-5, especially for those coming from the Greenwood, Phinney Ridge, Fremont or Wallingford neighborhoods. If you travel to the airport often from any of these neighborhoods, there is a shortcut to the airport, which includes Highway 99, Highway 509, and then Highway 518. This can save you 30 minutes during rush hour.
- The main east-west freeway is **Interstate 90**. The I-90 bridge is usually the better of the two Lake Washington bridges, because it has several lanes in each direction as well as a reversible H.O.V. lane. Because it begins near Safeco Field

and the new football stadium, I-90 does back up before and after Mariners and Seahawks games, so give yourself extra time when traveling on those days.

- The other east-west thoroughfare, **Highway 520**, runs from I-5 just north of Capitol Hill to the Eastside. The 520 Bridge is one of the worst stretches of road during rush hour. Even if there is no accident on the bridge, the amazing view of the lake and Mount Rainier, as well as bright sunlight, slows traffic on the bridge decks. The "high rises" (the high portions of the bridge) at the west end also cause traffic backups because drivers have to slow for the curves and accelerate for the incline. If you can't use I-90 as your regular route over the lake, set up a carpool and take advantage of the H.O.V. lanes or try to use an on-ramp as close to the bridge as possible.
- Another route from Seattle to the Eastside is **Interstate 405**, which generally runs north-south on the east side of Lake Washington. Interstate 405 goes through Renton, Bellevue, Kirkland, and Bothell, connecting with I-5 south of Seattle near Southcenter Mall, and north of Seattle in Lynnwood. Depending on your destination and the time of day, an I-5 to I-405 route might be the quickest way around the lake.
- The **West Seattle Freeway** starts at I-5 near Beacon Hill and heads west to the West Seattle peninsula, crossing Highway 99 on the way. This is the main thoroughfare in and out of the north end of West Seattle.

## CARPOOLING

High Occupancy Vehicle lanes or "diamond lanes" are located on Interstates 5, 405 and 90. These lanes are reserved for carpools (minimum two or three passengers, depending on the lane), buses and motorcycles. If you must travel over one of the Lake Washington bridges (I-90 or Highway 520) during rush hour, these lanes are the way to go. You'll be able to pass the rest of the traffic and cut to the front of the line at the bridge deck. For information on carpool parking permits, which can be used for discounted or free parking in downtown Seattle, call the city's **Carpool Parking/Permits** line at 206-684-0816.

If you don't have a carpool partner, Metro Transit offers **Rideshare**, a regional ride-sharing program that matches commuters with carpools. Visit www.rideshareonline.com to find a commuting partner in just minutes. Another option available through Metro and most other public transit services is a vanpool. **Vanpools** require 5 to 15 passengers and monthly fares vary depending on origin, destination, and number of riders. The advantages are that Metro provides the van, insurance, and gasoline. In addition, the carpool parking permit is free for vanpools. For more information on both the Ridematch and Vanpool programs, call 206-625-4500 or 800-427-8249, or visit Metro's web site, http://transit.metrokc.gov.

Free online services that match carpoolers are also an option. You can browse driver and passenger options and post your own offers and requests. Try www.AlterNetRides.com; www.Carpoolworld.com; and eRideShare.com.

## PARK & RIDES

Many drive to Park & Ride lots and then commute by bus to Seattle. For a complete and current listing of lots, go to www.wsdot.wa.gov/choices/parkride.cfm.

### AUBURN

- **All Saints Lutheran Church**, 27225 Military Rd S
- **Auburn Park & Ride**, "A" St NE and 15th St NE
- **Auburn Transit Center**, "A" St SW and 1st St SW
- **Peasley Canyon Park & Ride**, Peasley Canyon Rd

### BELLEVUE

- **Bellevue Christian Reformed Church**, 1221 148th Ave NE
- **Bellevue Foursquare Church**, 2015 Richards Rd
- **Bellevue Transit Center**, 108th Ave NE and NE 6th St
- **Bellevue Transfer Point**, 106th Ave NE and NE 6th St
- **Eastgate Park & Ride**, SE Eastgate Way and 141st Ave SE
- **Grace Lutheran Church**, NE 8th St and 96th Ave NE
- **Newport Covenant Church**, Coal Creek Pkwy and Factoria Blvd
- **South Bellevue Park & Ride**, Bellevue Way SE and 112th Ave SE
- **St. Andrew's Lutheran Church**, 2650 148th Ave SE
- **St. Luke's Lutheran Church**, Bellevue Way NE and NE 30th Pl
- **St. Margaret's Episcopal Church**, 4228 Factoria Blvd
- **Wilburton Park & Ride**, I-405 and SE 8th St

### BURIEN

- **Burien Transit Center**, SW 150th St and 4th Ave SW
- **Normandy Park Congregational Church**, 19247 1st Ave S

### BOTHELL

- **Bothell Park & Ride**, Woodinville Dr and Kaysner Way
- **Brickyard Road**, I-405 and NE 160th St

### DUVALL

- **Duvall Park & Ride**, State Route 203 and Woodinville-Duvall Rd

### FEDERAL WAY

- **Federal Way Park & Ride**, 23rd Ave S and S 323rd St
- **Federal Way Transit Center**, S 317th St and 23rd Ave S

- **Our Saviour's Baptist Church**, S 320th St and 8th Ave S
- **Redondo Heights Park & Ride**, Pacific Hwy S at S 276th St
- **South Federal Way Park & Ride**, 9th Ave S and S 348th St
- **St. Luke's Lutheran Church**, 515 S 312th St
- **Sunrise United Methodist Church**, 150 S 356th St
- **Twin Lakes Park & Ride**, 21st Ave SW and SW 344th St

## ISSAQUAH
- **Issaquah Highlands Park & Ride**, 1755 Highlands Dr NE
- **Issaquah Park & Ride**, 1740 NW Maple St
- **Klahanie Park & Ride**, SE Klahanie Blvd and 244th Pl SE
- **Tibbetts Lot**, 1675 Newport Way NW
- **Tibbetts Valley Park**, 12th NW and Newport Way

## KENMORE
- **Kenmore Park & Ride**, Bothell Way NE and 73rd Ave NE
- **Kenmore Community Church**, Bothell Way NE & 75th Ave NE

## KIRKLAND
- **Holy Spirit Lutheran Church**, NE 124th St and 100th Ave NE
- **Houghton Park & Ride**, I-405 and NE 70th Pl
- **Kingsgate Park & Ride**, I-405 and NE 132nd St
- **Kirkland Transit Center**, 3rd St and Park Ln
- **Lake Washington Christian Church**, 13225 116th Ave NE
- **Rosehill Presbyterian Church**, NE 90th St and 122nd Ave NE
- **South Kirkland Park & Ride**, 108th Ave NE and NE 38th Pl
- **SR-908/Kirkland Way Park & Ride**, NE 85th St and Kirkland Way

## KENT
- **Easthill Friends Church**, 22600 116th Ave SE
- **Kent Covenant Church**, 12010 SE 240th St
- **Kent-Des Moines Park & Ride**, I-5 and Kent-Des Moines Rd
- **Kent/James Street Park & Ride**, N Lincoln Ave & W James St
- **Kent Transit Center**, 301 Railroad Ave N
- **Kent United Methodist Church**, SE 248th St and 110th Ave SE
- **Lake Meridian Park & Ride**, 132nd Ave SE and SE 272nd St
- **St. Columba's Episcopal Church**, 26715 Military Rd S
- **Star Lake Park & Ride**, I-5 and 272nd St
- **Valley View Christian Church**, 124th Ave SE and SE 256th St

## MEDINA
- **Evergreen Point Bridge**, State Rte 520 and Evergreen Point Rd

- **St. Thomas Episcopal Church**, 84th Ave NE and NE 12th St

## MERCER ISLAND
- **First Church of Christ Scientist**, 8685 SE 47th St
- **Initial Tropical Plants**, 2441 76th Ave SE
- **Mercer Island Presbyterian Church**, 84th Ave SE and SE 39th St
- **Mercer Island United Methodist Church**, SE 24th St and 70th Ave SE
- **Mercer Island Park & Ride**, 80th Ave SE and N Mercer Way
- **QFC Village**, SE 68th St and 84th Ave SE

## REDMOND
- **Bear Creek Park & Ride**, 178th Pl NE and NE Union Hill Rd
- **Overlake Park & Ride**, 152nd Ave NE and NE 24th St
- **Overlake Park Presbyterian Church**, 1856 156th Ave NE
- **Redmond Park & Ride**, 161st Ave NE and NE 83rd St

## RENTON
- **Fairwood Assembly of God**, 131st Ave SE and SE 192nd St
- **First Baptist Church**, Hardie Ave SW and SW Langston Rd
- **Fred Meyer**, 365 Renton Center Way
- **Kennydale United Methodist Church**, Park Ave N and N 30th St
- **Nativity Lutheran Church**, 140th Ave SE and SE 177th St
- **New Life Church**, 152nd and Renton-Maple Valley Hwy
- **Renton Boeing Lot 6**, Garden Ave N and Park Ave N
- **Renton City Municipal Garage**, 655 S 2nd St, Flrs 4-7
- **Renton Highlands Park & Ride**, NE 16th St and Edmonds Ave NE
- **Renton Transit Center Park & Ride**, 232 Burnett Ave S
- **Renton Transit Center**, S 2nd St and Burnett Ave S
- **South Renton Park & Ride**, S Grady Way and Shattuck Ave S

## SEATTLE—CENTRAL
- **Calvary Christian Assembly Church**, NE 68th St and 8th Ave NE
- **Green Lake Park & Ride**, I-5 and NE 65th St

## SEATTLE—NORTH
- **South Jackson Park Park & Ride**, 5th Ave NE and NE 133rd St
- **North Jackson Park Park & Ride**, 5th Ave NE and NE 145th St
- **North Seattle Park & Ride**, 1st Ave NE and NE 100th St
- **Northgate Transit Center**, NE 103rd St and 1st Ave NE
- **Northgate Park & Ride**, NE 112th St and 5th Ave NE
- **Our Savior Lutheran Church**, NE 125th St and 25th Ave NE
- **Prince of Peace Lutheran Church**, 14514 20th Ave NE

## SEATTLE—SOUTH
- **Airport and Spokane Park & Ride**, Airport Way S and S Spokane St
- **Church by the Side of the Road**, South 148th St and Pacific Hwy S
- **Community Bible Church**, S 148th St and Pacific Hwy S
- **Holy Family Church**, SW Roxbury St and 20th Ave SW
- **Olson Place and Myers Way Park & Ride**, Olson Place SW and SW Myers Way
- **Sonrise Evangelical Free Church**, 610 SW Roxbury
- **Southwest Spokane Street Park & Ride**, 26th Ave SW and SW Spokane St

## SHORELINE
- **Aurora Church of the Nazarene**, 175th St and Meridian Ave N
- **Aurora Village Transit Center**, N 200th St and Ashworth Ave N
- **Bethany Baptist Church**, NE 181st and 62nd Ave NE
- **Bethel Lutheran Church**, NE 175th St and 10th Ave NE
- **Korean Zion Presbyterian Church**, 17920 Meridian Ave N
- **Shoreline United Methodist Church**, NE 145th St and 25th Ave NE
- **Shoreline Park & Ride**, Aurora Ave N and N 192nd St

## TUKWILA
- **Tukwila Interurban Investment**, 13445 Interurban Ave S
- **Tukwila Park & Ride**, Interurban Ave S and 52nd Ave S
- **Tukwila Surface Lot – Tukwila Commuter Rail Station**, 7301 S 158th St

## VASHON ISLAND
- **Episcopal Church of the Holy Spirit**, 15420 Vashon Hwy SW
- **Ober Park Park & Ride**, 99th Ave SW and SW 171st St
- **Tahlequah Park & Ride**, Vashon Hwy SW and SW Tahlequah Rd
- **Valley Center Park & Ride**, 99th Ave SW & SW 204th St

## WOODINVILLE
- **Cottage Lake Assembly of God**, 15737 Avondale Rd
- **Woodinville Park & Ride**, 140th Ave NE and NE 179th St
- **Woodinville Unitarian Universalist Church**, 19020 NE Woodinville-Duvall Rd

## FLEXCAR

Seattle and Eastside residents now have a car-sharing option, good for out-of-the-way errands or appointments. Called Flexcar, this car-sharing service offers the freedom of driving a car without the expense of owning one. Drivers pay for the time they use the car, and the company pays for gas, insurance, and maintenance. Flexcar members determine their monthly driving needs and then choose one of seven plans, which start at $10 per hour. An application fee and yearly membership apply and some plans have monthly fees. For more information, call 206-323-FLEX, or visit www.flexcar.com.

## CAR RENTAL

Those who need a weekend rental should reserve at least a week in advance.

- **Advantage**, 800-777-5500, www.advantagerentacar.com
- **Alamo**, 888-426-3299, www.alamo.com
- **Avis**, 800-831-2847, www.avis.com
- **Budget**, 800-527-7000, www.budget.com
- **Dollar**, 800-800-4000, www.dollar.com
- **Enterprise**, 800-736-8222, www.enterprise.com
- **Hertz**, 800-654-3131, www.hertz.com
- **National**, 888-868-6204, www.nationalcar.com
- **Thrifty**, 800-847-4389, www.thrifty.com

## TAXIS

Unless you are downtown, on Capitol Hill, or at the airport, you'll probably need to call ahead to arrange for a taxi. A few of Seattle's many taxicab companies are listed here; others can be found in the Yellow Pages.

- **Farwest Taxi**, 206-622-1717
- **Orange Cab**, 206-522-8800, www.orangecab.net
- **Yellow Cab**, 206-622-6500

# BY BIKE

Despite the hilly terrain and the wet, chilly fall and winter weather, a surprisingly large number of Seattle residents use bikes for recreation or transportation. The city estimates that the number of people commuting each day ranges between 4,000 and 8,000. To assist bicycle commuters, the **Seattle Transportation Bicycle Program** has created about 28 miles of bike trails and paths, 14 miles of on-street, striped bike lanes, and 90 miles of signed bike routes.

During the summer months, Seattle's Lake Washington Boulevard becomes a long, winding playground for the city's bike enthusiasts. On Bicycle Saturdays and Sundays, between 10 a.m. and 6 p.m., the city shuts down the lakeside thoroughfare to automobile traffic. For more information about the Seattle Bicycle & Pedestrian Program or to order a free Seattle bicycling guide map, call 206-684-7583 or visit www.seattle.gov/transportation/bikeprogram.htm.

Bicyclists can "bike and ride" at no extra cost, thanks to a Metro Transit program that allows riders to load their bikes onto racks installed on Metro buses. For details on the **Bike & Ride Program**, visit Metro's web site at http://transit. metrokc.gov or call 206-553-3000.

Bicycle helmets are mandatory in Seattle and all of King County. You will be ticketed if you're caught riding without one. King County maintains a list of organizations that offer free or low-cost helmets. Visit www.metrokc.gov/health/ injury/helmets.htm. For more information on helmets, visit the **Bicycle Helmet Safety Institute** web site (www.helmets.org).

## BY PUBLIC TRANSPORTATION

Traffic and public transportation issues have snarled recent legislative sessions in the state, and have taken center stage in local elections for many years. Unfortunately, lawmakers and residents continue to struggle with some of the worst traffic in the country. Major transportation issues affecting the Puget Sound region include replacing the aging 520 bridge and the Alaskan Way Viaduct, widening I-405, connecting Highway 509 to I-5, and creating some type of regional transit.

## LIGHT RAIL

In 1996, state voters passed a 21-mile light rail package for service from SeaTac to the University District, but due to funding issues, **Sound Transit**, the agency in charge of the project, had to scale back the plan. Construction is well underway on the first phase of the project: a 14-mile line that will run from downtown Seattle to Tukwila and will begin carrying riders in 2009. Shortly after that a 1.7 mile extension will be added, running to SeaTac Airport, which will start carrying passengers in December of 2009. Plans are still in the works for an extension northward to the University District to be opened in 2016, and the potential still exists for future extensions all the way north to Northgate. In the meantime, the new light rail line will make stops in Rainier Valley, Beacon Hill, and SODO on its way to and from the airport and downtown. A tunnel was created underneath Beacon Hill to carry the new trains, and construction continues to disrupt traffic in the Rainier Valley, so plan your travel routes accordingly. For more information, construction updates, and depot locations, visit www.soundtransit.org.

The city of Tacoma already has a short light rail line called **Tacoma Link**, running from the Tacoma Dome Station to the Theater District, with stops at Union Station and the Convention Center. Riding on Tacoma Link is free and more information can be found at www.soundtransit.org.

For the time being, until light rail is completed, buses are the primary means of mass transit in Seattle.

# BUSES

**Metro Transit** provides buses that are generally clean and on time, although they make frequent, time-consuming stops as they traverse the city. Express buses are much faster but go to fewer destinations. Crosstown buses are limited and transfers are often necessary when traveling between neighborhoods. The good news is that the bus fares are reasonable: adult fares are $1.25/off-peak, $1.50/one-zone peak, $2/two-zone peak; youth fares are $.50; seniors and persons with disabilities are $.25/off-peak and $.50/peak. In addition, most of downtown is part of a Ride Free zone, meaning that passengers can use the bus for free in the downtown area as long as they disembark before crossing Denny Way or Yesler Way—most bus drivers announce the end of the Ride Free zone. The Ride Free area in downtown is possible since fares are collected at the beginning of the ride if you're traveling toward downtown, or at the end of the ride if you're traveling away from downtown. A sign at the front of the bus will let you know when to pay your fare.

**Bus passes** and ticket books are available and can save a lot of money for regular passengers. Some employers, institutions, and community organizations provide free or discounted passes for employees and members, as part of the Employer Commute Services sponsored by King County Metro. Bus passes are available at over 100 locations in the city, including some drug stores and cash machines, or you can call Metro at 206-624-PASS or visit http://transit.metrokc.gov, and purchase with a credit or debit card.

**Bus schedules** are posted at all bus stops (but only for the buses that use that route), or you can call Metro's Automated Schedule Information Line at 206-BUS-TIME. Metro's 24-hour Rider Information Line at 206-553-3000 connects you to a Metro employee who can assist you with schedule and route information, as long as you can provide your starting point and destination. The online **Trip Planner** is a handy tool that lets you input your starting and ending destinations, and date and time of trip to get a customized route that will provide bus numbers and bus stop locations, and can be sorted by fastest trip, fewest transfers or least amount of walking. You can use the service for trips within King, Pierce, and Snohomish counties. It's located at http://tripplanner.metrokc.gov. Metro Transit also has an informative and comprehensive web site at http://transit.metrokc.gov.

In addition to buses, Metro runs two unique public transportation systems. A relic of the Seattle World's Fair, the **Monorail** runs between Westlake Center in the downtown shopping district and the Seattle Center. Numerous problems with the aging system make it mostly a tourist attraction with a doubtful future.

The **Waterfront Trolley** uses an old railroad track to travel from the International District to the north end of the Waterfront, making several stops along the way. Currently, the north end of the waterfront is undergoing redevelopment with the addition of the Seattle Art Museum's 9-acre Olympic Sculpture Park, a greenspace and beach offering outdoor art installations. Construction called for temporarily suspending the trolley service, which was replaced by a bus "wrapped" to look like the trolleys. The service is free and the old trolleys are expected to resume service in the summer of 2007.

Despite a shortened light rail line, Sound Transit has successfully initiated much of the service approved by voters in 1996, including **ST Express** bus service linking Seattle, Bellevue, Tacoma, and Everett. The buses operate on a three-zone fare system. The cost depends on the number of fare zones you traverse and your fare type (youth, adult or senior/disabled). Fares range from $1.25 to $2.50 for adults, $.75 to $2 for youth, and $.50 to $1.25 for senior/disabled passengers. For more information, call 800-201-4900 or visit www.soundtransit.org.

Outside Seattle, Community Transit covers most of Seattle's neighboring communities; Everett Transit covers the greater Everett area north of Seattle; Pierce Transit provides bus service in Tacoma.

- **Community Transit**, 425-353-RIDE or 800-562-1375, www.commtrans.org
- **Everett Transit**, 425-257-8803, www.everettwa.org/transit
- **Pierce Transit**, 253-581-8000, 800-562-8109, www.ptbus.pierce.wa.us

## COMMUTER TRAINS

The **Sounder** commuter trains offer rail service between Tacoma and downtown Seattle, with stops in Puyallup, Sumner, Auburn, Kent, and Tukwila. The north route serves Everett, Edmonds, and downtown Seattle. The trains offer service in peak directions only, so trains leave Tacoma at four different times of the morning heading for Seattle, and return to Tacoma four times in the afternoon. Sounder trains leave Everett for Seattle twice every morning and return twice in the afternoon. In a partnership with Amtrak, two more trains are offered on the Everett-Seattle route each morning and afternoon, although you must use one of the Sounder train passes for your fare, or pay full price Amtrak fares. For the schedule and more information about Sounder trains, call 800-201-4900 or visit www.soundtransit.org.

## FERRIES

Because there are no bridges connecting Seattle with the Olympic Peninsula, many area residents commute to and from work by ferry. The **Washington State Ferries** system is the largest in the United States and includes 10 routes that serve the Puget Sound area. To commute to the city, residents ride the **Seattle-Bremerton**, **Seattle-Bainbridge Island** routes or the **Seattle-Vashon Island** passenger-only route, which all dock at the Seattle waterfront terminal at Colman Dock. The **Fauntleroy-Vashon-Southworth** route serves West Seattle, Vashon Island, and the Olympic Peninsula, and the **Edmonds-Kingston** route departs from a terminal in Edmonds, 20 minutes north of Seattle. The **Anacortes-San Juan Islands** and **Anacortes-Sidney, BC** routes originate in Anacortes, about an hour north of Seattle.

Those routes used for commuting to Seattle can be very busy in the morning and evening hours. If you're walking on, you probably won't have any problem, even if you arrive just a few minutes before departure. If you're driving, however, you'll need to arrive early or be prepared to take a later ferry. This is also true for weekends or holidays. The wait time for those who want to ferry their vehicles on the San Juan Islands routes can be several hours on summer holiday weekends.

Schedules and fares vary according to season and route. The peak season is May through September when fares will be higher, and non-peak is October through April. Some routes only charge fares one way, generally westbound, like the Fauntleroy-Vashon route. Others charge vehicle/driver fares both ways, but passenger fares only one way. Fares also vary depending on size and type of vehicle. Discounted passes are available for frequent passengers, children, disabled persons, and senior citizens.

Ferry information pamphlets are available at all ferry terminals, as well as at some transit information booths in the city. For more information, call the Washington State Ferries' information line at 206-464-6400 or 888-808-7977 or visit www.wsdot.wa.gov/ferries, where you can also view webcams of the ferry docks, wait times, and use a fare calculator to find out how much your trip will cost.

## REGIONAL/NATIONAL TRANSPORT

## AMTRAK

King Street Station, which serves as Seattle's **Amtrak** station, borders the historic International District and Pioneer Square, near the new football stadium at the south end of downtown. The station is served by the Cascades (Eugene, Portland, Seattle, Vancouver, BC), Coast Starlight (Seattle, Portland, Oakland, Los Angeles), and Empire Builder (Chicago, Seattle or Portland) trains.

- **Amtrak National Route Information**, 800-USA-RAIL, www.amtrak.com
- **Amtrak Seattle Station**, 303 S Jackson St, 206-382-4125

## BUSES

The **Greyhound Lines** bus terminal is located at 8th Avenue and Stewart Street in downtown Seattle. For reservation information call the terminal directly at 206-628-5526, Greyhound's national reservation number at 800-231-2222, or visit www.greyhound.com. Another option for bus trips to some eastern Washington cities is **Northwestern Trailways**. Call 800-366-3830 for reservations and information, or visit www.northwesterntrailways.com.

## AIRPORTS/AIRLINES

The **Seattle-Tacoma International Airport**, known locally as Sea-Tac, is located south of Seattle at 17801 Pacific Highway South. For parking rates and information, airport weather conditions, and general information, call 206-433-5388 or visit www.portseattle.org/seatac.

Construction woes seem never-ending at Sea-Tac, and can affect everything from parking to drop-off and pick-up. A major renovation and expansion was completed in 2006, but a third runway and a light rail station will keep construction going for some time. And, as a result of September 11 and other terrorist acts around the globe, increased security has added to the confusion. Express security lines are available at security checkpoints for those in wheelchairs, passengers with no carry-on luggage, and for some frequent fliers and first- or business-class passengers, depending on the airline. Contact your airline to see if you qualify. Security regulations change frequently; one day you're allowed an item in your carry-on luggage and the next it is only allowed in checked baggage. The best ways to keep up with the changes and rules are to contact your airline, check the Sea-Tac airport web site for updates, or contact the **Transportation Security Administration** at 866-289-9673 or visit their web site at www.tsa.gov for the latest news and updates on security and travel-related issues.

Curbside check-in is available for domestic passengers only on the upper airport drive, but stopping your car is allowed only for picking up or dropping off passengers, and loading or unloading luggage. Passengers are not permitted to leave their cars while they check their bags curbside. Vehicles left unattended are ticketed even if the driver is nearby. At Sea-Tac, the upper drive is for departures, and baggage claim and pick-up are located on the lower drive. Note: when the upper drive is congested, passengers with few or no bags should consider being dropped-off on the lower drive. A new cell phone waiting lot is available just a couple of minutes away from the baggage claim area, where you can wait until you get a call that someone is ready to be picked up. It has space for 40 vehicles to wait at one time.

Finally, a word about delays. According to data from the National Weather Service, Sea-Tac Airport can only use one runway 44% of the time due to poor weather conditions. Rain, fog, and clouds are often to blame, reducing visibility so drastically that only one of the airport's two closely positioned runways can be used. This, of course, causes delays that have become notorious. Capacity is also a problem, but should be cleared up by the end of 2008 when a third runway that can be used in adverse weather is scheduled to open for incoming flights. Be sure to call your airline before you head to the airport.

These major airlines serve passengers at Sea-Tac:

- **Air Canada**, 800-247-2262, www.aircanada.ca
- **Alaska Airlines**, 800-426-0333, www.alaska-air.com
- **America West**, 800-235-9292, www.americawest.com
- **American Airlines**, 800-433-7300, www.americanairlines.com
- **Asiana Airlines**, 800-227-4262, http://us.flyasiana.com
- **British Airways**, 800-247-9297, www.british-airways.com
- **China Airlines**, 800-227-5118, www.china-airlines.com
- **Continental Airlines**, 800-525-0280, www.continental.com
- **Delta Airlines**, 800-221-1212, www.delta.com
- **EVA Air**, 800-695-1188, www.evaair.com.tw
- **Frontier Airlines**, 800-432-1359, www.frontierairlines.com
- **Hawaiian Airlines**, 800-367-5320, www.hawaiianair.com
- **Horizon Air**, 800-547-9308, www.horizonair.com
- **JetBlue Airways**, 800-JETBLUE, www.jetblue.com
- **Korean Air**, 800-438-5000, www.koreanair.com
- **Northwest Airlines**, 800-225-2525, www.nwa.com
- **Scandinavian Airlines**, 800-221-2350, www.scandinavian.net
- **Southwest Airlines**, 800-435-9792, www.iflyswa.com
- **Sun Country Airlines**, 800-359-6786, www.suncountry.com
- **United Airlines**, 800-241-6522, www.ual.com
- **US Airways**, 800-428-4322, www.usair.com

## TRAVELING TO SEA-TAC AIRPORT BY CAR

When traveling to the airport by car, use the following directions: from Seattle take I-5 south to the Southcenter/Sea-Tac Airport exit and follow the signs to get on Highway 518. From Highway 518 take the Sea-Tac Airport exit and stay to the left as you exit. This will put you on the main road into the airport, which is clearly marked with signs to baggage claim, airline counters, and parking.

**Alternate directions** from downtown Seattle, Ballard, Phinney Ridge, Greenwood, Fremont, and Broadview (these are just a little faster during rush hour): take Highway 99 south until it forces you left onto 1st Avenue South. Stay in the right lane and follow directions to the 1st Avenue South Bridge (only a few blocks). After you cross the bridge, the road you are on becomes Highway 509. Stay on Highway 509 to the Sea-Tac Airport and Highway 518 exit. Take Highway 518 east, then, from Highway 518, take the Sea-Tac exit. This exit puts you on the main road into the airport.

The parking garage at Sea-Tac is connected to the main terminal by sky-bridges on the 4th floor. To get a complete list of parking rates, visit the web site or call the Public Parking Office at 206-433-5308. The following **parking options** are available:

- Hourly parking, for people who plan to spend a few hours or less at the airport, is available on the fourth floor, skybridge level. Rates start at $2 for the first 30 minutes.
- Daily Parking, available on the top four floors of the garage (levels 5-8). These same floors serve as long term parking, where the daily rate is $22. A reduced, weekly rate of $99 that includes all taxes and fees is available for those parking more than four days.
- Disabled parking: more than 100 stalls are located on the 4th floor of the airport garage; hourly parking rates apply.
- Valet parking: $20 for up to 4 hours, $30 for 4 to 24 hours.

Sea-Tac uses an automated parking payment system to help travelers get out of the airport quickly. Automated pay kiosks on the 4th floor of the garage allow visitors to pay for both long- and short-term parking before they reach their cars. Simply take a ticket as you enter the parking garage, and keep it with you. When you're ready to retrieve your car, you can pay at the kiosks with either cash or a credit card and then feed your validated ticket into the machine at the garage exit as you are leaving. For additional parking details, call 206-433-5308 or visit the Port of Seattle's web site at www.portseattle.org/seatac.

Finally, there are several discount parking lots near Sea-Tac Airport that cost much less than the airport parking garage and offer quick shuttle service to and from their lots and the airport. Many have security services so your vehicle will be monitored while you are gone. Reservations can generally be made over the phone or online. The following will get you started, but check the Yellow Pages under "Parking Facilities" for a comprehensive list.

- **Extra Car Airport Parking**, 16300 International Blvd, 206-248-3452, 800-227-5397, www.extracar.com
- **Park N Fly**, 17600 International Blvd, 206-433-6767, www.parknflyseattle.com
- **SeaTac Park**, 2701 S 200th St, 206-824-2544, www.seatacpark.com
- **Thrifty Airport Parking**, 18836 International Blvd, 888-634-7275, www.thriftyparking.com

## TRAVELING TO SEA-TAC AIRPORT BY BUS & SHUTTLE VAN

The following public transportation bus routes provide airport service to and from Seattle and surrounding communities. Buses arrive at and leave from the far south end of the baggage claim area, outside Door 2. Departure times are posted at the bus stop and bus timetables can be picked up near Door 16 on the baggage claim level. For bus departure and arrival times, and route maps, check the web site at http://transit.metrokc.gov/tops/bus/flymetro.html.

- **Metro Route 140**: daily service to and from Southcenter, Renton, and Burien. Travel time is 15 minutes to Burien and 45 minutes to Renton.
- **Metro Route 174**: daily service to and from downtown Seattle, and to and from Federal Way. Travel time is 45 minutes. Also: daily early-morning service to and from downtown Seattle. Travel time is 30 minutes.
- **Metro Route 194**: daily service to and from downtown Seattle and Federal Way. Travel time is 30 minutes.
- **Metro Route 180**: weekday early morning service from Auburn and Kent to the airport; weekday morning and afternoon service to Burien; and weekday morning and afternoon service to Kent and Auburn.
- **Sound Transit Route 560**: daily service to and from Bellevue, Renton, Burien, and West Seattle. Travel time is 45 minutes to and from Bellevue, 15 minutes to and from Renton, and 40 minutes to and from West Seattle.
- **Sound Transit Route 574**: daily service to and from Lakewood, Tacoma, and Sea-Tac Airport.

**Shuttle van** or **bus**: most downtown hotels offer shuttle service to the airport; call ahead for times and costs (it may be free if you are a hotel guest). For door-to-door shuttle service, try one of the following:

- **Airport Express by Gray Line**, 206-626-6088, 800-426-7505, www.graylineofseattle.com
- **Airporter Shuttle**, 360-380-8800, 800-235-5247, www.airporter.com
- **Bremerton-Kitsap Airporter**, 360-876-1737, www.kitsapairporter.com
- **Capital Aeroporter**, Olympia: 360-754-7113, Tacoma: 253-927-6179, Sea-Tac Airport: 206-244-0011, outside Washington: 800-962-3579, www.capair.com
- **Centralia Sea-Tac Airporter**, 800-773-9490
- **Olympic Van Tours**, 360-452-3858
- **Shuttle Express**, 425-981-7000, 800-487-7433, www.shuttleexpress.com
- **Quick Shuttle**, 604-940-4428, 800-665-2122, www.quickcoach.com

There are two other airports in the Seattle area. **Renton Municipal Airport** (425-430-7471, www.rentonwa.gov), owned by the City of Renton, is located about 25 miles south of downtown Seattle. The airport is used primarily by single and twin-engine planes, a few corporate jets, and some private flying clubs. There is no commercial flight activity. **King County International Airport**, also known as Boeing Field, serves air cargo companies, recreational fliers, charter services, flight schools, and emergency services. **Kenmore Air** is the only passenger airline at the airport, offering service to the San Juan Islands, Oak Harbor, Port Angeles, and Campbell River Airport in Canada. Call 425-486-1257 or visit www.

kenmoreair.com for more information. The airport is also a major center for Boeing operations. For more information, visit www.metrokc.gov/airport.

# TRAVEL RESOURCES

There are a number of online travel sites where you can sometimes find good deals. They include, among others, **Travelocity.com**, **Expedia.com**, **Orbitz.com**, **Lowestfare.com**, **Hotwire.com** and **Cheaptickets.com**. If cost far outweighs convenience, check **Priceline** (www.priceline.com), where you may be able to pin down an inexpensive fare at inconvenient hours (often in the middle of the night). Their motto, "Name Your Price and Save" says it all. **Sidestep.com** is a travel search engine that offers comparison shopping—listing comparable routes, services, and prices from all the major sites like Expedia and Orbitz. Their search results also include listings directly from suppliers and cover some services the major sites don't offer, like JetBlue.

Many airlines post last-minute seats at reduced rates, usually on Wednesdays. In fact, booking with the airline of your choice, either online or by phone, often proves less expensive than booking with some so-called discount travel sites.

Have you ever wondered where the best seats are on a plane? A new web site, **Seatguru.com**, can tell you. You can choose the airline and the plane you'll be flying on and view a diagram of the plane with seats marked as good, be aware, or poor, and use that information when making a seat request with your airline.

**To register a complaint against an airline**, the Department of Transportation is the place to call or write: 202-366-2220, Aviation Consumer Protection Division, C-75, 400 7th Street SW, Washington, DC 20590. You can also use email to lodge complaints or concerns using this address: airconsumer@dot.gov.

Information about airport conditions, including weather and air traffic congestion which could create flight delays, can be checked online at www.fly.faa.gov.

I F YOU NEED TEMPORARY QUARTERS WHILE YOU ARE LOOKING FOR A place to live, Seattle offers a variety of options. Those planning on staying in temporary housing for more than a couple of weeks should consider a sublet or short-term lease. Apartment sublets are often advertised in classifieds, particularly during the spring and summer when college students head out of town. The apartment search firms listed in the **Finding a Place to Live** chapter can assist you with finding a short-term lease, or see below under the **Short Term Leases and Residence Hotels** and **Summer Only** sections. For additional lodging options, and to get a packet of information on accommodations in Seattle or surrounding communities, try **Seattle-King County Convention and Visitors Bureau** (520 Pike Street, 206-461-5800, 206-461-5840 [TDD], www.seeseattle. org) or **Washington State Department of Tourism** (800-544-1800, www.expe riencewashington.com).

## HOTELS AND MOTELS

As a port city, business hub, and tourist destination, Seattle has a large number of hotels and motels offering various levels of service and facilities. In general, the least expensive motels are those along Aurora Avenue North (Highway 99) north of downtown. These lodgings come with the security risks inherent to the high crime area of Aurora. They generally are not suitable for children or for adults uncomfortable with fast-paced urban settings, and for that reason are not listed here.

The following list of hotels and motels is by no means complete. For a more comprehensive listing, check the Yellow Pages under "Hotels and Other Accommodations." For up-to-the-minute room availability in Bellevue, Kent, Lynnwood,

Renton, and Seattle, call **Seattle Hotel Reservations** at 888-254-0637 or visit www.seattle-hotel-reservation.com. **Seattle Hotel Hotline** is another local reservation service. Call 800-361-1029 or visit http://seattle.hotel-hotline.com. **AAA** travel guides are a good source for hotel and motel recommendations. Free to members, their listings are useful because AAA weeds out those hotels that are not up to their standards. **Quikbook** is a national, discount room-reservation service that costs nothing to join. It offers reduced room rates for many hotels. For a list of cities and hotels, and information about them, call 800-789-9887 or visit www.quikbook.com. Other companies include **Hotels.com** (800-246-8357, www. hotels.com) and the online discount travel companies **Expedia** (800-397-3342, www.expedia.com), **Orbitz** (888-656-4564, www.orbitz.com), and **Travelocity** (888-872-8356, www.travelocity.com).

Hotel prices fluctuate, based on the season, special events, and vacancy rates. Call ahead for reservations, and be sure to ask about special discounts or business rates. Often, hotels will offer a special "internet only" rate, so be sure to check web sites before you book.

## LUXURY LODGINGS

A room at one of the following hotels costs $250 or more per night.

### SEATTLE
- **Alexis Hotel**, 1007 1st Ave, 206-624-4844, reservations: 866-356-8894, www. alexishotel.com
- **Crowne Plaza**, 1113 6th Ave, 206-464-1980, 877-227-6963, www.crowneplaza. com
- **Fairmont Olympic Hotel**, 411 University St, 206-621-1700, 800-257-7544, www.fairmont.com/seattle
- **Hotel Monaco**, 1101 4th Ave, 206-621-1770, 800-715-6513, www.monaco-seattle.com
- **Hotel Vintage Park**, 1100 5th Ave, 206-624-8000, 800-853-3914, www. hotelvintagepark.com
- **The Edgewater Hotel**, 2411 Alaskan Way, 206-728-7000, 800-624-0670, www. edgewaterhotel.com
- **The Sorrento Hotel**, 900 Madison St, 206-622-6400, 800-426-1265, www. hotelsorrento.com
- **W Hotel Seattle**, 1112 4th Ave, 206-264-6000, 877-WHOTELS, www.whotels. com
- **Red Lion Hotel on Fifth Avenue**, 1415 5th Ave, 206-971-8000 or 800-325-4000, www.redlion5thavenue.com

## MIDDLE-RANGE LODGINGS

These hotels charge between $150 and $250 per night.

### BELLEVUE
- **Hyatt Regency Bellevue**, 900 Bellevue Way NE, 425-462-1234, 800-233-1234, www.hyatt.com
- **Courtyard by Marriott**, 11010 NE 8th St, 425-454-5888, www.marriott.com/bvudt

### ISSAQUAH
- **Holiday Inn of Issaquah**, 1801 12th NW, 425-392-6421, 888-HOLIDAY, www.holiday-inn.com

### KIRKLAND
- **Comfort Inn**, 12202 NE 124th St, 425-821-8300, www.choicehotels.com
- **Courtyard by Marriott**, 11215 NE 124th St, 425-602-3200, www.marriott.com

### REDMOND
- **Redmond Inn**, 17601 Redmond Way, 425-883-4900, 800-634-8080, www.redmondinn.com

### RENTON
- **Holiday Inn Renton**, 1 S Grady Way, 425-226-7700, 888-465-4329, www.holiday-inn.com

### SEATTLE
- **Best Western Pioneer Square Hotel**, 77 Yesler Way, 206-340-1234, 800-780-7234, www.bestwestern.com
- **The Inn at the Market**, 86 Pine St, 206-443-3600, 800-446-4484, www.innatthemarket.com
- **Mayflower Park Hotel**, 405 Olive Way, 206-623-8700, 800-426-5100, www.mayflowerpark.com
- **Renaissance Madison Hotel**, 515 Madison St, 206-583-0300, 800-278-4159, www.renaissancehotels.com
- **Sheraton Seattle Hotel & Towers**, 1400 6th Ave, 206-621-9000, 800-325-3535, www.sheraton.com/seattle
- **Silver Cloud Inn Lake Union**, 1150 Fairview Ave N, 206-447-9500, 800-551-7207, www.scinns.com
- **Silver Cloud Inn University District**, 5036 25th Ave NE, 206-526-5200, 800-205-6940, www.scinns.com
- **WestCoast Vance Hotel**, 620 Stewart St, 206-441-4200, 800-325-4000

- **The Westin Seattle**, 1900 5th Ave, 206-728-1000, www.starwood.com/westin

## BUDGET STAYS

You can stay at one of these hotels for less than $150.

### BELLEVUE
- **Best Western Bellevue Inn**, 11211 Main St, 425-455-5240, 800-528-1234, www.bestwestern.com
- **Doubletree Hotel**, 818 112th NE, 425-455-1515, 800-222-8733, www.doubletree.com

### BOTHELL
- **Comfort Inn & Suites**, 1414 228th St SE, 425-402-0900, www.comfortinn.com

### EVERETT
- **Holiday Inn Everett**, 3105 Pine St, 425-339-2000, 888-465-4329, www.holiday-inn.com
- **Howard Johnson Plaza Hotel**, 3105 Pine St, 425-339-3333, 800-406-1411, www.the.hojo.com

### FEDERAL WAY
- **Best Western Federal Way Execartel**, 31611 20th S, 253-941-6000, 800-528-1234, www.bestwestern.com
- **Comfort Inn**, 31622 Pacific Hwy S, 253-529-0101, www.comfortinn.com

### KENT
- **Best Western Plaza by the Green**, 24415 Russell Rd, 253-854-8767, 800-648-3311, www.bestwestern.com
- **Comfort Inn**, 22311 84th S, 253-872-2211, www.comfortinn.com

### KIRKLAND
- **Best Western Kirkland Inn**, 12223 NE 116th, 425-822-2300, 800-332-4200, www.bestwestern.com

### LYNNWOOD
- **Hampton Inn & Suites**, 19324 Alderwood Mall Pkwy, 425-771-1888, www.hamptonseattlenorth.com

### SEATTLE
- **Ace Hotel**, 2423 1st Ave, 206-448-4721, www.theacehotel.com

- **Best Western Loyal Inn**, 2301 8th Ave, 206-682-0200, 800-351-9444, www. bestwestern.com
- **Hotel Seattle**, 315 Seneca St, 206-623-5110, www.thehotelseattle.com
- **Travelodge**, 2213 8th Ave, 206-624-6300, 888-515-6375, www.travelodge. com
- **Travelodge by the Space Needle**, 200 6th Ave N, 206-441-7878, 888-515-6375, www.travelodge.com
- **Travelodge University**, 4725 25th Ave NE, 206-525-4612, 888-515-6375, www. travelodge.com
- **University Inn**, 4140 Roosevelt Way NE, 206-632-5055, 800-733-3855, www. universityinnseattle.com

## TUKWILA
- **Best Western at Southcenter**, 15901 West Valley Hwy, 425-226-1812, 800-544-9863, www.bestwestern.com

# SHORT-TERM LEASES AND RESIDENCE HOTELS

The following hotels and leasing companies offer full suites for rent by the day, week or month. Rooms include a kitchen or kitchenette, living room, and bedroom. Often maid service and other amenities are available.

- **Aboda Corporate Housing**, 425-861-0500, www.aboda.com
- **Accommodations Plus**, 425-455-2773, www.aplusnw.com
- **Alternative Suites International**, 206-860-1616, 888-900-4050, www.asuites. com
- **Executive Residence Inc.**, 206-329-8000, 800-428-3867, www.executive residence.com
- **Oakwood Corporate Housing**, 425-861-1175, www.oakwood.com
- **Pacific Guest Suites**, 425-454-7888, 800-962-6620
- **University Hotel**, 4731 12th Ave NE, 206-522-4724, 800-522-4720, www. university-hotel.com

# BED & BREAKFASTS

If you're in the mood for quaint or cozy, consider a bed and breakfast. Most of Seattle's B&Bs are outside the downtown area, so this may also be a good way to check out prospective neighborhoods. You may contact the inn directly (listed below), or try one of the local or national bed and breakfast registries. Locally, call **Seattle Bed & Breakfast Association** (206-547-1020, 800-348-5630, www. lodginginseattle.com), **Bed & Breakfast Association of Suburban Seattle** (www.seattlebestbandb.com), or **Pacific Reservation Service** (206-439-7677,

800-684-2932, www.seattlebedandbreakfast.com). Other sites include **InnSite** (www.innsite.com) and **Bed and Breakfast Inns Online** (www.bbonline.com).

- **11th Avenue Inn**, 121 11th Ave E, 206-669-4373, 800-370-8414, www.11th avenueinn.com
- **Bacon Mansion**, 959 Broadway E, 206-329-1864, 800-240-1864, www. baconmansion.com
- **Chambered Nautilus Bed & Breakfast**, 5005 22nd Ave NE, 206-522-2536, 800-545-8459, www.chamberednautilus.com
- **Chelsea Station on the Park**, 4915 Linden Ave N, 206-547-6077, 800-400-6077, www.bandbseattle.com
- **Gaslight Inn**, 1727 15th Ave, 206-325-3654, www.gaslight-inn.com
- **Mildred's Bed & Breakfast**, 1202 15th Ave E, 206-325-6072, 800-327-9692, www.mildredsbnb.com
- **Salisbury House**, 750 16th Ave E, 206-328-8682, www.salisburyhouse.com
- **Villa Heidelberg Bed & Breakfast**, 4845 45th Ave SW, 206-938-3658, 800-671-2942, www.villaheidelberg.com
- **Wildwood Bed & Breakfast**, 4518 SW Wildwood Place, 206-819-9075, 800-840-8410, www.wildwoodseattle.com

## ALTERNATIVE LODGINGS

### HOSTELS

Hostels offer basic accommodations at low prices, but there are a few restrictions. Generally, you should expect to sleep in a shared room and use a common bathroom and shower, although some have private rooms at a higher price. Some hostels require membership in an international hostelling association, some restrict the number of nights you can stay, or limit the time that you can be in the hostel during the day. The wisest course is to call in advance to make sure that you qualify (and that you'll be happy with the house rules).

- **Green Tortoise Hostel**, 105-1/2 Pike St, 206-340-1222, 888-424-6783, www.greentortoise.net
- **Hostelling International**, 84 Union St, 206-622-5443, www.hiseattle.org

### WASHINGTON ATHLETIC CLUB

The Inn at the Washington Athletic Club offers hotel rooms for members of reciprocal clubs across the country, and their guests. Rates vary depending on membership status and time of year. For more information, or a list of reciprocal clubs, call 206-622-7900 or visit www.wac.net.

## SUMMER ONLY

Summer housing on Seattle-area campuses is restricted to students, visiting conference attendees, and special-interest groups. If you're looking for an apartment or rental house in which to spend the summer (which *is* the best time of year in Seattle), concentrate your efforts in university neighborhoods where students vacate from June to September. The University District, adjacent to the University of Washington, is a good place to start. Also consider the Fremont area near Seattle Pacific University. Short-term and seasonal housing opportunities are listed in the classifieds section of *The Seattle Times* (www.seattletimes.com) and *Seattle Post-Intelligencer* (www.seattlepi.nwsource.com) under "Vacation/Seasonal Rentals" and in the *Seattle Weekly* (www.seattleweekly.com) under "Short Term Housing."

A FTER YOU'VE FOUND A HOME AND HAVE SETTLED IN A BIT, YOU'LL probably want to explore outside Seattle. The communities of the Puget Sound area and western Washington are wonderful places to visit. Just a short drive away (five hours at most) you'll discover mountain peaks, lush valleys, azure lakes and streams, delightful fields of flowers, and picturesque farms. For general travel information and a tourism packet, call the Washington State Tourism Office at 800-544-1800 or visit www.experiencewashington.com.

Most of the locations listed in this chapter offer a variety of activities, lodgings and other attractions. For information on outdoor sports like hiking, fishing, and skiing, read the **Sports and Recreation** chapter of this book. See also **Outdoor Guides** in **A Seattle Reading List**.

## WHIDBEY ISLAND, SAN JUAN ISLANDS

**Whidbey Island**, northwest of Seattle, is one of the two longest islands in the United States (Long Island and Whidbey Island trade the honor back and forth as their measurements change with erosion). Whidbey Island is most easily reached by ferry from Mukilteo, but a longer route through Mount Vernon and Anacortes can save you the ferry fare. Whidbey has several picturesque towns, such as **Coupeville** and **Oak Harbor**. While visiting, make sure you try some mussels in a local seafood restaurant, and take the time to drive to **Deception Pass**, at the north end of the island. The view from the bridge is stunning, though not recommended for those afraid of heights. For a free **Island County Discovery Guide** and other tourist information, call 888-747-7777, or visit www.islandweb.org.

The **San Juan Islands** are reached by ferry, either from Anacortes or Bellingham, and are worth the trip. If possible, give yourself a long weekend or several days; the wait for the ferry can take several hours, especially on a holiday or summer weekend. There are several islands in the San Juans worth visiting, each with breathtaking views. Stay in a quaint bed and breakfast or hotel, or check for vacation rentals on the internet or in Seattle newspapers. Camping is also available in the breathtaking Moran State Park on Orcas Island. You'll find secluded beaches, cozy coffee shops, and charming towns. If possible, take your bike or kayak, and tour the islands that way. Ferry rides between islands, especially if you're walking or taking a bicycle, are inexpensive, but you'll want to make sure that the dock is close enough to town, or you might be in for a long haul. For more information, contact the **Orcas Island Chamber of Commerce** at 360-376-2273 or www.orcasislandchamber.com, **San Juan Island Chamber of Commerce** at 360-378-5240 or www.sanjuanisland.org, **Lopez Island Chamber of Commerce** at 360-468-4664 or www.lopezisland.com, or the **San Juan Islands Visitors Bureau** at www.visitsanjuans.com, where you can download a free visitors guide.

## SKAGIT VALLEY

**Skagit Valley**, located only a couple hours north of Seattle, is famous for its tulips, producing more of the flowers than the Netherlands. During the spring and summer, thousands of visitors come to the valley to see the colorful tulip fields. The entire month of April is given over to the Skagit Valley Tulip Festival. In addition to viewing acres of waving tulips, be sure to visit nearby **La Conner** or **Mount Vernon**. La Conner is a captivating village, with intimate cafés, homemade ice cream and candy shops, and scrumptious bakeries. A few antique malls on the edges of town attract Seattle collectors as well. Mount Vernon offers several antique malls, delicious eateries, and a local brewpub with excellent food. The Skagit Valley is also a well-known haven for artists, with the **Museum of Northwest Art** located in La Conner: 360-466-4446, www.museumofnwart.org. For more information, call the **Skagit Valley Tulip Festival Office** at 360-428-5959, or visit www.tulipfestival.org.

## VICTORIA, VANCOUVER, AND HARRISON HOT SPRINGS, B.C.

Located on the southern tip of Vancouver Island, **Victoria, B.C.,** is a direct ferry ride from the Seattle Waterfront on the *Victoria Clipper*. It's a small but appealing city, with a lively waterfront and beautiful gardens. The **Butchart Gardens** in particular are worth a visit. Bus tours leave for the gardens several times a day from the waterfront. Children will enjoy the wax museum with its replicas of famous and historical figures. A trip to Victoria isn't complete without high tea at the Empress Hotel, which presides over the waterfront. For visitor information call **Tourism Victoria** at 250-953-2033 or visit www.tourismvictoria.com.

A three-hour drive north of Seattle on I-5, **Vancouver, B.C.**, is a cosmopolitan port city offering great dining and shopping, including an extensive underground mall and Robson Street, which is lined with fashionable clothing boutiques, trendy cosmetics stores, and unique beauty and bath shops. Visit **Granville Island** for a bustling farmers' market during the day or live music and dancing at night. Rent bicycles and pack a picnic lunch to ride through beautiful **Stanley Park**, which overlooks the shipping activity in the bay. Music concerts and live theater performances draw many Seattle residents to Vancouver, since many tours stop at only one of the two cities. For more information, call 604-682-2222 or visit www.tourismvancouver.com.

If you're in the mood to relax and get away from the big city pace, consider a trip to the sleepy resort town of **Harrison Hot Springs, B.C.** From any point in this small town, you'll have a spectacular view of Harrison Lake and surrounding mountains. During spring and summer, you can charter a fishing boat, take a cruise on the lake, play golf, go parasailing, play tennis, swim in the lake or the public hot springs, hike, water ski, windsurf, or go horseback riding. Harrison Hot Springs is just a little more than four hours away from Seattle. A stay at the Harrison Hot Springs Resort offers a soak in private hot springs pools and complimentary high tea. For additional information on the town and neighboring communities call the **Harrison Hot Springs Chamber of Commerce** at 604-796-5581 or visit www.harrison.ca.

## EAST OF THE CASCADES

Located on Highway 2 on the east side of the Cascade Mountains, Washington's own Bavarian village, **Leavenworth,** attracts many visitors. During the summer, the town is a destination for novice rock climbers, who scale boulders along Icicle Creek. In the fall, Leavenworth presents the music-filled and beer-soaked Oktoberfest celebration. In winter, the village offers nearby skiing at Stevens Pass, as well as Christmas festivals and concerts. For more information, contact the **Leavenworth Chamber of Commerce** at 509-548-5807 or visit www.leaven worth.org.

Also east of the Cascades, **Lake Chelan** is a favorite among sun-seekers and water enthusiasts. The area is a favorite family destination, with plenty of water-based activities and houseboat rentals. At the southern tip of the lake, the town of Lake Chelan offers crowded bars, casual restaurants, and sporting goods shops. Condominiums and motels line the lakeshore, and there is public camping at nearby parks. Call ahead for reservations, though, because the area is usually packed during the summer months. At the northern tip of the lake, the tiny town of **Stehekin** is reachable only by ferry or boat from Chelan and is favored by hikers and those wishing a quieter vacation. For additional tourist information call 800-4-CHELAN or go to www.lakechelan.com.

## OLYMPIC PENINSULA AND MOUNTAINS

A short ferry ride across Puget Sound, the **Olympic Peninsula** has something for everyone. **Poulsbo** is a small Scandinavian-style village located 30 minutes east of the Bainbridge ferry terminal. Stop in for a fabulous donut at Sluys Poulsbo Bakery, home of the original recipe for Poulsbo Bread. Just outside of town, the Thomas Kemper microbrewery offers daily tours and a tasty pub menu.

Drive south on Highway 101 along **Hood Canal** for scenic little fishing towns like **Quilcene**, clamming and oyster beaches, and spectacular vistas from **Mt. Walker**. Heading north on Highway 101, you'll find **Port Townsend**, where *An Officer and a Gentleman* was filmed. It features historic buildings, antique stores, unusual boutiques, and kite shops, and you can also catch a ferry to Whidbey Island from downtown.

**Port Angeles**, at the northern tip of the peninsula, offers ferry service to Victoria, B.C. **Hurricane Ridge**, located only 15 minutes away from Port Angeles, is always worth a visit. The mountaintop views from the ridge are sensational, even if you only drive to the parking lot and visitors' center. **Sequim** is famous for its fields of lavender and as the sunniest town in Western Washington, receiving only 16 inches of rain a year.

Nestled in the Olympic National Park, **Sol Duc Hot Springs**, 866-476-5382, www.visitsolduc.com, has cabins and a campground for visitors. Soak in the beautiful outdoor pools, take a short hike to the Sol Duc waterfall, or arrange for a massage from on-site massage therapists. Another short drive takes you to secluded **Ruby Beach**, one of the nicest sandy beaches on the Washington Coast. For more information on the Olympic Peninsula, visit the **North Olympic Peninsula Visitor and Convention Bureau** at www.olympicpeninsula.org.

If you are interested in hiking or mountain climbing, get a copy of one of the many hiking guides to the Olympics. (See the **Literary Life** section of the **Cultural Life** chapter for a list of area bookstores.) If you enjoy mountain climbing, two mountains on the Peninsula are especially challenging: The Brothers is the twin-peaked mountain that is easily visible from Seattle, and Mount Olympus, while it cannot be seen from the city, is the tallest mountain in the Olympic range. To climb to the summit of either of these peaks, contact a local mountain climbing club or guide service (see the **Sports and Recreation** chapter for listings). Happily, there are many more hikes in the Olympics that are manageable for the average person. For information on **Olympic National Park**, call 360-565-3130 or visit www.nps.gov/olym.

## THE COAST

A popular summer destination along the coast is the tourist town of Ocean Shores. Hotels line the beach, and popular activities include horseback riding on the beach, driving on the beach, beachcombing, kite flying, and a Fourth of July fireworks show over the ocean. For a free visitors guide, call the **Ocean Shores Chamber of Commerce** at 800-762-3224 or visit www.oceanshores.org.

In the mood for a picturesque beach resort town and spectacular ocean view? Try either the southwest Washington coast or northern Oregon coast. **Long Beach**, at the far southwest tip of Washington, is said to be the world's longest beach. Several annual events are held in Long Beach, such as a state kite-flying festival, regional stunt kite competition, sand sculpture contest, and Fourth of July fireworks celebration. Contact the **Long Beach Peninsula Visitor's Bureau** at 360-642-2400 or 800-451-2542, or visit www.funbeach.com.

Across the mouth of the Columbia, the Oregon coast offers a stretch of beautiful beaches and ocean surf. **Seaside** is the best known destination, with affordable beach cottages and hotels and access to an expanse of white sandy beach. Other nearby towns attract fewer visitors, a plus for those in search of a private stretch of beach or a romantic getaway. If that's your preference, rent a cottage in **Gearhart** or reserve a room overlooking the ocean in **Cannon Beach**. For more information on these and other Oregon destinations, call the **Oregon Tourism Commission** at 800-547-7842 or visit www.traveloregon.com. The drive to Long Beach from Seattle is about four hours; Seattle to Seaside takes four to five hours, even in Friday rush hour traffic. If possible, give yourself a long weekend, but expect more crowds if it's a holiday.

## MOUNT RAINIER

Majestic **Mount Rainier** will be a familiar sight soon after you move here, and definitely worth a visit. During the winter, **Crystal Mountain Ski Resort** bustles with activity while the rest of the mountain is deserted. In early spring however, the roads begin to re-open and visitors flock to the area to hike, mountain climb, and camp. Many start their hikes from the mountain's most visited site, **Paradise,** which hosts a visitor center and historic lodge. Mount Rainier is a challenging hiking or climbing destination even for experienced climbers. Some short hikes near the base of the mountain are suitable for the average recreational hiker; look in a good hiking book or trail guide for details. For anything other than a day hike on a well-marked trail be sure to research your route carefully and take an experienced outdoorsman or guide with you. If you're interested in climbing to the summit, contact a local mountain climbing club or guide service (several are listed in the **Sports and Recreation** chapter). Don't let the beauty of the Cascades and Olympics fool you; people get lost and some die every year climbing mountains in Washington. For more information, call **Mount Rainier National Park** at 360-569-2211 or visit the National Park Service's Mount Rainier web site at www.nps.gov/mora.

S PEND A YEAR IN SEATTLE AND THE DELIGHTFUL MIX OF EVENTS THAT take place here will amaze you. Residents embrace the few months of sunshine and the long, wet winter months with a variety of music, food, and arts festivals, and sporting events. Below is a list of annual highlights you won't want to miss. Unless otherwise noted, all events are held in Seattle. To find smaller events, and happenings in communities outside of Seattle, check your local newspaper or visit www.nwsource.com.

## JANUARY

- **Martin Luther King, Jr. Celebration**—Central Area Motivation Program, 206-812-4940, www.mlkseattle.org; this annual celebration features a rally, march, workshops, music, and entertainment.
- **Seattle Boat Show**—Qwest Field Event Center, 206-634-0911, www.seattleboatshow.com; the Northwest Marine Trade Association sponsors this annual event for boat enthusiasts and prospective buyers.
- **Seattle Wedding Show**—Washington State Convention & Trade Center, 425-744-6509, www.weddingshow.com; prospective brides flock to this event showcasing everything from gowns to honeymoons.

## FEBRUARY

- **Chinese New Year**—International District, 206-382-1197, www.internationaldistrict.org; this traditional Chinese festival includes a colorful parade.
- **Festival Sundiata**—Seattle Center, 206-684-7200, www.seattlecenter.com; this annual celebration commemorates African and African-American culture, history, and art, with exhibits and live performances.

- **Mardi Gras**—Pioneer Square, 206-622-2563; Seattle's very own Fat Tuesday celebration takes place in bars throughout the city's historic district.
- **Northwest Flower and Garden Show**—Washington State Convention Center, 206-789-5333, www.gardenshow.com; a gardener's paradise, featuring seminars, displays, workshops, and vendors.
- **Seattle Home Show**—Qwest Field Event Center, 425-467-0960, www.seattlehomeshow.com; homeowners find thousands of ideas for improving their homes inside and out.
- **Seattle International Bicycle Expo**—Warren G. Magnuson Park, 206-522-3222, www.cascade.org/expo; cycling enthusiasts enjoy exhibits, demonstrations, and presentations on all aspects of the sport.
- **Seattle RV & Outdoor Recreation Show**—Qwest Field Event Center, 425-277-8132, www.mhrvshows.com; discover the biggest, newest, and best in recreational vehicles and outdoor recreation.
- **Vietnamese Lunar New Year Celebration**—Seattle Center, 206-706-2658, www.tetinseattle.org; the Vietnamese community celebrates Tet, its most important festival of the year.

## MARCH

- **Daffodils in Bloom Celebration**—La Conner, 888-642-9287, www.laconnerchamber.com; fields ablaze with yellow blossoms are found just a short drive from Seattle.
- **Irish Week Festival**—Seattle Center, 206-223-3608, www.seattlecenter.com; sponsored by the Irish Heritage Club, this family festival celebrates St. Patrick's Day by presenting Irish films, history, dancing, language workshops, and a festive parade through downtown Seattle.
- **Seattle Women's Show**—Qwest Field Event Center, 425-485-0285, www.nwwomenshow.com; fashion, fitness, and food combine to make this event a local favorite.
- **St. Patrick's Day Parade**—Bainbridge Island, 206-842-3700, www.bainbridgechamber.com; the island community of Bainbridge hosts a parade to celebrate the Irish in everyone.
- **Whirligig**—Seattle Center, 206-684-7200, www.seattlecenter.com; the Seattle Center presents a fun-filled family event, with carnival activities for children.

## APRIL

- **Daffodil Festival**—253-863-9524, www.daffodilfestival.net; the highlight of this festival is the large parade that winds through the cities of Tacoma, Puyallup, Sumner and Orting.

- **Earth Day Puget Sound**—dozens of groups hold a variety of events throughout the region in recognition of Earth Day, including exhibits, activities, and music along Seattle's waterfront. Check your local newspaper for information.
- **Friends of the Seattle Public Library Book Sale**—Magnuson Park, 206-386-4098, www.splfriends.org; twice a year an enormous warehouse is converted into the biggest book sale in the city. Proceeds from the sale of books, art, music, and movies benefit the Seattle Public Library. While you'll find a separate section for appropriately priced rare and antique books, most items are a dollar or less.
- **Seattle Cherry Blossom Festival**—Seattle Center, 206-723-2003, www.seattlecenter.org; this annual festival celebrates both contemporary and traditional aspects of Japanese culture with artists, stage performances, children's entertainment, and exhibits.
- **Seattle Jewish Festival**—206-443-5400, www.jewishinseattle.org; celebrates the culture and traditions of Judaism with food, entertainment, and art.
- **Skagit Valley Tulip Festival**—Mount Vernon, 360-428-5959, www.tulipfestival. org; during the month of April, the Skagit Valley hosts the annual Tulip Festival, featuring tours of brilliantly colored fields of silky tulips, set against a backdrop of Mount Baker and the Cascade Mountains. Enjoy local art exhibits and special events, dine in local restaurants, visit nearby antique malls in La Conner or Mount Vernon, or send bulbs in your favorite colors to loved ones.
- **Take Our Daughters and Sons to Work Day**—www.daughtersandsonstowork. org; organizations all over Puget Sound participate in this educational and fun day held on the fourth Thursday of every April.

## MAY

- **Bike to Work Month**—206-517-4826; sponsored by the Cascade Bicycle Club, challenges, events, and lots of bike commuting are featured all month, with many area employers participating.
- **MS Walk**—206-284-4236, www.nmsswas.org; the MS Walk supports national research and local programs for people living with Multiple Sclerosis in Western and Central Washington.
- **Northwest Folklife Festival**—Seattle Center, 206-684-7300, www.nwfolklife. org; held every Memorial Day weekend, the Folklife Festival celebrates the folk arts communities of the Northwest. This popular and free event offers a blend of world music and dance performance, arts and crafts exhibits, musical and artistic workshops, and films and demonstrations focusing on ethnic and folk heritage in the Northwest.
- **Opening Day**—206-325-1000, www.seattleyachtclub.org; on the first Saturday of May, the Seattle Yacht Club sponsors the Opening Day celebration, which

marks the first official day of the summer boating season, a Seattle tradition since 1909. Hundreds of gaudily decorated pleasure boats parade through the Montlake Cut and then tie up to one another in Lake Washington to watch the Windermere Cup rowing race. Even if you don't own a boat, you can enjoy the spectacle from the Montlake Bridge or from the sloping sides of the cut.

- **Pike Place Market Festival**—Pike Place Market, 206-682-7453, www. pikeplacemarket.org; held each Memorial Day weekend to celebrate the arrival of summer, this event features music stages, Northwest food and craft vendors, and beer and coffee gardens.
- **Seattle International Children's Festival**—Seattle Center, 206-684-7338, www.seattleinternational.org; this annual event—one of the largest of its kind in the United States—features appearances by performing troupes from around the world.
- **Seattle Maritime Festival**—Seattle Waterfront, 206-284-8285, www.seattle propellerclub.org; this annual event, held mostly on Pier 66, features the largest tugboat race in the world.
- **Syttende Mai**—Ballard, 206-789-5708, www.syttendemaiseattle.com; this annual Scandinavian festival is held in the Ballard neighborhood to commemorate Norwegian Independence Day.
- **University District Street Fair**—University District, 206-547-4417, http:// streetfair.udistrictchamber.org; several blocks of University Way are closed to traffic for this fair, which features arts and crafts kiosks, music and dance performances, and lots of great food.

## JUNE

- **Chinese Culture and Arts Festival**—Seattle Center, 206-684-7200, www. seattlecenter.com; the Seattle Center hosts two days of Chinese opera, dance, visual arts, ancient crafts, and children's activities.
- **Edmonds Arts Festival**—Frances Anderson Center, Edmonds, 425-771-6412, www.edmondsartsfestival.com; this free festival 20 miles north of Seattle attracts more than 75,000 spectators over Father's Day weekend.
- **Fremont Fair**—Fremont, 206-694-6706, www.fremontfair.com; located in "The Center of the Universe," as Fremont is fondly called, this festival features nude bicyclists and unusually costumed participants celebrating the summer solstice with a rowdy Solstice Parade, art booths, food, and music.
- **Komen Seattle Race for the Cure**—Qwest Field Event Center, 206-633-6586, www.komenseattle.org; proceeds from this popular 5K run fund research efforts and local breast health and breast cancer outreach efforts.

- **Lake Union Wooden Boat Festival**—the Center for Wooden Boats, 206-382-2628, www.cwb.org; maritime experts and wooden boats gather at the south end of Lake Union.
- **Out to Lunch Concert Series**—206-623-0340, www.downtownseattle.com; held at venues in downtown Seattle, this intimate concert series produced by the Downtown Seattle Association attracts many popular musicians.
- **Pagdiriwang**—Seattle Center, 206-684-7200, www.seattlecenter.com; a celebration of Philippine culture, this festival includes music, dance, and dramatic performances.
- **Seattle Pride**—Seattle Center, 206-322-9561, www.seattlepride.org; the Seattle Pride march, parade, and celebration are boisterous events that take place on the last weekend in June. The downtown parade ends at the Seattle Center where the celebration continues. Parade participants range from politicians to "dykes on bikes."

## JULY

- **Arab Festival**—Seattle Center, 206-684-7200; held every other year in odd numbered years, the Arab Festival features folk dancing, a traditional bazaar, food, cultural and educational booths, and children's activities.
- **Bellevue Arts and Crafts Fair**—Bellevue, 425-519-0770, www.bellevueart. org; artists from across the country exhibit their work at the most successful arts and crafts festival in the Pacific Northwest.
- **Bite of Seattle**—Seattle Center, 425-283-5050, www.biteofseattle.com; "The Bite" showcases local restaurants, microbreweries, wineries, and coffee houses. Local merchants and artisans open small booths to display and sell their wares, and musicians, jugglers, and other performers provide outdoor entertainment.
- **Chinatown International District Summer Festival**—Hing Hay Park, 206-382-1197, www.internationaldistrict.org; The ID, also known as the International District, celebrates summer with cultural entertainment, ethnic foods, arts and crafts, and community booths.
- **Fourth of Jul-Ivars**—206-587-6500, www.ivars.net; a fantastic show of fireworks over Elliott Bay, this Independence Day event is enjoyed from the Seattle Waterfront and Myrtle Edwards Park.
- **King County Fair**—King County Fairgrounds, Enumclaw, 206-296-8890, www. metrokc.gov/parks/fair; Washington's oldest county fair includes nationally known entertainers, a professional rodeo, and all the usual fair fixin's.
- **Seafair**—206-728-0123, www.seafair.com; the Seafair festival begins in mid-July but lasts well into August, and offers something for everyone. The Milk Carton Derby at Green Lake, which usually kicks off Seafair, is a race of

homemade boats kept afloat (or not) by milk cartons. A true community celebration, Seafair consists of numerous neighborhood festivals, kids' parades, and sidewalk sales. Athletic events include a triathlon and the Torchlight Run. Other events include the Annual Torchlight Parade, a performance by the Blue Angels, and the arrival of the Seafair Fleet—Naval and Coast Guard ships that can be toured on the Seattle Waterfront. The grand finale of this event is the Seafair hydroplane race (and qualifying races), which takes place on Lake Washington. During the races, Seward Park is packed, and everyone with access to a boat takes to the water to watch the excitement.

- **Seattle to Portland Bicycle Classic**—206-522-3222, www.seattletoportland. com; the Cascade Bicycle Club annual ride is one of the best cycling events in the country, and covers more than 200 miles between Seattle and Portland, with up to 9,000 participants from all over the country and world.
- **Summer Nights**—Gasworks Park, 206-281-7788; www.summernights.org; throughout the summer months, a series of concerts is held in a stunning outdoor Seattle setting. Previously located on downtown waterfront piers but moved due to construction, the series took a break in 2006 but expects to resume in 2007 at Gasworks Park. Big name musical acts in an intimate outdoor setting make this a favorite summertime activity.
- **WaMu Family 4th**—Gasworks Park, Lake Union, 206-281-7788, www. wamufamily4th.org; the annual fireworks spectacular that Time Magazine called one of the nation's "Top Five Fireworks Displays" takes place above Lake Union near downtown. Music blasting from large speakers in Gasworks Park accompanies the brilliant display. People fill the park to capacity, and other viewpoints along the lake are usually full of onlookers as well.

## AUGUST

- **BrasilFest**—Seattle Center, 206-684-7200, www.seattlecenter.com; this sultry celebration of South American soul and Brazilian style features performances, children's activities, workshops, and food.
- **Cambodian Cultural Heritage Festival**—Seattle Center, 206-684-7200, www. seattlecenter.com; through storytelling, traditional music, dance, and crafts, learn about the customs and traditions of Cambodia.
- **Danskin Triathlon**—800-452-9526, www.danskin.com/triathlon.html; thousands of women compete each August in the largest and longest-running triathlon series in multi-sport history. The annual event consists of a half-mile swim, 12-mile bike, and 3.1-mile run in and along Lake Washington.
- **Evergreen State Fair**—Monroe, 360-805-6700, www.evergreenfair.org; concerts and exhibits plus carnival and rodeo events pack twelve days in late August and early September.

- **Hempfest**—Myrtle Edwards Park, 206-781-5734, www.seattlehempfest.com; attendees rally in support of legalized marijuana at the north end of the Seattle Waterfront.
- **Night Out Against Crime**—206-684-7555; Seattle joins the rest of the country in promoting crime/drug prevention awareness. Residents turn on their porch lights and gather outdoors at block parties to strengthen neighborhood spirit and safety.
- **Seattle Music Fest**—Alki Beach, 206-632-4545, www.northwestarts.org; this three day festival on the beach showcases emerging artists in alternative rock.
- **TibetFest**—Seattle Center, 206-684-7200, www.seattlecenter.com; this festival showcases Tibetan and Himalayan cultural arts, folk music, and dance.

## SEPTEMBER

- **Blackberry Festival**—Bremerton, 360-377-3041, www.blackberryfestival. org; Bremerton's waterfront is transformed every year during this festival that includes a fun run, arts and crafts, music, and tons of blackberries.
- **Bumbershoot**—Seattle Center, 206-281-7788, www.bumbershoot.org; named after a slang term for umbrella, Bumbershoot is a Labor Day weekend event that has been a Seattle tradition since 1971. The festival that Rolling Stone magazine called "The Mother of All Arts Festivals" showcases more than 2,500 artists from all over the world. In addition to arts and crafts booths and dance performances, you'll find fortunetellers, street musicians, delicacies from local restaurants, and non-stop music concerts in multiple venues. The ticket price covers admittance to all of the exhibits and performances, but you'll need to stand in line to get seats for the headlining acts.
- **Commencement Bay Maritime Fest**—Tacoma, 253-318-2210, http://maritimefest.org; dragon-boat races, a salmon bake, art show, harbor tours, and a two-day boat-building contest highlight this celebration of Tacoma's working waterfront.
- **Fiestas Patrias**—Seattle Center, 206-903-0486, www.seattlefiestaspatrias.org; this Latin American cultural festival features traditional food, music, and dance performances.
- **Festa Italiana**—Seattle Center, 206-282-0627, www.festaseattle.com; this celebration showcases Italian food, music, art, and dance, including a bocce tournament, film festival, and a grape stomp competition.
- **Friends of the Seattle Public Library Book Sale**—Magnuson Park, 206-386-4098, www.splfriends.org; this is the fall installment of the popular biannual book sale, with over 200,000 items on sale.

- **Fremont Oktoberfest**—Fremont, 206-633-0422, www.fremontoktoberfest. com; as well as the mandatory beer garden, enjoy a fun run, live music, a carnival, and the highly popular chainsaw pumpkin carving contest.
- **Northwest AIDS Walk**—Volunteer Park, 206-323-9255, www.lifelong aidsalliance.org; this large and popular event supports the Lifelong AIDS Alliance.
- **PAWS Walk**—Magnuson Park, 425-787-2500, www.barkinthepark.com; this festival for dogs and the people who love them includes a fundraising walk for the PAWS animal shelter, off-leash areas, contests, and canine-inspired artwork. You can also adopt a dog or get your dog microchipped.
- **The Puyallup Fair**—Puyallup Fairgrounds, 253-841-5045, www. thefair.com; also known as the Western Washington Fair, this event has been held in Puyallup (PYEW-al-lup) since 1900. If you decide to "do the Puyallup," give yourself a whole day. You'll want to sample a famous onion burger, tour a cattle barn, ride the roller coaster, watch a concert, and savor fresh corn on the cob. Or perhaps you'll decide to try your hand at bungee jumping, marvel at the hypnotist's skill, visit the prize-winning vegetable exhibit, and have several hot buttery scones. Don't assume this is a little country affair or you'll miss out on one of the best events of the year, and the biggest in the state. Puyallup is near Tacoma, less than an hour's drive from Seattle. The fair lasts for 2-3 weeks in September.
- **Salmon Homecoming Celebration**—Magnuson Park, 206-386-4300, www.salmonhomecoming.com; The Salmon Homecoming Alliance hosts this celebration that aims to build bridges between tribal and non-tribal communities while supporting a healthy salmon population.

## OCTOBER

- **Earshot Jazz Festival**—Seattle, 206-547-6763, www.earshot.org; the city's best jazz festival features over 50 concerts and events over a 2-week period in venues all over the city. Internationally famous acts abound.
- **Issaquah Salmon Days Festival**—Issaquah, 425-392-0661, www.salmondays. org; Issaquah celebrates the return of salmon to its lakes, streams, and downtown hatchery with a parade, salmon bake, art, and music.
- **Seattle Home Show 2**—Qwest Field Event Center, 425-467-0960, www. seattlehomeshow.com; the popular spring event is duplicated in the fall, with tips on winterizing your home.

## NOVEMBER

- **Apple Cup**—206-543-2200, http://gohuskies.cstv.com; the state football rivalry of the season pits the University of Washington Huskies against the Washington State University Cougars. The venue alternates between Husky Stadium in Seattle and Martin Stadium in Pullman, east of the Cascades.
- **Green Lake Frostbite Regatta**—206-684-4074, www.cityofseattle.net/parks/boats/grnlake.htm; just as the weather gets a little too cold and the wind picks up the bite of winter, two annual rowing events are held in Seattle. The Frostbite Regatta is a series of fairly short races, easily watched from the side of the lake with a hot cup of coffee in hand.
- **Head of the Lake Regatta**—206-547-1583, http://lakewashingtonrowing.com; the Head of the Lake Race, which is held on a course that includes parts of both Lake Union and Lake Washington, is a three-mile race that tests the endurance of both rowers and spectators.
- **Hmong New Year Celebration**—Seattle Center, 206-684-7200, www.seattlecenter.com; this Laotian Hmong festival celebrates the lunar new year with art exhibits and dance performances.
- **Seattle International Auto Show**—Qwest Field Event Center, www.seattleautoshow.com; State Farm Insurance presents new and classic cars, trucks, motorcycles, SUVs and minivans, plus rare "supercars" and concept vehicles.
- **Seattle Marathon**—206-729-3660, www.seattlemarathon.org; this annual athletic event features a rolling course with scenic views, and a reputation for cold and rainy weather. The event also offers a marathon walk, half-marathon run and walk, and kids' marathon.
- **Winterfest**—Seattle Center, 206-684-7200, www.seattlecenter.com; an annual holiday event, this festival features school choirs, a public ice rink, a model train display, and all sorts of performances and shows. The five-week festival is a family favorite.
- **Yulefest**—Nordic Heritage Museum, Ballard, 206-789-5707, www.nordicmuseum.com; Ballard celebrates the holidays and its Scandinavian heritage the weekend before Thanksgiving.

## DECEMBER

- **Christmas Ship Festival**—206-623-1445, www.argosycruises.com; boaters in Seattle celebrate the holiday season with a festive parade of lighted boats that tour Puget Sound, Lake Washington, and Lake Union during the weeks before Christmas. Shoreside revelers gather around bonfires and are treated to Christmas carols sung by choirs on the boats as they stop at area parks and beaches.

- **Community Hanukkah Celebration**—Stroum Jewish Community Center, Mercer Island, 206-232-7115, www.sjcc.org; listen to music, and enjoy arts and crafts and a candle lighting ceremony at this community Festival of Lights.
- **New Year's Eve at the Space Needle**—Space Needle, 206-905-2100, www.spaceneedle.com; for many years, the Space Needle has been the site of the liveliest New Year's celebration in Seattle. From the formal dinner dance at the revolving restaurant level to the casual party at the base of the needle, it has become a destination for New Year's revelers. Even if you decide to spend a quiet New Year's Eve at home, consider driving (or walking) to one of the many parks overlooking the Space Needle just before midnight. The fireworks display, which is set off from the top and sides of the structure, is spectacular. If you can't see it in person, local news stations broadcast the extravaganza.
- **The Nutcracker**—Seattle Center Opera House, 206-441-9411, www.pnb.org; no Christmas in Seattle would be complete without the annual production of The Nutcracker by Pacific Northwest Ballet. With marvelous sets by Maurice Sendak, this unique production is popular with all age groups.
- **Zoolights**—Point Defiance Zoo and Aquarium, Tacoma, 253-591-5337, www.pdza.org; more than half a million lights shimmer in the shapes of animals, nursery rhymes, and local landmarks.

## ARCHITECTURE

- ***Classic Houses of Seattle: High Style to Vernacular, 1870-1950*** by Caroline T. Swope; covering the architectural styles and history of Seattle homes, from mansions to cottages.
- ***Made to Last: Historic Preservation in Seattle and King County*** by Lawrence Kreisman; outlines historical districts and landmarks.
- ***National Trust Guide Seattle: America's Guide for Architecture and History Travelers*** by Walt Crowley; in-depth guide to the famous and not so famous landmarks and buildings in Seattle, including maps and photographs.
- ***Shaping Seattle Architecture: A Historical Guide to the Architects*** by Jeffrey Karl Ochsner; traces the history of Seattle's architecture through biographies of the area's best known architects. Many famous Seattle buildings and houses are profiled in this book.

## ART

- ***Chihuly by Donald Kuspit***; a look at the career of internationally renowned glass artist Dale Chihuly in a coffee table–sized book full of stunning photos.
- ***A Field Guide to Seattle's Public Art*** edited by Steven Huss, contains five self-guided tours of Seattle's best-known public artworks, as well as essays by artists, writers, and historians.
- ***Seattle, Washington: A Photographic Portrait*** by Roger L. Johnson; the photographs of Seattle and the Puget Sound region are a visual feast of landscapes, people, and architecture.

## COMMUNITY

- *Gay Seattle: Stories of Exile and Belonging* by Gary Atkins; tells the stories of the gay community in Seattle and its trials and triumphs over the last century.
- *Neighbor Power: Building Community the Seattle Way* by Jim Diers; provides stories and practical methods for building stronger communities and citizen activists.

## FAMILY AND PETS

- *Best Hikes with Kids: Western Washington & the Cascades* by Joan Burton; an essential hiking guide for parents, this book describes day hikes and over-nighters suitable for the entire family.
- *Bringing Out Baby: Seattle and the Eastside: Places to Take Babies and Toddlers* by Julia Rader Detering; addresses where to go with the under-three set.
- *The Dog Lovers' Companion to the Pacific Northwest: The Inside Scoop on Where To Take Your Dog* by Val Mallinson; using a "4 paws" rating system and Pick of the Litter lists, find the best places to take your canine companion.
- *Out and About Seattle with Kids: The Ultimate Family Guide for Fun and Learning* by Ann Bergman and Virginia Smyth; this handbook can help families who are new to Seattle become acquainted with the city and its child-friendly diversions and resources.

## FICTION

- *The Art of Deception* by Ridley Pearson; the 2002 thriller featuring Seattle detective Lou Boldt. Earlier titles set in the Emerald City include *Middle of Nowhere*, *The First Victim*, and *The Pied Piper*.
- *Breach of Duty* by J.A. Jance; one in a 14-book series of mysteries featuring fictional Seattle detective J.P. Beaumont. Others include *Name Withheld*, *Lying in Wait*, and *Failure to Appear*.
- *Firetrap: A Novel of Suspense* by Earl W. Emerson; one of several mysteries by this author that take place in or around Seattle and feature firefighter sleuths. His previous series of books starring private eye Thomas Black still have a loyal following.
- *Half Asleep in Frog Pajamas* by Tom Robbins; a woman is in crisis in this typical Robbins wild ride set in Seattle.
- *The Highest Tide* by Jim Lynch; a 13-year-old boy's life is changed in a surprising way one summer in this beautiful novel set in the south end of Puget Sound.

- *Long for This World* by Michael Byers; in the late 1990s a Seattle doctor must cope with a startling and world-changing discovery.
- *Red Tide* by G.M. Ford; the fourth of a series following the investigative exploits of Seattle writer Frank Corso. Ford also wrote the successful Leo Waterman mystery novels about a Seattle private investigator.
- *Snow Falling on Cedars* by David Guterson; the author of this award-winning novel set in the Puget Sound area hails from Bainbridge Island. His other books include *East of the Mountains* and *The Country Ahead of Us, the Country Behind*.
- *Ten Little Indians* by Sherman Alexie; a compelling collection of short stories by the author of *The Lone Ranger and Tonto*, *Fistfight in Heaven*, *Indian Killer*, and *Reservation Blues*.

## FOOD & DINING

- *The Food Lover's Guide to Seattle* by Katy Calcott; a guide book to the city's freshest greens, best baguettes, and surliest fishmongers.
- *Pike Place Market Cookbook: Recipes, Anecdotes, and Personalities from Seattle's Renowned Public Market* by Braiden Rex-Johnson; with a forward by Tom Douglas, this little gem is part cookbook, part market history.
- *Tom Douglas' Seattle Kitchen* by Tom Douglas; Seattle's favorite chef and owner of several restaurants shares some of his inspired recipes.
- *Zagat Survey: Seattle/Portland Restaurants*; the annual edition of this indispensable survey will help you find the right restaurant for every occasion.

## HISTORY

- *Eccentric Seattle: Pillars and Pariahs Who Made the City Not Such a Boring Place After All* by J. Kingston Pierce; an amusing romp through the characters and events of Seattle's past.
- *Loser: The Real Seattle Music Story* by Clark Humphrey and Art Chantry; a history of Seattle music from the 1960s to the mid 1990s.
- *Nisei Daughter* by Monica Itoi-Stone; a Japanese-American woman's story of a Seattle childhood interrupted by the WWII relocation of Japanese-Americans to internment camps. This book is standard reading in many Seattle classrooms.
- *Skid Road* by Murray Morgan; the now-famous account of early Seattle, from which the phrase "skid row" was coined.
- *The World of Chief Seattle: How Can One Sell the Air?* by Warren Jefferson; a tribute to Chief Seattle and the Suquamish tribe.

## OUTDOOR GUIDES

- *100 Hikes in the Inland Northwest* by Rich Landers; the "100 Hikes" series published by Mountaineers Books also includes *100 Hikes in Washington's Alpine Lakes* by Vicky Spring, *100 Hikes in Washington's Glacier Peak Region, 100 Hikes in Washington's North Cascades National Park Region,* and *100 Hikes in Washington's South Cascades and Olympics* by Ira Spring.
- *Birds of Seattle and Puget Sound*, by Chris C. Fisher; essential field guide for Seattle bird watchers.
- *Don't Jump!; The Northwest Winter Blues Survival Guide* by Novella Carpenter and Traci Vogel; some silly—and some serious—tips to help Northwesterners through the winter doldrums.
- *Kissing the Trail: Greater Seattle Mountain Bike Adventures* by John Zilly; thorough descriptions of mountain bike trails in and near Seattle.
- *Nature in the City: Seattle: Walks, Hikes, Wildlife, Natural Wonders* by Maria Dolan and Kathryn True; fact-filled guide to the sometimes surprising places to experience the great outdoors in an urban environment.
- *Outside Magazine's Urban Adventure: Seattle* by Maria Dolan; discover the best spots for kayaking, hiking, biking, rock climbing, winter sports and more.
- *Seattle's Lakes, Bays & Waterways (Including the Eastside)* by Marge and Ted Mueller; the "Afoot & Afloat" series from Mountaineers Books also includes *Middle Puget Sound & Hood Canal, North Puget Sound, South Puget Sound* and *The San Juan Islands.*

## SPORTS

- *Hydroplane Racing in Seattle* by David D. Williams; summertime in Seattle means the hydroplane races during Seafair in August, and this chronicle is a fascinating look at the history and the present of the sport.
- *Out of Left Field: How the Mariners Made Baseball Fly in Seattle* by Art Thiel; from underdog team to the pride of a city, read about the rise of the Mariners.
- *Seattle Slew* by Dan Mearns; a biography of the city's most famous thoroughbred, from his Triple Crown glory to the illness that nearly took his life.

For help on finding 800 numbers, and especially for tips on how to reach an actual human being at hundreds of companies, go to www.gethuman.com.

## AGING

- **American Association of Retired Persons (AARP)**, 206-517-9348, 800-424-3410, 206-517-9344 (TTY), www.aarp.org
- **King County Aging Program**, 206-684-0660, www.metrokc.gov
- **Senior Information and Assistance Program**, 206-448-3110, www.metrokc.gov
- **Senior Services of Seattle/King County**, 206-448-5757, 206-448-5025 (TDD), www.seniorservices.org

## ALCOHOL AND DRUG ABUSE

- **Adult Children of Alcoholics Anonymous**, 206-722-6117, 800-562-1240
- **The Al-Anon & Alateen Information Service**, 206-625-0000
- **Alcohol/Drug 24-Hour Help Line**, 206-722-3700, 800-562-1240, www.adhl.org
- **Alcohol Drug Teen Help Line**, 206-722-4222, 877-345-8336, www.theteenline.org
- **Alcoholics Anonymous**, 206-587-2838; Bellevue, 425-454-9192; Edmonds, 425-672-0987, www.alcoholics-anonymous.org
- **Cocaine Anonymous**, 425-244-1150, 800-723-1923, www.ca.org
- **Highline Recovery Services**, 206-242-2260

- **King County Alcoholism and Substance Abuse Services & Information**, 206-296-5213, www.metrokc.gov
- **King County Chemical Dependency Civil Commitment**, 206-296-7612
- **Nicotine Anonymous**, www.nicotine-anonymous.org
- **Salvation Army Adult Rehabilitation Center**, 206-587-0503, www.nwarmy.org
- **Valley Medical Recovery Center**, 425-228-3450, www.valleymed.org
- **Women's Recovery Center**, 206-547-1955

## ANIMALS

- **Animal Bites**, 911
- **City of Seattle Animal Shelter**, 206-386-4254, www.cityofseattle.net/animalshelter
- **City of Seattle Pet Licenses**, 206-386-4262, www.cityofseattle.net/animalshelter
- **Humane Society for Seattle/King County**, 425-641-0080, www.seattlehumane.org
- **The Humane Society of the United States**, 206-526-0949, www.hsus.org
- **King County Animal Services**, 206-296-7387, www.metrokc.gov

## THE ARTS

- **4Culture**, 206-296-7580, www.4culture.org
- **Humanities Washington**, 206-682-1770, www.humanities.org
- **Seattle Arts Commission**, 206-684-7171, www.cityofseattle.net/arts
- **Washington State Arts Commission**, 360-753-3860, www.arts.wa.gov

## AUTOMOBILES

- **American Automobile Association (AAA) of Washington**, 206-448-5353; Bellevue, 425-455-3933; Everett, 425-353-7222; Lynnwood, 425-775-3571; Renton, 425-251-6040; www.aaawa.com
- **City of Seattle—Abandoned Automobiles/Public Areas**, 206-684-8763, www.seattle.gov
- **City of Seattle—Illegally Parked Vehicles**, 206-625-5011, www.seattle.gov
- **City of Seattle—Inoperative Automobiles/Private Property**, 206-684-7899, www.seattle.gov
- **Department of Ecology**, 800-272-3780, www.ecy.wa.gov

- **King County Vehicle/Vessel License Information**, 206-296-4000, 206-296-2709 (TTY), www.metrokc.gov/lars/autoboat
- **Municipal Court of Seattle** (parking tickets/traffic violations), 206-684-5600, 206-684-5210 (TTY), www.ci.seattle.wa.us/courts
- **Seattle Police Department Auto Impound**, 206-684-5444, www.cityofseattle.net/police
- **Washington State Department of Licensing**, 360-902-3600, www.dol.wa.gov

## BIRTH AND DEATH RECORDS

- **King County Vital Statistics**, 206-296-4769, www.metrokc.gov
- **State of Washington Department of Health Center for Health Statistics**, Birth/Death/Marriage/Divorce Certificates, 360-236-4300, www.doh.wa.gov

## CHAMBERS OF COMMERCE

### SEATTLE
- **Ballard Chamber of Commerce**, 206-784-9705, www.ballardchamber.com
- **Beacon Hill Chamber of Commerce**, 206-264-1996, www.beaconhillchamber.com
- **Central Area Chamber of Commerce**, 206-325-2864
- **Fremont Chamber of Commerce**, 206-632-7156, www.fremontseattle.com
- **Greater Seattle Chamber of Commerce**, 206-389-7200, www.seattlechamber.com
- **Greater University Chamber of Commerce**, 206-547-4417, www.udistrictchamber.org
- **Greenwood-Phinney Chamber of Commerce**, 206-789-1148, www.greenwood-phinney.com
- **Lake City Chamber of Commerce**, 206-363-3287, www.lakecitychamber.org
- **Magnolia Chamber of Commerce**, 206-284-5836, www.magnoliachamber.org
- **Northgate Chamber of Commerce**, 206-522-9400, www.northgatechamber.com
- **Queen Anne Chamber of Commerce**, 206-283-6876, www.qachamber.org
- **Southwest King County Chamber of Commerce**, 206-575-1633, www.swkcc.org
- **Wallingford Chamber of Commerce**, 206-632-0645, www.wallingford.org
- **West Seattle Chamber of Commerce**, 206-932-5685, www.wschamber.com
- **White Center Community Development Corporation**, 206-412-5376

## EASTSIDE

- **Bellevue Chamber of Commerce**, 425-454-2464, www.bellevuechamber.org
- **Greater Issaquah Chamber of Commerce**, 425-392-7024, www.issaquah chamber.com
- **Greater Kirkland Chamber of Commerce**, 425-822-7066, www.kirkland chamber.org
- **Mercer Island Chamber of Commerce**, 206-232-3404, www.mercerisland chamber.org
- **Redmond Chamber of Commerce**, 425-885-4014, www.redmondchamber. org
- **Woodinville Chamber of Commerce**, 425-481-8300, www.woodinville chamber.org

## WEST

- **Bainbridge Island Chamber of Commerce**, 206-842-3700, www.bainbridge chamber.com
- **Bremerton Chamber of Commerce**, 360-479-3579, www.bremertonchamber. org
- **Vashon Chamber of Commerce**, 206-463-6217, www.vashonchamber.com

## NORTH

- **Everett Area Chamber of Commerce**, 425-252-5181, www.everettchamber. com
- **Greater Edmonds Chamber of Commerce**, 425-670-1496, www.edmondswa. com
- **Greater Bothell Chamber of Commerce**, 425-485-4353, www.bothellchamber. biz
- **Shoreline Chamber of Commerce**, 206-361-2260, www.shorecham.org
- **South Snohomish County Chamber of Commerce**, 425-774-0507, www. sscchamber.org

## SOUTH

- **Auburn Area Chamber of Commerce**, 253-833-0700, www.auburnareawa. org
- **Greater Federal Way Chamber of Commerce**, 253-838-2605, www.federal waychamber.com
- **Greater Renton Chamber of Commerce**, 425-226-4560, www.gorenton.com
- **Kent Chamber of Commerce**, 253-854-1770, www.kentchamber.com
- **Tacoma Pierce County Chamber of Commerce**, 253-627-2175, www.tacoma chamber.org

## CITY GOVERNMENTS

### SEATTLE

- **Citizens Service Bureau** (complaints and information), 206-684-2489, www.seattle.gov/citizenservice
- **City Attorney**, 206-684-8200, 206-233-7206 (TTY), www.seattle.gov/law
- **City Auditor**, 206-233-3801, www.seattle.gov/audit
- **City Council**, 206-684-8888, 206-233-0025 (TTY), www.seattle.gov/council
- **City Information**, 206-386-1234, 206-615-0476 (TTY), www.cityofseattle.net
- **Crime Prevention**, 206-684-7555, www.seattle.gov/police
- **Office for Civil Rights**, 206-684-4500, www.seattle.gov/civilrights
- **Mayor's Office**, 206-684-4000, www.seattle.gov/mayor
- **Neighborhoods**, 206-684-0464, www.seattle.gov/neighborhoods
- **Seattle Chamber of Commerce**, 206-389-7200, www.seattlechamber.com

### EASTSIDE

- **Bellevue**, 425-452-6800, www.ci.bellevue.wa.us
- **Duvall**, 425-788-1185, www.cityofduvall.com
- **Issaquah**, 425-837-3020, www.ci.issaquah.wa.us
- **Kirkland**, 425-828-1100, 425-828-2245 (TTY/TTD), www.ci.kirkland.wa.us
- **Mercer Island**, 206-236-5300, www.ci.mercer-island.wa.us
- **Newcastle**, 425-649-4444, www.ci.newcastle.wa.us
- **Redmond**, 425-556-2900, www.ci.redmond.wa.us
- **Snoqualmie**, 425-888-1555, www.ci.snoqualmie.wa.us
- **Woodinville**, 425-489-2700, www.ci.woodinville.wa.us

### WEST

- **Bainbridge Island**, 206-842-2545, www.ci.bainbridge-isl.wa.us
- **Bremerton**, www.ci.bremerton.wa.us

### NORTH

- **Bothell**, 425-486-3256, www.ci.bothell.wa.us
- **Edmonds**, 425-775-2525, www.ci.edmonds.wa.us
- **Everett**, 425-257-8700, www.everettwa.org
- **Kenmore**, 425-398-8900, www.cityofkenmore.com
- **Lake Forest Park**, 206-368-5440, www.cityoflfp.com
- **Lynnwood**, 425-775-1971, www.ci.lynnwood.wa.us
- **Mountlake Terrace**, 425-776-1161, www.ci.mountlake-terrace.wa.us
- **Shoreline**, 206-546-1700, 206-546-0457 (TTY), www.cityofshoreline.com

### SOUTH

- **Burien**, 206-241-4647, 206-248-5538 (TTY), www.ci.burien.wa.us

- **Des Moines**, 206-878-4595, www.desmoineswa.gov
- **Federal Way**, 253-661-4013, www.ci.federal-way.wa.us
- **Kent**, 253-856-5200, www.ci.kent.wa.us
- **Normandy Park**, 206-248-7603, www.ci.normandy-park.wa.us
- **Renton**, 425-430-6400, www.ci.renton.wa.us
- **SeaTac**, 206-241-9100, www.seatac.wa.gov
- **Tacoma**, 253-591-5000, www.cityoftacoma.org
- **Tukwila**, 206-433-1800, www.ci.tukwila.wa.us

## CONSUMER COMPLAINTS AND SERVICES

- **Better Business Bureau of Alaska, Oregon and Western Washington**, 206-431-2222, www.thebbb.org
- **Citizens Service Bureau**, 206-684-2489, www.seattle.gov/citizenservice
- **US Consumer Product Safety Commission**, 800-638-2772, 800-638-8270 (TTY), www.cpsc.gov
- **Federal Trade Commission Northwest Regional Office**, 877-382-4357, www.ftc.gov
- **State of Washington Attorney General's Office**, 206-464-7744, 800-276-9883 (announcement line), www.atg.wa.gov
- **State of Washington Consumer Protection Complaints and Inquiries**, 206-464-6684, 800-551-4636, www.atg.wa.gov/consumer
- **State of Washington, Office of Insurance Commissioner**, 360-753-7300, 800-562-6900, www.insurance.wa.gov

## COUNTY GOVERNMENTS

### KING

- **King County Executive**, 206-296-4040, 206-296-0200 (TTY), www.metrokc.gov/exec
- **King County Department of Development and Environmental Services**, 206-296-6600, 206-296-7217 (TTY), www.metrokc.gov/ddes
- **King County Health Services**, 206-296-4600, www.metrokc.gov/health
- **Metropolitan King County Council**, 206-296-1000, 206-296-1024 (TTY/TDD), www.metrokc.gov/mkcc

### PIERCE

- **Pierce County Council**, 253-798-7777, 253-798-4018 (TDD), www.co.pierce.wa.us

- **Pierce County Executive**, 253-798-7477, www.co.pierce.wa.us
- **Tacoma-Pierce County Health Department**, 253-798-6500, 800-992-2456, www.tpchd.org
- **Pierce County Planning and Land Services Department**, 253-798-7210, www.co.pierce.wa.us

## SNOHOMISH

- **Snohomish County Executive**, 425-388-3460, www.co.snohomish.wa.us/executiv
- **Snohomish County Council**, 425-388-3494, www1.co.snohomish.wa.us/departments/council
- **Snohomish Health District**, 425-258-4227, www.snohd.org
- **Snohomish County Planning and Development Services**, 425-388-3311, www1.co.snohomish.wa.us/departments/pds

## CRIME

- **Crime in Progress**, 911
- **City of Seattle Crime Prevention**, 206-684-7555, www.seattle.gov/police

## CRISIS LINES

### CHILD ABUSE AND NEGLECT

- **New Beginnings for Battered Women and their Children**, (TTY/Voice) 206-522-9472, www.newbegin.org
- **State of Washington Department of Social and Health Services—Child Abuse Reporting**, (24-hours) 206-721-6500, (weekdays), 425-649-4110; East King County, 425-649-4110, 800-952-0073; South King County, 253-872-2665, 800-422-7880; North Seattle, 206-721-6500, 800-379-3395; South Seattle, 206-721-6500, 800-379-4139; www.dshs.wa.gov
- **State of Washington Domestic Violence Hotline**, 800-562-6025, www.courts.wa.gov

### CRISIS HOTLINE

- **Crisis Clinic 24-hour Crisis Line**, 206-461-3222, 206-461-3219 (TDD)

### DOMESTIC ABUSE

- **Domestic Abuse Women's Network**, 425-656-7867, www.dawnonline.org
- **King County Domestic Violence Automated Information Service**, 206-205-5555, www.metrokc.gov/dvinfo

- **National Domestic Violence Hotline**, 800-799-SAFE, 800-787-3224 (TTY), www.ndvh.org
- **New Beginnings for Battered Women and their Children**, (TTY/Voice) 206-522-9472, www.newbegin.org
- **State of Washington Adult Protective Services**, 206-341-7660, 800-346-9257, www.aasa.dshs.wa.gov
- **State of Washington Domestic Violence Hotline**, 800-562-6025, www.courts.wa.gov

## RAPE AND SEXUAL ASSAULT

- **Harborview Center for Sexual Assault and Traumatic Stress**, 206-521-1800, http://depts.washington.edu/hcsata
- **King County Sexual Assault Resource Center**, 425-226-7273, 800-825-7273, www.kcsarc.org

## DISABLED, SERVICES FOR THE

See the **Helpful Services** chapter.

## DISCRIMINATION

- **City of Seattle Office for Civil Rights**, 206-684-4500, 206-684-4503 (TTY), www.seattle.gov/civilrights
- **City of Seattle Office for Civil Rights**, Hate Crimes Hotline, 206-233-1080, www. seattle.gov /civilrights
- **State of Washington Human Rights Commission**, (Voice/TTY) 206-464-6500, www.hum.wa.gov

## EMERGENCY

- **Fire, Police, Medical**, 911
- **Federal Emergency Management Agency**, 425-487-4600, 800-525-0321, www.fema.gov

## FEDERAL OFFICES/CENTERS

- **Centers for Disease Control and Prevention**, 404-639-3311, www.cdc.gov
- **Consumer Product Safety Commission**, 800-638-2772, 800-638-8270 (TTY), www.cpsc.gov

- **Federal Consumer Information Center**, 888-878-3256, www.pueblo.gsa.gov
- **Federal Emergency Management Agency**, 425-487-4600, 800-525-0321, www.fema.gov
- **Federal Information Center**, 800-688-9889, 800-326-2996 (TTY), http://fic. info.gov
- **Small Business Administration**, 206-553-7310, 206-553-7349 (TTY), www. sbaonline.sba.gov
- **Social Security Administration**, 800-772-1213, 800-325-0778 (TTY), www. ssa.gov
- **US Attorney**, Western District of Washington, 206-553-7970, www.usdoj.gov
- **US Census Bureau**, 206-553-5837, www.census.gov
- **US Government Bookstore**, 206-553-4270, http://bookstore.gpo.gov

## GARBAGE

- **Seattle Public Utilities Household Hazardous Waste**, 206-296-4692, www. seattle.gov
- **Seattle Public Utilities Recycling and Disposal Station Information Line**, 684-8400, www. seattle.gov
- **Seattle Public Utilities Solid Waste Services**, **Missed Collection Hotline**, 206-684-7600, 206-233-7241 (TTY), www. seattle.gov

## HEALTH AND MEDICAL CARE

### STATE OF WASHINGTON
- **Washington State Healthcare Authority**, 800-826-2444, www.hca.wa.gov
- **Healthy Mothers, Healthy Babies**, 800-322-2588, www.hmhbwa.org
- **State of Washington Department of Social and Health Services**, 360-902-8400, 800-737-0617, www1.dshs.wa.gov

### SEATTLE
- **Children's Hospital & Medical Center Resource Line**, 206-526-2500, 877-526-2500, www.seattlechildrens.org
- **Columbia Public Health Center**, 206-296-4650, www.metrokc.gov/health
- **Community Health Access Program**, 206-284-0331
- **Downtown Public Health Center**, 206-296-4755, www.metrokc.gov/health
- **Harborview Medical Center Sexually Transmitted Disease Program**, 206-731-3590
- **King County Communicable Disease 24-Hour Report Line**, 206-296-4782, www.metrokc.gov/health

- **King County Health Services**, (TTY/Voice) 206-296-4600, www.metrokc.gov/health
- **King County HIV/STD Hotline**, 206-205-7837, www.metrokc.gov/health
- **King County HIV/AIDS Program**, 206-296-4649, www.metrokc.gov/health
- **King County Immunization Program Information**, 206-296-4774, www.metrokc.gov/health
- **King County Medical Society**, 206-621-9393, www.kcmsociety.org
- **North Seattle Public Health Center**, 206-296-4765, www.metrokc.gov/health
- **Northwest Hospital MED-INFO Physician Referral Line**, 206-633-4636, 206-368-1571 (TDD), www.nwhospital.org
- **Seattle Indian Health Board**, 206-324-9360, 800-367-5978, www.sihb.org

## SURROUNDING COMMUNITIES

- **Eastgate Public Health Center**, 206-296-4920, www.metrokc.gov/health
- **Federal Way Public Health Center**, 253-838-4557, www.metrokc.gov/health
- **Highline Community Hospital 24-NURSE Information Line**, 206-246-8773, www.hchnet.org
- **Kent Public Health Center**, 206-296-4500, www.metrokc.gov/health
- **Northshore Public Health Center**, 206-296-9787, www.metrokc.gov/health
- **Renton Public Health Center**, 206-296-4700, www.metrokc.gov/health
- **White Center Public Health Center**, 206-296-4646, www.metrokc.gov/health

## HOUSING

- **Central Area Motivation Program**, 206-812-4940, www.seattle.gov
- **King County Housing Authority**, 206-574-1100, 206-574-1108 (TDD), www.kcha.org
- **King County Housing Rehabilitation Programs & Repair Hotline**, 206-296-8672, www.metrokc.gov/dchs/csd/Housing
- **Seattle Housing Authority**, 206-615-3300, www.seattlehousing.org
- **Seattle Office for Civil Rights Housing Discrimination**, 206-684-4500, www.seattle.gov/civilrights
- **Tenants Union**, 206-723-0500, www.tenantsunion.org
- **Urban League of Metropolitan Seattle**, 206-461-3792, www.urbanleague.org
- **Department of Housing and Urban Development**, 206-220-5204, www.hud.gov

## LEGAL REFERRAL

- **City of Seattle Attorney**, 206-684-8200, 206-233-7206 (TTY), www.seattle. gov/law
- **King County Bar Association, Lawyer Referral and Information Service**, 206-623-2551, www.kcba.org
- **King County Prosecuting Attorney's Protection Order Advocacy Program**, 206-296-9547, www.metrokc.gov/proatty
- **Legal Action Center**, 206-324-6890, www.lac.org
- **Northwest Women's Law Center**, 206-621-7691, www.nwwlc.org
- **Unemployment Law Project**, 206-441-9178, www.unemploymentlawproject. org
- **Volunteer Legal Services**, 206-623-0281

## LIBRARIES

See the **Neighborhoods** chapter for branch libraries.

- **Everett Public Library**, 425-257-8000, www.epls.org
- **King County Library System**, 425-369-3200, 800-462-9600, www.kcls.org
- **Kitsap Regional Library**, 360-405-9100, www.krl.org
- **Pierce County Library System**, 253-536-6500, www.pcl.lib.wa.us
- **Seattle Public Library**, 206-386-4636, www.spl.lib.wa.us
- **Sno-Isle Regional Library System**, 425-778-2148, www.sno-isle.org
- **Tacoma Public Library**, 253-591-5666, www.tpl.lib.wa.us

## MARRIAGE LICENSES

- **King County Marriage Licenses**, 206-296-3933, www.metrokc.gov/lars/ marriage
- **Kitsap County Marriage Licenses**, 360-337-4935, www.kitsapgov.com
- **Pierce County Marriage Licenses**, 253-798-7030, www.co.pierce.wa.us
- **Snohomish County Marriage Licenses**, 425-388-3627, www.co.snohomish. wa.us

## PARKS

See the **Neighborhoods** chapter for community center locations, or the **Sports and Recreation** or **Greenspace and Beaches** chapters for individual parks.

## SEATTLE AND KING COUNTY

- **King County Parks and Recreation Department**, 206-296-4232, 206-296-4245 (TTY), www.metrokc.gov/parks
- **Seattle Parks and Recreation Department**, 206-684-4075, 206-684-4950 (TTY), www.seattle.govparks

## EASTSIDE

- **Bellevue Parks and Community Services Department**, 425-452-6881, www.ci.bellevue.wa.us/parks_homepage.htm
- **Issaquah Parks and Recreation Department**, 425-837-3300, www.ci.issaquah.wa.us
- **Kirkland Department of Parks & Community Services**, 425-828-1100, www.ci.kirkland.wa.us
- **Mercer Island Parks and Recreation**, 206-236-3545, www.ci.mercer-island.wa.us
- **Newcastle Parks Department**, 425-649-4444, www.ci.newcastle.wa.us
- **Redmond Parks and Recreation**, 425-556-2311, www.ci.redmond.wa.us
- **Snoqualmie Community Development**, 425-888-5337, www.ci.snoqualmie.wa.us
- **Woodinville Recreation and Parks**, 425-398-9327, www.ci.woodinville.wa.us

## WEST

- **Bainbridge Island Park and Recreation District**, 206-842-2302, www.biparks.org

## NORTH

- **Bothell Parks and Recreation**, 425-486-7430, www.ci.bothell.wa.us/departments/publicworks
- **Edmonds Parks, Recreation & Cultural Services**, 425-771-0230, www.ci.edmonds.wa.us
- **Everett Parks and Recreation**, 425-257-8300, www.everettwa.org/parks
- **Kenmore Parks**, 425-398-8900, www.cityofkenmore.com/local
- **Lake Forest Park Parks**, 206-368-5440, www.cityoflfp.com
- **Lynnwood Parks, Recreation and Cultural Arts Department**, 425-744-6475, www.ci.lynnwood.wa.us
- **Mountlake Terrace Recreation and Parks**, 425-776-9173, www.cityofmlt.com/departments/parks
- **Shoreline Parks**, 206-546-6517, www.cityofshoreline.com

## SOUTH

- **Burien Parks, Recreation and Cultural Services**, 206-988-3700, www. ci.burien.wa.us
- **Des Moines Parks**, 206-878-4595, www.desmoineswa.gov
- **Kent Parks, Recreation and Community Services**, 253-856-5100, www. ci.kent.wa.us/ParksRecreation
- **Renton Community Services**, 425-430-6600, http://rentonwa.gov
- **SeaTac Parks and Recreation**, 206-241-9100, www.ci.seatac.wa.us
- **Tacoma Metropolitan Park District**, 253-305-1000, www.metroparkstacoma. org
- **Tukwila Parks and Recreation Department**, 206-767-2342, www.ci.tukwila. wa.us

## POLICE

### STATE OF WASHINGTON

- **Emergency**, 911
- **Washington State Patrol Non-Emergency**, 425-649-4370, 425-649-4367 (TTY), www.wa.gov/wsp

### SEATTLE AND KING COUNTY

- **Emergency**, 911
- **King County Sheriff's Office Non-Emergency**, 206-296-3311, www.metrokc. gov/sheriff
- **Seattle Police Department Non-Emergency**, 206-625-5011, www.seattle. gov/police
- **Seattle Police Department East Precinct**, 206-684-4300, www. seattle. gov/police
- **Seattle Police Department North Precinct**, 206-684-0850, www. seattle. gov/police
- **Seattle Police Department South Precinct**, 206-386-1850, www. seattle. gov/police
- **Seattle Police Department West Precinct**, 206-684-8917, www. seattle. govpolice
- **Seattle Police Department Southwest Precinct**, 206-733-9800, www.seattle. govpolice

### EASTSIDE

- **Bellevue Police Department**, 425-452-6917, 877-881-2731, www.ci. bellevue.wa.us/police_home.htm
- **Issaquah Police Department**, 425-837-3200, www.ci.issaquah.wa.us/police

- **Kirkland Police Department**, 425-828-1183, 425-822-1244 (TDD), www. ci.kirkland.wa.us
- **Mercer Island Police Division**, 206-236-3500, www.ci.mercer-island.wa.us
- **Newcastle Police Department**, 425-649-4444, www.ci.newcastle.wa.us
- **Redmond Police Department**, 425-556-2500, www.ci.redmond.wa.us
- **Snoqualmie Police Division**, 425-888-3333, www.ci.snoqualmie.wa.us

## NORTH

- **Bothell Police Department**, 425-486-1254, www.ci.bothell.wa.us
- **Edmonds Police Department**, 425-771-0200, www.ci.edmonds.wa.us/police_dept.stm
- **Everett Police Department**, 425-257-8400, www.everettwa.org
- **Lake Forest Park Police Department**, 206-364-8216, www.cityoflfp.com/police
- **Lynnwood Police Department**, 425-744-6900, www.ci.lynnwood.wa.us
- **Mountlake Terrace Police Department**, 425-670-8260, www.cityofmlt.com
- **Shoreline Police Department**, 206-546-6730, www.cityofshoreline.com/cityhall

## SOUTH

- **Kent Police Department**, 253-856-5800, www.ci.kent.wa.us/Police
- **Renton Police Department**, 425-430-7500, http://rentonwa.gov/government
- **SeaTac Police Services**, 206-241-9100, www.ci.seatac.wa.us/department/policehomepage
- **Tacoma Police Department**, 253-5915905, www.cityoftacoma.org
- **Tukwila Police Department**, 206-433-1808, www.ci.tukwila.wa.us

## POST OFFICE

- **Addresses**—see the **Neighborhoods** chapter for branch stations.
- **US Postal Service**, 800-275-8777, www.usps.com

## ROAD CONDITION INFORMATION

- **Washington State Department of Transportation Highway Information Line**, 511, 206-368-HIWY, www.wsdot.wa.gov

## RECYCLING

- **City of Seattle Recycling Information**, 206-684-3000
- **State of Washington Recycling Information**, 800-732-9253

## SCHOOLS

### GREATER SEATTLE
- **Auburn School District**, 253-931-4900, www.auburn.wednet.edu
- **Bellevue School District**, 425-456-4111, 425-456-4211 (TTY), www.bsd405.org
- **Bremerton School District**, 360-478-5151, www.bremertonschools.org
- **Edmonds School District**, 425-670-7000, www.edmonds.wednet.edu
- **Federal Way Public Schools**, 253-945-2000, www.fwsd.wednet.edu
- **Highline School District**, 206-433-0111, www.hsd401.org
- **Issaquah School District**, 425-837-7000, www.issaquah.wednet.edu
- **Kent School District**, 253-373-7000, www.kent.wednet.edu
- **Lake Washington School District**, 425-702-3200, www.lkwash.wednet.edu
- **Mercer Island School District**, 206-236-3330, www.misd.k12.wa.us
- **Northshore School District**, 425-489-6000, www.nsd.org
- **Renton School District**, 425-204-2300, www.renton.wednet.edu
- **Shoreline School District**, 206-367-6111, www.shorelineschools.org
- **Tukwila School District**, 206-901-8000, www.tukwila.wednet.edu
- **Vashon Island School District**, 206-408-8100, www.vashonsd.wednet.edu

### SEATTLE PUBLIC
- **Administrative Center**, 206-252-0000, www.seattleschools.org
- **Automated Enrollment Services Line**, 206-252-0410
- **Bilingual Family Center**, 206-252-7750
- **Central Enrollment Service Center**, 206-720-3533
- **Customer Service Center**, 206-252-0010
- **Highly Capable Services**, 206-252-0130
- **North Enrollment Service Center**, 206-252-0765
- **School Board**, 206-252-0040
- **South Enrollment Service Center**, 206-252-7732
- **Superintendent's Office**, 206-252-0100
- **Special Education Services**, 206-252-0055
- **Transportation Services**, 206-252-0900
- **Wait List Automated Info Line**, 206-252-0212
- **West Seattle Enrollment Service Center**, 206-252-8660

## SHIPPING SERVICES

- **DHL Worldwide Express**, 800-225-5345, www.dhl-usa.com
- **FedEx**, 800-238-5355, www.fedex.com/us
- **FedEx Ground**, 800-238-5355, www.fedex.com/us

- **United Parcel Service (UPS)**, 800-742-5877, www.ups.com
- **US Postal Service Express Mail**, 800-222-1811, www.usps.com

## SOCIAL SECURITY

- **Social Security Administration**, 800-772-1213, 800-325-0778 (TTY), www.ssa.gov

## SPORTS

- **Everett Aqua Sox** (Northwest League Baseball), 425-258-3673, 800-GO-FROGS, www.aquasox.com
- **Seattle Mariners** (Major League Baseball), 206-346-4000, 206-322-HITS (tickets), http://mariners.mlb.com
- **Seattle Seahawks** (National Football League), 800-300-9540, 206-515-4791 (tickets), www.seahawks.com
- **Seattle Sounders** (A-League Soccer), 206-622-3415, 800-796-5425, www.seattlesounders.net
- **Seattle Sonics** (National Basketball Association), 206-283-DUNK, www.nba.com/sonics
- **Seattle Storm** (Women's National Basketball Association), 206-217-WNBA, www.wnba.com/storm
- **Seattle Thunderbirds** (Western Hockey League), 206-448-PUCK, www.seattle-thunderbirds.com
- **Tacoma Rainiers** (Pacific Coast League Baseball), 800-281-3834, www.tacomarainiers.com
- **University of Washington Huskies** (all teams), 206-543-2200, http://gohuskies.fansonly.com

## STATE OF WASHINGTON

- **Attorney General's Office**, 206-464-7744, 800-276-9883 (TTY), www.atg.wa.gov
- **General Information**, 800-321-2808, www.wa.gov
- **Governor's Office**, 360-753-6780, 360-753-6466 (TTY), www.governor.wa.gov
- **Legislative Hotline,** 800-562-6000
- **Secretary of State, General Information and Elections**, 360-902-4151, 800-422-8683 (TTY), www.secstate.wa.gov

## STREET MAINTENANCE

- **City of Seattle Street Repairs**, 206-386-1218 (asphalt and concrete), 206-386-1206 (emergency signs and signals), www.seattle.gov
- **King County Transportation Department Road Services Division**, 206-296-8100, 800-527-6237, 206-296-0933 (TTY), www.metrokc.gov/roadcon
- **State of Washington Department of Transportation**, 206-440-4000; Emergency Maintenance, 206-440-4490; Maintenance Administration, 206-440-4650, www.wsdot.wa.gov

## TAXES

### CITY
- **City of Seattle Finance Office**, 206-684-8300; City Business Tax, 206-684-8484, www.seattle.gov/financedepartment

### COUNTY
- **King County Assessor's Office**, 206-296-7300, 206-296-7888 (TTY), www.metrokc.gov/assessor
- **King County Personal Property Tax Line**, 206-296-4290, 206-296-4184 (TTY), www.metrokc.gov/assessor
- **King County Property Tax Advisor**, 206-196-5202, www.metrokc.gov/assessor
- **King County Real Estate Tax Information**, 206-296-0923 (automated), 206-296-3850, www.metrokc.gov/assessor

### FEDERAL
- **Internal Revenue Service**, Federal Tax Questions, 800-829-1040, 800-829-4059 (TTY); 24-hour Recorded Tax Help, 800-829-4477; www.irs.gov
- **Internal Revenue Service Local Taxpayer Advocate**, 206-220-6037, outside Seattle, 877-777-4778

### STATE (NO INCOME TAX)
- **Washington State Department of Revenue**, 425-277-7300, 800-647-7706, http://dor.wa.gov

## TAXIS

- **Farwest Taxi**, 206-622-1717
- **Orange Cab**, 206-522-8800, www.orangecab.net
- **Yellow Cab**, 206-622-6500

## TIME OF DAY/CURRENT TEMPERATURE, 206-361-TIME (8463)

## TOURISM

- **Canada, British Columbia**, 800-435-5622, www.hellobc.com
- **National Park Service**, 202-208-6843; Pacific West Region, 510-817-1300, www.nps.gov
- **National Park Service Campground Reservations**, 800-365-2267, www.nps.gov
- **Seattle–King County Convention and Visitors Bureau**, 206-461-5800, 206-461-5840 (TDD), www.seeseattle.org
- **State of Idaho**, 800-635-7820, www.visitid.org
- **State of Oregon**, 800-547-7842, www.traveloregon.com
- **Washington State Department of Tourism**, 800-890-5493, 360-725-5052, www.experiencewashington.com

## TRANSPORTATION

### AIRPORTS

- **Seattle-Tacoma International Airport**, 206-431-4444, www.portseattle.org/seatac
- **King County International Airport** (Boeing Field), 206-296-7380, www.metrokc.gov/airport
- **Paine Field Airport** (Everett), 425-353-2110, www.painefield.com
- **Renton Municipal Airport**, 425-430-7471, www.ci.renton.wa.us/pw

### BUSES

- **Community Transit**, 425-353-RIDE or 800-562-1375, www.commtrans.org
- **Everett Transit**, 425-257-8803, www.everettwa.org
- **Pierce Transit**, 253-581-8000, 800-562-8109, www.ptbus.pierce.wa.us
- **Greyhound Bus Line**s, 800-231-2222, www.greyhound.com
- **Metro Transit**, 206-553-3000, http://transit.metrokc.gov
- **Seattle Personal Transit**, (TTY/Voice) 206-860-8000
- **Senior Services Volunteer Transportation**, 206-448-5740, www.seniorservices.org
- **ST Express**, 800-201-4900, www.soundtransit.org

### TRAINS

- **Amtrak National Route Information**, 800-USA-RAIL, www.amtrak.com
- **Amtrak Seattle Station**, 206-382-4125

- **Sounder Commuter Trains**, 206-398-5000, 800-201-4900, 888-713-6030 (TTY), www.soundtransit.org

## FERRIES

- **Washington State Ferries**, 206-464-6400, 888-8087977, www.wsdot.wa.gov/ferries

## RIDE-SHARING PROGRAMS

- **Metro Transit Ridematch and Vanpool**, 888-814-1300, 800-833-6388 (TTY), www.rideshareonline.com

## UTILITY EMERGENCIES

- **Puget Sound Energy**, 888-225-5773, 800-962-9498 (TTY), www.pse.com
- **Seattle City Light**, 206-684-3000, 206-223-0025 (TTY), www.seattle.gov/light
- **Seattle City Light 24-Hour Power Outage Hotline**, 206-684-7400
- **Seattle City Light 24-Hour Electrical Emergency**, 206-706-0051
- **Seattle Public Utilities**, 206-684-3000, 206-233-7241 (TTY), www.seattle.gov/util
- **Seattle Public Utilities Emergency Resource Center** (activated during major emergencies), 206-684-3355
- **Seattle Public Utilities Missed Collection Hotline**, 206-684-7600
- **Seattle Public Utilities Sewer or Surface Drainage Emergencies**, 206-386-1800
- **Snohomish County Public Utility District**, 425-783-1000, www.snopud.com
- **Tacoma Power**, 253-502-8602, www.cityoftacoma.org.

## VOTING

- **King County Voter Registration**, 206-296-8683, www.metrokc.gov
- **Washington State Voting and Elections Information**, vote.wa.gov
- **Washington State Voter Registration Information**, 800-448-4881

## WASHINGTON STATE LOTTERY

- **Seattle Regional Office**, 206-764-6456
- **Winning Numbers**, 800-545-7510, www.walottery.com

## WEATHER

- **National Weather Service Forecast Office**, 206-526-6087, www.wrh.noaa. gov/sew
- **KING 5 TV Weather**, www.king5.com/weather
- **KIRO TV Weather**, www.kirotv.com/weather
- **KOMO TV Weather**, www.komotv.com/weather

## ZIP CODES

- **US Postal Service**, 800-275-8777, www.usps.com

AAA. . . . . . . . . . . . . . . . . . . . . . . . . . . . 144, 344, 372
AIDS . . . . . . . . . . . . . . . . . . 198, 317-318, 364, 380
ATM. . . . . . . . . . . . . . . . . . . . . . . . . . . . . . . . . . 153
Activity Clubs . . . . . . . . . . . . . . . . . . . . . . . . . . . 285
Address Locator. . . . . . . . . . . . . . . . . . . . . . . . .9-11
Admiral . . . . . . . . . . . . . . . . . . . . . . . . 72-73, 312
African American Academy . . . . . . . . . . . . . . . . . . .
Aging. . . . . . . . . . . . . . . . . . . . . . . . . . . . . . . . . . 370
Air Pollution. . . . . . . . . . . . . . . . . . . . . . . . . 299-300
Airlines . . . . . . . . . . . . . . . . . . . . . . . . . . . . 337-338
Airports 44, 65, 70, 107, 113-114, 299, 326, 331-333,
337-341, 388
Alcohol and Drug Abuse . . . . . . . . . . . .171, 318, 371
Alki. . . . . . . . . . . . . . . . . . . . . . . . . . . . . . . 72-75
Alki Beach Park . . . . . . . . . . . . . . . . . . . . . . . . . 201
Alternative Lodgings . . . . . . . . . . . . . . . . . . . . . . 348
Alternative Rock. . . . . . . . . . . . . . .37, 231, 236, 363
Amtrak. . . . . . . . . . . . . . . . . . . . . . . . 335-336, 388
Animals. . . . . . . . . .180-182, 292-293, 318, 366, 372
Antique Shops and Districts . . . . 20, 37, 40, 98, 216,
223-224, 353, 354, 359
Apartment Hunting. . . . . . . . . . . . . . . . 124-133, 141
Apartment Search Firms . . . . . . . . . . . . . . 127, 343
Apple Cup. . . . . . . . . . . . . . . . . . . . . . . . . . . .5, 365
Appliances . . . . . . . . . . 128, 131-132, 217, 219-220
Arab Festival. . . . . . . . . . . . . . . . . . . . . . . . . . . . 361
Architecture . . . . . . . . . . . . . . .16, 95, 99, 250, 367
Art Galleries . . . . . . . . . . . .20, 42, 68, 105, 243-244
Art Museums . . . . .5, 21, 29, 120-121, 241-243, 335
Art Walks. . . . . . . . . . . . . . . . . . 105, 231, 244-245
Au Pairs . . . . . . . . . . . . . . . . . . . . . . . . 182, 200-201
Auburn . . . . . . . . . . . . . . . . . . . . . . . . . . . . . . . 112
Aurora. . . . . . . . . . . . . . . . . . . . . . . . . . . . . . 53-54
Auto Impound. . . . . . . . . . . . . . . . . . . . . . . 167, 373
Automobile Insurance . . . . . . . . . . . . . . . . 170-171
Automobile Registration. . . . . . . . . . . . . . . . . . . 169
Automobile Repair. . . . . . . . . . . . . . . . . . . . . . . . 188
Automobile Safety . . . . . . . . . . . . . . . . . . 171, 189
Automobiles . . . . . . . . . . . . . . . . . . . 167-174, 372
Babysitting . . . . . . . . . . . . . . . . . . . . . . . . . . . . 201
Bailey Peninsula. . . . . . . . . . . . . . . . . . . . . . . . . 290
Bainbridge Island . . . . . . . . . . . . . . . . . . . . 104-105
Ballard. . . . . . . . . . . . . . . . . . . . . . . . . . . . . . 36-38
Ballet. . . . . . . . . . . . . . . . . . .3, 33, 234, 319, 366
Bank Accounts and Services. . . . . . . . . . . . . 153-155

Banking. . . . . . . . . . . . . . . . . . . . . . . . . . . . 153-155
Bars and Nightclubs. . . . . . . . . . . . . . . . . . 235-238
Baseball, College . . . . . . . . . . . . . . . . . . . . . . . . 258
Baseball/Softball, Participant. . . . . . . . . . . . . . . . 261
Baseball, Professional . . . . . . . . . . . . . . . . 256-257
Basketball, College . . . . . . . . . . . . . . . . . . . . . . . 259
Basketball, Participant . . . . . . . . . . . . . . . . 261-262
Basketball, Professional . . . . . . . . . . . . . . . . . . . 257
Bayside. . . . . . . . . . . . . . . . . . . . . . . . . . . . 102-103
Beaches . . . . 104, 113, 118, 266, 280, 287-295, 352,
254-255, 365
Beacon Hill . . . . . . . . . . . . . . . . . . . . . . . . . . 65-66
Bed & Breakfasts . . . . . . . . . . . . . . . . . . . . 347-348
Beds, Bedding & Bath . . . . . . . . . . . . . . . . . . . . 220
Bellevue . . . . . . . . . . . . . . . . . . . . . . . . . . . . 80-82
Bellevue Art and Crafts Fair. . . . . . . . . . . . . 242, 361
Belltown . . . . . . . . . . . . . . . . . . . . . . . . . . . . 20-24
Benson . . . . . . . . . . . . . . . . . . . . . . . . . . . 107-110
Better Business Bureau. . . . .145, 148, 188-189, 376
Bicycle Helmet Safety Institute . . . . . . . . . . . . . . 333
Bicycling . . . . . . . . . . . . . . . 262-263, 285, 332-333
Bike to Work Month . . . . . . . . . . . . . . . . . . . . . . 359
Bird Watching. . . . . . . . . . . . . . . 263, 288, 290-291
Birth and Death Records . . . . . . . . . . . . . . . . . . . 373
Bite of Seattle . . . . . . . . . . . . . . . . . . . . . . . . 33, 361
Bitter Lake. . . . . . . . . . . . . . . . . . . . 2, 54-56, 96
Blackberry Festival. . . . . . . . . . . . . . . . . . . . . . . 363
Block Watch . . . . . . . . . . . . . . . . . . . . . . . . . . . . 183
Blue Ridge . . . . . . . . . . . . . . . . . . . . . . . . . . . 36-40
Blues, Jazz. . . . . . . . . . . . . . . . . . . . . . . . . . . . . 236
Boating . . . . . . . . . . . . . . . . . . . . . 263-265, 360
Boeing. . 39, 70, 81, 95, 102-103, 107, 114, 117, 159,
246-247, 340-341, 388
Boeing Field . . . . . . . . . . . . . . . . . . . . .70, 340, 388
Bookstores . . . . . . . . . . . . . . . . . . . . . . 247-249, 379
Bothell. . . . . . . . . . . . . . . . . . . . . . . . . . . . . 98-99
Bowl, The . . . . . . . . . . . . . . . . . . . . . . . . . . . 99-100
Bowling. . . . . . . . . . . . . . . . . . . . .265, 288, 294
BrasilFest . . . . . . . . . . . . . . . . . . . . . . . . . . . . . 362
Bremerton. . . . . . . . . . . . . . . . . . . . . . . . . 105-106
Bridle Trails. . . . . . . . . . . . . . . . . . . . . . . . . . 80-82
Broadmoor . . . . . . . . . . . . . . . . . . . . . . . . . . 38-40
Broadview. . . . . . . . . . . . . . . . . . . . . . . . . . . 55-56
Brookside . . . . . . . . . . . . . . . . . . . . . . . . . . . 80-82
Brothers, The . . . . . . . . . . . . . . . . . . . . . . . . 2, 354

Bryant . . . . . . . . . . . . . . . . . . . . . . . . . . . . . . 48-51
Buddhism . . . . . . . . . . . . . . . . . . . . . . . . . . . . . 304
Budget Stays . . . . . . . . . . . . . . . . . . . . . . . . 346-347
Bulletin Boards . . . . . . . . . . . . . . . . . . . 124, 126-127
Bumbershoot . . . . . . . . . . . . . . . . . . . . . . . . 33, 363
Bureau of Consular Affairs. . . . . . . . . . . . . . . . . 176
Bureau of Educational and Cultural Affairs. . . . . . 201
Burien . . . . . . . . . . . . . . . . . . . . . . . . . . . . . .113-114
Burke-Gilman Trail . . . 44, 49, 56, 262, 271, 275, 289
Burke Museum. . . . . . . . . . . . . . . . . . . . . . . 48, 245
Bus Routes, Sea-Tac. . . . . . . . . . . . . . . . . . 339-341
Bus Service, National. . . . . . . . . . . . . . . . . . . . 337
Bus Service, Regional . . . . . . . . . . . . . . . . . 334-335
Buses . . . . . . . . . . . . . . . . . . . . . . . . . . . . . 334-335
Butchart Gardens. . . . . . . . . . . . . . . . . . . . . . . 352
Buying, Home. . . . . . . . . . . . . . . . . . . . . . . 133-142
Cable Television . . . . . . . . . . . . . . . . . . . . . . . . 176
Cambodian Cultural Heritage Festival . . . . . . . . . 362
Canoeing . . . . . . . . . . . . . . . . . . . . . . . . . . . . . 264
Cantergrove . . . . . . . . . . . . . . . . . . . . . . . . . 89-91
Capitol Hill. . . . . . . . . . . . . . . . . . . . . . . . . . . 28-30
Car Rental . . . . . . . . . . . . . . . . . . . . . . . . . . . . 332
Carkeek Park . . . . . . . . . . . . . . . . . . . .39, 55, 288
Carillon Point . . . . . . . . . . . . . . . . . . . . . . . . . . . 86
Carpets & Rugs . . . . . . . . . . . . . . . . . . . . . 220-221
Carpool Parking . . . . . . . . . . . . . . . . . . . . .172, 327
Carpooling . . . . . . . . . . . . . . . . . . . . . . . . 327-328
Cascade . . . . . . . . . . . . . . . . . . . . . . . . . . . 20-24
Cascade Mountains 5, 11, 37, 64, 269, 276, 353, 359
Cellular Phones . . . . . . . . . . . . . . . . . . . . . 163-164
Center School, The . . . . . . . . . . . . . . . . . . . . . 263
Central District . . . . . . . . . . . . . . . . . . . . . . . 61-63
Chambers of Commerce. . . . . . . . . . . . . . . 373-374
Champagne Point . . . . . . . . . . . . . . . . . . . . . 86-87
Chess . . . . . . . . . . . . . . . . . . . . . . . . . . . . . . . 265
Child Abuse and Neglect. . . . . . . . . . . . . . . . . . 377
Child Safety . . . . . . . . . . . . . . . . . . . . . . . 201-202
**Childcare and Education** . . . . . . . . . . . . . . 197-214
Childcare Resources . . . . . . . . . . . . . . . . . . . . . 199
Children and Culture . . . . . . . . . . . . . . . . . 251-254
Children and Moving . . . . . . . . . . . . . . . . . . 149-150
Children's Hospital & Regional Medical Center 56-57,
179, 202, 379
China Creek . . . . . . . . . . . . . . . . . . . . . . . . . . . 83
Chinatown. . . . . . . . . . . . . . . . . . . 25-26, 226, 361
Chinatown International District Summer Festival 361
Chinese Culture and Arts Festival. . . . . . . . . . . . 360
Chinese New Year . . . . . . . . . . . . . . . . . . . . . . . 357
Christianity . . . . . . . . . . . . . . . . . . . . . . . . 304-313
Christmas Ship Festival. . . . . . . . . . . . . . . . . . . 365
Churches . . . . . . . . . . . . . . . . . . . . . . . . . 303-316

City Government . . . . . . . . . . . . . . . . . . . . . 375-376
Classical Music. . . . . . . . . . . . . . . . . 232-235, 305
Classified Advertisements . . . . . . . . . . 125-126, 134
Climate . . . . . . . . . . . . . . . . . . . . . . . . . . . 287, 297-299
Co-housing . . . . . . . . . . . . . . . . . . . . . . . . 135-136
Coast Guard Museum Northwest. . . . . . . . . . . . 245
Coffeehouses . . . . . . . 17, 35, 37, 40, 42, 44, 48, 361
College Sports . . . . . . . . . . . . . . . . . . . . . . 258-259
Colleges and Universities . . . . . . . . . . . 211-214, 316
Columbia City . . . . . . . . . . . . . . . . . . . . . . . . 66-69
Comedy . . . . . . . . . . . . . . . . . . . . . . . . . . . . . . 240
Commencement Bay Maritime Fest. . . . . . . . . . . 363
Community Gardens . . . . . . . . . . . . . . . . . . .20, 228
Community Hanukkah Celebration. . . . . . . . . . . . 366
Community Theater . . . . . . . . . . . . . . . . . . . 239-240
Commuter Services . . . . . . . . . . . . . . . . . . . . . . 172
Computers . . . . . . . . . . . . .6, 133, 158, 175, 219-220
Concert Venues . . . . . . . . . . . . . . . . .103, 231, 235
Condominiums. . . . . . . . . . . . . . . . . . . . . . 135-136
Consumer Advocacy Programs . . . . . . . . . . . . . 190
Consumer Complaints . . . . . .147-148, 167, 189, 376
Consumer Complaints, Airlines. . . . . . . . . . . . . . 341
Consumer Complaints, Movers . . . . . . . . . 147-148
Consumer Protection. . 145, 148, 155-156, 161, 167,
188-189, 341, 376
Consumer Protection, Automobiles . . . . . . . . . . . 188
Consumer Protection, Rip-off Recourse. . . . 189-190
Consumer Protection, Utility Complaints . . . . . . . 167
Contemporary Music . . . . . . . . . . . . . . . . . . 235-238
Continuing Education. . . . . . . . . . . . . . 96, 212-214
Cooperative Apartment (Co-Op). . . . . . . . . . 135-136
Corner Market Building . . . . . . . . . . . . . . . . . . . . 21
Cougar Mountain Regional Wildland Park . . 83, 252,
292
Counties . . . . . . . . . . . . . . . . . . . . . . . . . . . 13-16
County Governments. . . . . . . . . . . . . . . . . . 376-377
Coupeville. . . . . . . . . . . . . . . . . . . . . . . . . . . . . 351
Courts . . . . . . . . . . . . . . . . . . . . . . . . . 372, 377-378
Cowen Park . . . . . . . . . . . . . . . . . . . . . . . . . . . 289
Credit Bureaus . . . . . . . . . . . . . . . . . . . . . . 139, 157
Credit Cards . . . . . . . . . . . . .154, 156-157, 168, 339
Credit Unions . . . . . . . . . . . . . . . . . . . 154-156, 170
Crime . . . . . . . . . . . . . . . . . . . 182-183, 363, 377-378
Crime Prevention . . . . . . . . . . . . .318, 363, 375, 377
Crisis Lines . . . . . . . . . . . . . . . . . . . . . . . . . 377-378
Crossroads. . . . . . . . . . . . . . . . . . . . . . . . . . 80-82
Crown Hill . . . . . . . . . . . . . . . . . . . . . . . . . . . 36-39
Crystal Mountain . . . . . . . . . . . . . . . . . . .277, 355
**Cultural Life.** . . . . . . . . . . . . . . . . . . . . . . . . 231-254
Culture for Kids. . . . . . . . . . . . . . . . . . . . . . 251-254
Daffodil Festival . . . . . . . . . . . . . . . . . . . . . . . . 358

Daffodils in Bloom Celebration . . . . . . . . . . . . . . 358
Dance . . 234-235, 237, 253, 266, 359, 363, 365-366
Daniel Bagley Elementary. . . . . . . . . . . . . . . . . . 203
Danskin Triathlon . . . . . . . . . . . . . . . . . . . . . 69, 362
Daybreak Star Cultural Center . . . . . . . . . . 288, 319
Daycare . . . . . . . . . . . . . . . . . . . . . 182, 197-201
Daycare, What to Look for In. . . . . . . . . . . . . . . 199
Death Records. . . . . . . . . . . . . . . . . . . . . . . . . . 373
Deception Pass . . . . . . . . . . . . . . . . . . . . . . . . . 351
Delridge. . . . . . . . . . . . . . . . . . . . . . . . . . . . . 72-75
Denny Blaine . . . . . . . . . . . . . . . . . . . . . . . . 58-60
Denny Regrade . . . . . . . . . . . . . . . . . . . . 8, 22-23
Denny Triangle. . . . . . . . . . . . . . . . . . . . . . . 20-24
Department of Early Learning . . . . . . . . . . . 198-199
Department of Fish and Wildlife . . . . . . . . . 267-268
Department of Licensing . . . . 159, 168-169, 173, 373
Department of Motor Vehicles, see Department of
    Licensing
Department of Neighborhoods . . . . . . . .17, 167, 189
Department of Parks and Recreation . .259-262, 268,
    272, 278, 280-281, 295, 381-383
Department of Transportation . . . 144-145, 189, 325,
    384, 387
Department Stores. . . . . . . . 114, 156, 216, 218-221
Des Moines . . . . . . . . . . . . . . . . . . . . . . . . . . .116
Diaper Services . . . . . . . . . . . . . . . . . . . . . . . . 185
Directory Assistance . . . . . . . . . . . . . . . . . . . . . 164
Disability Assistance. . . . . . . . . . . . . . . . . . . . . 319
Disabled, Services for the . . . . . . . . . . . . . . 190-192
Disaster Preparedness . . . . . . . . . . . . . . . . 300-301
Disc Golf. . . . . . . . . . . . . . . . . . . . . . . . . . . . . 268
Discount Stores . . . . . . . . . . . . . . . . . . . . . 216-217
Discovery Park. . . . . . . . . . . . 35, 268, 270, 288, 319
Discrimination. . . . . . . . . . . . . . . 131-132, 378, 380
Dockton Park . . . . . . . . . . . . . . . . . . . . . . . . . . 295
Doctors . . . . . . . . . . . . . . . . . . . . . 179-180, 380
Domestic Abuse. . . . . . . . . . . . . . . . . . . . 377-378
Domestic Services . . . . . . . . . . . . . . . . . . . 185-187
Downtown Parks . . . . . . . . . . . . . . . . . . . . 287-291
Downtown Seattle . . . . . . . . . . . . . . . . . . . . 20-24
Drinking Water . . . . . . . . . . . 37, 165-166, 229-230
Driver's License . . . . . . . . . . . . . . . . . . . . . 167-168
Drug Abuse. . . . . . . . . . . . . . . . . . . . 318, 371-372
Drug Dependency . . . . . . . . . . . . . . . . . 318, 371-372
Dry Cleaning Delivery . . . . . . . . . . . . . . . . . 185-186
Dunlap. . . . . . . . . . . . . . . . . . . . . . . . . . . . . 66-69
Dupre + Scott Apartment Advisors . . .31, 34, 46, 123
Duvall . . . . . . . . . . . . . . . . . . . . . . . . . . . . . 88-89
Duwamish District . . . . . . . . . . . . . . . . . . . . 70-72
Earshot Jazz Festival. . . . . . . . . . . . . . . . . . . . . 364
Earth Day Puget Sound. . . . . . . . . . . . . . . . . . . 359

Earthquakes . . . . . . . . . . . . . . . . . . 36, 297, 300-301
East Hill. . . . . . . . . . . . . . . . . . . . . . . . . . . . . . 111
Eastern Communities . . . . . . . . . . . . . . . . . . . 78-93
Eastlake . . . . . . . . . . . . . . . . . . . . . . . . . . . . 30-31
Eastside .4-5, 9-11, 33, 44, 50-52, 61, 74, 78-98, 137
Echo Lake. . . . . . . . . . . . . . . . . . . . . . . . . . . 95-97
Edmonds . . . . . . . . . . . . . . . . . . . . . . . . . . 99-100
Edmonds Arts Festival. . . . . . . . . . . . . . . . . . . . 360
Education . . . . . . . . . . . . . . . . . . . . 197-214, 385
Electricity. . . . . . . . . . . . . . . . . . . . . . . . . . 161-162
Electronics . . . . . . . . . . . . . . . . . . . . . . . . . 219-220
Emerald City. . . . . . . . . . . 1, 251, 269, 279, 297, 368
Emergency . . 183, 265, 300-301, 378, 383, 387, 389
Emissions Test Information . . . . . . . . . . . . . . 169-170
Employment . . . . . . . . . .128, 150, 190, 200-201, 381
Enrollment, Seattle Public Schools. . . . 203-205, 385
Entertainment, see also Cultural Life 100, 107, 112,
    193, 215, 232, 256-257, 357-366
Entertainment, Gay and Lesbian . . . . . . . . . . . . 193
Environment. . . . . . . . . . . . . . . . . . . . . . . . . . . 320
Ethics . . . . . . . . . . . . . . . . . . . . . . . . . . . . . . . 316
Ethnic Districts and Markets . . . . . . . . . . . . 226-227
Everett. . . . . . . . . . . . . . . . . . . . . . . . . . . . 102-104
Evergreen State Fair . . . . . . . . . . . . . . . . . . . . . 362
Experience Music Project . . . . . . . . . . . . . . . . . 245
Factory Discount Stores . . . . . . . . . . . . . . . . . . 217
Fairwood. . . . . . . . . . . . . . . . . . . . . . . . . . . 107-110
Farmers' Markets . . . . . . . . . . . 68, 215, 227-228, 353
Fauntleroy. . . . . . . . . . . . . . . . . . . . . . 72-75, 336
Federal Fair Housing Act. . . . . . . . . . . . . . . . . . 132
Federal Motor Carrier Safety Administration 144-145
Federal Offices/Centers. . . . . . . . . . . . . . . . 378-379
Federal Way. . . . . . . . . . . . . . . . . . . . . . . . .117-118
Fencing. . . . . . . . . . . . . . . . . . . . . . . . . . . . . . 266
Ferries. . . . . . . . . . . . . .7, 14, 123, 191, 335-36, 389
Festa Italiana . . . . . . . . . . . . . . . . . . . . . . . . . . 363
Festival Sundiata . . . . . . . . . . . . . . . . . . . . . . . 357
Fiction . . . . . . . . . . . . . . . . . . . . . . . . . . . . 368-369
Field Hockey. . . . . . . . . . . . . . . . . . . . . . . . . . . 266
Fiestas Patrias . . . . . . . . . . . . . . . . . . . . . . . . . 363
Film . . . . . . . . . . . . . . . . . . . . 240-241, 358-359, 363
Film Festivals . . . . . . . . . . . . . . . . . . . . . . .241, 363
Finding a Physician . . . . . . . . . . . . . . . . . . . 179-180
Finding a Place to Live . . . . . . . . . . . . . . . . 123-142
Finn Hill. . . . . . . . . . . . . . . . . . . . . . . . . . . . 86-87
First Hill. . . . . . . . . . . . . . . . . . . . . . . . . . 5, 26-28
Fishing . . . . . . . . . . . . . . . . . . . . . . . 266-268, 354
Flexcar . . . . . . . . . . . . . . . . . . . . . . . . . . . . 331-332
Folk Music . . . . . . . . . . . . . . . . . . . . . . . . . . . 237
Food . . . . . . . . . . . . . . . . . . . . . . . . . . . . . 224-228
Food Banks . . . . . . . . . . . . . . . . . . . . . . . . 228, 320

Football, Professional ...................... 257
Football, College .......................... 259
For Sale By Owner........................... 141
Forests ................................... 295
Fort Dent Park ............................ 293
Fourth of Jul-Ivars ....................... 361
Fremont ............................... 41-43
Fremont Fair........................... 42, 360
Fremont Oktoberfest ....................... 364
Fremont Outdoor Cinema .................... 42
Friends of the Seattle Public Library . . 247, 289, 322, 359, 363
Friends of the Seattle Public Library Book Sale. .359, 363
Frisbee ............................... 268, 288
Frostbite Regatta .......................... 365
Frye Art Museum ........................... 242
Furniture................................ 221-222
Gaelic Football ........................... 275
Garbage and Recycling............. 166-167, 379
Garden Centers ....................... 88, 223
Garlic Gulch .............................. 67
Gasworks Park.... 44, 235, 262, 268, 288-289, 362
Gay and Lesbian ................... 192-193, 321
Gazzam Lake Park ......................... 294
Gearhart, OR ............................. 355
Gene Coulon Memorial Beach Park.......... 293
Georgetown ............................ 70-72
Getting Around ....................... 11, 325
Getting Around By Bike ................. 332-333
Getting Around By Car.................. 325-332
Getting Around By Public Transportation ... 333-336
Getting Settled ...................... 161-183
Golden Gardens Park ...........38, 181, 282, 289
Golf .................................. 268-269
Graham Hill Elementary .................... 203
Grand Forest ............................. 294
Granville Island.......................... 353
Great Northern Railroad .................... 7
Great Seattle Fire........................ 7, 20
Green Lake............................. 45-47
Green Lake Frostbite Regatta............... 365
Green Lake Small Craft Center...........264, 288
Greenspace and Beaches ............. 287-296
Greenwood............................. 40-41
Greyhound Lines .......................37, 388
Grocery Stores........................ 224-225
Guggenheim Fountain....................... 49
Gymnastics................................ 269
Haller Lake .............................. 2
Harbor Steps ........................... 20-24

Hang Gliding........................... 269-270
Hardware & Garden Centers ............... 223
Harrison Hot Springs, B.C. ............. 352-353
Head of the Lake Regatta ................. 365
Health and Medical Care................... 379
Health Clubs........................... 284-285
Health Food Stores ....................... 225
Heat...................................... 162
Helpful Services ...................... 185-196
Hempfest ................................. 363
Henry Art Gallery ......................... 242
Higher Education ...................... 211-214
Highlands ............................. 95-97
Highway 99............................... 10-11
Highway 520............................... 10
Highway 522............................... 11
Hiking .................270, 354-355, 368, 370
Hinduism.................................. 313
Hip Hop................................... 237
History.................. 6-8, 245-246, 369
Hmong New Year Celebration................ 365
Hockey .............258-258, 266, 271, 288, 386
Homeless Services ........................ 321
Homeowner's Insurance ........ 132-133, 138-140
Homes Point.............................. 86-87
Homeschool Resource Center ............... 210
Homeschooling ........................... 210
Horse Racing ............................. 258
Horseback Riding..........260, 270, 353, 354-355
Hostels .................................. 348
Hotels ................................ 343-347
Houghton ............................... 86-87
Housecleaning ............................ 186
House Hunting ........................ 141-142
Household Shopping ................... 219-223
Housewares............................... 222
Housing................................... 380
Human Services........................... 322
Hurricane Ridge........................295, 354
Ice Skating .............................. 271
Improv.................................... 240
In-line/Roller Skating ..........271, 287-288, 291
Independence Day....30, 33, 44, 289, 355, 360-362
Inland Parks .......................... 287-291
Innis Arden ............................ 95-97
Insurance, Automobile................... 170-171
Insurance, Homeowner's and Renter's .... 132-133
Interbay................................ 32-34
Interlake ............................... 80-82
International District ................... 25-26
International Newcomers............... 194-196

Internet Banking . . . . . . . . . . . . . . . . . . . . . . 155
Internet Service Providers . . . . . . . . . . . . . . 164-165
Interstate 5 . . . . . . . . . . . . . . . . . . . . . . . . . . 10
Interstate 90 . . . . . . . . . . . . . . . . . . . . . . . . . 10
Interstate Moves . . . . . . . . . . . . . . . . . . 144-145, 148
Intiman Theater . . . . . . . . . . . . . . . . . . . . . 3, 3, 238
Intrastate Moves . . . . . . . . . . . . . . . . . . . . . 144, 147
Introduction . . . . . . . . . . . . . . . . . . . . . . . . .1-11
Irish Week Festival . . . . . . . . . . . . . . . . . . . . . . 358
Islam . . . . . . . . . . . . . . . . . . . . . . . . . . . .208, 313
Issaquah . . . . . . . . . . . . . . . . . . . . . . . . . . . 89-91
Issaquah Highlands . . . . . . . . . . . . . . . . . . . . 89-91
Issaquah Salmon Days Festival . . . . . . . . . . . . 364
Italian Festival . . . . . . . . . . . . . . . . . . . . . . . . . 363
Jackson Park . . . . . . . . . . . . . . . . . . . . . . . . 53-55
Japanese Tea Garden . . . . . . . . . . . . . . . . . . . . 290
Jefferson Park . . . . . . . . . . . . . . . . . . . .65, 269, 290
Jose Rizal Park . . . . . . . . . . . . . . . . . . . . . . . . 181
Juanita . . . . . . . . . . . . . . . . . . . . . . . . . . . . 86-87
Juanita Bay Park . . . . . . . . . . . . . . . . . . . . . . . 292
Judaism . . . . . . . . . . . . . . . . . . . . . . 313-315, 359
Judkins Park . . . . . . . . . . . . . . . . . . . . . . . . 61-63
Junk Mail . . . . . . . . . . . . . . . . . . . . . . . . . . . . 188
Kayaking . . . . . . . . . . . . . . . . . . . . . . . . .264, 370
Kelsey Creek Park . . . . . . . . . . . . . . . . . . . . . . 292
Kenmore . . . . . . . . . . . . . . . . . . . . . . . . . . . 98-99
Kent . . . . . . . . . . . . . . . . . . . . . . . . . . . .111-112
Kerry Park . . . . . . . . . . . . . . . . . . . . . . . . . . . 288
King County . . . . . . 13-14, 95-99, 107-119, 381-383, 387-389
King County Fair . . . . . . . . . . . . . . . . . . . . . . . 361
King County International Airport . . . . . . . . .340, 388
King County Library System . . . . .175, 250, 322, 381
Kingdome . . . . . . . . . . . . . . . . . . . . . . . . .20, 71
Kirkland . . . . . . . . . . . . . . . . . . . . . . . . . . . 86-87
Kitsap County . . . . . . . . . .14, 104-106, 259, 262, 381
Klondike Gold Rush . . . . . . . . . . . . . . . . . . . . 8, 48
Komen Seattle Race for the Cure . . . . . . . . . . . . 360
La Conner . . . . . . . . . . . . . . . . . . . . . . . . .352, 358
Lacrosse . . . . . . . . . . . . . . . . . . . . . . . . . . . . 266
Lake Chelan . . . . . . . . . . . . . . . . . . . . . . .282, 353
Lake City . . . . . . . . . . . . . . . . . . . . . . . . . . . 52-53
Lake Forest Park . . . . . . . . . . . . . . . . . . . . . . 97-98
Lake Hills . . . . . . . . . . . . . . . . . . . . . . . . . . . . 82
Lake Union . . . . .2-4, 9, 262-264, 268, 283, 288-289, 361-362, 365
Lake Union Wooden Boat Festival . . . . . . . . . . . 361
Lake View Cemetery . . . . . . . . . . . . . . . . . .272, 290
Lake Washington .2-11, 262-264, 267, 283, 289-293, 326-327, 360, 362, 365
Lamps & Lighting . . . . . . . . . . . . . . . . . . . . . . 222

Landlord Problems . . . . . . . . . . . . . . . . . . . 130-132
Landlord-Tenant Act . . . . . . . . . . . . . . . . . . 129-132
Landlord/Tenant Rights . . . . . . . . . . . . . . . . 131-132
Laurelhurst . . . . . . . . . . . . . . . . . . . . . . . . . . 56-58
Lease . . . . . . . . . . . . . . . . . . . .126, 129-131, 347
Leases/Rental Agreements and Security Deposits . . 130
Leavenworth . . . . . . . . . . . . . . . . . . . . . . .273, 353
Legal Aid . . . . . . . . . . . . . . . . . . . . . . . . . . . . 322
Legal Referral . . . . . . . . . . . . . . . . . . . . . . 380-381
Legal Resources . . . . . . . . . . . . . . . . . . . . . . . 190
Leschi . . . . . . . . . . . . . . . . . . . . . . . . . . . . 63-65
Leschi Park . . . . . . . . . . . . . . . . . . . . . . . . . . . 64
Libraries . . . . . . . . . . . . . . . .175, 249-250, 381
Library Cards . . . . . . . . . . . . . . . . . . . . . . . . . 175
Light Rail . . . . . . . . . . . . . . . . . . . . 333-335, 337
Lincoln Park . . . . . . . . . . . . . . . . .73, 263, 280, 291
Literacy . . . . . . . . . . . . . . . . . . . . . . . . . . . . . 322
Literary Life . . . . . . . . . . . . . . . . . . . . . . . . . . 247
Lodging . . . . . . . . . . . . . . . . . . . . . . . . . 343-349
Long Beach . . . . . . . . . . . . . . . . . . . . . . . . . . 355
Long Distance Service . . . . . . . . . . . . . . . . . . . 163
Lower Queen Anne . . . . . . . . . . . . . . . . . . . 32-34
Luther Burbank Park . . . . . . . . . . .79, 181, 291-292
Luxury Lodgings . . . . . . . . . . . . . . . . . . . . . . . 344
Lynnwood . . . . . . . . . . . . . . . . . . . . . . . . 101-102
MS Walk . . . . . . . . . . . . . . . . . . . . . . . . . . . . 359
Madison Park . . . . . . . . . . . . . . . . . . . . . . . 58-60
Madrona . . . . . . . . . . . . . . . . . . . . . . . . . . . 63-65
Madrona Park . . . . . . . . . . . . . . . . . . . . . . . . . 280
Magnolia . . . . . . . . . . . . . . . . . . . . . . . . . . 34-36
Magnuson Park . . . .56, 57, 181, 247, 271, 280, 282, 289, 358-359, 363-364
Mail Receiving Services . . . . . . . . . . . . . . . . . . 187
Major Expressways . . . . . . . . . . . . . . . . . . 326-327
Make-and-Take Meal Assembly . . . . . . . . . . . . . 229
Malls . . . . . . . . . . . . . . . . . . . . . . . . . . . 216-217
Manzanita Park . . . . . . . . . . . . . . . . . . . . . . . . 294
Maple Leaf . . . . . . . . . . . . . . . . . . . . . . . . . 45-47
Maps . . . . . . . . . . . . . 12, 18-19, 76-77, 94, 108-109
Mardi Gras . . . . . . . . . . . . . . . . . . . . . . . . 20, 358
Marriage Licenses . . . . . . . . . . . . . . . . . . . . . . 381
Martial Arts . . . . . . . . . . . . . . . . . . . . . . . . 271-272
Martin Luther King Jr. Celebration . . . . . . . . . . . . 357
Marymoor Park . . . . . . . . . .84-85, 181, 268, 274, 292
Matthews Beach Park . . . . . . . . . . . .56-57, 280, 289
Meal Assembly . . . . . . . . . . . . . . . . . . . . . . . . 299
Men's Services . . . . . . . . . . . . . . . . . . . . . . . . 322
Mercer Island . . . . . . . . . . . . . . . . . . . . . . . 79-80
Meridian Park . . . . . . . . . . . . . . . . . . . . . . . 95-97
Metro Transit . . . . . . 191-192, 327, 333-334, 388-389

Microsoft . . 2, 3, 23, 61, 78, 81, 84, 87, 89, 107, 208, 245
Microsoft (Neighborhood) . . . . . . . . . . . . . . . . . . . . 81
Middle Range Lodgings. . . . . . . . . . . . . . . . 345-346
**Money Matters** . . . . . . . . . . . . . . . . . . . . . . . 153-159
Monorail . . . . . . . . . . . . . . . . . . . . . . . . . . . . 5, 334
Montessori Schools . . . . . . . . . . . . . . . . . . . . . . . 209
Montlake. . . . . . . . . . . . . . . . . . . . . . . . . . . . 60-61
Montlake Cut . . . . . . . . . . . . . . . . . . . . . . . . 60, 360
Mortgages. . . . . . . . . . . . . . . . . . . . . . . . . 138-142
Motels . . . . . . . . . . . . . . . . . . . . . . . . 343-347, 353
Mount Baker. . . . . . . . . . . . . . . . . . . . . . . . . 65-66
Mount Baker Park . . . . . . . . . . . . . . . . . . . . 280, 290
Mount Baker Rowing and Sailing Center . . . 264, 290
Mount Olympus . . . . . . . . . . . . . . . . . . . . . . . . 354
Mount Rainier. . . . . . . 1, 2, 4, 262, 272, 295, 327, 355
Mount Rainier National Park . . . . . . . . . . . . 295, 355
Mount St. Helens . . . . . . . . . . . . . . . . . . . . . . . 278
Mount Vernon. . . . . . . . . . . . . . . 215, 351-352, 359
Mountain Biking . . . . . . . . . . . . . . . . . . . . 260, 263
Mountlake Terrace . . . . . . . . . . . . . . . . . . 100-101
Movers . . . . . . . . . . . . . . . . . . . . . . . . . . . 144-148
Movie Theaters. . . . . . . . . . . . . . . . . . 216, 240-241
**Moving and Storage** . . . . . . . . . . . . . . . . 143-151
Moving Within Seattle . . . . . . . . . . . . . . . . . . . . 147
Multiple Listing Service . . . . . . . . . . . . . . . . . . . 123
Municipal Court of Seattle . . . . . . . . . . . . . 173, 372
Museums . . . . . . . . . . . . . . . . . . . . . 241-247, 252
Museums, Art . . . . . . . . . . . . . . . . . . . . . . . 241-245
Museums, Culture and History . . . . . . . . . . 245-246
Museum of Flight . . . . . . . . . . . . . . . . . . . . . 70, 246
Museum of History and Industry . . . . . . . . . . . . . 246
Museums, Kids. . . . . . . . . . . . . . . . . . . . . . . . . 252
Museum of Northwest Art . . . . . . . . . . . . . . 242, 352
Museums, Science . . . . . . . . . . . . . . . . . . 246-247
Music, Classical . . . . . . . . . . . . . . . . . . . . . 232-235
Music, Contemporary. . . . . . . . . . . . . . . . . 235-238
Music, Kids. . . . . . . . . . . . . . . . . . . . . . . . 251-252
Nanitax . . . . . . . . . . . . . . . . . . . . . . . . . . . . . . 200
Nannies. . . . . . . . . . . . . . . . . . . . . . . . . . . 199-200
National Parks . . . . . . . . . . . . . . . . . . . . . . . . . . 295
Natural Gas . . . . . . . . . . . . . . . . . . . . . . . . . . . 162
Naval Station . . . . . . . . . . . . . . . . . . . . 56, 102, 289
**Neighborhoods** . . . . . . . . . . . . . . . . . . . . . . 13-121
New Holly . . . . . . . . . . . . . . . . . . . . . . . . . . 65, 68
New Year's Eve at the Space Needle. . . . . . . . . . 366
Newcastle. . . . . . . . . . . . . . . . . . . . . . . . . . . . . 83
Newspaper Classifieds . . . . . . . . . . . . . . . . . . . 141
Newspapers and Magazines. . . . . . . . . . . . 178-179
Newspapers, Gay and Lesbian. . . . . . . . . . . . . . 193
Nightclubs. . . . . . . . . . . . . . . . . . . . . . . . . 235-238

Night Out Against Crime . . . . . . . . . . . . . . . . . . 363
Nintendo . . . . . . . . . . . . . . . . . . . . . . . . . . . . . . 84
Non-Citizens . . . . . . . . . . . . . . . . . . . . . . . . . . . 174
Nordic Heritage Museum. . . . . . . . . 37, 246, 250, 365
Normandy Park . . . . . . . . . . . . . . . . . . . . . . 115-116
North Beach . . . . . . . . . . . . . . . . . . . . . . . . . 36-40
North Bend . . . . . . . . . . . . . . . . . . . . . . . . . . 92-93
North End . . . . . . . . . . . . . . . . . . . . . . . . . . 95-104
North Seattle Community College . . . . 54, 126, 212
Northacres Park. . . . . . . . . . . . . . . . . . . . . . . . . 181
Northeast Tacoma . . . . . . . . . . . . . . . . . . . 119-121
Northern Communities. . . . . . . . . . . . . . . . . 95-104
Northern Pacific Railroad. . . . . . . . . . . . . . . . . . . . 7
Northgate . . . . . . . . . . . . . . . . . . . . . . . . . . . 53-55
Northgate Mall . . . . . . . . . 53-54, 212, 216, 218, 247
Northwest AIDS Walk . . . . . . . . . . . . . . . . . . . . . 364
Northwest Chamber Orchestra . . . . . . . . . . . . . . 233
Northwest Flower and Garden Show . . . . . . . . . 358
Northwest Folklife Festival. . . . . . . . . . . . . . 33, 359
Northwest Multiple Listing Service . . . . . . . . . . . 123
Northwest Sinfonietta. . . . . . . . . . . . . . . . . . . . . 233
Northwestern Trailways. . . . . . . . . . . . . . . . . . . . 337
Nutcracker, The . . . . . . . . . . . . . . . . . . . . . . . . . 366
Oak Harbor. . . . . . . . . . . . . . . . . . . . . . . . 340, 351
Oak Tree. . . . . . . . . . . . . . . . . . . . . . . . . . . . 53-55
Ober Park . . . . . . . . . . . . . . . . . . . . . . . . . . . . . 295
Off-leash Areas. . . . . . . . . . . . . . . . . . . 181-182, 364
Oil Heat. . . . . . . . . . . . . . . . . . . . . . . . . . . . . . . 162
Oktoberfest. . . . . . . . . . . . . . . . . . . . . . . . . 353, 364
Old Town. . . . . . . . . . . . . . . . . . . . . . . . . . . 119-121
Olympic Mountains . 1, 274, 288-290, 291, 354-355, 370
Olympic National Forest . . . . . . . . . . . . . . . . . . . 295
Olympic National Park. . . . . . . . . . . . . . . . . 295, 354
Olympic Peninsula . . . . . . . . . . . . . . 5, 7, 295, 336, 354
Olympic Sculpture Park. . . . . . . . . . . . 242-243, 335
Online Banking. . . . . . . . . . . . . . . . . . . . . . 153, 155
Online Resources—Apartments and Roommates . . 127
Online Resources—Daycare . . . . . . . . . . . . . . . 199
Online Resources—House Hunting . . . . . . . . . . 141
Online Resources—Relocation. . . . . . . . . . . . . . 151
Online Schools. . . . . . . . . . . . . . . . . . . . . . . . . . 211
Online Service Providers. . . . . . . . . . . . . . . 164-165
Opening Day . . . . . . . . . . . . . . . . . . . . . . . . 60, 360
Opera . . . . . . . . . . . . . . . . . . . . . . . . . . . . 232-234
Oregon Coast. . . . . . . . . . . . . . . . . . . . . . . . . . 355
Othello Station . . . . . . . . . . . . . . . . . . . . . . . 65-66
Out to Lunch Concert Series. . . . . . . . . . . . . . . . 361
Outdoor Guides . . . . . . . . . . . . . . . . . . . . . . . . 370
Outdoor Wear. . . . . . . . . . . . . . . . . . . . . . . . . . 285

Outlet Malls. . . . . . . . . . . . . . . . . . . . . . . . 112, 217
Pacific Northwest Ballet. . . . . . . .3, 33, 234, 319, 366
Pacific Science Center. . . . . . . . . . . . . . . . . 8, 247
Package Delivery Services . . . . . . . . . . . . . . . . 187
Pagdiriwang . . . . . . . . . . . . . . . . . . . . . . . . . . . 361
Paragliding . . . . . . . . . . . . . . . . . . . . . . . . . 269-270
Paramount Theater . . . . . . . . . . . . . . . .48, 235, 238
Park & Rides . . . . . . . . . . . . . . . . . . . . . . . . 328-331
Parking . . . . . . . . . . . . . . . . . . . . . . . . . . . . 172-173
Parking Permits . . . . . . . . . . . . . . . . . . . . . 173, 327
Parking, Sea-Tac . . . . . . . . . . . . . . . . . . . . . . . . 339
Parking Tickets. . . . . . . . . . . . . . . . . .167, 173, 372
Parks, see **Greenspace and Beaches**,
    and **Community Resources** in individual
    **Neighborhood** listings
Parks and Recreation Departments . . . . . . .259-290,
    381-383
Parkwood . . . . . . . . . . . . . . . . . . . . . . . . . . . . 95-97
Participant Sports and Activities . . . . . . . . . 259-284
Passports . . . . . . . . . . . . . . . . . . . . . . . . . . 175-176
PAWS Walk . . . . . . . . . . . . . . . . . . . . . . . . . . . . 364
Pest Control . . . . . . . . . . . . . . . . . . . . . . . . 186-187
Pet Laws & Services . . . . . . . . . . . . . . . . . . 180-182
Phinney Ridge . . . . . . . . . . . . . . . . . . . . . . . . 40-41
Pierce County. . . . . . 3, 14-15, 119-121, 376-377, 381
Pike Place Market  5, 20-24, 228, 232, 242, 360, 369
Pike Place Market Festival . . . . . . . . . . . . . . . . . 360
Pill Hill . . . . . . . . . . . . . . . . . . . . . . . . . . . . . . 5, 26
Pioneer Building. . . . . . . . . . . . . . . . . . . . . . . . . 20
Pioneer Square . . . . . . . . . . . . . . . . 6, 8, 20-24, 358
**Places of Worship** . . . . . . . . . . . . . . . . . . 303-316
Point Defiance Park . . . . . . . . . . . . . . . . . . 121, 293
Police . . 182-183, 246, 318, 373, 375, 377, 383-384
Politics. . . . . . . . . . . . . . . . . . . . . . . . . . . . 322-323
Pollution . . . . . . . . . . . . . . . . . . . . . . . . . 2, 299-300
Pools. . . . . . . . . . . . . . . . . . . . . . . . . . . . . 280-281
Port Angeles. . . . . . . . . . . . . . . . . . . . .295, 340, 354
Port Townsend . . . . . . . . . . . . . . . . . . . . . . . . . 354
Portable Storage . . . . . . . . . . . . . . . . . . . . . . . . 148
Portage Bay . . . . . . . . . . . . . . . . . . . . . . . . . . 60-61
Portland. . . . . . . . . . . . . . . . . .263, 336, 362, 369
Postal and Shipping Services . . . . . . . . . . . 187-188
Poulsbo. . . . . . . . . . . . . . . . . . . . . . . . . . . . . . . 354
Prepaid Cellular Phone Service . . . . . . . . . . . . . 164
Prepaid Debit Cards. . . . . . . . . . . . . . . . . . . . . . 157
Preserve, The. . . . . . . . . . . . . . . . . . . . . . . 102-104
Private Schools . . . . . . . . . . . . . . . . . . . . . . 206-210
Proctor . . . . . . . . . . . . . . . . . . . . . . . . . . . . 119-121
Professional Sports . . . . . . . . . . . . . . . . . . 256-258
Property Taxes . . . . . . . . . . . . . . . . . . . . . . . . . 134
Pt. Robinson Park . . . . . . . . . . . . . . . . . . . . . . . 295

Public Health of Seattle & King County . . . . 201-202
Public Schools . . . . . . . . . . . . . . . . . . 202-206, 385
Public Transportation. . . . . . . . . . . . . . . . . . 333-336
Puget Sound  1-6, 9, 13-15, 247, 263, 267, 354, 359,
    365
Puget Sound Energy . . . . . . . . . . . . . . 161-162, 389
Purchase Agreements. . . . . . . . . . . . . . . . . 138-140
Puyallup . . . . . . . . . . . . . . . . . 7, 207, 335, 358, 364
Puyallup Fair. . . . . . . . . . . . . . . . . . . . . . . . . 7, 364
Queen Anne . . . . . . . . . . . . . . . . . . . . . . . . . 32-34
**Quick Getaways**. . . . . . . . . . . . . . . . . . . . 351-355
Quikbook . . . . . . . . . . . . . . . . . . . . . . . . . . . . . 344
Qwest. . . . . . . . . . . . . . . . . . . . . . . . 162, 164-165
Qwest Field. . . . 20, 256-258, 357-358, 360, 364-365
Racquet Clubs . . . . . . . . . . . . . . . . . . . . . . . . . 273
Racquet Sports . . . . . . . . . . . . . . . . . . . . . . 272-273
Racquetball. . . . . . . . . . . . . . . . . . . . . . . . . . . . 273
Radio Stations . . . . . . . . . . . . . . . . . . . . . . 177-178
Rainier Beach. . . . . . . . . . . . . . . . . . . . . . . . . 66-69
Rainier Valley . . . . . . . . . . . . . . . . . . . . 66-69, 333
Rape . . . . . . . . . . . . . . . . . . . . . . . . . . . . . . . . . 378
Ravenna. . . . . . . . . . . . . . . . . . . . . . . . . . . . . 48-51
Ravenna Park . . . . . . . . . . . . . . . . . . . . . 50-51, 289
Real Estate Resources . . . . . . . . . . . . . 127, 141-142
Realtors. . . . . . . . . . . . . . . . . . . . . . . . . . . . 136-138
Recycling . . . . . . . . . . . . . . . . . . 166-167, 379, 384
Red Tide . . . . . . . . . . . . . . . . . . . . . . . 2, 266, 369
Redmond . . . . . . . . . . . . . . . . . . . . . . . . . . . 84-85
Redmond Ridge. . . . . . . . . . . . . . . . . . . . . . . 84-85
Redondo Beach. . . . . . . . . . . . . . . . . . . . . .117-118
Refugee Assistance. . . . . . . . . . . . . . . . . . . . . . 323
Religious Studies . . . . . . . . . . . . . . . . . . . . . . . 316
Relocation Resources . . . . . . . . . . . . . . . . . . . . 151
Rent Control . . . . . . . . . . . . . . . . . . . . . . . . 130-131
Rental Agents. . . . . . . . . . . . . . . . . . . . . . . . . . 127
Rental Agreement . . . . . . . . . . . . . . . . 129-132, 168
Rental Publications . . . . . . . . . . . . . . . . . . . . . . 126
Renter's/Homeowner's Insurance . . . . . . . . 132-133
Renting . . . . . . . . . . . . . . . . . . . . . . . . . . . . 124-133
Renton . . . . . . . . . . . . . . . . . . . . . . . . . . . .107-111
Renton Municipal Airport . . . . . . . . . . . . . . 340, 388
Residence Hotels. . . . . . . . . . . . . . . . . . . . . . . . 347
Residential Parking Permits . . . . . . . . . . . . . . . . 173
Restaurants . . . . . . . . . . . . . . . . . . . . . . . .229, 369
Richmond Beach . . . . . . . . . . . . . . . . . . . . . . 95-97
Richmond Highlands . . . . . . . . . . . . . . . . . . . 95-97
Ridematch . . . . . . . . . . . . . . . . . . . . . . . . .327, 389
Rideshare. . . . . . . . . . . . . . . . . . . . . . . . . .327, 389
Road Condition Information. . . . . . . . . . . . . . . . . 384
Roanoke. . . . . . . . . . . . . . . . . . . . . . . . . . . . 79-80
Robinswood . . . . . . . . . . . . . . . . . . . . . . . . . 80-82

Robinswood Community Park . . . . . . . . . . . 82, 292
Rock Climbing . . . . . . . . . . . . . . . . . . . . 273-274, 370
Roller Skating . . . . . . . . . . . . . . . . . . . . . . . . . . . . . 271
Roommate Referral . . . . . . . . . . . . . . . . . . . . . . . . 127
Roosevelt . . . . . . . . . . . . . . . . . . . . . . . . . . . . . . . 48-51
Rose Hill . . . . . . . . . . . . . . . . . . . . . . . . . . . . . . . . 84-87
Rosemont Beach . . . . . . . . . . . . . . . . . . . . . . . . . 80-82
Rowing . . . . . . . . . . . . . . . . . . . . .264, 290, 360, 365
Rucker Hill . . . . . . . . . . . . . . . . . . . . . . . . . . . 102-104
Rugby . . . . . . . . . . . . . . . . . . . . . . . . . . . . . . . . . . . 275
Running . . . . . . . . . . . . . . . . . . . . . . . . . . . . . 275-276
SODO . . . . . . . . . . . . . . . . . . . . . . . . . . . . . . . . . 70-72
STP . . . . . . . . . . . . . . . . . . . . . . . . . . . . . . . . . 263, 362
Safeco Field . . . . . . . . . . . . . . . . . .10, 20, 256, 326
Safety and Crime . . . . . . . . . . . . . . . . . . . . . 182-183
Sailing . . . . . . . . . . . . . . . . . . . . . . .263-264, 288, 290
St. Patrick's Day Parade . . . . . . . . . . . . . . . . . . . 358
Sales Tax . . . . . . . . . . . . . . . . . . . . . . . . . . . . 157-158
Salmon Homecoming Celebration . . . . . . . . . . . 364
San Juan Islands . . . . . . . . . . .36, 340, 351-352, 370
Sand Point . . . . . . . . . . . . . . . . . . . . . . . . . . . . . 56-58
Schools . . . . . . . . . . . . . . . . . . . . . . . . . . . . . 202-211
Schools—Seattle Public . . . . . . . . . . . . . . . . 202-205
Schools—Surrounding Communities . . . . . . 205-206
Schmitz Preserve Park . . . . . . . . . . . . . . . . . . . . 291
Scuba Diving . . . . . . . . . . . . . . . . . . . . . . . . . . . . 276
Seafair . . . . . . . . . . . 69, 275, 288, 290, 361-362, 370
Seahurst Park . . . . . . . . . . . . . . . . . . . . . . . . . . . . 293
Seasonal Affective Disorder . . . . . . . . . . . . . 298-299
Sea-Tac Airport . . . . . .44, 65, 107, 113, 299, 337-340
SeaTac . . . . . . . . . . . . . . . . . . . . . . . . . . . . . .114-115
Seattle Address Locator . . . . . . . . . . . . . . . . . . .9-11
Seattle Animal Control Center . . . . . . . . . . . 181, 318
Seattle Area Counties . . . . . . . . . . . . . . . . . . . 13-16
Seattle Art Museum (SAM) . . . . . 5, 21, 242-243, 335
Seattle Asian Art Museum . . . . . . . . . . . 29, 243, 290
Seattle Boat Show . . . . . . . . . . . . . . . . . . . . . . . . 357
Seattle Center . . . 8, 3, 203, 235, 238-239, 247, 251-
   252, 257, 271, 281, 326, 334, 357-366
Seattle Central Community College . . . . 29, 126, 212
Seattle Cherry Blossom Festival . . . . . . . . . . . . . 359
Seattle Children's Museum . . . . . . . . . . . . . . . . . 252
Seattle Children's Theatre . . . . . . . . . . . . . . 253-254
Seattle Choral Company . . . . . . . . . . . . . . . . . . . 232
Seattle City Light . . . . . . . . . . . . . . . . . . . 161, 389
Seattle Fault Line . . . . . . . . . . . . . . . . . . . . . . . . . 301
Seattle Fire Department . . . . . . . . . . . . . . . 202, 378
Seattle Grid . . . . . . . . . . . . . . . . . . . . . . . . . . . . . . . 9
Seattle History . . . . . . . . . . . . . . . . . . . . . . . . . . .6-8
Seattle Home Show . . . . . . . . . . . . . . . . . . . 358, 364
Seattle Hotel Hotline . . . . . . . . . . . . . . . . . . . . . 344

Seattle Hotel Reservations . . . . . . . . . . . . . . . . . 344
Seattle International Auto Show . . . . . . . . . . . . . 365
Seattle International Bicycle Expo . . . . . . . . . . . . 358
Seattle International Children's Festival . . . . . . . 360
Seattle International Film Festival . . . . . . . . . . . . 241
Seattle Jewish Festival . . . . . . . . . . . . . . . . . . . . 241
Seattle Marathon . . . . . . . . . . . . . . . . . . . .275, 365
Seattle Maritime Festival . . . . . . . . . . . . . . 185, 360
Seattle Men's Chorus . . . . . . . . . . . . . . . . . . . . . 232
Seattle Music Fest . . . . . . . . . . . . . . . . . . . . . . . . 363
Seattle Neighborhoods . . . . . . . . . . . . . . . . . . 16-75
Seattle Opera . . . . . . . . . . . . . . . . . . . .3, 8, 232, 252
Seattle Pacific University . . 33, 43-44, 124, 126, 212,
   234, 349
Seattle Passport Agency . . . . . . . . . . . . . . . 175-176
Seattle to Portland Bicycle Classic . . . . . . . 263, 362
Seattle Pride . . . . . . . . . . . . . . . . . . . . . . . .193, 361
Seattle Public Library . . 175, 201, 247, 249-250, 289,
   322, 359, 363, 381
Seattle Public Schools . . . . . . . . . . . . . . . . . 202-205
Seattle Public Utilities . . . . . . . . . . . 165-167, 379, 389
**Seattle Reading List, A** . . . . . . . . . . . 351, 367-370
Seattle Repertory Theatre . . . . . . . . . . . . . .3, 33, 239
Seattle RV & Outdoor Recreation Show . . . . . . 358
Seattle Symphony . . . . . . . . . . . . . . . . . .3, 233, 252
Seattle-Tacoma International Airport, *see also* Sea-
   Tac Airport . . . . . . . . . . . . . . . . . . . . . 114, 337, 388
Seattle to Portland Bicycle Classic . . . . . . . 263, 362
Seattle Transportation Bicycle Program . . . . . . . 332
Seattle University . . .29, 62, 124, 127, 212, 238, 248,
   316
Seattle Wedding Show . . . . . . . . . . . . . . . . . . . . 357
Seattle Women's Chorus . . . . . . . . . . . . . . . . . . . 232
Seattle Women's Show . . . . . . . . . . . . . . . . . . . . 358
**Seattle Year, A** . . . . . . . . . . . . . . . . . . . . . . 357-366
Second-Hand Shopping . . . . . . . . . . . . . . . . 223-224
Security Deposits . . . . . . . . . . . . . . . . . . . . . . . . . 130
Senior Services . . . . . . . . . . . . . .323-324, 371, 388
Sequim . . . . . . . . . . . . . . . . . . . . . . . . . . . . . . 5, 354
Serve Our Dog Areas . . . . . . . . . . . . . . . . . . . 85, 181
Service Employees International . . . . . . . . . 198-199
Services for People with Disabilities . . . . . . . 190-192
Seward Park . . . . . . . . . . . . . . . . . . . . . . . . . . . 69-70
Seward Park Art Studio . . . . . . . . . . . . . . . . . . . . 69
Shellfish Gathering . . . . . . . . . . . . . . . . . . . . 266-268
Shilshole . . . . . . . . . . . . . . . . . . . . . . . . . . . . . . 36-40
Shipping Services . . . . . . . . . . . . . . . 187, 385-386
Shopping Districts . . . . . . . . . . . . . . . . . . . . 215-216
**Shopping for the Home** . . . . . . . . . . . . . . 215-230
Shoreline . . . . . . . . . . . . . . . . . . . . . . . . . . . . . 95-97
Short-Term Leases . . . . . . . . . . . . . . . . . . . . . . . 347
Skagit Valley . . . . . . . . . . . . . . . . . . . . . . . . . . . . 352

Skagit Valley Tulip Festival . . . . . . . . . . . . . 352, 359
Skateboarding . . . . . . . . . . . . . . . . . . . . . . . . . . 271
Skid Row . . . . . . . . . . . . . . . . . . . . . . . . . . . . . 7, 369
Skiing . . . . . . . . . . . . . . . . . . . . . . . . . . . . . . 276-278
Snohomish County . . 15-16, 99-104, 374, 377, 381,
389
Snoqualmie . . . . . . . . . . . . . . . . . . . . . . . . . . 92-93
Snoqualmie Pass. . . . . . . . . . . . . . . . . . . . 2, 5, 78
Snowboarding . . . . . . . . . . . . . . . . . . . . . . . 276-278
Snowmobiling. . . . . . . . . . . . . . . . . . . . . . . . 278-279
Soccer. . . . . . . . . . . . . . . . . . . . . . . . . . . . . . 279-280
Social Security . . . . . . . . . . . . . . . . . . . . . . 174, 386
Softball . . . . . . . . . . . . . . . . . . . . . . . . . . . . . . . . 261
Sol Duc Hot Springs. . . . . . . . . . . . . . . . . . 295, 354
Solstice Parade . . . . . . . . . . . . . . . . . . . . . . . 42, 360
Sound Transit. . . . . . . . . . . . . . . . . . . .333, 335, 340
South Beacon Hill. . . . . . . . . . . . . . . . . . . . . . 65-66
South End. . . . . . . . . . . . . . . . . . . . . . . . . . . 107-121
South Park . . . . . . . . . . . . . . . . . . . . . . . . . . . 70-72
South Seattle Community College . . . . . . . . 127, 212
Southern Communities . . . . . . . . . . . . . . . . 107-121
Space Needle. . . . . . . . . . . . . . . . . . . 8, 33, 347, 366
Sporting Goods . . . . . . . . . . . . . . . . . . . . . . . . . 285
Sports and Recreation . . . . . . . . . . . . . . . 255-285
Stadium District . . . . . . . . . . . . . . . . . . . . . . 119-121
Stanley Park. . . . . . . . . . . . . . . . . . . . . . . . . . . . 353
Starting or Moving a Business . . . . . . . . . . . . . . 159
State and National Parks. . . . . . . . . . . . . . . . . . . 295
State Identification . . . . . . . . . . . . . . . . . . . . 167-169
State of Washington Offices .373, 376-379, 383-384,
386-387
Stevens Pass . . . . . . . . . . . . . . . . .2, 274, 277, 353
Stimson-Green Mansion . . . . . . . . . . . . . . . . . . . 27
Stolen Automobiles . . . . . . . . . . . . . . . . . . . 173-174
Storage Facilities . . . . . . . . . . . . . . . . . . . . 148-149
Street Maintenance . . . . . . . . . . . . . . . . . . . . . . 387
Student Housing Affairs . . . . . . . . . . . . . . . . . . . . 50
Summer Nights . . . . . . . . . . . . . . . . . . . . . 235, 362
Summit . . . . . . . . . . . . . . . . . . . . . . . . . . . .203, 277
Surrounding Communities. . . . . . . . . . . . . . . 78-121
Suzzallo Library . . . . . . . . . . . . . . . . . . . . . . 48, 250
Swedish Medical Center . . . . . . . . . . . . . . . 180, 202
Swimming. . . . . . . . . . . . . . . . . . . . . . . . . . 280-281
Synagogues. . . . . . . . . . . . . . . . . . . . . . . . . 313-315
Syttende Mai . . . . . . . . . . . . . . . . . . . . . . . . . . . 360
TOPS . . . . . . . . . . . . . . . . . . . . . . . . . . . . . . . . . 203
Tacoma. . . . . . . . . . . . . . . . . . . . . . . . . . . . 119-121
Tacoma Link. . . . . . . . . . . . . . . . . . . . . . . . . . . . 333
Tacoma Power. . . . . . . . . . . . . . . . . . . . . . . 162, 389
Take Our Daughters and Sons to Work Day . . . . 359
Talbot. . . . . . . . . . . . . . . . . . . . . . . . . . . . . . 107-110

Taxes. . . . . . . . . . . . . . . . . . . . . . . . . . 157-158, 387
Taxis . . . . . . . . . . . . . . . . . . . . . . . . . . . . . . 332, 387
Telecommunications and Research and Action
Center . . . . . . . . . . . . . . . . . . . . . . . . . . . . . . . 163
Telephone, Long Distance. . . . . . . . . . . . . . . . . . 163
Telephone Numbers. . . . . . . . . . . . . . . . . . . 371-390
Telephone Service . . . . . . . . . . . . . . . . . 162-163, 300
Television . . . . . . . . . . . . . . . . . . . . . . . . . . . 176-177
Temporary Lodgings. . . . . . . . . . . . . . . . . . 343-349
Tenant Rights . . . . . . . . . . . . . . . . . . . . . . . . 131-132
Tenant/Landlord Relations. . . . . . . . . . . . . . 130-132
Tenants Union . . . . . . . . . . . . . . . 129-132, 190, 380
Tennis . . . . . . . . . . . . . . . . . . . . . . . . . . . . . . . . . 272
Terrace Creek Park . . . . . . . . . . . . . . . . . . . . . . . 294
Theater . . . . . . . . . . . . . . . . . . . . . . . . . . . . . 238-240
Theater, Community . . . . . . . . . . . . . . . . . . . 239-240
Theater, Kids . . . . . . . . . . . . . . . . . . . . . . . . 253-254
Theater, Professional. . . . . . . . . . . . . . . . . . 238-239
Three Tree Point . . . . . . . . . . . . . . . . . . . . . .113-114
Thrift Stores . . . . . . . . . . . . . . . . . . . . . . . . . 223-224
TibetFest. . . . . . . . . . . . . . . . . . . . . . . . . . . . . . . 363
Ticketmaster. . . . . . . . . . . . . . . . . . . . . . . . . 231-256
Tickets. . . . . . . . . . . . . . . . . . . . . . . . . . . . . . 231-232
Ticketweb . . . . . . . . . . . . . . . . . . . . . . . . . . . . . . 232
Time . . . . . . . . . . . . . . . . . . . . . . . . . . . . . . . . . . 388
Tourism. . . . . . . . . . . . . . . . . . .296, 343, 351-355, 388
Towed or Stolen Cars . . . . . . . . . . . . . . . . . . 173-174
Traffic Reports . . . . . . . . . . . . . . . . . . . . . . . . . . 325
Trains . . . . . . . . . . . . . . . . . . . . . 335-336, 388-389
Transportation . . . . . . . . . . . . . . . . . . . . . . . 325-341
Triathlon . . . . . . . . . . . . . . . . . . . . . . . .69, 79, 362
Truck Rentals . . . . . . . . . . . . . . . . . . . . . . . . 143-144
Tukwila . . . . . . . . . . . . . . . . . . . . . . . . . . . . .114-115
US Department of Transportation. . . . . . . . . . . . . 144
UW Husky Stadium . . . . . . . . . . . . . . . . .60, 259, 274
Ultimate Frisbee. . . . . . . . . . . . . . . . . . . . . . . . . 268
Underwater Park . . . . . . . . . . . . . . . . . . . . . . . . . 294
Union Station . . . . . . . . . . . . . . . . . . . . . . . . 120, 172
Universities. . . . . . . . . . . . . . . . . . . . . . . . . . 211-214
University District . . . . . . . . . . . . . . . . . . . . . . 48-51
University District Street Fair. . . . . . . . . . . . . 49, 360
University of Washington. . . 127, 191, 211, 213-214,
242, 245-246, 250, 258-259, 265, 271, 274, 290,
298, 316, 349, 365, 386
University Park. . . . . . . . . . . . . . . . . . . . . . . . . 48-51
Used Bookstores . . . . . . . . . . . . . . . . . . . .44, 247, 249
Useful Phone Numbers and Web Sites . . 371-390
Utilities. . . . . . . . . . . . . . . . . . . .129, 161-167, 379, 389
Utility Complaints . . . . . . . . . . . . . . . . . . . . . . . . 167
Utility Emergencies . . . . . . . . . . . . . . . . . . . . . . . 389
Vancouver, B.C. . . . . . . . . . . . . 276-277, 336, 352-353

Vanpools. . . . . . . . . . . . . . . . . . . . . . . . . . . . 327
Vashon Island. . . . . . . 13, 73, 118-119, 136, 295, 336
Vehicle/Vessel License Sub-Agents. . . . . . . 169-170
Veterinarians. . . . . . . . . . . . . . . . . . . . . . . . 180-183
Victoria, B.C. . . . . . . . . . . . . . . . . . . . . . . . 352-354
Video Arcades . . . . . . . . . . . . . . . . . . . . . 281-282
Vietnamese Lunar New Year Celebration . . . . . . 358
View Ridge, Seattle . . . . . . . . . . . . . . . . . . . . 56-58
View Ridge, Everett . . . . . . . . . . . . . . . . . . . 102-104
Volleyball. . . . . . . . . . . . . . . . . . . . . . . . . . . . . 282
Volunteer Park . . 28-30, 242-243, 268, 280, 289-290, 292, 364
**Volunteering** . . . . . . . . . . . . . . . . . . . . . . . . 317-324
Voter Registration. . . . . . . . . . . . . . . . . . . 174, 389
Vulcan Northwest. . . . . . . . . . . . . . . . . . . . . 23-24
Wading Pools. . . . . . . . . . . . . . . . .280, 289, 291, 294
Waldorf Schools. . . . . . . . . . . . . . . . . . . . . . . . 210
Wallingford . . . . . . . . . . . . . . . . . . . . . . . . . . 43-45
WaMu Family 4th. . . . . . . . . . . . . . . . . . . . . . . 362
Warehouse Stores. . . . . . . . . . . . . . . . . . . 217-218
Washington Athletic Club. . . . . . . . . . . . . . 285, 348
Washington Attorney General . . . 132, 148, 156, 189, 376, 386
Washington Center for Real Estate Research. . .123, 142
Washington Coast . . . . . . . . . . . . . . . . . . . 354-355
Washington Park . . . . . . . . . . . . . . . . . . . . . 58-60
Washington Park Arboretum . . . . . . . . . .61, 263, 290
Washington State Child Care Resource & Referral Network . . . . . . . . . . . . . . . . . . . . . . . . . . . . . 197
Washington State Department of Transportation. 296, 325, 384, 387
Washington State Ferries . . . . . . . . . . . 335-336, 389
Washington State Housing Finance Commission . . . 134, 142
Washington State Tourism Office . . . . . . . . . . . . 351
Washington Utilities and Transportation Commission 144, 147-148
Water Quality . . . . . . . . . . . . . . . . . . . . . . . 165-166
Water Service. . . . . . . . . . . . . . . . . . . . . . . 165-166
Waterfront. . . . . . . . . . . . . . . . . . . . . . . . . . . 20-24
Water-skiing . . . . . . . . . . . . . . . . . . . . . . . . 2, 282
**Weather and Disaster Preparedness** . . . . 297-301
Web Sites. . . . . . . . . . . . . . . . . . . . . . . . . . 371-390
Webcams. . . . . . . . . . . . . . . . . . . . . . . . . 326, 336
Wedgwood . . . . . . . . . . . . . . . . . . . . . . . . . . 56-58
West Edge . . . . . . . . . . . . . . . . . . . . . . . . . . 20-24
West Point Lighthouse. . . . . . . . . . . . . . . . . 35, 288
West Seattle. . . . . . . . . . . . . . . . . . . . . . . . . 72-75
West Seattle Freeway . . . . . . . . . . . .11, 72, 74, 327
West Seattle Junction . . . . . . . . . . . . . . . . . 72, 75
Westcrest Park. . . . . . . . . . . . . . . . . . . . . 181, 291

Western Communities. . . . . . . . . . . . . . . . 104-106
Western Regional Climate Center . . . . . . . . 298-299
Western Washington Fair . . . . . . . . . . . . . . . . . 364
Westlake. . . . . . . . . . . . . . . . . . . . . . . . . . . . 32-34
What to Bring . . . . . . . . . . . . . . . . . . . . . . . . . .5-6
Whidbey Island. . . . . . . . . . . . . . . . . . . . . 351, 354
Whirligig . . . . . . . . . . . . . . . . . . . . . . . . . . . . . 358
White Center . . . . 125, 170, 273, 310, 321, 373, 380
Wilburton Hill Park . . . . . . . . . . . . . . . . . . . . . . 292
Willows . . . . . . . . . . . . . . . . . . . . . . . . . . . . 84-85
Wind-surfing . . . . . . . . . . . . . . . . . . . . . . . . . . 283
Wines . . . . . . . . . . . . . . . . . . . . . . . . . . . . . . . 230
Winslow . . . . . . . . . . . . . . . . . . . . . . . . . . 104-105
Winterfest . . . . . . . . . . . . . . . . . . . . . . . . . . . . 365
Women's Services. . . . . . . . . . . . . . . . . . . . . . 324
Woodinville. . . . . . . . . . . . . . . . . . . . . . . . . . 87-88
Woodland Park. . . . . . . . . . . . . . . .45, 181, 268, 288
Woodland Park Zoo. . . . . . . . . . . . .40, 45, 253, 288
Woodway . . . . . . . . . . . . . . . . . . . . . . . . . . 99-100
Woodway Highlands . . . . . . . . . . . . . . . . . . 99-100
Worship. . . . . . . . . . . . . . . . . . . . . . . . . . . 303-316
Wright Park. . . . . . . . . . . . . . . . . . . . . . . . 293-294
Yacht Clubs . . . . . . . . . . .60, 64, 103, 264-265, 360
Yoga . . . . . . . . . . . . . . . . . . . . . . . . . . . . . 283-284
Youth. . . . . . . . . . . . . . . . . . . . .251-254, 261, 324
Yulefest. . . . . . . . . . . . . . . . . . . . . . . . . . . . . . 365
Zip Codes . . . . . . . . . . . . . . . . . . . . . . . . . . . . 390
Zoolights . . . . . . . . . . . . . . . . . . . . . . . . . . . . . 366
Zoos . . . . . . . . . 40, 45, 121, 252-253, 288, 293, 366

The Newcomer's Handbook for Seattle, first published in 1999, was written by Amy Bellamy. The second edition, published in 2002, was revised by Monica Fischer.

The most recent revision has been done by Maria Christensen, who describes herself as follows:

**MARIA CHRISTENSEN** was born in Seattle and grew up on Vashon Island, an island just a short ferry ride from Seattle, fondly known as "The Rock." She left the Rock to attend the University of Washington and eventually moved for several years to Savannah, Georgia, to work on a degree in history. A love of Seattle brought her back, and she has lived in the University District, Capitol Hill, West Seattle, Beacon Hill, and Eastlake. She currently resides in Wedgwood with her two children and works as a freelance writer and bookkeeper.

# READER RESPONSE

We would appreciate your comments regarding this third edition of the *Newcomer's Handbook® for Moving to and Living in Seattle: Including Bellevue, Redmond, Everett, and Tacoma*. If you've found any mistakes or omissions or if you would just like to express your opinion about the guide, please let us know. We will consider any suggestions for possible inclusion in our next edition, and if we use your comments, we'll send you a free copy of our next edition. Please e-mail us at readerresponse@firstbooks.com, or mail or fax this response form to:

**Reader Response Department**
**First Books**
**6750 SW Franklin, Suite A**
**Portland, OR 97223-2542**
**Fax: 503.968.6779**

Comments: _____

_____

_____

_____

_____

_____

_____

_____

_____

Name: _____

Address: _____

_____

_____

Telephone: (          ) _____

Email: _____

**6750 SW Franklin, Suite A**
**Portland, OR 97223-2542**
**USA**
**P: 503.968.6777**
**www.firstbooks.com**

# RELOCATION TITLES

## Moving with Kids?

Look into *The Moving Book: A Kids' Survival Guide*.

Divided into three sections (before, during, and after the move), it's a handbook, a journal, and a scrapbook all in one. Includes address book, colorful change-of-address cards, and a useful section for parents.

Children's Book of the Month Club "Featured Selection"; American Bookseller's "Pick of the List"; Winner of the Family Channel's "Seal of Quality" Award

And for your younger children, ease their transition with our brand-new title just for them, *Max's Moving Adventure: A Coloring Book for Kids on the Move*. A complete story book featuring activities as well as pictures that children can color; designed to help children cope with the stresses of small or large moves.

## Got Pets?

*The Pet Moving Handbook: Maximize Your Pet's Well-Being and Maintain Your Sanity* by Carrie Straub answers all your pet-moving questions and directs you to additional resources that can help smooth the move for both you and your pets.

"Floats to the top, cream of the crop. Awesome book; I'm going to keep one on the special shelf here." – Hal Abrams, Animal Radio

## NEWCOMER'S HANDBOOKS®

Regularly revised and updated, these popular guides are now available for Atlanta, Boston, Chicago, London, Los Angeles, Minneapolis–St. Paul, New York City, San Francisco Bay Area, Seattle, and Washington DC.

"Invaluable ...highly recommended" – Library Journal

If you're coming from another country, don't miss the *Newcomer's Handbook® for Moving to and Living in the USA* by Mike Livingston, termed "a fascinating book for newcomers and residents alike" by the *Chicago Tribune*.

### Introducing NEWCOMER'S HANDBOOKS® NEIGHBORHOOD GUIDES!

This new series provides detailed information about city neighborhoods and suburban communities, helping you find just the right place to live. The first volume is for Dallas-Fort Worth, Houston, and Austin. More locations to come!

**6750 SW Franklin Street**
**Portland, Oregon 97223-2542**
**Phone 503.968.6777 • Fax 503.968.6779**
**www.firstbooks.com**

FIRST BOOKS

**FIRST BOOKS**

Visit our web site at
www.firstbooks.com
for information about
all our books.